EVA MURPHY

Patrick Murray
Kevin McDermott
Mary Slattery
Karol Sadleir

GW00633230

New
Discovery

Leaving Certificate Poetry Anthology
for Higher and Ordinary Level 2015

Edco
The Educational Company of Ireland

First published 2013

The Educational Company of Ireland
Ballymount Road
Walkinstown
Dublin 12

www.edco.ie

A member of the Smurfit Kappa Group plc

ISBN 978-1-84536-568-4

Editor: Jennifer Armstrong
Design: Design Image
Layout: DTP Workshop
Cover Design: Graham Thew

09S13

Foreword

This anthology, which includes all the poems prescribed for the Higher and Ordinary Level English Leaving Certificate Examinations of 2015, has been prepared by four experienced teachers of English. Each of the contributors has been able to concentrate on a limited number of the prescribed poets and their work, thus facilitating a high standard of research and presentation.

Guidelines are given which set each poem in context. In addition, each poem is accompanied by a glossary and appropriate explorations, designed to allow the student to find his/her authentic response to the material. Relevant biographical details are provided for each poet. A list of examination-style questions is provided for each prescribed poet at Higher Level along with a snapshot of the poet's work and a sample examination-style essay to aid revision. A snapshot is provided for all Ordinary Level poems.

Guidelines are included for students on approaching the Unseen Poetry section of the course. There is also advice on approaching the prescribed question in the examination. Students will also find the glossary of poetic terms a valuable resource in reading and responding to poetry.

The poetry course for Leaving Certificate English demands a personal and active engagement from the student reader. We hope that this anthology makes that engagement possible and encourages students to explore the wider world of poetry for themselves.

Teachers can access the *New Discovery for Leaving Certificate Higher and Ordinary Level* e-book by registering on www.edcodigital.ie

Contents

Acknowledgements

The poems in this book have been reproduced with the kind permission of the publishers, agents, authors or their estates as follows:

'The Tuft of Flowers', 'Mending Wall', 'After Apple Picking', 'The Road Not Taken', 'Birches', 'Out, Out-', 'Spring Pools', 'Acquainted with the Night', 'Design', 'Provide, Provide' by Robert Frost from *The Poetry of Robert Frost* edited by Edward Connery Lathem, Copyright 1923, 1928, 1930, 1969 by Henry Holt and Company, Copyright 1936, 1951, 1956 by Robert Frost, Copyright 1964, 1967 by Lesley Frost Ballantine. Reprinted with permission of Henry Holt and Company.

'Killing the Pig', 'The Trout', 'The Locket', 'The Cage', 'Windharp', 'All Legendary Obstacles', 'The Same Gesture', 'The Wild Dog Rose', 'Like Dolmens Round My Childhood and 'A Welcoming Party' by John Montague in *New Collected Poems* (2012) by kind permission of the author and The Gallery Press, Loughcrew, Oldcastle, Co Meath, Ireland.

'Lucina Shynning in the Silence of the Nicht', 'The Second Voyage', 'Deaths and Engines', 'Fireman's Lift', 'All for You', 'Following', 'Kilcash', 'Street', 'The Bend in the Road' and 'Translation' by Eiléan Ní Chuilleanáin in *Selected Poems* (2008). 'On Lacking the Killer Instinct' and 'To Niall Woods and Xenya Ostrovskaia, married in Dublin on 9 September 2009' by Eiléan Ní Chuilleanáin in *The Sun-fish* (2009). By kind permission of the author and The Gallery Press, Loughcrew, Oldcastle, Co Meath, Ireland.

'Pheasant', 'Finisterre', 'Mirror', 'Child', 'Morning Song', 'Elm', 'The Arrival of the Bee Box', 'Poppies in July', 'Black Rook in Rainy Weather', 'The Times are Tidy' by Sylvia Plath from *Collected Poems* (1981) published by Faber and Faber Ltd.

'Funeral Blues' by W. H. Auden from *Collected Poems* published by Faber and Faber.

'Self-Portrait in the Dark (with Cigarette)' by Colette Bryce reproduced with the permission of Macmillan Publishers Ltd.

'After Viewing *The Bowling Match at Castlemary, Cloyne* (1847)' by Greg Delanty in *Collected Poems* 1986-2006 published by Carcanet Press.

Emily Dickinson

1830–86

'HOPE' IS THE THING WITH FEATHERS
THERE'S A CERTAIN SLANT OF LIGHT
I FELT A FUNERAL, IN MY BRAIN*
A BIRD CAME DOWN THE WALK
I HEARD A FLY BUZZ – WHEN I DIED*
THE SOUL HAS BANDAGED MOMENTS
I COULD BRING YOU JEWELS – HAD I A MIND TO
A NARROW FELLOW IN THE GRASS
I TASTE A LIQUOR NEVER BREWED
AFTER GREAT PAIN, A FORMAL FEELING COMES

Biography

Emily Dickinson's life reads like a detective mystery. As a young woman she lived a social life, meeting up with friends, attending parties in her home town of Amherst and attracting the attention of several young men. By all accounts she was high-spirited and witty. From about the age of thirty she increasingly withdrew from society, choosing to live almost the entirety of her time as a recluse in her father's house, communicating with the outside world through a voluminous correspondence. In accordance with her wishes, after her death, her sister and sister-in-law destroyed all her correspondence. Fortunately, the thousand or so poems her sister found hidden in Emily's writing desk were saved.

Amherst

Emily Elizabeth Dickinson was born on 10 December 1830 in Amherst, a Calvinist town in Massachusetts. Apart from a brief period at Mount Holyoke Female Seminary, a trip to Washington and Philadelphia and a stay in Boston to receive treatment for an eye problem, all her life was spent there. She was the second child of Emily Norcross and Edward Dickinson. Her mother came from a prosperous family and her father was a lawyer, a politician and, later, the treasurer of Amherst College. In a letter to Thomas Wentworth Higginson, Dickinson was less than flattering of her parents: 'My Mother does not care for thought – and, Father, too busy with his Briefs – to notice what we do – He buys me many Books – but begs me not to read them – because he fears they joggle the Mind.' She had an older brother, Austin, and a younger sister, Lavinia. All three children were very close throughout their lives and all started school in the one-room local primary school.

Education

Dickinson received a sound education at Amherst Academy and Mount Holyoke Female Seminary. When they were young, Edward Dickinson encouraged his children in their education. In a letter, written when Emily was seven, he exhorted them to 'Keep school, and learn, so as to tell me when I come home, how many new things you have learned, since I came away.' Amherst Academy was a progressive school. It had a broad curriculum, from the classics to science, and the teachers were well qualified and motivated. The school was connected to Amherst College and students could attend college lectures in astronomy, botany, chemistry, geology, natural history and zoology. This scientific emphasis is reflected in Dickinson's poetry: in her fascination with naming, her detailed descriptions, her choice of words and the range of her imagery.

At the age of seventeen Dickinson entered Mount Holyoke Seminary, a boarding school run by a devout Christian headmistress, Mary Lyon. Many of the graduates of the seminary became evangelical missionaries. Her stay there was not happy. Evangelical fervour swept through the college and the students were invited to declare their faith in God openly and publicly. Dickinson refused to do so and was put into a category of students who were 'without hope'. Unhappy and homesick, she returned to Amherst. Thereafter her attitude to Christian belief was one of positive doubt. In 1850, when Amherst was infected with a bout of revivalist fervour, the nineteen-year-old Emily wrote: 'I am standing alone in rebellion'. Her rebellion, such as it was, was more private and interior than public in nature and found expression in her poetry. **Although Dickinson never declared herself a Christian, she spent a lifetime exploring the nature of the soul and the spiritual life. Her poems are influenced by the rhythms of Protestant hymns and the Bible is a major source of her diction and imagery.**

Young adulthood

As was the case with many unmarried daughters after the completion of their formal education, the future for Dickinson was one of domestic work. Because her family was a prominent one in Amherst, there were many visitors to the house. Not only were visitors to be received and entertained, but there was also an obligation to return social visits. In a letter written in 1850 Dickinson exclaimed: 'God keep me from what they call households.' Although she baked bread and worked in the garden, Dickinson refused to clean and dust the house. She also declined to make social calls, although she did maintain an active social life with her siblings and friends and read widely. Among the novels that had an electric effect upon her was *Jane Eyre* and she may well have identified with the novel's heroine.

In 1855 Dickinson travelled to Washington to visit her father who, by this time, had been elected to the US House of Representatives. She went on to Philadelphia to visit a friend from school. There, it seems, she met Charles Wadsworth, a Presbyterian preacher. There is much speculation that Wadsworth was the great secret love of her life.

In the following year Austin, her brother, married Susan Gilbert and set up home in an adjoining house. Dickinson spent many evenings in their company and the company of their friends. One of these friends was Samuel Bowles, editor of the *Springfield Republican*, an influential newspaper in Massachusetts, who published some of her poems. Dickinson maintained a correspondence with Bowles and his wife over the course of twenty-five years. Some critics suggest it was Bowles, and not Wadsworth, who was the love of her life.

Emily Dickinson

Withdraws from society

When their mother's health began to decline in 1855, Emily and Lavinia took over the running of the house. Although she was still in her twenties, Dickinson began to withdraw from society. Gradually she became a recluse, rarely if ever leaving her home. The myth of the mysterious woman dressed in white, glimpsed in her garden, was formed during her lifetime. Mabel Loomis Todd, a writer who came to live in Amherst in 1881 and who became the lover of Dickinson's brother, Austin, wrote to her parents about the 'lady whom the people call the Myth: She has not been outside of her own house in fifteen years . . . she dresses wholly in white, and her mind is said to be perfectly wonderful. She writes finely, but no one ever sees her.'

There has been much speculation on the cause of her seclusion. Many early biographers favoured the explanation of disappointment in love. Charles Wadsworth visited her in 1860 and some biographers see a connection between this visit and her decision to withdraw from the world. The truth may have been more prosaic. Her brother, for example, suggested that her seclusion was simply a pose. Certainly, her family did not regard her behaviour as odd. Relieved of the necessity of visiting and entertaining, Dickinson pursued her interest in writing. She wrote poems and she wrote letters to friends. Indeed, she regarded letter writing as a form of visiting, although more focused and intense than the polite form of social visits that were common in Amherst at that time.

It is evident from the number of poems that she wrote in 1862 that Dickinson underwent some kind of personal crisis. Speculation suggests that this crisis was related to the failure of a love affair. Many of the poems written in this period explore despair and depressed states of mind.

Although Dickinson withdrew from society, she did have friends. Apart from her sister and brother, she was very close to her brother's wife, Susan Gilbert, whose family also came from Amherst. Susan was a trusted friend and one of Dickinson's most important readers. Indeed, she may well have read all of Dickinson's poetry and many poems were written for her. (Although they lived in neighbouring houses, Dickinson often preferred to write to Susan rather than meet face to face.) Helen Hunt Jackson was another literary friend who encouraged Dickinson to publish her work. And Dickinson was certainly romantically involved with Otis Lord, a family friend, to whom she wrote ardent letters, but whose proposal of marriage she declined in 1880.

An audience for her poetry

In 1862, when she was aged thirty-two, Dickinson wrote to Thomas Wentworth Higginson enclosing some of her poems. She wanted to know if her verse was alive and did it breathe. Higginson was widely known as a man of letters and a prolific essayist. An essay that Dickinson read in the *Atlantic Monthly* prompted her to write to him. He was also a radical theologian, an outspoken supporter of women's rights and an advocate for the abolition of slavery. Although he had a reputation for encouraging young writers, Higginson neither fully understood the nature of Dickinson's talent, nor recognised the scope of her achievement. Faced with her epigrammatic style, Higginson tried to regularise and smooth her poems. Determined and certain, Dickinson refused to compromise.

Despite not fully appreciating her peculiar genius, Higginson mentored and encouraged Dickinson for many decades and her correspondence with him was immensely important to her. Interestingly, fewer than twenty of her poems were published during her lifetime. However, Dickinson sent poems to nearly all her correspondents and, in this way, her poems were circulated among her friends. So, although little of her work was published, she did have an audience for her poetry.

After her death, Emily's sister, Lavinia, found a box containing 900 poems 'tied together with twine' in 'sixty volumes' or fascicles (bundles). A hundred poems were published in 1890, edited by Mabel Loomis Todd and Thomas Wentworth Higginson, with 'corrections' made by Higginson to rhymes, punctuation, rhythms and, in some cases, imagery. Because of problems with copyright and family feuds over the ownership of the poems, it was not until 1955 that her collected poems were published in the way that she had written them.

Final years

The three years between 1882 and 1885 were difficult for Dickinson. She lost her mother; her friends Otis Lord and Helen Hunt Jackson; and her young nephew, Gilbert. Austin began an affair with Mabel Loomis Todd, a family friend, and Emily was torn between her brother and her sister-in-law, Susan.

In 1884 Dickinson suffered the first attack of the kidney disease that eventually caused her death in 1886, at the age of fifty-five. She left precise instructions for her funeral, specifying the white dress she was to be buried in and the route to be taken from her house to the churchyard. At her funeral service, Thomas Wentworth Higginson read a line from her favourite Emily Brontë poem as her epitaph: 'No coward soul is mine.'

Social and Cultural Context

Although her father was a politician and she lived during the period of the American Civil War (1861–5), there is little indication that the war had any significant influence on the poetry of Emily Dickinson. Nor do the poems give much indication that the era in which she lived was one in which the campaign for the rights of women began or that the campaign for the abolition of slavery, which led to the Civil War, dominated national politics. Dickinson's poetry does, of course, speak to the cultural and literary context of her day. The Calvinist tradition of her family and the writings of Henry David Thoreau and Ralph Waldo Emerson are important influences. Equally important to an understanding of her poetry was the position of women in society in nineteenth-century New England.

The Calvinist tradition

The Calvinist tradition was brought to New England by the Pilgrim fathers who settled there in the seventeenth century. The Calvinist emphasis on sin and damnation led to a strict moral code and a focus on sinfulness. All life, it seemed, was directed at preparing for the Day of Judgement. For this reason, individuals were encouraged constantly to examine their conscience. Calvinism created an atmosphere in which individualism was curtailed and artistic expression was viewed as potentially proud and sinful. Although Calvinism was on the wane in the nineteenth century, its influence remained strong in Amherst. Indeed, when Dickinson was a student at Mount Holyoke Female Seminary, the headmistress instigated a series of Calvinist revivals, during which students were encouraged to declare their faith as Christians. Beset by doubts, Dickinson refused to do so and remained unconverted. Despite this, the language of Calvinism and of the Bible is evident in her poetry and provides a rich source of imagery. The question of everlasting life was one to which she returned often in her poetry.

Ralph Waldo Emerson

Dickinson was certainly influenced by the group of writers known as Transcendentalists, the most famous of whom was Ralph Waldo Emerson. The Transcendentalists believed that God dwelt or was immanent in nature and in humanity. This led to a celebration of the natural world as a sign of God's creative energy. If Dickinson did not convert to Calvinism, neither did she convert to Transcendentalism. She did, however, admire Emerson's emphasis on self-reliance, the primacy of individual experience over tradition and the importance of the interior life. Indeed, Dickinson's reclusive lifestyle and her exploration of what she referred to as 'the undiscovered continent' echo some of the themes she found in Emerson's writing.

Alone in rebellion

The position of women in New England society was one of subservience to men. Women were not expected to be full-time writers or intellectuals, or to be involved in public affairs. Their place was at home, living pious, domestic lives. At one level, the external facts of Dickinson's life suggest that she was content with a domestic role. However, her poetry speaks of extreme states of mind, hints at suppressed emotions and feelings, challenges religious orthodoxy and reveals an individual deeply at odds with the social and religious values of her day: one who stood alone in rebellion.

Punctuation and Capital Letters

Dickinson was very eccentric in her usage of punctuation and capital letters. Generally, her odd use has the purpose of emphasis. Her use of the dash is a device to indicate her own peculiar sense of rhythm, which she felt was not adequately served by regular punctuation such as the semi-colon and colon. The dash also works to create moments of suspense or dramatic pauses in the poems.

Timeline

1830	Born 10 December in Amherst, Massachusetts
1835	Attends local primary school
1840	Attends school in Amherst Academy
1847	Boarder at Mount Holyoke Female Seminary; declines to profess herself a Christian
1848	Withdraws from Mount Holyoke due to ill health and home sickness
1850	Back in Amherst: 'I am standing alone in rebellion'
1855	Travels to Washington to visit her father and then to Philadelphia; probable meeting with Charles Wadsworth; her mother's health begins to decline
1856	Her brother, Austin, marries her friend, Susan Gilbert; the couple live in an adjoining house
1858	Begins writing in earnest; assembles her poems into bound packets or fascicles
1861	Suggestion of a personal 'major crisis'; more and more withdrawn from the world
1862	Writes to Thomas Wentworth Higginson and encloses some poems; writes 366 poems
1863	Writes 141 poems
1864	Writes 174 poems; visits Boston for treatment for her eyes; may have met Judge Otis Lord, who later proposes to her
1874	Father dies
1882	Friendship with Susan strained by Austin's love affair with Mabel; mother dies; Charles Wadsworth dies
1883	Eight-year-old nephew, Gilbert, dies; Emily is heart-broken
1885	Bedridden with Bright's disease
1886	Writes to cousins 'Called Back' on 14 May; dies on 15 May
1890	First selection of her poems published
1955	First edition of her poems published as she wrote them

'Hope' is the thing with feathers

'Hope' is the thing with feathers –
That perches in the soul –
And sings the tune without the words –
And never stops – at all –

And sweetest – in the Gale – is heard –   5
And sore must be the storm –
That could abash the little Bird
That kept so many warm –

I've heard it in the chillest land –
And on the strangest Sea –   10
Yet, never, in Extremity,
It asked a crumb – of Me.

Emily Dickinson

Glossary

1   *the thing*: although she gives 'Hope' some of the characteristics of a bird, Dickinson also wishes to be true to its abstract nature of 'hope' as a quality or disposition

Guidelines

Dickinson wrote a number of 'definition poems' in which she uses physical details to define what an abstract experience is or is not. Often her definitions consist of a series of comparisons. However, she does not use the word 'like'. 'Hope' is not like a thing with feathers, it 'is the thing with feathers' (line 1). The directness and confidence of the statement makes her definition vivid and immediate. As in religious symbolism, Hope is imagined as having some of the characteristics of a bird. **Although Hope may seem something slight (it is only a 'little Bird', line 7), it is in fact something immensely powerful and comforting.** The poem, written in 1861, during what was a difficult period for Dickinson, has an optimistic, buoyant mood.

Commentary

Stanza 1

In the first stanza Dickinson introduces the metaphor (Hope is a feathered thing that resides in the soul) and develops it through the poem by telling us that Hope sings; that it is resilient in times of storm and distress; that it is found in all places; and that it seeks nothing for itself.

According to the first line, Hope is a thing with feathers, that is, something that can fly, and that can lift the spirit. The use of the word 'feathers' suggests the warm, comforting nature of Hope. Hope, the poem asserts, resides in the soul. By describing the song of Hope as 'the tune without the words' (line 3), Dickinson suggests that Hope goes beyond logic and reason and their limitations. Hope is resilient and unceasing. It never stops 'at all'.

Stanza 2

The comfort that Hope gives in times of distress and uncertainty – emotional, spiritual, psychological – is recorded in stanza 2. The comfort of Hope is known to many. The phrase 'the little bird' (line 7) suggests the poet's affection and admiration for Hope.

Stanza 3

Stanza 3 records the poet's personal experience of Hope, in times of personal anguish. Hope has come to her in the 'chillest land' (line 9) and on 'the strangest Sea' (line 10). In these periods of personal crisis, Hope offered comfort, without seeking anything in return. Hope, in other words, is generous and other-seeking, asking nothing for itself. This final stanza of the poem strikes a solemn note, as if the poet wants to give hope the dignified celebration she believes it deserves.

Form of the poem

The poem is written in four-line stanzas. The second and fourth lines rhyme. The metre is based upon the common metre of hymns and ballads. Dickinson's punctuation, her use of slant rhymes and enjambment, and her skilled use of repetition and alliteration work to eliminate the sing-song effect of this metre.

Thinking about the poem

1   What is the most important quality of Hope, as suggested by the first stanza? What words or phrases capture this?

2   Think about the description 'the tune without the words' (line 3). Why might a tune without words be appropriate to Hope? Explain your answer.

3   How is the strength of Hope suggested in the second stanza?

4   The poem becomes more personal in the final stanza.
    a) What has been the poet's experience of Hope?
    b) What is the effect of the words 'chillest' (line 9) and 'strangest' (line 10)? Explain your answer.

5   What, do you think, does the poet have in mind in her reference to 'Extremity' in line 11?

6   Do you think that this poem would offer consolation to a reader in some kind of distress? How do you think it might do this? Give reasons for your answer.

Personal response

1   Did you enjoy reading this poem? Give a reason for your opinion.

2   Based on the poem, what kind of person do you imagine the speaker is?

There's a certain Slant of light

There's a certain Slant of light,
Winter Afternoons –
That oppresses, like the Heft
Of Cathedral Tunes –

Heavenly Hurt, it gives us –   5
We can find no scar,
But internal difference,
Where the Meanings, are –

None may teach it – Any –
'Tis the Seal Despair –   10
An imperial affliction
Sent us of the Air –

When it comes, the Landscape listens –
Shadows – hold their breath –
When it goes, 'tis like the Distance   15
On the look of Death –

Glossary

3	*Heft*: weight
10	*the Seal Despair*: 'Seal' has the meaning of mark or sign, as in the wax seal placed on a letter. In the Calvinist tradition, the sacraments are seals of God's promise of salvation. In this poem, the hope of salvation is noticeably absent

Guidelines

'There's a certain Slant of light' explores a state of mind in which the comfort of hope is absent. In its place there is the despair associated with a certain kind of winter light falling on the landscape. The speaker in the poem sees the light, coming from heaven, as an affliction, affecting the inner landscape of the soul. The poem was probably written in 1861, during the period when it is believed Dickinson suffered a major personal crisis.

Commentary

Stanza 1

The fall of a certain kind of winter light is oppressive, according to the first stanza of the poem, as oppressive as the 'Heft / Of Cathedral Tunes' (lines 3–4). This is a striking simile. It links winter light and church music with a heaviness of the soul (the word 'heft' suggests weight). What starts off as a visual image is now described in terms of music, and the music is, in turn, described in terms of weight. This blurring of the distinction between the senses (synaesthesia) creates a feeling of disturbance.

Stanza 2

Dickinson states that this slant of winter light gives 'Heavenly Hurt' (line 5). This is a hurt that leaves no physical wounds or scars but which affects the inner life or soul of the person and brings despair. One can interpret this stanza as suggesting that the relationship between humanity and heaven is marked by a certain cruelty on the part of heaven.

Stanza 3

It is suggested that the hurt referred to in the second stanza cannot be understood, taught or explained away. It is without remedy. The slant of light is the mark or sign of despair ('Seal Despair', line 10), which is both a psychological and a spiritual condition. The word 'Seal' also suggests the message of a royal personage, a closed communication, something beyond contradiction. This meaning is reinforced by the phrase 'imperial affliction', which implies that the affliction associated with the winter light is sent by a higher or sovereign authority. Is the message of the winter light the message of human mortality that is beyond contradiction?

Stanza 4

The light causes the world to be still and hushed, as if nature itself is in awe of heaven's light, and passive in the face of it. In other words, the light impresses as much as it oppresses. Note how, in this stanza, the poem moves from the inner landscape back to the external one. The passing of the light does not lift the feeling of despair. On the contrary, the passing of the light leaves a chill, as if one had looked on the distance between the present and our death. It is only when the light disappears that its full meaning becomes clear. The final dash in the poem suggests the unknown into which we all face.

Form of the poem

The poem is written in four-line stanzas with a regular rhyming scheme. The sounds and rhyme of the poem add considerably to the feeling of seriousness and weighty matters. Note the use of final 't' sounds, which slow the rhythm and give a sense of definition and precision to the poem. The poem itself works as a seal – it is written in an authoritative style that brooks no contradiction.

Thinking about the poem

1   What is the effect of a certain kind of winter light, according to the first stanza of the poem?

2   What state of mind might regard 'Cathedral Tunes' (line 4) as heavy or oppressive? Explain your answer.

3   What, according to the second stanza, is the effect of the light? Where is the difference made by the light noticed or felt?

4   In the second stanza the words 'we' and 'us' are used by the poet. Do you think that 'I' and 'me' might have been more appropriate? Explain your answer.

5   a) What words or phrases in the third stanza suggest the powerlessness of those afflicted by despair?

    b) What, in particular, is the effect of the word 'Seal' (line 10) in relation to despair?

    c) Does the phrase 'imperial affliction' (line 11) suggest that the affliction is sent by a higher authority (God) or is the idea that affliction is itself majestic? Give reasons for your answer.

6   What, according to the speaker, is the feeling or situation when the light goes?

7   Examine the rhymes and the rhythm of the poem. In your view, how important are they in expressing the poet's concerns?

8   Consider the three phrases 'Heavenly Hurt' (line 5), 'An imperial affliction' (line 11) and 'the Seal Despair' (line 10). What view of providence or God emerges from them?

9   Discuss the poem as an expression of a religious crisis, in which the speaker feels betrayed by God.

10 What does this poem have in common with "Hope' is the thing with feathers'?

11 'internal difference, / Where the Meanings, are' (lines 7–8). What, do you think, does this statement suggest about Dickinson?

Personal response

1   Pick two phrases or images from the poem that you like and explain their impact on you.

2   Is this poem is suitable or unsuitable for inclusion in a school anthology? Give reasons for your answer.

Before you read 'I Felt a Funeral, in my Brain'

Emily Dickinson's poem 'I Felt a Funeral, in my Brain' is on page 15. Working in pairs, think about the kind of poem you expect to follow from the first line. Think of a possible time when you might use these words to describe an experience.

I Felt a Funeral, in my Brain

I Felt a Funeral, in my Brain,
And Mourners to and fro
Kept treading – treading – till it seemed
That Sense was breaking through –

And when they all were seated,   5
A Service, like a Drum –
Kept beating – beating – till I thought
My Mind was going numb –

And then I heard them lift a Box
And creak across my Soul   10
With those same Boots of Lead, again,
Then Space – began to toll,

As all the Heavens were a Bell,
And Being, but an Ear,
And I, and Silence, some strange Race   15
Wrecked, solitary, here –

And then a Plank in Reason, broke,
And I dropped down, and down –
And hit a World, at every plunge,
And Finished knowing – then –   20

Emily Dickinson

Glossary		
4	*Sense:*	waking consciousness or common sense
6	*Service:*	a church funeral service or ceremony
9	*Box:*	coffin
11	*Boots of Lead:*	the heavy tread of the mourners
12	*Space:*	the outside world into which the imagined funeral cortege moves
13	*Heavens:*	the sky or firmament
19	*World:*	the worlds which the poet imagines her soul passing through on its way to its final destination

Guidelines

In this celebrated poem we are given an account of the progress of a funeral from the startling perspective of the person lying in the coffin. The poem was probably written in 1861, during a difficult period in Dickinson's personal life, when she was beset by both religious and artistic doubts. In addition, there were also her complicated and disappointed feelings for Samuel Bowles, editor of the *Springfield Republican* newspaper.

Commentary

Stanzas 1 and 2

In the first line the speaker declares 'I Felt a Funeral in my Brain'. The verb 'Felt' and the noun 'Brain' suggest an experience that is intense and physical. By using these words, Dickinson abolishes the traditional boundary between experiences of the mind and those of the body. What the poet imagines is so vivid that it feels like a physical experience. The repetition of the word 'treading' in line 3, describing the impact of the activities of the mourners, emphasises this physicality.

The second stanza continues the first-person narrative account of the progress of the funeral. When the mourners were seated, the service began. The stanza emphasises how hearing became the sense through which the 'I' received the world. The transition from 'Brain' in line 1 to 'Mind' in line 8 suggests, perhaps, that the physical intensity of the experience lessened, and it became more psychological in character. However, Dickinson understood that there can be no absolute distinction between mind and body.

Stanzas 3 and 4

In stanza 3 the word 'Soul' is introduced (line 10). This suggests that the experience, which began as a physical one and became more psychological in character, developed a spiritual quality as it proceeded. This development did not make the experience any clearer. In fact the descriptions in stanzas 3 and 4 suggest that the 'I' became increasingly disoriented and the boundary between external and internal collapsed.

Furthermore, as it progressed, the experience was increasingly defined by a sense of contraction. Space was filled with the tolling of a bell and 'Being' (line 14) was reduced to just hearing. Just as bells mark time and differentiate one moment from another, so the tolling in the poem marks a decisive moment. The sense of contraction experienced by the 'I' was accompanied by an overwhelming sense of isolation. The 'I' is described as shipwrecked from life, cut-off, along with silence, and left 'here'. The effect of 'here', placed as the last word in stanza 4, is to give a startling immediacy to the experience.

Stanza 5

Before the 'I' and the reader can take stock of the situation and grasp the nature of stanza 4's 'here', the poem is on the move again. 'Reason', the faculty that could help to make sense of the experience, did not hold up ('And then a Plank in Reason, broke', line 17) and the 'I' underwent a new sensation, that of falling, plunging deeper into the experience, down to new levels or worlds. And at the end of this plunging, we are told that the 'I' 'Finished knowing – then' (line 20). This may mean that the poet's knowledge of the beyond is finished at this point; or that the poet has finished her imagined funeral with the knowledge of something that she cannot express; or that knowledge itself finishes.

Different interpretations

Some critics read the plunge as the coffin's descent into the grave and the 'here' of stanza 4 as death. (The word 'Plank' in line 17 may suggest the planks placed across the open grave, before the final interment.) Such readers see stanzas 4 and 5 as describing the experience of entering into death. Others interpret the final stanza as describing the descent into madness or despair, while yet more read the plunge as a description of the loss of consciousness.

The final line is highly regarded by critics even as they disagree on its meaning. Some interpret it as a declaration that the plunge beyond reason yielded a new, deeper knowledge, although this knowledge is not expressed. At the end or finish of the fall, the 'I' had learned something, but this something is not revealed. Others read the final line as suggesting that thought and knowledge are lost in the fall. Another reading suggests that the poet, on the verge of gaining an imaginative insight into the nature of death, fails. However much she might desire to experience death, imaginatively, it is beyond the imagination's capacity to do so.

Looking at the poem as a whole, some critics see the funeral described in the poem as a metaphor for the breakdown of consciousness, and relate the poem to Dickinson's personal crisis. They read the poem as one of Dickinson's definition poems, where the progress of a funeral is a comparison (the vehicle) for despair or a mental breakdown (the tenor). Others take the poem at face value, regarding it as an unusual exploration of one of Dickinson's favourite themes – the transition between life and death, which she also explores in 'I heard a Fly buzz'. Some readers regard the poem as charting the failure of her poetic imagination, during a period when she was unable to write. Whichever interpretation is given, the poem sees Dickinson straining her imagination to the limits of its power.

Reading aloud

Just as there are several ways of interpreting the poem, so too there are several possibilities for reading it aloud. On the one hand, it can be read as a narrative of a nightmarish, terrifying experience. In this reading, the dashes and punctuation may suggest the fragmented comprehension of the 'I'. On the other, the fact that the poem is narrated in the past tense may suggest that a tone of calm, puzzled wonder might be appropriate.

Style and form of the poem

Dickinson uses the four-line stanza of the ballad or the hymn. An interesting stylistic feature is the repeated use of 'And' in the poem, especially in stanzas 4 and 5. This creates a sense of forward motion, as if the 'I' was powerless before the experience. Another notable effect is the repetition of the words 'treading' (line 3) and 'beating' (line 7) and the use of the dash after each use of these words, which emphasises the insistent nature of the noise.

Thinking about the poem

1   The poem tells a story. What, according to the speaker, happens in the opening two stanzas of the poem?

2   What is the effect of the repetition of 'treading' in line 3 and 'beating' in line 7?

3   In the third stanza the speaker says that the Mourners creaked across her Soul with 'Boots of Lead' (lines 10–11). What feeling is created by this description?

4   In terms of a person in a coffin, does it make sense to suggest that the whole of one's being might be reduced to the sensation of hearing, as one moves from life into death (lines 13–14)? Explain your answer.

5   The most dramatic moment of the poem occurs in stanza 5. Explain in your own words what happens.

6   In line 1 the poet uses the word 'Brain'; in line 8 it is 'Mind'; and 'Soul' is used in line 10. In your opinion, how do these changes contribute to the meaning of the poem? Explain your answer.

7   What, in your view, is the effect of the repeated use of the word 'and' in the poem?

8   Which of the following statements is closest to your interpretation of the poem?
    ● It is a poem about a funeral.
    ● It is a poem about a nervous breakdown.
    ● It is a poem about the limits of the imagination.
    You may choose more than one but you must explain your choice.

9   Prepare a reading of the poem that is calm and reflective. Prepare another that is panic-struck. Which reading, in your view, best captures the spirit of the poem?

10 Consider the use of the words 'Felt' and 'Brain' in the first line of the poem. What other words might Dickinson have used? What is the effect of using these words? Explain your answer.

11 Consider **two** examples of the use of the dash in the poem and comment on their effectiveness.

12 'And Finished, knowing – then –' (line 20). What is your understanding of the final line of the poem?

Personal response

1   You have been asked to make a short film to accompany a reading of the poem. What music, sound effects, colour, images, etc. would you use to create the atmosphere of the poem? Explain your choices.

2   Suggest an alternative title for the poem. Explain your suggestion.

snapshot

Startling perspective

Description of funeral

Imagery of heaviness and contraction

Imagery of falling

Terrifying, isolating experience

I Felt a Funeral, in my Brain

Experience is physical, psychological and spiritual

Use of 'and' and repetition creates sense of being overwhelmed

Theme of death and dying

Theme of breakdown

Ends on a note of uncertainty

A Bird came down the Walk

A Bird came down the Walk –
He did not know I saw –
He bit an Angleworm in halves
And ate the fellow, raw.

And then he drank a Dew   5
From a convenient Grass –
And then hopped sidewise to the Wall
To let a Beetle pass –

He glanced with rapid eyes
That hurried all around –   10
They looked like frightened beads, I thought –
He stirred his Velvet Head

Like one in danger, Cautious,
I offered him a Crumb
And he unrolled his feathers   15
And rowed him softer home –

Than Oars divide the Ocean,
Too silver for a seam –
Or Butterflies, off Banks of Noon
Leap, plashless as they swim.   20

Glossary		
1	*Walk*: sidewalk, footpath
3	*Angleworm*: a worm used as fish bait in angling
7	*sidewise*: sideways, towards one side
18	*Too silver for a seam*: the ocean's surface is so silvery that no division (such as made by oars) can be seen
20	*plashless*: making no disturbance

Guidelines

The poet observes a bird. She offers him a crumb. The bird flies away. In her poetry, Dickinson describes many small moments in life, especially in meetings of the human and the animal world, which have a feeling of accident, surprise and favour about them.

Stanzas 1 and 2

In the first stanza the narrator tells us of the bird straying into the human realm by coming down 'the Walk' (line 1). The narrator is unobserved by the bird and registers an amused surprise at the bird eating a 'raw' worm (line 4).

The narrator continues to observe the bird in stanza 2. Having dined, the bird quenches his thirst by drinking from the dewy grass. By referring to 'a Dew', Dickinson particularises the image, and creates the impression of observing the event through a microscope, as a scientist might do.

Having eaten and drunk his fill, the bird courteously steps aside to 'let a Beetle pass' (line 8). This image captures the essence of Dickinson's technique in the poem. On one hand, she observes the bird with a scientist's eye. On the other, she treats the events in a whimsical manner, by attributing human qualities and motives to the actions of the bird.

Stanza 3

In the third stanza, there is a change in perspective. The bird is no longer the gentleman diner. Now his movements suggest the nervousness of one who might himself fall prey to a predator. The phrase 'Velvet Head' (line 12), accurately capturing the texture and appearance of the head feathers, also suggests the beauty of the bird.

Stanzas 4 and 5

Sympathetic to the bird's fears, the observer moves to allay them by offering him a crumb. In using the word 'Cautious' (line 13) to refer to both the bird and the observer, Dickinson creates a sense of identification between them. Despite this, the proffered gift is not taken and the bird flies away.

The flight is not undertaken in panic. The sense of grace and ease in the flight of the bird is mirrored in the language of these lines (15–20), creating an impression of gentle motion. Although the bird flies away, there is little sense of disappointment in the poem's conclusion. The observer takes pleasure in their accidental encounter. The vocabulary of the final stanza (Ocean, silver, Butterflies, Noon, Leap, swim) suggests a life of innocent, carefree pleasure. Like an Impressionist painting, there is harmony of air, water and light.

Emily Dickinson

Form of the poem

The poem is written in four-line, rhyming stanzas. The long vowel sounds create a sense of quiet and hush. In this poem the dash is used to create pauses but it does not have the jarring effect that is evident in other poems. The overall effect of the poem is one of dreamy gentleness.

Thinking about the poem

1   What words and phrases in the poem convey the bird as (a) a predator; (b) a gentleman; and (c) prey? What is the poet's attitude to the bird in each of these guises?

2   The use and placing of the word 'Cautious' in line 13 is often admired by critics. Why, do you think, is this so?

3   The poem concludes with images of rowing and swimming. What do they suggest about the flight of the bird? What do they tell us about Dickinson? Explain your answer.

4   a) Where, in your view, is the humour and amusement of the poet most evident? Explain your answer.

    b) Do rhyme and punctuation contribute to the humour of the poem? Explain your answer.

5   'In the poem, we see how Dickinson views the world with the eye of a scientist and the eye of an artist.' Give your response to this assessment of the poem.

6   What impression of Dickinson do you form from reading the poem? Explain your answer.

Personal response

1   Your class is preparing an anthology of poems about nature. Discuss, in pairs or small groups, why you would (or would not) choose to include this poem.

2   You are the speaker in the poem, write a diary account about your visit to the garden.

Before you read 'I heard a Fly buzz – when I died'

Emily Dickinson's poem 'I heard a Fly buzz – when I died' is on page 23. Think about a deathbed scene that you have seen in a film. Working with a partner, describe the atmosphere of the scene and the behaviour of the characters. Keep that scene in mind as you read the next poem.

I heard a Fly buzz – when I died

I heard a Fly buzz – when I died –
The stillness in the Room
Was like the Stillness in the Air –
Between the Heaves of Storm –

The Eyes around – had wrung them dry –   5
And Breaths were gathering firm
For that last Onset – when the King
Be witnessed – in the Room –

I willed my Keepsakes – Signed away
What portion of me be   10
Assignable – and then it was
There interposed a Fly –

With Blue – uncertain stumbling Buzz –
Between the light – and me –
And then the Windows failed – and then   15
I could not see to see –

Emily Dickinson

Glossary		
4	*Heaves:* wind surges of a storm	
5	*Eyes around:* the mourners around the bed keeping watch	
7	*last Onset:* final assault of death	
7	*the King:* God	
8	*Be witnessed:* inspired by their religious faith, all waited for the moment of death when, they believed, God would be present in the room (in the Calvinist tradition the moment of death is the moment the soul faces the judgement of God)	
9	*Keepsakes:* mementoes or souvenirs	
11	*Assignable:* could be left or bequeathed	
12	*interposed:* came between things; here, the fly got between the dying person and the solemn moment of death	
13	*Blue:* there is no noun to follow the adjective 'Blue' so it carries over to 'Buzz' at the end of the line and suggests a confused or disturbed apprehension of the world	

Guidelines

Dickinson's fascination with death again provides the subject matter of this poem. It is written in the past tense, in the voice of the dying person, and describes the moment of death.

Commentary

Stanza 1

The startling perspective in the poem is announced in the first line: 'I heard a Fly buzz – when I died – '. The poem explores the moment of death. This moment is dominated, from the dying person's perspective, by the buzzing of a fly in the death-room. The fly interrupted the temporary silence in the room.

Stanza 2

In the second stanza we are told that, as death approached, the mourners gathered themselves and, inspired by their religious faith, waited for the moment when their God ('the King', line 7) would 'Be witnessed – in the Room' (line 8). In the Calvinist tradition, the moment of death is the moment when the soul faces God's judgement. The mourners around the deathbed are filled with expectancy; the phrase 'Be witnessed' suggests the solemnity of a court.

Stanza 3

The dying person had tidied up her legal affairs and, thus prepared, waited for the moment of death. However, it was not the presence of God coming to claim her soul that filled her consciousness, but a Fly who 'interposed' (line 12). The arrival of the fly, a symbol of human decay and corruption, suggests that death cannot be managed, arranged or ordered. The word 'interposed' implies that the fly got between the dying person and the solemn moment of death.

Stanza 4

In the final stanza, as the moment of death is described, the syntax is fractured, suggesting the failure of consciousness as sight and sound blur and become one. As the last act in the drama of life, the buzzing fly suggests life as comedy rather than tragedy. The buzzing of the fly is unexpected, it is like a drunkard disturbing the solemnity of an important occasion. The stumbling, buzzing fly comes between the dying person's sight and the source of light. And then, as suggested by the imagery of light and darkness, the dying person was plunged into the darkness of death, and the moment had passed.

The poem is deliberately ambiguous on the nature of the light that the fly obscured. Was it natural or divine light? Were 'the Windows' of line 15 the eyes, the windows of the soul, or the windows of the room? The ending of the poem, and the anti-climax it describes, suggests that humans have no way of knowing if the immortal life with God that their faith professes actually exists. The final line implies that the dying person is robbed of both sight and understanding, a finality emphasised by the rhyme of 'me' and 'see' in this stanza. Is this the message of the voice from the dead – after dying all is darkness and emptiness? Is that the significance of the dash that ends the poem? For those who identify the narrator of the poem with Dickinson, the poem appears to offer evidence of her lack of faith in an afterlife with God.

Form of the poem

As befits a poem on a religious theme, 'I heard a Fly buzz' is written in the metre of a hymn, with a four-line stanza and a regular rhyming scheme. However, the use of the dash, with its jarring effect, and run-on lines takes away the sing-song effect of the form.

Thinking about the poem

1 What is the story that the poem tells?
2 In the second stanza what is the attitude of the mourners as they wait for the death of the narrator? Explain your answer.
3 What words and phrases in stanza 3 suggest that the speaker prepared carefully for her death?
4 What is the effect of the appearance of the fly in the room at the moment when 'the King' (line 7) is expected?
5 What happens at the end of the poem?
6 Given the ending, how would you describe the tone of the poem: amused, irritated, fearful, puzzled or disappointed? Explain your choice.
7 Consider each of these readings of the poem. Which of them, if any, corresponds to your own?
    ● The fly cheats the dying person of a glimpse of God before the moment of death.
    ● The appearance of the fly is a reminder that death cannot be controlled and managed.
    ● The poem calls into question faith in God and an eternal life.
    Explain your answer.
8 On the evidence of this poem, what kind of person do you imagine Dickinson to have been? Explain your answer.

9   Which of Dickinson's other poems bears the closest resemblance to this one? Explain your answer.

10 'I heard a Fly buzz – when I died –' (line 1). In your view, is this an effective opening to the poem? Explain your answer.

11 'when the King / Be witnessed' (lines 7–8). What view of death is suggested by these lines?

12 Comment on the use of the word 'stumbling' in line 13: 'With Blue – uncertain stumbling Buzz –'.

Personal response

1   Imagine that you are one of the mourners in the room. Write a letter to a friend in which you describe the moment of death and the feeling in the room afterwards.

2   You are asked to make a video version of the poem for YouTube. Describe as clearly as you can what your finished video will look and sound like.

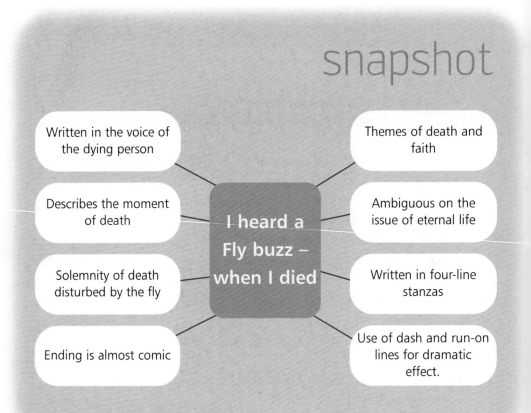

snapshot

Written in the voice of the dying person

Themes of death and faith

Describes the moment of death

Ambiguous on the issue of eternal life

I heard a Fly buzz – when I died

Solemnity of death disturbed by the fly

Written in four-line stanzas

Ending is almost comic

Use of dash and run-on lines for dramatic effect.

The Soul has Bandaged moments

The Soul has Bandaged moments –
When too appalled to stir –
She feels some ghastly Fright come up
And stop to look at her –

Salute her – with long fingers –   5
Caress her freezing hair –
Sip, Goblin, from the very lips
The Lover – hovered – o'er –
Unworthy, that a thought so mean
Accost a Theme – so – fair –   10

The soul has moments of Escape –
When bursting all the doors –
She dances like a Bomb, abroad,
And swings upon the Hours,

As do the Bee – delirious borne –   15
Long Dungeoned from his Rose –
Touch Liberty – then know no more,
But Noon, and Paradise –

The Soul's retaken moments –
When, Felon led along,   20
With shackles on the plumed feet,
And staples, in the Song,

The Horror welcomes her, again,
These, are not brayed of Tongue –

Glossary

7	*Goblin*: an ugly demon
10	*Accost*: to approach and speak to someone; and also to solicit sexually
13	*abroad*: in different directions; out of doors
16	*Dungeoned*: imprisoned
20	*Felon*: convict or prisoner
21	*shackles*: rings fixed around a prisoner's ankles and joined by a chain
21	*plumed feet*: feathered feet; the image calls to mind the figure of Mercury, the messenger of the Gods, who had winged sandals
24	*These*: refers back to the 'retaken moments' of line 19
24	*not brayed of Tongue*: not spoken about or publicised

Guidelines

'The Soul has Bandaged moments' explores the contrasting highs and lows of the inner life. Images of horror and fright are contrasted with images of fulfilled happiness. Images of imprisonment are contrasted with images of freedom. The poem begins with the figure of Fright and ends with the figure of Horror, suggesting that the soul experiences more anguish than joy.

The poem may be read in a number of different, if related, ways: in psychological terms as an exploration of depression and elation; in spiritual terms as an exploration of hope and despair; in sexual terms as an exploration of the conflict between freedom and restraint; or in artistic terms as an exploration of the absence and presence of inspiration.

Commentary

Stanzas 1 and 2

'The Soul' is portrayed in the poem as a terrified woman, helpless before the attention of an unwelcome other: many critics interpret the 'Fright' of stanza 1 as death or death's servant. In stanza 2 the Fright is described as saluting and caressing the Soul's 'freezing hair' (line 6). The 'freezing hair' indicates the chill of fear and the coldness of death that the Soul experiences as the Fright pays her unwanted attention. The dashes of the opening lines of stanza 2 capture the increasing fear of the soul. The placing of the word 'unworthy' in line 9 makes the subject uncertain. Does it refer to the Lover, the Fright or the Soul herself? Does the word refer to the erotic turn the poem takes at this point?

Stanzas 3 and 4

Stanzas three and four break free of the atmosphere of threat, dread, claustrophobia and death that dominates the first two stanzas. Now the images suggest sensuous pleasure, freedom, warmth and fulfilment. The simile 'like a Bomb' (line 13), however, strikes a note of caution. The Soul's escape is too exuberant, too ecstatic. Like a bomb, it will explode and leave a sense of desolation. These two stanzas suggest an intense period of psychological elation and, perhaps, artistic energy.

Stanzas 5 and 6

The moments of escape come to an end and, like a prisoner, the Soul is welcomed again by 'The Horror' (line 23). The imagery of shackles and staples is striking and contrasts with the imagery of flight often used by Dickinson to denote joy and happiness. The final two stanzas express the poem's despairing point of view: the interior life – psychological, spiritual, artistic, erotic – is characterised by feelings of oppression and despair, punctuated by periods of respite.

The final line states that these moments when the Soul is a prisoner 'are not brayed of Tongue'. In other words, they are not talked about. This may suggest that the subject of depression and despair is not one which is spoken of in public, and to do so would be to 'bray' or to speak in a way that might be considered rough and uncouth. Thus, the experience of depression is, essentially, a lonely and isolating one. However, the tone of the final line can be read as a proud declaration of strength and pride.

Form of the poem

The poem is divided into three sections, each containing two stanzas. Each section describes a condition of the soul. The first section (stanzas 1 and 2) suggests constraint and violation; the second (stanzas 3 and 4) celebrates the delirium of freedom; the third (stanzas 5 and 6) describes the soul's recapture.

The poem departs from Dickinson's usual four-line stanzas with one verse of six lines and a final concluding couplet. In the second stanza, the repetition of 'her', the alliteration and the hissing 's' sound combine to create a feeling of dread.

Thinking about the poem

1   'The Soul has Bandaged moments' (line 1). Consider the possible meanings of 'Bandaged'. What does the word suggest about the condition of the Soul?

2   How is the figure of Fright portrayed (lines 3–6)? What words capture the Soul's terror before this Fright?

3   The image of Fright, the cold stranger menacing the Soul (portrayed as a vulnerable young girl), is taken from the tradition of Gothic Romance. Do you think that the word 'Goblin' (line 7) adds or takes away from the atmosphere of horror?

4   a) Who, do you think, is the 'Lover' referred to in line 8?
     b) Who or what is 'Unworthy' (line 9)? Explain your answers.

5   In your view, what does the word 'Bomb' (line 13) suggest about the nature of the Soul's escape described in stanza 3?

6   In stanza 4 the words 'Noon' and 'Paradise' are used as shorthand for happiness and fulfilment. Do you think that they are effective? Explain your answer.

7   Explain, as clearly as you can, what Dickinson means by the 'retaken moments' (line 19) of the Soul?

8   a) What, in your view, does Dickinson have in mind in her reference to 'The Horror' in line 23 of the poem?
     b) Does the verb 'welcomes' work in this line? Explain your answer.

9   In your view, what does the final line suggest about the sufferer's experience of depression? Give reasons for your answer.

10   Some critics read the poem as expressing the poet's depression at the loss of her creativity. What parts of the poem most support this reading?

11   Read the poem aloud. Do you think that the rhythm suits the mood of the poem? Explain your answer.

12   There is no first-person pronoun in the poem and, in the eyes of some critics, this lessens the impact of the poem. Do you agree with their point of view? Give reasons for your answer.

Personal response

1   Complete the following statements to describe your response to the poem:
     ● I found the poem enjoyable because . . .
     ● I found the poem depressing because . . .
     ● I found the poem interesting because . . .

2   If you were asked to give a talk outlining the main ideas in this poem, what points would you emphasise?

I could bring You Jewels – had I a mind to

I could bring You Jewels – had I a mind to –
But You have enough – of those –
I could bring You Odors from St. Domingo –
Colors – from Vera Cruz –

Berries of the Bahamas – have I –   5
But this little Blaze
Flickering to itself – in the Meadow –
Suits me – more than those –

Never a Fellow matched this Topaz –
And his Emerald Swing –   10
Dower itself – for Bobadilo –
Better – Could I bring?

Glossary	
3	*St. Domingo*: San (or Santo) Domingo, capital of the Dominican Republic. The name is intended to suggest somewhere exotic. Like all the places mentioned in the poem, it is associated with the Spanish conquest of South America: the city was given its name by Christopher Columbus (1451–1506)
4	*Vera Cruz*: port in Mexico, founded by Hernán Cortés (1485–1547); an exotic place known for its colourful houses and tropical plants and flowers
5	*Bahamas*: a group of islands in the West Indies, where Columbus first made landfall in the New World in 1492; another exotic location
9	*Topaz*: a gem famous for its lustre and beautiful colours
10	*Emerald*: a precious stone, green in colour
11	*Dower*: gift, often used to describe the wealth brought to a man by a woman on their marriage
11	*Bobadilo*: Francisco de Bobadilla (d.1502), the Spaniard sent by Isabella and Ferdinand of Spain in 1499 to San Domingo to take over from Columbus as governor of the Indies. Bobadilla ordered Columbus to be returned to Spain in shackles and seized his gold and treasures

Guidelines

Although Dickinson is often described as a recluse, she had a wide circle of friends and corresponded with many of them throughout her life. Many of her letters took the form of poems, or were written to accompany small gifts that she enclosed. These poems, many of them written as riddles, show the playful and humorous sides of Dickinson's personality. Some of the letters/poems were clearly intended as tokens of her love, though she took considerable pains to disguise the identity of her beloved. 'I could bring You Jewels' is a good example of her letter-poems.

Commentary

Stanzas 1 and 2

The opening line of the poem strikes a note of confidence and playfulness, which is sustained to the end of the poem, making this the most joyful of Dickinson's poems on the Leaving Certificate course. The poem is also different in that it focuses on a relationship, rather than on the individual consciousness of the speaker.

In the first two stanzas the speaker considers the gift she will offer her beloved, the 'You' of the poem. She settles on a small meadow flower. The chosen gift is a mark of the speaker's freedom and uniqueness, and a reflection, perhaps, of her unshowy personality. The note of confidence and self-ease is striking in this choice. In the first stanza, the luxury of considering exotic gifts is reflected in the long lines that Dickinson employs. As she settles on her gift, the lines get shorter and the tone more decisive.

Stanza 3

A jaunty, confident tone is evident in the use of the word 'Fellow' in line 9. The concluding rhetorical question suggests that the flower is the best gift she could offer. Notice how, in this final stanza, the assured, confident tone is emphasised in the use of the word 'Never' (line 9) and in the rhyming of 'Swing' and 'bring', which closes her argument with a ring of authority. In its playful, assured way, the poem establishes that the true value of gifts and the true nature of riches cannot be measured in material terms.

Form of the poem

Dickinson employs the four-line stanza with the rhyme occurring between lines 2 and 4. Unlike other of her poems, there is a conversational feel to the opening lines, achieved by the length of the line and the phrase 'had I a mind to'. This is Dickinson at her most relaxed. As the poem proceeds, the tone becomes less conversational and concludes with the magisterial four-word last line.

Thinking about the poem

1 What do you learn about the 'You' of the poem, the person to whom the poem is addressed, from the first two lines? Explain your answer.

2 What, in your view, is the effect of the place names – St Domingo, Vera Cruz, Bahamas – used in lines 3 to 5?

3 In the first five lines a number of potential gifts are rejected. How does the gift that is eventually selected differ from them?

4 a) In your view, what does the choice of gift tell you about the speaker?
   b) What does it suggest about the nature of the relationship between the lovers?

5 What view of riches is suggested by the poem? Explain your answer.

6 'The voice of the poem shows an absolute certainty and confidence in herself, in her choice of gift and in her beloved.' Give your response to this assessment of the poem.

7 What, in your view, is the mood of the poem?

Personal response

1 Using 'I could bring You Jewels' as a model, write your own love poem.

2 You have been asked to find a poem to read at a school event. Would you choose this one? Explain your answer.

A narrow Fellow in the Grass

A narrow Fellow in the Grass
Occasionally rides –
You may have met Him – did you not
His notice sudden is –

The Grass divides as with a Comb –   5
A spotted shaft is seen –
And then it closes at your feet
And opens further on –

He likes a Boggy Acre
A Floor too cool for Corn –   10
Yet when a Boy, and Barefoot –
I more than once at Noon
Have passed, I thought, a Whip lash
Unbraiding in the Sun
When stooping to secure it   15
It wrinkled, and was gone –

Several of Nature's People
I know, and they know me –
I feel for them a transport
Of cordiality –   20
But never met this Fellow
Attended, or alone
Without a tighter breathing
And Zero at the Bone –

Glossary

6	*spotted shaft*: the long thin mottled body of the snake
13	*Whip lash*: the part of the whip used for striking or lashing
14	*Unbraiding*: untwining like the leather thongs of a lash
19	*transport*: a strong emotion

Guidelines

This was one of the few poems published during Dickinson's life. It was published under the title 'Snake', though the word is never used in the poem. (In a letter discussing the poem, written in 1866, Dickinson did, however, refer to 'my Snake'.) Dickinson wrote many poems on the birds and small creatures that she observed in her garden. Her attitude to animals is often one of amused absorption. However, the snake arouses a terrified fascination. Interestingly, the poem is written in the persona of a male.

Commentary

Stanza 1

The opening two lines of the poem strike an off-hand note, as if the reader has joined a casual conversation. The word 'Fellow', for example, creates a sense of easy familiarity. By the fourth line, the tone has altered. The abruptness of line 4: 'His notice sudden is', and the menacing 's' sounds it contains, indicate an absence of fellow-feeling in the speaker for the snake. On second reading, it may well be the figure of the Devil on horseback that is brought to mind by the stanza's imagery.

Stanzas 2 and 3

The imagery in stanza 2 hints at the secrecy, danger and unpredictability of the snake. The word 'shaft' (line 6) suggests the danger and speed of an arrow-shaft.

The third, eight-line, central stanza returns to the casual-seeming air of the opening line and describes the favoured habitat of the snake. The poem changes direction in this stanza. There is a switch to the past tense as the speaker recalls a boyhood memory. The word 'Barefoot' (line 11) suggests the vulnerability and simplicity of the boy, who is no match for the crafty snake.

Stanzas 4 and 5

In the fourth stanza the speaker states that he knows 'Several of Nature's People' (line 17) and they know him, and he professes for them 'a transport / Of cordiality' (lines 19–20). There is a whimsical, even comic, air to this stanza. However, the snake stands apart from the 'Several of Nature's People' and the speaker's attitude to the snake is caught in the celebrated final stanza.

The last line of the poem, 'And Zero at the Bone – ', catches the inner terror caused in the speaker by this animal. The combination of the abstract 'Zero', with its association of void and emptiness, and the concrete 'bone' captures the physical sensation of a terror that is almost beyond words. The use of the word 'Fellow' in the final stanza reads as a measured irony.

Adam and Eve

In responding to a poem about a snake, it is almost impossible to ignore the figure of the snake in the story of Adam and Eve. There, the serpent, the Devil in disguise, deceived Adam and Eve into acting against God's command. This story predisposes us to view the snake as an evil deceiver.

Form of the poem

Dickinson rarely strays from the four-line stanza of the ballad or the hymn. When she does, as in the third stanza of this poem, there is very little innovation in the stanza form. Her success as a poet comes in the dramatic use of the dash, and the change in tone she achieves through the sound of words and her startling imagery, as evident in the final line of the poem.

Thinking about the poem

1 The word 'Fellow' (lines 1 and 21) has a feeling of familiarity about it. Does it capture the speaker's attitude to the snake? Explain your answer.

2 In six lines (lines 3–8), Dickinson succeeds in suggesting the danger, unpredictability and secrecy of the snake. How, in your opinion, does she do this?

3 What, in your view, does the snake's habitat (lines 9–10) tell us about him?

4 In your view, which of the following ideas are associated with the adjective 'Barefoot' in line 11: hardiness, innocence, vulnerability and/or foolishness? Explain your choice.

5 What do the words 'Whip lash' (line 13) suggest about the snake? Explain your answer.

6 a) What is the speaker's relationship with 'Nature's People', as described in stanza 4?

   b) In your view, is there anything contradictory in the idea of 'a transport of cordiality'?

7 What, do you think, is the effect of the 'But' placed at the opening of the fifth stanza?

8 Dickinson substitutes her phrase 'Zero at the Bone' (line 24) for the more usual 'chilled to the bone'. In your view, what does she gain by doing so?

9 Show how Dickinson uses rhythm and sound to capture the movements of the snake.

10 What, if anything, does the snake symbolise in the poem? Explain your answer.

Personal response

1 Your class is publishing this poem on a website. In pairs, discuss the design of the page and what images should accompany the poem.

2 Imagine that you are editing this poem, you can make any changes to the poem you deem necessary. What changes would you make and why?

I taste a liquor never brewed

I taste a liquor never brewed –
From Tankards scooped in Pearl –
Not all the Vats upon the Rhine
Yield such an Alcohol!

Inebriate of Air – am I –   5
And Debauchee of Dew –
Reeling – thro endless summer days –
From inns of Molten Blue –

When 'Landlords' turn the drunken Bee
Out of the Foxglove's door –   10
When Butterflies – renounce their 'drams' –
I shall but drink the more!

Till Seraphs swing their snowy Hats –
And Saints – to windows run –
To see the little Tippler   15
Leaning against the – Sun –

Emily Dickinson

Glossary		
3	*Vats:*	vessels for storing liquid, for example, wine
3	*Rhine*:	a wine region of Germany on the banks of the River Rhine; there is another draft of this poem in which line 3 reads: 'Not all the Frankfort berries'
5	*Inebriate*:	intoxicated
6	*Debauchee*:	a person who pursues pleasure in a reckless way
8	*Molten*:	melted; presumably, the shimmering effect on the blue sky caused by the heat of the sun
10	*Foxglove*:	a tall purple or white flowered plant
11	*'drams'*:	a small measure of alcohol
13	*Seraphs*:	angels
15	*Tippler*:	a frequent drinker (of alcohol)
16	*Leaning . . . Sun*:	in the other draft of the poem, the final line reads 'From Manzanilla come.'

Guidelines

The poem was first published anonymously on 4 May 1861 in the *Springfield Republican* under the title 'The May Wine'. Two lines were altered by the editor to achieve an exact rhyme, and another line was changed to make the meaning clearer. Richard Sewell, Dickinson's biographer, describes it as 'a rapturous poem about summer'. The central metaphor of intoxication is ironic, given that Dickinson grew up in a Puritan household, and her father was a supporter of the Temperance League. A further irony is that the poem was written in the common rhythm of hymns.

Commentary

The central metaphor of the poem is one of intoxication brought on by a joyous appreciation of life. The poem describes the speaker's sense of delight in the beauty of the world around her. Dickinson strikes an exaggerated, playful tone, established from the first line, 'I taste a liquor never brewed'. The riddling quality of this line and the extravagance of the imagery capture the mood of dizzy happiness that infuses the poem. In the third stanza, the imagery of flowers as inns or taverns and bees as drunkards continues the vein of cartoon humour evident throughout the poem.

In the final stanza Dickinson does not present the world's beauty as a sign of God's creativity. The inhabitants of heaven are presented as faintly ridiculous, enclosed and, perhaps, envious of the freedom and of 'the little Tippler' (line 15), whose pose, leaning against the sun, strikes a note of comic rebelliousness, applauded by the angels as they swing their hats to honour her.

In many of her poems, the 'I' persona is shown as starving or thirsting. This poem is a rarity in Dickinson's work in that it celebrates the joy of excess, a reckless, indulgent joy captured in the word 'Debauchee' (line 6).

Christian interpretation

For some critics, the poem is not a celebration of excess and rebelliousness. They read the 'Sun' of the final stanza as a symbol of Christ. In this reading, the speaker announces an intention to enjoy the beauty of the world until she comes into the company of Christ, where her arrival will be greeted by the watching angels and saints.

Form of the poem

The poem is written in the common metre of hymns and flows along without any of the dramatic pauses or changes of tone evident in many of Dickinson's other poems.

1 a) What kind of tankards are, in your view, 'scooped in Pearl' (line 2)?

   b) What does this suggest about the liquor to be drunk from them? Explain your answer.

2 Identify the words and phrases in the poem that are associated with intoxication. What, according to the second stanza, is the cause of the speaker's intoxication?

3 In your opinion, is the association of drunkenness with bees (lines 9–10) apt? Explain your answer.

4 'I shall but drink the more!' (line 12). What, in your view, is the tone of this declaration?

5 What image of heaven is presented in stanza 4? In your view, is it an effective image?

6 One critic remarked that the Sun in stanza 4 is treated as a celestial lamppost. Would you agree that the entire poem is marked by a similar spirit of whimsy and joy? Explain your answer.

7 Comment on the use of comic exaggeration in the poem. What phrases strike you as being particularly humorous?

8 Compare the celebration of the summer sun, in this poem, with the meditation on winter light in 'There's a certain Slant of light'.

Personal response

1 Working in pairs, put together a collection of images that creates a similar mood to that of the poem.

2 You have been asked to review this poem for a literary magazine. In less than 300 words try to capture your thoughts.

Emily Dickinson

After great pain, a formal feeling comes

After great pain, a formal feeling comes –
The Nerves sit ceremonious, like Tombs –
The stiff Heart questions was it He, that bore,
And Yesterday, or Centuries before?

The Feet, mechanical, go round –   5
Of Ground, or Air, or Ought –
A Wooden way
Regardless grown,
A Quartz contentment, like a stone –

This is the Hour of Lead –   10
Remembered, if outlived,
As Freezing persons, recollect the Snow –
First – Chill – then Stupor – then the letting go –

Glossary	
3	*He*: the reference is ambiguous, it could refer to the 'stiff Heart' or to Christ, whose suffering is brought to mind by the experience of great pain
3	*bore*: has two possible meanings: to bear suffering or to accept blame
4	*And … before*: the 'stiff Heart' feels disoriented, not able to distinguish between recent time ('Yesterday') and past time ('Centuries before')
6	*or Ought*: or anything
7	*a Wooden way*: the phrase suggests the unnatural movements of a puppet; it also suggests Christ's stumbling on the Way of the Cross
9	*Quartz*: a very hard mineral
13	*Stupor*: a dazed condition

Guidelines

'After great pain' was written in 1862, a year in which Dickinson wrote 366 poems. Many commentators believe that she was on the edge of madness during this time. This is another poem that explores the effects of anguish upon the individual. The source of the pain referred to in line 1 is not disclosed. It may be the result of loneliness, separation or bereavement, all of which Dickinson experienced. The absence of personal statement gives the poem a universal quality, as if the poet is speaking for all who have suffered great pain.

Commentary

Stanzas 1 and 2

The opening line strikes a note of dignified solemnity. The nature of the 'great pain' is not described. Interestingly, the opening line suggests that such pain leads not to a loss of control but to the constraint of formality. However, the sense of control is lost in the second stanza with its fragmented phrases and incomplete meanings. The phrasing and punctuation of the second stanza suggest a series of unconnected sensations and thoughts, and reflect the way in which pain interrupts the mind's ability to make sense of experience and derive meaning from it. The final line of the stanza suggests that great pain results in a hard, stone-like insensitivity, which brings its own kind of contentment, 'A Quartz contentment, like a stone'. The word 'contentment' is almost ironic.

Stanza 3

The opening line of the third stanza defines the nature of this 'contentment': it is the 'Hour of Lead'. It is the period of heavy and deadening oppression when all human sensations become frozen. This period is not forgotten, even if the sufferer survives it. The memory of this oppression is likened to 'Freezing persons' recollecting 'the Snow' (line 12). The continuous present of the final line means that the reader cannot determine if the freezing person has survived the ordeal, or if it continues. Here, as in the rest of the poem, the thought is incomplete.

Form of the poem

In keeping with its theme, 'After great pain' moves away from the regularity of the ballad and hymn form. The long lines of the opening stanza, with their steady stoicism and harmonious sounds, are in contrast to the staccato movement of stanza 2. Although the thought of the poem may be incomplete, each stanza concludes with a full rhyme that mirrors the formality mentioned in the first line of the poem.

Emily Dickinson

Thinking about the poem

1 'After great pain, a formal feeling comes –' (line 1). Explain, as clearly as you can, what is meant by 'formal' in this context?

2 What, in your view, is the effect of comparing the nerves, which convey feelings and sensations from the body to the brain, to tombs (line 2)?

3 The meaning of lines 3 and 4 is hard to unravel, due to the conciseness of the language. Give careful consideration to each of the following questions.

   a) What does the adjective 'stiff' suggest about the Heart?

   b) Does the Heart feel in some way guilty?

   c) If 'He' does not refer to the Heart, does it refer to Christ? Could it refer to both?

   d) Does 'bore' suggest suffering or blame? Might it suggest both?

   e) Does the line 'And Yesterday, or Centuries before?' suggest the Heart's confusion, or the fact that Christ's suffering is both past and present?

   In each case, explain your answer.

4 How, in stanza 2, is the dazed condition of the victim of great pain suggested? What words are particularly effective?

5 In your view, what kind of contentment is a 'Quartz contentment' (line 9)?

6 How well, do you think, does the phrase 'Hour of Lead' (line 10) sum up the mental and physical condition of the sufferer?

7 The final image of the poem 'Chill – then Stupor – then the letting go –' (line 13) is much admired. Do you read it as a pessimistic or an optimistic ending? Explain your answer.

8 Read the poem aloud. What sounds contribute to the mood of the poem?

Personal response

1 Write a short letter to Emily Dickinson telling her about your thoughts and feelings on this poem. Refer to the text of the poem in your letter.

2 In pairs, create an interview set-up. Both partners write two questions each that they would like to ask Emily Dickinson. Take turns at being the interviewer and the poet. Write down two interesting things that arose from this process about either the poem or the poet. Discuss these in class.

3 'What Dickinson describes in "After great pain" is the numbed feeling that is caused by emotional or spiritual pain.' Give your response to this statement.

Exam-Style Questions

1   'Emily Dickinson's poetry explores extreme states of mind and emotion in an unusual way.' Discuss this statement.

2   Discuss the view that Dickinson's fascination with death leads to her best writing.

3   'It is less what Emily Dickinson has to say than her manner of saying it that is interesting.' Give your view of this statement.

4   From your reading of her poetry, do you agree that Dickinson's poetry offers us a glimpse into a fascinating mind and a fascinating writer?

5   'The loss of love and the loss of faith are dominant themes in Dickinson's poetry.' Discuss this view.

6   'Even when she is dealing with serious themes, Dickinson's poetry is marked by a sense of wit and a sense of humour.' Discuss this view of Dickinson's poetry.

7   'In Dickinson's poetry we see the world through the eye of an artist and the eye of a scientist.' Discuss this view of Dickinson's poetry.

8   'Dickinson's poetry is not hard to understand. It is, however, complex.' Give your response to this statement.

9   What, in your experience, is the effect of reading Dickinson's poetry?

10 'Dickinson's poetry is the poetry of small details and large ideas.' Discuss.

11 Write an introduction to Dickinson's poetry for readers new to her poetry. You should cover the themes and preoccupations of her poetry and how you responded to her use of language and imagery in the poems you studied.
    Some of the following areas might be covered in your introduction:
    ● Her exploration of extreme states of mind.
    ● Her exploration of death and dying.
    ● The importance of the soul.
    ● Her fondness for definition.
    ● Her observations of nature.
    ● The power and freshness of her language.
    ● Her epigrammatic style.
    ● Her creative use of the dash and capitalised nouns.

Emily Dickinson

43

12 'What Emily Dickinson's poetry means to me.' Write an essay in response to this title. You should include a discussion of her themes and the way she expresses them. Support the points you make by reference to the poetry on your course.

Some of the following areas might be included:

- Her treatment of hope and despair.
- Her search for definition.
- Her attitude to death and mortality.
- The psychological drama of her poems.
- The lack of a firm conclusion.
- Her sense of nature.
- The craft of her poetry.

13 Write a letter to a friend outlining your experience of studying the poetry of Emily Dickinson. You should refer to her themes and the way she expresses them. Support the points you make by reference to the poetry on your course.

Material might be drawn from the following:

- Her family and religious background.
- The contrast between her sedate life and the drama of her poetry.
- Her tone and style.
- Her interest in extreme emotions and psychological states.
- Her preoccupation with death.
- Her painter's eye for the details of nature.
- The lines and images that stay with you.

14 Write an essay in which you outline your reasons for liking or not liking the poetry of Emily Dickinson. You must refer to the poems on your course.

Some possible reasons for liking the poetry:

- The uniqueness of the poetic voice.
- The striking perspective of many of the poems.
- The vitality and energy of the writing.
- The impact of the poetry upon the reader.
- The wit and intelligence of Dickinson's writing.

Some possible reasons for not liking the poetry:

- The themes of death, isolation and despair.
- The absence of happiness in many of the poems.
- The sense of annihilation in many of the poems.
- The obsession with her own mind.
- The effect of the poems upon the reader.

Sample Essay

Write a letter to a friend outlining your experience of studying the poetry of Emily Dickinson. In your letter you should refer to her themes and the way she expresses them. Support the points you make by reference to the poetry on your course.

Dear Jane,

We have just finished reading the poetry of Emily Dickinson in class. What an amazing experience it has been. I feel I have been on an exhilarating but exhausting rollercoaster. What a fascinating poet and woman. I think Emily Dickinson proves the old saying true: never judge a book by its cover.

[Appropriate register used]

Viewing her life from the outside who could have guessed at the tumultuous seas of her mind? She came from a well-respected family in Amherst in New England. Her family were Calvinists. That makes me of think of a strict upbringing with a great deal of attention to saving your soul. But I don't think our idea of a religious tradition different from our own is ever really accurate, do you? It seems Emily enjoyed parties and visiting and dancing and several young men were interested in her. That doesn't seem too strict. In the school she attended, Mount Holyoke Female Seminary, she was a bit of a rebel, refusing to declare publicly her faith in God. That must have taken some courage. And I don't think she ever really settled the questions of belief in God and belief in the afterlife in her lifetime.

[Selective use of relevant biographical information]

She was a rebel in other ways, too. After she came home from boarding school, she opted out of some of the duties of someone in her position: receiving visitors and making endless social calls and doing mindless household chores. I like the sound of her – quietly determined and not bound by other peoples' rules. (She reminds me of you.) And then when she was around thirty, something must have happened to her, because she more or less withdrew into her own room, communicated with most of the outside world only through letters and began writing in a furious kind of way. I know I've often wanted to lock myself in my room but it doesn't last more than a few hours! And when I'm in a black mood I scribble in my diary, but she wrote 366 poems in 1862. What must have happened to her? We don't know and that adds to the fascination. Her sister and sister-in-law, Vinnie and Susan, destroyed all her correspondence after her death, as she had requested. I wish they hadn't! Luckily, they kept the thousand or more poems (a thousand poems!) they found in her writing desk.

[Personal response given]

And what poems they are – short sharp meditations on the world around her and the places she travelled to in her imagination. Those journeys were to the 'chillest land' and the 'strangest Sea' and she made them bravely and in solitude. I think I understand why hope was so important to her. If you undertake the kind of dangerous psychological journeys she took, you need to have something to fall back on, something that 'never stops – at all'. You want everything to turn out well for her. I almost cheered when I read 'I taste a liquor never brewed', how she drank in the happiness of summer days. Because those moments of happiness are rare enough in her poetry. And you hope that when she sent her beloved the little meadow flower, described in 'I could bring You Jewels – had I a mind to', her beloved sent her something equally charming back. Because more often than not the emotions in the poems are fearful and despairing. Even her little poem on the snake ends with the terrifying 'Zero at the Bone'.

[Good use of quotation in this paragraph]

The poems that made the greatest impact on me are the darker poems. 'After great pain, a formal feeling comes' is icy in its depiction of what I think was probably a broken heart and the numb feeling that comes with intense pain, so that you no longer want to cling to life: 'First – Chill – then Stupor – then the letting go – '. It is such a precise poem that you never doubt that Dickinson is writing about herself and her own experience even if she writes in an impersonal way. I think the impersonal style is a way of dealing with what would otherwise be too difficult to write about.

[More detailed discussion of a poem]

There is a similar feeling of chill in 'The Soul has Bandaged moments' (Isn't that the best title ever?!). I love the image of the 'freezing hair' and the dread caused by the unwanted advances of the Fright. Likewise the images of the 'shackles on the plumed feet' and the 'staples, in the Song'. It is like when Hope has been imprisoned and 'the little Bird that kept so many warm' is abashed in 'Hope' is the thing with feathers'. Is it a strange choice of word to say 'I love' such imagery? But that is the funny thing about a poem – even when it deals with psychological pain, you can admire the mind and the skill of the poet who created it. I feel a similar kind of admiration for the stately, stoical tone in which Emily describes the 'Heavenly Hurt' that comes with 'a certain Slant of light'. The light carrying the 'Seal Despair' cannot be countered or stopped and so must be endured. But she writes with such certainty and force that the poem carries Dickinson's own seal of authority. Her unusual punctuation adds to the sense that Dickinson will not be contradicted. She knows what she is talking about. It's as if she masters negative experiences by defining them so clearly.

[Uses several poems to make a point]

Of course, she doesn't always know what she is talking about. In her two great poems on death, she ends with the shuddering dash of 'I Felt a Funeral, in my Brain' and the darkness of 'I heard a Fly buzz – when I died'. That final dash is like a barrier that stops her and you from falling over a cliff. Somewhere beyond that dash is the place 'Where the meanings are', but despite her brave, maybe even her mad, effort, she cannot get there. When she pushes her imagination to 'Extremity', she still comes up short, at the end of knowing, facing the blank space beyond the dash, or a fly gets between her and the revelation she is waiting for. 'I heard a Fly buzz' is grimly comic, but I wonder how Emily felt when she finished 'I Felt a Funeral in my Brain'? I think she must have felt as 'wrecked' and 'solitary' as the persona of the poem. To put all that effort into imagining and understanding something and then to finish with that emptiness or 'Zero at the Bone'. I wonder did she take consolation from creating what I think is her finest poem? I hope she did.

[Opening sentence flows well from the previous paragraph and sets up this paragraph of comment and interpretation]

It's not the easiest poem to read or interpret. I think it is definitely an attempt to imagine a funeral from the perspective of the person in the coffin, before the moment when you are buried and lose the connection from the life you are departing. All your experiences contract and you can only hear the world ('And then I heard them lift a Box', 'Then Space – began to toll, As all the Heavens were a Bell, And Being, but an Ear') and then you lose even that connection and plunge into death. But it is also a description of Dickinson the poet undergoing the experience of imagining the funeral in her brain and persisting and succeeding, even if it is a terrifying and disturbing experience, until the point when the connection with life is severed and her imagination cannot travel any further:

> And then a Plank in Reason, broke,
> And I dropped down, and down –
> And hit a World, at every plunge,
> And Finished knowing – then –

I'm not sure I'd have the courage to make that kind of psychological and imaginative journey and record it as carefully as she has done. How it must have exhausted her and left her depleted.

[Personal response given to issues raised in the poem]

Please read these poems, Jane, and write back and let me know that you love them as much as I do! Having encountered them 'I feel for them a transport of cordiality'. I hope you will, too.

Your friend,

Sarah

[Keeps task in mind in concluding the essay]

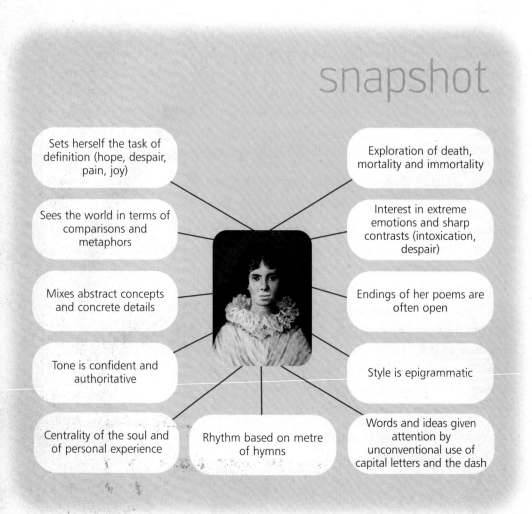

snapshot

Sets herself the task of definition (hope, despair, pain, joy)

Exploration of death, mortality and immortality

Sees the world in terms of comparisons and metaphors

Interest in extreme emotions and sharp contrasts (intoxication, despair)

Mixes abstract concepts and concrete details

Endings of her poems are often open

Tone is confident and authoritative

Style is epigrammatic

Centrality of the soul and of personal experience

Rhythm based on metre of hymns

Words and ideas given attention by unconventional use of capital letters and the dash

John
Donne

b. 1572 - 1631

Biography

Donne (pronounced 'done'), the son of a prosperous London merchant, was one of the most learned men in an age remarkable for learned men. His learning is constantly reflected in his poetry. He spent three years at Oxford University and three at Cambridge. He was also a student at the Inns of Court in London, where he studied law, language and theology.

As a young man, Donne was extremely ambitious, attaching himself to influential patrons as a means of advancing his career. He travelled in Europe and took part in two naval expeditions. He became secretary to Sir Thomas Egerton, a man of great power and influence. His hopes of worldly advancement were blighted, however, when he secretly married Anne More, Egerton's niece, in 1601. She was seventeen, he almost thirty. Her father, who was Lieutenant of the Tower of London, used his power to ruin Donne's career, compelling Egerton to dismiss him and have him imprisoned. On his release, Donne had to take legal action to be reunited with his wife. He summarised the consequences of his imprudent marriage in a rueful, witty epigram: 'John Donne – Anne Donne – Undone'.

Religion

Donne was born into an age of fierce, often deadly, religious controversy. During the long reign of Elizabeth 1 (1558–1603), Catholics were regarded as enemies of the state and many suffered torture, imprisonment and death for upholding their faith. Donne was brought up a Catholic. His mother was related by marriage to Sir Thomas More, the Lord Chancellor of England, who had been martyred in 1535 for refusing to acknowledge the claim of Henry VIII to be head of the English church. Four hundred years after his death, More was declared a saint by the Catholic Church. Donne's family suffered for their religion. His brother Henry died in 1593 after being arrested for concealing a priest.

When he was about thirty, Donne abandoned his Catholic faith and became an Anglican. In 1615 he was ordained to the ministry of the Church of England. He became a champion of his new religion, and wrote a good deal of anti-Catholic propaganda.

Literary career

His literary career has two broad divisions. His memorable secular poetry (love poems, elegies and satires) belongs to the first half of his life, when he enjoyed the society of women and was especially fond of the theatre. Almost all of his poems, even the Holy Sonnets, were written before his ordination in 1615. This event marked a new phase in his literary career. He abandoned poetry for the composition of sermons, achieving fame as one of the outstanding preachers of his time.

Fragments of these sermons, divorced from their original contexts, have long been part of popular discourse (for example, 'no man is an island' and 'never send to know for whom the bell tolls; it tolls for thee'). Donne's sermons are intensely personal, expressing remorse for past sins and, above all, reflecting his obsessive interest in his own death, which was the subject of his last sermon, preached before Charles 1. The point of the sermon was reinforced by what his first biographer called 'a decayed body and a dying face'. Death is also a major theme of his poetry.

Donne became Dean of St Paul's Cathedral in London in 1621. This promotion, as he himself put it, marked the rejection of 'the mistress of my youth, Poetry' for the wife of mine age, Divinity [Religion]'. The evidence suggests that Donne regarded himself as a writer of sermons rather than a poet. He published virtually nothing of his poetry and took no steps to collect or preserve it. On the other hand, he saw to it that his sermons were carefully preserved for publication.

His literary contemporaries saw things differently. When his poems were published after his death, some of the principal writers of his time composed impressive tributes to his originality and inventiveness. Then, for over two centuries, his poetry was not highly regarded. In the eighteenth century, when elegance and grace were among the desirable features of poetry, Donne's verse was seen as awkward, primitive and inelegant, partly due to the fact that his work was available only in poor, inaccurate versions.

Following the publication of T. S. Eliot's celebrated essay 'The Metaphysical Poets' in 1923, Donne came to be regarded as a major poet, admired above all for his unique blend of thought with feeling, his exciting use of argument and analogy, and his mastery of a lively, colloquial idiom. Donne is now valued for his wit, expressed in what became known as 'the metaphysical conceit', which depends for its success on the ability to discover resemblances between apparently unrelated facts and ideas. There is also recognition of his constant readiness to surprise and his use of learned ideas in support of the most daring conclusions. The Donne revival became a cult. Some important twentieth-century poets and critics, among them T. S. Eliot and Ezra Pound, were profoundly influenced by his poetry. The daring conceit with which Eliot opens 'The Love Song of J. Alfred Prufrock' is a famous example of this influence.

Donne's poetry is necessarily elitist, given his tendency to exploit his massive, wide-ranging store of knowledge. Donne appeals to the intelligence and knowledge of his readers, as well as to their imaginations. An appreciation of his poems depends ultimately on our ability to work at them in order to discover what their astonishingly broad range of reference meant to their author, and what it can mean four centuries later.

John Donne

Social and cultural context

Metaphysical poetry

Since Samuel Johnson's discussion of their work in his *Lives of the Poets* (1779–81), it has been customary to describe Donne, Herbert, Vaughan and Marvell (to mention only the greater figures) as the English metaphysical poets. To give an account of some of the distinctive features of Donne's poetry is a convenient method of describing the outstanding characteristics of metaphysical poetry.

One of the most remarkable things about Donne's poems is the extent to which they are taken up with arguments or attempts to persuade. Many of them are exercises in the use and abuse of logic. An astonishing example is 'The Flea', which consists of twenty-seven lines of witty, close-knit argument on the significance for two lovers of a fleabite. It is an argument designed to prove that if the speaker's mistress kills the flea, she will be committing murder, suicide and sacrilege.

In Donne's love poems, the speaker argues constantly with the woman he is addressing, trying to persuade her to share a point of view. In his religious poems, the 'Holy Sonnets' for example, he cannot refrain from arguing with God, to whom he addresses some outrageously witty and paradoxical appeals, such as in 'Batter My Heart'.

Much of Donne's poetry is dramatic, dealing vividly and directly with actual or imaginary experiences, situations and attitudes. His arresting, often startling, openings are one aspect of his dramatic manner, illustrated for example in 'The Sunne Rising', which opens 'Busie old foole, unruly Sunne'. Other dramatic features are the reader's sense of a situation, a speaker and someone being spoken to. As we read Donne's love poems and many of the sonnets, we have, more distinctly than in the case of almost any other poet, the impression of a living voice speaking from the page to us. The rhythms of Donne's verse are closer to those of living, colloquial speech than to those of most lyrical poems. Many of his poems are like performances by an actor enormously enjoying his brilliant displays of showmanship and virtuosity. The dramatic gifts displayed in the poems make it easy to understand why he was regarded as the greatest preacher of his age.

Donne is consistently witty, even in his very serious poems. Wit, arguably the essential feature of all metaphysical poetry, implies quickness of intellect, the ability to say brilliant or sparkling things that surprise or delight by means of unexpected thoughts or expressions. Donne's wit finds an outlet in outrageous arguments, paradoxes, puns and, above all, conceits.

A paradox is a statement that on the surface seems to be a contradiction but which turns out, on closer examination, to have a valid meaning that goes beyond the bounds of common sense and logic. The sonnet 'Batter My Heart' is built around a series of powerful paradoxes.

A conceit is a comparison, often extended, between things that at first sight seem to have little or nothing in common. A famous example is the comparison between lovers and compasses in 'A Valediction: Forbidding Mourning'. Those who do not like Donne's conceits tend to describe the comparisons they involve as far-fetched. Those who admire them stress the ingenuity, boldness and originality of the best examples.

Donne greatly extended the scope and subject matter of poetic imagery. He takes his images from a very wide range of subjects. The furniture of his love poems is not limited to the traditional properties employed by love poets, such as gardens, balconies and nightingales. His speakers stimulate (or puzzle) the minds of loved ones with an impressively daunting array of images drawn from learned sources. Some of his most famous conceits are theological, medical or scientific, or are drawn from geographical discovery and exploration, the law or medieval philosophy. They are deployed in a witty, knowing, subtle way as, for example, in the opening line of his sonnet on death and final judgement, where the reference to 'the round earths imagin'd corners' is a clever indication that the speaker is familiar with both the old and the new astronomy. In Donne's poetry, learned images are balanced by others that are homely and realistic, drawn from the routines of daily life.

Donne introduced a new tone into English love poetry. The Elizabethan love poet tended to idealise the beloved, presenting her as a paragon of beauty and virtue to be thought and spoken of with reverence. Donne's love poetry can be impudent and insolent, sceptical and mocking, cynical and flippant. It is seldom idealistic, tender or reverential. His speakers think of the women they address as people who can respond to witty arguments and who might enjoy elaborate fooling or outrageous paradoxes. The poet and critic John Dryden may have spoken for many puzzled readers when he declared that Donne 'perplexes the minds of the fair sex with nice speculations of philosophy when he should engage their hearts, and entertain them with the softness of love'. This comment suggests that Donne had a higher opinion of the intellectual capacities of women than Dryden did. It also indicates that these two great poets held widely differing views on the nature of love poetry.

Timeline

1572	Born in London, son of a rich merchant
1584–94	Studies languages, law and theology
1595–7	Searches for Spanish treasure ships with the navy
1601	Becomes a member of parliament
1601	Secretly marries Anne More, and is imprisoned
1606–14	Unsuccessfully seeks employment
1611	'The Anniversarie' appears
1615	Becomes a clergyman of the Church of England
1615–31	Becomes a famous preacher, and a chaplain to the king
1617	His wife dies
1619	Travels in Germany as a chaplain
1621	Elected Dean of St Paul's Cathedral
1631	Having preached his own funeral sermon, he dies in London
1633	First collected edition of his poems published

The Sunne Rising

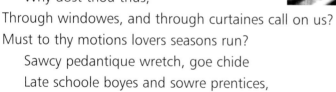

Busie old foole, unruly Sunne,
  Why dost thou thus,
Through windowes, and through curtaines call on us?
Must to thy motions lovers seasons run?
    Sawcy pedantique wretch, goe chide   5
    Late schoole boyes and sowre prentices,
  Goe tell Court-huntsmen, that the King will ride,
  Call countrey ants to harvest offices;
Love, all alike, no season knows, nor clyme,
Nor houres, dayes, moneths, which are the rags of time.   10

Thy beames, so reverend, and strong
  Why shouldst thou thinke?
I could eclipse and cloud them with a winke,
But that I would not lose her sight so long:
    If her eyes have not blinded thine,   15
    Looke, and to morrow late, tell mee,
  Whether both the'India's of spice and Myne
  Be where thou leftst them, or lie here with mee.
Aske for those Kings whom thou saw'st yesterday,
And thou shalt heare, All here in one bed lay.   20

She'is all States, and all Princes, I,
  Nothing else is.
Princes doe but play us; compar'd to this,
All honor's mimique; All wealth alchimie.
    Thou sunne art halfe as happy'as wee,   25
    In that the world's contracted thus;
  Thine age askes ease, and since thy duties bee
  To warme the world, that's done in warming us.
Shine here to us, and thou art every where;
This bed thy center is, these walls, thy sphaere.   30

John Donne

Glossary

1	*Busie old foole:* foolish old busybody
1	*unruly:* unmannerly
4	*Must . . . run?* Must lovers plan their lives according to the movements of the sun?
5	*Sawcy:* saucy, impertinent
5	*pedantique:* over-exact, insisting too much on rules and timetables
6	*sowre prentices:* bad-humoured apprentices
7	*Goe . . . ride:* James I liked to go stag-hunting in the early morning; the sun is being asked to wake those courtiers who are anxious to flatter the king by joining him
8	*countrey ants:* hard-working farmers
8	*offices:* work
9	*Love . . . clyme:* love is the same at all times, it does not depend on varying seasons or climates
10	*rags:* fragments, human divisions
11–12	*Thy beames . . . think?* Why should you imagine that your beams are so impressive in their strength?
14	*lose her sight:* lose sight of her
17	*the'India's . . . Myne:* the East Indies were famous for spice, the West Indies for goldmines
18	*or lie . . . mee:* Donne's witty way of saying that his mistress is as valuable as the spices and gold of the Indies
19–20	*Aske . . . lay:* his mistress is as great and noble as all the kings of the world
21	*She'is . . . I:* his mistress is every country, while he is king of every country
22	*Nothing else is:* the lovers are enough for each other; their world consists of nothing but themselves
24	*mimique:* mimic, a poor imitation
24	*alchimie:* alchemy (brass imitating gold), thus a mere pretence
25	*Thou . . . we:* since the sun is single, it is only half as happy as the lovers, each of whom enjoys the happiness of the other
29–30	*Shine here . . . spheare:* for the lovers, the world has contracted to a single room. The speaker imagines the bed as the Earth around which the Sun must revolve, and the walls of the room mark the boundaries of its revolution

Guidelines

In one sense, this is a traditional poem. Since ancient times, poets had been writing addresses to the sun. Donne continues in their tradition, but with a difference. His predecessors invoked the sun with reverence – as a beautiful life-giving god or goddess and as the centrepiece and glory of the universe. **Donne's speaker treats the sun with contempt, as an unmannerly intruder into his life and that of the woman whose love he is sharing. He displaces the sun from its central position in the scheme of nature, a position now occupied by himself and his mistress.**

Commentary

Like many poems by Donne, this one is designed to shock and surprise, as the speaker overthrows normal expectations. His contemporary audience was accustomed to hearing the sun described in flattering terms as the giver of delight and fruitfulness. Instead, Donne launches his poem with a serious of dismissive and insulting phrases directed against the sun, reducing it to the status of a silly, vain, ill-mannered busybody, a 'Busie old foole' (line 1), a 'Sawcy pedantique wretch' (line 5), with a mistaken sense of duty and a silly obsession with time.

Notice that this love poem is not addressed to the speaker's mistress, but to the sun as a disturber of his and her enjoyment. **The speaker sees the intrusive arrival of the sun in the morning as a challenge to be faced and dismissed.** Instead of disturbing lovers such as his mistress and himself, the speaker suggests that the sun should busy itself with the performance of humble, commonplace duties. He haughtily declares that lovers should be exempt from the control exercised by the sun over the passage of time, dismissing the notion that the lives of lovers should be governed by a timetable set by the sun's movements: 'Must to thy motions lovers' seasons run?' (line 4). The speaker scornfully observes that the sun would be better employed seeing to it that schoolboys, apprentices, courtiers and harvesters get up in time to fulfil their duties.

Donne does not persist with his impertinent, dismissive treatment of the sun. In the course of the poem, **the speaker undergoes a change of mind about what he would like the sun to do and about the role of the sun in relation to himself and his mistress.** In the first stanza, the sun was curtly dismissed from their lives: 'Goe tell Court-huntsmen', 'Call countrey ants' (lines 7 and 8). By the end, the speaker is prepared to invite the sun to participate in their lives: 'Shine here to us' (line 29). He dismissed the sun in stanza 1 because, presumably, he wanted to be left alone with his love. By stanza 3, he wants the sun to stay and warm him and her. The impatient, dismissive tone of his initial address to the sun gives way to sympathy for an ageing heavenly body needing rest: 'Thine age askes ease' (line 27).

However, there is a subtle motive behind his requests that the sun should shine on the bedchamber in which he and his mistress are. He wants the sun to be exclusively at their service, to shine on them alone: 'and since thy duties bee / To warme the world, that's done in warming us' (lines 27 and 28). **By means of a typically outrageous piece of logic, the speaker tries to convince the sun that by shining on the lovers it will be carrying out all the duties assigned to it by nature.** His argument depends on the notion that the lovers' bed constitutes the entire Earth ('thy center') and that the walls of the bedroom form the entire orbit ('spheare') of the sun (line 30). In turn, this idea depends on the belief of pre-modern astronomy that the Earth stood at the centre of the universe, with the sun and the planets orbiting around it.

The speaker's attention gradually drifts from the sun to his mistress. As it does, **he defines the quality of the love he shares with her. The love is absolute, all-sufficient and totally satisfying.** Even the sun is only 'halfe as happy' (line 25) as the lovers are (because the sun is single). This happiness, deriving from absolute love, is conveyed in images of royalty. The speaker tells the sun that he and his mistress are as happy and fortunate as all the kings of the world combined, because the absolute happiness the lovers enjoy is a concentration of all the highest forms of happiness that the most exalted versions of humanity (i.e. kings) enjoy: 'Aske for those kings whom thou saw'st yesterday, / And thou shalt hear, All here in one bed lay' (lines 19 and 20).

The lovers' happiness receives even more exaggerated treatment in the opening of stanza 3: 'She'is all States, and all Princes, I, / Nothing else is' (lines 21 and 22). The speaker sees his mistress as the whole world, over which he presides as sole, absolute monarch. The world in question is a world of love, with the speaker its only beneficiary as king of all that world's love. This extravagant boast is reinforced by the astonishing claim that nothing exists apart from the two lovers, 'Nothing else is'.

This poem is open to a few differing interpretations. On the surface, it appears that the speaker has found complete happiness, fulfilment and self-sufficiency in his relationship with his mistress. They form their own world, a world so complete as to make everything else seem irrelevant and meaningless. Those who read the poem in the light of Donne's biography, however, tend to see the speaker as less fulfilled than he is claiming to be. Donne was an extremely ambitious man, and would have enjoyed the life at the king's court that he dismisses with such contempt in the first stanza. Perhaps he compensated for his absence from this kind of life by pretending that it was of no importance when compared with the kingdom he had invented for himself and the woman he loved, in which each enjoyed exclusive power over the other, and to which the sun itself was a servant.

Tone of the poem

'The Sunne Rising' displays a variety of tones, ranging from the lively, impertinent dismissiveness and near contempt of the opening stanza to the note of satisfied love at the end of the same stanza ('Love, all alike, no season knows, nor clyme'). It combines wit and passion, angry impatience and emotional contentment.

Language of the poem

The language of the poem is informal and colloquial. There is a strong sense of living speech, highly individual and intimate, and avoiding formality. The diction is that of common life, plain and unpretentious. Simple words are, however, sometimes combined to produce effects of surprise, as new meanings emerge: 'Court-huntsmen', 'country ants,' 'the rags of time'. Assonance and alliteration, instead of being used simply for the sake of verbal melody, reinforce the feeling: 'Must to thy motions lovers seasons run?' The distinctive quality of 'The Sunne Rising' is defined by its blend of emotion, wit and lively argument, which are all communicated in flexible, subtle language.

Thinking about the poem

1 Suggest reasons why the whole poem is addressed to the sun.
2 Describe the speaker's attitude to the sun.
3 Explain the references to time in the poem.
4 Why, in your opinion, does the speaker refer to his mistress as 'all States' and himself as 'all Princes' (line 21)?
5 Discuss the function of the imagery in the poem.
6 'Busie old foole, unruly Sunne' (line 1). Is this an effective opening line? Give reasons for your answer.
7 'Why shouldst thou thinke?' (line 12). Comment on Donne's use of questions in this poem.
8 'Nothing else is' (line 22). What impression is created by this statement?
9 Many of Donne's poems are complex and difficult. Do you think that 'the Sunne Rising' is one such poem? Explain your answer.
10 'In this poem, Donne is arguing that losing the world and having it are the same.' Give your response to this comment.

John Donne

Personal response

1   Write a personal response to this poem, describing its impact on you.

2   Imagine that you have been commissioned to take a photograph to be placed alongside this poem on a website. Describe what you would include in your photo. What lighting would you use? What mood or atmosphere would you try to convey?

Before you read 'Song: Goe and Catche a Falling Starre'

What does the title of the poem below suggest to you? Should it be taken literally?

As a class, compile a list of any other impossible tasks that you can think of.

Song: Goe and Catche a Falling Starre

Goe, and catche a falling starre,
    Get with child a mandrake roote,
Tell me, where all past yeares are,
    Or who cleft the Divels foot,
Teach me to heare Mermaides singing,   5
    Or to keep off envies stinging,
        And finde
        What winde
Serves to advance an honest minde.

If thou beest borne to strange sights   10
    Things invisible to see,
Ride ten thousand daies and nights,
    Till age snow white haires on thee,
Thou, when thou retorn'st, wilt tell mee
All strange wonders that befell thee,   15
        And sweare
        No where
Lives a woman true, and faire.

If thou findst one, let mee know,
  Such a Pilgrimage were sweet;   20
Yet doe not, I would not goe,
  Though at next doore wee might meet,
Though shee were true, when you met her,
And last, till you write your letter,
    Yet shee   25
    Will bee
False, ere I come, to two, or three.

Glossary	
2	*Get . . . roote:* make a mandrake root pregnant. The mandrake, a plant with forked roots, was believed to have human qualities
4	*cleft the Divels foot:* the devil was often depicted in art as having a cloven hoof
12	*Ride . . . nights:* this recalls the story of a squire who engaged in a three-year countywide search for a chaste woman, and eventually found one: a plain countrywoman, whom he could not corrupt
15	*befell:* happened to
18	*true, and faire:* faithful as well as beautiful
20	*were:* would be
21	*doe not:* do not tell me
25–7	*Yet . . . three:* but she would have been unfaithful ('false'), before I got there, with two or three other men

Guidelines

The theme of this witty, extravagant poem is the infidelity of women, particularly beautiful women. It is, the argument of the poem goes, as hard to find a beautiful woman who is at the same time faithful and chaste as it is to perform traditionally impossible tasks.

In many contemporary love poems lists of impossible tasks were used for emphasis to enforce a point. In his epic poem *The Faerie Queene*, Edmund Spenser presents the Squire of Dames setting off on a countrywide search for a chaste woman. In the course of three years, he could find only one who was both beautiful and chaste. A similar quest is at the heart of this poem.

Commentary

This is a conventionally cynical poem. The speaker rejects the possibility that a woman can be both chaste and beautiful. To make his point, he considers a number of other supposed impossibilities.

Stanza 1

The logic of the poem is that the discovery of a beautiful yet chaste woman is likely to prove as difficult as the solution to a number of notoriously impossible tasks, which are set out in stanza 1. The tasks are: catching a falling star; causing a mandrake root to become pregnant; explaining what has become of all the years that have passed since creation; discovering the identity of the person who caused the devil's foot to be divided in two; learning to hear the songs of mermaids; finding a method of making people secure against the envy of others; and identifying a wind that will blow good fortune to an honest person.

Stanzas 2 and 3

Having listed these impossibilities in the first stanza, the speaker spends the rest of the poem dismissing the notion that a woman who is both beautiful and chaste is to be found anywhere. In stanza 2 he imagines an acquaintance going on a magical journey through the world, lasting ten thousand days and nights, and returning to swear that nowhere was there to be found 'a woman true, and faire' (line 18).

On the other hand, as stanza 3 suggests, perhaps the adventurer will reveal to the speaker that such a woman does exist. The possibility leads to the moving reflection that this discovery would make the 'Pilgrimage' to meet her a 'sweet' (line 20) and worthwhile event, like the revelation of some saint whose rare combination of chastity and beauty made her remarkable. The speaker finds it impossible, however, to maintain this faith in the existence of such a creature and lapses into cynicism. The woman reported by the pilgrim might have been both chaste and beautiful when he met her, but it will be futile for the speaker to go in quest of her. By the time of his arrival, he believes that she would have lost her honour 'to two, or three' (line 27) men.

This is one of Donne's typically witty poems. It is not simple in mood or tone. It is possible to read it as an irresponsibly flippant comment on female virtue. It may also be read as a cynical exercise based on personal experience of disillusionment or disappointment. It should be borne in mind that even **Donne's seemingly trifling poems can have serious implications**, as line 20, 'Such a Pilgrimage were sweet', may suggest.

Thinking about the poem

1   In your opinion, does the speaker really believe the argument he is advancing in this poem?

2   What is the mood of the poem? Is the speaker being cynical, sad, pessimistic, light-hearted or satirical for example? Or can he be serious?

3   What does the poem tell you about the kind of person the speaker is?

4   What is the significance of the reference to 'a Pilgrimage' in line 20?

5   Contrast the ideas and attitudes of this poem with those of 'The Sunne Rising'.

6   'finde / What winde / Serves to advance an honest minde' (lines 6–8). What impression of the speaker do these lines give?

7   Choose two images from the poem that you find impressive. Explain your choice.

8   'Yet shee / Will bee / False, ere I come, to two, or three' (lines 25–27). How do these final lines affect your reading of the poem?

9   Give an outline of the theme of this poem and of the way in which Donne develops it. Does he convince you?

10   What does the subject matter and the way it is treated tell you about the author of the poem?

Personal response

1   Imagine you are a woman living next door to the speaker. Write a letter to him, setting out what you like or dislike about this poem.

2   If everything the speaker says were true, what kind of a world would this be? In your comments make reference to key passages in the text.

3   With a partner, discuss whether attitudes to women have changed since Donne's time. Is it likely that a modern poet would write a similar poem?

snapshot

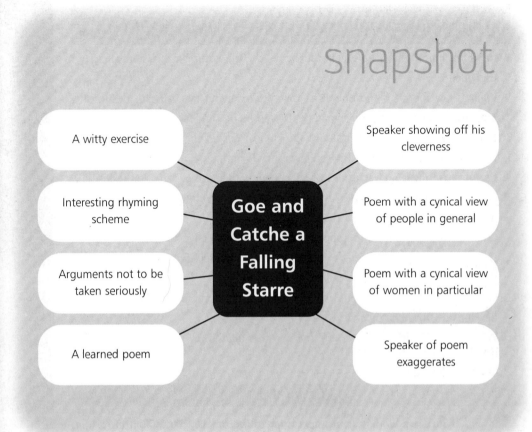

- A witty exercise
- Interesting rhyming scheme
- Arguments not to be taken seriously
- A learned poem

Goe and Catche a Falling Starre

- Speaker showing off his cleverness
- Poem with a cynical view of people in general
- Poem with a cynical view of women in particular
- Speaker of poem exaggerates

occasion
TIME PASSING

The Anniversarie

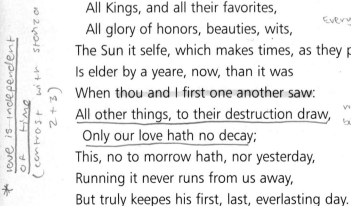

All Kings, and all their favorites,
    All glory of honors, beauties, wits,
The Sun it selfe, which makes times, as they passe,
Is elder by a yeare, now, than it was
When thou and I first one another saw: 5
All other things, to their destruction draw,
    Only our love hath no decay;
This, no to morrow hath, nor yesterday,
Running it never runs from us away,
But truly keepes his first, last, everlasting day.   10

Everything has aged

with time things decay but not their love

A YEAR SINCE THEY MET

love is eternal + timeless + faithful

love is-independent of time with stanza (contrast 2+3)

Two graves must hide thine and my coarse,

If one might, death were no divorce.

Alas, as well as other Princes, wee,

(Who Prince enough in one another bee,) *IMPORTANCE TO EACHOTHER*

Must leave at last in death, these eyes and eares,   15

Oft fed with true oathes, and with sweet salt teares; *tears of love + sadness*

But soules where nothing dwells but love → *love is the only*

(All other thoughts being inmates) then shall prove *permanent feeling*

This, or a love increased there above,

When bodies to their graves, soules from their graves remove.   20

go to heaven together

And then wee shall be throughly blest,

But wee no more, than all the rest; *everyone is happy, equal in heaven.*

Here upon earth, we'are Kings, and none but wee *conceits* *equality in love*

Can be such Kings, nor of such subjects bee;

Who is so safe as wee? where none can doe *vunerability*   25

Treason to us, except one of us two. *TRUST IN EACHOTHER.*

True and false feares let us refraine,

Let us love nobly, and live, and adde againe

Yeares and yeares unto yeares, till we attaine *live happily together as long as possible.*

To write threescore: this is the second of our raigne.   30

60 yrs

(side margins, rotated) *(contrast with stanza 1)*   *rhetorical question*

Glossary		
2	*All glory of honors:* all who enjoy honours	
2	*beauties, wits:* all beautiful and clever people	
3	*The Sun . . . passe:* the sun marks the passing of time as the great people of the world pass on on their journey to eternity	
10	*keepes . . . day:* their love will always be as strong as it was in the beginning	
11–12	*Two . . . divorce:* we will have to be buried in separate graves when we die. If we were permitted to share a single grave, our souls would not be allowed to leave our bodies, and death would not be able to separate our bodies from our souls as it should	
11	*coarse:* corpse	
12	*were:* would be	
18	*inmates:* lodgers (in contrast to permanent residents)	
18	*prove:* experience	

John Donne

Glossary

19	*This:*	the love they now enjoy
19	*above:*	in Heaven
20	*remove:*	leave (the souls leave their bodies)
21	*throughly:*	thoroughly, absolutely
22	*wee . . . rest:*	the disadvantage of being in Heaven is that the lovers will be no happier there than any of its other inhabitants
24	*nor . . . bee:*	nor can we be subjects of such kings (as ourselves)
27	*refraine:*	control, restrain
30	*threescore:*	sixty
30	*second . . . raigne:*	second anniversary of our reign (as kings of each other)

Guidelines

This poem should be read in conjunction with 'The Sunne Rising', where similar ideas are expressed, and where kingship is also a controlling metaphor. 'The Anniversarie' is based on an extended conceit, a set of comparisons and contrasts between the lovers and two royal persons. Each is the exclusive territory of the other and each is also governed exclusively by the other. **The central theme is the absolute importance of love in the lives of the lovers**. While everything else is doomed to decay, their love will endure, even beyond the grave.

Commentary

The title, 'The Anniversarie', refers to the anniversary of the lovers' first meeting. The lovers are happier and more secure than any earthly king because their love is so perfect and absolute that they never need to fear betrayal, as kings do. **Even heavenly happiness could not exceed their earthly joy in each other**. This explains the desire, expressed in the final stanza, for a long continuation of their lives. The detailed meaning of the poem becomes clearer if we work through it stanza by stanza.

Stanza 1

There are two main parts in this stanza. In the first five lines, the speaker records the fact that he and the woman he loves are celebrating the first anniversary of their meeting. He gives the two of them an exalted place in the world by setting this first anniversary against the background of the gradual passing of kings, those who enjoy honour, all beautiful and clever people and the passage of the sun through the heavens. The next five lines claim that in the midst of the universal destruction of the great people on Earth and even of the cosmos, one value will survive: the love the speaker and his mistress have for each other.

Stanza 2

In the second stanza the voice of **the speaker betrays uneasiness as he contemplates his death and that of his mistress** and the fact that their bodies will be buried in separate graves. If they could share one grave, their souls would not wish to leave their bodies and therefore death would not separate, or 'divorce' (line 12), their souls from their bodies as it should. One of the horrors of death for the speaker is that it involves bodily separation, and the destruction of the eyes and ears, which have often given and received tokens of true love. In the face of such a mournful prospect, the speaker tries to apply all the comfort he can. In death, he tells his lover, their souls, which now experience total love, will still experience the same love as they do on Earth, or even a higher and greater form.

Stanza 3

The opening of this stanza raises a troublesome question about the fate of the lovers in the next world. The speaker acknowledges in line 21 that in heaven ('then') they will be absolutely happy ('blest'). But he then admits that their happiness will be no greater than anybody else's (because all souls in heaven are equally happy). This provides the clue to the real theme of the poem, which is the speaker's desire for supremacy. **His alarm at the thought of death is not because it will separate the lovers or diminish their love, but because it will put an end to the supremacy they enjoy as kings on Earth** – a condition enjoyed by nobody else: 'and none but wee / Can be such Kings' (lines 23 and 24). By the end of the poem it has become clear that happiness is not what the speaker longs for, since if it was he would be looking forward to death, which would ensure perfect happiness for him, his mistress and everyone else. Since the afterlife can make him no happier than 'all the rest' (line 22) of heaven's inhabitants, he puts it aside in favour of his earthy reign: 'Here upon earth, we'are Kings' (line 23). Although this earthly supremacy is only temporary and will end in death, he is determined to enjoy it to the full.

The poem has undergone a significant change in direction. The speaker began by celebrating a timeless love: 'This, no to morrow hath, nor yesterday' (line 8). He ends by suggesting that all he and his mistress can do is to enjoy as many years as they can of supremacy over each other and hope to live long lives: 'To write threescore' (line 30).

Style and language of the poem

'The Anniversarie' illustrates most of the distinctive features of Donne's poetry. Even when, as in this case, he is being tender and passionate, he is still argumentative; his speaker is anxious to prove a point through the witty use (or abuse) of logical principles. His celebration of the perfection of his earthly happiness in stanza 3 is expressed in controlled, logical terms.

Like every other Donne poem, 'The Anniversarie' has a basic logical structure, the framework of which may be expressed as follows:

- All things pass and decay except our love.
- Even after death our love will increase rather than diminish.
- But, whereas in death we shall be no happier than other heavenly spirits, we are uniquely happy here on Earth.

The poem features conceits, ambiguities and paradoxes, all illustrating Donne's wit and inventiveness. While the entire poem is based on an extended conceit, there are also some local conceits. Lovers are seen both as rulers and territories (see also 'The Sunne Rising'). The lovers' triumphant and absolute command of each other's affections is seen as a 'reign' secure from treason. The second stanza uses a conceit to underline the absolute value of love in the souls of the lovers: their souls are seen as dwellings where love is the only tenant; all other feelings are mere lodgers or 'inmates' (line 18).

In the first stanza Donne uses a brilliant paradox to express the permanence of love in 'Running it never runs from us away' (line 9), and a clever, ingenious paradox to describe the movement of the sun, which is passing even as it measures time: 'The Sun it selfe, which makes times, as they passe' (line 3).

The poem demands a slow, deliberate reading. The opening stanza is stately and pompous in movement; the second, with its parentheses and qualifying clauses, is densely intricate; while the third combines passion with admirable restraint.

Thinking about the poem

1   In stanza 1 Donne creates a disturbing impression of the fate of earthly and heavenly things. How does he counteract this in the same stanza?
2   Consider the significance of the contrast between lines 3–4 and lines 9–10. What point is being made?
3   Is the speaker as confident in stanza 2 as he was in stanza 1? Give reasons for your answer.

4   Does the introduction of the lovers' deaths and their graves change the mood of the poem? Give reasons for your answer.

5   What reservations does the speaker have about death? Consider especially the final stanza.

6   Is there a touch of self-deception in the poem – an attempt to present things as better than they really are?

7   Is there evidence in the poem that the speaker does not really believe what he says at the beginning: that the love he is celebrating is independent of time? Does his attitude to this change in the course of the poem?

8   Do you think the adjectives are well-chosen in 'sweet salt teares' (line 16)? Give reasons for your answer.

9   Comment on the phrase 'But wee no more, than all the rest' (line 22).

10 Give your views on the effectiveness of the phrase 'Yeares and yeares unto yeares' (line 29).

11 Write about this poem as a treatment of love, death and time.

12 References to princes, kings and kingship, dominate 'The Anniversarie'. How do these images help to express the main theme of the poem?

Personal response

1   If you received this poem as a first anniversary gift, how would you respond to it?

2   Pick two lines from the poem that you like and explain their impact on you.

Song: Sweetest Love I Do Not Goe

Sweetest love, I do not goe,
  For weariness of thee,
Nor in hope the world can show
  A fitter Love for mee;
    But since that I   5
Must dye at last, 'tis best,
To use my selfe in jest
  Thus by fain'd deaths to dye;

Yesternight the Sunne went hence,
  And yet is here to day,   10
He hath no desire nor sense,

Nor halfe so short a way:
 Then feare not mee,
But believe that I shall make
Speedier journeyes, since I take   15
 More wings and spurres than hee.

O how feeble is mans power,
 That if good fortune fall,
Cannot adde another houre,
 Nor a lost houre recall!   20
  But come bad chance,
And wee joyne to'it our strength,
And wee teach it art and length,
 It selfe o'er us to'advance.

When thou sigh'st, thou sigh'st not winde,   25
 But sigh'st my soule away,
When thou weep'st, unkindly kinde,
 My lifes blood doth decay.
  It cannot bee
That thou lov'st mee, as thou say'st,   30
If in thine my life thou waste,
 That art the best of mee.

Let not thy divining heart
 Forethinke me any ill,
Destiny may take thy part,   35
 And may thy feares fulfill;
  But thinke that wee
Are but turn'd aside to sleepe;
They who one another keepe
 Alive, ne'r parted bee.   40

Glossary

4	*fitter:* more suitable
6	*dye:* to die, but also to part or separate
7	*To . . . jest:* to mock myself
8	*fain'd:* pretended
12	*Nor . . . way:* the sun has a longer journey ('way') than the speaker and still returns within a day
13	*Then . . . mee:* don't worry about my return
21–4	*But . . . advance:* but if bad luck strikes us, we do all we can to extend its effects and to teach it clever and long-drawn-out ways of casting us down
33	*divining:* foreseeing, anticipating
34	*ill:* misfortune
35–6	*Destiny . . . fulfill:* if you anticipate misfortune for me, fate may well bring this about

Guidelines

Superficially, this is a witty poem about parting; but **Donne uses the temporary departure of a lover from his beloved to make a serious point: such partings will help both of them to prepare for the inevitable final parting that will come with death.** Separation is a useful rehearsal for the ultimate separation of death, and if his beloved can bear separation from him calmly and nobly, she will rise above the condition of being a slave to fate.

Commentary

Like many of Donne's poems, this one involves some rapid changes of mood and tone. The first four lines, with their gentle rhythms and lyrical tone, suggest a conventional love poem, but the next four lines give a very different impression.

The real subject is not the speaker's sad parting from his lover, but his desire to accustom himself to the idea of death. Since he must die sometime, it is best to get used to death by practising a lesser form of it, and to use parting to remind them of the final separation that death will bring about. All these earthly partings, such as the one he is dealing with in the poem, are a series of 'fain'd' (line 8) or pretended deaths.

Notice that as the poem proceeds, it develops into a series of arguments designed to influence his lover's behaviour. The fourth stanza typifies the speaker's kind of argumentation. He tries to persuade her to refrain from sighing and weeping by invoking the traditional argument that a woman who wastes her body and soul in grief at the same time wastes the life and soul of her lover, since the two of them are so intimately involved with each other: 'in thine my life thou waste' (line 31).

The argument of the final stanza is a warning: by anticipating evil fortune (his death during absence) she may help to bring it about: 'Destiny may take thy part, / And may thy feares fulfill' (lines 35 and 36).

Thinking about the poem

1   This poem has often been described as an unusual kind of love poem. Do you agree or disagree with this point of view? Explain your answer.
2   Discuss the poem under the heading 'A rehearsal for death'.
3   Consider the role of fate in the poem.
4   Select your favourite image, line or phrase in the poem and say why you have chosen it.
5   What is the point of this poem? Analyse the speaker's arguments. Are they convincing?

Personal response

1   Imagine you are the wife of the speaker. It is the day after his departure and you are recording your thoughts in your diary. Write a diary entry in which you respond to his advice.
2   Has this poem altered your views of being separated from a loved one for an extended period? Give reasons for your response.

REASSURANCE

A Valediction: Forbidding Mourning
(farewell speech)

simile →
As virtuous men passe mildly away,
   And whisper to their soules, to goe,
Whilst some of their sad friends doe say,
   The breath goes now, and some say, no:

a dying man, happy to die → heaven

persuasion
So let us melt, and make no noise,
   No teare-floods, nor sigh-tempests move,
T'were prophanation of your joyes
   To tell the layetie our love.

5

metaphysical

Moving of th'earth brings harmes and feares,
  Men reckon what it did and meant, → don't be scared
But trepidation of the spheares,   of our seperation 10
  Though greater farre, is innocent.

ordinary, physical
Dull sublunary lovers, love
  (Whose soule is sense) cannot admit (allow)
Absence, because it doth remove   15
  Those things which elemented it.

↑ CONTRAST ↓

But we by a love, so much refin'd,
  That our selves know not what it is, True love
Inter-assured of the mind, (spiritual, not physical)
  Care lesse, eyes, lips, and hands to misse. → don't miss this   20

Persuasion
↓
Our two soules therefore, which are one,
  Though I must goe, endure not yet
A breach, but an expansion,
  Like gold to ayery thinnesse beate. → gold, stretched does not lose value

TRUE

SIMILE   metaphors

If they be two, they are two so   25
  As stiffe twin compasses are two,   ETERNAL LOVE
Thy soule the fixt foot, makes no show
  To move, but doth, if the'other doe.

DONNE   WIFE

And though it in the center sit,
  Yet when the other far doth rome,   30
It leanes, and hearkens after it,
  And grows erect, as that comes home.

↳ she stays, he goes. he will come back

Such wilt thou be to mee, who must
  Like th'other foot, obliquely runne;
Thy firmnes makes my circle just   SCIENTIFIC   35
  And makes me end, where I begunne.   ↳ feature of metaphysical

John Donne

Glossary

1–2	*virtuous . . . goe:* good people are happy to die, and do not struggle against death
5–6	*melt . . . move:* let us part quietly, avoiding floods of tears and windy sighs
7	*'Twere . . . joyes:* our love would be brought into disrepute
8	*layetie:* unlearned, ignorant people (lay people were traditionally contrasted with the more learned clergy); here, people who do not understand their love
9–12	*Moving . . . innocent:* relatively small movements on Earth, such as earthquakes, cause damage, and make people wonder how much damage has been caused and what it signifies. On the other hand, the far greater agitation ('trepidation') of the spheres circling the Earth are relatively harmless ('innocent'). In ancient astronomy, which Donne uses here for poetic purposes, the spheres were concentric hollow globes moving around the Earth and making music as they moved
13–16	*Dull . . . elemented it:* common, everyday earthly ('sublunary') love, being primarily sensual, does not survive the absence of the loved one, because absence removes the physical properties on which it was founded ('which elemented it')
18	*our selves . . . is:* Donne often suggests that true love cannot be defined in terms of any particular feature
24	*gold . . . beate:* gold was beaten out fine to make gold leaf. Absence will refine their love, making it achieve the highest spiritual quality. The more the gold is hammered, the thinner it gets, becoming almost as immaterial as souls and stretching out to span continents, thus keeping the lovers united
25	*they:* the souls of the lovers
26	*stiffe:* firm
26	*twin compasses:* a pair of compasses used for drawing circles; these were common emblems of constancy in the midst of change
34	*obliquely:* diagonally, at an angle
35	*firmness:* constancy
35	*makes my circle just:* makes me complete a true circle; the circle was an emblem of perfection and continuity

Guidelines

This is a poem of parting. In 1611 Donne's patron, Sir Robert Drury, persuaded Donne to accompany him on a trip to Europe, one purpose of which was to enhance his skills as a diplomat and consequently his prospects of entering the diplomatic service. Donne's wife was deeply troubled at the thought of his departure, and asked him not to go, but to no avail. According to Donne's first biographer, the poet marked his departure with this farewell poem, and left for Europe with Drury, Lady Drury, servants, hounds and hawks. To suit his purposes on this occasion, **Donne argues that continuous bodily contact is not necessary for the maintenance of the love between two people** (see stanza 5).

Commentary

This poem is a fine example of Donne's fondness for conveying deep feeling through difficult (and now obsolete) concepts. The speaker's concern is to suggest that the relationship between the two lovers is such that their separation as a result of his proposed journey is not only unimportant, but in fact impossible. **He tries to show, by the use of analogies, that the two of them are so strongly bound together that distance cannot keep them apart.** The analogies are drawn from **science** and craftsmanship.

Stanzas 1 and 2

In the opening lines, based on the familiar notion of separation as a death for lovers, Donne breathes new life into a commonplace image. The death described is so tranquil and gradual that those watching at the bedside cannot be sure when the dying person breathes his last: 'Whilst some of their sad friends doe say, / The breath goes now, and some say, no' (lines 3 and 4). **The speaker wants his parting from his loved one to be as quiet and imperceptible as the parting of a tranquil soul from a dead body, involving no loud demonstration of grief.** They are to 'melt' (line 5) away from each other, avoiding sighs and tears.

Stanza 3

The third stanza introduces a learned conceit for the purpose of further reinforcing his plea that the parting should be free from loud demonstrations of emotion. Their grief at parting is, paradoxically, too deep to be loudly expressed. The conceit here, stressing the difference between the harms and fears caused by earthquakes and the much greater consequences for the solar system caused by the quieter movement of the heavens, is an argument to suggest that **the deep feeling the lovers have for each other is best expressed in ways that attract little or no attention.**

Stanzas 4–6

The speaker develops the notion that the lovers share a single soul, and that since their love does not depend on sensual elements, it cannot be broken by physical separation. To illustrate the impossibility of separating their spiritual selves, Donne uses a wholly original and appropriate conceit, implying that **as the gap between their bodies grows larger (as the speaker moves further on his journey), the single soul they share will stretch to fill the gap.** They will thus not endure 'A breach, but an expansion, / Like gold to ayery thinnesse beate' (lines 23 and 24). This conceit provides a touch of imaginative genius. Gold is associated with beauty, value and nobility, appropriate to the kind of love being described, and it is also capable of being hammered into incomparably thin leaf, making its 'ayery thinnesse' a satisfying image of a soul stretching indefinitely.

Stanzas 7–9

Donne moves to another conceit in the final three stanzas. Perhaps the lovers do not share a common soul after all, but have separate ones. He deals with this possibility by suggesting that their souls are joined together. To illustrate this idea, **he pictures their souls as the legs of a pair of compasses. He is the foot that makes a circle as he moves around on his journey; she is the foot that remains fixed in one place.** Whatever the movement, the lovers, like the legs of the compass, remain aligned.

The compass conceit has further implications, suggested in the second to last line of the poem: 'Thy firmnes makes my circle just' (line 35). The idea here is that the moving leg of the compass is able to make a true ('just') circle only because the other maintains its position (its 'firmnes'). This firmness represents the woman's fidelity. The closing of the circle depicted in the final line of the poem – 'And makes me end, where I begunne' (line 36) – points to the **reunion of the lovers** when the journey is over.

Thinking about the poem

1. Donne uses metaphors to express much of his meaning in this poem. These metaphors are drawn from a wide variety of human activities. Examine each of these metaphors in turn, showing how they contribute to the speaker's argument.

2. Does the speaker supply convincing reasons for leaving his wife and going on an extended tour?

3. Donne's poems are notable for their many conceits (comparisons between things that at first might appear to have little in common). One of these involves the lovers as a pair of compasses. Can this comparison be justified?

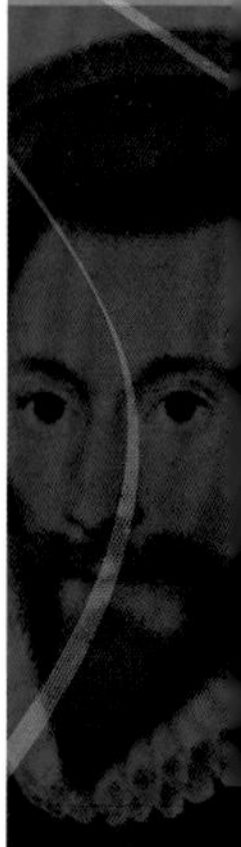

4 Donne was fond of reconciling opposites in his poetry: absence and presence, material and immaterial, for example. Show how 'A Valediction: Forbidding Mourning' illustrates this impulse.

5 Many of Donne's poems are extended arguments. Analyse each of Donne's arguments in this poem.

6 In the early twentieth century, Donne was greatly admired for his originality of thought and language. How does this poem illustrate these qualities?

Personal response

1 'A Valediction: Forbidding Mourning' features a number of ideas that a modern reader is bound to find unfamiliar and difficult to understand. Comment on the difficulties presented by the poem, and say whether you think, in spite of these difficulties, it can still appeal to a twenty-first century reader. Support your comments with reference to the poem.

2 Imagine you are the woman to whom this poem is addressed. Write a brief dialogue, involving you and the speaker, in which you respond to his argument.

[handwritten: seduction poem]

The Dreame

[handwritten: Like 'the Flea', addresses woman directly]

[handwritten: addressing her directly]

Deare love, for nothing lesse than thee   *[handwritten: flattering the woman]*
Would I have broken this happy dreame,
  It was a theame
For reason, much too strong for phantasie,   *[handwritten: she was in the dream]*
Therefore thou wakd'st me wisely; yet   5
My Dreame thou brok'st not, but continued'st it,
Thou art so truth, that thoughts of thee suffice,
To make dreames truths; and fables histories;
Enter these armes, for since thou thoughtst it best,   *[handwritten: IMPERATIVE (persuasion)]*
Not to dreame all my dreame, let's act the rest   10

    [handwritten: comparing her to light]
As lightning, or a Tapers light,
Thine eyes, and not thy noise wak'd mee;   *[handwritten: thought of her woke him]*
  Yet I thought thee
(For thou lovest truth) an Angell, at first sight,   *[handwritten: ANGEL → GOD]*
But when I saw thou sawest my heart,   15
And knew'st my thoughts, beyond an Angels art,

[handwritten: thought she was an angel, but she knows what he's thinking about]

When thou knew'st what I dreamt, when thou knew'st when
Excesse of joy would wake me, and cam'st then,
I must confess, it could not chuse but bee
Prophane, to thinke thee any thing but thee. *(angel)*   20
(blasphemy)

SHE'S LEAVING — Coming and staying show'd thee, thee,
But rising makes me doubt, that now,
   Thou art not thou.
That love is weake, where feare's as strong as hee;   *Her love is weak if she has fear, shame*
'Tis not all spirit, pure, and brave,   25
If mixture it of Feare, Shame, Honor, have,   *SOCIETY*
SIMILE — Perchance [as] torches which must ready bee,
TEASING — Men light and put out, so thou deal'st with mee,
Thou cam'st to kindle, goest to come; Then I   *PARADOX*
Hopeful tone — Will dreame that hope againe, but else would die. — *SIMILAR TO 'The Flea'*   30

Glossary		
1–2	*for nothing . . . dreame:* I would not have wanted this dream interrupted for anybody but you	
3–4	*It . . . phantasie:* the subject matter ('theame') of the dream was better suited to wakeful reality than to fantasy experienced in sleep	
7	*so truth:* so completely and absolutely the truth	
7–8	*thoughts . . . histories:* the thought of you is enough to turn dreams into realities, and to turn fables into true history	
9–10	*Enter . . . rest:* the dream has involved a love scene between the speaker and his mistress. Now that he is awake, he asks her to make the events of the dream real	
11	*a Tapers light:* the light of a candle	
13–14	*Yet . . . Angell:* an angel is associated with truth, and her devotion to truth causes him to identify her as an angel	
14	*at first sight:* when I awoke from my dream	
15–16	*when . . . art:* an angel cannot read the human mind, but God can. When he realises that she can read his thoughts, he realises that she is more God than angel	
20	*Prophane:* profane, unworthy	
20	*to thinke . . . thee:* to think that you were anybody but yourself	
21	*show'd thee, thee:* showed that you were yourself	

uses logic in arguments, combined with flattery

22	*doubt:* suspect
24–6	*That . . . have:* if fear, shame or honour are present, true love that is unmixed and sure of itself ('pure, and brave') is absent
27–8	*Perchance . . . out:* perhaps a torch that has already been used ignites more quickly than an unused one
29	*to kindle:* to arouse passion
29	*goest to come:* you go only to come back again
30	*will dreame . . . die:* the 'hope' he will dream about is a renewal of his experience of love

Guidelines

What Donne describes in this poem is a common theme of love poetry of his time. The subject matter was inherited by Donne and his contemporaries from ancient classical poetry. **The speaker dreams pleasantly and happily of the joys of love with his mistress. He wakes to find her at his bedside, and they proceed to enact what he has been dreaming about.** In 'The Dreame', waking and sleeping life are not distinguished from each other with absolute clarity: his lover blends into the dream, not breaking it but continuing it.

Commentary

This is an extremely subtle and difficult poem. Some of the difficulty arises from the fact that there is no clear or obvious distinction between waking and sleeping life in the way the speaker records these: **reality and dream blend imperceptibly into each other.**

Stanza 1

The opening stanza seems to make clear that the poem is half-dream and half-fact. The speaker has been dreaming of enjoying the act of love with his mistress. The sleeping images of this fantasy are so compelling that they rouse him to wakefulness: they were much too powerful to be confined to the speaker's imagination. At this point, it appears, the person who wakes the speaker blends into his dream, and so, as he puts it, 'My Dreame thou brok'st not, but continued'st it' (line 6). Thus, dream becomes reality as the lovers proceed to enact it: 'Enter these armes, for since thou thoughtst it best, / Not to dreame all my dreame, let's act the rest' (lines 9 and 10).

Stanza 2

The second stanza is based on theological distinctions between, for example, what God and the angels can know. On awakening from his dream, he imagined his mistress to be an angel, but then, on reflection, he realised that she had more than angelic knowledge, since she clearly knew the moment when 'Excesse of joy' (line 18) would wake him, and came to him just then. The contemporary doctrine of angels held that they could not discover the hidden secrets of the human heart in this way. She is thus more God than angel.

Stanza 3

The final stanza features a witty abuse of logical argument and is typical of Donne. Her coming to him at a vital stage in his dream, and her staying with him to act out the rest of that dream, suggest to him that the one who interrupted the dream was really his mistress: 'Coming and staying showed thee, thee' (line 21). However, now that she has departed, he has his doubts, or pretends to have: 'But rising makes me doubt, that now, / Thou art not thou' (lines 22 and 23). The paradox is easily explained. In the speaker's self-centred view of things, the mistress is defined in terms of her ability to gratify his desires. She is thus totally herself when she is doing this and not herself when she is not.

The speaker worries and wonders at her departure, musing, for example, whether 'Feare, Shame, Honor' (line 26) may have made her reluctant to give herself fully to him. At the end, he has a reassuring thought: perhaps she came only to inflame his feelings and will return to set them fully alight, just as torches which have been burning and then quenched ignite more easily the next time. He thus hopes that she has departed only to come back again: 'goest to come' (line 29). If that is the case, he can hope to be awakened from another dream, or dream that she will return to enhance his happiness. If not, he will be miserable.

Thinking about the poem

1   'To make dreames truths' (line 8) is a key phrase in the poem. What is its significance? What is the relationship in the poem between dreams and truths (or realities)?

2   What exactly is happening in this poem? Can its details be interpreted in more than one way?

3   Donne is fond of arguing, even in his love poems. Discuss some of the arguments he advances in 'The Dreame'.

4 In what respects is 'The Dreame' not a straightforward love poem?

5 Do you find 'The Dreame' a happy poem? Give reasons for your answer.

6 Donne is celebrated as a witty poet. How does this poem illustrate the nature of his wit?

7 On the evidence in the poem, how would you say the speaker regards his 'Deare love' of line 1?

8 Consider how the images of the poem help to convey its meanings.

9 In 'The Dreame', waking and sleeping life are not distinguished from each other, but girl blends into dream and dream into girl. Show how Donne achieves this effect in the poem.

Personal response

1 Did you enjoy reading this poem? Give a reason for your opinion.
2 Do you think that the person addressed in this poem is likely to be pleased by what the speaker is telling her? Explain your answer.

Before you read 'The Flea'

What do you expect a poem called 'The Flea' to be about? How does the fact that this poem was written about four hundred years ago affect your expectations?

The Flea

Marke but this flea, and marke in this,
How little that which thou deny'st me is;
It suck'd me first, and now sucks thee,   *womans + mans → blood*
And in this flea, our two bloods mingled bee;
Thou know'st that this cannot be said   5
A sinne, nor shame, nor losse of maidenhead,
　　Yet this enjoyes before it wooe,
　　And pamper'd swells with one blood made of two,
　　And this, alas, is more than wee would doe.
　　　persuasion

Oh stay, three lives in one flea spare,　　　　　　　　　　10
Where wee almost, yea more than maryed are.
This flea is you and I, and this　　　　*→ union in Flea*
Our mariage bed, and mariage temple is;
Though parents grudge, and you, w'are met,
And cloysterd in these living walls of Jet.　　　　　15

persuasion Though use make you apt to kill mee,　*→ flea holds her blood*
　Let not to that, selfe murder added bee,
　And sacrilege, three sinnes in killing three. *repetition, religious*
　　destroy a holy thing　　　　　**FLEA KILLED**

Cruell and sodaine, hast thou since　　　*exaggeration*
Purpled thy naile, in blood of innocence? *→ Christ*　20
Wherein could this flea guilty bee,
Except in that drop which it suckt from thee?
Yet thou triumph'st, and saist that thou
Find'st not thy selfe, nore mee the weaker now;　*alliteration*
　'Tis true, then learne how false, feares bee;　　25
Just so much honor, when thou yeeld'st to mee,
Will wast, as this flea's death tooke life from thee.

resourceful

Glossary		
1	*marke:* observe, note	
5	*said:* called	
6	*maidenhead:* virginity	
9	*more . . . doe:* they do not want a pregnancy	
10	*stay . . . spare:* refrain from killing the flea, and so spare three lives all at once (the flea's, yours and mine). Since their 'two bloods' are 'mingled' in the flea (because it bit both of them), he imagines both their lives are present in its body	
11	*maryed:* married	
15	*cloysterd . . . Jet:* lodged inside the walls of the flea's black body	
16	*use:* habit, custom	
17–18	*Let . . . three:* do not add suicide and sacrilege to murder. She will be guilty of sacrilege if, by killing the flea, she destroys the temple in which they were married	
19	*sodaine:* sudden, impulsive	

a conceit is a comparison, often extended between things that at first sight seem to have little or nothing in common.

hypocritical - religious references used to try and commit a sin.

19	*since:* already
20	*Purpled thy naile:* she has crushed the flea to death with her fingernail
21	*Wherein:* in what way
26–7	*Just . . . thee:* she will lose no more of her honour by yielding to him than the flea took from her when he sucked her blood

Guidelines

Flea poems were very common in European Renaissance literature. They were generally indecent. Here Donne deflects attention from the woman's body and focuses instead on the body of the flea. By sucking the speaker's blood and the blood of his mistress, the flea becomes a symbol of the union he desires with her. Donne displays extraordinary ingenuity and skill in his witty exploration of the implications of a fleabite.

Commentary

This poem is a brilliant exercise in imaginative wit. Donne organises his poem, which is a series of ingenious arguments addressed to the speaker's mistress, in three stages, each based on a nine-line stanza.

Stanza 1
The speaker draws a moral or lesson from the flea's actions and tries to incite his mistress to follow its example. The flea has bitten both of them and thus mingled their bloods inside its body. The speaker uses the flea as an image of the physical union of a man and a woman, something he would like to enjoy with the woman he is addressing. He envies the flea who, as he fancifully imagines, can enjoy her body without having to woo her first.

Stanza 2
As the woman prepares to kill the flea that has just bitten her, he warns her of the consequences of doing this. The argument of this stanza is wonderfully ingenious and, if we accept its astonishing premise, perfectly logical. It is founded on the notion that because the flea has sucked blood from both the speaker and his mistress, it now incorporates three lives: his, hers and its own. Since their bloods are mixed inside its body, within its 'living walls of Jet' (line 15), the flea has been transformed into their marriage bed and their marriage temple or church, the places where they are united as one.

John Donne

Having used the presence of their mingled bloods in the flea's body to arrive at the outrageous conclusion that this makes the flea their place of residence, the speaker wittily, and equally outrageously, deduces that 'This flea is you and I' (line 12). This allows him to propose a further argument. If his mistress kills the flea, she will be guilty of three major offences. First, she will be committing murder by killing him inside the flea. Second, by killing herself inside it, she will be committing suicide. Third, she will be destroying the temple in which they were married (as he sees it), thus committing sacrilege.

Stanza 3

As the third stanza makes immediately clear, the speaker's attempts to save the flea's life have been futile. The woman has killed it and so shed innocent blood. Donne's speaker extracts what advantage he can from the woman's argument that neither he nor she has suffered from what she has done to the flea. From this, he draws the odd conclusion that if she yields to him, she will lose no more honour than she did when 'the flea's death tooke life' from her (line 27).

Thinking about the poem

1   Here the flea appears in a variety of guises. List these. How appropriate are they to Donne's theme?
2   What is Donne trying to achieve in the poem?
3   Discuss 'The Flea' as an example of Donne's astonishing ingenuity and verbal dexterity.
4   Is the flea the central character of this poem?
5   Outline the argument of the poem in your own words.
6   On the evidence of the poem, what kind of woman is Donne addressing?
7   In this poem, Donne treats the flea as no flea has been treated in English before. Comment on the original elements in 'The Flea', and on the role Donne assigns to the flea in the lives of the two people who are the other subjects of the poem.
8   'living walls of Jet' (line 15). Comment on whether this is an effective description of a flea.
9   'Purpled thy nail' (line 20). Discuss this description and how it affects your impression of the woman.

Personal response

1 Choose two lines from the poem that especially appeal to you and explain your choice.

2 'The Flea' is generally regarded as an extremely clever and entertaining poem. Explain why you agree or disagree with this view of the poem.

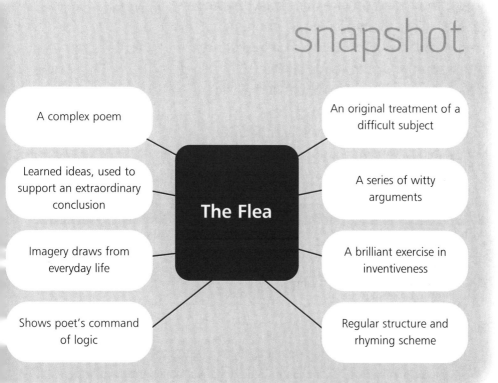

snapshot

The Flea

A complex poem

Learned ideas, used to support an extraordinary conclusion

Imagery draws from everyday life

Shows poet's command of logic

An original treatment of a difficult subject

A series of witty arguments

A brilliant exercise in inventiveness

Regular structure and rhyming scheme

John Donne

[handwritten: SONNET — Petrachan / Italian Sonnet]

Batter My Heart
[handwritten: SOUL above "Heart"]

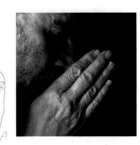

[handwritten: Direct order]

Batter my heart, three person'd God; for, you *[A]*
As yet but knocke, breathe, shine, and seeke to mend; *[B]*
That I may rise, and stand, o'erthrow mee'and bend *[B]*
[handwritten: reform/ renew] Your force, to breake, blowe, burn and make me new. *[A]*
[handwritten: simile] I, like an usurpt towne, to'another due, *[5]*
Labour to'admit you, but Oh, to no end, *[octet]*
Reason your viceroy in mee, mee should defend,
But is captiv'd, and proves weake or untrue.
Yet dearely I love you, and would be loved faine, *[sestet]*
[handwritten: engaged] But am betroth'd unto your enemie: *[→ devil]*
[handwritten: against his will] Divorce mee'untie, or breake that knot againe, *[10]*
Take mee to you, imprison mee, for I
[handwritten: captured] Except you'enthrall mee, never shall be free,
Nor ever chast, except you ravish mee.

Glossary		
1	*three person'd God:* the Trinity: Father, Son and Holy Ghost	
5	*like . . . due:* the usurped town owes its loyalty to somebody other than the one who occupies it. The speaker is the town: he owes loyalty to God, but is in the possession of God's enemy, the devil	
6	*labour:* work, toil	
6	*to no end:* to no purpose, without success	
7	*Reason . . . defend:* reason should be able to defend me from evil acts or impulses. A viceroy is a monarch's representative. Donne imagines reason representing God in the human mind to help in the struggle against evil	
9	*be loved faine:* dearly wish to be loved	
10	*betroth'd:* engaged to be married	
10	*your enemie:* the devil	
11	*Divorce . . . againe:* he is asking God to separate him from the devil by untying or breaking the bond that unites him to evil	
13–14	*Except . . . ravish mee:* these two lines are based on two startling paradoxes. The speaker is telling God that he will never be free from sin unless God makes him his prisoner ('enthralls' him) and that he will never be chaste unless God possesses his body and soul	

Guidelines

This poem belongs to a group of Holy Sonnets, written at a dismal period in Donne's life after the death of his wife in 1617. This event deeply affected his outlook and robbed him of the security and fixity his wife had provided. In his adversity, he looked to God for some compensating assurance of love and comfort. The tension evident in 'Batter My Heart' and 'At the Round Earth's Imagin'd Corners' arises from the speaker's anxiety that his sinful life may not dispose God to grant him salvation. This anxiety sometimes betrays the speaker's terror, particularly as he contemplates an unfavourable judgement from God.

Commentary

Two emotions dominate this sonnet: the speaker's overpowering sense of guilt and his obsessive desire to be liberated from the tyranny of sin. The task of liberation is to be performed by God. Up to now, as the second line indicates, God has been gentle in his attempts to win the speaker's heart: he has been content 'to knocke, breathe, shine, and seeke to mend'. These quiet attempts to persuade the speaker to reform are doomed. Stronger measures are demanded. God must 'batter' (line 1) instead of knock. The speaker cries out to be overwhelmed by God's power, or 'force' (line 4), so that he may be shattered and then re-created, like base metal transformed into gold.

In lines 5 to 8 the soul is imagined as a conquered city, willing to admit the dispossessed prince (God) who is besieging it. The images of siege and warfare seem natural in the context created by the violent movement of the opening four lines. Now the speaker is explaining to God that he cannot resist sin without divine help. His reason on its own is incapable of conquering the assaults of evil.

Lines 9 and 10 introduce a new metaphor. The speaker presents his relationship with God in terms of the unsatisfied longings of a lover. He speaks as a woman about to be forced into a marriage against her will, looking wistfully towards the man she loves in the hope that he may still claim her from her hateful partner. The loved one is God; the one who holds the speaker in bondage is the devil.

So far the poem has featured strongly contrasted images of physical violence and romantic love. In the final four lines, these images are combined in a powerful, if somewhat startling, plea to God. If the speaker is ever to feel safe from the evil enemy, God must take possession of his entire being as a besieger might overwhelm a town, or as a ravisher might violate a woman.

John Donne

Tone and language of the poem

The first four lines are urgent, even violent, in tone. The explosive effect is achieved by an unusually dense accumulation of heavily stressed verbs. Continuous alliteration enhances the sense of urgency and power ('batter', 'breathe', 'bend', 'breake, blowe, burn').

Lines 5 to 8 involve a major change of tone. The speaker abandons his imperative mood and becomes apologetic as he explains his problems to God. To reinforce the plaintive mood, gentler sounds (as in 'usurpt', 'reason', 'viceroy' and 'proves') displace the explosive ones of the first four lines. Line 9 is gentle and wistful. The fierce demands of the opening are by now moderated to the tenderness of 'Yet dearely I love you, and would be loved faine'.

The last four lines are dominated by the same violent and passionate feeling with which the poem opened, as the speaker renews his tormented request to be possessed by God.

Like Donne's other poems, 'Batter My Heart' is argumentative in tone and is dominated by the poet's powerful wit. The speaker argues urgently and persistently with God with the aim of forcing him to accept his point of view and his answer to the difficult problems he is facing.

The major figures of speech in the poem are those found in all of Donne's major poems: the conceit and the paradox. Some of the conceits are telescoped, such as the one in line 4 where the image ('breake, blowe, burn') is of an alchemist turning base metal to gold. Others are more elaborate, as when Donne compares his soul to a captured town and to an unhappily engaged woman, both seeking liberation.

There are three particularly impressive paradoxes. The first of these – 'That I may rise, and stand, o'erthrow mee'and bend / Your force . . . and make me new' – suggests that he can never stand firm unless God first overthrows him. This has its parallel in the double paradox of the final two lines: the speaker can never be free until God has taken him prisoner, nor chaste until God has ravished him.

Form of the poem

The poem is a traditional Petrarchan sonnet. Its fourteen lines are divided into an octave (the first eight lines) and a sestet (the final six lines). It has a traditional rhyming pattern: *abba abba cdcdee* and is written (more or less) in iambic pentameter. Donne uses this controlled form to contain the various emotions expressed in the poem. He uses the same form for the next two sonnets on the course: 'At the Round Earth's Imagin'd Corners' and 'Thou Hast Made Me'.

Thanks Eva! ◡◠

Thinking about the poem

1   How does the speaker treat God in this poem? What kind of relationship does he imagine he has with God?

2   The poem is <u>densely metaphorical</u>. Examine Donne's use of <u>metaphor as an expression of meaning</u>. <u>Why</u> are metaphors more effective here than literal expression might have been?

3   By line 9 the mood and tone of the poem, as well as the key metaphors, have <u>changed</u>. Comment on this change. why? octer - sester

4   In the final four lines, Donne brings the conflicting images (violence and love) of the previous ten lines together. Is this an effective way in which to end the poem?

5   Paradox is a key figure in 'Batter My Heart'. Analyse its use. What does it achieve?

6   Would you agree that the sonnet reveals a troubled mind? What are the details that suggest this idea?

7   Reading this sonnet makes us feel that both God and the devil are familiar acquaintances, close at hand. Comment on this observation, with reference to the poem.

8   This sonnet is not merely an exercise in powerful rhetoric, or a showing-off of Donne's talent for paradox. It is also an impressive testimony of the poet's deep religious conviction, his fear of losing God's friendship. Do you think both parts of this statement represent the truth about 'Batter My Heart'. Refer to the poem in support of your response.

Personal response

1   Did you enjoy reading this poem? Give a reason for your answer.

2   Try to write a Petrarchan sonnet, keeping to the structure, rhythm and rhyming scheme used in 'Batter My Heart'.

John Donne

At the Round Earth's Imagin'd Corners

At the round earths imagin'd corners, blow
Your trumpets, Angells, and arise, arise
From death, you numberlesse infinities
Of soules, and to your scattred bodies goe,
All whom the flood did, and fire shall o'erthrow,   5
All whom warre, dearth, age, agues, tyrannies,
Despaire, law, chance, hath slaine, and you whose eyes,
Shall behold God, and never tast deaths woe.
But let them sleepe, Lord, and mee mourne a space,
For, if above all these, my sinnes abound,   10
'Tis late to aske abundance of thy grace,
When wee are there; here on this lowly ground,
Teach mee how to repent; for that's as good
As if thou hadst seal'd my pardon, with thy blood.

Glossary		
1	*imagin'd corners:* the Book of Revelations refers to 'the four corners of the earth'
2	*trumpets:* St Paul tells the Corinthians that angels will play trumpets to herald the resurrection of the dead
4	*soules . . . goe:* the orthodox Christian teaching is that between death and the final resurrection of the dead, human souls exist in isolation from their bodies. Donne suggests here that the soul dies with the body, and that both will be resurrected on the Last Day
4	*scattred bodies:* the bodies of the dead scattered about the world as dust and bones
5	*the flood:* the Book of Genesis describes the destruction of almost the entire human race in a great flood
5	*fire:* some people believe that the final destruction of the world will be through fire
6	*dearth:* famine
6	*agues:* fevers

7–8	*you . . . woe:* those who survive until the Last Day will not have to experience the pain of death. Donne would like to avoid this and the prospect of rotting away in the grave, which is why he would like the Last Day to come while he is still alive
9–12	*But . . . there:* Donne is having second thoughts. He now realises that if he were to face the Last Judgement immediately, he might not be saved because of the great number of sins he has committed
12	*lowly ground:* Earth
14	*As . . . blood:* if he can repent, he can be sure of earning the pardon that Christ's death has won for humankind

Guidelines

During much of his later life, Donne showed a deep interest in the fate of those who would be alive on the Last Day, and liked to imagine that he himself might be counted as one of them. If he were, he would be able to avoid what he dreaded most: the corruption of his body and its dissolution in the grave. In one of his sermons, he numbered himself among the fortunate mortals who, by living till the end of the world, would avoid having to die, or if they did die for a brief time, would not taste the corruption of the grave. He said: 'We shall die, and be alive again, before another could consider that we were dead'. This urgent desire to be alive on the Last Day explains why he asks in this sonnet that the Last Judgement should take place now (lines 1–4) rather than at some indefinite point in the future.

Commentary

Donne was fascinated by death and dying and he liked to think that he and his contemporaries were the Earth's last inhabitants. It is to such people that he addresses the closing words of the octave of this sonnet: 'and you whose eyes / Shall behold God, and never tast deaths woe' (lines 7 and 8). **The people who will never experience the pain of death are those who will still be alive on the Day of Judgement.** They will come face to face with God without having to endure the death that all other mortals endured.

For Donne, the single most revolting aspect of death was the thought of his body and the bodies of those he loved rotting away in the grave. If he could be one of those fortunate enough to survive until the Last Day, he could avoid this gruesome fate. He would also escape another fate that he found distasteful: the period between death and resurrection, during which human souls had to exist in isolation from their bodies. He finds this last idea so difficult to accept that he rejects the orthodox Christian teaching on the subject and suggests that the soul will die with the body and be resurrected with it on the Last Day. He makes souls as well as bodies 'arise / From death' (lines 2 and 3).

The speaker asks that the Last Judgement should take place at once. To achieve this desirable result, he is prepared to call for the immediate end of the world, and of everybody and everything in it, provided that he is given enough time to repent for his many sins.

In the last six lines of the poem, however, **the speaker has second thoughts about the imminent end to his and all other human lives. He decides that if he were to face the Last Judgement now he might not be saved because of the multitude of his sins.** It would therefore be better for him if the dead were allowed to sleep on a while ('a space', line 9) so that he may learn to repent of his sins while he is still on Earth ('this lowly ground', line 12). It will be too late to ask God's pardon when he is facing him on the Day of Judgement.

Rhythm and tone of the poem

There is an effective contrast in rhythm and tone between the octave and the sestet of this sonnet. The Day of Judgement is evoked in the exciting, almost breathless, rhythms of the first eight lines. In the final six lines, when consideration of the fate of the multitudes of the dead gives way to the speaker's own plight, the rhythm becomes quieter, gentler and less complex. The tone of the first eight lines is insistent and rhetorical; that of the final six is humble and submissive.

Thinking about the poem

1. In what ways might this sonnet be regarded as an extremely self-centred poem?
2. In the course of the sonnet, the speaker experiences a change of mind. Identify this and try to account for it.
3. Describe the state of mind emerging from the sonnet. What is the speaker's primary emotion?
4. What is the speaker's attitude to death?
5. Consider the contrast between the first eight lines of the sonnet and the final six.

6   The speaker refers to 'you whose eyes, / Shall behold God, and never tast deaths woe' (lines 7 and 8). Show how central these lines are to the meaning of the poem.

7   How does Donne use the sonnet form to organise or give structure to his thoughts in this poem?

8   'At the round earths imagin'd corners' (line 1). Comment on the impact of this opening phrase.

Personal response

1   'This sonnet tells us something interesting about Donne's outlook, and about the kind of person he was.' What impression do you get of the poet from your reading of this poem?

2   You are publishing this poem on a website and you have been asked to create or find a suitable photograph or picture to accompany it. Describe the image you would use.

John Donne

Thou Hast Made Me

Direct statement   *Rhetorical Question*

Thou hast made me, And shall thy worke decay?
Imperative
Repaire me now, for now mine end doth haste,   *Death is imminent*
I runne to death, and death meets me as fast,   *personification*
                                                 URGENCY
And all my pleasures are like yesterday;
I dare not move my dimme eyes any way,   5
Despaire behind, and death before doth cast   → *not confident*
                                  alliteration
Such terrour, and my feeble flesh doth waste   → *thinks he's going*
By sinne in it, which it t'wards hell doth weigh;   *to hell*
Onely thou art above, and when towards thee
permission
By thy leave I can looke, I rise againe;   10
inclusive unite
But our old subtle foe so tempteth me,   *DEVIL*   SESTET
That not one houre my selfe I can sustaine;
                     lift
Thy Grace may wing me to prevent this art,
And thou like Adamant draw mine iron heart.
         magnet   *cold*   → *weight to hell /*
                                          draw to god.

CONCEIT
god as a
magnet

OCTET

93

Glossary		
2	*mine end doth haste:* my death approaches fast	
5	*dimme eyes:* his eyes have been dimmed by age	
8	*which . . . weigh:* the weight of his sins drags him towards hell	
11	*subtle foe:* cunning enemy; here, the devil, who tempts him to despair in his hour of distress	
12	*not . . . sustaine:* the poet cannot sustain himself for even an hour against the devil's temptations	
13	*Thy . . . art:* God's grace may draw him upward (towards God) and so frustrate the devil's tricks	
14	*like Adamant . . . heart:* like a magnet, God may attract the speaker's iron heart (a hard heart that is unresponsive to God)	

Guidelines

Like the other Holy Sonnets, this is a poem depicting a struggle. The speaker is in a state of spiritual terror, looking anxiously to God to save him from despair as the devil, the clever old enemy of humankind, tempts him to lose hope. He is sure that God can save him from his despair, but not so sure that God will. Behind his despair, and feeding it, is the speaker's fear of imminent death, and the danger that he will be damned for his past sins.

This is a further expression of the anxiety that haunts Donne's Holy Sonnets, and should be read along with 'Batter My Heart' and 'At the Round Earth's Imagin'd Corners'.

Commentary

As in 'Batter My Heart', the speaker acknowledges his inability to help himself. This time, he has to fight the temptation to despair, which haunts him as the prospect of death and possible damnation looms before him. When he looks up to God he can rise above his despair, but only for a while. The 'old subtle foe' (line 11) of humankind, Satan, works to ensure that despair returns.

The emphasis of the poem is on the power of God to defeat the devil's efforts against him. The speaker knows that God must take the initiative if he is to be redeemed, but also knows that God has not yet done this. As is his usual practice, Donne uses a conceit to make his point. The unrepentant heart of the sinner is made of iron; God must become a magnet ('Adamant', line 14) to draw in this unresponsive metal and redeem it. However, the poem offers no assurance that God will actually take this necessary action. It closes on a note of doubt. All the speaker can hope for is that God's grace 'may' (line 13) raise him in the end.

The critic John Carey has compared the speaker of this poem to a drowning man. This man tells a mysterious bystander on the bank of the river that if he tosses a lifebelt he can save him from death by drowning. However, no lifebelt is forthcoming. Worse still, the man in the water knows that he does not deserve to be saved.

Thinking about the poem

1   The sonnet reveals the speaker as a helpless dependent creature. In what ways is this dependency suggested?
2   What are the speaker's main fears? Are these justified?
3   What image of God emerges from the sonnet? Is the God imagined by the speaker benevolent or punitive? Is he to be loved or to be feared? Is he the friend or the enemy of sinners?
4   How would you describe the mood of the poem?
5   Are the speaker's problems solved at the end?
6   In this sonnet Donne declares that 'death before doth cast / Such terrour' (lines 6 and 7). Consider this statement as expressing the key sentiment of the poem. In your opinion, why does death hold such terror for the speaker? Support your comments with evidence from the poem.
7   Is this a poem about guilt as well as about death? Explain your answer.

Personal response

1   Did you enjoy reading this poem? Give a reason for your opinion.
2   Suggest an alternative title for this poem. Explain your thinking.

Exam-Style Questions

1   Donne's poems are filled with mixed emotions, ranging from playful irreverence and cynicism to profound reverence and sincerity. Examine the variety of moods displayed in the poems on your course..

2   Examine the notion that Donne is a very original love poet. Support the points you make with reference to the poems on your course.

3   In your opinion, what kind of audience did Donne address his poems to?

4   Consider the propositions that Donne's love poems are composed exclusively from the viewpoint of the man, and that whatever the woman does is in response to him – to his urging, pleading, arguing, bullying, weeping.

5   Discuss Donne as a witty, learned, argumentative poet.

6   Explore the idea that Donne's religious poetry reveals an insecure temperament and a profound sense of fear.

7   Much of Donne's poetry, whether secular or religious, is dominated by the need to convince whomever is being addressed. Examine this aspect of the poems.

8   Discuss Donne's treatment of death.

9   Consider some unusual and distinctive aspects of Donne's use of imagery.

10   Donne's poetry is sometimes remarkable for its witty misuse of logical arguments in support of absurd conclusions. Explore this idea.

11   Outline and discuss some features of Donne's poems that make them difficult to understand. You might refer, for example, to his learned references, his comparisons and his use of obscure sources.

12   What appeal might Donne's poems have for a young, modern reader?

13   In many of Donne's poems we can detect a strong impulse to bind opposites together. This impulse can be found in single images or in whole poems. Use some of the poems on your course to show this impulse at work.

Sample essay

The most impressive feature of Donne's poetry is the manner in which he uses all kinds of learned ideas in support of his arguments.

Discuss this comment with reference to some of the poems on your course.

Donne's learned ideas, which feature in almost all his poems on our course, are drawn from many fields of human knowledge. His poems give the impression that he was familiar with the latest developments in geographical exploration, science, theology and philosophy. He was also a master of rhetoric (the science of argument), and familiar with a range of mythologies. It was thus possible for him to draw on this vast store of learned information and illustration to support whatever kind of argument he wanted to engage in.

[Introduction agrees with and expands on the statement]

The arguments that form the substance of so many of his poems can be with anyone, human or divine, or with non-human entities. Donne seems to enjoy arguing for its own sake. Many of his arguments can appear odd or far-fetched. For example, throughout 'The Sunne Rising' Donne is arguing with the sun that it has no business shining through his windows and curtains in order to wake him and the woman he loves. By doing this, he maintains, the sun is acting like a foolish old busybody, a 'busie old foole', and displaying an 'unruly' attitude. Instead, he argues, the sun would be better employed at other tasks, such as waking schoolboys who would otherwise be late, or alerting bad-humoured apprentices that it is time to go to work. He also tells the sun that it should alert courtiers who like to flatter the king by hunting with him that it is time for them to rise. Donne's learning comes to the fore in the clever use of his geographical knowledge:

> Looke, and to morrow late, tell mee
>
> Whether both th'Indias of spice and Myne
>
> Be where thou leftst them . . .

In these lines, Donne is showing that the East Indies were noted for spices, and the West Indies for their goldmines. At the same time he urges the sun to make its next visit later in the day than it has made the present one.

[Discussion of first poem supports the statement]

The argument in 'Song: Goe and Catche a Falling Starre' is quite different from that advanced in 'The Sunne Rising'. The speaker addresses his argument to an unidentified person. The point of the argument this time is to suggest that, as the speaker says, 'no where lives a woman true, and faire'. In other words, it is not possible to find a woman who is both attractive and chaste. The speaker has obviously made up his mind that beautiful women cannot be virtuous, and that he does not need to prove this. Instead, he makes a list of impossible tasks, including: catching a falling star, making a mandrake root pregnant, explaining where past years have gone, revealing who caused the devil to have a cloven foot, and making it possible for the singing of mermaids to be heard. The point is that it will prove equally impossible to discover a beautiful chaste woman.

[Note how first sentence of the above paragraph links with the previous paragraph]

In 'Song: Sweetest Love, I Do Not Goe', Donne comes up with another kind of argument, this one based on the quaint idea that if his love sighs while he is away, she is really sighing his soul away, and if she weeps, she is causing his life's blood to decay. In either case, she will be doing him harm, and proving that she does not love him. The point of his argument is that she should patiently endure separation from him until he returns. Another part of the argument is that if she worries about him coming to harm while he is away ('Forethinke me any ill'), her fears may be justified as 'Destiny' may bring him to the harm she worries about.

[Third poem is introduced to widen the discussion]

In another poem of parting, 'A Valediction: Forbidding Mourning', Donne tries to reassure the woman he loves by arguments drawn from science and geometrical drawing. The scientific argument is stated in lines that require knowledge of the process required to make gold leaf:

> Our two soules therefore, which are one
>
> Though I must goe, endure not yet
>
> A breach, but an expansion,
>
> Like gold to ayery thinnesse beat.

The argument here is based on the suggestion that absence will not involve a breach between him and his beloved. On the contrary, it will keep them united. He uses a far-fetched comparison to demonstrate this. The more gold is hammered, the thinner it becomes, eventually stretching out to span continents. Similarly, he argues, absence will refine and stretch out the love two people feel for each other, so that this love also spans continents and overcomes distance.

In the same poem, Donne draws on imagery from geology and astronomy to make another point:

> Moving of th'earth brings harmes and feares,
>
> Men reckon what it did and meant,
>
> But trepidation of the spheares,
>
> Through greater farre, is innocent.

In the second and third of these lines, Donne is drawing on an ancient view that the Earth was circled by spheres, whose movements were far greater than those of the Earth itself when earthquakes occurred.

[Fourth poem is introduced and quotes are used to illustrate the points made]

The argumentative, learned poems I have so far considered are addressed to women. Donne, however, was also prepared to argue with God, sometimes using violent language, as in the sonnet 'Batter My Heart'.

[A short paragraph informs the reader that the focus is moving from Donne's love poems to his religious sonnets]

A good example of the way in which Donne calls on his learning to support his arguments is the sonnet 'At the Round Earth's Imagin'd Corners'. Even the title of this sonnet displays the poet's familiarity with the newest developments in scientific thought. The 'imagined corners' refer to the long-standing view that the Earth was flat and thus had four corners. Reference to the 'round earth' is Donne's way of showing that he is familiar with the displacement by later astronomers of the old view.

This poem also demonstrates Donne's expert handling of theological views, especially those concerning the end of the world and the coming of Christ to judge humankind. These views form the context of the sonnet, which condenses a good deal of biblical teaching, featuring Angelic trumpets, the 'numberlesse infinities of soules' joining their 'scattred bodies'. Donne introduces the novel idea that he may survive until the Last Day and 'never tast deaths woe', asking God to let him repent of his sins in time to save his soul. The final line of the poem is based on the Christian doctrine of redemption: that Christ redeemed sinful humankind with his own blood.

[Sonnet used to demonstrate Donne's scientific learning and to illustrate his religious thinking]

A third sonnet, 'Thou Hast Made Me', is an eloquent argument on the Christian idea of sin and temptation, and the power of God to overcome these. The speaker is weighed down with fear of hell and of his own weakness in failing to resist the urge to sin and in failing to resist the snares of the devil's tricks. He urges God to draw him struggling towards heaven, using a magnetic force: 'And thou like Adamant draw mine iron heart'.

[Sonnet used to expand discussion of Donne's theological knowledge]

There are many impressive features of Donne's poetry, including his witty arguments, his clever use of language, his dramatic style and his inventiveness. But these features rely on and are enhanced by his use of learned ideas. All the examples I have given in this essay show that Donne has mastered a wide range of knowledge and is able to use this knowledge easily and naturally to illustrate his arguments. I therefore agree with the statement that this is the most impressive feature of his poetry.

[Conclusion refers back to the question and summarises response to the statement]

John Donne

snapshot

Blends wit with seriousness

Ability to surprise

Poems remarkable for their witty paradoxes

Obsessed with death

Extremely learned, reveals knowledge of science, medicine, astronomy, geography and theology

Some critics find his poetry difficult and over-elaborate

Uses startling effects

Fond of logical argument

Love poems are often insolent, mocking and cynical rather than tender or adoring

Imagery drawn from everyday life, as well as from books

Deeply interested in religion

Balances reason with emotion

Robert Frost

b. 1874-1963

Biography

Robert Frost was born in San Francisco in 1874. His father died from tuberculosis when Robert was eleven years of age, leaving the family with just eight dollars to live on. His mother then moved the family to Massachusetts, where his grandparents lived. Robert attended Lawrence High School and later Dartmouth College, but failed to finish his undergraduate course, taking a job at a mill instead. He started to study again in 1897, at Harvard University, but left without taking a degree. He tried shoemaking, teaching, editing a local paper and then farming.

Frost the farmer

In 1895 he married Elinor White. They had six children, one of whom died in infancy. For a number of years the family lived on a farm that Frost had inherited from his grandfather. He also supplemented his income by teaching, which he enjoyed. In 1911 Frost sold the farm and moved to England, where he hoped to find literary success.

Frost and his family returned to America in 1915 and settled on a farm in New Hampshire. The life of a farmer appealed to him. He combined farming with family life, writing and lecturing. This pattern would continue for the rest of his life. He was a gifted speaker, with his mixture of homespun Yankee wisdom, poetic insights and sense of humour. Invitations for him to speak and read his poems around the country poured in.

Frost's public success was not mirrored by his personal life. His sister Jeanie suffered from mental illness. One of his daughters, Marjorie, had a nervous breakdown and died at the age of twenty-nine from tuberculosis. Another daughter, Irma, also suffered from mental illness. His son Carol took his own life in 1940. Frost's wife, Elinor, died of a heart attack in 1938; they had been married for forty-three years. Although Frost does not refer directly to these events in his work, it may be that the trauma of these experiences is reflected in the occasional darkness of his poems. We know that he also suffered from depression at periods in his life. ('Acquainted with the Night' hints at these experiences.)

Following Elinor's death, Frost may have gained some consolation from his long relationship with Kay Morrison, his secretary and manager, for whom he wrote some appreciative poems.

Literary career

His first book of poems, *A Boy's Will,* was published in England in 1913. This collection contained 'The Tuft of Flowers'. His originality was recognised by leading poet and fellow American Ezra Pound, who praised Frost for having 'the good sense to speak naturally and to paint the thing, the thing as he sees it'. W. B. Yeats called the volume 'the best poetry written in America for a long time'. Frost began to enjoy the friendship and acceptance of the English literary society of the time. His second collection, *North of Boston* (1914), in which 'Mending Wall' was published, received excellent reviews.

Back in America, his experience of rural life is reflected in his third collection, *Mountain Interval* (1916), in which several of his most famous lyrics appear, including 'Out, Out–'. This sad poem was based on a true story: the death in a farm accident of a neighbour's son.

The collection *New Hampshire* (1923) consolidated his already formidable reputation, and in 1924 he was awarded the first of his four Pulitzer Prizes for Poetry – a record number for any poet. *West-Running Brook* (1928) was followed by the *Collected Poems* in 1931. In the same year he was elected to the American Academy of Arts and Letters. Many honorary degrees and public awards followed. His other published collections were *A Further Range* (1936), *A Witness Tree* (1942), *Steeple Bush* (1947) and his last collection, *In the Clearing* (1962).

Frost could be said to have been a 'celebrity' in his lifetime. He was a gifted speaker and was often invited to address the public. He recited one of his poems, 'The Gift Outright', at the inauguration of John F. Kennedy as US President in 1961, watched by a television audience of around sixty million people. As a celebrated poet, he travelled to places as far apart as Brazil and Ireland. In a visit to Soviet Russia in 1962, he read his poem 'Mending Wall'.

When Frost died in 1963, at the age of eighty-nine, he was considered one of the finest American poets of the twentieth century.

Robert Frost

Social and cultural context

Modernism

Poets of the Modernist movement were influenced by the great developments in human thought in philosophy and science that had taken place at the end of the nineteenth century, notably the work of Sigmund Freud in psychoanalysis and Charles Darwin in science. The experience of the First World War, too, altered social attitudes and structures. It no longer seemed artistically credible to write poems in the traditional metres and forms. Indeed, the central tenet of the Modernist movement, articulated by Ezra Pound, was 'make it new'.

Although Frost was part of the literary circle in London that included Pound, and he was a contemporary of many of the other great Modernist poets of the twentieth century (including T. S. Eliot and Wallace Stevens), Frost's work differs from theirs in certain important respects. His poetic practice was not unduly influenced by ideas current at the time and his career took a different path. Much of the work of Modernist poets was so experimental that it could be obscure, resulting in low sales figures for their books. Frost, on the other hand, set out to be understood.

Frost was a traditionalist in form and metre. He avoided writing in free verse. The settings of his poems are for the most part rural, whereas the Modernists saw themselves as the poets of the metropolis. Their works allude constantly to classical literature, while Frost's poems were praised for their accessibility. He was nonetheless a learned man who wished to develop his art in an independent and ambitious way. Early in his career he had a self-confident sense of purpose. As he wrote to his friend John Bartlett, 'To be perfectly frank with you I am one of the most notable craftsmen of my time. That will transpire presently.'

Sound of sense

Frost developed a sophisticated theory of poetic language, which he called the 'sound of sense'. By this he meant that language in poetry should reproduce the exact tone of meaning in human speech. He recognised that his theory was not altogether original – the Romantic poets, as far back as the late eighteenth century, had put forward the idea that literary language should be as close as possible to 'the language of men'. But by the end of the nineteenth century, the diction of poetry had ceased to have common currency, and Frost, like Modernist poets also, searched for a new idiom in which to write.

The American way of life

The story of Frost's subsequent career as a poet is interesting for the light it throws upon cultural attitudes in America. His success can be partly explained by the way he deliberately built up a public persona of himself as a typical Yankee: a plain man living in rural New England, a man for whom the hard work of farming was a real inspiration. Poems such as 'Mending Wall' and 'After Apple-Picking' reflect this image of his life.

Biographers and critics have discussed the extent to which this persona was real or invented. They point out that he was a distinguished teacher and intellectual. His poems are not the simple 'nature' poems that they seem to be on the surface. As he said himself, 'I'm not a nature poet. There's always something else in my poetry.' But he continued to play a role that appealed to the public, as an essentially American poet rooted in rural values. Caribbean poet Derek Walcott described him as 'the icon of Yankee values, the smell of wood-smoke, the sparkle of dew, the reality of farm-house dung, the jocular honesty of an uncle'.

Social historians point out that in the twentieth century the American way of life became increasingly urbanised and remote from the rustic idylls that Frost's poems seem to depict, for example in 'Birches'. It may be that nostalgia played a part in the public acclaim of Frost.

In social and cultural terms he certainly had a prominent role in American public life. During the Second World War 50,000 copies of one of his poems were distributed to US troops stationed overseas to boost morale. Honours and awards were heaped upon him during the course of his long life. His standing in American society can be seen clearly by his participation in Kennedy's inauguration in 1961, while in 1962 he was asked to visit Russia on a good will mission for the US Department of State.

His place in the canon of American literature is assured, both as a poet who influenced the course of the lyric poem as written by American poets, and as a best-selling poet whose work is part of the cultural birthright of the American people.

Robert Frost

Timeline

1874	Born San Francisco, USA
1885	Moves with family to New England
1887–9	Attends Dartmouth College
1895	Marries Elinor White
1897	Attends Harvard University
1901	Moves to grandfather's farm in Derry, New Hampshire
1911	Moves to England, hoping for literary success
1913	Publishes first book of poems, *A Boy's Will*
1914	Second collection, *North of Boston*, appears
1915	Returns to America, settling on a farm in New Hampshire
1916	Publishes *Mountain Interval*
1917	Joins Amherst College as poet in residence
1920s	Divides time between farming, lecturing and literary activities
1923	Publishes *New Hampshire*
1924	Wins first of four Pulitzer Prizes for Poetry
1928	Publishes *West-Running Brook*
1931	*Collected Poems* appears. Elected to the American Academy of Arts and Letters
1936	Publishes *A Further Range*
1938	Elinor dies
1942	Publishes *A Witness Tree*
1947	Publishes *Steeple Bush*
1961	Reads poetry at the inauguration of President John Fitzgerald Kennedy
1962	Visits Russia on a good will mission for the US Department of State. Last collection, *In the Clearing*, appears
1963	Dies in Boston

Some people believe that we can learn a lot by observing nature. What might we learn from a tuft of flowers?

The Tuft of Flowers

I went to turn the grass once after one
Who mowed it in the dew before the sun.

The dew was gone that made his blade so keen
Before I came to view the leveled scene.

I looked for him behind an isle of trees;   5
I listened for his whetstone on the breeze.

But he had gone his way, the grass all mown,
And I must be, as he had been – alone,

'As all must be,' I said within my heart,
'Whether they work together or apart.'   10

But as I said it, swift there passed me by
On noiseless wing a bewildered butterfly,

Seeking with memories grown dim o'er night
Some resting flower of yesterday's delight

And once I marked his flight go round and round,   15
As where some flower lay withering on the ground.

And then he flew as far as eye could see,
And then on tremulous wing came back to me.

I thought of questions that have no reply,
And would have turned to toss the grass to dry;   20

But he turned first, and led my eye to look
At a tall tuft of flowers beside a brook,

Robert Frost

107

A leaping tongue of bloom the scythe had spared
Beside a reedy brook the scythe had bared.

The mower in the dew had loved them thus,   25
By leaving them to flourish, not for us,

Not yet to draw one thought of ours to him,
But from sheer morning gladness at the brim.

The butterfly and I had lit upon,
Nevertheless, a message from the dawn,   30

That made me hear the waking birds around,
And hear his long scythe whispering to the ground,

And feel a spirit kindred to my own;
So that henceforth I worked no more alone;

But glad with him, I worked as with his aid,   35
And weary, sought at noon with him the shade;

And dreaming, as it were, held brotherly speech
With one whose thought I had not hoped to reach.

'Men work together,' I told him from the heart,
'Whether they work together or apart.'   40

Glossary	
title	*Tuft:* cluster or clump
1	*turn the grass:* turn the grass over so that it will dry
3	*keen:* sharp-edged
6	*whetstone:* stone used for sharpening tools
18	*tremulous:* quivering
23	*scythe:* a long curving, sharp-edged blade for cutting grass

Guidelines

'The Tuft of Flowers' is from Frost's first collection of poems, *A Boy's Will*, published in England in 1913 when he was thirty-nine years old. These are the poems that made him famous. The collection of poems was praised by reviewers, among them Ezra Pound, for their 'simplicity', but as Frost himself remarked, 'if they are [simple] they are subtle too'.

Commentary

Frost said that this poem is 'about fellowship' (companionship). **Nature is seen to teach the poet an important lesson about human beings and their relationships with one another.** The poem is in a long tradition of nature poems that see nature not only as a source of delight, but also as containing lessons that can be learned, as if nature is a text that can be read in many ways. Nature, it was suggested, can illumine human feelings and situations.

Frost takes a simple situation – the speaker goes out to turn the grass after it has been mown earlier in the day – and from there he allows natural images to create atmosphere and symbolise human experience.

At the beginning of the poem the speaker seems to feel rather lonely and isolated. The man who had mown the grass has long gone. The place is empty and silent. He seems to accept his feelings of loneliness as part of the experience of being human.

The word 'But' (line 11) introduces a different mood, as the speaker begins to observe a butterfly in full flight, going 'round and round' (line 15). Words such as 'bewildered' (line 12) and 'tremulous' (line 18) capture its zigzag flight, but the speaker sees it as having a purpose. It is seeking out the flowers it had visited the previous day, of which it had some memories of 'yesterday's delight' (line 14). At first it seems to fail, landing on a flower that 'lay withering on the ground' (line 16) before resuming its search. This reminds the speaker that there are 'questions that have no reply' (line 19).

The speaker follows the butterfly's flight into a 'tall tuft of flowers' (line 22) that the previous mower had not cut down. These flowers had been left uncut by the previous mower purely for his own pleasure – 'sheer morning gladness' (line 28) – and not as a message to anyone else. The speaker feels a sense of connection with him nevertheless. Now he feels as if he 'worked no more alone'(line 34). In contrast with his earlier lonely feelings, he takes comfort in the idea that he and the previous mower are communicating with each other in 'brotherly speech' (line 37).

The final couplet contradicts the idea that people are alone 'Whether they work together or apart' (line 40). **In fact, the speaker says, even if people must work separately, companionship and understanding is possible between them. This paradox (or seeming contradiction) is the main theme of the poem.**

Robert Frost

Viewpoints

Some readers have suggested that we can read 'The Tuft of Flowers' as Frost's way of describing the situation of the modern poet who must find his own way of writing poems. This is a lonely enterprise at first, until the poet, like the speaker who finds the flowers, realises that he is not writing alone but in a continuous tradition of poetry. In later life Frost admitted that the poem contained 'a definition of poetry'. You might take into account that there are many images of speech and communication used throughout the poem, such as the speaker 'said', he 'listened', he had 'questions', he 'held brotherly speech', etc. These images would suggest that the poem itself is communicating with previous poems and reaching out to those poems that will come afterwards.

Frost's nature poems

'The Tuft of Flowers' illustrates some of Frost's characteristic poetic methods in his nature poems. There is the figure of the speaker-poet at his solitary labour. There are the observations and loving descriptions of real situations and natural scenes. We also see how Frost moves from describing a scene to recognising its underlying significance for human beings. This is also seen in 'Mending Wall', where Frost questions and explores the meaning of another ordinary situation.

Personification

The butterfly is personified as a creature whose role it is to lead the speaker to the flowers and thus to 'teach' him the social lesson of the poem. The image of the butterfly seems to arise naturally from the poem's setting, but it belongs also to the literary tradition of the fable, in which a helpful creature points a human being in the right direction. (Butterflies had from the time of the Greeks been associated with Psyche, or the soul). Other objects are personified – the flowers as messengers, for instance – so that the speaker's interpretation of the scene leads to the positive lesson of the final couplet, which contradicts the earlier, bleaker view of human life.

Form of the poem

The poem is organised in couplets, each expressing a single thought. The rhyme scheme is regular throughout: *aa, bb, cc.* This makes the poem sound pleasantly harmonious, which contributes to the optimistic attitude that is finally expressed.

Thinking about the poem

1. Why does the speaker say at first that all people must be alone, 'Whether they work together or apart' (line 10)?

2. What would you say is the mood of the speaker in the first five couplets?

3. How would you describe the setting of the poem: peaceful, lonely, bleak? Perhaps you would suggest another word. Explain your answer.

4. What role does the butterfly play in the poem?

5. What does the speaker realise when he sees the tuft of flowers?

6. Why, in your opinion, does the speaker refer to the previous mower as a 'spirit kindred to my own' (line 33)?

7. What does the speaker have in common with the earlier mower?

8. How does the speaker's mood change in the last four couplets?

9. From your reading of the poem, would you agree that Frost had a positive attitude to nature? Give reasons for your answer.

10. Do you agree with the view suggested in the guidelines that the poem is about writing poetry? Give reasons for your answer.

11. 'The butterfly and I had lit upon, / Nevertheless, a message from the dawn' (lines 29 and 30). What, in your opinion, is the 'message from the dawn'?

12. 'A leaping tongue of bloom the scythe had spared' (line 23). Comment on the image of flowers as a 'leaping tongue'. Do you find it an effective image?

Personal response

1. Do you like poems that contain a 'message', as this one does? Give a reason for your answer.

2. Your class is preparing an anthology of poems about nature. Discuss, in pairs or small groups, why you would (or would not) choose to include this poem.

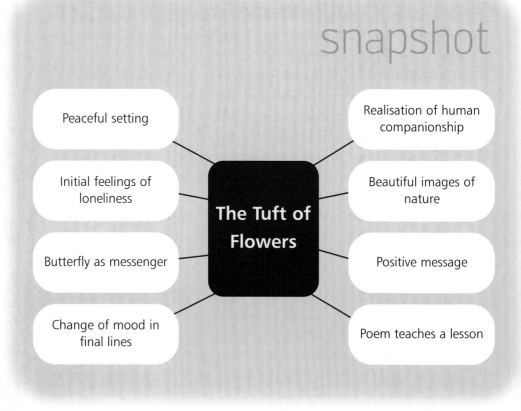

snapshot

Peaceful setting

Initial feelings of loneliness

Butterfly as messenger

Change of mood in final lines

The Tuft of Flowers

Realisation of human companionship

Beautiful images of nature

Positive message

Poem teaches a lesson

Before you read 'Mending Wall'

What expectations would you have about a poem with the title 'Mending Wall'? Do you see mending a wall as an act of co-operation? Does it suggest a desire to keep someone or something inside? Or is it a necessary means of keeping someone or something out of your property?

Mending Wall

Something there is that doesn't love a wall,
That sends the frozen-ground-swell under it
And spills the upper boulders in the sun,
And makes gaps even two can pass abreast.
The work of hunters is another thing: 5
I have come after them and made repair
Where they have left not one stone on a stone,

But they would have the rabbit out of hiding,
To please the yelping dogs. The gaps I mean,
No one has seen them made or heard them made, 10
But at spring mending-time we find them there.
I let my neighbor know beyond the hill;
And on a day we meet to walk the line
And set the wall between us once again.
We keep the wall between us as we go. 15
To each the boulders that have fallen to each.
And some are loaves and some so nearly balls
We have to use a spell to make them balance:
'Stay where you are until our backs are turned!'
We wear our fingers rough with handling them. 20
Oh, just another kind of outdoor game,
One on a side. It comes to little more:
There where it is we do not need the wall:
He is all pine and I am apple orchard.
My apple trees will never get across 25
And eat the cones under his pines, I tell him.
He only says, 'Good fences make good neighbors.'
Spring is the mischief in me, and I wonder
If I could put a notion in his head:
'*Why* do they make good neighbors? Isn't it 30
Where there are cows? But here there are no cows.
Before I built a wall I'd ask to know
What I was walling in or walling out,
And to whom I was like to give offense.
Something there is that doesn't love a wall, 35
That wants it down.' I could say 'Elves' to him,
But it's not elves exactly, and I'd rather
He said it for himself. I see him there,
Bringing a stone grasped firmly by the top
In each hand, like an old-stone savage armed. 40
He moves in darkness as it seems to me,
Not of woods only and the shade of trees.
He will not go behind his father's saying,
And he likes having thought of it so well
He says again, 'Good fences make good neighbors.' 45

Guidelines

'Mending Wall' is from *North of Boston* (1914). One of Frost's most famous poems, it established him as an authentic rural poet, familiar with the ways of farming and with the rugged landscape of New England.

We know from his biographers that Frost sometimes felt alienated from other people. In 'Mending Wall' he seems to be very aware of the differing ideas he and his neighbour have about whether a wall between their properties is really necessary. But he appears to lack the confidence to express his views openly, as if he is not really sure of the response he would get if he did.

The poem took on a wider political significance, as a comment on East–West relations, when Frost recited it to Nikita Khrushchev, the leader of Russia, on a visit to the USSR in 1962. The symbolism of the 'wall', between the West and the Soviet Union, was immediately obvious. In later years the poem has also been used to symbolise other political and social barriers between peoples and countries.

Commentary

Each spring the narrator arranges to meet his neighbour to mend the wall, but it becomes clear that there are differences of opinion between them about whether or not a wall is really needed.

Lines 1–34

The speaker of the poem begins rather mysteriously by saying 'Something there is that doesn't love a wall', and then giving examples of how much nature seems to dislike walls. The ground swells under them in frosty weather (there may be a pun on Frost's name implied here), rocks fall from the top and gaps appear, not only those caused by hunters but strange gaps: 'No one has seen them made or heard them made' (line 10).

The atmosphere at first is co-operative and light-hearted. The speaker playfully tells us that both neighbours resort to a 'kind of outdoor game' (line 21) as they place the fallen boulders back on the wall, talking to them as though they have taken on a life of their own and do not want to remain fixed: 'Stay where you are until our backs are turned!'(line 19). It is as if the wall has been influenced by the 'something' that does not want it built in the first place.

The speaker now makes his views known. **There is really no need for a wall, he says, since his neighbour grows pine trees and he has apple orchards.** He jokes that his apple trees will never eat the pine cones on the other side. But the neighbour does not agree. He simply repeats the saying: 'Good fences make good neighbours' (line 27). This well-known saying is found in many languages and cultures.

The speaker refuses to let this go, and in a spirit of mischief he questions his neighbour about the old saying. Fences are only needed where there are cows that may wander, he suggests. He tries to make the neighbour think about the idea of a wall and what its purpose is. Are you walling yourself in or walling others out? By building a wall (excluding other people) or not building a wall (including them), who are you likely to offend? (lines 32–34).

Lines 35–45
The line 'Something there is that doesn't love a wall' is repeated (line 35), and the speaker continues the sense of mystery he has created from the beginning. He suggests that perhaps 'elves' (line 36), mischievous little creatures from folklore, had a role in knocking down the wall. **But his neighbour has no such ideas, playful or otherwise. Seen now holding one of the stones, he is presented rather threateningly** as an 'old-stone savage armed' (line 40), someone who 'moves in darkness' (line 41). All he can think of to say is 'his father's saying' (line 43) that he will not go against, which suggests that **he cannot and will not change his mind that 'Good fences make good neighbours'** (line 45).

Metaphor of wall
Frost often used ordinary and everyday activities – turning the grass, mending a wall – to reveal deeper meanings. In other words, **Frost saw the metaphorical significance of many seemingly unimportant events.**

The two farmers mending the wall between their lands seem also to be erecting human barriers between themselves. At first they are seen to agree about the necessity of the wall. But a certain amount of tension appears as the speaker allows another point of view to surface. The wall seems to take on a life of its own, influenced perhaps by the 'something' that does not want it built in the first place. There are hints of elemental, even supernatural, energies that seem to comment unfavourably on human attitudes, especially those of the unresponsive neighbour. His unthinking repetition of his father's saying suggests that he is unable to move beyond what has always been thought and said. The rather depressing implication is that the human desire for co-operation (a theme also in 'The Tuft of Flowers') is often thwarted by people themselves. **The neighbours are working together to keep themselves apart.**

Form and language of the poem

In 'Mending Wall' we can see Frost's theory of the 'sound of sense' in the language of poetry. He believed that poems should be able to reproduce the exact tone and nuance of meaning of human speech. In this poem the language is conversational, as if the speaker is thinking aloud. But it is important to note that although the poem does not rhyme, and sounds deceptively casual, Frost uses a strict poetic metre for the entire forty-five lines: iambic pentameter, or five main stresses within the line. Frost famously said once that for him writing poems in so-called 'free verse' would be 'like playing tennis with the net down'.

Thinking about the poem

1   'Something there is that doesn't love a wall' (lines 1 and 35). How, according to the poem, do walls get broken down?

2   Describe how the speaker and his neighbour go about repairing the wall.

3   What difference of opinion exists between the speaker and his neighbour about the wall?

4   Based on evidence from the poem, what sort of person is the neighbour?

5   What 'notion' (line 29) does the speaker want to put in his neighbour's head?

6   Ideas of destroying and mending are found in the poem. Can you find any other contradictions? Explain your answer.

7   What lines or phrases in the poem best capture the conversational style used by Frost?

8   Do you agree that Frost paints an interesting picture of rural life in the poem? Give reasons for your answer.

9   'Oh, just another kind of outdoor game, / One on a side. It comes to little more' (lines 21 and 22). Do you think Frost sees mending the wall as 'just another kind of outdoor game'? Give a reason for your answer.

10   Compare this poem to any other poem by Frost that you have studied as part of your course.

Personal response

1   Complete the following statements to describe your response to the poem:
   ●   I found the poem enjoyable because . . .
   ●   I found the poem depressing because . . .
   ●   I found the poem realistic because . . .

2   Is the saying 'good fences make good neighbours' true, in your opinion? Contribute to a class discussion on this topic. At the end, have a class vote on whether the statement is true.

3   You are Frost's neighbour. Write an entry in your diary in which you describe mending the wall and give your opinion of your neighbour, Robert Frost.

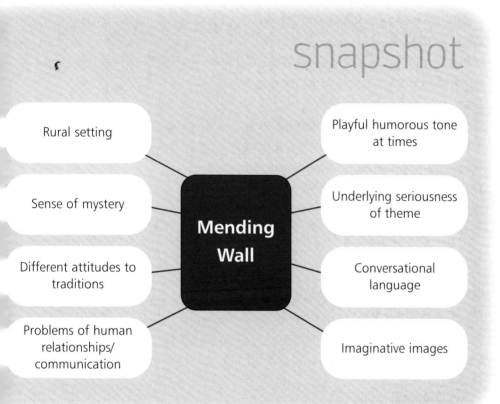

snapshot

Rural setting

Sense of mystery

Different attitudes to traditions

Problems of human relationships/ communication

Mending Wall

Playful humorous tone at times

Underlying seriousness of theme

Conversational language

Imaginative images

After Apple Picking

My long two-pointed ladder's sticking through a tree
Toward heaven still,
And there's a barrel that I didn't fill
Beside it, and there may be two or three
Apples I didn't pick upon some bough.   5
But I am done with apple-picking now.
Essence of winter sleep is on the night,
The scent of apples: I am drowsing off.

I cannot rub the strangeness from my sight
I got from looking through a pane of glass   10
I skimmed this morning from the drinking trough
And held against the world of hoary grass.
It melted, and I let it fall and break.
But I was well
Upon my way to sleep before it fell,   15
And I could tell
What form my dreaming was about to take.
Magnified apples appear and disappear,
Stem end and blossom end,
And every fleck of russet showing clear.   20
My instep arch not only keeps the ache,
It keeps the pressure of a ladder-round.
I feel the ladder sway as the boughs bend,
And I keep hearing from the cellar bin
The rumbling sound   25
Of load on load of apples coming in.
For I have had too much
Of apple-picking: I am overtired
Of the great harvest I myself desired.
There were ten thousand thousand fruit to touch,   30
Cherish in hand, lift down, and not let fall.
For all
That struck the earth,
No matter if not bruised or spiked with stubble,
Went surely to the cider-apple heap   35
As of no worth.
One can see what will trouble
This sleep of mine, whatever sleep it is.
Were he not gone,
The woodchuck could say whether it's like his   40
Long sleep, as I describe its coming on,
Or just some human sleep.

Glossary

7	*essence:* scent
12	*hoary:* white or greyish-white frost
20	*russet:* a reddish-brown colour
40	*woodchuck:* a North American species of marmot or burrowing rodent that hibernates during the winter

Guidelines

'After Apple-Picking' is from Frost's second published book of poems, *North of Boston* (1914). Along with 'Mending Wall' and 'Birches' it was written in the autumn of 1913, while Frost and his family lived at Beaconsfield in England. The setting and imagery are undoubtedly those of the farms in New England (hence the north of Boston of the title of the collection) that Frost had temporarily left behind. The poem evokes beautifully and lyrically the abundant apple-harvest of a New England farm.

Commentary

Lines 1–8

The speaker of the poem, either Frost himself or the farmer persona he often adopted, depicts himself at the moment between being awake and falling asleep.

The long day's labour is over, although the speaker may feel that he has not entirely finished it. His ladder is still 'sticking through a tree' (line 1) and he did not quite pick all of the apples. He is drowsy and prepares for sleep. **The voice is that of a practical farmer looking over his day's work,** pleased to be 'done with apple-picking now' (line 6).

From the earliest lines of the poem there is a contrast between the down-to-earth tone and the poetic imagery used. The ladder is pointing 'Toward heaven' (line 2), a phrase that suggests aspirations and thoughts beyond those of a merely practical man. The metaphor he uses is richly evocative and sensuous: 'Essence of winter sleep is on the night, / The scent of apples' (lines 7 and 8). Here he seems to link the sleep that is coming upon him with the scent of apples that surrounded him as he worked. This gives a dream-like quality to his reveries as the poem proceeds, and leads to the poem's central metaphors of sleep and dreaming.

Lines 9–20

Images of what he has experienced during his day's work enter his mind. **Reality and dream begin to merge.** At this point in the poem, the speaker is confusing times and tenses, as one does in a dream-like state. He is falling asleep, but he recalls how that morning he had skimmed the ice from a drinking trough and held it for a moment like a 'pane of glass' (line 10), which caused him to see things with 'strangeness' (line 9), as if it is happening again.

This is an interesting and important idea in the poem. The action is rooted in the real world of the farmer, looking after the drinking trough for his animals on a cold morning. But it also implies that **his imagination causes him to see the world in a different way**. Now he sees the apples as 'magnified' (line 18), appearing and disappearing as in a vision. He notices every 'fleck of russet' (line 20) on them.

Lines 21–40
Sensuous images re-create the experience of apple-picking. He feels the pressure of the ladder on his instep. He feels the movement of the ladder as it sways with the branches of the trees. He hears the 'rumbling sound' (line 25) of the apples as they tumble into the cellar bin. The images suggest abundance and extravagance, as do the repetition in phrases such as 'load on load' (line 26) or 'ten thousand thousand' (line 30). This was indeed a 'great harvest' (line 29) as he had himself hoped it would be. There was joy in the work, certainly. He had to touch each of the apples – 'Cherish in hand' (line 31) – and look after them carefully.

But he also experienced weariness – he is 'overtired' (line 28) – and anxiety. Any apple that fell to the ground would be discarded on the 'cider-apple heap' (line 35). All these things, he suggests, will figure in the troubled sleep that is coming over him, 'whatever sleep it is' (line 38). This phrase and the lines that follow are vague and unspecified, appropriately enough in a poem in which reality and unreality are deliberately blurred.

Lines 41 and 42
The speaker cannot say for sure whether the sleep he feels 'coming on' (line 41) and which he is so looking forward to will be like the long sleep of the hibernating woodchuck, or 'just some human sleep' (line 42).

Like many of Frost's seemingly simple statements, these last lines can be interpreted in different ways. Is he talking about the sound sleep that follows long labour, which gives human beings such comfort? Since the harvesting of apples has ceased, might this sleep suggest the inactivity of winter on the farm that resembles the hibernation of animals like the woodchuck? Or, since sleep and death have long been associated, might this line point us to a metaphorical reading of the whole poem?

Interpreting the poem

The voice in the poem is that of the farmer engaged in hard physical toil. We know from the facts of Frost's life that farming was important to him, but we cannot ignore his ambitions to be a great poet. As we read 'After Apple-Picking' we can sense that the poem is grounded in real life. We really believe that this man has harvested apples.

The reader can visualise the scene, with its ladder, the few remaining apples and the ice that melted earlier in the morning. The speaker even has the ache in his instep to remind him of how hard he worked.

But it is also true that the whole poem is concerned with what is happening in the apple-harvester's mind as it moves back and forth over his experiences. It is then that the reader is reminded that this is what a poet does. The metaphor of sleep and dreaming that runs through the poem, the merging of reality and strangeness, suggests the transforming vision of the poet.

It is possible to read the poem, as the critic and biographer Jay Parini does, as a poem that is about how the imagination works. In such a reading the work of the imagination is the 'great harvest' that needs to be cherished and developed. The work of the imagination, in this case writing poetry, involves anxiety and loss. In this context the reader can see the anxiety that must trouble the sleep of any creative artist: that his or her imagination will cease to bear fruit, perhaps forever, which is in itself a kind of metaphorical death.

The poem has also been given a wider metaphorical interpretation. The apple-picking could be seen as a metaphor for life itself, the tasks and effort involved, the successes and failures – not all the apples have been harvested, and some are of little value, as Frost reminds us. In this context, the 'human sleep' might suggest human death (the 'long sleep'), which comes almost as a relief to the 'overtired', overburdened human being.

Frost on metaphors

Frost himself pointed the way for readers of his poems to interpret them metaphorically, as Parini and others have done. In a speech he made on one occasion he discussed the place of metaphor in poems:

> Poetry provides the one permissible way of saying one thing and meaning another. People say, 'Why don't you say what you mean?' We never do that, do we, being all of us too much poets. We like to talk in parables and in hints and in indirections.

Mood of the poem

However they choose to interpret the meaning of the poem, readers have always responded to the mood Frost creates. Apple-picking takes place at the end of the summer, at the transitional time of autumn. It has been pointed out that the mood of the poet is autumnal, weary and sleepy and yet aware of change. Frost creates this mood as he moves in his mind from past to present, morning to evening, waking to sleep. He expresses uncertainty about his situation in images of drowsiness and dreaming: 'I cannot rub the strangeness from my sight'. He accepts that he will never know whether his own sleep will be like the woodchuck's 'long sleep', and leaves us with a doubt about the meaning of the term 'human sleep'.

Language and sound patterns

Readers also respond to the attractive sounds Frost uses throughout the poem. As in many of his other poems, Frost uses a mixture of plain matter-of-fact language, for example: 'And there's a barrel that I didn't fill . . . But I am done with apple-picking now', and poetic images and phrases in the poem, for example: 'Magnified apples appear and disappear . . . And every fleck of russet showing clear'.

Unlike some of his other poems, Frost chose to use end-rhyme throughout 'After Apple-Picking': 'tree' / 'three', 'still' / 'fill', 'bough' / 'now', etc. But appropriately in a poem concerned with change and uncertainty, these rhymes are not heard as predictable and stale. He varies the line lengths and occasionally separates the rhymes, for example 'break' / 'take' (lines 13 and 17).

Other sound patterns echoed through the poem are assonance, for example the short 'i' sound is repeated in the opening lines ('sticking' / 'didn't') and in the end-rhymes. Frost also uses consonance: 'Essence of winter sleep is on the night / The scent of apples . . .'.

The word 'sleep' seems to echo through the poem, occurring six times, and it is the last word we hear.

Thinking about the poem

1 Explore the sensuousness of the images in the poem.
2 Would you agree that there is a contrast between the poetic and the real in the language of the poem? Examine the language with this in mind.
3 How does Frost convey the dream-like atmosphere of the poem?
4 Some metaphorical readings of the poem have been suggested in the commentary above. Which reading do you prefer? Explain your answer.
5 Is it significant that the speaker has been picking apples and not some other fruit? In your response you might remember the biblical story of the Tree of Knowledge and the Garden of Eden.
6 Explore the sound patterns of assonance, consonance and rhyme throughout the poem and say what effect they had on you as a reader.
7 What significance does the woodchuck have in the poem, in your opinion?
8 The poem has been called a 'lyric idyll'. The word 'idyll' suggests a happy, ideal situation. Comment on this description and say whether you think the mood of the poem is entirely happy.

Personal response

1   If you were asked to choose your favourite poems of Robert Frost, would you include this one among them? Give reasons for your answer.
2   Would you prefer to see the poem as a purely descriptive nature poem? Give a reason for your view.

Before you read 'The Road Not Taken'

Most people have had to make some important decisions in their life. Before you read Frost's poem 'The Road Not Taken', you might recall how you arrived at a decision you took and how you felt afterwards.

The Road Not Taken

Two roads diverged in a yellow wood,
And sorry I could not travel both
And be one traveler, long I stood
And looked down one as far as I could
To where it bent in the undergrowth;   5

Then took the other, as just as fair,
And having perhaps the better claim,
Because it was grassy and wanted wear;
Though as for that, the passing there
Had worn them really about the same,   10

And both that morning equally lay
In leaves no step had trodden black.
Oh, I kept the first for another day!
Yet knowing how way leads on to way,
I doubted if I should ever come back.   15

I shall be telling this with a sigh
Somewhere ages and ages hence:
Two roads diverged in a wood, and I—
I took the one less traveled by,
And that has made all the difference.   20

Glossary		
1	*diverged:* went in different directions
5	*undergrowth:* bushes, ferns, etc. growing beneath taller trees in a wood

Guidelines

'The Road Not Taken' is from *Mountain Interval* (1916). It is one of Frost's most popular and often-quoted poems. It is said to have been inspired by Frost's friend, the poet Edward Thomas, whom he had met in England and who was subsequently killed in the First World War. Thomas was apparently in the habit of expressing regret at whatever decision he had taken.

Commentary

The poem dramatises the choices we are presented with in life and their consequences.

Lines 1–12
The poet uses the metaphor of two roads, one of which the speaker must take. In the first three stanzas we can see the speaker's mind working as he tries to decide between them. First, there is the human desire to avoid deciding in the first place: he is 'sorry I could not travel both' (line 2). He tries to establish what choosing one over the other might entail, by looking as far down the road as he can. Then, almost it seems on impulse, he 'took the other, as just as fair' (line 6), suddenly deciding that it seems less worn and more grassy. However, even then he changes his mind about that: both roads were equally worn, and both were covered in leaves on that autumn morning.

Lines 13–15
The word 'Oh', which Frost often uses so expressively (see 'Mending Wall'), signals a note of regret as the speaker says 'I kept the first for another day!' (line 13). Yet, **as he takes the final decision to choose one road rather than the other, he is aware that he may never again have the opportunity to travel the second one.** He knows how the direction of his life may change or, as he says, how 'way leads on to way' (line 14).

Stanza 4
In the final stanza the speaker is looking back and reflecting on the choice he made. Not only does he review the reasons for his decision, such as they were, but he visualises himself examining it at some time in the future, 'ages and ages hence' (line 17). He sees himself remembering the situation 'with a sigh' (line 16). Is this a sigh of real regret? If it is, then the final line, 'And that has made all the difference' (line 20),

might suggest that his decision has involved suffering and loneliness, as the image of the road 'less traveled by' (line 19) might indicate. We know from the facts of Frost's life that he experienced suffering and tragedy. On the other hand, the sigh could suggest a resigned acceptance of the choice he had made, and in this case the 'difference' might have improved his life, rather than caused him pain.

We should take into account, too, the contradiction expressed in the poem. If both roads are the same, as the speaker has told us earlier, how is the one chosen 'the one less traveled by' (line 19)? The reader might come to the conclusion that it did not matter which road he took or did not take. Whatever choice he made was surely bound to make a difference in his life. From this point of view, the final line can be seen as ironic in tone.

Interpreting the poem

A number of interpretations have been put forward. Is the poem concerned with choice of career in life? (We may remember that Frost left his life as a farmer in New England to develop his gifts as a poet.) Or does the poem hint at a moral struggle that has to be confronted, in which the least popular and most difficult option is chosen? And how do we interpret the closing lines of the poem?

Readers have responded to the poem's attractive setting, with the 'yellow wood' evoking the famous New England fall. As in many of Frost's poems, images of nature are described not merely for their own sake but to suggest an analogy with human concerns.

Language and sounds of the poem

The language of the poem is simple and direct. The impression is given of someone thinking aloud about an immediate experience. Yet, the poem is carefully crafted in terms of sound patterns that create a musical effect. There is assonance in the repeated short 'e' sound throughout, sibilance (as in 'grassy', 'passing'), alliteration (as in 'wanted wear', 'lay in leaves') and of course end-rhyme.

Thinking about the poem

1 How are the two roads presented, as they appeared to the speaker?

2 Trace the speaker's train of thought as he makes his decision.

3 Do you think the poet has dramatised the process of decision-making effectively? Give a reason for your opinion.

4 Do you think the speaker is happy with his decision? How can we tell from the tone of the poem? Look especially at the final stanza.

5   Speculate about the choices in Frost's life (or anyone else's) that may be symbolised in this poem.

6   Suggest what the poet means by the final line: 'And that has made all the difference'.

7   'yellow wood' (line 1). Comment on the poem's setting.

8   'Frost seldom wrote about nature for its own sake.' Write a short paragraph in which you discuss this statement with reference to 'The Road Not Taken'.

Personal response

1   Can you understand why this is a well-loved poem in America and elsewhere? Explain your answer.

2   With a partner, discuss suitable music and images to accompany a reading of this poem. Share your ideas with the class and be prepared to explain/defend your choices.

Before you read 'Birches'

Would the title 'Birches' lead you to expect a straightforward poem about birch trees? As in any Frost poem, be prepared to be led in many different directions.

Birches

When I see birches bend to left and right
Across the lines of straighter darker trees,
I like to think some boy's been swinging them.
But swinging doesn't bend them down to stay
As ice-storms do. Often you must have seen them   5
Loaded with ice a sunny winter morning
After a rain. They click upon themselves
As the breeze rises, and turn many-colored
As the stir cracks and crazes their enamel.
Soon the sun's warmth makes them shed crystal shells   10
Shattering and avalanching on the snow crust—
Such heaps of broken glass to sweep away
You'd think the inner dome of heaven had fallen.
They are dragged to the withered bracken by the load,
And they seem not to break; though once they are bowed   15

So low for long, they never right themselves:
You may see their trunks arching in the woods
Years afterwards, trailing their leaves on the ground
Like girls on hands and knees that throw their hair
Before them over their heads to dry in the sun.   20
But I was going to say when Truth broke in
With all her matter-of-fact about the ice-storm,
I should prefer to have some boy bend them
As he went out and in to fetch the cows—
Some boy too far from town to learn baseball,   25
Whose only play was what he found himself,
Summer or winter, and could play alone.
One by one he subdued his father's trees
By riding them down over and over again
Until he took the stiffness out of them,   30
And not one but hung limp, not one was left
For him to conquer. He learned all there was
To learn about not launching out too soon
And so not carrying the tree away
Clear to the ground. He always kept his poise   35
To the top branches, climbing carefully
With the same pains you use to fill a cup
Up to the brim, and even above the brim.
Then he flung outward, feet first, with a swish,
Kicking his way down through the air to the ground.   40
So was I once myself a swinger of birches.
And so I dream of going back to be.
It's when I'm weary of considerations,
And life is too much like a pathless wood
Where your face burns and tickles with the cobwebs   45
Broken across it, and one eye is weeping
From a twig's having lashed across it open.
I'd like to get away from earth awhile
And then come back to it and begin over.
May no fate willfully misunderstand me   50
And half grant what I wish and snatch me away
Not to return. Earth's the right place for love:

I don't know where it's likely to go better.
I'd like to go by climbing a birch tree,
And climb black branches up a snow-white trunk   55
Toward heaven, till the tree could bear no more,
But dipped its top and set me down again.
That would be good both going and coming back.
One could do worse than be a swinger of birches.

Glossary

9	*crazes their enamel:* makes small cracks in the hard ice-coated birches
11	*avalanching:* hurtling down
14	*bracken:* ferns

Guidelines

'Birches' is found in *Mountain Interval* (1916). Frost agreed with his readership in ranking 'Birches' among his strongest poems. Set in New England, the poem is based on the children's game of swinging birches, which involves climbing birch trees until your weight brings the trunk plunging down to the ground. Frost enjoyed doing this as a child at his uncle's farm in New Hampshire. **As is the usual pattern in a Frost poem, however, the act of swinging birches takes on a metaphorical significance.**

Commentary

Lines 1–20

The poem begins with a deceptively simple comment. When he sees birches with their trunks bent, the speaker says he likes to think that some boy's been bending them. At once we are introduced to the idea of both nature and the boy who delights in it. But he knows that swinging on them would never make them arch permanently as 'ice-storms do' (line 5). He then goes on to describe the effect these ice-storms have on the slender branches and trunks of the trees. He assumes his readers' familiarity with the sight: 'Often you must have seen them' (line 5).

He takes care to be as precise as possible in describing them, while using highly imaginative language and imagery that appeals to our senses. Onomatopoeic words such as 'click' (line 7) and the hard 'c' sounds repeated in 'cracks and crazes' (line 9) make us almost hear the sound of the ice beginning to melt on the trees as the breeze and the sun do their work. Vivid visual images create the scene. Only 'crystal shells' (line 10) and 'heaps of broken glass' (line 12) remain as the ice melts further. We can almost feel the movement as the crystals are described as 'Shattering and avalanching' (line 11) across the snow. These lovely images are quickly followed by the ordinary phrase 'Such heaps of broken glass to sweep away' (line 12), which leads on to the poetic metaphor of the glass as 'the inner dome of heaven' (line 13).

We can see **a blend of poetic and down-to-earth images** in these lines. The language is at times plain as it gives a precise description of the branches laid low by the storms (lines 14–18) but then there is a gloriously romantic simile: the leaves on the trees are 'Like girls on hands and knees' throwing their hair out to dry in the sun (lines 18–20).

Lines 21–40

The speaker describes the previous passage as being a moment when 'Truth broke in / With all her matter-of-fact' (lines 21 and 22). We can see how ironic the comment is when we recall that the 'facts' were written in highly imaginative language. In contrast, the boy who swings birches in these next lines is depicted in ordinary everyday terms. (Nonetheless, he is a creature of Frost's imagination.) He is an ordinary boy, living in the country with its usual country chores.

The actual swinging of the birches is described in detail and with great care. And **the lessons he learns can be applied to life situations**. Images of conquest suggest determination and the necessity for persistence. Climbing carefully to the top and 'not launching out too soon' (line 33) teaches him the values of control and the joy of achievement, ending with the tremendous happiness of landing successfully on the ground.

The image of filling 'a cup / Up to the brim, and even above the brim' (lines 37 and 38), which requires that you take considerable pains, seems to suggest a desire to reach beyond what is possible. Placed side by side with images of joyful freedom, it could be said to crystallise in a metaphorical way the two contrasting ideas mentioned earlier: the idea of facts and truth, and the imaginative expression of those facts, which is poetry itself. Poetry may begin with natural fact, but it soon learns to transcend the limitations of fact, and delight in so doing.

Lines 41–59

The speaker continues to invite us to connect the action of swinging birches with the writing of poems – both offer a dream of escape from the harshness of reality. He recalls nostalgically that he was once 'a swinger of birches' (line 41). Life was different then, he seems to suggest, unlike adult life with its problems and sufferings. He would like to escape 'from earth' (line 48) into the world of the imagination. Climbing a birch tree as he used to do, suggests the speaker, would be like going '*Toward* heaven' (line 56): a movement of aspiration towards the spiritual world of the imagination but not a complete departure from reality (earth).

The line that could be said to comment on the entire process is: 'That would be good both going and coming back' (line 58). The words are simple, but, as in many of Frost's poems, there is an underlying complexity in the thought. It is as if the speaker-poet is affirming both strands of poetic endeavour: the engagement with the facts of the natural world and the point of departure these facts offer the poetic imagination. But in no sense is he rejecting the real world, for 'Earth's the right place for love' (line 52). The images of 'heaven' he has introduced are metaphorical and not to be taken literally by any 'fate' that would 'misunderstand' him (line 50) and bring about his actual death. The poem has moved from description to philosophical meditation in these lines.

The final line of the poem reads like an aphorism (a brief, pithy saying), but its wisdom has been borne out by the poet's description of swinging birches and the lessons it provides for life.

Language of the poem

The language of the poem echoes the rhythm of the spoken voice. It is as if the speaker is thinking aloud, addressing an imaginary companion, perhaps. He uses ordinary conversational phrases such as 'I like to think', 'you must have seen them', 'and begin over'. As in many conversations, he rambles from his main point, describing the effect of the ice-storm, before bringing himself back with 'But I was going to say'. For Frost, achieving what he called 'the sound of sense' was crucial and, as in 'After Apple-Picking' and 'Mending Wall', we can certainly hear the spoken voice in 'Birches'.

We also see in this poem how Frost moves between straightforward description in factual, exact terms (the ice-storm passage, the precise description of how the boy swung on the birches) and more lyrical passages that seem to have more 'poetic' qualities. He uses highly sensuous images, simile and metaphor when he describes the birch branches and the experience of swinging on them. Throughout the poem, too, he writes in classic blank verse with its traditional iambic pentameters.

By blending down-to-earth and imaginative language Frost affirms what he is suggesting in the poem – that poetry must engage with both the real world and the world of the imagination.

Thinking about the poem

1   In lines 5 to 20 Frost describes the birches after an ice-storm. Do you think the images he uses convey the scene effectively? Explain your answer.

2   In what way does the swinging of birches take on a metaphorical significance? Where in the poem does this occur? What is the first lesson a boy learns from swinging birches, for example?

3   Does the poem invite a number of further metaphorical readings as it progresses? For instance, you could take into account especially the lines where the speaker refers to himself: 'So was I once myself a swinger of birches. / And so I dream of going back to be' (lines 41 and 42). What might this 'dream' suggest about the work of a poet?

4   'The poem enacts the desire to escape, to move beyond the here and now of the real world to the world of the imagination.' In what lines is this most evident?

5   Does the poet find this world of the imagination ultimately satisfying, or does he express reservations about it? Explain.

6   One critic has said that 'Birches' is 'not only a poem about trees but also a celebration of spiritual thirst'. Explain how the poem might be interpreted in this way.

7   Discuss the view that the form and language of 'Birches' mirror the poet's awareness of the tension between the human desire to withdraw from the world and longing to remain a part of it.

8   Would you agree that the language of the poem echoes the rhythms of the spoken voice? Explain your answer. You might look at the use of colloquialisms (everyday phrases), the pauses within the lines (caesuras) and the impression created of someone thinking aloud.

9   'One could do worse than be a swinger of birches' (line 59). In your view, has the poet proved the truth of this statement?

10 Frost once said that poetry 'begins in delight and ends in wisdom'. Does this remark help you to appreciate the theme and mood of 'Birches'?

Personal response

1   It has been said that 'Birches' is a poem likely to appeal to young people. Explain why you agree or disagree with this view.

2   Lines 29 to 40 describe the young boy swinging birches. Choose your favourite lines from this section and say what it is that you like about it.

Before you read 'Out, Out–'

'Out, Out–' by Robert Frost on page 132 tells the story of a fatal accident on a farm. Is that the sort of topic that you expect poetry to deal with? What tone do you expect such a poem to have?

'Out, Out—'

The buzz saw snarled and rattled in the yard
And made dust and dropped stove-length sticks of wood,
Sweet-scented stuff when the breeze drew across it.
And from there those that lifted eyes could count
Five mountain ranges one behind the other   5
Under the sunset far into Vermont.
And the saw snarled and rattled, snarled and rattled,
As it ran light, or had to bear a load.
And nothing happened: day was all but done.
Call it a day, I wish they might have said   10
To please the boy by giving him the half hour
That a boy counts so much when saved from work.
His sister stood beside them in her apron
To tell them 'Supper.' At the word, the saw,
As if to prove saws knew what supper meant,   15
Leaped out of the boy's hand, or seemed to leap—
He must have given the hand. However it was,
Neither refused the meeting. But the hand!
The boy's first outcry was a rueful laugh,
As he swung toward them holding up the hand,   20
Half in appeal, but half as if to keep
The life from spilling. Then the boy saw all—
Since he was old enough to know, big boy
Doing a man's work, though a child at heart—
He saw all spoiled. 'Don't let him cut my hand off—   25
The doctor, when he comes. Don't let him, sister!'
So. But the hand was gone already.
The doctor put him in the dark of ether.
He lay and puffed his lips out with his breath.
And then—the watcher at his pulse took fright.   30
No one believed. They listened at his heart.
Little—less—nothing!—and that ended it.
No more to build on there. And they, since they
Were not the one dead, turned to their affairs.

Glossary

title	*'Out, Out–':* these words echo Macbeth's 'Out, out, brief candle!' (*Macbeth*, Act 5, Scene 5), found in a speech in which Macbeth refers to how short and sad life is
1	*buzz saw:* a circular saw
2	*stove-length:* the right size to fit in a stove
6	*Vermont:* a state in New England in the United States
19	*ruefu:* sorrowful
28	*ether:* an anaesthetic
34	*affairs:* activities, things to do

Guidelines

This poem is from Frost's collection *Mountain Interval* (1916). One of Frost's most affecting poems, it is based on a true story. In 1910 the child of a neighbour of Frost's in Vermont, New England, was killed in an accident on his father's farm. The boy, called Raymond Tracy Fitzgerald, was helping his father to saw wood when his hand was caught in the sawing machine. He died from the effects of shock, which caused heart failure.

Commentary

The title of the poem is part of a quotation from Shakespeare's *Macbeth*. When Macbeth hears about the death of his wife, he says: 'Out, out, brief candle! Life's but a walking shadow'. The speech he goes on to make is a moving comment on how short life is. As such it is relevant to the story told in Frost's poem.

Lines 1–18
The poem sets the scene almost like a play does. The tragedy takes place in the yard of a farm from where there is a view of the mountains of Vermont. It is a peaceful rural scene, but from the beginning we are made aware of the unpleasant noise made by the saw as it 'snarled and rattled' (line 1). It also 'made dust', an image which hints at the death that will take place.

The boy's life is shown as hard-working, perhaps even harsh – the speaker regrets that he could not have finished work earlier, for instance. His sister plays her role in the drama as she arrives to call him to supper. Here **we see the saw almost as a living thing, another character in the drama,** as the speaker suggests that it deliberately reached for the boy's hand, as if it understood the word 'supper' and was hungry. There is also a suggestion that the boy somehow reached out to the saw: 'Neither refused the meeting' (line 18). **The accident is the moment of crisis in the drama.**

Lines 19–34

Next we hear of the boy's reaction. It is both sad and chilling. His first response is to give 'a rueful laugh' (line 19), as if in shock. Then he begs for help, for his hand to be spared: 'Don't let him cut my hand off' (line 25). The words suggest that he also realises that he is facing death: 'Then the boy saw all' (line 22). All the doctor could do was to give him an anaesthetic until he died.

His death seems to come as a surprise to 'the watcher at his pulse' (line 30). We do not know who this refers to, perhaps the doctor, or the boy's sister or parents. **His moment of death is described with no expression of grief or even much comment to console us.** But it is the reaction of those who are left alive that takes us aback. They seem to accept the situation and calmly go on with their lives: 'And they, since they / Were not the one dead, turned to their affairs' (lines 33 and 34). Even the word 'affairs' seems rather cold and unfeeling.

Responses to the poem

Readers have been divided in their responses to this poem. Some critics suggest that Frost is merely being realistic in accepting that accidents can and do happen on a farm. They argue that Frost is showing the courage of the family in coming to terms with their loss. They point out that by using the quotation from *Macbeth*, one of Shakespeare's most moving plays, as his title, Frost is certainly not dismissing the boy's death as something unimportant.

Other readers feel that there is something cold and even cruel about the ending of the poem. It is as if the boy must be forgotten about now that he is no longer of use on the family farm. Frost's neighbours would not have been rich farmers, so an extra worker would now be necessary, and this would cause financial hardship. Be that as it may, the lack of any expression of grief for the death of a son seems strange.

The reader must make up his or her own mind about how to respond to the ending of the poem.

Language of the poem

Frost makes use of sound to communicate the drama of the scene. Words such as 'buzz', 'snarled' and 'rattled' are onomatopoeic (echoing the sounds made by the saw) and repetition of these words throughout the poem adds to their effect. Other sound effects include alliteration such as 'sweet-scented stuff', and assonance such as 'count' and 'mountain'. For the most part the language of the poem is simple and straightforward. Images of natural peace and beauty such as the 'sunset far into Vermont', and domestic details such as the sister 'in her apron', contrast with horrific images of the boy trying to prevent the 'life from spilling' from his hand.

Thinking about the poem

1   Tell the story of the poem in your own words.
2   Describe the place where the poem is set.
3   How does the poet prepare us for the tragedy from the beginning?
4   What impression of country life do you get when you read this poem?
5   Are there any lines in the poem that you find puzzling or disturbing? Explain your answer.
6   In your opinion, what is the poet suggesting in the passage beginning: 'Then the boy saw all . . .' (line 22).
7   'At the word, the saw, / As if to prove saws knew what supper meant, / Leaped out of the boy's hand' (lines 14–16). What picture do these lines create for you?
8   'Little—less—nothing!—and that ended it' (line 32). Do you like this line in the poem? Explain your answer.
9   'And they, since they / Were not the one dead, turned to their affairs' (lines 33 and 34). What impression is created by these final lines?
10 People have said that this is a very dramatic poem. Do you agree? Explain your answer.
11 Which of the following words best describes the tone of the poem: cruel, unfeeling, sympathetic, realistic? Explain your choice.

Personal response

1   Write the diary entry of the boy's sister in which she records her experiences and feelings on the day the accident happened.
2   You are a reporter for the local newspaper in Vermont. Write a report of the accident.

3   Your class wants to make a short film based on the poem. In pairs or groups, discuss the sort of atmosphere you would create, and say what music, sound effects and images you would use.

snapshot

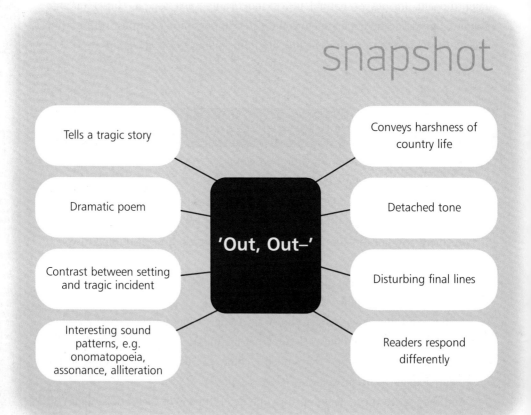

Tells a tragic story

Dramatic poem

Contrast between setting and tragic incident

Interesting sound patterns, e.g. onomatopoeia, assonance, alliteration

'Out, Out–'

Conveys harshness of country life

Detached tone

Disturbing final lines

Readers respond differently

Spring Pools

These pools that, though in forests, still reflect
The total sky almost without defect,
And like the flowers beside them, chill and shiver,
Will like the flowers beside them soon be gone,
And yet not out by any brook or river,   5
But up by roots to bring dark foliage on.

The trees that have it in their pent-up buds
To darken nature and be summer woods—
Let them think twice before they use their powers
To blot out and drink up and sweep away   10
These flowery waters and these water flowers
From snow that melted only yesterday.

Glossary

2	*defect:* flaw
6	*foliage:* green leaves

Guidelines

The lyric 'Spring Pools' is the opening poem in the volume *West-Running Brook* (1928). The poem describes the natural phenomenon of how leaves and flowers are 'brought on' by the act of sucking up spring pools through the roots of trees.

Commentary

Stanza 1

The images in the first stanza create an impression of peace and tranquillity. The spring pools reflect the 'total sky almost without defect' (line 2). But there is an underlying bleakness in the language that suggests change and death: the pools 'chill and shiver' (line 3). The poet reminds us starkly that they will 'soon be gone' (line 4). Ironically, it is nature itself that brings about such destruction: the roots of the trees, images of growth, will destroy the pools.

Stanza 2

The **theme of natural process and organic change** continues in the second stanza. Images of the trees portray them as creative and powerful, as the phrase 'pent-up buds' (line 7) suggests. But their power can also destroy. They can 'darken nature' (line 8), 'blot out and drink up and sweep away' (line 10). The tone is regretful and sombre as the poet, perhaps rather helplessly, urges the trees to 'think twice' (line 9) before destroying the pools. He leaves us with the thought that the pools were themselves once the 'snow that melted only yesterday' (line 12). The image recalls winter and the unrelenting cycle of the seasons.

Metaphorical reading

As with most of Frost's poems, metaphorical readings of 'Spring Pools' have been suggested. Nature has often been used as an emblem of human life, a tradition with which Frost was familiar. We saw in 'The Tuft of Flowers' how Frost sees in nature a lesson that can be learned. Whereas in that poem nature is seen as benign and the lessons it offers hopeful, in this poem there is a much less optimistic mood. **The cycle of birth and death depicted in the poem may symbolise the cyclical nature of human life**, with words such as 'dark' (line 6) and 'darken' (line 8) underlining the shadow of death.

Frost's biographer Jay Parini suggests that 'Spring Pools' is about writing. He points to the fact that water, for Frost, often signified a source of poetic inspiration. **The image of the pools that reflect the sky becomes a metaphor for the power of the artist to reflect the world in all its beauty.** But this world, Parini goes on to say, must be transformed by the poet's imagination before he can make of it a new work of art – the work of the artist involves a certain destructiveness as well as creativity. Such work is both beautiful and frightening at the same time. We can see how this reading has a great deal to recommend it when we consider that Frost contemplated the power of the imagination in other poems such as 'After Apple-Picking' and 'Birches'.

Mood of the poem

The mood of 'Spring Pools' is regretful and sombre. Nature is seen as something beyond the understanding and influence of human beings. 'Let them think twice' has a futile, helpless tone in the face of the underlying realisation in the poem that nature never thinks at all. There is dark irony in the fact that Frost presents spring, a time of renewal, as also a time of decay.

Form of the poem

The two stanzas of the poem are patterned in exactly the same way, mirroring each other as the pools mirror the sky. Each has six lines, with the first two lines rhyming and the other four lines having alternate rhymes. The continuity of nature is echoed in the many run-on lines that carry the images like a chain from beginning to end. Repetition of words and whole phrases also reinforces the theme of continuity. For these reasons and others Parini has referred to the poem as one of Frost's most intricately made poems.

Thinking about the poem

1 How is the beauty of the spring pools suggested in the early lines of the poem?
2 What irony is there in the manner in which their beauty will be soon destroyed?
3 Would you agree that the poem recognises the inevitable process of nature while at the same time lamenting that it must be so? Explain your answer.
4 Describe the mood or atmosphere of the poem.
5 How do the sound patterns of the poem – rhyme, assonance, repetition –convey the mood of the poem?
6 Would you agree that 'Spring Pools' is an intricately-made poem? Give reasons for your response.

7   In your view, is the poem purely concerned with nature, or does it have a relevance to human life?

8   Compare the attitude to nature implied in this poem with that in 'The Tuft of Flowers'.

Personal response

1   Write a personal response to this poem, describing its impact on you.

2   Imagine that you have been commissioned to take a photograph to be displayed beside this poem on a website. Describe what you would include in your photo. What lighting would you use? What mood or atmosphere would you try to convey?

Before you read 'Acquainted with the Night'

What comes to mind on reading the title 'Acquainted with the Night' in the poem below? In thinking about this, consider all the possible implications of both the key words, 'acquainted' and 'night'.

Acquainted with the Night

I have been one acquainted with the night.
I have walked out in rain – and back in rain.
I have outwalked the furthest city light.

I have looked down the saddest city lane.
I have passed by the watchman on his beat   5
And dropped my eyes, unwilling to explain.

I have stood still and stopped the sound of feet
When far away an interrupted cry
Came over houses from another street,

But not to call me back or say good-bye;   10
And further still at an unearthly height
One luminary clock against the sky

Proclaimed the time was neither wrong nor right.
I have been one acquainted with the night.

Guidelines

This short lyric, a sonnet, is from *West-Running Brook* (1928). The poem is unusual among Frost's work in that it is set in the city rather than in rural surroundings. **It depicts the dark, alienating side of urban existence.** The speaker in the poem experiences a sense of deep depression and loneliness as he walks through the city streets.

Commentary

The title of the poem and the first line set up a rich association of ideas for the reader. **It appears that the 'night' is not only to be read literally but also reflects the 'dark night of the soul' that the speaker has experienced. Nature itself seems to echo his sadness and despair, with images of darkness and rain.**

The speaker records what he sees and hears as he comes and goes in the city. There is a suggestion of hidden violence in the urban landscape – 'an interrupted cry' (line 8) can be heard coming 'from another street' (line 9). These cries are disembodied, almost surreal, like 'the sound of feet' (line 7) that is also heard.

But what strikes the reader most perhaps is the sense of isolation that the poem expresses. There is no attempt to make any human contact. Indeed the speaker 'dropped' his eyes (line 6) when he met another person, 'the watchman on his beat' (line 5). No one is crying out 'to call me back or say good-bye' (line 10). We can detect a note of self-pity here, but if we take into account the speaker's admission that he himself is 'unwilling to explain' (line 6), we may accept that his alienation is self-induced and deliberate. Words such as 'outwalked', 'furthest', 'passed by' (lines 3 and 5) seem to emphasise how he has left the comfort of human society (or perhaps wished to).

It may be that the 'luminary clock' (line 12) he sees (the moon or an actual clock?) symbolises, in a general way, the passage of time. Its message – 'the time was neither wrong nor right' (line 13) – is slightly mysterious. Is it saying that time is indifferent to those who live in the isolation of the city? That right or wrong (or time) is irrelevant in urban life? It may also echo Hamlet's expression of despair in Shakespeare's play of the same name: 'The time is out of joint'.

Form and sounds of the poem

The poem is a sonnet of fourteen lines, but it is not structured in either of the traditional forms (octave and sestet or three quatrains and a couplet). Instead there are four tercets (three-line stanzas) and a couplet, with the rhyming pattern *aba, bcb, cdc, dad, aa*. Apart from the rhyming couplet, this rhyme pattern corresponds to what is called *terza rima*. The Italian poet Dante, who invented the form, wrote in his *Inferno* about a descent into hell. Frost would have had this in mind when he chose the form in which to express his own sense of despair. The rhyme scheme is regular to the point of monotony, which contributes to the tone of melancholy.

The sound patterns also echo the mood of alienation expressed. Long-drawn-out vowel sounds predominate in the rhymes. For example, 'lane' and 'explain', 'beat' and 'feet' have an almost onomatopoeic effect as they echo the sound of lament. By ending the poem with the same line as it began, the suggestion is that we have come full circle, and nothing has changed.

Themes of the poem

Critics have pointed out that 'Acquainted with the Night' shows Frost's awareness of the themes and poetic techniques of modernist poets of the early twentieth century, such as T. S. Eliot and Ezra Pound, for whom the city was an image of alienation. Certainly the poem offers a contrast in the work of a poet whose social vision seems so optimistic, as expressed in 'The Tuft of Flowers' or 'Mending Wall'.

It may be that in this poem Frost reveals some of his darkest fears about living – fears that were reflected in his frequent bouts of depression and psychosomatic illness during his lifetime. One of Frost's critics, Lionel Trilling, caused quite a stir when he once referred to Frost as 'a tragic poet whose work conceived of a terrifying universe'. Poems such as 'Acquainted with the Night', 'Design' and 'Provide, Provide' would bear out this perception of Frost's vision.

Thinking about the poem

1 In your opinion, what is the poet suggesting when he says that he has been 'acquainted with the night'? How do the images that follow develop this opening statement?

2 Which image is the most effective in illustrating the poet's theme, in your opinion?

3 How is the indifference of the city suggested in the imagery of the poem?

4 Seven of the poem's fourteen lines begin with 'I'. Write a paragraph commenting on the effect of this.

5   What insight does the poem give us into Robert Frost as a person, in your view?

6   Do you find this poem different in tone from other poems by Frost on your course? Explain your answer.

7   Describe the theme and mood of the poem, and the impact they have on you.

8   Do you agree with the critic Lionel Trilling's description of Frost as a 'tragic poet'? Give reasons for your response.

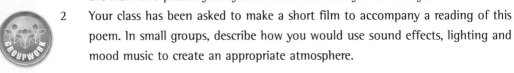

Personal response

1   Imagine that you are the 'watchman on his beat' (line 5). Write a paragraph on the man who passed you by and would not look you in the eye.

2   Your class has been asked to make a short film to accompany a reading of this poem. In small groups, describe how you would use sound effects, lighting and mood music to create an appropriate atmosphere.

Before you read 'Design'

In groups or pairs, discuss what the word 'design' means to you. Think about all the possible aspects of the word. (Use a dictionary if possible.) Then keep these meanings in mind as you read the poem.

Design

I found a dimpled spider, fat and white,
On a white heal-all, holding up a moth
Like a white piece of rigid satin cloth—
Assorted characters of death and blight
Mixed ready to begin the morning right,   5
Like the ingredients of a witches' broth—
A snow-drop spider, a flower like a froth,
And dead wings carried like a paper kite.

What had that flower to do with being white,
The wayside blue and innocent heal-all?   10
What brought the kindred spider to that height,
Then steered the white moth thither in the night?
What but design of darkness to appall?—
If design govern in a thing so small.

Glossary

1	*dimpled spider:* the spider has a small dent on its body, rather like a dimple
2	*heal-all:* a type of plant in the mint family, once used for medicinal purposes; usually the flowers are violet-blue
3	*rigid satin cloth:* satin is often used to line coffins
4	*blight:* disease
6	*witches' broth:* soup or potion concocted by witches
12	*thither:* in that direction
13	*appall:* literally, 'to make pale'; to horrify

Guidelines

The sonnet 'Design' was collected in the volume *A Further Range* (1936). However, it had been written much earlier, around 1911/12.

Commentary

Lines 1–8 (the octave)

The poem moves naturally from a description of a scene to a meditation on its significance. In the octave (eight lines) **the speaker describes how he finds a spider on a flower holding up a moth it has captured.**

At first the scene seems innocent, as the repetition of 'white', the colour of purity, suggests. The spider is described in the first line as 'dimpled', seemingly harmless, but 'fat and white' has less charming connotations. The moth is white, too. The images become more menacing as the poem proceeds, with connotations of deceit and death. The moth has been lured to its death by the heal-all, and is compared now to a 'white piece of rigid satin cloth' (line 3), such cloth is used to line coffins.

All these specimens of nature – the spider, the moth, even the heal-all – play their part in nature's destructiveness. They are 'assorted characters of death and blight' (line 4). Indeed they are compared to the horrible ingredients of a 'witches' broth' (line 6). The metaphors and similes the speaker uses to describe them in the last two lines of the octave are grimly ironic. The 'flower like a froth' (line 7) has connotations of poison or venom. The 'dead wings' of the moth are compared to a 'paper kite' (line 8) – a child's plaything, but also a bird of prey.

Lines 9–14 (the sestet)

As in most sonnets, there is a change of focus in the sestet (six lines). The situation described in the octave is now commented upon. The tone becomes angry as **the speaker questions the motives of the plant that helped the spider kill the moth.** The question seems to imply that the flower is not so 'innocent' (line 10) after all, since it changed its colour from blue to white to trap the moth to its death. It had entered into a conspiracy with the 'kindred' (line 11) spider – the word is heavily ironic.

The answer the speaker gives is that it was nature's design all along to bring about this chain of events. It is a 'design of darkness', in other words, evil, and is meant to horrify: 'appall' (line 13).

The tone of the final line is a little uncertain. It can be read as a question or a statement. If it is a question, it completes the speculative tone in which the poem is written and the speaker's puzzlement at nature's ways. If it is a statement, it may imply that the question of design in nature does not really arise at all. If there is no design, it follows logically that there may be no designer. This is the final disturbing vision of the poem.

Themes of the poem

'Design' speculates about a number of issues that have interested philosophers for centuries. Since the time of the medieval philosopher Thomas Aquinas, one of the arguments often put forward for the existence of a benevolent deity is the 'argument from design'. Aquinas argued that God had made each detail in nature with some particular function and purpose in mind. In this sonnet Frost speculates on the possibility that nature is not only an impersonal force that offers no guidance in human affairs, but that the very force that drives it may in fact be evil.

Another aspect of the problem has been how to account for the presence of evil in the world. Frost takes an ironic approach to the theme. The title is heavily ironic in view of the discovery the speaker makes at the end. Throughout the sonnet, words that suggest goodness turn out to be evil: the 'innocent' heal-all that is obviously not innocent, the 'white' spider and moth that are part of the powers of 'darkness', and the apparent 'design' in nature that turns out to be an illusion.

Many of Frost's poems have been read in terms of their metaphorical significance. For this poet, nature has rarely been seen as an end in itself, but as a means whereby human beings can learn something about themselves. Might this poem suggest in its final lines that our lives are governed by chance rather than by the plan of a loving creator?

Some commentators have read the poem as a comment on the nature of poetic design as well as theological or scientific design. From this point of view the final line, 'If design govern in a thing so small', might refer to the poem itself as an artefact. This is an interesting viewpoint, particularly as we have seen that many of Frost's poems are concerned with the nature of artistic creation and the power of the human imagination.

Form of the poem

The sonnet form allows the poet to deal with a large and important theme in a controlled way. Frost has chosen to keep to a traditional Petrarchan rhyme scheme in the octave: *abbaabba.* In the sestet he varies the tradition slightly: *acaacc.* Unusually, he repeats the rhymes of the octave, drawing attention to the long 'i' sound.

The expert 'design' of the sonnet has been noted. There is a pattern of three rhymes that reflect the three characters in the story, namely the spider, the heal-all and the moth. Words are used cleverly to bring out their full connotations. For example, 'white' takes on different meanings as the poem progresses. There are other instances of wordplay, too. Heal-all is the name of a flower, but ironically this flower destroys rather than heals. The word 'appall' reflects its literal meaning of becoming white (as in paleness/pallor), but also takes on a more sinister meaning.

Thinking about the poem

1. Explore the imagery of the octave, paying special attention to Frost's use of the colour white and the connotations of his similes.
2. Having considered the imagery, how would you describe the tone of the octave?
3. What emotions are conveyed in the sestet?
4. How are the octave and the sestet linked together?
5. Structurally, a sonnet is often said to move from 'sight to insight' (i.e. from description to contemplation). In what way might this be true of 'Design'?
6. What point is the speaker making in the poem's final line, in your opinion?
7. What vision of nature is suggested by this poem? How does it compare with that expressed in 'The Tuft of Flowers' and 'Spring Pools'?
8. The critic James Dickey has said that the best of Frost's poetry has to do with 'darkness, confusion, panic, terror'. Do you think this comment is relevant to a poem like 'Design'?
9. Do you think 'Design' is a well-made poem? Explain your answer.
10. 'The poem 'Design' raises a number of interesting questions.' Write a short essay in response to this statement.

Robert Frost

Personal response

1   Choose two lines from the poem that especially appeal to you and explain your choice.
2   'Design' is generally regarded as a very clever poem. Explain why you agree or disagree with this view.

Provide, Provide

The witch that came (the withered hag)
To wash the steps with pail and rag,
Was once the beauty Abishag,

The picture pride of Hollywood.
Too many fall from great and good   5
For you to doubt the likelihood.

Die early and avoid the fate.
Or if predestined to die late,
Make up your mind to die in state.

Make the whole stock exchange your own!   10
If need be occupy a throne,
Where nobody can call *you* crone.

Some have relied on what they knew;
Others on being simply true.
What worked for them might work for you.   15

No memory of having starred
Atones for later disregard,
Or keeps the end from being hard.

Better to go down dignified
With boughten friendship at your side   20
Than none at all. Provide, provide!

Glossary

1	*hag:* ugly old woman
2	*pail:* bucket
3	*Abishag:* an allusion to the biblical story of Abishag, a beautiful girl who came to attend the dying King David and who tried but failed to arouse the ageing king's desire (*1 Kings 1.3*)
8	*predestined:* determined beforehand
12	*crone:* withered old woman
17	*Atones:* makes up for
20	*boughten:* a regional word meaning something shop-bought, as against something naturally acquired

Guidelines

'Provide, Provide' was written in 1933 and appeared in the collection *A Further Range* (1936). Frost said that the central character of the poem, the witch who came to wash the steps, was based on a real woman whom he had seen cleaning the steps of a university building.

The poet Derek Walcott has speculated that the poem had its origin in Frost's childhood experience. When his father died at the age of thirty-four, Frost's mother had exactly eight dollars to pay for her husband's funeral. Understandably, this would have created an anxiety in him about money throughout his life.

It has also been suggested that Frost's vehement opposition to the New Deal policies of Franklin D. Roosevelt in 1930s America sparked off a cynical reaction in him, which finds expression here. Frost was opposed to the new social welfare policies, preferring the more conservative policies of self-sufficiency and individualism. Whatever the possible personal background to the poem, its stark phrases and bitter tone are unlike anything else in Frost's work.

Commentary

The language of the poem is straightforward and direct, as if the speaker is addressing a public audience. The moral is clear: the old woman who is reduced to cleaning the steps may once have been young and successful. Once she was like 'the beauty Abishag' (line 3), a famous biblical beauty. Perhaps she was a successful Hollywood star. By placing images of the old and the modern side by side, Frost seems to suggest that the lesson is true for all time. Now the woman is a 'witch', a 'withered hag' (line 1). **Like many of the great and beautiful, she failed to provide for herself financially.**

The speaker has some mock-advice: to 'Die early' (line 7); if we cannot do that, we ought at least to try to be self-sufficient. **He counsels us to recognise the value of both money and power.** His advice here is exaggerated and not completely serious: 'Make the whole stock exchange your own!' (line 10) or 'occupy a throne' (line 11) so that no-one can treat you with disrespect. We could also rely on experience, or our sense of truth, as others have done; however, these may be of limited value in the end: 'What worked for them might work for you' (line 15). Memories of past glories simply are not enough. It is better to finish our days surrounded by paid – 'boughten' (line 20) – friendship rather than by none at all. The imperative tone of the last words – 'Provide, provide!' – adds an urgency to the poem.

Viewpoints

'Provide, Provide' has been called 'an immortal masterpiece'. With unsentimental honesty it faces the fact that old age brings with it diminishing beauty and success. It accepts that much of our experience of love, power and friendship is illusory. It offers us advice on how to live out our lives in some dignity. Although it is impersonal – no 'I' figure appears in it – it seems to reveal a great deal about Frost himself. It raises questions about his personal happiness at a time when he was at the height of his fame in America.

The critic Frank Lentricchia suggests that Frost is talking directly to himself in the poem:

> Hollywood's poet, talking contemptuously to and at himself, looking down the road at a possible fate that he would not be able to say he hadn't chosen, were it to turn out to be his – because he had made the decision to commit himself to fame's course.

From this point of view, the poem is even more honest and revealing. Although he enjoyed giving performances of his poems and speaking in public, Frost may have felt ambivalent about his experience of being famous. Lentricchia's comment throws some light, in retrospect, on a poem such as 'The Road Not Taken', which dramatises such a decision-making process.

Rhythm of the poem

The poem is written in four-beat (tetrameter) rhyming tercets (stanzas of three lines each) that give it a strong forward thrust. Frost referred to this metre as having 'plenty of tune'.

Thinking about the poem

1   What advice does the speaker give to people who wish to avoid the fate of people like Abishag? In what tone is the advice given?

2   Does the tone of the poem change as it progresses? Explain your answer.

3   What significance may there be in the fact that Frost does not use the first person 'I' in the poem?

4   What sort of person does this poem reveal the speaker to be? Do you think you would like him?

5   The critic Randolph Jarrell described this poem as 'an immortal masterpiece'. What qualities of the poem might have led him to this conclusion?

Personal response

1   What is your response to this poem and to the speaker's advice? Would you agree that the view of life expressed in 'Provide, Provide' is darkly cynical?

2   The poem is unlike most of Frost's other poems. Would you include it in a personal selection of Frost's poems for an anthology? Explain your answer.

Exam-Style Questions

1   Write an introduction to a short collection of poetry chosen from the poems of Robert Frost on your course.

You are free to choose whatever poems you like to answer this question. Some possible areas for discussion include:

- Frost's themes: nature and what we can learn from it about human experience, etc.
- What his poems reveal about him as a person – his poetic 'voice'.
- His use of language, in particular his use of metaphor.
- His choice of traditional forms in which to write.
- The emotions underlying his best poems.

Always support the points you make with relevant quotation or reference.

Robert Frost

2   Write a response to the view that Robert Frost's poems reflect the poet's own life and reveal his personality.

Possible points include:

- His poems are almost always set in the rural surroundings of New England that he lived in and loved.

- His poetic 'voice' reveals his personality, his love of nature, his interest in its deeper significance, etc.

- Many of his poems deal with particular times and emotions he experienced such as childhood, decision-making, depression, cynicism of old age.

- He reveals that he is aware of the darker side of human existence as well as its beauty.

Remember to support your points with relevant quotation or reference

3   Robert Frost was one of the most popular and best-selling of American poets in the twentieth century. Can you suggest why?

Possible points include:

- His choice of themes, while personally expressed, have a universal appeal (illustrate with examples).

- His use of language is attractive and accessible, his images and phrases are memorable, etc.

- The imagery of his poems is rooted in the American landscape and experience.

- His poems reveal his personality to the reader.

- His poems appeal to the reader both intellectually and emotionally.

- The reader can always gain some insight or learn some lesson from his poems.

You must support the points you make with relevant quotation or reference to the poems on your course.

4   Robert Frost accepted the view of the poet and critic Ezra Pound that his poems were 'simple', but added 'if they are they are subtle too'. Do you think Frost's assessment is true of the poems that are on your course?

5   The critic James Dickey has said that the best of Frost's poetry has to do with 'darkness, confusion, panic, terror'. Another critic, Lionel Trilling, spoke of him as a 'terrifying poet'. How do you respond to these views?

6   W. H. Auden described the characteristic voice of Frost's poems as 'always that of the speaking voice, quiet and sensible'. Examine this statement in the light of your reading of Frost's poems.

7   'Many of Robert Frost's poems begin with straightforward description and move towards meditation and commentary.' Discuss this view.

8   'It begins in delight and ends in wisdom.' This is how Frost described the process of composing a poem. How far might this reflect the imaginative structure of a typical Frost lyric?

9   'In his poems Robert Frost sees the beauty of nature, but there is also an awareness of its menace.' Do you agree with this view?

10   'Robert Frost seldom describes nature merely for its own sake. He uses it also as analogy for human and even artistic concerns.' Discuss this statement with reference to the poems on your course.

11   Frost said of his poetry that it provided a 'momentary stay against confusion'. To what extent might this statement illuminate the feelings behind the poems on your course?

12   What qualities of Robert Frost's poetry made him one of the most popular and best-selling poets of twentieth century America? You must support the points you make with relevant quotation or reference to the poems on your course.

Sample essay

'Frost's simple style is deceptive and a thoughtful reader will see layers of meaning in his poetry.'

Do you agree with this assessment of his poetry? Write a response, supporting your points with the aid of suitable reference to the poems on your course.

[This question is from the 2011 Leaving Certificate exam]

Robert Frost said that his poems were both 'simple' and 'subtle'. He admitted that although his poems were about nature, 'there is always something else in them'. In a clear indication to the reader not to take his poems at face value, he spoke of the place of metaphor in poetry, saying, 'Poetry provides the one permissible way of saying one thing and meaning another.' With these pointers from the poet himself, it is clear that the thoughtful reader will be alert to the possibility of layers of meaning within Frost's apparently simple poems.

[Introductory paragraph makes general comment relevant to question]

'The Road Not Taken' is one of Frost's most famous poems. The language in this poem is simple and clear as Frost dramatises the process of making a decision. He presents the reader with a straightforward image: two paths in a yellow wood, one of which the poet says he must choose to travel. We can visualise the traveller looking down 'as far as I could' to see which road would be better. We can follow his train of thought as he weighs up his options. One road seems 'grassy and wanted wear', but the speaker sees too that both roads that morning 'equally lay in leaves no step had trodden black'. As people do, he promised himself he would return and take the other road one day, yet knew in his heart that he would not.

To this point the poem seems simple and uncomplicated. But as suggested in the opening paragraph, simplicity in Frost's poems can be deceptive. The final stanza of the poem leaves the reader somewhat puzzled. Why does the speaker see himself as regretting his choice at the very moment he takes it? Is he suggesting that his choice has resulted in suffering and isolation, as the phrase 'less traveled by' might indicate? A thoughtful reader may see that this phrase is contradictory in the poem because he has told us that both roads were in fact the same. And what is the 'difference' it has made to his life? Perhaps his tone is ironic here, since whichever choice he made was surely bound to make a difference in his life. We are left with a number of questions to which there is no obvious answer – and this is before we begin to wonder what the speaker's 'choices' actually involved. Could he be thinking of his career (we know Frost was a farmer and a poet), or actual choices he had to make as a writer trying to make his own way?

[Discussion of first poem looks at how it appears simple yet has underlying meanings. Note how quotations are integrated into sentences]

Frost's apparent simplicity can be seen in many of his other poems also. 'Birches' begins directly with a simple statement, when Frost says that when he sees birch trees he likes 'to think some boy's been swinging them'. The setting is rural New England, where Frost was familiar with this game. It involves climbing trees until your weight brings the trunk plunging down to the ground, and then jumping off. Frost goes on to describe how ice-storms cause the branches to bend down in a way that swinging on them does not do. He describes them in a blend of conversational language ('often you must have seen them') and sensuous images (the trunks arching on the ground 'like girls on hands and knees that throw their hair before them over their heads to dry in the sun'). When he eventually gets to the picture of the boy who swings birches, he describes him in factual, down-to-earth language as 'some boy too far from town to learn baseball'. He describes the process of the game accurately and precisely. But the careful reader soon begins to see the rich metaphorical significance of the description. By swinging birches, the boy learns a great deal that can be applied to life: determination, persistence, choosing the right moment to do things and knowing when to stop. These are important lessons for a successful life.

[Introduction of second poem and consideration of its meanings]

There are further layers of meaning in the poem, however. Frost personalises the poem when he says 'So was I once myself a swinger of birches.' We cannot ignore the fact that Frost, as a poet, may have learned some useful lessons from his childhood game, lessons that he used in writing poems. Metaphorically speaking, the 'pains' the boy took in climbing the trees can relate to the hard work necessary in writing poetry, knowing when to start and stop and conquering the rules of verse (which to Frost were always important). Frost goes on to say that he would 'like to get away from earth awhile' by 'climbing a birch tree . . . toward heaven.' Here he seems to be linking in an even deeper way the experience of climbing trees (the world of reality) and writing poetry (entering into the world of the imagination). Yet, as he makes clear, he does not desire to leave the real world for ever ('may no fate wilfully misunderstand me'), but to enjoy both parts of the journey: 'That would be good both going and coming back.' The words are simple, but they have an underlying complexity of meaning given what Frost has said before in the poem. It is as if he is affirming both aspects of poetic endeavour: the engagement with the facts of the natural world, and the point of departure these facts present to the poetic imagination.

[More detailed discussion of second poem. References to both elements of question. Quotations and/or references used in support of points made]

Another example of Frost's apparent yet deceptive simplicity can be seen in the poem 'After Apple-Picking'. Once again the setting is rural New England, the activity an ordinary seasonal one: picking and harvesting apples. As is usual in his poetry, Frost evokes beautifully the abundant harvest, using rich sensuous images of sight and sound. There are so many apples that the drowsy farmer seems to see them as in a dream, 'magnified apples appear and disappear'. He hears the 'rumbling sound of load on load of apples coming in'. It is as if 'there were ten thousand thousand fruit to touch, cherish in hand, lift down, and not let fall'. As we read the poem we can really believe that this speaker has harvested apples – he even has the ache in his instep to prove it – and that he desires sleep, above all else. But it is also true that the whole poem is concerned with what is happening in the apple-harvester's mind as it moves back and forth over his experience, and it is then that the thoughtful reader may remember that the speaker is also a poet. Many readers have been aware that the 'great harvest' Frost 'desired' was to produce memorable poems. They then begin to realise that there is an analogy between the labour of the apple-harvester and that of the poet who has to work with his imagination. The 'fruit' then becomes the poetic themes and metaphors that a poet must 'cherish'. Like apple-picking, the work of a poet involves anxiety and loss that may trouble one's sleep, causing one to fear the 'long sleep' of death – death perhaps of the creative imagination.

[Third poem introduced and discussed in similar terms]

Robert Frost

'Mending Wall' takes another straightforward rural activity and yet moves beyond its surface simplicity to question long-held views and values. The speaker describes the yearly ritual of meeting 'at spring mending-time' to repair the wall that divides their properties. At first there is an easy, social tone to the poem. He and his neighbour both seem to be aware of the necessity to mend the wall, each taking care to look after the stones that have fallen on his own side. A thoughtful reader may notice, however, that the repeated phrase 'between us' can suggest both sharing and division at the same time. As the poem progresses, the reader can see how the speaker's attitude to mending the wall differs from that of his neighbour. The speaker seems to be aware of the irony of the wall's existence, since, as he says, his neighbour has pine trees, he has an apple orchard, and so the 'apple trees will never get across and eat the cones' under the neighbour's pines. But when he queries the need for a wall, the neighbour quotes the old saying, 'Good fences make good neighbours.'

[Introduction of fourth poem; note how link is made to preceding discussion]

At this point in the poem a certain tension appears. The narrator seems to join forces with the destructive energy he has mentioned before that destroys walls. 'Spring is the mischief in me' he says, and so he begins to question his neighbour's views. He describes him now in rather menacing images as holding a stone 'like an old-stone savage armed'. Instead of the co-operation that had existed between them there now seems to be division, even hostility. This suggests that the neighbourly relationship is only surface-deep. When the neighbour merely repeats his father's saying about fences, it is clear that there is no more to be gained from the exchange. The gulf between them is impassable. The implications are rather depressing: that human desire for co-operation is often thwarted by people themselves. So the apparently simple situation of mending a wall has led Frost to contemplate the theme of alienation and the complexity of human relationships.

[Fourth poem discussed in similar terms]

Frost's evident love of nature, the gift he had of observing the natural word, sometimes led him to contemplate the meaning of existence itself. In the sonnet 'Design' the thoughtful reader can see this process at work. In the octave Frost describes how he found a spider on a flower (a heal-all) holding up a moth it had just captured. Everything is white, the colour of innocence and purity. But this seemingly innocent scene takes on suggestions of deceit and evil. The moth is being held up 'like a white piece of rigid satin cloth', similar to that inside a coffin. Each of the poem's three 'characters' – spider, moth and flower – has a role in the grim drama of nature's destructiveness.

In the sestet the focus changes as the speaker comments on the situation. He becomes passionately angry as he questions the motives of the plant, which became white in order to trap the moth, in a sort of conspiracy with the spider. He answers his own question when he says that it was nature's design to bring about this chain of events, and that this was a 'design of darkness', in other words, evil. However, having reached this conclusion, he then wonders tentatively in the final line, 'if design govern in a thing so small'. A thoughtful reader may see underlying complexity of meaning in such a simple statement. If there is no design in nature, it follows logically that there is no designer, which implies that there may not be a greater purpose to life as religion suggests. If this is what Frost means to suggest, he is speculating about a problem that has interested philosophers for centuries: how to explain the meaning of existence. In a simple 'nature' poem, he has raised profound questions.

[Fifth poem used to support discussion of simplicity and levels of meaning]

The poetry of Robert Frost, rooted in the rural world he loved and dealing with apparently simple situations, leaves the thoughtful reader with a sense of wonder, plenty to think about and occasional puzzlement, but always with enjoyment.

[Brief concluding paragraph refers back to the question]

Robert Frost

snapshot

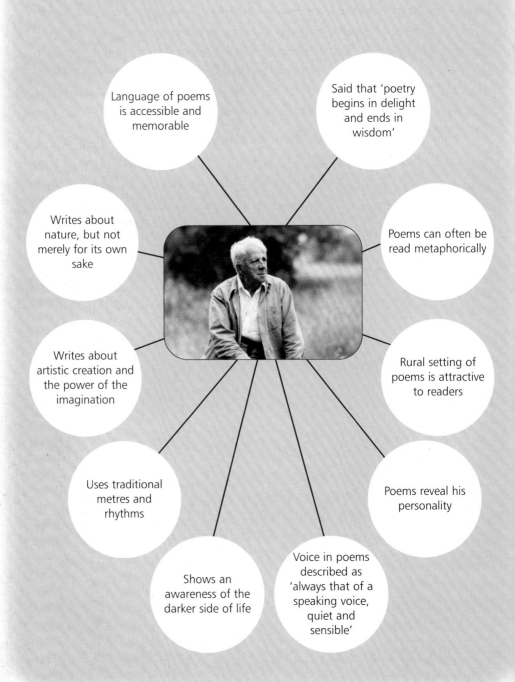

Language of poems is accessible and memorable

Said that 'poetry begins in delight and ends in wisdom'

Writes about nature, but not merely for its own sake

Poems can often be read metaphorically

Writes about artistic creation and the power of the imagination

Rural setting of poems is attractive to readers

Uses traditional metres and rhythms

Poems reveal his personality

Shows an awareness of the darker side of life

Voice in poems described as 'always that of a speaking voice, quiet and sensible'

Thomas Hardy

1840–1928

Biography

Thomas Hardy was born on 2 June 1840 at Higher Bockhampton, a village in Dorset, in a house built by his great-grandfather. He was the first child born to Thomas Hardy, a stonemason and builder, and Jemima Hand, a cook and servant-maid. His father was a talented musician, and his mother encouraged her son to read and pursue his education. The warmth of his home life, his extended family, and the surrounding heath and woodland ensured that Hardy had a lifelong affection for his home place. When he was ten, he was sent to school in nearby Dorchester to learn Latin and Greek.

Early career

At seventeen, Hardy was apprenticed to a local architect and church-restorer, John Hicks, who had offices in Dorchester. Then, when he was twenty-two, he went to London. There, he attended operas and the theatre, and visited museums and galleries. He also began to read and write in a serious way. Influenced by the thinkers and writers of his day, he abandoned his belief in God, though, in his own words, he remained 'churchy; not in an intellectual sense, but in so far as instincts and emotions ruled'. Hardy stayed in London for five years, until, exhausted by long hours of study, disappointed in his literary ambitions and in love, and undergoing a crisis of faith, he returned to his parents' home and resumed work with his former employer.

Emma Gifford

In 1870 Hardy visited Cornwall to prepare a report on the restoration of St Juliot's Church, near Boscastle. There, he met and fell in love with Emma Gifford. Their courtship, amid the wild and beautiful landscape of Arthurian Cornwall, was idyllic. Emma encouraged Hardy to pursue his writing and, in 1874, after the success of *Far from the Madding Crowd*, his fourth book, they married. The early years of the marriage were happy but the couple grew steadily apart. Emma disapproved of the themes explored by her husband in his writing, and her religious beliefs were offended by his agnosticism.

In 1885 Hardy designed and built a large house, 'Max Gate', on the outskirts of Dorchester, not far from his parents' home. This closeness highlighted the growing estrangement between Hardy's wife and his family. Although she entertained lavishly, she considered her husband's family to be her social inferiors and never invited them to visit. Within a few years, the couple lived separate lives within their large and lonely house.

Career as a poet

Hostile reaction to the novel *Jude the Obscure*, published in 1895, which some critics read as the imaginative response to his unhappy marriage, caused Hardy to abandon the writing of novels and turn to his first love, poetry. By any standards, this was a remarkable decision.

Hardy was, by that time, a successful writer, who had built his country mansion; travelled extensively in Europe; and socialised within London's fashionable society. He was also approaching his sixtieth year. Suddenly, he gave up writing novels and devoted himself to poetry, launching a new career that was to last over thirty years and which produced over nine hundred poems. There is no other poet in the English language who began his poetic career so late in life. And this may be a key to Hardy's poetry. It is the poetry of a man looking back on his life, often, though not always, in a spirit of regret and loss.

In 1889 he published his first collection, *Wessex Poems*. Nine further books of poetry were published during his lifetime.

Emma Hardy died suddenly in 1912. Hardy was overcome with feelings of remorse for neglecting the woman he had once loved so passionately. The poems he wrote to, and about, her in the next two years are among the finest love poems ever written. In 1914 Hardy married Florence Dugdale, his secretary and companion, who was forty years his junior. After their marriage, Florence was not pleased that nearly all the poems her husband wrote continued to be about his first wife.

The couple lived in Dorchester, with Hardy writing incessantly up to a few weeks before his death in 1928. His ashes were buried, with great pomp and ceremony, in Poet's Corner, in Westminster Abbey, London, with a handful of Dorset earth sprinkled on the casket. His heart, however, was buried in Stinsford Churchyard in the grave of his first wife, under the tombstone he himself had designed. For all his success, Hardy remained modest and unassuming about his literary successes.

Thomas Hardy

Social and cultural context

During Hardy's long life, England and Europe underwent enormous social, cultural and economic changes. Hardy witnessed the rapid expansion of cities and the growth of the middle class in England; he was aware of the advances in science and engineering; he observed the struggle of the suffragette movement; he lamented the disappearance of the English system of farming, which had gone on unchanged for hundreds of years, and the related decline in traditional crafts; he viewed with dismay the progress of the First World War.

In his early years Charles Dickens and Lord Alfred Tennyson were in their prime, and Gladstone, Disraeli, Bismarck and Garibaldi were the leading political figures of the day. When he died T. S. Eliot, James Joyce and Virginia Woolf were the leading writers, while Hitler, Stalin and Mussolini were in the ascendant. In his early lifetime Hardy saw the rise of railways; towards the end he travelled in a motorcar. By any standards, Hardy lived in a time of remarkable and profound change.

The England he had been born into, and which he loved and celebrated in his Wessex novels, had disappeared by the time of his death. Writing in 1940, on the centenary of Hardy's birth, W. H. Auden remarked: 'He is dead, the world he knew has died too, and we have other roads to build, but his humility before nature, his sympathy for the suffering and the blind, and his sense of proportion are as necessary now as they ever were.'

Anti-war stance

One major change was the rise of the British Empire. Queen Victoria was proclaimed Empress of India in 1876 and England was involved in a war in South Africa in 1899. Hardy had little sympathy for the militarism of the British Empire. His opposition to imperialist war is expressed in the poem 'Drummer Hodge'.

During the First World War Hardy expressed compassion for the ordinary English and German soldiers, whom he regarded as victims of the German 'war-lords'. Indeed, in one poem he suggested that the English and the German people were related by both race and language. He believed that the slaughter of ordinary men served no cause other than the ambition of the 'war-lords'. Although distressed by the war, and hostile to the military establishment in England, he believed that it was England's duty to face down the arrogance and evil of those who waged war.

Throughout his life he maintained an anti-war stance, which was not an easy thing to do in a period of such intense national and imperial rivalry. However, he had little faith that his poems could change matters, an attitude expressed in 'Afterwards', in the statement, 'But he could do little for them; and now he is gone'. There is a similar feeling of powerlessness in the face of human evil in 'Channel Firing'.

Science and philosophy

Hardy came from the 'lower social classes' and was largely self-educated. He had a lifelong interest in both science and philosophy. Influenced by Charles Darwin's theory of evolution and the philosophical writers of his day, in particular John Stuart Mill, he abandoned his belief in God. His attitude to faith and belief is evident in 'The Oxen' and 'The Darkling Thrush'. The loss of faith in God was replaced, in part, by a belief in evolutionary progress. He sometimes referred to himself as a 'meliorist'; that is, someone who believed in the gradual improvement and advancement of humankind. However, Hardy viewed an individual's life as minute and almost inconsequential compared with the vastness of time and the universe. This outlook gave him a fatalistic attitude that many characterise as pessimism, and this pessimistic strain may well have deepened under the stress of his personal unhappiness in his marriage to Emma.

While Hardy's poetry reflects some of the philosophical debates of the age, he was not a systematic thinker or a philosopher. As Samuel Hynes puts it, 'his poetry is philosophical in so far as the problems with which he was obsessed might also concern a philosopher, but it does not contain a philosophy'.

Power of nature

Hardy's fiction and poetry both chart the power of nature and set it against the pretensions and vanity of human beings, as in 'The Convergence of the Twain'. In this poem, as elsewhere, Hardy is didactic. The destructive progress of time is explored most vividly in 'During Wind and Rain'. Indeed a sense of loss is probably the most characteristic feature of Hardy's poetry, though this sense is due as much to personal temperament as to the spirit of the age.

The Victorian age was one in which economic self-interest and selfishness, allied to strict moral orthodoxy and an obsession with 'respectability', informed the lives of many members of the middle classes. Hardy, too, was an individualist, but one with a strong attachment to his native place and to his family, as evident in 'The Self-Unseeing'. Furthermore, he believed in the virtues of kindness and compassion. In fact, in 'Afterwards' he expresses the hope that he will be remembered for his concern for all living creatures.

In his fiction Hardy engages and challenges the dominant attitudes of contemporary society towards issues of class, gender and sexuality, but his poetry does not reveal the same level of engagement. Indeed his fondness for narrative and traditional stanza

Thomas Hardy

forms gives his poetry an old-fashioned feel. The poetry for which he is most remembered is personal and lyrical, most especially the love poems written after the death of his first wife, Emma.

In the many selections of Hardy's poetry currently available, he emerges as a poet of nature, of love, of death and of loss. He appears as a man of compassion, mindful of life's ironies and nostalgic for his rural boyhood. In a time of war and uncertainty, his poetic voice was reassuring and comforting when set against the modernist poetry of his contemporaries, most notably T. S. Eliot. If Eliot is regarded as an urban, intellectual, even obscure, modern poet, then many readers see Hardy as provincial, sentimental and traditional, though this view is not an adequate account of his poetic achievement, or of the tragic scepticism that pervades much of his writing.

Biographical element

Despite living through an age burdened with conflicting beliefs and ideas on religion, science, nature and economic and social advancement, Hardy's poetry stays close to his personal experience. Indeed the personal quality of his poetry may well have been Hardy's response to the challenge of making poetry meaningful in a post-Darwin age, when belief in God seemed unsustainable.

Whatever the reason, in almost all his lyrical poetry, it is possible to trace the biographical event that give rise to the poem. In the poems written after Emma's death, Hardy not only remembers the past but also imbues his remembrance with the passionate promise of their early years together. In effect, he remakes their love. Perhaps it is his exploration of the old theme of love, its promise and disappointment, that made Hardy popular in his day and accounts for his continued popularity.

Notwithstanding the changing times through which he lived, or perhaps because of them, Hardy returned to familiar themes. As he himself said shortly before his death, 'All we can do is write on the old themes in the old style, but try to do it a little better than those who came before us.' The very familiarity of his themes gives Hardy's readers a sense of comfort and continuity, even when he views the world through his ironic eyes and notes what Samuel Hynes calls 'the disparity between the way things ought to be and the way they are', and the sadness that this brings.

Timeline

1840	Born at Higher Bockhampton, Dorset
1848	Attends local schools
1850	Attends school in Dorchester and learns Latin and Greek
1856	Becomes apprenticed to Dorchester architect John Hicks
1857	Meets the classical scholar Horace Mole and begins to write poetry
1862	Moves to London
1865	Loses his religious beliefs
1867	Moves back to Dorchester to his parents' house
1870	Visits Cornwall and meets Emma Gifford
1871	Publishes his first novel
1872	Moves back to London
1874	His novel *Far from the Madding Crowd* is a big success; marries Emma Gifford
1885	Moves to Max Gate, in Dorset, a house he designed himself
1891	*Tess of the d'Urbervilles* is a major success; marriage begins to deteriorate
1895	*Jude the Obscure* is met with public outrage; Emma increasingly unhappy
1896	Abandons novel writing and devotes himself to poetry
1904	Meets Florence Dugdale
1910	Florence Dugdale moves to Max Gate as his secretary
1912	Death of Emma
1913	Revisits Cornwall and Plymouth and the places where he first met Emma
1914	Marries Florence Dugdale
1919	*Collected Poems* published
1928	Dies on 11 January; his heart is buried in Dorset and his ashes in Westminster Abbey

Drummer Hodge

I

They throw in Drummer Hodge, to rest
  Uncoffined – just as found:
His landmark is a kopje-crest
  That breaks the veldt around;
And foreign constellations west   5
  Each night above his mound.

II

Young Hodge the Drummer never knew—
  Fresh from his Wessex home—
The meaning of the broad Karoo,
  The Bush, the dusty loam,   10
And why uprose to nightly view
  Strange stars amid the gloam.

III

Yet portion of that unknown plain
  Will Hodge for ever be;
His homely Northern breast and brain   15
  Grow to some Southern tree,
And strange-eyed constellations reign
  His stars eternally.

Glossary	
2	*Uncoffined:* without placing his body in a coffin
3	*kopje:* hill or headland. Like 'veldt' and 'karoo', 'kopje' comes from Afrikaans, the Dutch-based language spoken by the Boers. All three words refer to the landscape
4	*veldt:* grassland, unenclosed pasture
5	*constellation:* group of stars
8	*Wessex:* an Anglo-Saxon kingdom in south-west England. Hardy applied the name to a region comprising Dorset and neighbouring counties, which was the setting for his novels and many of his poems
9	*Karoo:* a high plain
10	*loam:* a dark soil with a texture like wet sand
12	*gloam:* twilight

Guidelines

'Drummer Hodge' was included in the collection *Poems of the Past and the Present* (1901). The poem was written in 1899, during the time of the Second Boer War in South Africa (1899–1902). When it was first published, it was entitled 'The Dead Drummer' and an explanatory note was added, which read: 'One of the Drummers killed was a native of a village near Casterbridge.' As a native of Dorset, who loved his home place, Hardy would have felt for the young man buried unceremoniously so far from his home. Here, as in other of his poems, Hardy expresses his dislike for the military establishment, and his fondness for the ordinary people of his native Dorset.

Commentary

The poem looks at the subject of war from the perspective of one young boy. There are no grand statements against war, yet the poem succeeds in suggesting the sacrifice of a young life by the machinery of war. In place of heroic sentiments we have humane sympathy for the young drummer.

Stanza 1

The first line of the poem suggests that the burial detail treat their fallen comrade as a piece of rubbish to be discarded, 'They throw in Drummer Hodge . . .'. The words 'throw in' seem particularly brutal. In Hardy's eyes, the army authorities had little regard for the soldiers in their care. The drummer's name is also significant. 'Hodge' was the nickname given to country boys, often considered dull-witted and unsophisticated by town and city dwellers.

The drummer lies 'uncoffined' (line 2). In this word, Hardy suggests a lack of respect for the young soldier. In all his writing, the churchyard, with the graves of the local community, is an honoured place. Hardy described the churchyard, where many of his ancestors were buried, as the 'most hallowed spot on earth'. The importance he attached to the commemoration of the dead is evident in the five chapters devoted to the death, burial and tombstone of Fanny Robin in *Far from the Madding Crowd*. Therefore, by Hardy's standards, the treatment of Drummer Hodge is barbaric.

The use of the Dutch-Afrikaans words – 'kopje-crest' and 'veldt', (lines 3 and 4) – to describe the landscape emphasises the foreignness of the surroundings where Drummer Hodge dies and is buried. For Hardy, who loved his home place and was a frequent visitor to the graves of his ancestors, the idea of lying 'uncoffined' in alien soil under 'foreign constellations' (line 5) is a dreadful prospect.

Thomas Hardy

Stanzas 2 and 3

In the second stanza there is a sense not only of displacement but of incomprehension. Hodge could not understand or read the landscape or, by implication, the reason or meaning for his being there and dying there.

Yet, the third stanza states, he will lie eternally, lost and alone, in this strange and alien place. The 'homely' (line 15) young man from the northern hemisphere has been absorbed in the southern soil, rooted and, perhaps, imprisoned eternally in a tree, under strange stars. As in stanza 1, both stanzas 2 and 3 conclude with an image of the strange constellations in the southern sky.

From other of his poems and from his novels we know how much Hardy prized knowledge of nature, knowledge of both land and sky. For Hardy, knowledge and love go hand in hand. It is his love for his native place that the young Hodge brings with him to his grave in a distant land. It is arguable that the idea of the body being absorbed into nature has none of the consoling effects often associated with this idea. There is no consolation because the soil is southern and the 'Northern breast and brain' (line 15) will not rest there comfortably.

Form and language of the poem

Although the poem is written to commemorate a young boy from Wessex and has a traditional stanza form with a simple, song-like rhyming scheme and rhythm, the language is not condescending or artificially 'rustic'. On the contrary, the poem demonstrates Hardy's fondness for inventing or coining words. Frequently positive words were made negative by prefixing 'un' or 'dis', as in 'uncoffined'. Moreover, the use of foreign words gives the poem an exotic feel. Some of Hardy's early critics pointed to a lack of elegance in his poetry, but in doing so they missed the extent to which his poetry frees itself from class-bound conceptions of 'poetic diction' and avoids false sentiment.

Thinking about the poem

1   What is the effect of the description, 'They throw in Drummer Hodge' in the first line of the poem? Does it make the act seem: casual, respectful, brutal or caring? Explain your choice.

2   How is the foreignness of Hodge's resting place emphasised in the first stanza?

3   How does the second stanza emphasise the idea of displacement?

4   Which of the following words do you think best describes the mood of the final stanza: regretful, sad, sympathetic or angry? Explain your choice.

5   'His homely Northern breast and brain / Grow to some Southern tree' (lines 15 and 16). Is this suggestion, that Drummer Hodge will be absorbed into nature, presented as a consolation in the poem? Explain your answer.

6   Would you agree with the view that 'Drummer Hodge' is an anti-war poem? Explain.

7   'What the poem shows is how the lives of ordinary, decent people are destroyed by wars that have nothing to do with them.' Write a short essay supporting or challenging this view of the poem.

8   Examine the stanza form of the poem. Does it suit the subject matter and theme of the poem? Explain.

Personal response

1   Working in pairs, consider why, in your view, Hardy includes so many references to the sky and the landscape in the poem.

2   Create a multimedia presentation, with images and sound, to accompany a reading of the poem.

3   Based on your impression of the young drummer, write a letter that he might have sent home to his family, telling how he feels about being in South Africa.

Before you read 'The Darkling Thrush'

Before you read Thomas Hardy's 'The Darkling Thrush', consider these questions. Do you like New Year's Eve? Do you look forward to the year ahead with optimism or pessimism? Do you look back on the year just gone with pleasure or regret? Do you like the cold, dark nights of winter or do you find them a little depressing?

Share your thoughts with a partner before reading this poem, set at the end of the day, at the end of the year, at the end of a century.

The Darkling Thrush

I leant upon a coppice gate
  When Frost was spectre-gray,
And Winter's dregs made desolate
  The weakening eye of day.
The tangled bine-stems scored the sky   5
  Like strings of broken lyres,
And all mankind that haunted nigh
  Had sought their household fires.

The land's sharp features seemed to be
    The Century's corpse outleant,   10
His crypt the cloudy canopy,
    The wind his death-lament.
The ancient pulse of germ and birth
    Was shrunken hard and dry,
And every spirit upon earth   15
    Seemed fervourless as I.

At once a voice arose among
    The bleak twigs overhead
In a full-hearted evensong
    Of joy illimited;   20
An aged thrush, frail, gaunt, and small,
    In blast-beruffled plume,
Had chosen thus to fling his soul
    Upon the growing gloom.

So little cause for carolings   25
    Of such ecstatic sound
Was written on terrestrial things
    Afar or nigh around,
That I could think there trembled through
    His happy good-night air   30
Some blessed Hope, whereof he knew
    And I was unaware.

31st December 1900

Glossary		
title:	*Darkling:* a word used in poetry and meaning shrouded or covered in darkness. It refers to a thrush singing in the dark, and to the poet's mind, which is shrouded in darkness	
1	*coppice gate:* a gate made from cut branches	
2	*spectre-gray:* in the fading light, the frost is a ghostly shade of grey	
3	*dregs:* deposits, waste	
3	*desolate:* bleak, miserable	

5	*tangled bine-stems:* this could refer to the stem of the hop, or common bindweed, which wraps itself around other plants and strangles them
6	*lyres:* small string instruments (like a harp) that were popular in ancient Greece. The image of a broken lyre was used on tombstones to symbolise the end of life
7	*nigh:* near, nearby
10	*outleant:* this may mean laid out (like a dead body)
13	*germ:* beginning, seed
16	*fervourless:* without feeling or passion
19	*evensong:* a service of evening prayer and hymns in the Anglican church. Hardy was raised an Anglican and retained a lifelong love of the hymns and rituals of the church
20	*illimited:* limitless, endless
22	*blast-beruffled plume:* the wind is ruffling the bird's feathers
25	*carolings:* singing carols or hymns of praise
27	*terrestrial things:* things of this world (as opposed to things of heaven)

Guidelines

The poem was written at the end of 1900 and appeared in the collection *Poems of the Past and the Present* (1901). The poem is intended to be read as if the darkness is falling on the final hours of the century. It was originally entitled 'By the Century's Deathbed'. It is one of the most anthologised of all Hardy's poems, though whether it expresses hope or pessimism is open to debate. At the time of writing, it had been thirty years since Hardy had first met his wife, Emma, and the couple were very distant from each other.

Commentary

The title of the poem is interesting. 'Darkling' is a word used in poetry, with the general meaning of 'shrouded in darkness'. It had been used in three great poems known to Hardy: John Keats's 'Ode to a Nightingale', Matthew Arnold's 'Dover Beach', both written in the nineteenth century, and John Milton's 'Paradise Lost', which was written in the seventeenth century. These three poems deal with large themes: hope and despair, faith and reason. The dramatic flourish of dating the poem '31st December 1900' creates the impression of Hardy summing up these weighty issues on the eve of a new century.

Stanza 1

Hardy's poem opens with the word 'I'. All else that follows is narrated by the speaker of the poem and seen through his or her eyes. The imagery of the opening stanza is bleak and desolate. The winter's day drawing to an end is presented in terms of disintegration and death. The frost is 'spectre-gray' (line 2); the 'eye of day' is 'weakening' (line 4). The plants are compared to 'broken lyres' (line 6), a traditional grave emblem, symbolising the end of life, and 'mankind' seems to 'haunt' the world (line 7). Other words such as 'dregs' and 'desolate' (line 3) create an air of pessimism, while 'the tangled bine-stems' and the verb 'scored' (line 5) suggest that life is being strangled and cut to pieces.

Stanza 2

There is a change in perspective in the second stanza. Not only is the day drawing to a close, but the century is also coming to an end. The change in perspective leads to an intensification of the images of death. The landscape, as seen by the speaker, is compared to 'the Century's corpse' (line 10); the sky is the Century's 'crypt' (line 11); while the wind is described as the Century's 'death-lament' (line 12). In the eyes of the speaker, the natural forces of birth and death have 'shrunken hard and dry' (line 14). Projecting his or her despair upon the world, the speaker suggests that 'every spirit upon earth / Seemed fervourless as I' (lines 15 and 16). If, as many commentators suggest, the 'I' of the poem is identified with Hardy, this stanza implies that, at the turn of the century, the poet was in despair that human beings were left in a bleak world where the traditional comforts of religion had been lost and the basic meaning of life was unintelligible to the mind.

Stanza 3

There is a sudden change of mood in the third stanza, captured in the word 'joy' in line 20. The joy comes from the voice of a thrush. The bird's song is described as 'evensong' (line 19), a comparison that invokes images of a congregation singing hymns, united in faith. It is an image that contrasts with the solitary fervourlessness of the speaker. The bird is not an abstract principle, but a real 'thrush, frail, gaunt, and small' (line 21). In spite of his age and the cold, the bird is able to 'fling' (line 23) his song upon the air. There is a sense of energy and defiance suggested by the verb 'fling'. Despite the 'growing gloom' (line 24), the joy of the bird is without limit.

Stanza 4

The speaker tries to make sense of the bird's song. In the words 'carolings' (line 25) and 'ecstatic' (line 26), the speaker recognises the joy of the song but cannot see how any 'terrestrial' (line 27) thing, 'Afar or nigh around' (line 28), could be the source of the joy. Instead of identifying with the bird, the final stanza seems to emphasise the speaker's difference from it. In using the word 'terrestrial', is the speaker implying that, for him or her, there is nothing beyond this world?

The final four lines of the poem are intriguing. Here the speaker states that, 'I could think' (line 29) that the joy of the bird is accounted for by 'Some blessed Hope' (line 31). Note how tentative the phrase 'could think' is. It hovers ambiguously between a positive and a negative statement. And even if the poet does think that the joyful song of the bird is caused by hope, it is a hope of which the speaker is 'unaware'.

So how is a reader to read this stanza? Certainly, given the poem's popularity, many readers read the final stanza as a statement of hope. The bird teaches humanity to trust and hope, despite all indications to the contrary. However, if the focus is on the narrator, then it is possible to read the stanza as a statement of despair. The narrator recognises that the bird is sustained by a hopeful force to which he or she has no access. This realisation can only be seen as intensifying the sorrow of the speaker.

Form and language of the poem

The poem is written in four eight-line rhymed stanzas. The tone of the poem is solemn and serious, while the choice of words, the use of alliteration, and the rhythm give it a hymn-like quality. (This may be an ironic twist by the poet.) The language of the poem is spare and hard-edged; for example, 'shrunken hard and dry'; 'fling his soul'; 'bleak twigs overhead'.

Thinking about the poem

1   Explain, as clearly as you can, the setting for the poem.
2   In your view, which of the following words best describes the atmosphere of the poem: bleak, lonely, joyless, beautiful, joyful, hopeful? Explain your choice.
3   Select two phrases from the first and second stanzas that help create the atmosphere of the poem. Explain your choice.
4   The narrator describes the thrush as 'frail, gaunt, and small' (line 21). Choose three words of your own to describe how you picture the thrush in this poem.
5   What makes the song of the thrush so striking to the listener?
6   Which two options from the following list are closest to your view of the bird in the poem?
    ● The thrush symbolises hope.
    ● The thrush symbolises the beauty of the world.
    ● The thrush symbolises the promise of spring.
    ● The thrush symbolises the wonder of God's creation.
    ● The thrush symbolises despair.
    Explain your choices.

7   The poem is interpreted in many different ways. In the case of each of the following statements, select quotations (words, phrases or lines) from the poem to support the view expressed:

●   The speaker of the poem is only an observer of life, cut off from living and from his fellow humans.

●   The song of the thrush causes the narrator to feel sorrow.

●   What the speaker recognises in the song of the bird is that there may be hope for the world, even if he is unaware of it.

8   Which of the readings of the poem in question 7 is closest to your own? Give reasons for your choice.

9   What impact do the words 'evensong' (line 19) and 'carolings' (line 25) have in the poem?

10   How do the stanza form, rhyme and choice of words contribute to the religious-like atmosphere of the poem?

11   What is the effect of using the verb 'fling' (line 23) to describe the song of the bird?

12   Comment on the use of the word 'terrestrial' (line 27) and its contribution to the meaning of the poem.

Personal response

1   What music and images would you use to accompany a reading of this poem? Explain your choice.

2   Did you enjoy reading 'The Darkling Thrush'? Give a reason for your opinion.

3   Based on the poem, what kind of person do you imagine the speaker is? Hardy received many visitors at his home, Max Gate. Imagine you had visited him in the run up to New Year's Eve 1900. Write a short description of the man you met.

The Darkling Thrush

Marks the end of a century

Title reflects the day and the speaker's mind

The speaker is alone

Barren, frozen landscape

Gloomy mood and images of death

Hymn-like rhythm

Sudden song of the old thrush

Bird seems to be full of hope, unlike the speaker

Thomas Hardy

Before you read 'The Self Unseeing'

Before reading Thomas Hardy's 'The Self Unseeing' consider these questions. Have you a favourite song or tune to which you like to dance? What mood or feeling does the music cause you to experience? Do you associate the music with any particular person, place or time? Share your thoughts with a partner.

The Self Unseeing

Here is the ancient floor,
Footworn and hollowed and thin,
Here was the former door
Where the dead feet walked in.

She sat here in her chair,   5
Smiling into the fire;
He who played stood there,
Bowing it higher and higher.

Childlike, I danced in a dream;
Blessings emblazoned that day;   10
Everything glowed with a gleam;
Yet we were looking away!

Glossary

3	*the former door:* the poem is set in Hardy's childhood home in Higher Bockhampton, at one point the front door had been moved
4	*dead feet:* this phrase recalls all Hardy's dead family and friends who walked through the door
5	*She:* the poet's mother
7	*He:* the poet's father, a noted fiddle player, from whom Hardy inherited his love of music
10	*emblazoned:* adorned, embellished

Guidelines

The poem was included in the 1901 collection, *Poems of the Past and the Present*. It was composed between 1898 and 1901. Hardy wrote 'The Self-Unseeing' after a visit to his childhood home and it recalls a typical scene from his family life. His father, a stonemason by trade, plays the violin; the young Hardy dances to the music; and his mother sits by the fire. Hardy's father died in 1892. The poem is an exercise in memory and nostalgia.

Commentary

Stanza 1

The narrator, Hardy himself, goes back to his family home and remembers his childhood there. The reader is like a companion to whom Hardy points out different things. The building carries the traces of the dead generations in its 'ancient floor / Footworn and hollowed and thin' (lines 1 and 2) and in his memory of a 'former door / Where the dead feet walked in' (lines 3 and 4). The house commemorates the dead while attesting to the destruction wrought by time. Not surprisingly, the tone is elegiac, expressed through the simple diction and the long vowel sounds, 'footworn', 'hollowed', 'thin' (line 2). While many of Hardy's poems are marred by clumsy phrasing or rhythm, this one is word perfect.

Stanza 2

The narrator points out where 'She' (line 5) and 'He' (line 7) positioned themselves as 'He' played music. These characters are almost certainly Hardy's father and mother. The image of his mother 'Smiling into the fire' (line 6) evokes both a special moment and a special warmth.

Stanza 3

The third stanza reunites the narrator and his young self: 'Childlike, I danced in a dream' (line 9). Now the memories are more specific and refer to one particular day, a day 'emblazoned' by 'blessings' (line 10), a day of perfect happiness when 'Everything glowed with a gleam' (line 11). The irony is that the realisation of that happiness comes to the poet when his parents are long dead.

The use of the word 'Yet' at the beginning of the final line is typical of how Hardy qualifies moments of happiness. The joyful imagery of the final stanza is undercut by the failure of the participants to understand or acknowledge the happiness they shared, as they shared it. They enjoy the music but each in his or her own way. Despite this failure, the poem still stands as a celebration of family life.

Title

The title of the poem is interesting. There is a sense that Hardy apportions blame to himself for being 'unseeing', for dancing 'in a dream' (line 9), and for understanding too late the happiness he enjoyed with his parents. 'The Self-Unseeing' is typical of many poems in which a remembered past speaks more forcefully to the poet than the present reality. Of course, it can be argued that in celebrating the past, as he does so often, Hardy continues to 'look away' from the present and continues, therefore, to undervalue it.

Form of the poem

The poem is written in a traditional ballad form. Each stanza has four lines and rhymes *abab*. The simple style and diction suit the celebration of ordinary people, who were without airs or graces. Note how the alliteration (on the letters 'h', 'd', 'g' and 'b') echoes the music of the fiddle. Note also how the word 'emblazoned' shines out of the poem, perfectly capturing the idea of the remembered scene glowing in the poet's memory.

Thinking about the poem

1   What mood is created by Hardy's description in stanza 1?

2   What picture of Hardy's family and childhood is conveyed in this poem?

3   'Everything glowed with a gleam; / Yet we were looking away!' (lines 11 and 12). Explain, as clearly as you can, the meaning of the final line and the 'yet' it contains.

4   The poem is written in a simple style. Does this simplicity contribute or detract from its power?

5   Comment on the use of the word 'emblazoned' (line 10) and the range of meanings it conveys.

6   In pairs, consider these five readings of the poem. Comment on each and then choose the two that are closest to your own. Share your ideas with the rest of the class.

(a)   The poem celebrates family life.

(b)   The poem teaches that the present is often less vivid than the memory of it.

(c)   The poem captures the inevitability of loss and the isolation of the person who remembers.

(d)   The poem expresses a simple truth: people rarely value the happiness of their lives until it is too late.

(e)   What the poem suggests is that happiness is not self-conscious. There is no ingratitude in the couple or the boy, just a simple enjoyment of the present.

Personal response

1   Working in pairs, put together a collection of images that creates a similar mood to that of the poem.

2   Write a brief account of what the speaker of the poem tells us, this time from the mother's point of view.

Before you read 'The Convergence of the Twain'

Thomas Hardy's poem 'The Convergence of the Twain' is on page 177. Everyone knows the story of the *Titanic*, the 'unsinkable' ship that sank on its first trip across the Atlantic. In pairs, discuss what, if anything, you think the tragedy teaches us. Share your ideas with the rest of the class.

The Convergence of the Twain

Lines on the loss of the **Titanic**

I

In a solitude of the sea
Deep from human vanity,
And the Pride of Life that planned her, stilly couches she.

II

Steel chambers, late the pyres
Of her salamandrine fires,   5
Cold currents thrid, and turn to rhythmic tidal lyres.

III

Over the mirrors meant
To glass the opulent
The sea-worm crawls — grotesque, slimed, dumb, indifferent.

IV

Jewels in joy designed   10
To ravish the sensuous mind
Lie lightless, all their sparkles bleared and black and blind.

V

Dim moon-eyed fishes near
Gaze at the gilded gear
And query: 'What does this vaingloriousness down here?'   15

VI

Well: while was fashioning
This creature of cleaving wing,
The Immanent Will that stirs and urges everything

VII

Prepared a sinister mate
For her — so gaily great —   20
A Shape of Ice, for the time far and dissociate.

VIII

And as the smart ship grew
In stature, grace, and hue,
In shadowy silent distance grew the Iceberg too.

Thomas Hardy

IX

Alien they seemed to be: 25

No mortal eye could see

The intimate welding of their later history,

X

Or sign that they were bent

By paths coincident

On being anon twin halves of one august event,   30

XI

Till the Spinner of the Years

Said 'Now!' And each one hears,

And consummation comes, and jars two hemispheres.

Glossary	
title	*Twain:* two
4	*pyres:* piles of combustible material, especially for the cremation of corpses
5	*salamandrine fires:* the meaning may be 'furnace' fires. The word 'salamander' also refers to a mythical creature who lived in fire without being harmed; the owners of the Titanic believed the ship could endure all trials
6	*thrid:* to thread or move carefully through
6	*lyres:* ancient stringed instruments
15	*vaingloriousness:* boastfulness, vanity, ostentation
18	*Immanent Will:* Hardy uses this term in various writings to describe the underlying force in the universe. Although he did not believe in God, he believed that there was a Will or an energy within nature and the universe (though his views on the precise nature of this Will were not clearly defined or consistent). What is consistent in the concept of the Immanent Will is an attempt to find an underlying pattern to, or explanation of, life. In an early poem, 'Hap', Hardy suggests that he could bear his suffering if 'some vengeful god' admitted to causing it. What seems unbearable is that there is no explanation for it. In 'The Convergence of the Twain', the 'Immanent Will' resembles Fate, the agency that predetermines the course of events
21	*dissociate:* regarded as unconnected, separate
27	*welding:* union, especially the fusing of pieces of metal (as in shipbuilding)
29	*paths coincident:* the same course
30	*anon:* soon

30	*august:* high ranking, major
31	*Spinner of the Years:* time
33	*consummation:* perfect completion; when applied to a marriage it means sexual intercourse

Guidelines

On 15 April 1912 the SS *Titanic* sank, with the loss of 1,513 lives, after colliding with an iceberg during her maiden voyage. This poem was originally written for a gala concert in aid of the Titanic Disaster Fund in May 1912. It was subsequently revised and expanded. Although Hardy was acquainted with two of the victims of the disaster, the poem is less concerned with mourning the dead than with rebuking the vanity that believed the ship unsinkable, which may explain why the ship's owners failed to provide enough lifeboats. At the time of the disaster, prominence was given to the reply made by a deckhand to a question put by a wealthy passenger. The deckhand is reported to have said: 'God Himself could not sink this ship.' 'The Convergence of the Twain' comments on the disastrous folly of such arrogance. The poem appeared in Hardy's 1914 collection, *Satires of Circumstance.*

Commentary

In the first five stanzas the ship is presented as lying on the bottom of the ocean. The poem then suggests that, as the ship was being built, its fate was already determined because the iceberg that would destroy it was also taking shape in the north Atlantic. The inevitable collision is described in the final stanza. The poem presents the sinking of the *Titanic* as something similar to Greek tragedy in which human pride or hubris is punished by the gods. The ship, the material object, symbolises human pride and vanity. The sinking of the ship is portrayed as a rebuke to human pride by the 'Immanent Will' (line 18).

Stanzas 1 and 2
The long vowel sounds and the alliteration of the opening line create a solemn tone: 'In a solitude of the sea'.

The *Titanic* is referred to as 'she' (line 3) and we are told that she lies at the bottom of the ocean, far from the human vanity and pride that planned her. The introduction of the notions of vanity and pride strike the moral tone of the poem, which regards the sinking of the ship as a lesson, a warning against human arrogance in the face of nature or some other shaping force.

Thomas Hardy

In the solitude of the sea, the ship remains as a symbol of human vanity, her purpose altered from that intended by her human creators. On the ocean bed her fires have been quenched and her steel parts rotate to the movement of the tide.

Stanza 3

The third stanza introduces the image of mirrors, traditional symbols of vanity. The mirrors were intended to allow the rich and glamorous passengers to admire themselves. Now sea-worms crawl over them, ugly creatures indifferent to their reflected image. Line 9, 'The sea-worm crawls – grotesque, slimed, dumb, indifferent' is savage in its effect, betraying, perhaps, Hardy's deep hostility to the vanity of the ship's owners and the builders who declared the ship unsinkable and made it a monument to conspicuous wealth. Perhaps in this line, and throughout the poem, we catch the voice of the countryman, with a dislike for idle displays of wealth.

Stanzas 4 and 5

The ironic contrasts between the intention to impress and the fate of the ship is continued in stanzas 4 and 5. The rich and sensuous diction has captured the opulence of the ship – 'steel' (line 4), 'salamandrine' (line 5), 'sensuous' (line 11) – but, without any human eye to gaze upon these, the jewels and 'gilded gear' (line 14) lose all meaning. With grim humour, Hardy imagines moon-eyed fishes asking, 'What does this vaingloriousness down here?' (line 15).

Stanzas 6–10

The remaining six stanzas give an answer to the fish's question. The 'vaingloriousness' (line 15) rests on the seabed because, as the ship was in preparation, the 'Immanent Will' (line 18), portrayed as a vengeful god, prepared a sinister mate to consummate a violent union. The sexual imagery of 'mate' (line 19), 'intimate welding' (line 27) and 'consummation' (line 33) is developed from the convention of referring to a ship as feminine and her first trip as 'a maiden voyage'. The ship is, in the words of J. O. Bailey, 'ornamented as if for marriage, "gaily great" to meet a bridegroom'. In stanza 8 Hardy skilfully creates the parallel preparation of the ship and the iceberg, each destined for the other, though unaware of each other.

As Hardy presents it, the iceberg, the 'Shape of Ice' (line 21) was destined for the *Titanic*, though 'No mortal eye could see / The intimate welding of their later history' (lines 26 and 27). Implicit in these lines is the suggestion of an immortal eye that could see and shape history. The idea of foreseeing an event is also suggested in Hardy's use of the adjective 'august' (line 30), which is related to the noun 'augury' (an omen). The word 'convergence' in the title of the poem further advances the idea that the two elements, the natural iceberg and the manmade ship, were brought together by an act of will.

Stanza 11

The final stanza of the poem, in which time is personified as 'the Spinner of the Years' (line 31), adds a dramatic flourish and creates a sense of immediacy, most notably in the use of the word 'Now!' (line 32). Here Hardy borrows from Greek mythology, where the Fates were sister goddesses who presided over the birth, life and death of humans. One fabricated the thread of an individual's life, one measured its length and determined its character and the third cut it off with her shears. The Fates were unappeasable and unrelenting. As with the idea of the Fates, the poem offers a deterministic view of the disaster. The personification of the forces governing the universe makes them appear closer to the Old Testament conception of a vengeful God than to any unconscious and impersonal forces of the kind Hardy wrote about elsewhere.

The change of rhythm in the final stanza suggests the sudden and unexpected impact. The 'Spinner of the Years' (line 31) is like a film director, dictating the action. The use of the word 'jars' (line 33) is particularly effective.

Universal meaning

Clearly Hardy was attracted to the story of the *Titanic*. Yet what the poem reveals is less the meaning of the event than Hardy's need to order and arrange experience into a symmetrical form, into a moral pattern. In creating the neat symmetries of the poem, some critics argue that Hardy sacrificed the individual human meaning of the event for an impersonal, universal one. (There are no individual people portrayed in the poem.) The poem is less about the sinking of the *Titanic* than it is about Hardy's reaction to the universe.

On the other hand, the unusual perspective of the poem – its remote, general and ironic perspective – is what other critics value. In common with many other poems, this poem has the theme of what Michael Schmidt calls 'unfulfilment' (i.e. the thwarting of human intention or desire). Mostly this theme is presented in personal terms, but here it works on a more abstract level, though mediated through language and imagery that is sensuous and concrete.

As Hardy presents it, the emphasis in the story is on the ship as a symbol, not on the people who lost their lives on board her.

Hardy's beliefs

The poem casts some light on Hardy's beliefs. He turned away from the Christian God, believing that if the world was governed by some force it was an indifferent and impersonal one. However, his beliefs were not systematic. At times, as in 'The Convergence of the Twain', the Immanent Will is portrayed as a God-like figure, not unlike a Greek god or the vengeful God of the Old Testament. And it is the presence in the poems of such mythic figures that point to the tension in Hardy between the world of faith and the world of reason, between religion and science. Hardy can see no reason for believing in God, yet he is not prepared to reject the possibility of a superior force governing human life. In a diary entry he described himself as 'a harmless agnostic' rather than 'a clamorous atheist'.

Form of the poem

The rhythm of the poem is ponderous and weighty, as ponderous and weighty as the ship and the 'shape of ice' that collided. The rhyming scheme, the use of alliteration, the unusual diction and the shape of the three-line stanza, all create the impression that the poem is deliberately crafted and artificial, so that the form of the poem mirrors the ship about which it is written.

Thinking about the poem

1   Which words and phrases in stanzas 1 to 5 capture the opulence of the ship? How is this opulence shown in an ironic light in these stanzas?

2   What drama is described in stanzas 6 to 10?

3   What is the effect of personifying the 'Spinner of the Years' (line 31)?

4   Hardy uses the convention of referring to a ship as feminine and the first trip as a 'maiden voyage' in the sexual imagery of the poem. In your opinion, is this imagery successful?

5   Show how the poem works by way of a series of contrasts.

6   'The ponderous language and rhythm captures, in an ironic way, the movement of the huge ship towards its tragic end. The change of rhythm, at the end of the poem, communicates the sudden impact.' Do you agree with this reading of the poem?

7   Comment on the view that the poem reads the *Titanic* disaster as the inevitable outcome when human folly pits itself against natural forces.

8   Do you think that the poem is callous or is it an understandable attempt to find some meaning, however unpalatable, in the disaster? Explain your answer.

9   'The poem demonstrates Hardy's attraction to a good story, and his interest in what might be termed cinematic narrative techniques.' Discuss this view of the poem.

10 Here are three readings of the poem. Which one is closest to your understanding?

- The poem is about the tragic sinking of the Titanic and the great loss of life.
- The poem is an attack on human vanity.
- The poem expresses a pessimistic view of human life, governed as it is by forces beyond human control.

Explain your thinking.

11 What does the poem tell us about Hardy's religious beliefs? Refer to the poem in answering.

Personal response

1 Select a piece of music that you think would make a suitable accompaniment to a reading of the poem. Explain your choice.

2 How has this poem affected your view of the Titanic disaster?

Channel Firing

That night your great guns, unawares,
Shook all our coffins as we lay,
And broke the chancel window-squares,
We thought it was the Judgment-day

And sat upright. While drearisome   5
Arose the howl of wakened hounds:
The mouse let fall the altar-crumb,
The worms drew back into the mounds,

The glebe cow drooled. Till God called, 'No;
It's gunnery practice out at sea   10
Just as before you went below;
The world is as it used to be:

'All nations striving strong to make
Red war yet redder. Mad as hatters
They do no more for Christés sake   15
Than you who are helpless in such matters.

'That this is not the judgment-hour
For some of them's a blessed thing,
For if it were they'd have to scour
Hell's floor for so much threatening . . .   20

'Ha, ha. It will be warmer when
I blow the trumpet (if indeed
I ever do; for you are men,
And rest eternal sorely need).'

So down we lay again. 'I wonder,   25
Will the world ever saner be,'
Said one, 'than when He sent us under
In our indifferent century!'

And many a skeleton shook his head.
'Instead of preaching forty year,'   30
My neighbour Parson Thirdly said,
'I wish I had stuck to pipes and beer.'

Again the guns disturbed the hour,
Roaring their readiness to avenge,
As far inland as Stourton Tower,   35
And Camelot, and starlit Stonehenge.

Glossary	
3	*chancel:* part of a church containing the altar, sanctuary and choir
9	*glebe:* land, often belonging to a church parish
15	*Christés:* Christ's
22	*blow the trumpet:* signal of the Last Judgement
35	*Stourton Tower:* site of a monument dedicated to Alfred the Great and his victory over the invading Danes
36	*Camelot:* the legendary court of King Arthur, who led the Britons against the invading Saxons, the race of Alfred the Great
36	*Stonehenge:* a stone circle that was the centre of an ancient civilisation that pre-dated the coming of the Celts and the Romans

Guidelines

The poem was written three months before the outbreak of the First World War. The firing described in the poem was gunnery practice on battleships in the English Channel, near Portland Harbour. In a letter to a friend, Hardy's second wife said that 'The buried people at Stinsford [where Hardy's ancestors were buried] hear the guns being fired at Portland.' The poem appeared in Hardy's 1914 collection, *Satires of Circumstance*.

Commentary

Stanzas 1 and 2

The poem begins dramatically with the dead addressing the gunners on the battleships. The situation is humorous and the tone of complaint adds to it. The language is the language of the country, plain and unadorned. So great was the din, the dead tell us, that they believed that it marked Judgement Day and they sat up, awaiting God's judgement. They go on to relate that they were not the only ones to be disturbed. The noise upset the animals: hounds howled, the church mouse was so frightened it let fall the crumb from its mouth, the worms retreated and the parson's cow 'drooled' (line 9). All these images suggest a tall tale, where exaggeration is part and parcel of the enjoyment. In keeping with the tradition of the tall tale, the usual divisions cease to be, so that the dead speak to the living, animals speak to humans and God speaks to all.

Stanzas 3–5

In stanza 3 we are told of God's intervention. He soothes the dead with an explanation of the noise: 'No; / It's gunnery practice out at sea' (lines 9 and 10). God speaks in the same no-nonsense manner as the dead. This is God as he might have been portrayed in a medieval mystery play, recognisably human and ordinary. God describes the living as 'Mad as hatters' (line 14) and suggests that were it Judgement Day, many of the living would be cast into hell 'for so much threatening' (line 20). The tone and tenor of God's language is amusing (the verb 'scour' in line 19 is particularly so), but amid the amusement there is the serious observation that the world has not grown wiser since the dead departed it and nations still 'strong to make / Red war yet redder' (lines 13 and 14).

Stanzas 6 and 7

The rough humour continues when God jokes that it will be considerably warmer when he calls Judgement, but adds, more gently, that he might let the dead rest eternally. In the seventh stanza the dead wonder if the world will ever be a saner place. Little hope is held out for such a prospect as 'many a skeleton shook his head' (line 29). Even the parson, Parson Thirdly, despairs of humankind, suggesting that his forty years of preaching and encouraging people to lead better lives might just as well have been spent on 'pipes and beer' (line 32). This comment catches what many consider to be Hardy's pessimistic view of humanity.

Stanza 8

There is a change of tone in the final stanza, as the humour of the poem disappears and the noise of the guns is interpreted as 'their readiness to avenge' (line 34). Their noise reaches inland as far as Stourton Tower, Camelot and Stonehenge. The place names represent three civilisations, each one overthrown violently by the succeeding one. Their inclusion in the final line of the poem points to the unending cycle of war that has marked the history of humanity and indicates a collective failure to learn anything from history. The meaning of the gunnery practice is established by relating it to the collapse of ancient civilisations.

Although humorous and sarcastic, the poem touches on serious issues: the prevalence of war; the futility of faith; the powerlessness of God; the absence of hope. Given that Britain was preparing for war, the poem might be considered a brave one, as it refuses to make war in any way glorious or noble.

Form of the poem

The poem is written in a traditional ballad form, in rhyming four-line stanzas. It has something of the quality of a tall tale told in a pub using everyday language.

Thinking about the poem

1   Describe the setting and the situation in 'Channel Firing'.

2   How do the dead view the living in the poem?

3   How is God portrayed in the poem? Is the portrayal blasphemous? Consider:
    - God's attitude to the living and the pursuit of war.
    - What God intends to do to the gunners on Judgement Day.
    - God's attitude to the dead.

4   What is the point of Parson Thirdly's regret that he had not stuck to 'pipes and beer' (line 32)?

5   What is the significance of the place names in the final stanza, in the context of history and war?

6   'Although the tone of the poem is humorous and it has the quality of a tall tale, it is not a frivolous poem and reveals the poet's genuine fears.' Do you agree with this reading of the poem? Give reasons for your answer.

7   What does this poem reveal about Hardy's attitude to war?
8   One critic suggests that the poem deals with (a) the futility of war, (b) the futility of faith, (c) the foolishness of God, and (d) the shapelessness of the future. Comment on each of these claims, supporting your remarks with relevant quotations.

Personal response

1   Do you like poems that use humour to make a serious point, as this one does? Give a reason for your answer.

2   Your class is preparing an anthology of poems about war. Discuss, in pairs or small groups, why you would (or would not) choose to include this poem.

When I Set Out for Lyonnesse

When I set out for Lyonnesse,
   A hundred miles away,
   The rime was on the spray,
And starlight lit my lonesomeness
When I set out for Lyonnesse   5
   A hundred miles away.

What would bechance at Lyonnesse
   While I should sojourn there
   No prophet durst declare,
Nor did the wisest wizard guess   10
What would bechance at Lyonnesse
   While I should sojourn there.

When I came back from Lyonnesse
   With magic in my eyes,
   All marked with mute surmise   15
My radiance rare and fathomless,
When I came back from Lyonnesse
   With magic in my eyes!

Glossary

title	*Lyonnesse:* the name given to the area of north Cornwall in Arthurian legend
3	*rime:* the white frost that forms on plants, as dew freezes
3	*spray:* the shoot of a plant that spreads out into branches or flowers
7	*bechance:* happen
8	*sojourn:* visit, stay temporarily
9	*durst:* dared to
15	*mute surmise:* silent guessing
16	*fathomless:* beyond measure and understanding

Guidelines

On 7 March 1870 Hardy travelled from Dorset to St Juliot in Cornwall to make recommendations for the repair and improvement of the local church. There, he met Emma Gifford, whose sister was married to the local rector. During the three days of his visit, Emma and Hardy spent much time in each other's company, and fell in love. When he returned to his family home in Dorset, his mother noticed that something had happened to him. St Juliot was a romantic place. Nearby was King Arthur's ruined castle.

In 1913, a few months after Emma's death, Hardy revisited the scenes of their courtship in Cornwall. He wrote this poem in 1914, forty-four years after the events described in it. He considered it one of his sweetest lyrics. Hardy said of himself, 'I have a faculty . . . for burying an emotion in heart or brain for forty years, and exhuming it at the end of that time as fresh as when interred.' This faculty is in evidence in the poems that recall his courtship of Emma Gifford.

Despite the promise and magic of their first years together, their marriage became increasingly unhappy. After Emma died, Hardy found among her papers two personal manuscripts. One of them contained bitter denunciations of his behaviour towards her. The other contained recollections of her youth up to the time they met and became engaged. This second manuscript revived memories that had lain buried for more than forty years and which surfaced with extraordinary clarity. Hardy described the poems he wrote after her death as an atonement for his neglect. Certainly, his love poems to Emma are characterised by both love and remorse.

'When I Set Out for Lyonnesse' is one of the most lyrical of all Hardy's poems. It is marked by a sweetness and lightness of tone. It recalls less the beloved than the journey into love and the effect of love upon the younger self.

Stanza 1

The poet refers to the 'lonesomeness' (line 4) of his younger self, setting out on the journey. The place is distant, a 'hundred miles away' (line 2), so distant that he was forced to rise early and leave before sunrise in the frost and cold. Taken out of context these details suggest a journey made in reluctance and with no sense of anticipation. Yet, the soft sounds of the sibilant 's', the verbal echoes and repetition, and the invocation of 'Lyonnesse', the mythical kingdom associated with King Arthur, give an impression of dreamy romanticism as much as cold isolation.

The key to the poem, perhaps, lies in the realisation that it was written after the completion of the journey and the sudden discovery of overwhelming love, so that the lonesomeness of the poet is viewed from the perspective of discovered love. The remarkable, even ironic, feature of the poem is that the events described are viewed from a distance of forty-four years after their occurrence.

Stanza 2

The second stanza plays on the concepts of expectation and discovery, and suggests the extraordinary nature of the transformation brought about by his stay in 'Lyonnesse'. Neither 'the wisest wizard' (line 10) nor a 'prophet' (line 9) could have foreseen 'What would bechance at Lyonnesse / While I should sojourn there' (lines 7 and 8). The exact nature of the event is left unstated. It is as if Hardy is saying that we do not need the details to understand what happened. Love's mysteries need no explanation.

Stanza 3

The transformation wrought by love is captured in the third stanza. The 'magic' (line 14) in his eyes and the 'radiance' (line 16) of love is noticed by all those around him who 'surmise' (line 15) the reason for the change. His radiance is described as 'rare and fathomless' (line 16). The words 'magic', 'radiance', 'fathomless' and 'Lyonnesse' establish love as something mysterious and magical that befalls people and alters them in perceptible ways.

A beautiful illusion?

Thomas Hardy and Emma Gifford met under romantic circumstances in a place that was itself romantic. Everything about the meeting was magical. It is possible that the very magic of their new-found love blinded them to the reality of each other. Perhaps, more than any of the poems he wrote, 'When I Set Out for Lyonnesse' reveals that

Thomas Hardy

their love was a beautiful illusion. What is remarkable is that, after more than forty years, Hardy was able to capture so vividly the feeling of magic that accompanied his first journey to St Juliot in 1870.

Form of the poem

Hardy structures the poem through repetition, giving it an incantatory quality in keeping with the theme of magical transformation. Each stanza deals with one part of the journey: the departure, the visit, the return. Each stanza has the structure of a rondeau, where the last two lines repeat the first two. Although the poet refers to his lonesomeness in stanza 1, the poem is written after the event, so that the magical transformation he experienced during his time in St Juliot colours everything.

Thinking about the poem

1   How does the poet describe himself as he set out on his journey? What words or phrases are particularly striking?

2   What change has taken place in the poet, on his return, as described in the third stanza?

3   What is the purpose of stanza 2? How does it contribute to the story of the poem?

4   Does Hardy, in your view, succeed in creating a sense of magic in the poem? Explain your answer.

5   Working in pairs, examine one stanza carefully and describe how Hardy creates the music of the stanza.

6   Describe the stanza form and the structure of the poem.

7   Does the stanza form, rhyme and rhythm suit the theme and mood of the poem? Explain your thinking.

8   'This is an unusually tender and optimistic poem for Hardy.' Based on the Hardy poems you have read so far, do you agree with this view of the poem?

9   Here are three views of the poem. Which one is closest to your own understanding?

    ●   The poem establishes Lyonnesse or Cornwall as a place of romance.

    ●   The poem describes the magical effect of love.

    ●   The poem tries to change a real journey into a medieval quest.

    Explain your thinking.

10   The poem was written over forty years after the event it celebrates. Which of the following, in your view, motivated Hardy to write it: deep love, regret or guilt? Explain your thinking as clearly as you can.

Personal response

1   If you were asked to make a short film to accompany a reading of this poem, what music, sound effects, colour, images and other background material would you use to create an appropriate atmosphere for the reading? Comment on your choices.

2   Did you enjoy reading this poem? Give a reason for your opinion.

Before you read 'Under the Waterfall'

Before you read 'Under the Waterfall', consider the following questions. What is it about waterfalls that attracts us? In pairs, discuss the attraction of waterfalls and what, in your view, they can be used to symbolise.

Under the Waterfall

'Whenever I plunge my arm, like this,
In a basin of water, I never miss
The sweet sharp sense of a fugitive day
Fetched back from the thickening shroud of gray.
    Hence the only prime   5
    And real love-rhyme
    That I know by heart,
    And that leaves no smart,
Is the purl of a little valley fall
About three spans wide and two spans tall   10
Over a table of solid rock,
And into a scoop of the self-same block;
The purl of a runlet that never ceases
In stir of kingdoms, in wars, in peaces;
With a hollow, boiling voice it speaks   15
And has spoken since hills were turfless peaks.'
'And why gives this the only prime
Idea to you of a real love-rhyme?
And why does plunging your arm in a bowl
Full of spring water, bring throbs to your soul?'   20

'Well, under the fall, in a crease of the stone,
Though where precisely none ever has known,
Jammed darkly, nothing to show how prized,
And by now with its smoothness opalized,

    Is a drinking-glass: 25
    For, down that pass
    My lover and I
    Walked under a sky

Of blue with a leaf-wove awning of green,
In the burn of August, to paint the scene,   30
And we placed our basket of fruit and wine
By the runlet's rim, where we sat to dine;
And when we had drunk from the glass together,
Arched by the oak-copse from the weather,
I held the vessel to rinse in the fall,   35
Where it slipped, and sank, and was past recall,
Though we stooped and plumbed the little abyss
With long bared arms. There the glass still is.
And, as said, if I thrust my arm below
Cold water in basin or bowl, a throe   40
From the past awakens a sense of that time,
And the glass we used, and the cascade's rhyme.
The basin seems the pool, and its edge
The hard smooth face of the brook-side ledge,
And the leafy pattern of china-ware   45
The hanging plants that were bathing there.

'By night, by day, when it shines or lours,
There lies intact that chalice of ours,
And its presence adds to the rhyme of love
Persistently sung by the fall above.   50
No lip has touched it since his and mine
In turns therefrom sipped lovers' wine.'

Glossary

9	*purl:* flow with a rippling movement and a murmuring sound
10	*spans:* a span is the width of an extended hand, usually taken as nine inches
13	*runlet:* a little stream
24	*opalized:* made to shine like a jewel by the action of the water
37	*abyss:* very deep gorge; here, the seemingly bottomless water
40	*throe:* sudden pang or pain; shock of feeling or pleasure
47	*lours:* darkens; when the weather turns dark or threatening
48	*chalice:* drinking vessel

Guidelines

'Under the Waterfall' was first published in Hardy's 1914 collection, *Satires of Circumstance*; his first book of poetry after the death of his first wife, Emma, in 1912. The incident, described in the poem, dates from the period of their courtship. After her death, Hardy found two personal manuscripts, among his wife's papers. In one, he read the following:

> Often we walked to Boscastle Harbour down the beautiful Valency Valley where we had to jump over stones and climb over a low wall by rough steps, or get through a narrow pathway, to come on great wide spaces suddenly, with a sparkling little brook going the same way, in which we once lost a tiny picnic-tumbler, and there it is to this day no doubt between two of the boulders.

Hardy drew a sketch of Emma reaching for the glass, dated 1870. As it was Emma who recorded the incident in her manuscript, *Some Recollections*, Hardy makes her the speaker who recalls the scene whenever she plunges her arm into a basin of water.

Commentary

At one level this is a narrative poem telling the story of a wine glass lost by the lovers on a picnic, told in the voice of the woman. At another level, the poem celebrates the power of memory to recover moments of emotional intensity and save them from forgetfulness. This theme is expressed clearly and memorably in the opening lines of the poem, which are, arguably, among the finest ever written by Hardy.

Lines 1–4

The opening lines describe a common occurrence – the way in which a physical action or sensation can trigger a memory. In this case, the act of plunging her arms into a basin of water restores the 'sweet sharp sense' (line 3) of a day that is otherwise slipping from consciousness, or shrouded in the grey of forgetfulness. The words 'fugitive' (line 3) and 'shroud' (line 4) raise a common theme in Hardy's work: the transient nature of human experience in time.

These lines are admired for the naturalness of the voice; for the interplay of sound and sense; and for the beauty of the phrasing as in 'sweet sharp sense' (line 3). In this phrase, the slight intake of breath that accompanies a shock is reproduced in the sounds of the poem.

Lines 5–20

In the remainder of the opening stanza the narrator makes a connection between the plunging of her arms into a basin and the sound of a stream going over a small waterfall and flowing away. She says that the sound of the stream is the 'the only prime / And real love-rhyme / That I know by heart, / And that leaves no smart' (lines 5–8). For the lover, this love-rhyme, sung by the stream, is constant and unceasing and speaks through wars and peace. Why the lover makes this association is not clear, so Hardy introduces a second speaker who addresses the lover and asks her what the reader wants to know (lines 17–20).

Stanza 2

The lover then describes the idyllic scene of the picnic – the basket of fruit and wine; the wine drunk from the same glass; the blue of the August sky; the canopy of trees and the stream and waterfall where they dined. As the poem gathers narrative momentum, the lover sketches the scene as the glass slipped and they 'plumbed the little abyss / With long bared arms' (lines 37 and 38) to no avail. It is for this reason, she explains, that plunging her arm in a basin recalls the past to her.

Stanza 3

In the final stanza the sacramental associations of the words 'wine' and 'chalice' reveal the true significance of the events of that day to the woman. The glass, the chalice, lying there untouched since her lips and those of her lover drank from it, remains as an enduring symbol of their love. Its presence gives a personal meaning to the love-rhyme of the flowing stream.

Ambiguity

There is an interesting ambiguity in the lover's words in lines 5 to 8. The word 'prime' (line 5) suggests both the first and the most valuable. Is she suggesting that this love rhyme, the first, is the only one associated with pure happiness? Is she suggesting that this first love-rhyme is the only one she can recall without hurt or 'smart' (line 8)? Does the 'thickening shroud of gray' (line 4) suggest that the intervening years have not fulfilled the promise of that day? Or are these only shadows that do not obscure the poem's celebration of first love, or diminish its testimony to the power of that love to endure?

In this context, the glass itself is worth considering. It is, after all, lost in a 'little abyss' (line 37) and is 'past recall' (line 36). Taken on their own, these images suggest the idea of love lost as much as immortalised. However, the lost glass is transformed into a chalice and comes to symbolise the moment of love that will never be lost.

Narrative voice

'Under the Waterfall' is one of the few poems about his relationship with his first wife that is not written from Hardy's point of view. And, despite the ambiguities of the poem, it is not marked by the same degree of loss, regret and waste that characterise the love poems written after Emma's death. It is worth reading the poem aloud a number of times before deciding if you think Hardy has caught the flow of the woman's voice. You might also consider if all the rhymes and choice of words are successful. Some critics read it as wholly successful; others see some clumsiness in the rhymes and phrasing. In the same way there is some disagreement on the need for the second speaker. What is commonly agreed is that 'Under the Waterfall' succeeds in creating images of romance and happiness that combine physical sensation with a spiritual sensibility.

Thinking about the poem

1   What is the story that the poem tells?
2   Consider carefully the nature and significance of remembering, as described in the first four lines of the poem. Pay attention to key words and their connotations.
3   'The first four lines of the poem are among the finest Hardy ever wrote.' Give your response to this opinion.
4   Comment on the imagery in lines 13 and 14, and the theme suggested by them.
5   What idyllic images of love are created by the woman speaker in the third stanza, between lines 21 and 38?
6   How does the woman regard the glass in the final stanza? Comment on the use of the words 'chalice' and 'wine' and their significance.
7   What might the glass symbolise in Hardy's life?
8   Does Hardy capture the flow of the woman's voice in the poem? Explain your answer.
9   In your view, is the second voice (lines 17–20) necessary to the poem? Give reasons for your answer.

Thomas Hardy

10   In terms of style, music and rhyme, is the poem successful in your view? (One critic refers to 'one ridiculous rhyme' in the poem.)

11   'In 'Under the Waterfall' we see both Hardy's gift for making a phrase as well as his clumsiness in doing so.' Comment on this assessment of the poem.

12   Do you agree that the poem succeeds in creating images of romance and happiness? Give reasons for your answer.

Personal response

1   Emma Gifford, Hardy's first wife, kept a diary. Writing in her voice, make an entry describing the day of the picnic at the waterfall. The entry should describe the loss of the glass, as well as giving Emma's thoughts about it.

2   You have been asked to find a poem to read at a school event. Would you choose this one? Explain your answer.

Before you read 'During Wind and Rain'

Before you read 'During Wind and Rain', consider these questions. Have you seen old photographs of now dead grandparents or great-grandparents? Are there family photographs of houses where they once lived? What mood do these photographs create? How do you feel when you view them?

Share your thoughts with a partner before reading Hardy's poem, in which each stanza is like an old family photograph.

During Wind and Rain

They sing their dearest songs —
He, she, all of them — yea,
Treble and tenor and bass,
   And one to play;
With the candles mooning each face. . . .   5
   Ah, no; the years O!
How the sick leaves reel down in throngs!

They clear the creeping moss —
Elders and juniors — aye,
Making the pathways neat   10

And the garden gay;
And they build a shady seat. . . .
      Ah, no; the years, the years;
See, the white storm-birds wing across.

They are blithely breakfasting all —   15
Men and maidens — yea,
Under the summer tree,
      With a glimpse of the bay,
While pet fowl come to the knee. . . .
      Ah, no; the years O!   20
And the rotten rose is ript from the wall.

They change to a high new house,
He, she, all of them — aye,
Clocks and carpets and chairs
      On the lawn all day,   25
And brightest things that are theirs. . . .
      Ah, no; the years, the years;
Down their carved names the rain-drop ploughs.

Glossary		
1	*They:* the family of Hardy's first wife, Emma
1	*sing . . . songs:* Emma's father played the violin and her mother played the piano and sang
3	*Treble . . . bass:* their different singing voices: treble is a high female voice, tenor a high adult male voice and bass a low male voice
7	*reel down:* stagger, whirl about
7	*throngs:* crowds, swarms
15	*blithely:* casually, in a carefree manner
28	*carved names:* the names carved on the tombstones

Guidelines

'During Wind and Rain' had its origins in scenes described in *Some Recollections*, the personal manuscript of Hardy's first wife, Emma, which he found after her death in November 1912. It is likely that the poem was written in early 1913. It is not difficult to imagine how the themes of change, and of the loss of happiness and hope, came to the poet, who, in his mid-seventies, read the vivid accounts of the girlhood of his dead wife.

After Emma's death, Hardy visited Cornwall, where the couple first met. He also went to Plymouth and visited the graves of her family. The poem appeared in Hardy's 1917 collection, *Moments of Vision*. The publication of the collection, which featured so many poems about his dead wife, caused his second wife, Florence, to feel lonely, jealous and resentful.

Commentary

Each stanza presents a double perspective – the scenes of happiness, taken from Emma's account of her childhood and early adulthood in Plymouth, and Hardy's mournful cry at the wreckage brought by the years.

Stanza 1
The image of family life in the first stanza is one of togetherness and happiness. The family are gathered around the piano singing. There are men and women, whose voices intermingle and complement each other. The songs they sing have meaning and significance for they are 'their dearest songs' (line 1). The scene is deftly sketched in four lines. The present tense adds to the immediacy of the scene. Then in the fifth line there is a hint of a change – the candlelight illuminates their faces but casts everything else in shadow. In the sixth line, the speaker of the poem cries out in protest at the years and the effect of time. The 'O' of the line is a cry of suffering. The seventh line gives an image of the decay brought by time: 'How the sick leaves reel down in throngs!'

The double perspective of past and present (summer and winter; optimism and regret) established in stanza 1 is maintained throughout the poem. It is interesting to note Hardy's use of the pronouns, 'he', 'she' and 'they' and the nouns 'treble', 'tenor' and 'bass' (lines 1–3) to refer to the family members. Hardy maintains this impersonal mode of representation throughout the poem. Yet, somehow, this does not lessen the impact of the poem. It is as if every reader can supply the faces from his or her own family.

In the second stanza the scene is of the family, young and old, working in the garden of the family home. There is a sense of the family looking forward to the future, preparing the garden for summer days to come: 'and they build a shady seat' (line 12). As in the first stanza the fifth line speaks of shadows in the adjective 'shady'. Thirty years before he wrote this poem, Hardy noted that he lived in a world 'where nothing bears out in practice what it promises incipiently'. In the sixth line the speaker again cries out in protest at the passing of time, which casts a shadow over all human activity. The second stanza repeats the pattern of the first by ending with an image of storm and change: 'See, the white storm-birds wing across.' The storm-birds presage a change in the seasons from the sunshine of summer to the uncertainty of winter.

By framing the scene of the family working in the garden with an image of decay and a cry of protest against the passing of time, the poet invites us to view with sympathy and sadness their human endeavour and their human hopes, frail as these seem against the relentless march of time.

Stanza 3

The third stanza presents an idyllic picture of an open-air breakfast in the garden 'Under the summer tree' (line 17). The garden has a view of the sea. The imagery suggests happiness and prosperity. The garden is a familial version of paradise, with the pet birds suggesting luxury and ease. However, like the other scenes of family life, this one is counterbalanced by an image of violent decay: 'And the rotten rose is ript from the wall' (line 21). The alliteration and the echoing 't' sound emphasise the force of the action conveyed in the striking verb 'ript'. The word 'rose' works by way of its association with love. Time, the line says, destroys love.

Stanza 4

The final stanza captures the family in the business of moving house. As the poem progresses the scenes from family life have a narrative quality that trace a story of increasing happiness and prosperity, the latter suggested here in the list of possessions: 'clocks and carpets and chairs' (line 24). The family members have reached some high point of happiness and the 'brightest things' are theirs. The phrase 'brightest things' (line 26) may refer to health, happiness, friendship and love, as much as to material possessions. Yet, as the double perspective of the poem reminds us, we cannot hold happiness for long. The cry of protest, in the final stanza, seems more anguished than the others, 'Ah, no; the years, the years' (line 27).

The final image of decay is a devastating one. Not only does it juxtapose death with life, it suggests that even the names of the dead can be worn away by time and the elements: 'Down their carved names the rain-drop ploughs' (line 28). Memory

Thomas Hardy

and our efforts to commemorate it are subject to the erosion of time. As Shakespeare highlighted in his sonnets, poetry celebrating a person can offer some defence against the working of time. Despite this, however, the dominant feelings of this poem are those of loss.

Form of the poem

Hardy liked to experiment with different stanza forms and rhyme schemes. The rhyme in this poem is complicated: *abcbca*. However, between lines 5 and 6, Hardy inserts a refrain. In stanzas 1 and 3 the refrain is 'Ah, no; the years O!' In stanzas 2 and 4 it changes to 'Ah, no; the years, the years'. The refrain helps create the double perspective in the poem. Note, too, the long line that concludes each stanza. These lines are dominated by long vowels and images of destruction and decay. They contrast with the short lines and joyful rhythm of the first five lines of each stanza.

Thinking about the poem

1   Tell the story of the family, as described in the first five lines of each stanza.
2   'He, she, all of them—yea, / Treble and tenor and bass' (lines 2 and 3). What is the effect of describing the family members in this way and of not using personal names?
3   'The four pictures of family life paint a picture of love, happiness and hope.' Give your opinion of this view of the poem.
4   Look at the last line of each stanza. Based on these lines, what, in your opinion, is the theme of the poem?
5   'Each of the scenes of happiness is viewed through the regret that time and change have brought.' Discuss this view of the poem.
6   In your view, which of the following is the moral of the poem?
    ● Enjoy life while you may.
    ● Time ruins everything.
    ● All good things come to an end.
    ● It is hard to be the one who survives.
    Explain your choice.
7   Choose one stanza. Read the first five lines aloud and write a note on their rhythm, mood and language. Now read the last two lines aloud and write a note on their rhythm, mood and language. Note the differences.
8   What impression of Hardy do you get from reading the poem?

9 Compare the three poems, 'Under the Waterfall', 'When I Set Out for Lyonnesse' and 'During Wind and Rain', that Hardy wrote shortly after Emma's death. What do they reveal to the reader about the couple?

10 Write a short essay explaining why, in your opinion, this poem is admired by many readers.

Personal response

1 Florence, Hardy's second wife, was upset when her husband wrote poems about his dead wife. Write a diary entry in which Florence records her reaction to reading 'During Wind and Rain'.

2 Imagine you were asked to select a piece of music to accompany a public reading of this poem. Describe clearly the music you would choose and your reasons for choosing it.

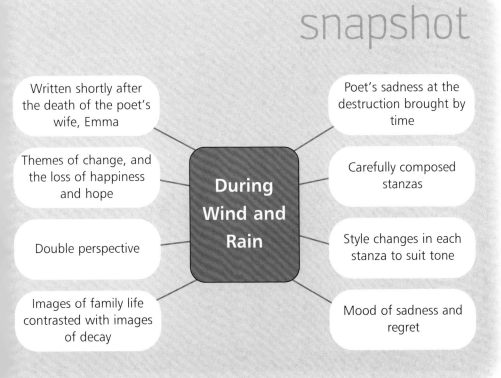

snapshot

Written shortly after the death of the poet's wife, Emma

Themes of change, and the loss of happiness and hope

Double perspective

Images of family life contrasted with images of decay

During Wind and Rain

Poet's sadness at the destruction brought by time

Carefully composed stanzas

Style changes in each stanza to suit tone

Mood of sadness and regret

Before reading 'The Oxen' by Thomas Hardy, join up into small groups and share your favourite part of the Christmas story. You might also compare your response to the Christmas story as a young adult to that of your childhood self.

The Oxen

Christmas Eve, and twelve of the clock.
  'Now they are all on their knees,'
An elder said as we sat in a flock
  By the embers in hearthside ease.

We pictured the meek mild creatures where   5
  They dwelt in their strawy pen,
Nor did it occur to one of us there
  To doubt they were kneeling then.

So fair a fancy few would weave
  In these years! Yet, I feel,   10
If someone said on Christmas Eve,
  'Come; see the oxen kneel

'In the lonely barton by yonder coomb
  Our childhood used to know,'
I should go with him in the gloom,   15
  Hoping it might be so.

1915

Glossary	
3	*elder:* older member of the community (a term of respect)
13	*barton:* farmyard
13	*coomb:* short valley

Guidelines

This poem was first published in *The Times* on 24 December 1915, during the First World War. The miraculous is associated with Christmas in all of Hardy's writing. It was from his mother that Hardy heard the legend of the oxen kneeling in their stable at midnight on Christmas Eve. At a time of war, Hardy wishes that the old comforts of his childhood beliefs were still available to him.

Commentary

The poem expresses the conflict between Hardy's intellectual beliefs and his emotions. Hardy does not believe in the Christmas story. Intellectually, he has left Christianity behind. Emotionally, however, he wishes that the magical Christmas story of his childhood were true.

Stanza 1

The poem is written in a simple stanza form. As often in Hardy's poetry, the past and the present are contrasted. It begins with a memory of the past. The community is gathered together on Christmas Eve 'in hearthside ease' (line 4) when an elder remarks that 'Now they are all on their knees' (line 2). There is no need for elaboration for all understand the reference to the oxen and to the Christmas legend that at midnight on Christmas Eve the oxen kneel.

The gathering is described as a 'flock' (line 3) suggesting a close-knit rural community, sharing the same beliefs, but also, perhaps, an unquestioning attitude to those beliefs. As an adult, Hardy broke free from the flock and its beliefs, but at Christmas and in a time of war, he looks back with nostalgia to simpler times. The 'embers' of line 4 refer both to the warmth of the fire and to its dying, reflecting Hardy's own warm response to a belief that he no longer carried.

Stanza 2

The words of the elder conjure a picture of 'the meek mild creatures' (line 5) for those seated together. The phrase is perfect, portraying both the language of child-like belief and the humility at the heart of the story. Among this community, no one doubted the truth of the oxen kneeling at midnight in honour of Christ's birth.

Stanza 3

In the third stanza the contrast between the innocent past and the war-torn present is caught in the phrase 'In these years' (line 10). The verb 'weave' (line 9) is interesting, suggesting, perhaps, that the old belief was originally woven and is now unravelling.

Then Hardy adds an afterthought, 'Yet, I feel' (line 10). He imagines someone inviting him to go to the farmyard in the valley of his childhood to see if the oxen are kneeling.

The dialect words 'barton' and 'coomb' (line 13) suggest the tight-knit community of his childhood. Although Hardy no longer believes, he says he would go hoping that the legend might be true. Hardy awaits an invitation that he knows will never come so his hope can continue a little longer.

Narrative voice

By any standards, this is a beautifully judged poem. Hardy speaks in a very personal voice. There is no distance between the 'I' of the poem and Hardy himself. Like other poets such as Patrick Kavanagh, Hardy longs for the comfort of those childhood beliefs that his intellect now rejects. The poem is marked by an understated sense of personal loss and alienation. Hardy accepted the theories of the nineteenth century on the origins of the world while retaining a fondness for the religion of his childhood.

Form and language of the poem

Hardy's training as an architect is sometimes evident in the elaborate stanza forms of his poetry, but in 'The Oxen' he follows the common metre found in ballads and hymns. These consist of a four-line stanza, rhyming *abab*. The form is suited to the thought and feeling of the poem. The inclusions of dialect words adds a rural flavour.

Thinking about the poem

1   'as we sat in a flock' (line 3). In your view, what is the significance of the word 'flock', in this context?

2   Why does the phrase 'meek mild creatures' (line 5) work so well in the poem? Which other words or phrases are suited to the theme?

3   What is the implied contrast between past and present in the phrase 'In these years' (line 10)?

4   'Hoping it might be so' (line 16). What does the final line of the poem tell us about the narrator's attitude to the legend of the oxen?

5   The poem is written using a simple ballad stanza and rhyme. Is this form suited to the theme of the poem? Explain your answer.

6   'The poem is marked by an appreciation of and a nostalgia for the Christian belief that it ultimately rejects.' Do you agree with this reading of the poem? Explain your answer.

7   The poem was written during the First World War. How does this context help us to understand the poem and the attitudes it expresses?

8   Here are three readings of the poem. Which one is closest to your own?

The poem expresses nostalgia for the religious beliefs of the poet's childhood.

The poem celebrates the life of a vanishing rural community.

In a time of war, the poem expresses a wish for a return to a simpler life.

Give reasons for your choice.

Personal response

1   Select a piece of music that you think would make a good accompaniment to 'The Oxen' and explain your choice.
2   Write a short letter to Thomas Hardy telling him about your thoughts and feelings on this poem. Refer to the text of the poem in your letter.

Before you read 'Afterwards'

Having read a number of Hardy's poems, how, in your opinion, would he like to be remembered? What appear to be his best qualities?

Share your thoughts with a partner, before hearing the views of the rest of the class.

Afterwards

When the Present has latched its postern behind my tremulous stay,
   And the May month flaps its glad green leaves like wings,
Delicate-filmed as new-spun silk, will the neighbours say,
   'He was a man who used to notice such things'?

If it be in the dusk when, like an eyelid's soundless blink,   5
   The dewfall-hawk comes crossing the shades to alight
Upon the wind-warped upland thorn, a gazer may think,
   'To him this must have been a familiar sight.'

If I pass during some nocturnal blackness, mothy and warm,
  When the hedgehog travels furtively over the lawn,   10
One may say, 'He strove that such innocent creatures
  should come to no harm,
  But he could do little for them; and now he is gone.'

If, when hearing that I have been stilled at last, they stand at the door,
  Watching the full-starred heavens that winter sees
Will this thought rise on those who will meet my face no more,   15
  'He was one who had an eye for such mysteries'?

And will any say when my bell of quittance is heard in the gloom,
  And a crossing breeze cuts a pause in its outrollings,
Till they rise again, as they were a new bell's boom,
  'He hears it not now, but used to notice such things'?   20

Glossary

1	*postern:*	back door or gate, small private door
1	*tremulous:*	trembling, sensitive
10	*furtively:*	in a sly or secretive way
17	*bell of quittance:*	funeral bell

Guidelines

This poem was written in 1917 and was the concluding poem in Hardy's collection, *Moments of Vision*. Hardy was seventy-seven years of age and living through the First World War. Conscious that he might not publish another collection, 'Afterwards' describes how he would like to be remembered. There is no mention of literary fame, and none of the pessimism that is evident in other of his poems. Instead, he hopes to be remembered as a countryman, who noticed the changes in nature and felt compassion for 'innocent creatures' (line 11). (As it turned out, Hardy went on to publish two more collections before he died.)

Looking ahead to his own death, Hardy hopes that he will be remembered for his sensitive observation of nature and his kindness to all living things. The poem has a tentative, questioning quality, reflected in the repeated use of words such as 'If', and 'may'. Hardy makes no claims for himself or his place in literary history. His modest hope is that he will be remembered by his neighbours as they notice the changes in nature, like the trees coming into bloom, or the winter skies, or the movements of birds and animals. Although a celebrated man of letters, Hardy is more interested in the regard of his neighbours than in the judgement of the reading public. Like a shepherd or a ploughman, he hopes to be remembered as someone with an eye for nature.

Stanza 1

Because the poem is a thoughtful meditation, even an elegy, spoken by an old man, it moves slowly. From the opening line, it is clear that the concentration of consonants and the high number of stressed vowels make those lines hard to recite. This is particularly true of the second line: 'And the May month flaps its glad green leaves like wings'. Here the language is as sticky and clogged as the leaves it describes. And the first line captures the slow speech of the old man: 'When the Present has latched its postern behind my tremulous stay'. The word 'postern' suggests a small gate or exit used for unimportant guests, while the adjective 'tremulous' suggests the frailty and insecurity of an individual life, especially in a time of war. The poem is not marked by a fear in the face of the death. On the contrary, it is a remarkably composed and detached meditation, slow and deliberate in its progress and its effects.

The first three lines and their somewhat laboured movement are in sharp contrast to the simplicity of line 4: 'He was a man who used to notice such things'. How successful is this change of style within the stanza, a change that is repeated in the other four stanzas of the poem? Critics are divided. As David Wright states, 'It is . . . difficult to make up one's mind how good, and/or how bad, almost any particular poem of Hardy's is.'

What is clear is that the halting slowness of the opening lines catches the voice of the old man, facing up to death, and this voice contrasts with the simpler but more vigorous voice of the neighbours. What is also clear is Hardy's realisation that, after his death, nature will continue to renew itself. The new leaves will appear in May, marking a new cycle of regeneration. This is a familiar theme in Hardy. The individual human life is mortal, just as the hawk and hedgehog mentioned in the poem are mortal, but nature and time continue. It is no coincidence that the word 'when' is repeated in the poem.

Thomas Hardy

Stanza 2

In the second stanza the scene is set at dusk 'Upon the wind-warped upland thorn' (line 7). The setting and the image of the gliding hawk suggest a bleaker season than the May of the first stanza. The comparison of the hawk's flight to 'an eyelid's soundless blink' (line 5) is often cited as an example of Hardy's real eye for nature. (The description might also refer to the moment when he himself passes from life to death.) However, there is a sense of nature viewed from a distance, in a passive way. And that sense of distance and passivity suggests that the speaker is growing away from the world. He is an observer rather than a participant in life, though there is no hint of self-pity.

In a celebrated passage in his biography, which he co-wrote with his second wife, Hardy describes an attitude to life which is evident in this poem:

> To think of life as passing away is sadness; to think of it as past is at least tolerable. Hence, even when I enter a room to pay a simple morning call I have unconsciously the habit of regarding the scene as I were a spectre not solid enough to influence my environment, only fit to behold.

The habit of assuming the identity of a spectre (ghost) is evident in the manner in which the poem highlights the things observed rather than the observer. Even the hope of remembrance is linked to the observed world.

Stanza 3

In the third stanza the 'nocturnal blackness' is not frightening, but 'mothy and warm' (line 9). And the hedgehog is not a garden pest but 'an innocent creature' (line 11) in need of protection. His hope is that his neighbours will remember him as someone who 'strove that such innocent creatures should come to no harm' (line 11). There is a characteristic Hardyesque touch in 'But he could do little for them' (line 12). This line catches Hardy's philosophical outlook that little could be changed in life. The line is striking because of his lifelong campaign against cruelty to animals. It suggests a realisation that his efforts were ineffectual.

Stanza 4

In the fourth stanza the scene is set in winter. Hardy imagines his neighbours 'watching the full-starred heavens that winter sees' (line 14) and remembering him as 'one who had an eye for such mysteries' (line 16). Hardy makes no attempt to describe or interpret the mysteries suggested by the stars. He is content to be remembered as someone who was aware of them. The tone in this stanza is mellow and thoughtful, the sounds of the soft 's', the rich 'r', the whispering 'w' and the long vowels create a sweet, melancholic music.

Stanza 5

In the final stanza Hardy wonders if anyone will speak of him after his death and remember him as someone who used to notice how the breeze interrupts the waves of sound emanating from the church bell. There is a gentle irony in this stanza. Hardy refuses to invest 'the bell of quittance' (line 17) with any religious or divine significance. It is simply a marker of time, a way of signalling his death.

The sounds of the stanza rise to a crescendo in the penultimate line, 'Till they rise again, as they were a new bell's boom' (line 19). There is an onomatopoeic effect in the phrase 'new bell's boom'. It works, like a dramatic drum roll or trumpet flourish, to prepare for the final statement. The comma after 'boom' imitates the breeze interrupting the flow of sound. This pause heightens our expectation of the final line, but when it comes it is almost an anti-climax: 'He hears it not now, but he used to notice such things' (line 20).

Remembrance

As the poem presents it, life after death is dependent upon a neighbour or friend remembering the characteristics of the dead person. Beyond remembrance, there is no after-life. Although a stoical and dignified meditation, the poem makes no great or compelling claims for the meaning or purpose of either life or death. Perhaps, in the end, what the poem most reveals is Hardy's love for his home place and for his own people. It is their estimation of him that matters most. He hopes that they will remember him and approve him as the 'one who had an eye for such mysteries' (line 16).

Thinking about the poem

1 How does Hardy view the hawk, the hedgehog and the darkness in the poem?
2 Do you agree that Hardy's view is the view of a country-dweller rather than a city-dweller? Explain your answer.
3 How does the poem create a sense of the unfolding seasons and the passage of time in its structure? Refer to individual words and phrases in your answer.
4 Here are two opposing views about the sounds of the poem. Which do you most agree with?
   ● The long lines and slow movement of the poem suit the mood and theme.
   ● The poem is too rich and cloying in its sounds.
   Explain your choice.
5 What picture of Hardy emerges from the poem? Do you find his self-portrait an appealing one? Explain your answer.

Thomas Hardy

6   What kind of after-life does the poem suggest or presume? In your opinion, is it a comforting view?

7   What view of death emerges from 'Afterwards' and where is it most evident in the poem?

8   Here are three views of the poem. Which one is closest to your own reading of the poem?
   ● In this poem Hardy identifies the things that matter most to him.
   ● In this poem Hardy identifies his unique qualities.
   ● In this poem Hardy paints a dishonest picture of himself.
   Explain your choice.

9   Working in pairs, examine one stanza of the poem and identify the sound patterns that are evident to you.

Personal response

Write an answering poem to 'Afterwards', addressed to Thomas Hardy and using details from the poem, in which you say how you will think of Hardy and remember his poetry after you complete the Leaving Certificate.

Exam-Style Questions

1   'What makes Hardy great as a poet is his ability to articulate feelings with which everyone can identify, in a style that is easy to understand.' Do you agree with this assessment of Hardy? Support the points you make with reference to the poems on your course.

2   'What is most evident in Hardy's poetry is his tenderness for all living things, expressed in the ordinary language of a country man.' Discuss this statement in relation to the poems on your course.

3   'Hardy's poetry is remarkable for its range of themes and its range of verse forms.' Give your opinion of this statement.

4   'Hardy's poems commemorating his love for Emma Gifford are both personal and universal.' Write a response to the poetry of Thomas Hardy in light of this statement.

5   'There is in Hardy's poems an affection for the old certainties of Christianity without any accompanying intellectual consent.' Give your response to this assessment of Hardy.

6   'Hardy's poetry moves between celebrations of natural phenomena, evocative elegies of the past and philosophical musings on the meaning of life.' Give your response to this view of Hardy's poetry.

7   Do you agree that by using traditional and innovative rhymed forms, Hardy's poetry retains an old-fashioned quality, even when he deals with contemporary and modern issues?

8   'In Hardy's poetry we encounter the individual isolated within his or her memories, for whom the happiness of the past remains unrealised.' Discuss this assessment of Hardy's poetry.

9   'Hardy's language is not elegant, the lines do not flow and the rhymes seemed strained. Nevertheless, despite the awkwardness and clumsiness of the writing, his poems move us because in them we hear the voice of an old man struggling honestly with the ironies and sufferings of life.' Discuss this assessment of Hardy's poetry.

10 'The failure of hopes, the destructiveness of time, the inevitability of loss and the persistence of memory. These are the themes that dominate Hardy's poetry.' Do you agree with this view of Hardy's work?

11 'Hardy's style makes it difficult for a reader to decide if a poem is well or badly written.' Discuss this statement in relation to the poems you have read.

12 Give your personal response to the poetry of Thomas Hardy. Your answer might address some or all of the following:

- The themes of love and regret
- The anti-war stance
- The craft of poetry
- The picture of Hardy that emerges in the poems
- Poetry that is both personal and universal
- The impact of the poems upon you.

Sample essay

'Hardy can write deceptively simple poetry, but a careful reading will reveal layers of deeper meaning.'

Do you agree with this assessment?

I agree that Thomas Hardy can write simple poetry, which, when examined closely, reveals further layers of meaning. Hardy came to poetry late in life and many of his poems look back to an earlier, simpler time. They are mostly written in the traditional forms of ballads and hymns. However, the poems are rarely just snapshots of the past. Beneath the surface simplicity, we see Hardy struggling with the big questions of life: time, mortality and loss, including the loss of faith.

[Introduction addresses the question asked and sets out areas to be developed]

A prime example of a deceptively simple poem is 'The Self-Unseeing'. The poem is an exercise in nostalgia, as Hardy recalls a childhood memory. As described in the poem, the young Hardy dances to the music of his father's fiddle, while his mother sits by the fire, looking on. On one level, it is a simple poem, written in a plain, unadorned style. On another level, it is a meditation on the themes of time and mortality, from a very personal perspective. In the style of a documentary film-maker, Hardy invites the reader to view his old family home, pointing out different features. 'Here is the ancient floor,' he tells us and then, 'here was the former door'. However, the door is 'where the dead feet walked in' and the floor is 'footworn and hollowed and thin'. This is more than simple description. The house bears the traces of his dead relatives who walked through the door, while the floor, where once he danced as a young boy, is changed and worn by time. In other words, a happy memory is overshadowed by death and the changes wrought by time.

[First poem introduced and analysis begins to answer the question asked]

In the final stanza of the poem, Hardy tells us that 'blessings emblazoned that day' and 'everything glowed with a gleam'. However, the final line introduces a qualification, 'yet we were looking away'. As presented by Hardy, we are seldom aware of happiness as it happens, and only come to appreciate it when it is too late and those we love are gone. The use of the word, 'yet' in the final line uncovers a new layer of meaning in the poem. This new meaning helps us to understand the title of the poem, 'The Self-Unseeing'. It is as if Hardy is chiding himself for his failure to appreciate the fullness and happiness of the moment with his parents. This simple, twelve-line poem manages to celebrate his family, while addressing the question of mortality and the effects of time and, more specifically, the failure to appreciate our moments of happiness until it is too late and those we love are gone.

[Discussion of first poem is developed without losing sight of the question. Relevant quotations from the poem are distributed throughout the discussion]

'During Wind and Rain' is another poem that can be described as deceptively simple, though it is more complex than 'The Self-Unseeing'. Like 'The Self-Unseeing', it recalls memories from childhood. In this instance, the memories are those of Hardy's first wife, Emma Gifford, as recorded in the journal that Hardy read shortly after her death. As a love poem to his late wife, Hardy creates four snapshots from her family album. In the first one, the family are shown as a tight-knit group, gathered around the piano, singing 'their dearest songs'. There is a triumphant note of contented happiness in the line, 'He, she, all of them—yea'. In the next stanza, the family are shown working together in the garden, clearing a path and building 'a shady seat'. The third stanza portrays the family at leisure, 'blithely breakfasting all'. In these snapshots, there is no sense of threat or doubt or worry. Whether working or at leisure the family is united and happy. In the final picture, the family move 'to a high new house' and are surrounded by the marks of prosperity, 'clocks and carpets and chairs'.

Hardy's real genius in this poem is to take these images from the past and introduce into them his own anguished cries at the changes brought by time. The cries are those of an old man grieving for his dead wife, 'Ah, no; the years O!' and 'Ah, no; the years, the years'. The effect is heightened by the final line in each stanza, which, in simple, clear language, and in the style of the refrain in a ballad, uses the symbolism of wind and rain to convey the destruction brought by time: 'How the sick leaves reel down in throngs', 'See, the white storm-birds wing across', 'And the rotten rose is ript from the wall' and 'Down their carved names the rain-drop ploughs'.

There are no difficult words in 'During Wind and Rain' and the stanza form is not complex. However, the effect of the poem is startlingly dramatic and emotionally draining. Into these short sketches of family life, Hardy manages to introduce the contrast between the past and the present; between hope and despair; between order and chaos; between human effort and the forces of nature. He writes a poem that is a love poem and a poem of mourning, a poem in which human hopes, energy and love seem to be washed away by the storms of time. It is a poem rich in meaning.

[Smooth transition in discussion from first to second poem. Good discussion of a second poem, with a mixture of comment and interpretation]

Another poem which draws on Emma's memoir is 'Under the Waterfall'. The poem recalls a picnic in the Valency Valley when the young lovers (Emma and Hardy) lost a tumbler between two boulders in the stream. In her journal, Emma remarked that the tumbler was probably still there, where they had left it. According to the poem, Emma recalls the occasion whenever she plunges her arm into a basin of water. The opening lines of the poem are quite beautiful:

Whenever I plunge my arms like this,
In a basin of water, I never miss
The sweet sharp sense of a fugitive day
Fetched back from its thickening shroud of gray

These lines do more than tell the story of the lost tumbler. They introduce the idea that a physical sensation can prompt the memory to recall past events and save them from forgetfulness. Memory captures the fugitive day of the picnic. The voice of the narrator is natural and fluent, and the poem flows along as merrily as the stream where the glass was lost:

Over a table of solid rock,
And into a scoop of the self-same block;
The purl of a runlet that never ceases

On first reading, the poem is a slightly whimsical account of a small event in the life of the young lovers. However, as the poem proceeds, there are a number of unsettling notes. Having both drank from the same glass, the tumbler is accidentally dropped into the stream and there it remains, 'Jammed darkly, nothing to show how prized, and by now with its smoothness opalized'. If the tumbler symbolises their love, then is the meaning of the poem that their love, too, is jammed darkly in the past, with nothing to show how prized it once was? When, late in the poem, the narrator says that 'By night, by day, when it shines or lours, there lies intact that chalice of ours', the reader wonders if the intact but lost chalice, which cannot be retrieved, is a symbol of the love lost between Emma and her husband? Is their love something which cannot be retrieved? The chalice is, after all, described as 'past recall' in a 'little abyss'. And so a poem that begins as a celebration of a memorable day ends with the suggestion that the promise of the day was lost along with the tumbler, never to be retrieved.

[Always aware of question, the essay manages the difficult balancing act of recounting enough of the story of the poem to be able to comment and interpret it]

Hardy's poetry often deceives us as readers. 'The Oxen', for example, appears to be simply a recounting of a beautiful folk tradition about the animals kneeling in their stalls at midnight on Christmas Eve. But then the use of the word 'might' in the final line transforms it into a poem about the loss of religious faith, and a longing for the comfort of childhood beliefs that are no longer available to the adult poet. The fact that the poem was first published on Christmas Eve 1915 adds poignancy to the loss of faith. Another example is 'Channel Firing', a blackly humorous poem, set in a graveyard, which is changed into something altogether more serious and disturbing by the naming of places that stretch back far into history (Stourton Tower, Camelot, Stonehenge) and which suggest the inability of humans to learn from the past.

[Candidate shows awareness of other poems that support the argument]

In conclusion, throughout Hardy's poetry, we encounter lines of beautiful simplicity: 'Here is the ancient floor', 'Hoping it might be so', 'They change to a high new house', 'No lip has touched it since his and mine', etc. Beyond this simplicity, however, Hardy leads us to consider questions of loneliness and disappointment, the loss of belief, the destruction wrought by time, and the despair of losing love. This mix of surface simplicity and an underlying sophistication is one of the reasons why Hardy's poetry endures.

[Conclusion goes back to terms of the question in summing up the argument]

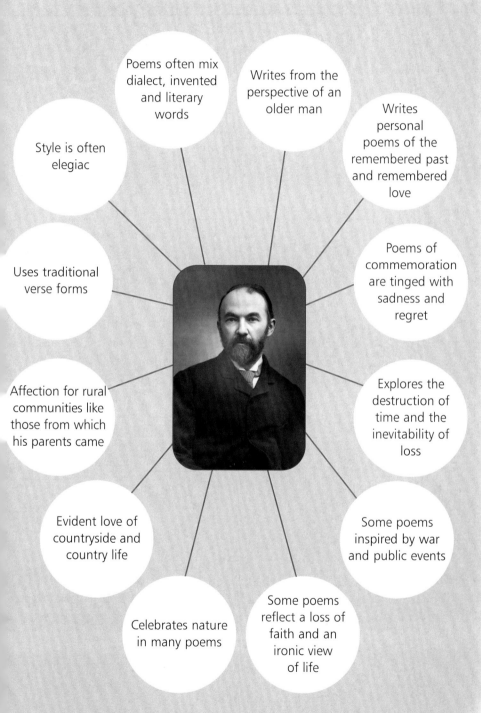

Poems often mix dialect, invented and literary words

Writes from the perspective of an older man

Writes personal poems of the remembered past and remembered love

Style is often elegiac

Poems of commemoration are tinged with sadness and regret

Uses traditional verse forms

Explores the destruction of time and the inevitability of loss

Affection for rural communities like those from which his parents came

Some poems inspired by war and public events

Evident love of countryside and country life

Some poems reflect a loss of faith and an ironic view of life

Celebrates nature in many poems

Thomas Hardy

215

John Montague

b. 1929

Biography

John Montague was born in Brooklyn, New York on 28 February 1929. His parents were Irish emigrants. During the War of Independence, his father, James, was a Volunteer whose activities included participation in ambushes and house-burning. He emigrated to New York in 1925. In Ireland he had been unsuccessful in business ventures financed from the sale of his farm. He became a ticket collector in the New York subway. His wife and two young sons joined him later.

Growing up in Ireland

John left New York at the age of four with his mother and two brothers when his father could no longer support the family. They returned to Co. Tyrone, where his mother took little or no part in his upbringing. He was reared by two aunts who lived in his father's home in Garvaghy and he grew up without knowing his father.

He was educated at Garvaghy Primary School and later at St Patrick's College in Armagh. One of his teachers at St Patrick's College was Sean O'Boyle, a leading authority on Ulster folksong and Irish poetry. O'Boyle gave him a love of the Gaelic tradition, which was to have a profound influence on his life and on his poetry. In 1946 he won a scholarship to University College Dublin. He later studied at Yale and Berkeley, two famous American universities.

Literary and academic career

Montague published his first collection of poems, *Forms of Exile*, in 1958. In the 1960s he taught Anglo-Irish literature at University College Dublin and in 1967 he issued *A Chosen Light*. In the late 1960s he responded with enthusiasm to the Northern Ireland Civil Rights Movement and dedicated a collection of poems, *A New Siege*, to Bernadette Devlin, one of the leaders of the movement.

In 1972 he published *The Rough Field*, in which he explored Ulster and family history. Other important collections of his poetry include *A Slow Dance* (1975), *Poisoned Lands* (1977), *The Great Cloak* (1975), *Selected Poems* (1982) and *The Dead Kingdom* (1984). *A Slow Dance* is particularly interesting for its treatment of the Northern Ireland conflict. In one of the poems in that collection, 'Falls Funeral', there is a chillingly realistic account of the burial of a murdered Catholic child. In another, 'Northern Express', Montague shows how the horrors of the struggle can affect ordinary people. Some of the poems in *The Dead Kingdom* deal with his father's lonely life in Brooklyn.

John Montague

Montague has held a wide variety of positions throughout his adult life. He has been a film critic, a proofreader, an editor, a university lecturer and a writer in residence at many American universities. In 1998 he was appointed to the Ireland Chair of Poetry, which is supported by the Ireland Fund. Since the 1970s he has been based in Cork, lecturing at University College Cork and running poetry workshops. He was the first significant twentieth-century poet writing from a Northern Irish Catholic background. He established a tradition that has been followed by others from a similar background, including Seamus Heaney.

Social and cultural context

Family history

Many of Montague's poems are based on his family history and are strongly autobiographical. Memories of his father are a major theme. In 'The Cage', for example, he recalls his father's unhappy life in New York, trying to preserve his identity as 'a traditional Irishman' by drinking 'neat whiskey'. His father's ultimately successful struggle with his addiction to alcohol made Montague proud. After his father's death, he paid envious tribute to his freedom from addiction for fifteen years, remarking that 'if you're an alcoholic that's quite heroic'. A second quality he admired in his father was that he was 'an intensely believing Catholic'. Montague remembered thinking his 'poor old battered father quite noble' when he saw him laid out in a Franciscan habit. He believed that the power of his religious faith 'enabled him to surmount in himself a life which, he said himself, he had frittered away'.

In 'The Locket', the poet's relationship with his mother is affectionately explored. Montague constructs his poem out of the miserable life endured by his mother, partly the result of his father's inability to support a wife and family, and partly the result of adverse circumstances: she had arrived on her husband's New York doorstep just in time for the Great Depression of 1929.

Local history

Montague's poetry reflects his lifelong interest in the history, mythology and landscape of his ancestral home in Co. Tyrone. It was natural for a poet born in exile to display more than an ordinary interest in the world in which his father and mother grew up, as well as in their neighbours and relatives. In one of his most distinguished early poems, 'Like Dolmens Round My Childhood, the Old People', he combines references to the ancient landscape of Tyrone and its prehistoric burial customs with an exploration of the mysterious old characters who fired his imagination during his childhood in Tyrone. In this poem, the people and their way of life are of much greater interest to the poet than the relics of ancient times. Montague does, however, suggest an intimate link between past and present. His old and eccentric neighbours have inherited ancient customs from their primitive past. This makes it possible for him to feel that the past still lives through them.

National history

Montague's consciousness of the degradation of cultural values in Ireland is at the heart of his work. His sense of cultural and geographical dispossession is also pervasive and manifests itself in many ways and in many poems. 'The Grafted Tongue', for example, is about the British imposition of a foreign language and an alien culture on nineteenth-century Ireland, which was, in Montague's words, obliged 'To grow a second tongue, as harsh a humiliation as twice to be born.' In 'The Wild Dog Rose', the theme of cultural and linguistic loss is more obliquely suggested by the plight of a woman subjected to an attempted rape. With Montague's sanction, this incident may be interpreted as a backward glance at a period in Irish history when the cultural and material heritage was violated by a powerful foreign aggressor.

Montague draws impressively on the tradition of *dinnseanachas*, which dwells on the significance of place names and their resonance. The title of one of his collections, *The Rough Field*, makes a subtle reference to this tradition, since it is an English translation of Garvaghy, his parental home.

'A Welcoming Party' suggests a broader vision of the world. Here, Montague ironically explores the detachment of Irish children from the realities of total war, his own 'parochial brand of innocence' in the face of a film showing a Second World War concentration camp. In this poem, an individual experience takes on a universal meaning.

Timeline

1925	His father emigrated to New York
1928	His mother and his two older brothers moved to New York
1929	Born in Brooklyn, New York
1933	Returns to the family home in Garvaghy, Co. Tyrone, where he is reared by his aunts
1941	Enrols as a student (boarder) at St Patrick's College, Armagh, where Sean O'Boyle, one of his teachers, gives him a love of the Gaelic tradition
1946	Wins a scholarship to UCD; and later studies in the United States
1952	His father returns to Ireland
1958	Publishes first collection of poems, *Forms of Exile*
1972–88	Lectures at University College Cork, influencing a generation of poets and publishing his most important work
1987	Honoured by the State of New York for his literary achievements
1998	Becomes Ireland Chair of Poetry

Killing the Pig

He was pulled out, squealing,
an iron cleek sunk in the roof
of his mouth.

(Don't say they are not intelligent;
they know the hour has come   5
and they want none of it:
they dig in their little trotters,
will not go dumb or singing
to the slaughter.)

That high pitched final effort,   10
no single sound could match it –
a big plane roaring off,
a *diva* soaring towards her last note,
the brain-chilling persistence of an electric saw,
scrap being crushed.   15

Piercing and absolute,
Only high heaven ignores it.

Then a full stop.
An expert plants
a solid thump of a mallet   20
flat between the ears.

Swiftly the knife seeks the throat;
swiftly the other cleavers work
till the carcass is hung up
shining and eviscerated as   25
a surgeon's coat.

A child is given the bladder to play with.
But the walls of the farmyard still
hold that scream, are built around it.

Glossary

2	*cleek:* large hook or crook for catching hold of something; an iron-headed club with a straight narrow face and a long shaft
7	*trotters:* pig's feet
13	*diva:* famous female opera-singer
14	*brain-chilling . . . saw:* the poet is comparing the effect of the doomed pig's squealing with the effect on the human brain of the constant buzzing of an electric saw
16	*absolute:* complete, unlimited
17	*Only . . . it:* the squeals of the pig disturb human listeners, but the heavenly powers seem uninterested (there is also a suggestion that heaven is too far away to hear the noise made by the pig)
20	*mallet:* a hammer with a wooden head
23	*cleavers:* heavy choppers used to divide large sections of meat
24	*carcass:* dead body of an animal, usually with the head, limbs and entrails removed
25	*eviscerated:* with the intestines or bowels removed

Guidelines

For centuries, poets have been writing about living, dead and dying birds, animals and fish. Those who write such poems achieve their effects mainly by means of realistic, almost clinical, descriptions. This particularly applies to those poems dealing with the slaughter of animals. In such poems you will find that the emphasis is on description – even minute details are dwelt upon. These poets are generally reluctant to evaluate or make judgements on what is happening, leaving this to the reader's imagination. 'Killing the Pig' is different in this respect. **The poem resonates beyond the immediate situation and Montague raises some profound questions for the reader to grapple with.**

Commentary

The poem consists of two strands. One embodies a detailed, vivid description of the procedure involved in slaughtering a pig: 'An expert plants / a solid thump of a mallet / flat between the ears' (lines 19–21). **In the other, Montague tries to interpret the event from the pig's point of view.** For example, he tells us that when pigs are being led to the slaughter, 'they know the hour has come / and they want none of it' (lines 5 and 6). He supports his claim by describing the terrible scream,

'Piercing and absolute' (line 16), which signals the pig's consciousness of its approaching fate: the blow to the head, the knife in the throat and the cleavers dismembering the carcass.

The most striking figures in the poem are metaphors. The ones in which Montague conveys the disturbing sound of the pig's scream are especially powerful. There are four such metaphors in all: a plane taking off with a roar, an opera star reaching her final high note, the persistent buzz of an electric saw and the sound of a crusher grinding metal down into scrap. Two of these metaphors, those of the electric saw and the scrap crusher, are the most obviously appropriate ones. The other two, however, show the poet's fertile imagination at work. The jet plane gives the impression of tremendous sound soaring towards the heavens as the pig's scream does. The opera singer's final note may be interpreted as a human cry of protest, having the same tragic finality as the pig's scream. It is worth noting that all those cries, whether they are uttered by the singer, the machines or the pig, are futile. In the scheme of Montague's poem, 'high heaven' (line 17) pays no attention to signals from Earth, whether these are signals of distress or protest.

In the final two lines Montague extends the poem's scope backwards and forwards in time, beyond the central incident of slaughter. The idea that 'the walls of the farmyard still / hold' (lines 28 and 29) the scream of the pig after it has died raises a number of possibilities. The poet is suggesting that he will always associate this farmyard with the pig's scream or hear it in his mind whenever he visits the place. There is a further layer of meaning in the last two lines: the poet is inviting us to imagine a time before the farmyard walls were built and to enter the mind of the builder. We can imagine this builder thinking that in some future time, pigs, like this one, would go screaming to their deaths in this farmyard. Thinking like this, he plans the wall as a way of confining the scream and its terrible significance.

Thinking about the poem

1   How does this poem encourage the reader to feel sympathy for the pig? Give details from the poem in support of your answer.
2   Mention three details from the poem that you found disturbing. Say how the poet achieves this effect.
3   Why does the poet dismiss the idea that pigs are not intelligent?
4   Before it dies, the pig utters a high-pitched sound. The poet tries to convey this sound in four different ways. List these and say how effective each one is.

223

5   In your opinion, why does the poet say that 'Only high heaven ignores' (line 17) the pig's scream?

6   Is the poet suggesting that the killing of the pig is unnecessarily cruel? Give reasons for your answer.

7   Why, in your opinion, does the poet describe the person who thumps the pig's head with a mallet as an 'expert' (line 19)?

8   How does the poet suggest that the killing of the pig is an impersonal ritual? How does he distance those who kill the pig from their actions?

9   Does the poem give us any idea of how the poet feels about what he is describing?

Personal response

1   Give your response to the poem, recording its effect on you, the feelings it arouses in you, and your views on the kind of event it describes.

2   You have been asked to make a short film of the events described in this poem. Explain how you would use sound effects, lighting and mood music to create an appropriate atmosphere.

3   Imagine you are a newspaper reporter. You have been assigned to visit the farmyard in which this pig is killed and to write a report on what you see and hear. Prepare your report.

The Trout

Flat on the bank I parted
Rushes to ease my hands
In the water without a ripple
And tilt them slowly downstream
To where he lay, tendril light,   5
In his fluid sensual dream.

Bodiless lord of creation
I hung briefly above him
Savouring my own absence
Senses expanding in the slow   10
Motion, the photographic calm
That grows before action

As the curve of my hands
Swung under his body
He surged, with visible pleasure.   15
I was so preternaturally close
I could count every stipple
But still cast no shadow, until

The two palms crossed in a cage
Under the lightly pulsing gills.   20
Then (entering my own enlarged
Shape, which rode on the water)
I gripped. To this day I can
Taste his terror on my hands.

Glossary		
5	*tendril light:* a tendril is a leaf or stem used by climbing plants to attach themselves to a support. This phrase suggest that the trout seems almost weightless	
6	*fluid:* the fluid dream may be one in which each part merges easily into the next; 'fluid' may also mean 'watery'	
6	*sensual:* giving pleasure to the senses	
7–8	*Bodiless . . . above him:* the poet hovered above the trout like a god	
16	*preternaturally close:* closer than is normal in nature	
17	*stipple:* dot, fleck	

Guidelines

Like 'Killing the Pig', this poem deals with one aspect of the relationship between human beings and other creatures. 'The Trout' also has some affinity with 'The Cage' as the subjects of both poems feel imprisoned. In 'Killing the Pig' Montague becomes a somewhat troubled commentator on the ritual of slaughter. In 'The Trout' he is more restrained. It is not until the last two lines that he conveys deep feeling for the fish whose terror he can still feel to this day.

Commentary

A central theme of the poem is the speaker's presentation of himself in relation to the trout. We find the essence of this relationship in stanza 2. The speaker visualises himself hovering directly above the trout as a 'Bodiless lord of creation' (line 7). These lines imply that in his confrontation with the trout, **the speaker sees himself as a divine being with the power to control the created world.** This sense of the speaker as a god is conveyed by the image of a bodiless being who is able to hover over the trout and to experience a sense of physical absence. The divine image is also used in stanza 3, where the speaker describes himself as being 'preternaturally close' (line 16) to the trout just as he is on the point of capturing it.

The speaker is not entirely objective in his presentation of the trout. Twice in the course of the poem **he projects his own feelings and emotions onto the fish.** In the first stanza he imagines it lost in a 'fluid sensual dream' (line 6). In the final stanza he attributes human emotion to the captured trout: 'To this day I can / Taste his terror on my hands' (lines 23 and 24). In 'Killing the Pig' Montague also conveys the sense of terror experienced by creatures at the hands of human beings. The speaker's sympathetic identification with the feelings of the trout is part of a pattern that may be found in many of Montague's poems. Such poems suggest that he lives in harmony with the natural world. **He is able to catch the trout because he is in tune with its habitat and understands its way of life.**

The poem needs to be read slowly and deliberately. Its movement is relaxed, in keeping with the leisurely pace of the event it describes. Rhythm and meaning are in close harmony. The second stanza gives a good description of the way in which movement reflects meaning: 'Senses expanding in the slow / Motion, the photographic calm / That grows before action' (lines 10–12). Notice how the movement of the poem is constantly arrested by the poet's use of breaks in the meaning at the ends of lines: 'Flat on the bank I parted / Rushes to ease my hands / In the water without a ripple' (lines 1–3).

Thinking about the poem

1   In this poem, what happens is partly seen from the speaker's point of view and partly in terms of what the trout might have felt. Comment on this idea with reference to the poem.

2   Describe the speaker's feelings as he stalks the trout and catches it.

3   Explain the speaker's progress from his 'own absence' (line 9) to his 'own enlarged / Shape' (lines 21 and 22).

4   What might the speaker mean by 'the photographic calm / That grows before action' (lines 11 and 12)?

5   The speaker tells us that the trout 'surged, with visible pleasure' (line 15) just before it was caught. What do you think is meant here?

6   Write about two images from the poem that you find particularly impressive. Explain your choice.

7   Discuss the ways in which Montague makes a simple incident exciting.

8   Does stanza 4 provide an effective ending for the poem? Give your reasons for agreeing or disagreeing.

9   The poem is about more than the capture of a trout. Suggest some other issues it raises.

Personal response

1   Imagine you are the fish described in this poem. Describe how you feel about your encounter with the speaker in the poem.

2   Based on your reading of 'Killing the Pig' and 'The Trout', write a short piece on the relationship between human beings and animals.

Before you read 'The Locket'

Many of Montague's poems feature members of his family. 'The Locket' is about his mother and his relationship with her. In small groups, discuss the images and themes you would expect to find in a poem written by a child about his or her mother.

memories
valuable
precious
sentimental
love

The Locket

Sing a last song   *rhyme*
for the lady who has gone,   *saying goodbye*
fertile source of guilt and pain.   *feels guilty*
The worst birth in the annals of Brooklyn,   *(quote from his mother)*   *Birth*
that was my cue to come on,   5
my first claim to fame.

Naturally, she longed for a girl,
and all my infant curls of brown
couldn't excuse my double blunder   *birth + boy*
coming out, both the wrong sex,   10

227

and the wrong way around.
Not readily forgiven.

So you never nursed me   *she didnt love him*
and when all my father's songs
couldn't sweeten the lack of money,   *love dies when*   15
personification
(when poverty comes through the door   *they dont have*
money
love flies up the chimney,)
Your favourite saying.

Then you gave me away,
might never have known me,   20
if I had not cycled down   *trying to gain*
her love back
to court you like a (young man,)
teasingly untying your apron,   *~ suiter. taking the*
drinking by the fire, yarning   *place of his father.*

Of your wild, young days   *language is*   25
which didn't last long, for you,   *descriptive*
lovely Molly, the belle of your small town,   *+ narrative*
landed up mournful and (chill   *simile*   *+ conversational*
as the constant rain that lashes it,)   *at times.*
(wound into your cocoon of pain.)   30
Metaphor

Standing in that same hallway,
don't come again, you say, roughly,   *pushing him away.*
I start to get fond of you, John,
and then you are up and gone:
the harsh logic of a forlorn woman   35
resigned to being alone.

And still, mysterious blessing,
I never knew, until you were gone,   *she did love him*
that, always around your neck,
you wore an oval locket   40
with an old picture in it,
of a child in Brooklyn.

Narrative structure
evident in poem

Glossary

2	*the lady:* the poet's mother, Molly
3	*fertile source:* the poet's mother inspired strong feelings in him
4	*annals:* chronicles, historical records
4	*Brooklyn:* New York borough where the poet was born
6	*claim to fame:* his troublesome birth was the first remarkable thing about him
12	*Not readily forgiven:* his mother did not easily forgive him for being a boy and for having caused her such pain at his birth
15	*sweeten:* compensate for
19	*gave me away:* from the age of four, the poet was raised, not by his mother, but by two aunts
24	*yarning:* telling stories
27	*lovely Molly:* a reference to 'The Rose of Mooncoin', a famous Irish ballad
28	*landed . . . chill:* ended up or turned out sad and cold
30	*cocoon:* a protective covering; here it means a retreat from the sorrows of life
35	*forlorn:* pitifully sad and lonely
38	*gone:* dead

Guidelines

This is one of a number of poems in which Montague deals with members of his family. His mother is the main subject of 'The Locket' and the poem looks at the unusual relationship between mother and son. The background of the poem is a sad one. His mother, having given birth to two boys, resented John's birth because she wanted a girl. He thus felt, and was made to feel, that he should carry a burden of guilt for having been born, particularly as his birth was a difficult one for his mother. Following their return to Ireland, his mother refused to let him live with her; he was obliged to live with his aunts seven miles away and endure the emotional consequences of his parents' broken marriage.

Commentary

The poem is a lament for the poet's dead mother. It is not a conventional lament for a dead person: the poet is much more interested in the influence of his mother on his life than in her significance as a woman. **The emphasis is on the damaging influence of his mother on his life and development.** She did not welcome his birth and found it hard to forgive him for it. She never nurtured him, and gave him away rather than rear him. She discouraged his visits in order to avoid growing fond of him. In this she follows 'the harsh logic of a forlorn woman / resigned to being alone' (lines 35 and 36).

Rejection is not, however, the entire story of the poem, which ends with the poet's experience of what he calls a 'mysterious blessing' (line 37). After her death, it transpires that his mother always wore an oval locket containing an old picture of the poet as a child.

In 'The Locket', as in many of Montague's poems, among them 'Like Dolmens Round My Childhood, the Old People' and 'The Wild Dog Rose', outward appearances can be profoundly deceptive.

On a first reading, the fourth stanza of the poem may seem odd. The poet claims that his mother might never have known him if he had not cycled the seven miles separating his home and hers. The purpose of his visit was: 'to court you like a young man, / teasingly untying your apron, / drinking by the fire, yarning' (lines 22–24). These ritual visits are best explained by the idea that the young Montague is not making them merely in an attempt to heal the wound of being an unwanted child.

There is a sense in which he sees himself as his father's double, as he does in 'The Cage', and even more obviously in a poem called 'The Same Fault', where he remarks that he and his father have 'the same scar / in the same place / as if the same fault ran through us both'. The child's mental anguish at being a displaced, unwanted child is mirrored in his father's anguish at losing his family, since, as a husband, he is unwanted. His wife, having instinctively rejected their child, engages in a double rejection when she refuses to live in New York as an immigrant wife and leaves her husband in order to return to Ireland. The boy's understanding of his father's predicament may well help to explain why he is willing to assume the role of his father's double, wooing his mother as if on his father's behalf and vainly trying to heal the wounds of family division.

Thinking about the poem

1 The title of the poem and the final stanza emphasise the importance of the locket. Why is the locket so important to the poet?

2 Describe the tone of the first stanza.

3 When the poet has his mother describe his coming into the world as '*The worst birth in the annals of Brooklyn*' (line 4), are we to take him seriously? Explain your answer.

4 Montague describes his mother as a 'fertile source of guilt and pain' (line 3). How is this description illustrated in the rest of the poem?

5 Show how the poet explores the theme of rejection throughout the poem.

6 The poem gives us an idea of the poet's attitude to his mother. How would you describe this attitude?

7 What does the poem tell us about the mother's life?

8 How does the young Montague try to win his mother's affection? Does he succeed?

9 Write an account of the young Montague's relationship with his mother, based on this poem.

10 What has happened to make the mother of the poet 'a forlorn woman' (line 35)? You might look particularly at stanza 3.

11 Is the poet sorry for himself? Give reasons for your answer.

12 What is the happiest moment of the poem, and what is the saddest?

Personal response

1 Imagine you are the speaker of the poem. Write a short account of your feelings about the circumstances outlined in the poem.

2 You have been chosen to speak to your class about this poem. Write out the talk you would give. Your talk should include a summary of the content of the poem, and of your own views on it.

3 Write a brief account of what the speaker of the poem tells us, this time from the mother's point of view.

John Montague

snapshot

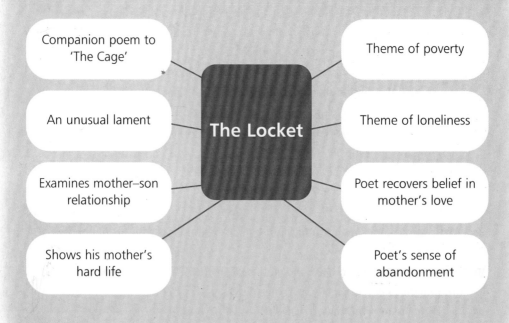

Companion poem to 'The Cage'

An unusual lament

Examines mother–son relationship

Shows his mother's hard life

The Locket

Theme of poverty

Theme of loneliness

Poet recovers belief in mother's love

Poet's sense of abandonment

Before you read 'The Cage'

'The Cage' by John Montague is partly about being trapped in a miserable job. In a small group, draw up a list of the things that might make someone feel unhappy at work or feel that their job is like a cage.

[handwritten:] · trapped · isolated · restricted · wanting to escape

The Cage

[handwritten:] striking / impression

My father, the least happy
man I have known. His face
retained the pallor *(pale)*
of those who work underground:
the lost years in Brooklyn

[handwritten:] Reference to the oddyssy and to his fathers deathly complexion having worked underground.

[line 5]

listening to a subway   *feels sorry for his father.*
shudder the earth.

But a traditional Irishman
who (released from his grille   *(the cage)*
in the Clark Street I.R.T.)   *station*   10
drank neat whiskey until
he reached the only element
he felt at home in
any longer: brute oblivion.

And yet picked himself   *redeeming thing about his*   15
                         father
up, most mornings,
to march down the street   *pride*
extending his smile
to all sides of the good,
(all-white) neighbourhood   20
belled by St Teresa's church.

came out of exile (retired)
When he came back
we walked together
across fields of Garvaghy
to see hawthorn on the summer   25
hedges, as though
he had never left;
a bend of the road

which still sheltered
primroses. But we   30
did not smile in
the shared complicity
of a dream, for when
weary Odysseus returns
Telemachus should leave.   35

[handwritten: Montague in NY]

Often as I descend *[handwritten: suggestion of going to something negative.]*

into subway or underground

I see his bald head behind

the bars of the small booth;

the mark of an old car *[handwritten: haunted by sad images of his father]*   40

accident beating on his

ghostly forehead.

	Glossary
3	*pallor:* an unnatural paleness
5	*Brooklyn:* a borough of the City of New York
6	*subway:* the New York underground rail system
9	*grille:* a metal screen with bars in the subway ticket office
10	Clark Street I.R.T. Clark Street is a New York subway station in Brooklyn. I.R.T. stands for the Interborough Rapid Transit Company, a private rail company that operated the subway line until 1940
11	*neat:* undiluted (no water added)
14	*brute oblivion:* total forgetfulness
21	*belled by:* served by or called to worship at
22	*came back:* returned to Ireland
24	*Garvaghy:* the Co. Tyrone birthplace of Montague's father, who returned to Ireland in 1952, nineteen years after John had been sent back from New York
33–5	*for when . . . leave:* the references to Odysseus and Telemachus come from Homer's Greek epic poem *The Odyssey*. Odysseus (also known as Ulysses) travelled on land and sea for twenty years. He had left his wife and son, Telemachus, to wait at home for him in Ithaca. When he returned, Telemachus left Ithaca. The story told by Homer in his epic reminds Montague of the story of his own family. Like Odysseus, Montague's father is separated for a long period from his wife and son. Like Telemachus, the younger Montague left for New York almost as soon as his father returned home

Guidelines

The poem is about Montague's father, James. **It is also about the father–son relationship, and about the effects of exile and return on a man described in stanza 2 as 'a traditional Irishman'.** Montague's father had reasons to be unhappy. His militant patriotism induced him to flee Ireland. Shortly after he arrived in New York, America was hit by the Great Depression. His failure to earn an adequate living and his fondness for alcohol alienated his wife. His wife and family abandoned him in the early 1930s. He remained in New York until his retirement in 1952. He then returned to Ireland to live out the last seven years of his life in Omagh, Co. Tyrone.

Commentary

The first three stanzas provide a concise account of James Montague's life as an Irish emigrant in New York. It is significant that the poet describes his father's time in New York as 'the lost years' (line 5). The suggestion here is that exile from the place of his ancestors deprives his life of its essential meaning and robs him of his identity. **The title of the poem is a metaphor for James Montague's plight. He spends his working life underground in a subway ticket office, a kind of miniature prison in which he dispenses tickets through the bars of a grille.** He is pale-faced from a lack of natural light and fresh air, his ears are assaulted by the noise of the subway trains as they 'shudder the earth' (line 7). His pale colour suggests death, which is also brought to mind by the image of the underground. This word invokes thoughts of Hades, the home of the dead in Greek mythology. Compare the parallel imagery in 'All Legendary Obstacles'.

What he has lost through exile is suggested in stanzas 4 and 5: the fields of his native Garvaghy, 'hawthorn on the summer / hedges' (lines 25 and 26) and primroses sheltered by a bend in the road. Life in the infernal underground cage can be relieved only in the 'brute oblivion' (line 14) of drunkenness, another kind of imprisonment. The contrast between these forms of physical and mental captivity and the freedom of the open fields of Garvaghy is central to the meaning of the poem. James Montague's underground life behind the grille of the Clark Street subway station becomes a metaphor for his life as an exile who cannot feel at home in New York and who tries to find a substitute home in a state of forgetfulness induced by neat whiskey. **The image of a cage suggests another kind of double life. He is visible through its bars and at the same time cut off from a world to which he does not fully belong.**

Stanzas 4 and 5 refer to James Montague's return to Ireland in 1952. The end of the father's exile does not, however, mark the beginning of a happy relationship between father and son. They 'did not smile in / the shared complicity / of a dream' (lines 31–33). They had been apart for so long that they did not have the same plans or dreams. When James Montague, like the weary Odysseus of Homer's ancient epic, came home, his son John, like Telemachus, felt he himself had to go into exile. His place of exile is New York, the one originally chosen by his father.

The final stanza of the poem is based on the notion that the father is a double for his son, just as the son is a double for him. To reinforce this point, Montague uses an image of his dead father behind the bars of a subway booth: 'the mark of an old car / accident beating on his / ghostly forehead' (lines 40–42). Elsewhere in his work, Montague is at pains to stress the physical resemblance between his father and himself, in particular the detail of a facial scar common to both as a means of suggesting that he sees his father as an image of himself (see the reference to 'The Same Fault' in the commentary on 'The Locket').

Thinking about the poem

1   In your opinion, why did the poet choose 'The Cage' as the title of this poem? Explore the ideas associated with the image of the cage throughout the poem.

2   How would you describe the poet's attitude to his father? Refer to words or phrases in the poem.

3   Explain the reference to 'the lost years in Brooklyn' (line 5).

4   Why did the poet's father seek comfort in 'brute oblivion' (line 14)?

5   The poet tells us that his father extended his smile 'to all sides of the good, / (all-white) neighbourhood' (lines 19 and 20). Explain this reference.

6   How is the idea of imprisonment suggested in stanza 2 of the poem?

7   In stanza 5 we are told that father and son 'did not smile in / the shared complicity / of a dream' (lines 31–33). Why was this so? What was the dream?

8   Comment on the reference to Odysseus and Telemachus in stanza 5.

9   On the evidence of the poem, does the father's life seem to have served any purpose?

10   The poem features some significant examples of contrast. Discuss some of these, for example the contrast between Brooklyn and Garvaghy.

11   What do the images in the final stanza of the poem ('I descend'; 'underground'; 'bars'; 'ghostly forehead') suggest to you?

12   'This poem is about Montague's father, but it is also about Montague himself.' Comment on this interpretation, referring to the text in support of your answer.

Personal response

1   Imagine you are the poet's father. Compose an account of your life during your 'lost years in Brooklyn' working in the underground. Describe also how you felt about yourself and the kind of work you had to do, and how you coped with this.

2   Write your own response to 'The Cage', as if the man at the centre of the poem was your father.

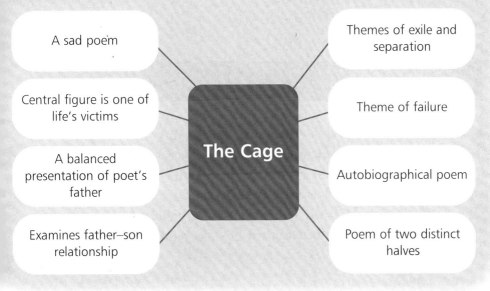

- A sad poem
- Central figure is one of life's victims
- A balanced presentation of poet's father
- Examines father–son relationship

The Cage

- Themes of exile and separation
- Theme of failure
- Autobiographical poem
- Poem of two distinct halves

John Montague

INSTRUMENT

Typical images

Windharp

The sounds of Ireland,
that restless whispering
you never get away
from, seeping out of
low bushes and grass,   5
heatherbells and fern,
wrinkling bog pools,
scraping tree branches,
light hunting cloud,
sound hounding sight,   10
a hand ceaselessly
combing and stroking
the landscape, till
the valley gleams
like the pile upon   15
a mountain pony's coat.

onomatopoeia

Assonance

personification

Glossary

2	*restless whispering:* sound of the wind
15	*pile:* soft projecting surface of hair on the pony's back

Guidelines

This poem was dedicated to the Irish artist Patrick Collins, whose atmospheric landscape paintings find a poetic equivalent in 'Windharp'. The title of the poem is an allusion to ancient Greek mythology. Montague has in mind Aeolus (whom Zeus appointed keeper of the winds) and the harp named after him, the Aeolian harp or windharp. This harp was much favoured by the English Romantic poets. Its strings, of varying thickness, were all tuned to the same note. When the wind blew across the strings, it played the music of nature, much as it does when it blows across the Irish landscape in the poem.

The title may have another significance for Montague. The seal of the Society of United Irishmen, founded in Belfast in 1791, featured a harp. Montague linked this harp not only to the harp of Aeolus, but 'more immediately to the events of my own country'.

Commentary

The structure of the poem is interesting: it consists of a single extended sentence. **The rushing, onward movement of the verse perfectly reflects the restless activity of the wind.** The poem is a sensitive response to the natural world: **Montague evokes its many voices and varied musical sounds in familiar, commonplace images.** For example, in lines 4 and 5 the breeze comes through the bushes and the grass in the same way as water leaks slowly from porous materials. The wind has a 'wrinkling' (line 7) effect on water, causing ripples on the surface of the water in bog holes.

The music of the landscape is not particularly pleasing to the ear. It has an unsettling effect on the listener, suggested by its 'restless whispering' (line 2). The dominant sounds are disturbing: 'seeping' (line 4), 'wrinkling' (line 7) and 'scraping' (line 8). At one point, the images of the wind's activity become menacing, even predatory: 'light hunting cloud, / sound hounding sight' (lines 9 and 10). The wind blows the clouds across the sky in its hunt for light and sight. The image is based on a hound chasing after its prey.

At line 11, tactile and visual imagery replace the imagery of sound. The 'hand ceaselessly / combing and stroking / the landscape' (lines 11–13) represents the care nature takes of that landscape. The image of the hand humanises the action of the wind. The entire landscape is like a great harp that the wind is constantly playing on. The hand that strokes the landscape is seen, by means of a charming simile, to comb the pony's back as well. Nature's fostering activity prepares us for the revelation of the full glory of the landscape as 'the valley gleams' (line 14).

As is often the case in Montague's poetry, **this poem has implications that go deeper than the surface meaning.** Montague, with the imagery of music in mind, has indicated that this music might be able to suggest, in a Northern Ireland context, an inclusive, unpartitioned attitude in which all Irish people 'should be able to accept, or listen to, many voices, agreeable or disturbing, which haunt our land', and in that way 'blend, as a symphony contains its dissonances, structures of healing'.

Thinking about the poem

1   The poem is dedicated to a famous landscape painter. In what ways might this poem appeal to such a painter?
2   Is this poem an entirely happy one? Does it suggest any criticisms of the Irish landscape?
3   Comment on the poet's choice of 'Windharp' as his title.
4   How do the final five lines contrast with what has gone before?
5   Do you think the poet captures some essential features of the Irish landscape? Explain your answer by referring to significant details in the poem.
6   Why does the poet refer to a hand 'combing and stroking / the landscape' (lines 12 and 13)? Is there a connection between this image, the title of the poem, and the pony's coat?
7   How does the poet suggest the ceaseless movement of the wind?

Personal response

1   This poem would make an ideal subject for a short video or film. If you were asked to make such a film to accompany a reading of the poem, what music, sound effects, colour, images and other background material would you use to create an appropriate atmosphere for the reading? Comment on your choices.
2   You have been asked by the Irish Tourist Board to compile a brochure highlighting the attractions of the Irish landscape. How would you use the details of this poem as inspiration for your brochure?

All Legendary Obstacles

All legendary obstacles lay between
Us, the long imaginary plain,
The monstrous ruck of mountains
And, swinging across the night,
Flooding the Sacramento, San Joaquin,   5
The hissing drift of winter rain.

All day I waited, shifting
Nervously from station to bar
As I saw another train sail
By, the San Francisco Chief or   10
Golden Gate, water dripping
From great flanged wheels.

At midnight you came, pale
Above the negro porter's lamp.
I was too blind with rain   15
And doubt to speak, but
Reached from the platform
Until our chilled hands met.   *uncertainty of new love.*

You had been travelling for days
With an old lady, who marked   20
A neat circle on the glass
With her glove, to watch us
Move into the wet darkness
Kissing, still unable to speak.

Glossary	
2	*plain:* a large area of low, generally flat, land
3	*ruck:* heap or pile
5	*Sacramento, San Joaquin:* rivers in California
10–11	*San Francisco Chief or Golden Gate:* trains operating in California

12	*flanged wheels:* wheels protected by metal rims or flanges that keep them in place
14	*negro:* old-fashioned term for a person of African origin or descent (the term was more widely accepted when the poem was written in 1966 than it is today)
23	*wet darkness:* dark night with rain falling

Guidelines

Many of Montague's poems can be adequately understood only with the help of information on the circumstances of the poet's life, his family background, the neighbourhoods in which he grew up and the cultural, social and political history of Ireland. In particular, plantation, dispossession and emigration are matters that influenced Montague's thinking. Such poems include 'Like Dolmens Round My Childhood, the Old People', 'The Windharp', 'The Locket' and 'The Cage'.

'All Legendary Obstacles' is an account of separated lovers coming together. The woman has travelled across the American continent to where the speaker of the poem waits for her in San Francisco.

Commentary

'All Legendary Obstacles' is a love poem, which helps to explain why its language is richer and less matter of fact than that in many of Montague's other poems.

Stanza 1

The opening stanza is grandly rhetorical and urgent in its rhythms. Lines 4 to 6 impressively reflect the movement of the rain across a wide geographical expanse. The 'legendary obstacles' (line 1) separating the lovers are the great natural barriers, the long plain and the huge pile of mountains, and to a lesser extent, perhaps, 'The hissing drift of winter rain' (line 6).

Montague does not want his high rhetorical flight to get out of control, which is why he places the word 'Us' at the beginning of line 2 rather than at the end of line 1. He temporarily slows the movement of the verse, only to quicken its pace again in the remainder of the stanza. The second line, with its reference to 'the long imaginary plain' poses a problem. The plain referred to is clearly a real one. It is being imagined by the waiting lover rather than being an imaginary thing. To make sense, the poet should have written 'the long-imagined plain'. It seems that Montague allowed his desire to achieve impressive sound effects to overrule the demands of meaning: 'imaginary' is rhythmically superior and provides a pleasant verbal echo of 'legendary' in line 1.

Stanza 3

The opening lines of Stanza 3 call for comment: 'At midnight you came, pale / Above the negro porter's lamp' (lines 13 and 14). The key word here is 'pale'. It is a word that Montague uses very often in his poetry. Here it is used with impressive effect. It contrasts sharply with the darkness of the porter's skin and with the midnight darkness. The word has another significance. Montague, like many of the Romantic poets, thought of 'pale' as a symbol of death. Keats, for example, describes the dying knight in 'La Belle Dame Sans Merci' as 'palely loitering'. With this in mind, we may think of the woman of the poem as being surrounded by an aura of death; perhaps she is recovering from an illness that brought her near to death.

This kind of interpretation is reinforced by the general melancholy of the midnight scene, the 'hissing drift of winter rain' (line 6), the 'chilled hands' (line 18) of the lovers and the 'wet darkness' (line 23). There is also a sense of uncertainty: the speaker could not see properly due to the falling rain and, not sure what to say, he said nothing.

At one level, the poem deals with the ordinary experience of two separated lovers. At a deeper level, as some of its details suggest, the woman's journey has disturbing implications. Are we, for example, to see a sinister meaning in the black porter? Is he a figure from the underworld? Or is the transcontinental crossing in which the pale woman participates a journey to the underworld, and has the train arriving at midnight, the fateful hour, been part of a funeral procession?

The 'legendary obstacles' of the title are the obstacles that, in legend and fable, fate places between lovers as a means of separating them. Of such obstacles, the ultimate one is death. Images of death seem to hover around the platform, which is the stage on which the events of the poem are enacted. The ending of the poem, however, may suggest a contrary view. The lady with her circle on the glass (duplicating what the porter does with his lamp, when he sheds a circle of light on the lovers' meeting) is an image of age, from which the two lovers slip away into the darkness. The moving train is an image of transience, from which the lovers retreat into what they must hope will be a permanent state of love.

[handwritten margin note: use of contrast. black + white adds to cinematic approach]

Thinking about the poem

1 What does the poem tell us about the speaker's relationship with the person he is waiting for? How does he feel about her?

2 Why is the speaker uneasy and nervous as he waits?

3 The poem features some striking contrasts. Comment on these.

4 Choose two images from the poem that appeal to you. Explain why you like them.

5 Why does the speaker find it impossible to speak?

6 Do you think the old lady in the final stanza adds to the meaning of the poem? Explain your answer.

7 Write your own account of the poem, explaining what it means to you.

8 What does the title of the poem suggest? How does it relate to the overall impact of the poem?

9 Is this a sad or a happy poem?

10 Does this poem have a single theme? Explain your answer.

Personal response

1 Suggest an alternative title for this poem. Explain your suggestion.

2 The poem does not provide much detail about the 'you' of the poem. Using details from the poem, supplemented with other details from your imagination, provide an account of the events depicted in the poem from this person's point of view.

The Same Gesture

There is a secret room
of golden light where
everything – love, violence,
hatred is possible:
and, again love.   5

Such intimacy of hand
and mind is achieved
under its healing light
that the shifting of
hands is a rite   10

like court music.
We barely know our
selves there though
it is what we always were
– most nakedly are –   15

and must remember
when we leave, re-
suming our habits
with our clothes:
work, 'phone, drive   20

through late traffic
changing gears with
the same gesture as
eased your snowbound
heart and flesh.   25

Glossary

10	*rite:* sacred ritual
11	*court music:* elegant, graceful music played for royal persons
15	*nakedly:* obviously, essentially; there is also a pun on its literal meaning of 'without clothes' (see lines 19 and 20)

Guidelines

This is a love poem. In traditional love poetry, it is possible to identify two distinct interpretations of the meaning of love. In many poems, we find a tension between them. The tradition of Platonic poetry emphasises the spiritual dimension of love, as an image of God's love for human beings, and underplays its physical expression. In this poem, Montague is an anti-Platonic love-poet, who finds the fullest meaning of love only in its physical expression.

Commentary

The 'secret room' (line 1) imagined in the poem is the room shared by the two lovers. **In this room, love, in its purely physical sense, excludes everything else from their consciousness.** A 'healing light' (line 8) shines on the lovers as they embrace and caress each other. Their love gestures are seen by the speaker as equivalent to a sacred ceremony or 'rite' (line 10) in which sense and intelligence are intimately linked.

The speaker sees the room in which he imagines the most intimate physical contact between himself and his lover as a sacred space or place of worship, in which the two lovers become closest to their true selves. For a while, the room they share becomes the whole world: it is a place where 'everything . . . is possible' (lines 3 and 4) and it contains everything that matters. A similar idea is at the heart of John Donne's poem 'The Sunne Rising'.

There are realities other than the intimacies described in the first three stanzas. These intimacies are passing, temporary events in a temporary space. They can linger only in the memory. **The lovers must leave their sanctuary and return to the routines of everyday life:** 're- / suming our habits / with our clothes / work, 'phone, drive' (lines 17–20). **The same hands that expressed loving gestures must soon be put to more everyday use.** The same kind of gesture that eased and melted the woman's 'snowbound / heart and flesh' (lines 24 and 25) is soon used by the speaker to change gears as he drives through traffic.

Thinking about the poem

1. Why does the poet describe the light in the room as 'golden' (line 2)?
2. Why is the room called 'secret' (line 1)?
3. What is the significance of the 'healing light' (line 8)?
4. Is the kind of love described in the poem permanent? Base your answer on evidence offered by the poem.
5. Discuss the meaning of the poem's title, 'The Same Gesture'.
6. There is a contrast between the first three stanzas of the poem and the final two. Comment on this.
7. What is the theme of the poem?
8. Do you find this poem optimistic? Give reasons for your answer.
9. What does the poem tell us about the meaning of love? Do you share the point of view it expresses?
10. It has been suggested that this is an escapist poem, dealing with people who try to find a refuge from reality. Would you agree? Give reasons for your answer.

Personal response

1   If you were asked to suggest appropriate music to accompany a reading of 'The Same Gesture', what kind of music would you choose? Comment on your choice.

2   Write a short piece entitled 'Escaping from reality'.

The Wild Dog Rose

I

I go to say goodbye to the *Cailleach*
that terrible figure who haunted my childhood
but no longer harsh, a human being
merely, hurt by event.

The cottage,   5
circled by trees, weathered to admonitory
shapes of desolation by the mountain winds,
straggles into view. The rank thistles
and leathery bracken of untilled fields
stretch behind with – a final outcrop –   10
the hooped figure by the roadside,
its retinue of dogs

which give tongue
as I approach, with savage, whining cries
so that she slowly turns, a moving nest   15
of shawls and rags, to view, to stare
the stranger down.

And I feel again
that ancient awe, the terror of a child
before the great hooked nose, the cheeks   20
dewlapped with dirt, the staring blue
of the sunken eyes, the mottled claws
clutching a stick

but now hold
and return her gaze, to greet her,   25
as she greets me, in friendliness.
Memories have wrought reconciliation
between us, we talk in ease at last,
like old friends, lovers almost,
sharing secrets   30

of neighbours
she quarrelled with, who now lie
in Garvaghy graveyard, beyond all hatred;
of my family and hers, how she never married,
though a man came asking in her youth   35
'You would be loath to leave your own'
she sighs, 'and go among strangers' –
his parish ten miles off.

For sixty years
since she has lived alone, in one place.   40
Obscurely honoured by such confidences,
I idle by the summer roadside, listening,
while the monologue falters, continues,
rehearsing the small events of her life.
The only true madness is loneliness,   45
the monotonous voice in the skull
that never stops

because never heard.

                                    II

And there
Where the dog rose shines in the hedge   50
she tells me a story so terrible
that I try to push it away,
my bones melting.

Late at night
a drunk came beating at her door   55
to break it in, the bolt snapping
from the soft wood, the thin mongrels
rushing to cut, but yelping as
he whirls with his farm boots
to crush their skulls   60

In the darkness
they wrestle, two creatures crazed
with loneliness, the smell of the
decaying cottage in his nostrils
like a drug, his body heavy on hers,   65
the tasteless trunk of a seventy year
old virgin, which he rummages while
she battles for life

bony fingers
reaching desperately to push   70
against his bull neck. 'I prayed
to the Blessed Virgin herself
for help and after a time
I broke his grip'.

He rolls   75
to the floor, snores asleep,
while she cowers until dawn
and the dogs' whimpering starts
him awake, to lurch back across
the wet bog.   80

III

And still
the dog rose shines in the hedge.
Petals beaten wide by rain, it
sways slightly, at the tip of a
slender, tangled, arching branch   85

which, with her stick, she gathers
into us.

'The wild rose
is the only rose without thorns,'
she says, holding a wet blossom   90
for a second, in a hand knotted
as the knob of her stick.
'Whenever I see it, I remember
the Holy Mother of God and
all she suffered.'   95

Briefly
the air is strong with the smell
of that weak flower, offering
its crumbled yellow cup
and pale bleeding lips   100
fading to white

at the rim
of each bruised and heart-
shaped petal.

Glossary		
1	*Cailleach:* Irish and Scots Gaelic for an old woman, a hag
3	*harsh:* cruel, severe
6	*admonitory:* warning
8	*straggles:* comes gradually into view
9	*untilled:* not cultivated
10	*outcrop:* the part of a rock formation that is visible on the surface
12	*retinue:* group of followers
13	*give tongue:* express themselves
16–17	*stare . . . down:* look with a fixed expression at the stranger until he is forced to look away
19	*awe:* feeling of great respect mixed with fear
21	*dewlapped:* having folds of skin hanging from the neck or throat
22	*mottled:* spotted

John Montague

27	*wrought reconciliation:* brought about friendly relations
36	*loath:* unwilling, reluctant
41	*Obscurely . . . confidences:* in some vague way he was flattered that the old woman shared her private thoughts with him
43	*monologue:* a long speech made by one person during a conversation
43	*falters:* slows down
44	*rehearsing:* repeating
46	*monotonous:* boring, tedious
50	*dog rose:* delicately scented wild rose with pink or white flowers
52	*I . . . away:* I don't want to hear it
58	*cut:* bite
77	*cowers:* crouches in fear
78	*lurch:* stagger
99	*crumbled:* crushed
100–101	*pale . . . white:* the dog rose is pink at the edges and white at the centre
102	*rim:* outer edge

Guidelines

'The Wild Dog Rose' is best read in conjunction with 'Like Dolmens Round My Childhood, the Old People'. The old woman who is the subject of the former poem has much in common with the old people of the latter, who made Montague fearful in his childhood and who troubled his dreams. In both poems, people are not what they seem. The early description of the old woman as a *cailleach*, the Irish word for hag, suggests that she was widely regarded as a sinister creature, almost a witch, because of her hideous appearance, her 'great hooked nose', her cheeks 'dewlapped with dirt' and 'her mottled claws' (lines 20–22). As the poet explores her character and situation, we learn that she is in fact a lonely, suffering human being, harshly treated by circumstances.

Commentary

Contrast is at the heart of 'The Wild Dog Rose'. For example, the contrast between past and present, between the poet's childhood view of the old woman as an object of terror and his mature view of her as an unfortunate victim in need of sympathy. This sympathy is strongly evoked by the poet. Instead of cowering in terror before her, he can now greet her in friendliness. The two of them can talk easily and naturally, 'like old friends, lovers almost / sharing secrets' (lines 29 and 30). He is honoured by her willingness to share the small events of her life with him, particularly the cause of her present loneliness: her refusal as a young woman of a proposal of marriage from a man who lived ten miles away. The poet who was terrified of her in his childhood now learns that she had to confront her own terrors, above all her isolation: 'The only true madness is loneliness, / the monotonous voice in the skull / that never stops / because never heard' (lines 45–48).

The climax of the poem is the terrible story of an attempt by a drunken man to rape her one night in her cottage. The incident is presented in realistic detail and the effect is shocking. There is a touch of ambiguity in the account, as the poet tries to understand the motives of the drunken aggressor and his way of life: 'they wrestle, two creatures crazed / with loneliness, the smell of the / decaying cottage in his nostrils / like a drug' (lines 62–65).

It is important to note that the woman's terrible ordeal does not result in madness or in the destruction of her will to survive. At the heart of her account of the attempted rape and her battle for life, she recalls that she prayed to the Blessed Virgin for help. She believes that as a result of this prayer she was able to break the assailant's grip. The reference to the Blessed Virgin becomes part of the symbolic meaning of the poem and of its title. The old woman gives the clue to this when she suggests an association between the wild dog rose and the Blessed Virgin. Whenever she sees the flower, she remembers 'the Holy Mother of God and / all she suffered' (lines 94 and 95). **Her cruel history of fear, attempted rape and isolation based on superstition is transformed by the dog rose. It still shines in the hedge, reminding her of her stubborn faith in the Mother of God, which permits her to survive the monotony of her life as well as her suffering.**

Montague's comment on the central episode of the poem is worth bearing in mind. He points to a crucial distinction between the woman's interpretation of her experience and the more ambiguous way in which he, as the poet, may have intended to present it. Montague writes:

> After she is almost raped, the woman prays to the Blessed Virgin. The Blessed Virgin is symbolised for her by the Wild Dog Rose, but the end of the poem describes that as a 'weak flower'. This is her comfort. The poem doesn't say that it accepts that comfort, just that she has been able to draw strength from it as people do from whatever they can manage to believe in.

'The Wild Dog Rose' necessarily takes on a political dimension, as an implied comment on an imperial rape of a weak subject people. In 1980, when *The Rough*

Field was performed in a theatre, Montague approved of the playing of the traditional Irish patriotic tune 'Róisín Dubh' (Little Black Rose) as background music to the description of the rape. Montague remarked:

> And so, as she's describing her rape or her attempted rape, you get this lovely song of Ireland's betrayal and Ireland's loss and Ireland's wrong. And it's very very moving. Terribly moving.

Thinking about the poem

1. What happened to make the poet see the old woman as 'no longer harsh' but as 'a human being / merely, hurt by event' (lines 3 and 4)?
2. Do you think the woman's environment has influenced the young Montague's attitude to her?
3. Is there a suggestion in the poem that the woman's physical appearance caused the poet to judge her harshly? Explain your answer with reference to the poem.
4. The woman in the poem is a lonely person. Is this important? Give reasons for your answer.
5. Why is the poet honoured as the old woman tells him about the small events of her life?
6. Discuss two images from the poem that you find impressive. Give reasons for your choices.
7. Contrast the child's view of the old woman with the adult's view.
8. In your opinion, why did the old woman greet the poet 'in friendliness' (line 26)?
9. Give your impression of the old woman as she appears in the poem.
10. What does the woman's account of the attempted rape tell us about her?
11. In part II of the poem it is clear that the wild dog rose has a symbolic meaning. How is this suggested in the poem? Give your interpretation of the symbolism of the rose.
12. The Blessed Virgin plays an important part in the woman's account. Comment on this and her association with the rose.

Personal response

1. Imagine you are one of the old woman's neighbours and you are familiar with her story. Write a short account of your feelings about her.
2. You are a newspaper reporter assigned to report the old woman's story, following an interview with her in her own home. Write your report, accompanied by a suitable headline.

Find out all you can about dolmens and standing circles of stones: their appearance, construction, purpose and meaning. The information you get should help you to understand more fully some aspects of this poem by John Montague.

Like Dolmens Round My Childhood, the Old People

Like dolmens round my childhood, the old people.

Jamie MacCrystal sang to himself,
A broken song without tune, without words;
He tipped me a penny every pension day,
Fed kindly crusts to winter birds.   5
When he died, his cottage was robbed,
Mattress and money box torn and searched.
Only the corpse they didn't disturb.

Maggie Owens was surrounded by animals,
A mongrel bitch and shivering pups,   10
Even in her bedroom a she-goat cried.
She was a well of gossip defiled,
Fanged chronicler of a whole countryside;
Reputed a witch, all I could find
Was her lonely need to deride.   15

The Nialls along a mountain lane
Where heather bells bloomed, clumps of foxglove.
All were blind, with Blind Pension and Wireless,
Dead eyes serpent-flicked as one entered   *metaphor*
To shelter from a downpour of mountain rain.   20
Crickets chirped under the rocking hearthstone
Until the muddy sun shone out again.

John Montague

simile

Mary Moore lived in a crumbling gatehouse,
Famous as Pisa for its leaning gable.
Bag-apron and boots, she tramped the fields   25
Driving lean cattle from a miry stable.
A by-word for fierceness, she fell asleep
Over love stories, Red Star and Red Circle,
Dreamed of gypsy love rites, by firelight sealed.

Wild Billy Eagleson married a Catholic servant girl   30
When all his Loyal family passed on:
We danced round him shouting 'To Hell with King Billy,'
And dodged from the arc of his flailing blackthorn.
Forsaken by both creeds, he showed little concern
Until the Orange drums banged past in the summer   35
And bowler and sash aggressively shone.

Curate and doctor trudged to attend them,
Through knee-deep snow, through summer heat,
From main road to lane to broken path,
Gulping the mountain air with painful breath.   40
Sometimes they were found by neighbours,
Silent keepers of a smokeless hearth,
Suddenly cast in the mould of death.

Ancient Ireland, indeed! I was reared by her bedside,
The rune and the chant, evil eye and averted head,   45
Fomorian fierceness of family and local feud.
Gaunt figures of fear and of friendliness,
For years they trespassed on my dreams,
Until once, in a standing circle of stones,
I felt their shadows pass   50

Into that dark permanence of ancient forms.

Glossary

1	*dolmens:* tombs usually consisting of several great stone slabs supporting a flat capstone; most date from the Neolithic period (4000 to 2400 BC)
10	*mongrel bitch:* female dog of mixed breed (may also be a term of abuse directed at Maggie)
12	*She . . . defiled:* she told foul stories about others
13	*Fanged chronicler:* teller of bitter, biting stories
14	*Reputed:* having the reputation of
15	*deride:* mock other people
18	*All . . . Wireless:* they were all blind and entitled to a pension and a radio from the social welfare services
23	*gatehouse:* a house that would have been occupied by the gatekeeper or caretaker of a larger house or estate
24	*Pisa:* a reference to the leaning tower in that Italian city
24	*gable:* the upper part of a wall at the side of a building, usually shaped like a triangle to fit under the roof
25	*Bag-apron:* apron made out of an old bag or sack
26	*miry:* muddy
27	*by-word for:* perfect example of
28	*Red Star and Red Circle:* magazines featuring love stories
29	*rites:* customs, rituals
31	*Loyal family:* family that supported the political connection between Northern Ireland and Great Britain and was loyal to the British monarch
32	*King Billy:* William of Orange (1650–1702), a Dutchman who became King of England in the Protestant Revolution of 1688 and who remains a loyalist hero
33	*arc:* curve
33	*flailing:* swinging, thrashing (with a stick)
34	*Forsaken . . . creeds:* abandoned by the Catholic and the Protestant communities
35	*Orange . . . past:* bands paraded by as part of the Orange Order marching season
36	*bowler and sash:* items worn by members of the Orange Order
37	*Curate:* Catholic priest
43	*cast in the mould:* shaped into a model
45	*rune and the chant:* a rune was a song or set of words believed to have magic properties; 'chant' has a similar meaning
45	*averted:* looked or turned away

46	*Fomorian:* the Fomorians were a savage tribe of ancient settlers in Ireland
46	*feud:* long-standing dispute often involving several generations of the same families
47	*Gaunt:* very thin
48	*trespassed on:* invaded
49	*standing circle:* in ancient Ireland, stone circles were associated with the worship of the sun
50–51	*I . . . forms:* the ancient forms that haunted him have passed away into mythology

Guidelines

This poem, written in 1959, deals with some of the more unusual people who inhabited the world of Montague's childhood. Like many of Montague's poems, this one features fully human individuals, scarred by misery and suffering but also possessing faith and enjoying life. The main characters in the poem are isolated, lonely people. For the young Montague, their main significance was that they haunted his childhood dreams, conjuring up sinister and grotesque images associated with ancient pagan customs. In early adult life, when childhood gave way to manhood, the dark dreams no longer troubled him. He traces his liberation from their fearful grip to a single experience. Standing as a young man in a circle of stones, he felt the terrible shadow cast by the old people pass away and the nightmare transformed into myth.

Commentary

The dolmens mentioned in the title and in the first line of the poem have a symbolic meaning. **By imagining the old people as dolmens, the poet is suggesting why Jamie MacCrystal, Maggie Owens and the others dominated his life and troubled his dreams. He was imprisoned by their influence in much the same way as the body of an ancient inhabitant of Ireland was buried beneath a dolmen.** There is a further dimension to the comparison between dolmens and old people. To the poet's eye, the human figures are scattered around the landscape like figures of stone.

The poem, however, is one of liberation as well as of imprisonment. This becomes clear in the final stanza. Just as the dolmens represent the child's captivity, the standing circle of stones is associated with his release from the fearful dreams inspired by the old people. The final stanza tells us that his escape from the shadow cast on his young life by his elderly neighbours coincides with his entry into manhood. The act of making the old people present in his poetry serves a purpose similar to exorcism. They become external to his mind and find their permanence in stone.

To the child's imagination, the characters of the poem are forbidding, abnormal and sometimes grotesque. Jamie MacCrystal's song without tune and without words is sung to himself. Maggie Owens is thought to be a witch and keeps a she-goat in her bedroom. The Nialls are all blind. Mary Moore is remarkable for her fierceness. Billy Eagleson is wild and wields a flailing blackthorn. **These primitive people carry on some of the pagan traditions of ancient Ireland.**

There is, however, more to them than this. They may be 'Gaunt figures of fear' (line 47), but **they also appeal to the poet's imagination as figures of friendliness.** In spite of their forbidding appearance, the poet is able to feel sympathy for them and to understand the motives behind their behaviour. Jamie MacCrystal is a poor man but still gives a penny to the young Montague every pension day and feeds hungry winter birds. Maggie Owens is a notorious gossip but the poet feels able to explain this by suggesting that frustration and loneliness cause her to speak ill of her neighbours. We find a similar attitude in 'The Wild Dog Rose', where the woman described as a hag is really an ordinary human being who has suffered much in her isolation.

Thinking about the poem

1. In the title and in the first line, the poet relates the old people to dolmens. What is the significance of this relationship?
2. The old people mentioned in the poem have a few things in common. Mention as many of these as you can.
3. What is the poet's attitude to the people he is describing. Explain your answer by referring to words or phrases from the poem.
4. Which of the people, in your opinion, had (a) the happiest life and (b) the saddest life. Refer to the poem for examples.
5. Maggie Owens is not the woman she seems. Explain this idea.
6. The old people are described as 'Silent keepers of a smokeless hearth / Suddenly cast in the mould of death' (lines 42 and 43). What does this mean? Has 'mould' more than one meaning in this context?
7. Is the poem sad, or comic, or both? Explain.
8. Choose your favourite character from the poem. Give reasons for your choice.
9. Why has Billy Eagleson been 'Forsaken by both creeds' (line 34)? What effect do the 'Orange drums' (line 35) have on him?
10. What does the poet mean when he claims that he was 'reared' by the 'bedside' of 'Ancient Ireland' (line 44)? Develop your answer by referring to the poem.

11 In your opinion, why does the poet describe his neighbours as 'Gaunt figures of fear and of friendliness' (line 47)?

12 How did the old people trespass on the poet's dreams? How did he free himself from the influence of these dreams?

Personal response

1 Imagine you are the poet as a child. Compose a piece describing your neighbours and your feelings about them.

2 Based on the details provided in the poem, write a piece about the environment in which the poet grew up.

3 Compose a piece entitled 'All the lonely people'.

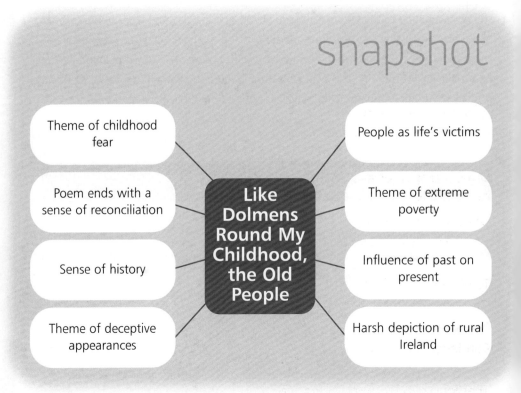

snapshot

Theme of childhood fear

Poem ends with a sense of reconciliation

Sense of history

Theme of deceptive appearances

Like Dolmens Round My Childhood, the Old People

People as life's victims

Theme of extreme poverty

Influence of past on present

Harsh depiction of rural Ireland

Before you read 'A Welcoming Party'

John Montague's 'A Welcoming Party' on page 259 records the brutality meted out to certain kinds of people in wartime concentration camps. Find out what kinds of people suffered and died in these camps, and why.

A Welcoming Party

Wie war das möglich?

That final newsreel of the war:
A welcoming party of almost shades
Met us at the cinema door
Clicking what remained of their heels.

From nests of bodies like hatching eggs   5
Flickered insectlike hands and legs
And rose in ululation, terrible, shy;
Children conjugating the verb 'to die'.

One clamoured mutely of love
From one mouth like a burnt glove;   10
Others upheld hands bleak as begging bowls
Claiming the small change of our souls.

Some smiled at us as protectors.
Can these bones live?
Our parochial brand of innocence   15
Was all we had to give.

To be always at the periphery of incident
Gave my childhood its Irish dimension;
Yet doves of mercy, as doves of air,
Can falter here as anywhere.   20

That long dead Sunday in Armagh
I learned one meaning of total war
And went home to my Christian school
To kick a football through the air.

Glossary	
Wie war das möglich? How could this happen?	
1	*newsreel:* type of news programme shown in cinemas before television became popular
1	*the war:* Second World War (1939–45); the final newsreel shows the discovery of death camps by Allied forces in 1945
2	*shades:* ghostly figures; the skeletal figures shown on the screen are little more than ghosts
4	*Clicking . . . heels:* in the context of a German camp, clicking the heels may be interpreted as a token of respect on the part of the inmates for their liberators. The heels of the welcoming party, however, have been worn down by starvation so that they can only click what is left. Notice the cruel irony of the title.
5	*nests of bodies:* the bodies of the dead and dying were piled in heaps
6	*Flickered . . . legs:* the poet imagines that the heaps of bodies are newly hatched eggs and that the twitching arms and legs of the camp victims are like the chicks emerging from the breaking shells
7	*ululation:* loud cries of sorrow
8	*conjugating:* listing the various forms of [death]
9	*One . . . love:* the silent attempt of the child to express love spoke more loudly and was more appealing than if the child had been able to shout
11–12	*Others . . . souls:* other victims held up their skinny hands as if they were begging for the small amount of pity that we could offer them
13–16	*Some . . . give:* the surviving victims in the newsreel could expect nothing from the audience in the cinema except an innocent response based on a lack of understanding
17–18	*To . . . dimension:* Irish children did not experience the horrors of the Second World War. Their only experience of it was based on newsreel films. The Irish dimension to the poet's wartime childhood was his ignorance of the realities of the conflict
17	*at . . . incident:* not directly involved in the war
19	*doves of mercy:* people with kind feelings and intentions
19	*doves of air:* doves that fly
21	*long dead Sunday:* Sunday long ago. Given the nature of the film, is there a pun on 'dead'?
22	*total war:* during the Second World War innocent civilians on both sides suffered as much as soldiers

In this poem Montague recalls a visit he made to a cinema with fellow-students when he was a pupil at St Patrick's College, Armagh. He was about sixteen when the newsreel described in the poem was shown. At the end of the war, cinemas throughout the Western world showed similar newsreels depicting the horrors of German concentration camps. The question raised in German following the title of the poem is the kind of one that a young audience might ask: **How could a great people like the Germans have descended to the barbarities depicted in the newsreel?**

Commentary

The poem combines description with reflection on what the details shown in the newsreel might have meant to a boy who had been insulated from the brutality of the Second World War. Earlier newsreels had shown the progress of the war, the victorious and defeated armies, navies and air forces, the bombed cities and the millions of fleeing refugees. **The final newsreel of the war shows the ultimate result of the combat: innocent civilians are degraded to a sub-human condition, most of them facing death from starvation and neglect.** Montague presents the realities of the death-camps as depicted in the newsreel with frank realism in stanzas 2 and 3.

The poet reflects on the meaning of what his younger self experienced on 'That long dead Sunday in Armagh' (line 21). The troubling question raised in the final three stanzas concerns the inability of the young audience to do anything for the dying children in the newsreel. The latter hold their hands out and plead for help. In response, all that the audience can offer is sympathy. The poem gives an insight into the position taken by most Irish people during the Second World War. The southern Irish state remained neutral. Participation in the war remained optional for citizens of Northern Ireland. **The poem reflects the detachment of people like the young Montague**: 'To be always at the periphery of incident / Gave my childhood its Irish dimension' (lines 17 and 18). The final stanza of the poem offers an ironic reflection on the boy's experience. On the playing-field of his 'Christian school' (line 23) he enjoys the luxury of a game of football while his contemporaries in Europe are raising 'insectlike hands and legs' (line 6), begging for survival.

John Montague

Thinking about the poem

1 Comment on the poet's choice of 'A Welcoming Party' as his title.

2 In the first stanza the poet conveys a sinister and disturbing atmosphere. Explain how he does this.

3 Why are the hands and legs described as 'insectlike' (line 6)?

4 What do the animal images in stanza 2 suggest?

5 What was the response of the cinema audience to what was shown on the screen?

6 How does the poet suggest that the cinema audience might have been as helpless as the victims?

7 Why did the victims suffer the fate described in the poem?

8 In the fifth stanza the poet talks about the 'Irish dimension' (line 18) of his childhood. Explain this reference. What has the 'Irish dimension' to do with the subject matter of the poem?

9 What does the poet mean when he is talking about being 'at the periphery of incident' (line 17)?

10 Why is the epigraph to the poem in German?

11 Does the final stanza convey the idea that what he had seen on the cinema screen did not affect the young Montague very deeply? Explain your answer.

12 Why might the poet choose to mention going back to his 'Christian school' (line 23)? How would you describe the tone of the final stanza?

Personal response

1 The question asked as an introduction to the poem – *Wie war das möglich?* (How could this happen?) – refers to the scenes relayed in the newsreel and described by the poet. Write a piece in which you reflect on this question.

2 'Man's inhumanity to man makes countless thousand mourn' (Robert Burns). Consider this as an appropriate comment on the poem.

Exam-Style Questions

1 Select two poems by Montague that deal with similar themes and issues. Discuss the poet's treatment of his subject matter in each case. Comment on any contrasts in approach between the two poems.

2 Name your favourite Montague poem. Give an account of the poem, its theme(s), language and imagery, indicating the qualities you most admire.

3   Do you find that Montague has a sad outlook on life? Base your answer on reference to a selection of his poems.

4   Montague's poems are notable for their descriptive qualities. Discuss two poems that you find outstanding in this respect.

5   Discuss Montague's treatment of women in his poetry. Support the points you make with reference to the poems on your course.

6   Many of Montague's poems deal with the past. Discuss one of the poems in light of this comment and explain why the past means so much to him.

7   Personal themes play a large part in Montague's poetry. Consider the autobiographical element in two of his poems.

8   Montague's poems give us a good picture of the kind of man who wrote them. Based on your reading of the poems you have studied, give your impression of the poet.

9   Discuss the theme of exile in the poetry of Montague.

10 In Montague's poetry there are numerous victims (a) of society, (b) of other people and (c) of circumstance. Using these headings, write an essay on Montague's victims.

11 You are asked to give a talk on Montague's poetry. What would you say?

12 Montague's poetry displays an understanding of the problems people have to face in their daily lives and in their relationships. Explore this idea.

13 Montague's poems move easily between ancient and modern settings. Discuss this aspect of his work using appropriate quotations.

14 Consider Montague as a nature poet.

15 Write an essay on Montague's exploration of the theme of love.

16 'Montague is an Irish poet, but much more than that.' Discuss this statement.

17 The cruelties of life loom large in Montague's poetry. Examine the poet's treatment of these.

18 What does Montague's poetry have to offer the young, modern reader? Your answer should refer to the poems by Montague on your course, and quote from them where necessary.

19 Discuss Montague's treatment of (a) the father–son relationship and (b) the mother–son relationship. In your discussion you should make detailed reference to poems by Montague on your course, and quote where necessary.

20 'Although Montague's poetry deals mainly with the sadder aspects of life, it also sounds many notes of hope.' Examine this verdict, supporting your answer with quotation from, and reference to, relevant poems by Montague on your course.

Sample essay

In his poetry Montague deals with many of the sad aspects of life. Discuss this comment with reference to some of the poems on your course.

The sad aspects of life dealt with in Montague's poetry include exile, separation, cruelty, suffering and disappointment. These themes are prominent because they arise naturally from the autobiographical nature of Montague's poetry in general, and from the fact that his experience of life was marked by many of the things he wrote about. Sometimes Montague himself was the victim of life's cruelties; at other times his parents were the victims, or he observed the suffering inflicted by powerful people on innocent victims.

[Introduction responds to the question and sets out the areas to be discussed in the remainder of the essay]

The theme of the sad aspects of life is prominent in the two poems Montague wrote about his parents: 'The Cage' and 'The Locket'. The first of these is about his father. The sad tone of the poem is set in the first two lines: 'My father, the least happy man I have known'. The sadness of 'The Cage' is derived from the circumstances of his father's life as an exile in New York. The poem conveys the sense that he is trapped like an animal in an underground cage, denied the light of day, 'his face', as Montague puts it, 'retained the pallor of those who work underground'. The poem's reference to 'the lost years in Brooklyn' is appropriate. When, like some prisoner, he is daily 'released from his grille', he gets no relief from his unhappiness except by drinking 'neat whiskey' and thus trying to ease his sad condition through drunken forgetfulness: the 'only element' he feels 'at home' in is 'brute oblivion'.

The return of Montague's father to Ireland after his long exile does not bring much relief. Father and son have been separated so long that they have little in common. They do not 'smile in the shared complicity of a dream'. They are soon fated to separate, 'for when weary Odysseus returns Telemachus should leave'. When the father (Odysseus) comes home from New York, the son (Telemachus) leaves home for that city. These sad circumstances are compounded in the final stanza, when the son descends into the New York underground and has visions of his father's 'bald head behind the bars of the small booth'.

[First poem used to comment on personal sadness; quotations support points made]

In 'The Locket' the sad themes of exile and separation are also prominent. This time, the victims are the poet and his mother. Even the poet's arrival in the world has proved a source of misery to both his mother and himself, when it should have been a source of joy. His mother liked to remind him that, for her, his was 'the worst birth in the annals of Brooklyn'. For him, because of these reminders, she became a 'fertile source of guilt and pain'. She also made him feel guilty because he was a boy when she would have preferred a girl. The result was a sad one. His mother never nursed him, and gave him away to relatives to be reared.

To add to his misery, and despite her rejection of him, he retained an affection for her, cycling down to their home to win her attention, 'to court' her 'like a young man', but all in vain: 'don't come again, you say, roughly, I start to get fond of you, John'. There is a sad twist in the final stanza, when the poet reveals that his mother always wore a locket around her neck 'with an old picture in it, of a child in Brooklyn'. This may be a 'mysterious blessing', but the sad aspect is that while his mother lived he never knew the significance of the locket.

[Second poem used to further illustrate sadness at the personal level]

Another poem which deals with the sadness arising from human relationships is 'The Wild Dog Rose'. The subject here is the poet's encounter with the 'Cailleach', or hag, 'that terrible figure who haunted my childhood'. The sad aspect of his childhood attitude to this woman is his misunderstanding of her real nature, his understandable failure to see that she was not harsh or terrible, but 'a human being merely, hurt by event'. At the heart of the poem is a profoundly and disturbingly sad episode in which the old woman tells him 'a story so terrible that I try to push it away, my bones melting'. This episode concerns a brutal sexual assault on her by a drunken man, and may be said to represent the depressing world in which many of Montague's characters live out their sad lives. Another poem 'Like Dolmens Round My Childhood, the Old People' features a number of these characters: Jamie MacCrystal, the poor, kind old man whose cottage is robbed when he dies; the Nialls, all of whom are blind and live in misery; Mary Moore who lives in a crumbling house and drives 'lean cattle from a miry stable'; and others.

[Two more poems introduced and used to comment on sadness at the community level]

The Montague poem that conveys the ultimate in human sorrow and the suffering of the innocent is 'A Welcoming Party', dealing with the poet's youthful experience of a post-war newsreel depicting the fate of Jewish victims of German concentration camps. Here we have a horrifying description of what people with power can do to destroy other people's lives and degrade men, women and children to the level of animals:

From nests of bodies like hatching eggs

Flickered insectlike hands and legs

And rose in ululation, terrible shy;

Children conjugating the verb 'to die'.

[Fifth poem used to broaden the focus and consider sadness at the international level]

Montague's poetry also looks at what human beings can do to animals. 'Killing the Pig' is sad because Montague presents the slaughter of a pig in a way in which readers' feelings are bound to become engaged and emotions aroused. The pigs are not presented as passive victims going to the slaughter. Instead, 'they know the hour has come and they want none of it'. Their scream is a 'high pitched final effort' that no other sound can match; it is 'piercing and absolute', but 'high heaven ignores it'. In this way we get the impression that the destiny of the pig at the hands of humans is a pitiless one. This pig's death-scream is muted when an expert plants 'a solid thump of a mallet flat between the ears' and a knife swiftly 'seeks the throat'. The cruelty of the process is intensified when we remember that before the pig is dragged out to be killed, an iron hook has been sunk into the roof of his mouth. For those who perform the killing operation, it is simply part of a day's work, but for the poet, 'the walls of the farmyard still hold that scream'.

[Sixth poem used to discuss a further aspect of the question]

The emphasis in all these poems is on the sadness of life and on the part played by human beings in causing this sadness, whether to themselves, to other people, or to animals.

[Brief conclusion brings together the areas explored in the essay]

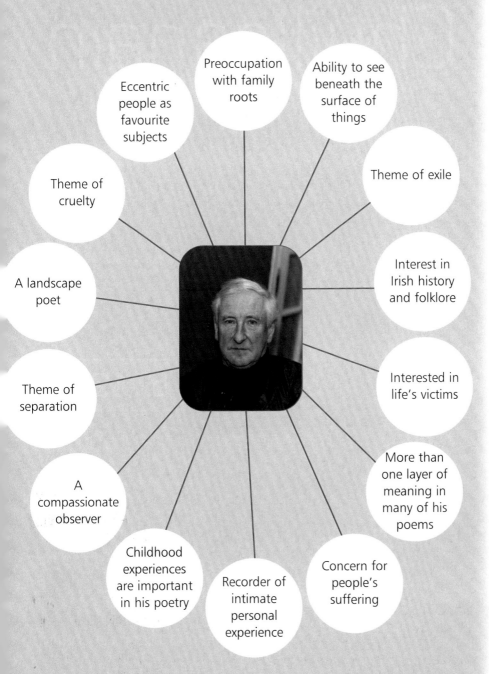

Eccentric people as favourite subjects

Preoccupation with family roots

Ability to see beneath the surface of things

Theme of cruelty

Theme of exile

A landscape poet

Interest in Irish history and folklore

Theme of separation

Interested in life's victims

A compassionate observer

More than one layer of meaning in many of his poems

Childhood experiences are important in his poetry

Recorder of intimate personal experience

Concern for people's suffering

John Montague

Eiléan Ní Chuilleanáin

b. 1942

Biography

Eiléan Ní Chuilleanáin was born in Cork in 1942. She was one of three children born to Cormac Ó'Cuilleanáin, a Professor of Irish Literature in University College Cork, and Eilís Dillon, a classic children's author. In one interview Ní Chuilleanáin said that she became a poet because her mother wrote prose and she thought that poetry was more difficult. Folklore is important in her poetry and this may be attributed to the folkloric elements in her mother's fiction and her father's vast collection of folklore.

Family life

Ní Chuilleanáin grew up in a strongly republican household. Her father fought in the War of Independence and was captured during the Civil War. Her great uncle Joseph Mary Plunkett was one of the seven signatories of the Proclamation of the Irish Republic. He was executed at the end of the 1916 Easter Rising in Kilmainham Gaol. His younger brothers were imprisoned and his parents were deported to England. These events inspired Ní Chuilleanáin with a great sense of national pride. She describes herself as a 'Gaelic-speaking female papist whose direct and indirect ancestors, men and women, on both sides, were committed to detaching Ireland from the British Empire.' They were a bilingual family.

Music is important in her family life, her mother played the cello and her sister Máire was a violinist with the London Philharmonic Orchestra. Her son, Niall, is also a keen musician. Ní Chuilleanáin's love of music is reflected in her poetry, not only as subject matter but also in its texture and form.

She spent much of her childhood on the campus of UCC (her mother ran the university nursery) and this appears to have instilled in her an appreciation for architecture. In many of the poems that we will be looking at we will see how she uses architecture for its imagistic and metaphorical possibilities.

Her father had six unmarried sisters – three of whom were nuns, two joined a French order and the third was a Sister of Nazareth. Ní Chuilleanáin has remarked that her aunts who went to live in convents had far more interesting lives than the ones who stayed at home. We can see the influence of their religious life through the images of buildings, churches, convents and monasteries in her poetry. Ní Chuilleanáin's interest in some of these buildings may have stemmed from her early visits to European convents with her father.

Education and career

Ní Chuilleanáin was educated in the Ursuline Convent in Cork, she did her undergraduate degree in UCC where she was awarded a Bachelor of Arts in 1962 and a Master of Arts in 1964. She also attended Oxford and received a Bachelor of Literature (1968) in Elizabethan prose, concentrating on the field of religious writing. She was appointed to a junior lectureship in English in Trinity College Dublin in 1966, where she later became an Associate Professor of English and Head of the Department. She specialises in the literature of the English Reformation and European Renaissance.

As a young woman in Dublin in the 1960s, she shared her interest in poetry with some like-minded young poets, including Pearse Hutchinson, Michael Hartnett and MacDara Woods. In 1966 she won the Irish Times Poetry Award for her poem 'Ars Poetica'. Encouraged by this success, she published her first poetry collection, *Acts and Monuments*, in 1972. This collection won the prestigious Patrick Kavanagh Poetry Award.

In 1975 she co-founded the literary magazine *Cyphers* (named after her cat). Initially it focused on publishing Irish and international poetry but later began to feature criticism and fiction. One of her co-founders was MacDara Woods, whom she married three years later in 1978. They both continue to edit the magazine and it has become the most distinguished literary magazine in Ireland.

Ní Chuilleanáin continued to receive critical acclaim for her poetry, she published her second collection in 1975, *Site of Ambush*, which received the Irish Publishers Award. She published four more books of poetry and in 1992 she won the Lawrence O'Shaughnessy Prize for poetry awarded by the Irish American Cultural Institute, which named her 'among the very best poets of her generation'. Her most recent publications are *The Girl Who Married the Reindeer* (2001) and *The Sun-Fish* (2009). The latter was nominated for the T. S. Eliot Award and won the 2010 International Griffin Poetry Prize. She received $65,000 and international recognition of her poetry. Despite winning many awards, Ní Chuilleanáin does not believe that poetry should be about winning prizes and has remarked that she was initially depressed about the T. S. Eliot nomination, stating that 'there are good poets who never get nominated for things'.

She is regarded as one of Ireland's most accomplished contemporary poets. Her poetry can be opaque and enigmatic, mysterious and indirect, yet with time and consideration it unravels, and the mystery, while never fully absent, engages us and draws us in to a folkloric world that collapses the distance between the past and the present. She lovingly records nature and transforms it with a powerful imagination. She contrasts stillness and motion, life and death and always with an air of secrecy.

According to one critic, 'Eiléan Ní Chuilleanáin does many expert things in her poems but does them so quietly that often she remains unheard except by those who have returned many times to listen.'

As readers of her poetry we need to listen, to give ourselves up to each poem's voice and allow ourselves to be led to strange and mystical places.

Ní Chuilleanáin is also a gifted translator. She knows Italian, French, Latin, Romanian and Irish. She has translated Nuala Ní Dhomhnaill from Irish, Michele Ranchetti from Italian and Ileana Melancioiu from Romanian.

Social and cultural context

Interest in the English Renaissance

When in Oxford Ní Chuilleanáin spent a lot of time reading religious sermons and wrote her thesis on Thomas Nashe. Nashe was a famous Elizabethan satirist. He satirised contemporary literature and was known for writing scathing pamphlets criticising writers who plagiarised classical works. In Elizabethan England there was no such thing as author's copyright, so when you sold your work to a publisher, the publisher kept all the profits (even if it was a bestseller). Inevitably writers were not wealthy; the lucky ones had patrons who paid the writer to dedicate the book to them. When they began *Cyphers* – despite having very little funds – the co-founders agreed that every writer whose work they published would receive some payment, however little.

Ní Chuilleanáin admires the poetry of the English Renaissance. These poets provided different ways of using imagery and language. Interestingly, she has remarked that Irish, Latin, French and Italian poetry offer her 'alternate rhythms and perspectives'. As a young girl she translated 'pages and pages of French novels into English, totally preoccupied by prose style and her choice of words'.

Richard Crashaw

Richard Crashaw was part of the seventeenth-century group of Metaphysical poets. It is said that 'there is no religious poetry in English so full at once of gross and awkward images and imaginative touches of the most ethereal beauty'. This can be seen in his poem 'Hymn to the Name and Honour of the Admirable Saint Teresa', which has phrases such as 'the milky soul of a soft child'. In his poetry he uses images and phrases that would appear incongruous and unseemly to excess. His influence can be seen in some of Ní Chuilleanáin's peculiar phrasing and strange imagery. For example, in 'The Second Voyage' she describes the waves as follows: 'The ruffled foreheads of the waves crocodiling and mincing past'. Here and in the 'scribbles' of seaweed we can see her powerful imagination at work.

The historical sense

Ní Chuilleanáin acknowledges Constantine Cavafy as having played a special role in the formation of her work. Cavafy was a renowned Greek poet who was instrumental in the revival and recognition of Greek poetry. He wrote about historical figures real or imaginary who played a role in Greek history. He had an immense knowledge of history, as is clear from his poetry. In 1911 he wrote a poem called 'Ithaca', which gives an account of Odysseus's return journey home. In 'Kilcash' we can see a similar determination to revive and recognise Irish poetry, and in 'The Second Voyage' Ní Chuilleanáin also uses the figure of Odysseus and explores his psychological journey.

Many of her poems invoke historical figures (such as Odysseus, Mary Magdalene, Oliver Cromwell and Lady Iveagh) and play around with the concept of the past and the present. For example, in 'Lucina Schynning in Silence of the Nicht' we are transported from a 'ruin by a sour candle' to a chapel floor in post-Cromwellian Ireland. This may be what T. S. Eliot called 'the historical sense'. For Eliot, this sense 'involves a perception not only of the pastness of past, but of its presence'. It requires the poet to write about the present, but with a parallel feeling for the past, and in so doing the poet creates 'a simultaneous order'. We will see this 'simultaneous order' in many of the poems on this course, including 'Lucina Schynning in Silence of the Nicht', 'Fireman's Lift', 'Following', 'Translation', 'The Bend in the Road' and 'On Lacking the Killer Instinct'.

W. B. Yeats

William Butler Yeats also had a great impact on Ní Chuilleanáin, not only for his symbolic poetry but also for his monumental contribution to the Irish Literary Revival. This literary movement was associated with the revival of interest in Ireland's Gaelic heritage and the growth of Irish nationalism from the mid-nineteenth century. Both poets make strong use of symbols: usually something physical that is both itself and representative of something else, something immaterial with timeless qualities.

Yeats draws heavily on folklore and Irish myth in his writing and even with the limited selection of Ní Chuilleanáin's poetry on the course we will see how he may have influenced her poetic writing. In 1972 she organised an exhibition called 'Irish Poetry Now', which represented poetry since the death of Yeats. While Yeats experimented with free verse, he was a master of the traditional form. Interestingly, Ní Chuilleanáin distances herself from this form of writing.

Ní Chuilleanáin also admires the work of her Irish contemporary Medbh McGuckian, stating that her poetry is 'authentically mysterious in the way a poet has a right to be, revealing with deliberation what she chooses and convincing us that the mystery of the poem corresponds to a mystery in human existence' (*Cyphers*, Summer 1981).

Other comments Ní Chuilleanáin made on some poetry in Northern Ireland, 'Drawing Lines' (*Cyphers*, Spring 1979), help us to better understand her own poetry. She affirms that when a poem succeeds it 'creates its own meagre, mysterious context, its present moment in which it exists fully'; and that 'To think about what a poem is you need to consider the nature of the poet's self which in turn must be part of the content'. Ní Chuilleanáin sees the intentional mystery in her poems as her 'right' to include and that as a poet she can create her unique vision of the world in whatever way she chooses.

Eiléan Ní Chuilleanáin

Timeline

1942	Born in Cork
1962	Graduates with a Bachelor of Arts degree from UCC
1964	Graduates with a Master of Arts degree from UCC
1966	Becomes a junior lecturer in English in Trinity College, Dublin
1966	Wins the Irish Times Poetry Award for 'Ars Poetica'
1968	Receives a Bachelor of Literature degree from Oxford University
1972	Publishes her first book of poetry, *Arts and Monuments*, and wins the Patrick Kavanagh Poetry Award
1975	Co-founds the literary magazine *Cyphers* and publishes her second collection, *Site of Ambush*, which received the Irish Publishers Award
1977	Publishes *The Second Voyage*
1978	Marries the poet MacDara Woods
1981	Publishes *The Rose Geranium*
1983	Her son Niall is born
1989	Publishes *The Magdalene Sermon*, which was shortlisted for the Irish Times/Aer Lingus Award
1990	Her sister Maíre dies
1992	Wins the prestigious O'Shaughnessy Poetry Award from the Irish American Cultural Institute
1994	Publishes *The Brazen Serpent*. Her mother dies
2001	Publishes *The Girl Who Married the Reindeer*
2007	Was the subject of a full issue of *Irish University Review*
2008	Publishes *Selected Poems*
2009	Publishes *The Sun-Fish*, which was shortlisted for both the T. S. Eliot Prize and Poetry Now Award
2010	Wins the International Griffin Poetry Prize for *The Sun-Fish*

Before reading 'Lucina Schynning in Silence of the Nicht' try to recall a time in your life when you needed to escape from something. Describe the place where you went and the relief that you got from going there.

Lucina Schynning in Silence of the Nicht

Moon shining in silence of the night
The heaven being all full of stars
I was reading my book in a ruin
By a sour candle, without roast meat or music
Strong drink or a shield from the air   5
Blowing in the crazed window, and I felt
Moonlight on my head, clear after three days' rain.

I washed in cold water; it was orange, channelled down bogs
Dipped between cresses.
The bats flew through my room where I slept safely.   10
Sheep stared at me when I woke.

Behind me the waves of darkness lay, the plague
Of mice, plague of beetles
Crawling out of the spines of books,
Plague shadowing pale faces with clay   15
The disease of the moon gone astray.

In the desert I relaxed, amazed
As the mosaic beasts on the chapel floor
When Cromwell had departed, and they saw
The sky growing through the hole in the roof.   20

Eiléan Ní Chuilleanáin

Sheepdogs embraced me; the grasshopper
Returned with lark and bee.
I looked down between the hedges of high thorn and saw
The hare, absorbed, sitting still
In the middle of the track; I heard   25
Again the chirp of the stream running.

Glossary

title	*Lucina . . . Nicht:* alludes to the opening line of William Dunbar's poem 'The Birth of Antichrist' (written in the early sixteenth century), where the speaker is dreaming of a terrible fight between good and evil. Fortune, the persona of the poem, offers a vision of the struggle between the forces of God and the devil. Dunbar's poem opens with the shining moon and the silence of the night. The moon is referred to as Lucina, the pagan goddess of childbirth, often associated with witchcraft and the occult. She is deemed a suitable guardian spirit to give birth to the Antichrist
6	*crazed:* wildly insane or excited; also a network of fine cracks produced on a surface
9	*cresses:* any of several edible plants with sharp-tasting leaves
18	*mosaic:* image made out of small pieces of coloured glass, stone, tile, etc.
19	*Cromwell:* Oliver Cromwell (1599–1658) was an English general and politician who led a ruthless and brutal military campaign to reconquer Ireland for the English Parliament

Guidelines

This poem is in Ní Chuilleanáin's first collection, *Acts and Monuments*, which was awarded the prestigious Patrick Kavanagh Poetry Award. She was twenty-six when she wrote it, her father was very ill in hospital and things were getting on top of her. Her cousin had a cottage in the hills and Ní Chuilleanáin visited it on her own to escape. She went there to calm down, to relax and to try to come to terms with what she was experiencing. She was reading William Dunbar's poetry at this time.

Commentary

The poem is a dramatic monologue of a woman re-emerging after a trauma. Ní Chuilleanáin notes that her female characters are often isolated and in motion, doing something that theoretically might be considered dangerous. They are not passive and they very often act on their own, moving beyond stereotypes. The speaker in this poem is a female, on her own, presenting a different response to the vicissitudes of fortune.

This poem can be read in many ways depending on what the reader brings to the poem and what it stirs in them. It could be a response to where Ní Chuilleanáin was at the time of writing it. It may be read as a reflection on the restorative power of nature or the resilience of women in the face of adversity. Or it could be read as one woman's re-emergence into a post-Cromwellian Ireland. It is up to each reader to decide which interpretation makes most sense, all are equally valid.

Stanza 1

This poem is set in 'a ruin' (line 3). Ní Chuilleanáin went there for three days when her father was very ill. When she arrived there were holes in the roof, there were no supplies, there was a candle and not much else. However, it was there that she began to come to terms with her personal situation.

It may also have reminded her of what post-Cromwellian Ireland may have been like. In 1649 Cromwell landed in Ireland in response to the Irish Confederate Wars. Cromwell's forces, known as the New Model Army, defeated the Confederate and Royalist coalition and occupied the country. Cromwell was excessively cruel and the impact of the war was indisputably severe. Known among the Irish as the Antichrist, he butchered countless Irish men, women and children. However, in stark contrast to that violent time, there is a stillness and tranquillity about the figure in this poem. She is sitting under the silent moonlit sky, peacefully reading by candlelight. She does not have 'roast meat or music / Strong drink or a shield from the air' (lines 4 and 5), but her head is 'clear' (line 7) after a three-day deluge of rain.

The 'three days' rain' (line 7) may represent the combatant Cromwell, spreading his wave of darkness and destruction as he crosses the country, razing the land and crushing the spirit of the Irish. Or it may represent the deluge of emotion and confusion the poet felt during her father's illness.

Stanza 2

A wash 'in cold water' (line 8) seems to have had a cleansing and redemptive effect on the poet. She is emerging from her sleep and encounters nature anew: 'bats flew through my room' (line 10), 'Sheep stared at me when I woke' (line 11).

Stanza 3

She remains still and leaves the darkness of the deluge behind her: 'Behind me the waves of darkness lay' (line 12). She rejects the temptation to challenge and delve into whatever has happened before. She does not journey but finds herself in a pure space, at one with nature. She has woken up. In this stillness she relaxes and bathes in moonlit channels.

The listing of the plagues in the third stanza – of mice, beetles and faces – reminds us of the plagues of Egypt. She states that these are behind her. 'The disease of the moon gone astray' (line 16) could be a reference to the madness that seemed to have taken over a once peaceful place, or the loss of control she may have felt on foot of her father's illness.

Stanza 4

In the fourth stanza we see the poet identifying with the 'mosaic beasts on the chapel floor' (line 18) that outlasted the warrior. Their chapel may have been destroyed but they have survived, like the poet in the 'ruin', to see the 'sky growing through the hole in the roof' (line 20). This is a sight they never would have seen if the chapel had remained intact. Perhaps the still and unwavering power of nature is something that the poet may have been blind to before her awakening.

Stanza 5

The fifth stanza describes the kinship that the poet shares with the animals, 'Sheepdogs embraced me' (line 21), and the wildlife. The hare shares her stillness; both are 'absorbed' (line 24) until their trance is broken by the first sound of the poem: 'the chirp of the stream running' (line 26). The movement of a delicate stream is a beautiful image; she is hearing it 'again' (line 26). It never disappeared but perhaps her ability to hear its eternal flow and life wavered for a while.

In this poem the poet seems to gain entry into a world that she might have missed. She is surrounded by animal life and the open sky and becomes an extension of animate and inanimate nature.

Tone and language of the poem

The poem has a peaceful, serene and otherworldly tone. This is in contrast to its themes of survival, resilience, nature, stillness and war.

The language used is concrete, yet strange images are created. The imagery is vivid and dark but ultimately hopeful. It makes use of various symbols, including water, the night sky, the hare and books.

Thinking about the poem

1   In your opinion, why has Ní Chuilleanáin chosen this particular title?
2   In a couple of sentences, write the story of the poem.
3   The first two lines of the poem are very peaceful and serene. How does the poet achieve this?

4   The poet has said that she needed to escape from her father's illness. Is there any
    evidence in the poem to suggest this?

5   Ní Chuilleanáin often refers to windows and doors as gateways into other worlds.
    In this poem she writes 'without . . . a shield from the air / blowing in the crazed
    window' (lines 4–6). Comment on the use of the word 'crazed' in this line.

6   The speaker identifies herself with the 'mosaic beasts on the chapel floor' (line
    18). Comment on the possible reasons why she does this.

7   The poet uses concrete language to create strange and unusual images. Identify
    three examples of this and try to explain them.

8   How would you describe the speaker in the poem?

    ● She is confused and afraid.

    ● She is deeply sad and lonely.

    ● She is independent and contemplative.

    ● She is peaceful and relaxed.

    Explain your choice.

9   Based on your reading and study of the poem, which of these statements best
    describe it?

    ● It is a poem about the devastation of war.

    ● It is a poem about re-emergence and hope.

    ● It is a poem about being at one with nature.

    ● It is a poem about coming to terms with life.

    Explain your choice.

10 Throughout the poem the poet uses the pronoun 'I' and the possessive pronoun
    'my'. What is the effect of this for us as readers?

11 Water is a reoccurring symbol in Ní Chuilleanáin's poetry and it represents many
    different things. Identify where she refers to water in this poem and what you
    think it represents.

Personal response

1   In pairs, take turns to read the poem aloud. As you listen, note down
    your favourite phrases, words, sounds or images. Explain to your
    partner why these stood out for you.

2   Create an audio-visual aid to accompany the poem. It must include images (still
    or otherwise) and music. It cannot be any longer than two minutes. You must
    be prepared to answer questions on your production afterwards.

3   You are the speaker in the poem, write a diary account about your emergence
    from the ruin.

4   Imagine that you are the antithesis of the figure in the poem, write a short poem
    describing your response to the devastation around you.

Before reading 'The Second Voyage' ask yourself this question: if you could identify yourself with any mythological or historical figure, who would it be and why?

The Second Voyage

Odysseus rested on his oar and saw
The ruffled foreheads of the waves
Crocodiling and mincing past: he rammed
The oar between their jaws and looked down
In the simmering sea where scribbles of weed defined   5
Uncertain depth, and the slim fishes progressed
In fatal formation, and thought
                If there was a single
Streak of decency in these waves now, they'd be ridged
Pocked and dented with the battering they've had,   10
And we could name them as Adam named the beasts,
Saluting a new one with dismay, or a notorious one
With admiration; they'd notice us passing
And rejoice at our shipwreck, but these
Have less character than sheep and need more patience.   15

I know what I'll do he said;
I'll park my ship in the crook of a long pier
(And I'll take you with me he said to the oar)
I'll face the rising ground and walk away
From the tidal waters, up riverbeds   20
Where herons parcel out the miles of stream,
Over gaps in the hills, through warm
Silent valleys, and when I meet a farmer
Bold enough to look me in the eye
With 'where are you off to with that long   25
Winnowing fan over your shoulder?'
There I will stand still
And I'll plant you for a gatepost or a hitching-post

And leave you as a tidemark. I can go back
And organise my house then.   30
                        But the profound
Unfenced valleys of the ocean still held him;
He has only the oar to make them keep their distance;
The sea was still frying under the ship's side.

He considered the water-lilies, and thought about the fountains   35
Spraying as wide as willows in empty squares,
The sugarstick of water clattering into the kettle,
The flat lakes bisecting the rushes. He remembered spiders
and frogs
Housekeeping at the roadside in brown trickles floored   40
with mud,
Horsetroughs, the black canal, pale swans at dark:
His face grew damp with tears that tasted
Like his own sweat or the insults of the sea.

Glossary		
1	*Odysseus:* an ancient Greek mythical hero	
3	*mincing:* moving in an affectedly elegant manner	
11	*Adam:* the first man created by God	
17	*crook:* bend; here, it suggests that the pier is shaped like a hook	
26	*Winnowing fan:* tool for generating air to separate the grain from the chaff	
28	*gatepost:* a post usually set up to support a gate that allows entry onto a person's land	
28	*hitching-post:* a post to which a horse (or other animal) may be tethered to prevent it from straying	
29	*tidemark:* mark or line showing the highest or lowest point reached by the tide	
31	*profound:* very deep	

Eiléan Ní Chuilleanáin

Guidelines

The Second Voyage is the title of Ní Chuilleanáin's 1986 collection of poems. As its title suggests, she ventures further into unsure places in her poetry.

Ní Chuilleanáin wrote this poem while she was in Oxford, where she was not particularly happy. She was writing a thesis and living a rather isolated life. She did, however, enjoy taking a punt out on the river. When she came back she had to tie up the punt and put away the punt pole. She would get a key and lock the oar into a big shed with a thatched roof. One day she noticed the pole leaning against the thatched roof and for some reason this sight reminded her of Odysseus and the prophesy that he would have to set out on a second voyage. She realised quite a long time afterwards that what she was really thinking about was going home to Ireland. That is how she identified with Odysseus.

Odysseus is a Greek mythic hero renowned for his cunning and strength. He is the hero of *The Odyssey*, an epic story that describes his adventures as he tries to return home after the Trojan War to re-establish his place as the King of Ithaca. He is away for twenty years, ten of which are spent at sea trying to get home to Ithaca. He angered Poseidon, who punished him by killing his men and making Odysseus's time at sea longer and more arduous. Nonetheless, Odysseus survives all that happens to him. His courage, wits and endurance enable him to come through each and every difficulty and arrive home safely.

Ní Chuilleanáin describes herself as having an 'Odysseus complex': from about the age of thirteen she wanted to be an explorer, free to go off to all sorts of places and discover new things. In 'The Second Voyage' she takes Odysseus and enables the reader to see a very different man to the mythological hero presented in *The Odyssey*. He appears confused, beaten and unsure of himself. In this reimagining of Odysseus the emphasis shifts from the conventional image of a hero to the final vision of a man caught in a trap and broken.

Commentary

It could be said that in this poem Ní Chuilleanáin undoes the mythical figure of Odysseus and attempts to harness the power of the myth to a new end. She blends the classical with the biblical in the form of Odysseus and Adam. She pits the intractable feminine sea against Odysseus's masculine attempt to control, name and order its power.

Stanza 1

In the first stanza we meet Odysseus at sea, he is not in control as we would expect but is angrily protesting at the irrepressible sea. The classical hero is 'rested on his oar' (line 1), looking at the waves. The sea seems characteristically feminine: 'The ruffled foreheads of the waves / Crocodiling and mincing past' (lines 2 and 3). The phallic connotations of the oar being 'rammed' (line 3) between the 'jaws' (line 4) of the waves can hardly be ignored. It may be read as a metaphor for sexual domination. The harsh language of 'he rammed' indicates a level of frustration. This is in direct contrast to the 'ruffled' waves and the 'simmering sea' with 'scribbles' of seaweed (line 5). The sea appears indifferent and autonomous. The repetition of 's' sounds here further enhances this effect. Odysseus ominously watches the fish progressing but they swim in 'fatal formation' (line 7): they will die at sea.

Stanza 2

Odysseus then confronts the waves and tries to 'name them as Adam named the beasts' (line 11). This reference is from Genesis 2:20, which states, 'And Adam gave names to all cattle, and to the fowls of the air, and to every beast of the field, . . . As they came before him, and passed by him, paying as it were their homage to him, their lord and owner.'

Odysseus, like Adam, tries to assert himself and gain control of the waves. His attempt to dent, batter and name them has had no effect whatsoever and the waves remain impervious to him. They are described in terms that have often been applied to the scandalous female: without a 'Streak of decency' (line 9), these 'notorious' (line 12) ones would 'rejoice at our shipwreck' (line 14). These insults are futile and serve to illustrate Odysseus's impotence against the power of the sea.

Stanzas 3 and 4

According to some critics, Odysseus projects a journey inland to stabilise the boundary between the uncontrollable ocean and the named, ordered and owned land. He intends to 'park my ship in the crook of a long pier / (and I'll take you with me he said to the oar)' (lines 17 and 18). If you have ever seen the film *Castaway* starring Tom Hanks, the oar here is beginning to take on a similar role to Wilson the football in the film. Hanks personifies and communicates with the football to preserve his sanity.

Odysseus wants to 'walk away' (line 19) from the shoreline, 'From the tidal waters, up riverbeds / Where herons parcel out the miles of stream' (lines 20 and 21). He wants to journey as far away as he can from the influence of the ocean. He will finally reach a place where the oar will be mistaken for a harvesting tool: 'that long / Winnowing fan' (lines 25 and 26). This is where he will 'stand still' (line 27) and his oar will mark his territory, his conquest: 'I'll plant you for a gatepost' (line 28). It is noteworthy that the oar would be useless here on the land, whether as a gatepost or a hitching post. The mention of a 'tidemark' reminds us that Odysseus is still at sea and only imagining his escape to the land. His hopes to 'go back / And organise my house' (lines 29 and 30) are dashed.

Odysseus realises that the 'Unfenced valleys of the ocean' (line 32) still hold him and that the oar is his only means of protection from the 'frying' (line 34) sea.

Stanza 5

Odysseus then pauses, overcome with a nostalgic longing, to imagine water in its tamed, feminine and cultivated form. He considers the domesticated forms of water – artificial attempts that people make to contain its power: water-lilies, fountains in squares, kettles, lakes, troughs, canals and 'pale swans at dark' (line 42). In listing them, we can see parallels with Adam naming the beasts. In these images water is a contained element, flowing through things; it is not a force to conquer.

He becomes overwhelmed by his inability to escape from or control the powerful ocean: 'His face grew damp with tears that tasted / Like his own sweat or the insults of the sea' (lines 43 and 44). He is confused and can no longer distinguish signs of his own distress, 'tears' and 'sweat', from the sea.

Comparison with 'Lucina Schynning in Silence of the Nicht'

We can read Ní Chuilleanáin's poem as a major revision of the classic hero Odysseus. It highlights the folly of man in his attempt to control the world and in many ways it reclaims the validity of the female experience. In light of this it would be remiss not to draw a comparison between Odysseus and Lucina (from the previous poem). Lucina identifies with the mosaic beasts who have outlasted the warrior, and enjoys kinship with the wildlife. She has achieved the peace that Odysseus longs for in this poem.

Thinking about the poem

1 What do you think is the significance of the poem's title, 'The Second Voyage'?
2 Describe Odysseus's mood in the first stanza? Explain why he feels this way.
3 Ní Chuilleanáin uses unusual verbs to describe the sea. Identify some of these and say what effect they have.
4 Why is it so important to Odysseus that he names the waves? What does he hope to achieve by doing this?
5 In the second stanza Odysseus imagines himself on land. Why, in your opinion, does he do this?
6 Odysseus's oar represents different things at different stages in the poem. Discuss what it represents, stating when and why.
7 'I can go back / And organise my house then' (lines 29 and 30). In your opinion, what is Odysseus saying here?

8   Odysseus lists various water features in the last few lines. What is significant about them?

9   The last two lines of the poem are very effective in summing up Odysseus's mood. Why?

10 Select one image in this poem and comment on it.

11 What, in your opinion, is the main theme of the poem?

12 Ní Chuilleanáin reimagines the myth of Odysseus in this poem. What reasons might she have for doing this? Is it effective?

Personal response

1   Imagine that you are Odysseus trapped at sea, write a letter to your wife describing your voyage.

2   Choose another mythical hero or legend and reimagine their story. Write a short poem about them.

Before you read 'Deaths and Engines'

The title of this poem is 'Deaths and Engines'. Can you recall a time in your life or an occurrence from recent history for which this title might be appropriate? Share your stories with a partner, explaining why this title suits them.

Deaths and Engines

We came down above the houses
In a stiff curve, and
At the edge of Paris airport
Saw an empty tunnel
– The back half of a plane, black   5
On the snow, nobody near it,
Tubular, burnt-out and frozen.

When we faced again
The snow-white runway in the dark
No sound came over   10
The loudspeakers, expect the sighs
Of the lonely pilot.

The cold of metal wings is contagious:
Soon you will need wings of your own,
Cornered in the angle where   15
Time and life like a knife and fork
Cross, and the lifeline in your palm
Breaks, and the curve of an aeroplane's track
Meets the straight skyline.

The images of relief: 20
Hospital pyjamas, screens round a bed
A man with a bloody face
Sitting up in bed, conversing cheerfully
Through cut lips:
These will fail you some time.   25

You will find yourself alone
Accelerating down a blind
Alley, too late to stop
And know how light your death is;
You will be scattered like wreckage,   30
The pieces every one a different shape
Will spin and lodge in the hearts
Of all who love you.

Glossary

7 | *tubular*: the form of a cylinder or tube

Guidelines

In 'Deaths and Engines' Ní Chuilleanáin recalls glimpsing the wreckage of an aeroplane at the edge of Paris airport. Her father had only recently died and this sight prompted her to contemplate the inevitability of death and its aftermath. She uses the imagery and language of aeroplanes and crashes to talk about life and death and what is left behind when we die.

Commentary

This is a lyric poem written using first-person and second-person narrative. Lyric poetry tends not to tell a story, or portray characters or actions; it generally addresses the reader directly and gives us an insight into the speaker's state of mind, perceptions and/or feelings. In this poem we gain an insight into Ní Chuilleanáin's thoughts on the inescapability of death and of what remains of us when we are gone. Ní Chuilleanáin employs this form without any trace of the usual sentimentality that accompanies lyric poetry.

Stanza 1

The first and second stanzas employ the first-person plural narrative: 'We came down above the houses' (line 1) and 'When we faced again' (line 8). The use of 'we' here makes the experience of being in the aeroplane more immediate and personal, causing the reader to empathise with the speaker in the poem. She is on a flight looking out the window at the 'back half' (line 5) of a 'burnt-out' (line 7) plane. We are never told what happened, or even that the wreckage is the result of a crash, but through her use of contrast, punctuation and rhythm we get the impression that it was a desolate and broken image.

Many people would find this an unnerving sight to behold if they were descending 'In a stiff curve' (line 2) to land. It highlights the possibility of what could happen and what is left after it does. The use of the dash (–) in the fourth line encourages us to pause, perhaps like the speaker did when she saw this sight. The contrast of the black plane against the white snow gives us a sense of how stark this image must have appeared to her. The end of the stanza, 'nobody near it, / Tubular, burnt-out and frozen' (lines 6 and 7), may indicate the isolation, emptiness and stillness she associates with the scene below her. Indeed Ní Chuilleanáin may have been feeling this way herself in light of her father's recent passing.

Stanza 2

The plane seems to be on course for landing and they are facing the runway 'in the dark' (line 9), with no sound over the loudspeakers. This silence is in stark contrast to the panic and fear that may have been experienced by the passengers on the plane she viewed earlier. She is still very much a passenger here, viewing the wreckage from a distance. She is safe. She describes the pilot as being lonely and it is not clear why. As readers, we are left to suggest our own reasons for this.

Stanza 3

Stanza 3 opens up with two unusual lines, 'The cold of metal wings is contagious: / Soon you will need wings of your own' (lines 13 and 14). Ní Chuilleanáin changes to the second-person narrative ('you') and it now seems that the speaker knows more than the reader and may appear instructional in her tone. Something has changed; it is as if the speaker has woken up to the certainty of death.

The use of the colon in line 13 notifies the reader that the information in the stanza will support, explain or elaborate upon the statement that 'The cold of metal wings is contagious'. The wings are cold and inanimate and perhaps it is these traits that are contagious: we are both cold and inanimate when we die. We are told that we will soon need our own wings; there is a certainty about this statement and the word 'will' makes it definite and assured. Perhaps it is a reference to our angelic ascension into heaven or it could be a reference to the spiritual and emotional lift that we will need when we are nearing our end, when 'the lifeline in your palm / Breaks' (lines 17 and 18). The use of the word 'cornered' (line 15) points to the inevitability of death when 'Time and life like a knife and fork / Cross' (lines 16 and 17).

Stanza 4

The speaker lists some 'images of relief' (line 20) or of escaping death. We are shown a man in a hospital bed after a trauma. His face is bloody but he is able to sit up and chat 'cheerfully / Through cut lips' (lines 23 and 24). The important thing is he is alive and it is a 'relief' (line 20). However, the last line of the stanza undermines the first one. We are told that these images of relief 'will fail you some time' (line 25). Again the speaker is definite here, there is no ambiguity: there will come a day when there will be no consoling images, no escape.

Stanza 5

The speaker describes what will happen on that day. We will find ourselves 'alone / Accelerating down a blind / Alley' (lines 26–28). This reminds us of the plane in the first stanza coming down 'In a stiff curve'; and the blind alley is reminiscent of the 'empty tunnel'. The difference is that on this journey we will be 'alone' and we will be unsure of the destination. It is 'too late to stop' (line 28), death is inevitable and we will not be in control anymore.

In line 29 the speaker outlines 'how light your death is'. This interesting statement perhaps refers to how unremarkable the moment of death actually is. We live for years with the knowledge that we will one day die but when we do it is over in an instant, we will leave our corporeal bodies and the mystery will begin. Lines 30 and 31 note that the journey will end with devastation and destruction and we 'will be scattered like wreckage' (line 30). Just like the plane on the runway in Paris, we will be broken, lifeless and cold.

The last two lines are transformative, however, and set us apart. We, unlike the plane wreckage, are unique and our many dimensions and facets, 'every one a different shape' (line 31), will be forever remembered by the people who knew us and loved us. We achieve immortality of sorts in the memories of others.

Thinking about the poem

1   In a couple of sentences explain what the poem is about.

2   In the first stanza the speaker describes what she saw at the edge of Paris airport, explain what you think is the significance of this sight.

3   Throughout the poem Ní Chuilleanáin uses aeroplane imagery. Find examples of this and say whether you find them effective.

4   Which of these statements best describes your view of what the poem is about?
   ● The poem is about surviving a plane crash.
   ● The poem is about life and death.
   ● The poem is about the inescapability of death and how parts of us remain.
   Explain your choice.

5   Which of the following choices best describes the tone of the poem?
   ● sentimental
   ● apathetic and distant
   ● restrained and controlled
   ● instructive and assured.
   Explain your choice.

6   'Soon you will need wings of your own' (line 14). What, in your opinion, is the speaker referring to here?

7   In your opinion, what does the speaker mean when she says that the 'images of relief' (line 20) will 'fail' us some times (line 25)?

8   The rhythm of the final stanza is different to the others. Why is this and how is it achieved?

9   Select your favourite image, line, phrase or sequence in the poem and say why you have chosen it.

10 In your view, is 'Deaths and Engines' a good title for the poem? Explain your answer.

11 Comment on line 13, 'The cold of metal wings is contagious'.

12 What is significant about the last four lines of the poem?

Personal response

1   Imagine that you are editing this poem, you can make any changes to the poem you deem necessary. What changes would you make and why?

2   In pairs, use the title 'Deaths and Engines' to write a poem based on some of the stories that were discussed in the 'Before you read' exercise.

Before you read 'Street'

The poem 'Street' is about a man falling in love with a woman he sees on the street. Think of a person who you saw or met once and who made a lasting impression on you. Discuss this person with the student beside you, outlining why you still remember the encounter.

MYSTERY + DANGER

Street

CINEMATIC

BLUNT

He fell in love with the butcher's daughter
When he saw her passing by in her white trousers
Dangling a knife on a ring at her belt. *CONTRAST*
He stared at the dark shining drops on the paving-stones.

RECKLESS / CARELESS

One day he followed her   5
Down the slanting lane at the back of the shambles. *varying line lengths*
A door stood half-open   *suspense*
And the stairs were brushed and clean,
Her shoes paired on the bottom step,
Each tread marked with the red crescent *(moonlight, romance)*   10
Her bare heels left, fading to faintest at the top.

enjambment

alliteration

no resolution at end (left dangling, like knife)

Glossary

6	*shambles:* butcher's slaughter house
10	*tread:* step

Guidelines

This poem could be described as a vignette of unrequited love with a gothic twist. It is beautifully cinematic and was based on a real girl who worked in a butcher's shop that the poet saw and never forgot. She was magnificently stunning in her white uniform and the image of this girl stirred the poet to write this poem.

When she was young Ní Chuilleanáin read a novel by Joseph Conrad called *The Rover*, which was set in the time of the French Revolution. It features a beautiful girl who has something mysterious about her but nobody knows what it is. The girl's aunt says that she can never marry anybody because she went out with the mob when they were killing people. When she came back her skirt was bloody up to the knee. That image stuck with the poet and we can see how it may have inspired the danger and mystery in this poem.

Commentary

The poem is written in the third-person narrative and this enables us to take a voyeuristic look at the world of the characters in the poem.

Stanza 1

We are introduced to a strange and unusual combination of themes: romance, butchery, beauty and danger. We are transported into the moment when the man first saw the butcher's daughter. We are told that that he has fallen in love at first sight with this woman. She is dressed in white and dangling a knife from her belt that is dripping with blood. It is fair to assume that she is a striking beauty, given the inspiration for the poem.

The opening line draws the reader in, we sense that there is something edgy about this situation. Butchery is a male-dominated profession and the nature of the work (slaughtering animals) is one not readily associated with women. Her white trousers provide the perfect contrasting backdrop to the bloody knife, still dripping with blood. The male character is staring at the 'shining' fresh 'drops on the paving-stones' (line 4), as if entranced or in awe of what she does for a living. We get the sense that the butcher's daughter is not aware of his feelings or that she is the object of his attention. What is it about this vision of her that has captivated him so?

Stanza 2

In the second stanza we find him following her down a lane at the back of the slaughter house. This further intensifies the mystery and reminds the reader that this place is where she butchers animals. The 'half-open' (line 7) door may illustrate that the man is not a part of her world, he can only glimpse into the unknown. The sight that he beholds is 'clean' and 'brushed' (line 8), which is not what we might expect to see inside a slaughter house.

Her shoes are all that he can see of her, they are neatly 'paired on the bottom step' (line 9). The woman has disappeared up the stairs and all that remains of her presence is the 'red crescent' (line 10) of blood that her heels have left behind. We are aware throughout this stanza that she appears unattainable and very separate to the man who has fallen in love with her. He is following her, watching her, longing for her, but she keeps moving further away from him and finally disappears like her bloody footprints that fade 'to faintest at the top' (line 11).

The world of the butcher's daughter is secret, unknown and unfamiliar and this may be what draws him to her. We, like the man in the poem, are left wondering about her footprints and what further mystery lies at the top of the stairs.

Thinking about the poem

1   Is 'Street' is an appropriate title for the poem? Give reasons for your answer.

2   The poem tells a story. In a short paragraph, outline what happens.

3   What type of atmosphere is created in the first stanza? How is this achieved?

4   In your opinion, which of the following phrases best reveals the thoughts of the man as he stares at the blood on the paving-stones?

- Could this beautiful creature have just slaughtered an animal?
- If only she wasn't a butcher.
- What a woman!
- How can I be at once attracted and repelled by this girl.

Explain your choice.

5   Choose two images from the poem that appeal to you and give reasons for your choices.

6   We get the impression that the girl did not know that this man has fallen in love with her. What do you think creates this impression?

7   In your opinion, what is the most mysterious moment in the poem and why?

8   Which of the following options is closest to your view of the man in the poem?

- a stalker
- a hopeless romantic
- a weird man.

Explain your choice.

9   The poem has a rich cinematic quality. In your opinion, how is the atmosphere of the poem created?

10   The word 'blood' is never mentioned in the poem yet it is referred to twice. Identify these references and outline why you think the poet chose not to use the word.

11   Comment on the use of the word 'dangling' (line 3).

12   Find and discuss specific examples of how the poet plays around with the notion of attraction.

Personal response

1   Imagine that the man follows her up the stairs. Write a paragraph on what happens next.

2   You have been asked to adapt this poem into a short film. Create a storyboard for the poem.

snapshot

A vignette of mysterious love		Free verse
Man falls in love with an unlikely character	**Street**	Plays around with notions of attraction
Inspired by a real memory		Third-person narrator
Cinematic and atmospheric		Unusual portrayal of a desirable woman

Before you read 'Fireman's Lift'

Before reading Eiléan Ní Chuilleanáin's poem 'Fireman's Lift' look at the picture of Correggio's *Assumption of the Virgin* on page 294. Write down any words that strike you about it. Share these words with the student beside you and together compose a ten-line response to what you see.

P.R. → STYLE

STRENGTH + EFFORT

Fireman's Lift

DEATH (SOME IMAGES REFER TO CHILDBIRTH)

Metaphor for the dome

I was standing beside you looking up *pushing*
Through the big tree of the cupola *heaving supporting*
Where the church splits wide open to admit
Celestial choirs, the fall-out of brightness. *verbs suggest MOVEMENT*

The Virgin was spiralling to heaven, 5
Hauled up in stages. Past mist and shining,
Teams of angelic arms were heaving,
Supporting, crowding her, and we stepped

Back, as the painter longed to
While his arm swept in the large strokes. 10
We saw the work entire, and how the light

IMAGES OF THE PAINTING

Melted and faded bodies so that
Loose feet and elbows and staring eyes
Floated in the wide stone petticoat
Clear and free as weeds. 15
affection → *personification*

This is what love sees, that angle:
The crick in the branch loaded with fruit,
A jaw defining itself, a shoulder yoked,

NURSES ARE LIKE ANGELS

The back making itself a roof *could be people looking after her Mother*
The legs a bridge, the hands *lifting + supporting* 20
A crane and a cradle.

MOTHERLY IMAGES LOVE

(angels)
Their heads bowed over to reflect on her
Fair face and hair so like their own
As she passed through their hands. We saw them
Lifting her, the pillars of their arms 25

* *images are physical although we associate heaven as not very physical*

description

love

(Her face a capital leaning into an arch)
As the muscles clung and shifted
For a final purchase together *strength – born into new life*
Under her weight as she came to the edge of the cloud.

Parma 1963–Dublin 1994 → TRASIENCE

Glossary		
title	*Fireman's Lift:* a technique used to lift and carry a powerless person; the person is carried across the shoulders of the carrier	
2	*cupola:* a dome-like structure on the top of a building	
17	*crick:* a bend or painful muscle spasm	
26	*capital:* the top or head of a column or pier	

Guidelines

This poem was written in response to the death of Ní Chuilleanáin's mother. Ní Chuilleanáin felt that this poem had to be a success as she knew that her mother would want her to write a poem about her dying. Her mother had written a children's book in response to her sister's death and so Ní Chuilleanáin saw this poem as maintaining a family tradition.

Her mother was ill in a nursing home and she remarked that one of the great things about that place was all the beautiful young nurses. This struck a chord with Ní Chuilleanáin. The image of all these young bodies lifting and moving her mother reminded her of the time she and her mother visited the cathedral in Parma whose dome features Correggio's fresco of the Virgin's Assumption into heaven, lifted up by the saints and angels. Both the poem and the fresco remember a dying mother.

Commentary

Stanza 1

The poet describes a scene in the cathedral in Parma. Ní Chuilleanáin recalls standing with her mother looking up into the dome. It is a Romanesque church and as such would not have originally featured a dome. During the Renaissance, however, a dome was added. This may be what the poet is referring to when she says that 'the church splits wide open' (line 3). If you look at the picture you will see the natural light flooding in through the circular windows, and also the light within the picture that Correggio has depicted coming from beyond the clouds and that illuminates the scene: 'the fall-out of brightness' (line 4). She describes the angels and saints – 'Celestial choirs' (line 4) – perched on the spiralling clouds.

Stanza 2

Our attention is drawn to the Virgin rising into heaven. She is being 'Hauled up' (line 6) at each stage of the ascension by the teams of angels. Ní Chuilleanáin uses a series of verbs – 'heaving, / Supporting, crowding' (lines 7 and 8) to highlight the huge effort that these teams were making to ensure her safe passage into another life. The poet has noted that on seeing the fresco she 'could only concentrate on one aspect, the way it shows bodily effort and the body's weight'.

Stanza 3

In this stanza the painter has been imagined into the poem. Correggio's toil and creativity in painting this fresco may also be seen as an act of worship. We could view the poem in a similar way, a daughter's mark of respect for her mother. She writes that the painter longs to step back and see 'the work entire' (line 11).

People can see the fresco in many different ways and this raises interesting questions about the role of the spectator in creating meaning. The poet is writing from the perspective of an observer but she is also a collaborator in meaning-making. She and her mother could step back and see 'the work entire' – a vision of the work that the painter may never have seen while he was painting it. The painting never leaves the poet. Perhaps as she watched her mother fading away she 'stepped back' and her mind flashed back to their shared experience in Parma. This momentary connection provided Ní Chuilleanáin with a creative outlet to express her sense of loss of her mother after she dies.

Stanza 4

Ní Chuilleanáin describes the effect that the real and depicted light has on the vortex of bodies, feet, elbows and faces populated around the clouds, 'Clear and free as weeds' (line 15). The painting does not contain many whole bodies, but there are lots of body parts. These parts interact and complement each other, giving the impression of weight, power and stress. In the fifth and sixth stanzas Ní Chuilleanáin's language and imagery mirrors this stress and weight.

The poet has remarked that she sees this fresco as a maternal image. She playfully reflects that looking up into the dome was like 'looking up under someone's skirt'. The swathes of fabric and the exposed limbs dangling stand in stark contrast to some of the depictions of Christ's ascension into heaven. The reference to the 'petticoat' in line 14 may be seen as mischievous or may reflect and celebrate the feminine body.

Stanzas 5 and 6

The poet's point of view changes from an authorial stance fixed in space and time to the perspective of memory and it becomes more personal: 'This is what love sees, that angle' (line 16). At this point in the poem, perhaps, the images of the Virgin and the poet's mother merge. The language and imagery capture the physicality of the Virgin's Assumption into heaven and also the struggle that the nurses may have experienced when lifting her dying mother.

Ní Chuilleanáin creates a verbal masterpiece. We get a sense of weight in her description of 'the branch loaded with fruit' (line 17), and of the absolute relinquishing of the earth in the image of the 'jaw defining itself' (line 18) as it looks up towards the light. There is also a sense of submission and trust in the 'yoked' (line 18) shoulder.

Like Correggio's fresco, the body is divided into parts and these parts become metaphors for structure and support: the back is like an arched roof, the legs are a bridge and the hands can be seen as a crane hauling up the body while simultaneously acting as a cradle to support it.

Stanza 7 and 8

We get a sense here that the nurses have become synonymous with Correggio's angels and saints. They are attending to the poet's mother just like the angels attended to Mary. She 'passed through their hands' (line 24) with absolute trust and belief. Their arms then become the pillar holding her up and her face is like a 'capital' (line 26). In other words, they are working together. Then, in one 'final purchase together' (line 28), she disappears behind 'the edge of the cloud' (line 29). While Correggio's fresco is an artistic re-creation of the Assumption of Mary, Ní Chuilleanáin's poem may be read as a poetic re-creation of her mother's spiritual ascent to the place beyond the clouds.

Thinking about the poem

1   Ní Chuilleanáin names two places and dates at the end of the poem. In your opinion, why does she do this? What might it be about Correggio's *Assumption of the Virgin* that makes it so important to the poet at this time?
2   What is the most striking image in the first stanza? Explain your choice.
3   Discuss Ní Chuilleanáin's description of figures in the dome. Is it effective? Explain your answer.
4   Do we get a sense of the poet's mother from this poem? If so, where and how?
5   Find two examples from the poem of how the language mirrors the image of the fresco?

6 Which of the following statements do you agree with most and why?

- This poem is a strange and unique way of marking her mother's death.
- This poem is a beautiful way of marking her mother's death.
- This poem is an overly complicated way of marking her mother's death.
- This poem is an interesting way of marking her mother's death.

Explain your choice.

7 At what point in the poem do the image of the Assumption and the image of the mother in the nursing home merge? How is this achieved?

8 Discuss the poet's choice of language and imagery in the fifth and sixth stanzas.

9 Are notions of trust and faith important in this poem? Explain your answer.

10 Contrast and compare the angels and saints in the picture with the nurses that cared for the poet's mother.

11 Describe the tone and atmosphere of the final stanza.

12 Which of the following statements best describes your view of the poem?

- It is a poem about a daughter trying to remember her mother.
- It is a poem about the relationship between art and real life.
- It is a poem that celebrates the mystery of life.

Explain your choice.

13 Some critics have said that this poem intellectualises the death of the poet's mother. Do you agree with this viewpoint? Explain your answer.

14 The poet compares looking up into the dome to looking up a 'wide stone petticoat' (line 14). In your opinion, why does she do this?

15 'This is what love sees, that angle' (line 16). What might the poet be referring to here?

16 Do you think that 'Fireman's Lift' is a good title? Explain your answer.

Personal response

1 You have been asked to review this poem for a literary magazine. In less than 300 words try to capture your thoughts.

2 If you had to choose a poem, a song, a piece of art, a place to remember someone special, which would you choose? Describe it and say what it is about it that makes it so important.

3 In pairs, create an interview set-up. Both partners write two questions each that they would like to ask the poet. Take turns at being the interviewer and the poet. Write down two interesting things that arose from this process about either the poem or the poet. Discuss these in class.

Before reading 'All for You' interview the person next to you, asking 'If you could have anything in the world, what would it be?' Ask them to describe what they would ask for and to explain why. Then ask what would happen if they actually got it.

All for You

NARRATIVE STYLE

→ *2 people*

Once beyond the gate of the strange stableyard, we dismount.
The donkey walks on, straight in at a wide door
And sticks his head in a manger.

The great staircase of the hall slouches back,   *Personification*
Sprawling between warm wings. It is for you.   5
As the steps wind and warp
Among the vaults, their thick ribs part; the doors   *sense of comfort + security*
Of guardroom, chapel, storeroom
Swing wide and the breath of ovens
Flows out, the rage of brushwood,   10
The roots torn out and butchered.

It is for you, the dry fragrance of tea-chests   *Heaven?*
The tins shining in ranks, the ten-pound jars   *god's house*
Rich with shrivelled fruit. Where better to lie down   *key*
And sleep, along the labelled shelves,   15
With the key still in your pocket?

Glossary	
3	*manger:* trough or box for feeding animals such as horses or cattle
6	*warp:* twist, turn
10	*brushwood:* cut or broken-off branches and twigs

Eiléan Ní Chuilleanáin

Guidelines

Ní Chuilleanáin has stated that she strongly dislikes the words 'you' and 'your', particularly the way they are used in advertising. For example, the ad that tells you the CD has 'all your favourite songs' – do advertisers know what our favourite songs are? How can they make these assertions? This is the irritant that inspired this poem.

The poet imagined a poem capturing what it would be like if everything was given to you, and everything was ready for you. We are told in the title that it is 'All for You' and we read in the poem what 'all' entails. However, despite elaborate details, we are never fully convinced as to whether it really is 'all' for the speaker in this poem, the title may therefore be ironic.

Commentary

Stanza 1

This very cinematic poem starts with an arrival – the speaker is introduced to an unknown 'strange stableyard' (line 1). This person is not alone, 'we dismount' (line 1); someone led him or her in. The speaker describes how the 'donkey walks on, straight in at a wide door' (line 2) to his manger. He, unlike this person, is no stranger here and he knows exactly where his place is. The opening stanza has a medieval feel to it – with its gate, stable yard, donkey and manger – and it brings to mind settings from some classic fairy tales.

Stanza 2

We are now in a huge hall with a 'great staircase' (line 4). The staircase 'slouches back' and is 'sprawling' between the wings of the 'warm' house (lines 4 and 5). These are unusual verbs to associate with an inanimate staircase. We more readily associate them with what people do on a comfortable couch or bed that they are familiar with. We could infer that the place is extremely inviting or that all the elements that make up this scene belong here and share a sense of ownership that the person is separate from, despite being told in line 5 that 'It is for you.' We are not told how this person feels about it 'all' or whether they actually want it or not. Could it be that this is someone else's vision of what this person wants? Or what reality is like when you get what you asked for?

The 'steps wind and warp / Among the vaults' (lines 6 and 7), the alliterative verbs enhance the gothic medieval atmosphere and tone. Ní Chuilleanáin has described this poem as having a kind of 'Jane Eyre' feel to it, stating that behind the many doors of the house – the 'guardroom, chapel, storeroom' (line 8) – 'there are things that you will only find out in time but they are dangerous things also'. She has said that the parting of the 'thick ribs' (line 7) is when 'the house stops being a place and starts being a body'. This throws the reader into a surreal place in the poem. Are we in a body, a house or a memory?

A clue may be contained in the 'storeroom' (line 8), which the poet has described as 'very important'. She grew up in an enormous and official house that formed part of a hostel for students on the grounds of UCC. There was a door that led into the storeroom of the hostel. Her mother, having charge of the stores, went there every Monday and gave out jam, raisins and tea to the students. It was a Victorian world, where the precious things were kept behind lock and key. In this poem the 'storeroom' is a place of abundance and warmth – 'breath of ovens' (line 9). The initial 'warmth' experienced in the house is contrasted with its source – the fire in the vaults. It burns with 'rage' from 'torn out and butchered' brushwood (lines 10 and 11). The language here suggests violence and danger. This is a house of many rooms and this person is perhaps discovering what lies within them and where she belongs within it all.

Stanza 3

This stanza repeats 'It is for you' (line 12) and then lists the contents of the storeroom. The storeroom may be seen as a place of order: it has 'labelled shelves' (line 15) and 'tins shining in ranks' (line 13). The speaker seems at home here and sees it as an appealing place to 'lie down / And sleep' (lines 14 and 15). Ní Chuilleanáin has said that she associates the storeroom with childhood and with the maternal body.

It is interesting that despite being in a huge house with many rooms, which we are told are 'all' for this person, the speaker chooses to lie down in the storeroom. Perhaps this is where this person feels in control: 'the key still in your pocket?' (line 16), or feels closest to the source of food and heat. One could make an association here with the maternal body, also a source of abundance and heat for a child. Perhaps, despite the huge house, this is all that the speaker wants. We are left guessing.

The question mark in the final line is intriguing. Keys can symbolise various things such as control, escape, ownership, power or freedom. We need to ask ourselves which meaning the poet wants to imply here. Does it mean the speaker can go wherever she wants? That she can escape? Does she even have the key or is she referring to her mother's pocket? Does the key mean that she is now in control? This line adds to the mysterious atmosphere of the poem.

Recurring symbols, setting and themes

We see in this poem some of the recurring symbols, setting and themes in Ní Chuilleanáin's poetry. The symbol of the key as in 'Translation', sleeping in unusual and strange places as in 'Lucina Schynning in Silence of the Nicht', the notion of order as in her father's library in 'Following' and the medieval, gothic and fairy tale setting that we see in almost all of the poems on this course. The poet moves between and within worlds, real and imaginary and we see that in this poem too.

Thinking about the poem

1   Do you agree that the poem has a medieval or gothic feel to it? Identify the features that give it this atmosphere.

2   Is the title ironic? Explain your answer.

3   We are not given a direct insight into how the speaker is feeling. Say how you think she responded to her new surroundings.

4   This poem has been described as very cinematic. Do you agree? Explain your answer.

5   Many critics have wondered whether the person in the poem is a nun, a bride, a servant . . . Write down who you think the speaker is and describe why.

6   Comment on the repetition of the phrase 'all for you'.

7   Which of these statements do you agree with most and why?
    ●   This poem is about what happens when you get what you want.
    ●   This poem is about ownership and belonging.
    ●   This poem is about what other people want for you.

8   Comment on the description 'Rich with shrivelled fruit' (line 14).

9   The final line is ambiguous. Discuss what you think the line means.

10 Choose your favourite image from the poem and describe why you chose it.

Personal response

1   Imagine you are the speaker in the poem, write a diary account of your first night in the house.

2   In pairs, using Animoto or Photo Story to create an audio-visual interpretation of the poem. Present it to the class.

Before you read 'Following'

Eiléan Ní Chuilleanáin's poem 'Following' on page 303 reads like a dream sequence. Dreams do not always make sense, yet in a strange and disjointed way, elements of them can be very significant. They do not necessarily have a narrative. Write down a dream that you remember and try to make sense of some of the elements of it.

Following

So she follows the trail of her father's coat through the fair
Shouldering past beasts packed solid as books,
And the dealing men nearly as slow to give way –
A block of belly, a back like a mountain,
A shifting elbow like a plumber's bend –   5
When she catches a glimpse of a shirt-cuff, a handkerchief,
Then the hard brim of his hat, skimming along,

Until she is tracing light footsteps
Across the shivering bog by starlight,
The dead corpse risen from the wakehouse   10
Gliding before her in a white habit.
The ground is forested with gesturing trunks,
Hands of women dragging needles,
Half-choked heads in the water of cuttings,
Mouths that roar like the noise of the fair day.   15

She comes to where he is seated
With whiskey poured out in two glasses
In a library where the light is clean,
His clothes all finely laundered,
Ironed facings and linings.   20
The smooth foxed leaf has been hidden
In a forest of fine shuffling,
The square of white linen
That held three drops
Of her heart's blood is shelved   25
Between the gatherings
That go to make a book –
The crushed flowers among the pages crack
The spine is open, push the bindings apart.

Glossary

10	*wakehouse:* place where people can come and visit the dead before they are buried
11	*white habit:* traditional robe worn by dead people
20	*facings:* collar, cuffs and trimmings of a coat
21	*foxed leaf:* well-worn page of a book
29	*spine:* the edge of the book where the pages are held together, it usually faces outwards when books are lined up on a shelf
29	*bindings:* coverings that bind the pages into a book and keep them together

Guidelines

Ní Chuilleanáin wrote this poem after attending a prize-giving ceremony in Dublin's RDS. She was following her friend, pushing through the people, searching for the material of his suit (he was the only man there wearing one) and this reminded her of following her late father, who had always worn a suit and hat. When she got home, she looked at a print she had in her bedroom of Jack Yeats's 'A Fair Day'. The picture is crammed with people at a fair and these two events inspired the following poem. This poem was written long after her father's death and in it she appears to be trying to recapture her father from memories she has of him. She takes us on a dream-like journey to a fair, into fairy tales with ghosts moving across bogs and finally to a library where she reconnects with her father.

While it is interesting for us to hear what inspired this poem and why the poet wrote what she did, it is also important to remember that our interpretation and response to the poem are equally relevant. Elements of this poem may appeal to our imaginations differently than the poet intended them. We may see things in this poem that she never saw and so it is important for us to respond in our own unique way and make meaning of the various strands that stand out for us.

Commentary

Stanza 1

This stanza is very much grounded in the concrete world of a fair. It is a word picture full of rich imagery, simile, metaphor, alliteration and symbolism. It is a busy fair day and a little girl has become separated from her father. She is catching glimpses of his coat as she passes the animals and the other men, who do not seem to regard her and are 'nearly as slow to give way' (line 3) as the animals. They block her vision with their bellies, huge backs and 'shifting' (line 5) elbows. The perspective that she describes the fair from allows us to imagine a slightly panicked little girl who is uncomfortable in this male world where both the men and the animals are indifferent to her. She 'follows the trail of her father's coat' (line 1) hoping to find him and feel safe in his close presence.

It is interesting that when she catches glimpses of him she recognises his shirt-cuff, handkerchief and hat. These may be seen as symbols of refinement that contrast with the earlier descriptions of the market scene: the 'beasts' (line 2), the 'block of belly' and the 'back like a mountain' (line 4). She may have perceived her father as being different from these 'dealing men' (line 3).

Stanza 2

The concrete world of stanza 1 dissolves into a gothic one. She moves from following her father's hat 'skimming along' (line 7) the hectic marketplace to 'tracing light footsteps / Across the shivering bog' (lines 8 and 9). We feel the palpable presence of the spiritual. She is now following a 'dead corpse' (line 10) in a very different realm.

Many of the images in this poem are allusions to folktales that Ní Chuilleanáin may have heard from her father, who was a great collector of them. She has stated that the 'dead corpse' here is taken from a folktale that tells the story of a girl who is out seeking her fortune and arrives at a wake house. The woman there asks her to sit up and watch the corpse. The lady informs her that the last two girls who watched the corpse fell asleep and terrible things happened to them. The girl assures the lady that she will not fall asleep. In the middle of the night the corpse rises and asks the girl to follow him and she follows the corpse across the bog.

Possibly the poet sees herself as this girl following the corpse, which may be an invocation of her father. The gothic landscape may be an imaginative space where she can spend time with her father who is no longer with her. Perhaps the poem itself becomes like a story of the wake: the girl stayed with the corpse and it came to life. Perhaps Ní Chuilleanáin feels that by remembering her father in this poem he too will come back to life.

The last four lines of the stanza are enchanted with disjointed images, the trunks of the trees are 'gesturing' (line 12; reminiscent of scenes from haunted forests in fairy tales), there are hands of women 'dragging needles' (line 13; perhaps referring to the suit mentioned earlier), there are 'Half-choked heads' (line 14; maybe a reference to cut flowers trying to sustain life in water) and 'Mouths that roar like the noise of fair day' (line 15; linking this place to the fair in stanza 1). Here the poet has created an otherworldly place, informed by elements from folktales, which works like a dream. This poem provides the reader with a great opportunity to respond imaginatively to the obscure imagery and descriptions.

Eiléan Ní Chuilleanáin

Stanza 3

We arrive in a library, where her father is given back to her. She can now see her father, she goes 'to where he is seated' (line 16) and there are two glasses of whiskey. (In his later years Ní Chuilleanáin's father suffered from terrible arthritis and he drank well-watered whiskey to help relieve the pain.) She presents him as being perfectly groomed, with clothes 'finely laundered, / Ironed' (lines 19 and 20). This is in keeping with the image of him in the first stanza. The poet has remarked that in this description she was trying to recapture her father and the men of his generation.

It is no coincidence that they are reunited in a library. Ní Chuilleanáin's father was a learned man, a professor, and she followed in his footsteps. The library would have been a space that they were both familiar with and comfortable in, a place where they frequently met and talked. She now has many of her father's books in her library, placed in exactly the same order as he had them in his own library.

There are memories in these books. She refers to the 'smooth foxed leaf' as being 'hidden' (line 21), waiting to be discovered in 'a forest of fine shuffling' (line 22; perhaps a reference to her father's collection of books in the library). We could also interpret these lines more literally: the leaf on the forest floor symbolises change and transformation, it reminds us of nature's cycle of constant regeneration.

She talks about a 'shelved' (line 25) book that holds not just this well-worn page but also a 'square of white linen' (line 23) that has 'three drops / Of her heart's blood' (lines 24 and 25) on it. We are not clear what exactly the three drops of blood represent. Three is a mystical and spiritual number featured in many fairy tales, and blood, the essence of life, is considered in folklore to have magical qualities. The poet has said that the girl had to do something to bring her father back. This is similar to many fairy tales: the protagonists usually must retrieve something or carry out some task before they get what they are looking for. Perhaps the journey thus far in the poem is the task and the reward is seeing her father again.

The poet comments:

> I find the idea of hiding something in a book really interesting; you can't see it but it is there. You don't have to look at it every day but now and again at appropriate times you can take it down and look at it. Hiding these things in a book is a bit like tucking things away in your memory. One of the functions of memory is not just to remind you that this or that happened but that it is in the past, it isn't now, except it doesn't work like that, things keep coming back.

This notion of memories coming back is clearer in the last two lines of the poem. The past will not stay past, it is alive. The crushed flowers between the pages in the book start to grow and, just like her memories, come to life again. The flowers 'push the bindings apart' (line 29). The memories can no longer be held or hidden in the book, they 'crack' (line 28) open the spine. Her father is dead and she is left with only her memories of him. In a sense she is trying to retrieve him in this poem, she searches for him, follows his lead, hoping that in the end she can revive him. Ní Chuilleanáin has said of this poem, 'I suppose I am really trying to bring my father back to life.'

Thinking about the poem

1 How does the poet describe the fair in stanza 1? How is the little girl feeling? Explain you answer.
2 The poet uses many poetic devices in the first stanza, choose two of these and describe their effect.
3 Describe the atmosphere of the second stanza? How is it created?
4 'The imagery in this poem is disjointed and obscure.' Do you agree with this statement? Explain your answer.
5 What impression do you get of the father in the poem? Explain your answer.
6 What impression do you get of the girl in this poem? Explain your answer.
7 Each stanza is set in a different place. What in your opinion is the significance of the different settings in the poem?
8 Which of the following statements best describes your view of the poem?
    ● It is a poem about loss.
    ● It is a poem about following in your father's footsteps.
    ● It is a poem about memory.
    ● It is a poem about the living and the dead.
    Explain your choice with reference to the text.
9 Do you agree that this is a gothic poem? Explain your answer.
10 There are many allusions to folklore in this poem. Identify two of these and explain why you think the poet decided to include them.
11 Comment on the poet's use of punctuation in the first stanza.
12 The poem is called 'Following'. Do you think it is an appropriate title? Explain your answer.
13 What do you think is the significance of the 'three drops / Of her heart's blood' (lines 24 and 25)?
14 What might the poet be referring to in the last two lines of the poem?

Personal response

1   You have been asked to put a soundtrack together for 'Following'. In groups, choose up to three songs that you think would enhance the poem. Share your choice with the class, stating why you picked these songs and what effect you were looking for.

2   We are never told what was written on the 'smooth foxed leaf' (line 21) that was hidden in the book. Create whatever document you think it was and share it with you partner.

3   Suggest an alternative title for the poem. Explain your suggestion.

Kilcash

From the Irish, c1800

What will we do now for timber
With the last of the woods laid low –
No work of Kilcash nor its household,
The bell is silenced now,
Where the lady lived with such honour,   5
No woman so heaped with praise,
Earls came across oceans to see her
And heard the sweet words of Mass.

It's the cause of my long affliction
To see your neat gates knocked down,   10
The long walks affording no shade now
And the avenue overgrown,
The fine house that kept out the weather,
Its people depressed and tamed;
And their names with the faithful departed,   15
The Bishop and Lady Iveagh!

The geese and the ducks' commotion,
The eagle's shout, are no more,
The roar of the bees gone silent,
Their wax and their honey store   20
Deserted. Now at evening

The musical birds are stilled
And the cuckoo is dumb in the treetops
That sang lullaby to the world.

Even the deer and the hunters   25
That follow the mountain way
Look down upon us with pity,
The house that was famed in its day;
The smooth wide lawn is all broken,
No shelter from wind and rain;   30
The paddock has turned to a dairy
Where the fine creatures grazed.

Mist hangs low on the branches
No sunlight can sweep aside,
Darkness falls among daylight   35
And the streams are all run dry;
No hazel, no holly or berry,
Bare naked rocks and cold;
The forest park is leafless
And all the game gone wild.   40

And now the worst of our troubles:
She has followed the prince of the Gaels –
He has borne off the gentle maiden,
Summoned to France and to Spain.
Her company laments her   45
That she fed with silver and gold:
One who never preyed on the people
But was the poor souls' friend.

My prayer to Mary and Jesus
She may come home safe to us here   50
To dancing and rejoicing
To fiddling and bonfire
That our ancestors' house will rise up,
Kilcash built up anew
And from now to the end of the story   55
May it never be laid low.

Eiléan Ní Chuilleanáin

Glossary

title	*Kilcash:* castle (now ruined) and lands in south Tipperary, near Ballydine, that once belonged to the Butler dynasty
16	*Lady Iveagh:* Margaret Butler, Viscountess Iveagh, who died in 1744

Guidelines

Ní Chuilleanáin was asked to translate this poem by one of her graduate students and his mother. They were writing a book about the history of Kilcash and had re-edited the poem 'Caoine Cill Chais'. They then asked the poet to translate it and it has now become the official translation of the poem. It was first published in 1999 in a book called *Kilcash*, and was then included in Ní Chuilleanáin's *Selected Poems* in 2001. Some of your grandparents may have sung the original poem in school *as Gaeilge*. It was written around 1800, and its authorship is unknown. Until 1999 it was widely believed that Fr Lane (who benefited from Lady Iveagh's generosity in educating him for the priesthood) wrote the poem, but this is now refuted.

Ireland at that time had been profoundly affected by the plantations. The native ruling classes were replaced by the Protestant Ascendancy and the Penal Laws denied political and most land-owning rights to Catholics. In this poem, the focus is on the ecological and ideological alteration of Ireland as a result of this period. In the 1600s Ireland was heavily wooded, but by the end of the 1700s the native woodlands had been decimated as a result of settlers exploiting the land for commercial ventures. The clearing of the woods also meant that the dispossessed Irish had no place to hide and it prevented surprise attacks on the planters.

This poem laments Ireland's loss, typified in the collapse of Kilcash after the passing of its owner Lady Iveagh. Kilcash is now a ruin but it has a long association with Irish history. The lady referred to in the poem was Margaret Butler, Lady Iveagh. She was from a staunchly Catholic Derry family and married Colonel Thomas Butler of Kilcash Castle. The poem captures the demise of Kilcash and its family. They symbolise the decline of many great Irish families. After Lady Iveagh died, the woods were sold off. It had a devastating effect on not only the local Irish people but also on the land and the animals. The poem waits in hope for the return of the glory days of old, but Kilcash remains a ruin.

This poem looks at the impact of colonialism on nature and heritage. It captures the demise of a great estate and the sense of abandonment felt by the Irish. It has a simple form and rhyming scheme, but is rich in imagery and symbolism.

Stanza 1 and 2

In the first stanza we hear the voice of the desperate Irish asking what will happen now that the woods have been destroyed and the occupants of Kilcash have disappeared. It laments the loss of Lady Iveagh, the heroine of the song, who was greatly admired: 'Earls came across oceans to see her' (line 7). There is a reference here to her faith, when the Earls came they could hear the 'sweet words of Mass' (line 8). She died and is buried in Kilcash and at her funeral her piety, charity and universal benevolence were praised. Fr Lane described her as a 'lady of great personal charm and a bright example of every female virtue'.

It was with great despair and anguish that the Irish watched the gradual disintegration and deterioration of the gardens and the house. This decline was mirrored in the people as they became 'depressed and tamed' (line 14) under the new rule.

Stanza 3 and 4

These stanzas look at the effect of the social and political change on the flora and fauna of Kilcash. The birds and the bees are silenced and stilled. The bee hives that once were so active have been deserted and the birds whose song once soothed all who heard them are now 'dumb' (line 23). The people and animals that moved on and followed 'the mountain way' (line 26) look on in pity at the diminished house. The once well-maintained lawns are overgrown and exposed; the paddock, once a place of order and refinement, is now a dairy.

Stanza 5

In this stanza we see that where there was light there is now darkness, streams are no longer gushing with water but run dry. No fruit grows on the trees and nature's cycle appears to be corrupted. The leafless park bears witness to chaos, even the game has 'gone wild' (line 40). Nature is now spoiled and thwarted.

Stanza 6

This stanza is probably the most puzzling of the poem. The previous stanzas outline the catastrophic effect on Kilcash of her departure and here we reach the climax, the 'worst of our troubles' (line 41), which is that 'She has followed the prince of the Gaels' (line 42). One commentator states that this stanza moves from the local interest of Lady Iveagh to an unspecified national Irish leader. In an inverse manner the specifically local poem has been given national significance as the cutting down of the woods had a deeper symbolic resonance with the Irish. There is the possibility that two similar poems were combined and that would explain the different focus within the stanza.

Stanza 7

The final stanza appeals to Mary and Jesus to bring Lady Iveagh back home. Lady Iveagh has passed on and they do not really expect her back but the motif of the leader who will return is a common one among oppressed nations. This final vision is apocalyptic: 'our ancestors' house will rise up' (line 53), order will be restored, and 'Kilcash built up anew' (line 54). This outcome will be celebrated and Kilcash will 'never be laid low' (line 56) again.

Thinking about the poem

1   The first two lines of the poem give us an insight into the plight of the people of Kilcash at this time. Based on the poem, describe the position that they are in.
2   What impression do you get of Lady Iveagh? Explain using examples from the poem.
3   This was a very popular poem/song in its time. Suggest possible reasons for this.
4   Which of the following statements do you think best describes how the speaker of the poem is feeling?
   ● The speaker is bewildered.
   ● The speaker is angry.
   ● The speaker is afraid.
   ● The speaker is forlorn.
   ● The speaker feels abandoned.
   Explain your choice.
5   'In this poem all our senses are stimulated.' Do you agree with this statement? Give a reason for your opinion.
6   We do not know the authorship of the original poem. Is that important? Explain your opinion.
7   Describe the tone of the poem.
8   The sixth stanza stands out from the others. What makes it different?
9   Select your favourite image from the poem and state why.
10 Comment on the reference to the line 'She may come home safe to us here' (line 50).

Personal response

1   Imagine that you are a newspaper reporter. Using details from the poem write an account of Kilcash since the passing of Lady Iveagh.
2   Imagine you are an estate agent. Write a description for the brochure of Kilcash prior to its demise.

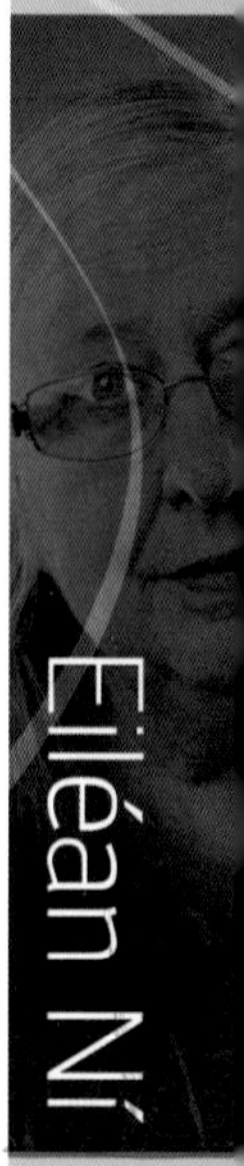

In small groups, gather as much information as you can from each other's knowledge of the Magdalen laundries. Share the information with the class, then read 'Translation' by Eiléan Ní Chuilleanáin.

Translation

for the reburial of the Magdalenes

The soil frayed and sifted evens the score –
There are women here from every county,
Just as they were in the laundry.

White light blinded and bleached out
The high relief of a glance, where steam danced
Around stone drains and giggled and slipped across water.

Assist them now, ridges under the veil, shifting,
Searching for their parents, their names,
The edges of words grinding against their nature,

As if, when water sank between rotten teeth
Of soap, and every grasp seemed melted, one voice
Had begun, rising above the shuffle and hum

Until every pocket in her skull blared with the note –
Allow us now to hear it, sharp as an infant's cry
While the grass takes root, while the steam rises:

    Washed clean of idiom • the baked crust
    Of words that made my temporary name •
    A parasite that grew in me • that spell
    Lifted • I lie in earth sifted to dust •
    Let the bunched keys I bore slacken and fall •
    I rise and forget • a cloud over my time.

5

10

15

20

Eiléan Ní Chuilleanáin

Handwritten annotations:
- sarcasm? irony?
- buried properly
- funeral / actual women (effects people everywhere)
- youth gone
- alliteration. Identity gone
- girls seen as unclean
- sad image – girls have lost their youth
- burial / nuns
- sharp names → all the names they were called
- image of scrubbing
- hands + soap melting
- assonance
- (babies) simile alliteration
- don't forget
- more people speak out
- badness of nuns = parasite
- NUN
- power gone
- I rise and forget → regret
- negative

Guidelines

The women (around 30,000) who were admitted to the Magdalen institutions (laundries) over a period of about 150 years were known as the Magdalenes. They were incarcerated, many against their will, at the request of the state, their family and priests, for a variety of reasons including growing up in care, stealing, prostitution and getting pregnant outside marriage. In some cases, young girls who were considered too promiscuous were sent to the Magdalen asylum. In 1993 an order of nuns in Dublin sold part of their convent to a property developer. Not long after the building works commenced, the remains of 155 women were discovered on the grounds of the convent. The discovery became a huge public scandal. Their bodies, in unmarked graves, were exhumed. They were later cremated and reburied together in Glasnevin. This poem was read at that ceremony.

Ní Chuilleanáin's poetry regularly features nuns. She refers to them affectionately and is usually very respectful towards them. This poem is different; here, she addresses a darker side and explores the role that many of them played in oppressing and institutionalising thousands of helpless women, women whose lives were stolen and whose deaths were hidden. This poem seeks to elicit speech from these silenced women, to 'translate' their silence into expression. It also gives a voice to the nuns who were responsible for this atrocity.

Commentary

Stanza 1

This stanza refers to the communal grave where the women who came 'from every county' (line 2) and worked in the laundry were buried. The opening line is macabre and powerful: 'The soil frayed and sifted evens the score'. It is left hanging. The soil that they were and are a part of has been 'sifted' and 'frayed'. The line is ambiguous as we do not know whether this 'evens the score' or whether it is even possible to right such a terrible wrong. One critic comments that the word 'score' here could suggest the aggressive imposition of an imprint. The power balance between the nuns and these women is also hinted at here. The nuns had absolute power in the laundries and the women were totally subservient and impotent.

Line 3, 'Just as they were in the laundry', compares the laundry and the gravesite, as though the grave has become an extension of the laundry. On entry into these laundries women's past lives were erased, they were given new names and they became anonymous. This is exactly how they remain in the grave: abandoned and anonymous but together.

Stanza 2

We get a glimpse of the happiness that these women could have enjoyed, the 'high relief' (line 5), the dancing and giggling that might be associated with young women. These women were deprived of such simple joys. 'White light' may symbolise their innocence and hope but it is 'blinded', they neither see it nor are exposed to it, it is 'bleached' out of their lives (line 4). Bleach is a very strong chemical that may have been used in the laundry as a stain remover and as a disinfectant. The alliteration of these verbs, 'blinded and bleached', conveys the horrific treatment that the women had to endure as atonement for their supposed transgressions. It enables us to further empathise with them. There is something arbitrary about how they were treated, similar to the dirty linen that passed through the laundry. The alleged stain on their past lives was being bleached out and their happiness was erased in the process.

The natural liveliness of the young women is poignantly displaced onto the steam, which unlike them is free to dance around, giggle and slip across the water. It disappears like the hopes and happiness of the girls. Ironically, it is the objects of labour that express the women's lost ability to dance and laugh.

Stanza 3 and 4

The girls are now mere 'ridges under the veil' of the anonymous earth, but they are 'shifting' (line 7). They are unsettled spirits: in death they are 'Searching for their parents, their names' (line 8), their stolen identities and lives. 'The edges of words grinding' (line 9) may be referring to the harsh and humiliating manner in which the girls were spoken to, which ground them down. In a sense the poem itself offers a counter to these sharp words as it highlights the corruption that forced these women into labour.

There is a prayer-like note of invocation at the start of stanza 3: 'Assist them now' (line 7). The appeal is not directed at anyone in particular. It could be intended for us, asking us to remember them, or it could be asking God to let them finally rest in peace.

The 'rotten teeth / Of soap' (lines 10 and 11) is a curious image and we could see the soap as a metaphor for the victims' souls that have become eroded from the daily labours. The teeth may symbolise the negligent treatment of the women (many of the skeletal remains displayed signs of abuse and neglect).

In the poem, as in the grave, the women's identities merge. Their choral voice has been communicating from beyond the grave in a 'shuffle and hum' (line 12). At this point, however, 'one voice' (line 11) is about to be given the last word.

Stanza 5 and 6

The last word is given to one of the nuns. Her voice is compared to 'an infant's cry' (line 14): shrill and hard to ignore. It speaks 'While the grass takes root' (line 15); that is, as time moves on. The speaker in the poem asks the reader to hear this voice: 'Allow us now to hear it' (line 14) – it is important that this nun is given a voice too.

Her speech is a 'note' of disgust that blares in her own 'skull' (line 13). She recognises the 'parasite' – power – that had grown inside her, the 'spell' that was cast on her (line 18). She speaks as if she was possessed by something evil or brainwashed by 'the baked crust / Of words' that are now 'Washed clean of idiom' (lines 16 and 17). Perhaps this corrupted and altered self that she speaks of only happened after she joined the order. The nuns, like the Magdalenes, were given new names and identities when they entered the convent. Many were asked to break contact with their families and devote their whole existence to God. She refers to her name as 'temporary' (line 17); perhaps she returned to her true self and her true name when she died, when she too lay 'in earth sifted to dust' (line 19).

Her 'bunched keys' (line 20) are a sign of her gatekeeping function and her authority, but they have no meaning now. She is no longer in control. She rises and forgets like the steam in the air, but the fact that the 'cloud' (line 21) remains makes the reader wonder whether she could ever forgive herself or forget the ignominy and impact of her actions.

This poem ensures that we do not forget 'a cloud over our time' (line 21) – this very dark period in Irish social history. The poet does not offer us any healing at the end. We do not know whether the 'score' is even (line 1). There is no attempt to wrap this one up nicely. The poem simply demands recognition of this event. One critic remarked that their story is exhumed here and (in a literal act of translation) reburied with dignity. In doing this Ní Chuilleanáin exposes the deeds of the unjust, no less than the sufferings of the just.

Thinking about the poem

1. Describe in five to ten lines what you think the poem is about.
2. The poem makes many comparisons throughout, pick two and explain them.
3. Do you agree that there is a real sense of unrest among the souls in the grave? Explain your answer.
4. Is it fair that the nun gets the last word in the poem? Explain your thinking.

5 The nun refers to the 'parasite' (line 18) that grew in her and the 'spell' (line 18) that was cast on her. In your opinion, is this an adequate attempt at explaining her actions?

6 Is the score ever settled in the poem? Explain your thinking.

7 Describe the tone of the poem.

8 Ní Chuilleanáin gives expression to silence. Do you agree with this claim? Give reasons for your answer.

9 Which of the following statements is closest to your view of the poem?
- It is a poem about injustice and oppression.
- It is a poem about shame and regret.
- It is a poem about evil and power.

Give reasons for your choice.

10 'ridges under the veil' (line 7) could have several meanings. Discuss what this phrase may be referring to.

11 Steam is a reoccurring motif in the poem. Explain when and why the poet uses it.

12 Comment on the phrase 'the baked crust / Of words' (lines 16 and 17).

13 Is the title appropriate? Give reasons for your view.

Personal response

1 Imagine you are one of the Magdalenes, write an account of why you are in the convent and how different it is from your previous life.

2 Imagine that you have arrested the nun in the poem. In pairs, write out the interrogation and act it out for the class (one person taking the role of the nun and the other the detective inspector).

3 Imagine you are a journalist at the reburial of the Magdalenes. With an account of the event for the evening edition of the newspaper.

Before you read 'The Bend in the Road'

Before reading 'The Bend in the Road' on page 318, think of a place from your childhood that you remember clearly. Describe it to the student beside you and list four big changes that have happened in your life since then.

The Bend in the Road

This is the place where the child
Felt sick in the car and they pulled over
peaceful And waited in the shadow of a house.
personification A tall tree like a cat's tail waited too.
They opened the windows and breathed 5
Easily, while nothing moved. Then he was better.

TRANSCIENCE

Over twelve years it has become the place
Where you were sick one day on the way to the lake.
You are taller now than us. *marvelling*
alliteration The tree is taller, the house is quite covered in 10
assonance With green creeper, and the bend } *some things*
In the road is as silent as ever it was on that day. } *don't change*

memories
everything Piled high, wrapped lightly, like the one cumulus cloud
growing In a perfect sky, softly packed like the air, ← *simile*
Is all that went on in those years, the absences, 15
The faces never long absent from thought,
The bodies alive then and the airy space they took up
HER When we saw them wrapped and sealed by sickness
SISTER Guessing the piled weight of sleep
PEOPLE
We knew they could not carry for long; *AROUND*
HER 20
This is the place of their presence: in the tree, in the air.
calm, still *in nature*
(like road)

Glossary	
13	*cumulus cloud:* a small or medium-sized puffy cloud, flat on the bottom with rounded towers on top

Guidelines

This poem was written after the death of Ní Chuilleanáin's sister in 1990. The poet remembered one day when her sister was ill but was still moving around in her dressing gown. She had looked at her and thought that there is a space that is going to be empty, and so it proved.

The poem was set and written in Italy. Her sister loved Italy and they bought a house there, but she became too ill to travel and never got to fully enjoy it. The episode of Ní Chuilleanáin's son feeling sick in the car happened a couple of years after her sister's death. It reminded her of time passing and of empty spaces left behind.

Commentary

Stanza 1

The first stanza opens with 'This is the place' and we immediately get a sense that the poet is taking us on a journey. We stop at the bend in the road and the poet recalls the place where they pulled over and opened the car window to get some air for their son, who was feeling sick. There was stillness: 'nothing moved' (line 6). The tree and the house remained still. The 'shadow of a house' (line 3) and the inventive simile of the 'tall tree like a cat's tail' (line 4) enhance the imagery of this scene. When their son felt better, they moved on. The subject matter is instantly relatable: the child was momentarily travel-sick but recovered after some fresh air.

Stanza 2

The poet now moves on twelve years and recalls the place in a reflective way. It is no longer just a bend in the road. In memory, this event became associated with just that particular part of the road where her boy felt sick. She reflects on all the changes that have happened since then: her son and the tree are taller and the house is now covered with a creeper. Yet the road is as silent as it was.

Stanza 3

The memory is not static and it becomes interwoven with other recollections. The final stanza widens the scope of description from the house, the tree and the bend in the road, to the sky. The speaker accumulates past experiences and organises them in language. The experiences listed in the poem are 'Piled high' (line 13) upon each other, like clouds 'In a perfect sky' (line 14), giving a spatial dimension to the telling of the story.

As well as the accumulation of external experience, we also gather feelings of absence and loss, and memories of loved ones who suffered illness and have passed away. These are now brought together and given witness to in the voice of the speaker. Thus the poem stands as a monument to place and time, to absence and presence, to past and present, to the 'faces never long absent from thought' (line 16). These are firmly placed in a spatial context in the language of the poem, as expressed in the final line: 'This is the place of their presence: in the tree, in the air' (line 21). The poem also pays tribute to the invisible, the unseen presence of other things that – like the bend in the road – wait in silence to be discovered and brought to life.

Thinking about the poem

1. In the first stanza the poet describes a place where 'the child' felt ill and 'they' stopped the car until 'he' recovered. Give a possible reason for the poet's decision to use the third-person narrative here.
2. 'nothing moved' (line 6). Why is stillness important here?
3. In the second stanza the poet changes to the second-person narrative: 'you' were sick, 'you' are taller. Is this important? Give reasons for your answer.
4. List all the things that have changed since that day twelve years ago. Which ones do you think had a bigger effect on the poet and why?
5. Create one sentence that sums up the main message of the final stanza.
6. There is a very airy feel to the final stanza. Comment on two ways that this has been achieved.
7. Choose your favourite image from the poem and say why you have chosen it.
8. Do you agree with the final line of the poem? Give two reasons why or why not.

Personal response

1. In pairs, make a short two- or three-minute presentation on any aspect of this poem using Animoto, PowerPoint, etc. for your class. You can add music, images and sound effects to enhance the presentation.
2. Write a poem about a place you remember fondly from when you were a child and try to include some changes that have happened since then.

snapshot

The Bend in the Road

- Set and written in Italy
- Based on a real incident: poet's son getting travel sick
- Reminds us of time passing
- Captures the stillness of the scene
- Imagery enhances the scene
- Focus widens as poem progresses
- Change of narrative voice during poem
- Pays tribute to unseen presences

Before you read 'On Lacking the Killer Instinct'

The poem below could be read as a companion piece to 'Lucina Schynning in Silence of the Nicht'. In pairs, discuss what you remember about that poem.

On Lacking the Killer Instinct

One hare, absorbed, sitting still,
Right in the grassy middle of the track,
I met when I fled up into the hills, that time
My father was dying in hospital—
I see her suddenly again, borne back   5
By the morning paper's prize photograph:
Two greyhounds tumbling over, absurdly gross,

While the hare shoots off to the left, her bright eye
Full not only of speed and fear
But surely in the moment a glad power,   10

Like my father's, running from a lorry of soldiers
In nineteen twenty-one, nineteen years old, never
Such gladness, he said, cornering in the narrow road
Between high hedges, in summer dusk.

     The hare   15
Like him should never have been coursed,
But, clever, she gets off; another day
She'll fool the stupid dogs, double back
On her own scent, downhill, and choose her time
To spring out of the frame, all while   20
The pack is labouring up.

    The lorry was growling
And he was clever, he saw a house
And risked an open kitchen door. The soldiers
Found six people in a country kitchen, one   25
Drying his face, dazed-looking, the towel
Half covering his face. The lorry left,
The people let him sleep there, he came out
Into a blissful dawn. Should he have chanced that door?
If the sheltering house had been burned down, what good   30
Could all his bright running have done
For those that harboured him?

    And I should not
Have run away, but I went back to the city
Next morning, washed in brown bog water, and   35
I thought about the hare, in her hour of ease.

Glossary	
16	*coursed:* hunted (by hounds using sight rather than scent)

Guidelines

As mentioned above, this poem can be read as a companion piece to 'Lucina Schynning in Silence of the Nicht', which was written at the time of her father's illness. Ní Chuilleanáin escaped to the hills where she experienced the cathartic effects of nature. She found stillness and peace among the flora and fauna and she began to come to terms with her father's situation.

This poem was written after her father's death. She took a year off to revisit west Cork and be in the places where her father had lived and frequented. In this poem she reminisces about her father's past and the type of man he was. She recalls her earlier escape to the hills and she interrogates it. She comes to terms with her response and faces the reality of her father's passing.

Commentary

Stanza 1

The poet is reading the morning papers and she sees a photograph of two greyhounds, but it is the hare in the picture that grabs her attention. It prompts her to recall her escape to the hills when her father was sick. The hare in the picture is running for its life, she is petrified full of 'speed and fear' (line 9) and also what Ní Chuilleanáin calls 'a glad power' (line 10).

Stanza 2

Ní Chuilleanáin then recalls a story from her father's past. We are brought back to 1921, when her father was fighting for Ireland's independence. In this scene he is a nineteen-year-old boy being chased by the Black and Tans, who were notorious for their unnecessary violence and brutality towards the Irish. Their ferocious behaviour in Ireland led to them being dreaded and despised throughout the land. Her father was running from a group of them; like the hare, he was running for his life. In this moment he shared the hare's 'gladness' (line 13). This may well have been the effects of the adrenalin but it was accompanied by a strange knowingness that they could escape.

Stanza 3

Both the poet's father and the hare were aware of the injustice of being 'coursed' (line 16). They both knew the lay of the land and were 'clever' (line 17) enough to be able to evade the 'stupid dogs' (line 18). This stanza focuses on the hare's tale of pursuit. She will have to face this chase again but she has worked out strategies to confuse them for now and knows when to 'spring out of the frame' (line 20), making fools of the pack of hounds 'labouring' (line 21) behind.

Stanza 4

We return to the world of her father being pursued. The lorry is now like the dogs, it is 'growling' (line 22). Sharing the hare's cunning, he runs into the kitchen of a house, throws water over his face, grabs a towel and starts drying his face. The soldiers follow his trail and burst in the door of the same unsuspecting household. They are met with a family, one of whom looks a little 'dazed' (line 26) but that was to be expected given the surprise intrusion. The family became complicit in the high-stake ruse and so the soldiers, like the dogs, left unsuccessful in their pursuit.

The family let him stay the night and he emerges 'Into a blissful dawn' (line 29). This is followed by some important and revealing questions, which the poet has said that he directed towards himself. He questions whether he should have risked going into the house. For all his 'bright running' (line 31), things could have gone terribly wrong. It was a huge gamble; if the Black and Tans had recognised him they would have killed everyone in the house. In his heightened state, however, he thought only of his own survival.

Stanza 5

The focus then turns to the poet: 'I should not / Have run away' (lines 33 and 34). Here she may be referring to the time she left her father when he was ill initially. Perhaps she, like the hare and her father, did what she had to do to get past this really difficult situation. We get the sense that she had to ask herself difficult questions around this time. Was she selfish to leave? Should she have stayed with her family?

She appears to let herself off the hook, however: 'but I went back to the city / Next morning, washed in brown bog water, and / I thought about the hare, in her hour of ease' (lines 34–36). The important thing was that she went back to her father, she did not stay away. She had momentarily escaped to gather herself and when she returned, replenished from the healing power of nature, she became like the hare she had seen there, still and serene in a place where she was at 'ease' (line 36) with herself.

Thinking about the poem

1 In a few sentences describe what this poem is about.
2 Is the title appropriate? Give reasons for your view.
3 What does the hare have in common with her father and with the poet?
4 Was the poet's father selfish in his action of running into the house? Explain your answer.
5 There is great energy and movement in the descriptions of the chasing of the hare and of the poet's father. How is this achieved?
6 Does Ní Chuilleanáin forgive herself for leaving her father when he was ill? Support your view with evidence from the poem.

7 Which of these statements do you most agree with?
- The speaker is honest and upfront about her father.
- The speaker is annoyed and ashamed of her father.
- The speaker is very clear-eyed about her father.

Give reasons for your view.

8 What is your understanding of the term 'glad power' (line 10)?

9 Write down one line or phrase that you particularly like and state why.

10 Choose your favourite image from the poem and say why you chose it.

Personal response

1 Imagine that you are a member of the household that the poet's father escaped into. Write a diary account of that day.

2 We are not told what specific incident or situation the poet's father is running away from. Look up some of the events that took place around this time in Cork and imagine him into one of them. Write an account, from his perspective, of what it was and what part he played in it.

Before you read 'To Niall Woods and Xenya Ostrovskaia, married in Dublin on 9 September 2009'

Imagine that your future son or daughter is getting married like in the poem below. Compose a poem as a gift to them wishing them well in their future lives together.

To Niall Woods and Xenya Ostrovskaia married in Dublin on 9 September 2009

NB. SPELLING

When you look out across the fields
And you both see the same star harmony
Pitching its tent on the point of the steeple—
That is the time to set out on your journey,
With half a loaf and your mother's blessing. HOPE   5

assonance
Leave behind the places that you knew:
All that you leave behind you will find once more,
You will find it in the stories;
The sleeping beauty in her high tower
With her talking cat asleep   10
Solid beside her feet – you will see her again.

When the cat wakes up he will speak in Irish and Russian
And every night he will tell you a different tale
And the firebird that stole the golden apples,
Gone every morning out of the emperor's garden, 15
And about the King of Ireland's Son and the Enchanter's
Daughter. King of ireland won hand of enchanters daughter but
fell asleep and lost her to the king of the island of Mists

The story the cat does not know is the Book of Ruth
And I have no time to tell you how she fared
When she went out at night and she was afraid, 20
In the beginning of the barley harvest,
Or how she trusted to strangers and stood by her word:

You will have to trust me, she lived happily ever after.

Glossary

3	*steeple:* church tower or spire
18	*Book of Ruth:* a Bible story from the Old Testament

Guidelines

Ní Chuilleanáin composed this poem for, and read it on the occasion of, the wedding of her son, Niall Woods, and his bride, Xenya Ostrovskaia. Poems like this, written to celebrate a wedding, are called epithalamiums.

The wedding was a civil ceremony and as such precluded religious readings or religious iconography. Both parents were asked to speak for two minutes at the ceremony and Ní Chuilleanáin began to write a speech without much success. She decided to write this poem instead. She had initially wanted to read from the Book of Ruth but, as she could not, she decided to disguise it in her poem among the many other references to the folktales and fairy tales that she read to her boy as he was growing up. Many of the tales she alludes to involve a son or young man going out on a quest, overcoming adversity and finally getting the girl and living happily ever after. She also included some Russian folktales for his bride and her family.

The poem captures stories from both cultures but more importantly it highlights the unity of cultures in folktales. The names and places in these stories are different but the messages and the journeys are often very similar.

comment on how you find it refreshing that this one is overwhelmingly positive.

The poem is ultimately a mother's blessing to her son and daughter-in-law as they embark on a new life together.

Stanza 1

The poet is directly addressing her son and his bride. She tells him that when two people look out and 'see the same star' (line 2), then that is the right time to set out on a new 'journey' (line 4), in this case marriage. Stars are one of the most beautiful and enchanting symbols. They can symbolise our hopes and dreams and Ní Chuilleanáin outlines that when you have found someone who sees the same star, 'Pitching its tent on the point of the steeple' (line 3), you know your time has arrived.

Line 5 alludes to an old folktale in which three sons head out to fulfil a quest. Their mother asks them before they leave: 'Do you want the whole loaf and no blessing or half the loaf and my blessing?' The first and second sons say the whole loaf, it is a long journey and they feel they will need the food. However, when they come to a test of character they fail. The third son says half the loaf and your blessing. Then he meets a hungry person and gives the bread to him, receiving valuable advice on how to pass the test.

The first two sons do not trust the journey. They do not realise that they will be looked after and they guard their possessions from fear. The third son is the eternal optimist, the hopeful and trusting one who lives from an open heart and is taken care of. He ends up getting the princess, the kingdom and rescuing his two older brothers along the way. Her son was very familiar with this folktale and would have appreciated the sentiments that she was expressing here.

Stanza 2

She instructs the couple to embark on their own journey. She reassures them that whatever they leave behind they 'will find it once more . . . in the stories' (lines 7 and 8). She then lists some well-known characters from fairy stories: 'sleeping beauty' (line 9) in her high tower and a 'talking cat' (line 10). She highlights once more that they will see them again. This repetition is important. She may be referring to the time when they have their own children and will pass on these stories. Or she may be saying something more profound about the nature of stories, that there are truths and eternal messages in folktales and fairy tales that will always be there. This sentiment was eloquently expressed by Morpheus in Shakespeare's *A Midsummer Night's Dream*, when he states, 'Things need not have happened to be true. Tales and dreams are the shadow-truths that will endure when mere facts are dust and ashes, and forgot.'

Stanza 3

In this stanza she marries both the Irish and Russian folktale traditions. She speaks of the 'firebird that stole the golden apples' (line 14) from the garden of the emperor. This is a reference to the Russian fairy tale of 'Ivan Tsarevich, the Firebird, and the Grey Wolf'.

Eiléan Ní Chuilleanáin

327

Long ago, in a distant land, there lived a tsar who owned a wonderful orchard. The trees in this orchard grew golden apples, but every night a firebird would steal the best apples. Having been informed by his youngest son, Ivan, that the firebird is stealing the apples, the tsar ordered his three sons to catch the firebird alive and bring it to him.

Ivan, assisted by a grey wolf, managed to get not only the firebird but also a wonderful horse and a princess named Elena the Fair. At the border of his father's kingdom, Ivan and Elena stop to rest. Ivan's two older brothers, returning from their unsuccessful quest, come across them while they are sleeping. They kill Ivan and threaten to kill Elena if she tells anyone what happened.

Ivan lies dead for thirty days until the grey wolf revives him with magic water. He arrives at the palace on the wedding day of Elena and his brother. The tsar askes for an explanation and Elena tells him the truth. The tsar is furious and throws the older brothers into prison. Ivan and Elena are married, inherit the kingdom, and live happily ever after.

Ní Chuilleanáin then chooses an Irish folktale, 'King of Ireland's Son and the Enchanter's / Daughter' (lines 16 and 17), which contains many of the same elements of storytelling: a hero, a villain, a quest, a magical helper, a princess, and a happy ever after.

Stanza 4

Ní Chuilleanáin refers to the Book of Ruth in this stanza. This story from the Old Testament is about a woman called Ruth who is rewarded for her faithfulness, kindness and integrity with protection and prosperity. This may be the poet's hope for her son and daughter-in-law: she wishes that they remain faithful and kind towards each other and that this will be rewarded with protection and prosperity.

The final line indicates that Ní Chuilleanáin is giving them her blessing and her belief that they will live happily ever after.

Thinking about the poem

1   According to the poem, what is the significance of both Niall and Xenya seeing the 'same star' (line 2)?

2   From your reading of the poem, what sort of mother do you imagine the poet might be?

3   What might the poet mean when she writes, 'All that you leave behind you will find once more' (line 7)?

4   The poet includes both Russian and Irish folktales in the third stanza. Outline two reasons why you think she does this.

5   Look up the Book of Ruth and explain 'how she trusted to strangers and stood by her word' (line 22).

6   Which of the following statements is closest to your interpretation of the poem?
- It is a poem about folktales and the messages that they have for us.
- It is a poem written from a mother to her son wishing him well on his wedding day.
- It is a poem about romantic love and motherly love.

Explain your choice.

7   Having read an outline of the folktale featuring 'half a loaf', what messages might the poet be sending to her son?

8   In your opinion, what will her son and daughter-in-law find 'in the stories' (line 8)?

9   What is the effect of the word 'Daughter' as the only word placed on line 17?

Personal response

1   Imagine you are the son or daughter-in-law whom the poem is dedicated to. Write a thank you letter to your mother/mother-in-law for the wedding poem.

2   Imagine your mother was to write you a poem for your wedding day. What things might she include and why?

3   In small groups, draw up a list of suggestions for a successful marriage.

snapshot

Written to celebrate a wedding

Dedicated to poet's son and his bride

Mother wishing her son well as he embarks on his new life

Uses folktales and stories to convey messages to the couple

To Niall Woods and Xenya Ostrovskaia, married in Dublin on 9 September 2009

Theme of trust: she trusts her son and asks her son to trust her

Illustrates the kindness and wisdom of the mother

Free verse

Unites Irish and Russian cultures

Eiléan Ní Chuilleanáin

Exam-Style Questions

1   Give your personal response to the poetry of Eiléan Ni Chuilleanáin, describing the impact of the poems upon you. Support your answer by relevant quotation from the poems you have studied.

Here are some possible areas that you might focus on in your answer:
- Her themes
- The influence of folklore and fairy tales
- The gothic imagery and rich symbolism of her poems
- Her style and voice as a poet.

2   What in your opinion are the emotions and the emotional experiences explored in Ní Chuilleanáin's poetry and how are these conveyed in the language and imagery of the poems? Support the points you make by quotation from the poems you have studied.

3   'While critics grapple to capture themes and styles, they all agree that the beauty of the verse stands alone.' In the light of this statement, discuss the beauty of Ní Chuilleanáin's poetry.

4   'Ní Chuilleanáin's poetry uses the language of history, religion, landscape and myth to unlock those categories of experience for which poetry is the proper language.' Do you agree with this reading of the poet's work? Support the points you make by quotation from the poems on your course.

5   'Ní Chuilleanáin's poetry is deeply reflective and personally revealing.' Discuss this statement in relation to the poems on your course.

6   The poet has remarked about her poetry: 'Quite often when I use visual imagery I am hoping that the reader will think themselves into the poem and see; that the eye will visualise it as a moving presence in the poem, rather than just looking at a picture.' Comment on her view of her poetry. Do you agree with it? Support the points you make with reference to the poems on your course.

7   Write an essay in which you outline your reasons for liking or not liking the poetry of Ní Chuilleanáin. You must refer to the poems of Ní Chuilleanáin on your course.

8   'The roles of nature and of landscape in her poetry are rich in meaning.' In the light of this statement, discuss the role of nature and landscape in Ní Chuilleanáin's poetry.

9   'Ní Chuilleanáin's poetry is informed by the theme of crossing: the crossing from one realm of experience to another, from the realms of the everyday and ordinary to the realms of the spirit world and the world of the other.' From your study of her poetry, would you agree with this statement?

10 Select your favourite poems by Ní Chuilleanáin and explain what it is that you admire about them.

Sample essay

'Ní Chuilleanáin's poetry has a transformative force that gives voice to the unspoken stories of our lives and pays witness to the mystic spaces of the human soul.'

From your study of her poetry, do you agree with this statement? Support the points you make with reference to the poems on your course.

I agree with this statement about Ní Chuilleanáin's poetry. There are elements of this 'transformative force' present from her earliest poems right through to her most recent work. This transformation occurs through nature in 'Lucina Schynning in Silence of the Nicht' and through memory in 'Following'. It is inspired by art and love in 'Fireman's Lift' and it is attempted from beyond the grave in 'Translation'. The 'unspoken stories' that are given voice are generally her own but they can extend to people who may not have had a voice or whose voices were silenced, as in the case of the Magdalenes. In many of her poems 'the mystic spaces of the human soul' refers to the human condition that is filled with mystery, wonder and unanswered questions.

[Introductory paragraph refers to the question asked and indicates areas that will be developed]

'Lucina Schynning in Silence of the Nicht' was written while the poet's father was seriously ill and it describes how she temporarily escapes the pain of the situation by running away for three days. The unspoken story is the guilt and pain that she must have been experiencing around this time and the soul searching she needed to engage in to come to terms with her father's failing health. We see the transformative force of nature when she emerges from the 'ruin'. She saw the 'moon shining' and the heaven 'full of stars' and she 'felt moonlight on [her] head, clear after three day's rain'. She 'washed in cold water', cleansing her body and soul, washing away her guilt and fear. She hears the 'chirp of the stream running', reminding her of the constant flow of life and the redemptive power of water. She is now transformed: 'behind me the waves of darkness lay', she can move forward and face her reality, 'relaxed'. She has a fresh perspective and can see things anew. She compares herself to 'mosaic beasts on the chapel floor' whose church was destroyed during Cromwell's reign of terror, yet 'through the hole in the roof' they too 'saw the sky growing'. In this poem we see the transformative forces of nature, how they 'embraced' and bolstered her during her dark period, and provided her with a new outlook on life's mysteries.

[Discussion of the first poem refers to themes in the question posed; note how quotations are incorporated into the sentences]

In her poem 'Following' we hear the unspoken story of her longing to be with her father again. She wrote this after he died and in it she is chasing him through the labyrinth of her childhood and her fondest memories of him (she even takes us to the imagined after-world in search of him). The poem's transformative force rests in the invocation of her father's spirit. It is through the process of remembrance and recollection that he comes back to her. The poem begins with her following 'the trail of her father's coat through the fair'. The place is 'packed solid' with 'dealing men' and 'beasts', she can only catch glimpses of her father. His 'shirt-cuff', 'handkerchief' and 'hat' – all symbols of refinement – give the reader a sense of the father. We then slip into a gothic spiritual world where she is following a 'dead corpse risen from the wakehouse'. This is a mystical space full of strange allusions and images that the poet may have associated with her father. Finally we arrive in the father's library, he is waiting for her and has 'whiskey poured out in two glasses'. She has found him. She describes him proudly in his 'finely laundered' clothes sitting where 'the light is clean'. This is in stark contrast to the eerie imagery of the previous stanza, where she was skimming 'across the shivering bog by starlight' searching for him. In this library she has metaphorically found her father. He is in her heart and her soul, where the memories, like the 'crushed flowers' in the books, are stored. Through this transforming process of recollection and searching, 'the pages crack the spine' open, pushing the 'bindings apart'. Her father's spirit is palpable and she is at peace in his presence.

[Discussion of a second poem, referring to the key terms of the question and using quotations to support points being made]

In 'Fireman's Lift' we really get a sense of the mystery of life and death and the transforming power of love. This poem was written after her mother's death. Like 'Following', she begins by recalling a memory: the cathedral in Parma in 1963 where she and her mother looked up at Correggio's 'Assumption of the Virgin'. When her mother was dying in hospital she commented that the sight of all the beautiful nurses lifting and moving her reminded her of the angels and saints that lifted and supported the Virgin Mary as she rose to heaven. In Parma in 1963, they both glimpsed Correggio's 'edge of the cloud' and were still left guessing as to what lies beyond. In Dublin in 1994, the mystery would be revealed to her mother as she left this world and entered the next. Ní Chuilleanáin hopes for a similar spiritual ascension for her mother, who is approaching the 'edge of the cloud' where the mystery begins. The transforming power of art enabled Ní Chuilleanáin to deal with the mystery surrounding death and it enabled her to express her love for her mother. Correggio expressed his love of Mary by painting this fresco, the angels and saints expressed their love for Mary by assisting her Assumption, and Ní Chuilleanáin here expresses her love of her mother by writing this beautiful poem.

[Third poem discussed in response to question]

Another poem that gives voice to an unspoken story is 'Translation'. This poem is different from the others mentioned so far in that what happens is more a translation than a transformation. This poem attempts to give expression to the silenced Magdelenes of the laundries and to their tormentors. The Magdalenes' voices are from beyond the grave, united by their painful past and their shared resting place: 'There are women here from every county, just as they were in the laundry'. The poem describes how the potential joy and happiness of these girls was 'blinded and bleached out' and how their lives, devoid of dancing or giggling, slipped away from them. The poet makes two prayer-like incantations: one to 'Assist them now' referring to the 150 women buried unceremoniously and anonymously and the other to 'Allow us now to hear it' referring to the solitary voice of a nun. It is questionable whether there is any transformation possible when it comes to the Magdalenes. Perhaps the best 'assistance' we can give is by remembering them and the atrocities they endured and this poem certainly ensures that. As for the nun, she appears transformed by death, she is now 'washed clean' of responsibility and free from the 'parasite that grew' inside her. With her 'bunched keys' now slackened and the control and 'spell' removed from her, she can 'rise and forget'. Ultimately, however, no one can forget the 'cloud over [our] time' that will remain a permanent stain in Irish social history and the poem records this. There is no neat wrapping up or resolution at the end of this poem. It reminds us of the unfathomable capacity for cruelty that we humans have.

[Fourth poem discussed in response to question; suitable quotations included]

In conclusion there are many instances of transformative forces at work in Ní Chuilleanáin's poetry. They enable us to hear not only the poet's unspoken story but also many of our own stories. Her poetry leans to the mystic spaces in the human soul and explores and examines them in an attempt to understand and come to terms with them. In doing this we see her capacity for fine detail, precise, delicate language and the creation of vivid and unforgettable poetry.

[Concluding paragraph revisits the key terms in the question and summarises the response]

Eiléan Ní Chuilleanáin

snapshot

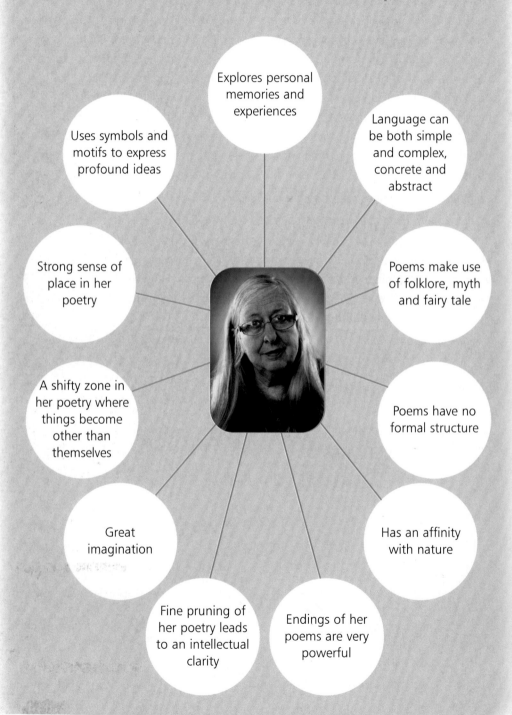

Explores personal memories and experiences

Language can be both simple and complex, concrete and abstract

Uses symbols and motifs to express profound ideas

Poems make use of folklore, myth and fairy tale

Strong sense of place in her poetry

Poems have no formal structure

A shifty zone in her poetry where things become other than themselves

Has an affinity with nature

Great imagination

Fine pruning of her poetry leads to an intellectual clarity

Endings of her poems are very powerful

Sylvia Plath

1932–63

Biography

Sylvia Plath was born in a seaside suburb of Boston, Massachusetts, in 1932. Both her parents, Otto Plath and Aurelia Schober, were academics and had German ancestry. They believed in the virtues of hard work and were committed to education. Sylvia was a bright, intelligent child and won many school prizes and awards.

When she was eight years old, her father died. On learning of his death, Plath declared, 'I'll never speak to God again.' Anxious to spare Sylvia and her younger brother, Warren, any unnecessary upset, Aurelia did not bring them to the funeral. Her father's death haunted Plath for the remainder of her life.

Otto's death left the family in straitened circumstances. Aurelia took up a full-time teaching job to support her children and Sylvia's grandparents moved in with the family in a house in the prosperous suburb of Wellesley. Plath later wrote that the move to Wellesley marked the end of her idyllic childhood by the sea.

The young writer

All through High School, Plath published poems and stories in local and national newspapers and in her school magazine. In her final year at school *Seventeen*, a national teen magazine, published her short story 'And Summer Will Not Come Again'. It was an important landmark in the young writer's life.

In 1951 Plath won two scholarships, which allowed her to attend Smith College, an exclusive women's college in Massachusetts. Her talent and intelligence were nurtured by the teaching staff there and she continued to have her work published. During her second year at Smith she was awarded a fiction prize by *Mademoiselle*, a fashionable, upmarket magazine for young women.

Personal insecurity

Despite academic, personal and social success, Plath was deeply insecure. The beginning of her third year in college saw her beset by many doubts and uncertainties. A four-week guest editorship at *Mademoiselle* in New York did little to improve matters.

Failure to secure a place on a summer writing course run by Frank O'Connor at Harvard in 1953 caused a crisis, and she was sent for psychiatric treatment. A poorly supervised and administered series of electric shock treatments worsened her condition and she made an attempt to take her own life. She was missing for three days, unconscious in a narrow space under the family home. She recovered her health over a period of six months with the help of a sympathetic psychiatrist.

Smith College offered Plath a scholarship to allow her to finish her degree, and she returned to the college in spring 1954, graduating with distinction. By then she had acquired a growing reputation as a writer.

Cambridge and early career

More success came her way in the form of a prestigious Fulbright scholarship to study at Cambridge University in England. Plath entered Newnham College in October 1955. It was in Cambridge that Sylvia Plath met the poet Ted Hughes. After a whirlwind romance, the couple married on Bloomsday, 16 June 1956. Following a two-month honeymoon in France and Spain, Plath returned to Cambridge to complete her studies. She continued to write, while, at the same time, helping Hughes to organise and send out his work. 'Black Rook in Rainy Weather' was written in this period.

The couple moved to the United States in summer 1957, and Plath taught for a year at Smith College. She found the job taxing and considered herself to be a poor teacher. She was also frustrated that she had so little time to devote to her writing. At the end of the academic year in summer 1958 she resigned her teaching position.

Plath rented an apartment in Boston. It did not go well. She suffered from writer's block and depression. 'The Times Are Tidy' was one of the few poems she completed. She was worried by financial concerns and tried to supplement their income by taking part-time secretarial work.

By summer 1959 things had improved. Hughes continued to write and publish and Plath, too, completed some poems and short stories. The couple then decided to return to England. First, however, they spent two months at a writer's colony in New York state. Relieved of domestic duties, Plath wrote freely and finished a number of the poems that are included in *The Colossus*, the only collection of her work published during her lifetime.

Mother, wife and poet

Frieda Rebecca Hughes, the couple's first child, was born in April 1960 in London. By this time Heinemann had agreed to publish *The Colossus* and Hughes had won the prestigious Somerset Maugham Award. Plath, however, was disappointed by the lack of reaction to *The Colossus* and, while she loved her husband and new daughter, found that the roles of mother and wife took her away from her writing.

1961 was a topsy-turvy year for Plath. It began with the sadness of a miscarriage, followed by an operation to remove an appendix. She likened her recovery from this to a resurrection. A contract with the *New Yorker* magazine boosted her morale and she began work on her novel, *The Bell Jar*.

When Plath became pregnant the couple decided to look for a house in the country, eventually moving, in autumn, to Court Green in Devon, a rambling, crumbling old house with three acres of lawn, garden and orchard. Despite her pregnancy, the care of a young daughter and the practicalities of setting up home in an old house, Plath wrote with great energy in her first months in Devon, though the poems she completed, including 'Finisterre' and 'Mirror', are marked by a sense of threat, fear and menace.

In January 1962 Plath gave birth to her second child, Nicholas. Her experience of birth and her remembrance of her miscarriage in the previous year inform her radio play *Three Women*, which she wrote for the BBC in spring 1962. The poems written later in 1962, most notably 'Elm', are dark meditations on love and self-knowledge.

By summer 1962 Plath's marriage to Hughes had begun to unravel. Hughes became involved with Assia Wevill, the wife of a Canadian poet. He left Court Green. A holiday in Ireland in September failed to save Plath's marriage.

Failing health

Back in Court Green in October and November 1962, Plath, working early each morning, wrote forty of the poems that make up the collection *Ariel*, including 'Poppies in July' and 'The Arrival of the Bee Box'. *Ariel* was published after her death. By any standards, these are remarkable poems.

Writing to a friend, she said, 'I am living like a Spartan, writing through huge fevers and producing free stuff I had locked in me for years.' The strain of writing these intense, personal poems began to affect her health. Her letters to her mother, from this period, are touched with desperation.

In November Plath decided to move back to London. She found a flat in the house where W. B. Yeats had once lived. By December she had closed up Court Green and moved into her new home with her two young children.

In January 1963 some of the worst weather seen in London for decades, allied to the delay in obtaining a phone, and the colds and flu she and the children suffered, cast her down and left her feeling isolated. She was further disheartened by the fact that her new work was, on the whole, rejected by the editors to whom she sent it. The publication of her novel, *The Bell Jar*, under a pseudonym, did little to lift the gloom.

Plath's final poems (including 'Child'), written in late January and early February 1963, reveal that her will to live was almost spent. She sought medical help and was put on a course of anti-depressants. Arrangements were made for her to see a psychiatrist. However, in the early hours of Monday 11 February 1963, overcome by a despairing depression, she took her own life.

Ariel, a collection of her final poems, was published in 1965. Since that time, it has sold over half a million copies. Plath's life, death and poetry have been the subject of much controversy. Understandably, given the tragic circumstances of her death, much of the response to her poetry has sought to relate her work to her life – to find clues in her poetry to explain her suicide or to attribute blame.

The difference between the personality that Plath reveals in her letters home to her mother and the darker personality of her journals has also attracted the attention of critics. Rarely has a poet left such a disputed body of work.

Social and Cultural Context

Plath was born into a male-dominated world. Her father ruled the family. Her mother was the wife and homemaker. Plath attended a college for girls, where she wanted to achieve and be a perfect American girl. Magazines like *The Ladies Home Journal* defined this ideal. A woman should be a wife, a homemaker and a mother, but she was not expected to be a professional or to have her own career. She was to be respectable. There was, in this middle-class culture, a tolerance of male promiscuity but girls were expected to be modest and virginal. Not to marry was to risk being labelled 'unfeminine'.

Plath struggled to escape this ideal of perfection. Her letters to her mother are full of references to her attempts to make a home for herself and Hughes and to win her mother's approval. She was conscious of this tendency in herself, noting in her journal: 'Old need of giving mother accomplishments, getting reward of love.' Her biographer, Anne Stevenson, says of the letters Plath wrote to her mother:

> Letters Home can be seen as one long projection of the 'desired image' (the required image) of herself as Eve – wife, mother, home-maker, protector of the wholesome, the good and the holy, an identity that both her upbringing and her own instinctive physical being had fiercely aspired to.

Search for an identity

Much of Plath's poetry can be seen as a struggle to create a new identity for herself that transcended the cultural limitations imposed upon women. Given society's view of women, Plath found it difficult to find acceptance as a writer outside of women's books and magazines. In her lifetime, her work won serious admiration from only a small number of people. She was more famous for being the wife of the poet Ted Hughes than for being a talented, ambitious and dedicated poet, novelist and short story writer, in her own right.

Plath's desire to fit in at school and be an all-American girl was deepened by her consciousness of her German ancestry. Plath's use of Holocaust imagery and her reference to her father as a Nazi in her poem 'Daddy' indicate a feeling of displacement, a fear that she might, somehow, be tainted by her origins. She also employed Holocaust imagery to speak of the suffering of women.

More than is sometimes acknowledged by critics, Plath was attuned, in a personal way, to the major historical issues of her time. She lived during the period of the Cold War and the ever-present threat of nuclear warfare between the United States and the Soviet Union. She was conscious of the dangers of a nuclear conflict and concerned for the future safety of her children. Plath wrote of these fears in a letter to her mother in December 1961:

> The reason I haven't written for so long is probably quite silly, but I got so awfully depressed two weeks ago by reading two issues of *The Nation* all about the terrifying marriage of big business and the military in America . . . and the repulsive shelter craze for fallout, all very factual, documented and true, that I simply couldn't sleep for nights with all the warlike talk in the papers . . . I began to wonder if there was any point in trying to bring up children in such a mad, self-destructive world. The sad thing is that the power for destruction is real and universal.

The fears expressed here find their way into her poetry in the terrifying imagery of her last poems.

Displacement

For Plath, the opportunity to live and study in England was a partly liberating experience. From England she could view with clarity the consumerism and militarism of US culture. However, she did not always feel at home in England and disliked the shabby inefficiency that she saw in English life. Plath was caught between the two cultures, feeling ambivalent towards both. Her feelings of displacement are important in shaping the poetry she wrote.

Timeline

1932	Born on 27 October in Boston, Massachusetts
1940	Her father dies. Sylvia declares, 'I'll never speak to God again'
1950	*Seventeen* publishes her story 'And Summer Will Not Come Again'
1951	Wins scholarship to the exclusive Smith College for women
1953	Wins guest editorship at *Mademoiselle* magazine; attempts suicide after failing to gain a place on writing course in Harvard
1954	Graduates with distinction from Smith College
1955	Wins Fulbright Scholarship and goes to Cambridge; meets the poet Ted Hughes
1956	Marries Hughes on Bloomsday
1960	Gives birth to Frieda Rebecca Hughes, the couple's first child; publishes first collection, *The Colossus*
1961	Moves to Devon; writes with great energy in first months there; concerned by talk of nuclear warfare
1962	Gives birth to her son, Nicholas; Plath and Hughes separate; writes over 40 poems in October and November; moves to London
1963	Publishes her novel, *The Bell Jar*; takes her own life in February
1965	*Ariel*, a collection of her last poems, is published

Black Rook in Rainy Weather

On the stiff twig up there
Hunches a wet black rook
Arranging and rearranging its feathers in the rain.
I do not expect miracle
Or an accident   5

To set the sight on fire
In my eye, nor seek
Any more in the desultory weather some design,
But let spotted leaves fall as they fall,
Without ceremony, or portent.   10

Although, I admit, I desire,
Occasionally, some backtalk
From the mute sky, I can't honestly complain:
A certain minor light may still
Leap incandescent   15

Out of kitchen table or chair
As if a celestial burning took
Possession of the most obtuse objects now and then –
Thus hallowing an interval
Otherwise inconsequent   20

By bestowing largesse, honour,
One might say love. At any rate, I now walk
Wary (for it could happen
Even in this dull, ruinous landscape); sceptical,
Yet politic; ignorant   25

Of whatever angel may choose to flare
Suddenly at my elbow. I only know that a rook
Ordering its black feathers can so shine
As to seize my senses, haul
My eyelids up, and grant   30

A brief respite from fear
Of total neutrality. With luck,
Trekking stubborn through this season
Of fatigue, I shall
Patch together a content   35

Of sorts. Miracles occur,
If you care to call those spasmodic
Tricks of radiance miracles. The wait's begun again,
The long wait for the angel,
For that rare, random descent.   40

Glossary

8	*desultory*: changing in a random way
10	*portent*: omen, a sign or indication of a future event
15	*incandescent*: red hot or white hot, shining, luminous
17	*celestial*: heavenly
18	*obtuse*: dull, insensitive
19	*hallowing*: to make holy or sacred
20	*inconsequent*: trivial, insignificant
21	*largesse*: generosity
23	*Wary*: alert, vigilant
25	*politic*: discreet, prudent
31	*respite*: rest, temporary relief
33	*Trekking*: making a long, hard journey
37	*spasmodic*: in sudden, brief spells

Guidelines

'Black Rook in Rainy Weather' is contained in Plath's first collection, *The Colossus* (1960). It was originally published in the English journal *Granta*, while she studied at Cambridge.

The poem alerts us to many features of Plath's style:

- The confident handling of rhyme and stanza form.
- The exploration of emotions and states of mind.
- The use of weather, colours and natural objects as symbols.
- The dreamlike or surreal world of the poem.

Although Plath uses 'I' in the poem, there is no simple relationship between this 'I' (the persona or speaker) and the writer. In fact many of her poems can be read as Plath trying out different identities. This poem explores the nature of poetic inspiration, and the necessity of such inspiration to ward off the speaker's fear of total neutrality.

Commentary

Describing the world

The poem begins with a clear description of the rook, sitting 'Arranging and rearranging feathers in the rain' (line 3). The sight is ordinary. The speaker of the poem tells us that she does not expect a 'miracle / Or an accident / To set the sight on fire' (lines 4–6). The words 'miracle' and 'fire' set up a contrast between the damp weather (the reality) and the fire of vision (the poet's imagination). The speaker is not expecting anything to happen. Her muse, her inner vision, seems to have deserted her. So she describes what she sees, content to let the world be as it is.

The word 'portent' (line 10) suggests the tradition of seeing the weather as a warning of things to come. The colour black is also associated with the ancient art of divination or prediction. In pre-Christian times a poet was considered to be a seer, a person possessed with the supernatural power of vision. This idea informs the poem's exploration of inspiration.

Inspiration

In stanza 3 the poet confesses that although she would like the sky to speak to her, she is not complaining. The reason for this is that the speaker believes that even the most ordinary object, such as a 'kitchen table or chair' (line 16), may appear transformed as if it was possessed by some heavenly fire. This visionary experience is described, in lines 19 to 22, in terms of heavenly generosity and love.

Although not stated directly, the poem suggests that poetic inspiration is like a gift from heaven. It is not within the control of the poet. It is not a matter of will or determination. **Inspiration, when it happens, has the quality of accident, favour and giftedness about it.** Nor is it that the poet is inspired, but rather that the world is transformed in the poet's presence. The adjectives 'incandescent' (line 15) and 'burning' (line 17) suggest the force and power of the experience of inspiration.

The speaker tells us that she is waiting for the angel, the symbol of heavenly visitation and inspiration, 'to flare / Suddenly at my elbow' (lines 26–27). The description of the landscape as 'dull, ruinous' (line 24) suggests how much the poet wants the angel to appear, while the adjective 'sceptical' in the same line implies that she is trying not to hope too much.

Fear and hope

Yet, the rook gives her reason to hope, for in catching a sight of him, she feels a lifting of her spirit and 'A brief respite from fear / Of total neutrality' (lines 31–32). These two lines are key to understanding the emotional centre of the poem. **Without vision, without the inspiration to write, the poet fears 'total neutrality'.** The words suggest a state of non-being, a blank. (This kind of fear is expressed in a number of other poems, including 'Poppies in July'.)

In lines 32 and 36 the speaker's voice falters, overcome by fatigue but hoping, 'With luck', to 'Patch together a content / Of sorts'. **The final stanza is balanced between faith and scepticism, between 'miracles' and 'tricks' (line 38). However, the poet's belief, or desire to believe, or need to believe, is expressed in the beautiful ending.** The image of the angel's 'rare, random descent' (line 40) calls to mind Pentecost, when, according to the biblical account, tongues of fire appeared over the apostles and they were filled with the Holy Spirit.

It is clear from this poem that for the speaker/poet, the threat to her well-being is posed by a fear of 'neutrality' (line 32). She is afraid that without moments of vision and the reassurance of her creativity, life and identity will be intolerable.

Style and form of the poem

The poem is written in unrhymed five-line stanzas, a form that Plath also uses in 'The Times Are Tidy' and 'The Arrival of the Bee Box'. The form allows for flexibility in rhythm and pacing. Reading the poem aloud allows you to hear the intricate sound patterns that Plath creates and the way in which she marries sound to the emotional tone of the poem. Consider, for example, the long, vowel sounds and the alliteration in line 33, which capture the effort and drudgery in going on: 'Trekking stubborn through this season'.

Thinking about the poem

1   What attitude to the rook and the weather does the speaker of the poem express in the first two stanzas? What do these stanzas suggest to you about the speaker?

2   How do you understand the idea of celestial burning, as presented in the poem? In your experience can ordinary objects be seized in the way described in lines 14 to 22 of the poem?

3   Consider the character of the speaker of the poem, as suggested by the adjectives ('wary', 'sceptical', 'politic') in lines 23 to 25. Having read the poem, what additional adjectives would you use to describe the speaker?

4   What is the fear referred to at the outset of stanza 7? Consider the possible meanings of the word 'neutrality' (line 32). How might the rook allay this fear? What is the relationship between the rook and the celestial burning referred to in the fourth stanza?

5   What is it that the speaker hopes to achieve, 'With luck' (lines 32–35)? What is your reaction to this hope?

6   What belief is expressed in the final stanza? How is the belief qualified?

7   'The wait's begun again' (line 38). Comment on the word 'again'.

8   'Trekking stubborn through this season / Of fatigue' (lines 33–34). Write a note on these lines and the way in which sound and sense combine.

9   The beauty of the last two lines of the poem has been remarked on by critics. What, in your view, makes them beautiful?

10   Examine the stanza form employed by the poet and comment on it.

11   Comment on the images of heat and light in the poem, and their relevance to the theme of the poem.

12   Consider the title of the poem and its relevance to the theme of the poem.

13   What does the poem say to you about imagination and the vision of the poet?

14   'The speaker of the poem is poised between hope and despair.' Comment on this view of the poem, supporting your answer by reference to the poem.

15   'Behind the controlled language of the poem there is a glimpse of a fearful and nightmarish personal world.' Is this a fair assessment? Support your answer by reference to the poem.

Personal response

1   Do you think that this poem is suitable or unsuitable for inclusion in a school anthology? Give reasons for your answer.

2   Using the title of this poem as your inspiration, write a poem that deals with weather and human moods and feelings.

The Times Are Tidy

Unlucky the hero born
In this province of the stuck record
Where the most watchful cooks go jobless
And the mayor's rôtisserie turns
Round of its own accord.   5

There's no career in the venture
Of riding against the lizard,
Himself withered these latter-days
To leaf-size from lack of action:
History's beaten the hazard.   10

The last crone got burnt up
More than eight decades back
With the love-hot herb, the talking cat,
But the children are better for it,
The cow milk's cream an inch thick.   15

	Glossary
2	*province*: here, a historical period; the word also carries the derogatory suggestion of a place that is culturally backward
2	*stuck record*: something that is going nowhere, as when a needle on a record player gets stuck on the vinyl surface of a record
3	*watchful cooks*: from the Middle Ages onwards the poisoning of food was common in attempts on the lives of the powerful; thus, cooks had to be vigilant, wary and politic
4	*rôtisserie*: traditionally, a pointed rod with a turning handle on which meat is skewered and roasted; today, an electric cooking apparatus, with a rotating spit
7	*lizard*: used here as a synonym for dragon
10	*hazard*: danger, risk; here, personal adventure
11	*crone*: withered old woman, witch

Guidelines

'The Times Are Tidy' was published in the 1960 collection, *The Colossus*. The poem was written during the summer of 1958, after Plath had resigned from her job as a teacher at Smith College.

This is one of the few Plath poems in which the 'I' persona does not appear. **The poem is a straightforward social comment on the blandness of contemporary culture compared with the fairy-tale world of the past.** (As a way of keeping up her German, the language of her ancestors, Plath read *Grimm's Fairy Tales*.)

Commentary

Stanza 1

The tone of the poem is ironic. It begins with a statement: 'Unlucky the hero born / In the province of the stuck record'. The suggestion is that the present is an unheroic age, with little opportunity for adventure or valour.

Stanza 2

The second stanza introduces the figure of the knight riding to battle the dragon ('lizard', line 7). There is no career, we are told, in such heroism. The word 'career' (line 6) suggests the difference between the heroic age of the past (not specified in time or place) and the career-minded world of the late 1950s. The stanza concludes with the statement: 'History's beaten the hazard' (line 10). Adventure is dead. It is impossible to read Plath's assessment of the bland safety of public life without thinking of the hazards that she feared in her private world.

Stanza 3

There is an ironic edge to the regret that announces: 'The last crone got burnt up / More than eight decades back' (lines 11–12). Magic and mystery, it seems, have died with her. The 'but' that introduces the two last lines is unconvincing; the speaker does not really believe that 'the children are better for it' (line 14) or that the thick cream is compensation.

Interestingly, around the time Plath wrote 'The Times Are Tidy', she and Ted Hughes were experimenting with a Ouija board. Plath found these sessions both intriguing and entertaining. She also shared Hughes' interest in tarot cards and horoscopes. **The consumer culture, rapidly developing in urban America, was too sanitised and removed from the superstitious beliefs that attracted her.** Perhaps the poem hints at the difference between Hughes' home county of Yorkshire in northern England, where superstitions still survived, and the urban culture of the United States, where they had disappeared.

Form of the poem

The poem shows Plath's attention to the craft of poetry. In each stanza there are interesting patterns of sound. Look, for example, how the vowel sounds 'o' and 'u' are woven into stanza 1. The 'k' sound in the first word of the poem is repeated at intervals and concludes the poem. The stanzas and rhymes are carefully worked. You might like to consider if all the rhymes are successful. Consider the lizard / hazard rhyme of stanza 2. Are the words well chosen?

Thinking about the poem

1 How is the disappearance of the world of fairy-tale adventure suggested in the first stanza?

2 Comment on the phrase 'the stuck record' (line 2) and the attitude it conveys.

3 Give examples of the people of whom it might be said they rode 'against the lizard' (line 7).

4 What is the meaning of the statement 'History's beaten the hazard' (line 10)?

5 How do you interpret the references to 'the love-hot herb' and 'the talking cat' (line 13)?

6 In your opinion, does the speaker believe that the gains referred to in the last two lines compensate for the losses mentioned in the rest of the poem? Support your answer by reference to the poem.

7 Describe the tone and mood of the poem and the attitude it expresses towards the contemporary world. Refer to the title of the poem, in your answer.

8 Is this a well-crafted poem? Explain your answer.

9 The poem is dismissed by some critics as a mere 'exercise'. What is your assessment of the poem?

Personal response

1 Your class has decided to make a video version of this poem for YouTube. In pairs or groups, discuss the sort of atmosphere you would like to create, and say what music, sound effects and images you would use.

2 You have been asked to find a poem to read at a school event. Would you choose this one? Explain your answer.

1961 *1961*

Morning Song

health *value* *life begins*

Love set you going like a fat gold watch. *harsh* *life is cruel*
The midwife slapped your footsoles, and your bald cry
Took its place among the elements. *vunerable*

BIRTH

Our voices echo, magnifying your arrival. New statue. *open to the elements now.* 5
In a drafty museum, your nakedness *lack of confidence*
Shadows our safety. We stand round blankly as walls.
dont know what to do. *fears for their relationship* *looking* *no words*

NEGATIVE

vunerable

detachement I'm no more your mother *puddle*
Than the cloud that distils a mirror to reflect its own slow
Effacement at the wind's hand. *sees her own destruction*

fragile *positive, gentle*
All night your moth-breath 10
onomatopoeic? Flickers among the flat pink roses. I wake to listen: *natural maternal instinct* *wall paper*
A far sea moves in my ear.
happy childhood memory.
realistic portrayl of new mother *awkword*
One cry, and I stumble from bed, cow-heavy and floral
hemmed in
In my Victorian nightgown.
Your mouth opens clean as a cat's. The window square 15

morning comes
Whitens and swallows its dull stars. And now you try
2nd cry Your handful of notes; *music crying*
The clear vowels rise like balloons. *gentle*
admiring the childs efforts to talk.
body taking its place in a more positive way.

POSITIVE

Glossary	
3	*elements*: earth, air, water and fire
9	*Effacement*: obliteration, erasure
11	*flat pink roses*: presumably the patterned wallpaper
13	*cow-heavy*: the poet's amused reference to her breasts heavy with milk

Guidelines

Plath wrote 'Morning Song', a poem on the birth of her daughter, in spring 1961, ten months after Frieda's birth, and shortly after a miscarriage. It was first published in *The Observer* newspaper in May 1961 and was later included in her posthumous collection *Ariel*, published in 1965. In November 1962 Plath arranged the poems for her collection, placing 'Morning Song' first so that the manuscript would begin with the word 'love' and end with the word 'spring' from the poem, 'Wintering'. (The published collection does not follow her wishes.)

'Morning Song' is clearly a celebration of birth, but there is also a suggestion of loss and separation in the imagery of the poem. The poem begins with the word 'love' and ends with the music of the child's cry rising 'like balloons'. In between it charts the mother's journey from her initial disorientation to her joyful acceptance of her baby.

Commentary

Estrangement

'Morning Song' opens with a bold statement and a striking image: 'Love set you going like a fat gold watch.' There is little sense of the miraculous or the mysterious in the slap that sets the child crying. The child's cry is described as 'bald' (line 2). It seems to express a basic instinct and, therefore, takes 'its place among the elements' (line 3). **The voice of the narrator, the mother, seems puzzled by what is happening, even as she speaks to her child. The sense of estrangement is captured in the imagery of the second stanza, where things seem out of proportion.** For example, 'Our voices echo, magnifying your arrival' (line 4).

The baby is like an exhibit in a museum, around whom the adults stand, unable to make sense of what it is they are looking at. The museum imagery is striking. The description of the baby as a 'New statue' (line 4) may indicate that the baby resembles a perfect work of art. The baby's fragility, her 'nakedness' in the 'drafty museum' (line 5), causes the parents to feel anxious about their ability to protect and safeguard the child they have brought into the world. This doubt is suggested in the phrase 'Shadows our safety' (line 6); *a* line that will support many interpretations. The word 'blankly' (line 6) is particularly significant as it implies that the experience of birth has somehow robbed the parents of their identity.

The sense of estrangement leads to a declaration in stanza 3, which rehearses an often-expressed fear in Plath's work: the fear of effacement, of annihilation. She fears that the birth of her child will rob her of her identity, just as the rain creates a mirror (in the form of a puddle or pool of water) in which the cloud is reflected and can see its own dispersal by the wind. This is a complex image of the relationship between mother and daughter.

Mother's protective response

There is a change in tone in the fourth stanza. The sound of the child's breath, symbolising its fragile, though insistent, hold on life, evokes the mother's protective response. After the estrangement of the opening stanzas, where the mother's response was frozen into an attitude of a blank wall in a museum setting, a more recognisable, domestic world appears. In contrast to the immobility of the second stanza, the child's cry stirs the mother into activity. Having regained her composure and her sense of self, she can laugh at herself: 'cow-heavy and floral / In my Victorian nightgown' (lines 13–14).

The speaker is now involved with her child, filled with wonder as her 'mouth opens clean as a cat's' (line 15). The image resonates with amused delight. The quality of happiness continues in the imagery of the growing light. The poem ends on a note of elation as the child's 'clear vowels rise like balloons' (line 18).

Form of the poem

The poem is written is unrhymed three-line stanzas. The first line has ten syllables, which is the standard line length in English poetry. What is interesting in the poem is how Plath breaks the line to achieve certain effects. Look, for example, how the short line 10 creates a space that is filled by 'flickers' on line 11, so that that we almost hear the child's breath in the sound and rhythm of the stanza.

Thinking about the poem

1. Comment on the importance of the words 'love' and 'elements' in the first stanza of the poem.
2. In what way is the child a 'New statue' (line 4)?
3. Explain, as clearly as you can, the museum imagery in stanza 2. What does it suggest about the relationship between the adults and the new-born child?
4. Tease out the meaning of the statement, 'your nakedness / Shadows our safety' (lines 5–6).
5. What is the tone of the declaration, 'I'm no more your mother' (line 7)?
6. What kind of relationship between mother and child is described in the cloud, mirror and wind imagery of the third stanza? Is it a distinctive view or does it express a general truth?
7. What does the moth imagery in stanza 4 suggest about the child?
8. What picture of the new mother is created in stanzas 4 and 5?
9. What is your favourite image in the poem? Explain your choice.

10 'Although tender in tone, the poem is clear-sighted and unsentimental.' Discuss this view of the poem.

11 'Even though the poem celebrates motherhood, the mother appears as an isolated and estranged figure.' Do you agree with this assessment of the poem? Support your answer by reference to the poem.

12 How do you imagine Frieda Hughes reacting to this poem about her birth?

Personal response

1 Frieda Hughes, Plath's daughter, is also a poet. Adopting her voice, write an answering poem to 'Morning Song', addressed to her mother and using details from the poem. You could begin with the line: 'You were the first to hear my handful of notes'.

2 You have been chosen to speak to your class about this poem. Write out the talk you would give. Your talk should include a summary of the content of the poem, and of your own views on it.

Before you read 'Finisterre'

Before reading 'Finisterre' by Sylvia Plath consider these questions: what kind of place do you imagine Land's End to be? If you were making a science fiction or horror film, how would you represent the place where the land ends? How would you feel if you arrived at such a place? Share your thoughts with a partner before reading the poem.

Finisterre

This was the land's end: the last fingers, knuckled and rheumatic,
Cramped on nothing. Black
Admonitory cliffs, and the sea exploding
With no bottom, or anything on the other side of it,
Whitened by the faces of the drowned.   5
Now it is only gloomy, a dump of rocks –
Leftover soldiers from old, messy wars.
The sea cannons into their ear, but they don't budge.
Other rocks hide their grudges under the water.

The cliffs are edged with trefoils, stars and bells   10
Such as fingers might embroider, close to death,
Almost too small for the mists to bother with.
The mists are part of the ancient paraphernalia –
Souls, rolled in the doom-noise of the sea.
They bruise the rocks out of existence, then resurrect them.   15
They go up without hope, like sighs.
I walk among them, and they stuff my mouth with cotton.
When they free me, I am beaded with tears.

Our Lady of the Shipwrecked is striding toward the horizon,
Her marble skirts blown back in two pink wings.   20
A marble sailor kneels at her foot distractedly, and at his foot
A peasant woman in black
Is praying to the monument of the sailor praying.
Our Lady of the Shipwrecked is three times life size,
Her lips sweet with divinity.   25
She does not hear what the sailor or the peasant is saying –
She is in love with the beautiful formlessness of the sea.

Gull-coloured laces flap in the sea drafts
Beside the postcard stalls.
The peasants anchor them with conches. One is told: 30
'These are the pretty trinkets the sea hides,
Little shells made up into necklaces and toy ladies.
They do not come from the Bay of the Dead down there,
But from another place, tropical and blue,
We have never been to.   35
These are our crêpes. Eat them before they blow cold.'

Glossary		
title	*Finisterre*: English name for Finistère, the westernmost part of Brittany, France	
1	*land's end*: the literal meaning of 'Finisterre'; from earliest times it was believed that the horizon marked the end of the created world	
1	*fingers*: here, rocks jutting into the sea; the imagery suggests the desperate clinging of a drowning person	

3	*Admonitory*: warning
7	*Leftover soldiers*: maimed veterans of the Algerian war
10	*trefoils, stars and bells*: wildflowers, identified by shape rather than name
13	*paraphernalia*: bits and pieces, miscellaneous items; here Plath is referring to the belief that the mists are the souls of the dead and associating this superstition with Finisterre
19	*Our Lady of the Shipwrecked*: statue commemorating lives lost at sea

Guidelines

'Finisterre' was among a group of poems that Plath wrote in autumn 1961, shortly after moving to Devon with her husband, Ted Hughes, and their daughter, Frieda. **Although this was one of the happiest periods of her personal life, the poems she wrote are dark.**

In June 1960 Plath and Hughes drove through Brittany, swimming along the rocky coastline of Finisterre. They also stopped at Berck-Plage, a seaside resort with a sanatorium for soldiers wounded in the Algerian war. Plath saw maimed soldiers limp among the holiday makers. The experience made a profound impression and called to mind her father's death, following the amputation of his leg. **The poems she wrote about Brittany – 'Finisterre' and 'Berck-Plage' – share a sense of death and menace, contrasting images of permanence and stability with those of formlessness and annihilation.** In this regard, it is worth bearing in mind that 'Finisterre' was written during a period when there was a serious risk of nuclear conflict between the Soviet Union and the United States. Plath wrote of her fears in a letter to her mother in December 1961.

The ocean played an important part in Plath's childhood and is a constant in the imagery of her poems. In a letter to her mother, written in 1958, she said, 'I am going back to the ocean as my poetic heritage.' She also wrote in her journal a note on the title of another of her poems, 'Full Fathom Five', which gives an insight into the importance of the sea for her:

> 'Full Fathom Five' . . . has the background of *The Tempest*, the association of the sea, which is a central metaphor for my childhood, my poems and the artist's subconscious, of the father image . . . and the pearls and coral highly wrought to art; pearls sea-changed from the ubiquitous grit of sorrow and routine.

As a twelve-year-old, Plath saw Shakespeare's *The Tempest*, a play that begins with a shipwreck, and she later associated Ariel's song, 'Full fathom five, thy father lies; / Of his bones are coral made', in that play with her own dead father.

Commentary

Different interpretations

At one level, 'Finisterre' is a description of a seaside resort. It depicts the rocky shoreline and the cliffs that surround the bay known as the Bay of the Dead. It describes the mists that rise from the sea, and the statue of Our Lady of the Shipwrecked, a memorial to the sailors who died at sea. The poem concludes with a description of the stalls and the trinkets sold by the local peasants. At another level, **'Finisterre' is a symbolic poem, in which the meeting of ocean and land is presented in terms of the recurrent drama of death and rebirth, of entrapment and freedom, and of form and formlessness.** As with other Plath poems, the symbolic language sends the reader off in many directions. Thus, 'Finisterre' can support different interpretations.

Form and formlessness

The vocabulary of the opening stanza suggests a pattern of force – 'knuckled', 'cramped', 'exploding' and 'cannons' – and of annihilation – 'end', 'last', 'nothing', 'Black' and 'bottom'. It is as if the Bay of the Dead is a site of battle between the sea and the land.

In the second stanza Plath sees, in the relationship between the sea mist and the rocks, an archetype or symbol of death and resurrection. **In describing the rocks and the sea mist, the poem juxtaposes the fixed and the fluid. The fixed forms of the rocks seem threatened by the formlessness of the sea and the mist, but they survive.**

The imagery of fixed forms and formlessness appears in the third stanza where the statue of Our Lady of the Shipwrecked is said to be 'in love with the beautiful formlessness of the sea' (line 27).

Final stanza

There is a shift of tone in the fourth stanza. We are back in the world of the living, on firm land. The peasants sell 'pretty trinkets' (line 31) to the tourists. The locals do not want their souvenirs to be associated with the Bay of the Dead. They tell her that the trinkets come from 'another place, tropical and blue' (line 34).

This place is like the world of Plath's childhood or the world of her poetry. She takes elements from the sea of her unconscious and makes them into poems. The poem ends with the peasants offering her some sustenance. They urge her to eat before the food goes cold. Although eating is associated with nurture, the final word of the poem, 'cold', returns to the idea of death that haunts the poem.

Thinking about the poem

1. The first five lines give a vivid account of the beliefs/fears once held about the sea. Describe these. Is there a relationship between these fears/beliefs and the private fears of speaker of the poem?

2. How is Finisterre regarded now, according to lines 6 to 9? Comment on the rock imagery in these lines.

3. Examine the description of the flowers and the mist in stanza 2. How are both associated with death?

4. Comment on Plath's use of the verb 'bruise' in line 15. Is it effective?

5. 'I walk among them, and they stuff my mouth with cotton. / When they free me, I am beaded with tears' (lines 17–18). What do you make of these lines and the drama they describe? (Are the mists/souls presented as hostile? Do they prevent her from speaking? Is the speaker in the poem more in sympathy with the ancient or the modern view of the place . . . ?)

6. How is Our Lady of the Shipwrecked presented in the third stanza? Is it a surprising representation?

7. Comment on the phrase, 'the beautiful formlessness of the sea' (line 27).

8. In lines 31 to 35 the peasants speak of 'the pretty trinkets that the sea hides', which come from a place far away. How do you interpret these lines?

9. Does the poem end on a hopeful note? Give reasons for your answer.

10. In your view, is the speaker of the poem attracted to the sea? Plath regarded the sea as an image of the artist's subconscious. What does the description of the sea in the poem suggest about Plath's subconscious and its concerns?

11. The poem arose from a holiday visit to a seaside resort. What does her treatment of this visit in the poem suggest to you about the personality and imagination of the poet? Support the points you make by quotation from the poem.

12. Choose one stanza from the poem and write a response to the sounds and imagery of the stanza.

Personal response

1. You have been asked to review this poem for a literary magazine. In less than 300 words try to capture your thoughts.

2. Imagine that you have been asked to make a webpage for this poem. Describe what the page should look like. What colours, fonts, images, etc. would you use? What mood would you try to convey?

Sylvia Plath

Mirror

I am silver and exact. I have no preconceptions.
Whatever I see I swallow immediately
Just as it is, unmisted by love or dislike.
I am not cruel, only truthful –
The eye of a little god, four-cornered.   5
Most of the time I meditate on the opposite wall.
It is pink, with speckles. I have looked at it so long
I think it is a part of my heart. But it flickers.
Faces and darkness separate us over and over.

Now I am a lake. A woman bends over me,   10
Searching my reaches for what she really is.
Then she turns to those liars, the candles or the moon.
I see her back, and reflect it faithfully.
She rewards me with tears and an agitation of hands.
I am important to her. She comes and goes.   15
Each morning it is her face that replaces the darkness.
In me she has drowned a young girl, and in me an old woman
Rises toward her day after day, like a terrible fish.

Glossary		
1	*preconceptions*: opinions or ideas formed in advance but not based on real knowledge or experience
14	*agitation of hands*: hand wringing; a similar symbol of distress is used in 'Child' to convey the speaker's anguish

Guidelines

'Mirror' was one of a group of poems written in Autumn 1961, days before Plath's twenty-ninth birthday and shortly after she and Ted Hughes moved to Court Green in Devon. Plath was pregnant with her second child at the time. This was one of the last poems she wrote before the birth of her baby, Nicholas.

As in 'Elm', Plath employs the technique of personification to achieve a sinister effect. She was well read in folk and fairy tales and may have taken the idea of a talking mirror from this tradition. Mirrors occur in many of Plath's poems. Perhaps, they suggest the dangers of judging ourselves too harshly, or of seeking perfection. Or they may suggest the lonely drama of living and dying, as it was, in the end, for Plath herself.

Commentary

Opening statement

The poem begins with a precise statement: 'I am silver and exact.' 'Silver' connotes something valuable but it also suggests something inanimate and, therefore, heartless. The adjective 'exact' is ambiguous. It suggests accuracy and correctness. However, there is a more sinister meaning to the verbal form of the word. 'To exact' is to extort or demand payment. **So the opening statement can be read in quite different ways. The surface meaning: I am valuable and accurate. Or the implied meaning: I am heartless and demand payment. The opening statement succeeds in expressing both meanings simultaneously, moving back and forth between the ordinary and the symbolic.**

If we identify the mirror with the perceiving self, then the opening statement suggests a harsh and unforgiving way of viewing the self. It suggests a lack of self-love. Is the voice of the mirror to be interpreted as the voice of the woman whose image the mirror reflects? Is the voice of the poem an aspect of Plath's own voice? Or should we keep a distance between the poet and the speaker of the poem? There are no correct answers to these questions. Different readers read the poem in different ways. Moreover, Plath's poetry succeeds in communicating on a number of levels, in any individual poem, without losing its sense of focus.

Final image

In the final image of the poem (the 'old woman' rising 'like a terrible fish', lines 17 and 18), **Plath suggests many fears and insecurities: the fear of time and old age; the fear of annihilation; the fear of entrapment and alienation; and the fear of losing control.** The image may also perhaps suggest a daughter's fear of her mother, which is the reading that the critic David Holbrook gives to these lines.

World of the poem

The world of the poem is a bleak and unloving one. The perceiving and recording intelligence is cold and inhuman. It gives nothing creative, warm or assuring to the woman. The image of the lake in the second stanza is striking. Like the bottom in 'Elm', the sea in 'Finisterre' and the bee box in 'The Arrival of the Bee Box', the lake represents the dark and fearful inner life. The woman is alone and has no one else to turn to, except the moon and the candles.

Form of the poem

Plath uses the nine-line stanza, which she also used in 'Finisterre'. The line length is irregular but the lines are mostly long. On the page, the two stanzas of the poem appear to mirror each other. The cold tone of the poem is reflected in the carefully phrased statements and the harsh 'k' sounds of the first stanza.

Many of the lines form complete sentences. This contributes to the impression of exactitude that the mirror claims for itself. A sense that is also reflected in the many short words with final voiced consonants ('exact', 'just', 'god', 'pink', 'part' and so on), which create an impression of cold precision. For some readers, the controlled accuracy of the language of the poem emphasises the agitation and disturbed feelings that lie behind the carefully chosen words and phrases.

The run-on line (line 17) that continues with 'rises' in the last line of the poem works brilliantly to mirror the shock of the 'old woman' rising like a 'terrible fish'.

Thinking about the poem

1   What qualities does the mirror attribute to itself in the first four lines of the poem? What is your reaction to the claims the mirror makes for itself? What is your reaction to the tone of these lines?

2   In what sense might a mirror be said to 'swallow' what it sees (line 2)?

3   'I am not cruel, only truthful' (line 4). Consider this statement. Is the voice of the poem cruel? Is it a masculine or a feminine voice? Are mirrors always truthful? What governs what a person may or may not see in a mirror?

4   Why does the mirror refer to the moon and candles as 'liars' (line 12)?

5   What is the woman's attitude to the mirror and the mirror's attitude to the woman? What is your attitude to the woman?

6   Comment on the images of the final lines of the poem and the impact they have on you. Where else is there a sense of dread or panic in the poem?

7   What does the poem say to you about fear and insecurity and the prospect of growing old?

8   'The exact and precise nature of the mirror is reflected in the language and structure of the poem.' In the light of this statement, comment on the language and form of the poem.

9   'The world reflected by the mirror is one in which the female persona suffers and is alone.' Do you agree with this reading of the poem? Support the points you make by quotation from the poem.

10   'The voice of the mirror is the harsh inner voice that every woman carries within herself.' Give your response to this statement, supporting the points you make by quotation from the poem.

Personal response

1   Suggest three songs or pieces of music that you think capture the mood and atmosphere of this poem. Explain your choice of music.

2   In pairs, create an interview set-up. Both partners write two questions each that they would like to ask Sylvia Plath. Take turns at being the interviewer and the poet. Write down two interesting things that arose from this process about either the poem or the poet. Discuss these in class.

Before you read 'Pheasant'

Before reading 'Pheasant' by Sylvia Plath consider this – have you ever been captivated or moved by the beauty and majesty of an animal? If so, share your experience with your class and explain, as best you can, the impact that the experience had on you.

Pheasant

You said you would kill it this morning.
Do not kill it. It startles me still,
The jut of that odd, dark head, pacing

Through the uncut grass on the elm's hill.
It is something to own a pheasant,   5
Or just to be visited at all.

I am not mystical: it isn't
As if I thought it had a spirit.
It is simply in its element.

That gives it a kingliness, a right.   10
The print of its big foot last winter,
The tail-track, on the snow in our court –

The wonder of it, in that pallor,
Through crosshatch of sparrow and starling.
Is it its rareness, then? It is rare.   15

But a dozen would be worth having,
A hundred, on that hill – green and red,
Crossing and recrossing: a fine thing!

It is such a good shape, so vivid.
It's a little cornucopia.   20
It unclaps, brown as a leaf, and loud,

Settles in the elm, and is easy.
It was sunning in the narcissi.
I trespass stupidly. Let be, let be.

Glossary		
3	*jut of that odd, dark head*: jerky, forward movement of the head; the way the head of the pheasant leaned forward	
12	*our court*: courtyard; Court Green is the name of the house in Devon where the poem is set; also suggests a royal court and picks up on the mention of the kingliness of the bird	
13	*pallor*: paleness	
14	*crosshatch*: shading by a series of intersecting lines; here, the prints left by the pheasant overlap those left by other birds to create a crosshatch pattern	
20	*cornucopia*: treasure; literally means horn of plenty, a Roman symbol of abundance	
23	*narcissi*: daffodil-like plants, with white or yellow flowers; there were thousands of bulbs planted around Court Green	

Guidelines

Plath wrote 'Pheasant' in April 1962, in a period of enormous creativity in which she wrote a number of fine poems within days of each other. The poem had its origins in Plath's glimpse of a pheasant standing on a hill at the back of her house.

Some critics read the poem in terms of the relationship between the speaker and the person she addresses. The 'you' of the poem is often identified with Ted Hughes, Plath's husband, who came from a Yorkshire family that was well used to hunting and fishing.

Commentary

Dramatic opening

The poem opens in a dramatic fashion. The speaker reports the intention of 'you' to kill the pheasant, which she has seen on the hill behind their house. The opening line has the quality of an accusation: 'You said you would kill it this morning.' The repetition of the pronoun 'you' and the use of the verb 'kill' are striking. **'You' is associated with death, is a killer or a potential killer.**

The plea

The speaker pleads for the pheasant's life. The plea in line 2 is direct and simple, 'Do not kill it.' This is not an order as the speaker feels obliged to supply reasons for this request. She says that the pheasant has the capacity to startle her, as it paces through the grass on the hill. She is fascinated by the movement and shape of its head. And because the pheasant is on their land, she feels a pride of ownership. She feels it is an honour to be visited by this kingly bird. The adjective 'dark' (line 3) suggests that the pheasant is unknowable and therefore remains a mystery to her.

The speaker continues her plea for the bird in the third stanza, arguing that the pheasant 'is simply in its element' (line 9). To the speaker's mind, this naturalness gives the bird a kingly quality, a right to exist, without fear or favour. **The implicit argument is that it is the 'you' and the 'I' who are the outsiders, the interlopers.** In stanza 6 the speaker indulges in a flight of fancy, wondering what it would be like to have a hundred (dozen) pheasants 'green and red' (line 17) on the elm's hill. **The green and red hues of the pheasant are symbols of life and passion.**

Anguished voice

In stanza 7 the focus returns to the pheasant. This one alone is a source of delight. It is a 'cornucopia' (line 20), with its fine shape and vivid colouring. She watches as it unclaps its wings and makes itself comfortable in the tree. **There is almost envy in the statement that the pheasant 'Settles in the elm, and is easy' (line 22). This ease is not shared by the speaker.**

The tone of the poem takes on an edge as the speaker describes herself as trespassing stupidly on the pheasant, sunning itself in the narcissi. And then the emotion, which has been controlled throughout 'Pheasant', breaks out in the urgent plea that concludes the poem: 'Let be. Let be.' **The repeated phrase captures the anguish of the speaker, while the echoing rhyme of the final two lines captures the intensity of the plea.** This is a trace of the anguished voice that we hear in 'Elm', 'Child', 'Mirror' and 'Poppies in July'.

Critical interpretation

For some critics, the plea is not for the pheasant but for the poet herself. Plath wrote 'Pheasant' in April 1962 during a tense period in her relationship with Ted Hughes. **Some critics read the poem as being about Plath's marriage.** She is the narrator and Hughes is the 'you' whom she addresses. **The pheasant represents the marriage itself, under threat from the male. It is he who is intent on destroying it.** Plath pleads for it. She pleads for its beauty and wonder, and for the life and passion that animate it. **The fact that it is the female who makes the plea suggests that the relationship of power is an unequal one, with the male possessing the authority to take or spare life, as he wills.** (In 'The Arrival of the Bee Box', the narrator says she will be a sweet god and spare the lives of the bees.) For the critic Linda Wagner-Martin, 'Pheasant' rests on the fear that the male will not listen to the female's plea for the life that deserves to exist. The male is a silent, powerful presence in the poem. The female is the pleading supplicant.

Form of the poem

'Pheasant' is a beautifully achieved poem. It has a conversational quality. Yet, apart from the final line, Plath uses a nine-syllable line, and there are subtle rhymes and half-rhymes throughout the poem. The rhyme scheme is a version of terza rima, a form in which the last word in the middle line of each stanza provides the rhyme for the next stanza. What is so impressive about 'Pheasant' is the way Plath follows a strict form while never losing the conversational feel of the poem.

Thinking about the poem

1 What is the dramatic situation suggested by the opening and closing of the poem?

2 What reasons does the 'I' give to support her plea, in stanzas 1 and 2?

3 From the evidence of stanzas 3 to 5, is the speaker sure of her reasons for wanting the pheasant spared? Quote from the poem in support of your answer.

4 In stanzas 7 and 8, what is the speaker's attitude to the pheasant and where is it most evident?

5 'At the end of the poem, it is the speaker who feels like an outsider.' Do you agree with this reading of the poem? Give reasons for your answer.

6 'The difference between "Pheasant" and "Black Rook in Rainy Weather" is that in the former there is no movement from the outside to the inside. It is the bird, rather than the poetic persona who is the centre of the poem.' *Or* 'In "Pheasant" the poetic persona pleads for herself in pleading for the bird.' Which of these two readings of the poem is closest to your own. Support the points you make by quotation from the poem.

7 In writing about 'Pheasant', Ted Hughes speaks of Plath achieving a 'cool, light, very beautiful moment of mastery'. Write a note on the kind of mastery achieved by Plath in 'Pheasant'. You might like to consider some or all of the following in your answer: the choice of verbs and their effect; the descriptions of the pheasant; the dramatic language; line length and syllable count; the stanza form. In considering these, be alert to the sounds of the poem and their effect.

8 If, as some critics suggest, the poem describes the relationship between the poet and her husband, what kind of relationship is portrayed? (In the above Commentary it is assumed that the speaker of the poem is a woman. Is this a fair assumption? Does the poem support it?)

9 If you were encouraging someone to read 'Pheasant' for the first time, how would you describe the poem and your reaction to it?

Personal response

1 Imagine you are the speaker of the poem. Write a short account of your feelings about the circumstances outlined in the poem.

2 If you were encouraging someone to read 'Pheasant' for the first time, how would you describe the poem and your reaction to it?

Sylvia Plath

Elm

for Ruth Fainlight

I know the bottom, she says. I know it with my great tap root;
It is what you fear.
I do not fear it: I have been there.

Is it the sea you hear in me,
Its dissatisfactions?   5
Or the voice of nothing, that was your madness?

Love is a shadow.
How you lie and cry after it
Listen: these are its hooves: it has gone off, like a horse.

All night I shall gallop thus, impetuously,   10
Till your head is a stone, your pillow a little turf,
Echoing, echoing.

Or shall I bring you the sound of poisons?
This is rain now, this big hush.
And this is the fruit of it: tin-white, like arsenic.   15

I have suffered the atrocity of sunsets.
Scorched to the root
My red filaments burn and stand, a hand of wires.

Now I break up in pieces that fly about like clubs.
A wind of such violence   20
Will tolerate no bystanding: I must shriek.

The moon, also, is merciless: she would drag me
Cruelly, being barren.
Her radiance scathes me. Or perhaps I have caught her.

I let her go. I let her go   25
Diminished and flat, as after radical surgery.
How your bad dreams possess and endow me.

I am inhabited by a cry.
Nightly it flaps out
Looking, with its hooks, for something to love. 30

I am terrified by this dark thing
That sleeps in me;
All day I feel its soft, feathery turnings, its malignity.

Clouds pass and disperse.
Are those the faces of love, those pale irretrievables? 35
Is it for such I agitate my heart?

I am incapable of more knowledge.
What is this, this face
So murderous in its strangle of branches? –

Its snaky acids hiss. 40
It petrifies the will. These are the isolate, slow faults
That kill, that kill, that kill.

Glossary

	dedication *Ruth Fainlight*: writer and friend of Plath
1	*the bottom*: the furthest point that can be reached; here, the deepest point in the subterranean world
1	*tap root*: the main root that goes deep into the soil
6	*voice of nothing*: silence, the absence of inspiration
19	*clubs*: stout-ended sticks used as weapons

Guidelines

'Elm' is a poem that went through numerous drafts before Plath completed it in April 1962. It follows on from the last line of 'Pheasant', in which the bird settles in the elm tree at the back of their house 'and is easy'. Plath took up the word 'easy' at the end of 'Pheasant' and began to explore the elm as something that is not easy.

Commentary

Title

The title refers to a wych elm that grew on a prehistoric mound at the back of Court Green, the house in Devon that Plath shared with Ted Hughes before the break-up of their marriage. In silhouette, the branches of the wych elm make strange, tangled shapes. Plath described the branches of the tree as an 'intricate nervous system'. She plays upon the visual appearance of the elm and its great age in giving it human characteristics. As Anne Stevenson, one of Plath's biographers, observes, the wych elm becomes 'witch' elm in the poem, a frightening, sinister presence.

Stanza 1

In the opening stanza the elm declares her knowledge. It is a dark and deep knowledge, one that has explored 'the bottom' (line 1), the thing that 'you' (the narrator) fears – implying the journey into the deepest part of the self or to the worst periods of one's life. The phrase also suggests the bed of a lake or river where the mud and sludge gather. The imagery here is reminiscent of that in 'Mirror'. The elm shows no sympathy and offers no comfort to the narrator. **The elm resembles an inner voice that is harsh and mocking.**

Stanza 2

In the second stanza the elm asks if the narrator hears the 'dissatisfactions' (line 5) of the sea, as the wind sounds in its branches. The sea is an important and complex symbol in Plath's poetry. It often represents formlessness and annihilation, as in 'Finisterre', or her childhood before the death of her father. After he died, Plath thought of him as drowned and described the creation of pearls as coming from the 'grit of sorrow and routine'. Thus, for Plath, the sea represents creativity and the subconscious of the artist.

The questions posed by the elm seem intended to taunt the narrator. The elm suggests that perhaps the sound is the 'voice of nothing' – the sound of silence, which it equates with the narrator's 'madness' (line 6). Silence – the absence of inspiration – was the cause of severe depression in Plath, who constantly feared that her poetic gift had deserted her.

Stanzas 3 and 4

Stanza 3 continues in a mocking vein. The elm compares its sounds to the pounding of horses' hooves. These hooves, it says, are the sound of love running away from the narrator. **The elm mocks the abandoned narrator's need and desire for it. Love's absence is a 'shadow' (line 7) that hangs over her life.** There is also an interesting ambiguity in the verb 'lie'. As with 'Pheasant', written during the same month, it is worth bearing in mind that Plath's marriage was in crisis at the time she wrote 'Elm'.

Stanza 5
The elm offers the narrator an alternative to the sound of the horse's hooves: 'the sound of poisons' (line 13). The movement from unattainable love to poison is similar to the movement in 'Poppies in July', where poison and annihilation are opposed to a life of intensity. Like the sound of madness, the sound of poisons is silent. Plath worried about the threat of nuclear warfare and the poisoning of the environment. Her fear is reflected in the imagery of this stanza, with its suggestions of acid rain and nuclear dust. The 'big hush' (line 14) may be the deathly silence induced by chemicals (arsenic is a component in many weed and insect killers) in the atmosphere and in the soil or it may be the hush following a nuclear explosion.

Stanzas 6 and 7
The nuclear imagery is continued into stanzas 6 and 7, where the sunset and the violent wind seem to characterise the flash and blast of a nuclear bomb. **The references to suffering – 'scorched', 'wires', 'violence', 'shriek' – speak as much to the suffering endured by Plath's body in the electric shock treatment she received for depression, as they do to the violence endured by the body of the elm.**

The difference established between the elm and the narrator in the first stanza becomes less apparent. In speaking of itself, the elm speaks for the narrator, and the narrator, increasingly, seems identifiable with Plath herself. This, in turn, leads to an intensifying of the emotional strain in the poem.

Stanzas 8 and 9
The elm/narrator continues to describe her suffering. Now it is the 'merciless' moon who is responsible. There are sixty-one references to the moon in Plath's poetry and none of them is benevolent. The moon is sterile and mocking. It is associated with women but it cannot create life (it is 'barren', line 23). 'Barren' is an adjective Plath uses often to indicate a strong dislike or horror of someone. A barren woman is, Plath suggests in another poem, like an empty museum. '*Diminished and flat, as after radical surgery' is a* startling and disturbing image that suggests a woman after a mastectomy.

Line 27 is a key line in interpreting the poem: **the elm suggests that the narrator's nightmares have taken them over and made them what they are: 'How your bad dreams possess and endow me.' From this point on, the elm and the narrator speak with one voice.** In 'The Moon and the Yew Tree', Plath says that the trees of the mind are black. The elm is black and expresses some of the dark, incomprehensible fears that occupy the narrator's mind.

Stanzas 10 and 11

The litany of the narrator's fears begins in stanza 10 and continues in stanza 11. **A bird-like predatory cry, 'this dark thing' (line 31), seems to represent the unconscious of the narrator.** It is fearful, threatening and malignant. It is as if she is a stranger to herself, terrified by forces that she cannot control and a destructive need for love. The imagery reminds us of the incomprehensible sounds in the box in 'The Arrival of the Bee Box'.

Stanzas 12 to 14

Stanza 12 returns to the need for love and the feeling that love, like the passing clouds, is unattainable. There is something pitiful in the question that concludes this stanza: 'Is it for such I agitate my heart?' (line 36).

But this question is not pursued, as the narrator admits she is incapable of more knowledge. However, even as she confesses to her inability to bear more knowledge, more knowledge must be borne. The elm's face forces itself into her consciousness bringing the knowledge of what that face represents. It is a Medusa-like face. Medusa symbolises duality, a double nature that is beautiful and horrifying, seductive and destructive. Is the narrator seeing her own nature in this face?

The 'snaky acids' of the branches 'hiss' (line 40) and the face freezes the will. Anyone who looked on Medusa (whose hair was a tangle of snakes) was turned to stone. The imagery also recalls the serpent in the Garden of Eden and suggests a correspondence between the elm and the Tree of Knowledge. The 'acids' of line 40 are the poisons that kill over time. The repetition of 'kill' in line 42 suggests both a violent frenzy and a hysterical fear of that violence.

The end of the poem, with its nightmarish imagery, a product of the narrator's imagination, suggests that it is the individual poisons ('the isolate, slow faults', line 41) that build up over time within the body (and the mind) that kill. **The repetition in the last line creates a feeling of inevitability, as if the narrator feels doomed, unable to escape the faults that kill.** It is interesting to note that the verb 'kill' also appears in the first line of 'Pheasant'.

Voice of the poem

In the poem, as in many others, Plath personifies a natural object (the elm) and gives it a voice. The voice is at once the 'voice' of a tree, as reported by the narrator, and the voice of the narrator herself.

The voice of the elm is knowledgeable, distressed and, at times, cruel and taunting. The elm addresses a 'you', the poetic persona of the poet, on the subject of fear, love, suffering and despair. Many critics read the second half of the poem as spoken by this 'you' and read the voice as anguished and fearful. The second part of the poem speaks of the need for love, its absence and a destructive inner force. However, to describe the poem in this way is, arguably, misleading. In each utterance of the tree, we can catch a trace of the woman's voice and, in effect, the voices blur and merge, as if the voice of the elm is the inner voice of the woman.

As with many of Plath's poems, the poetic persona seems very harsh in her view of herself. The end of the poem suggests the recognition of some inner faults that will lead to her death. The absence of love intensifies the activity of the dark owl-like thing, whose malignity she fears. As in 'Child', 'Mirror' and 'Poppies in July' the poetic persona is anguished and speaks in a voice that is, by the end of the poem, anguished and fearful.

Atmosphere of the poem

The technique of personification creates a surreal, even nightmarish effect. The world of 'Elm' is not unlike the world of a Brothers Grimm fairy tale, or the world of the subconscious: it is dark and frightening. The vocabulary of the poem captures this nightmarish world: 'terrified', 'dark' 'malignity', 'murderous', 'acid', 'kill'. It is also worth bearing in mind that, in the heightened atmosphere of the Cold War, there was much discussion about the prospect of nuclear warfare, so much so that Plath wrote to her mother a couple of months before she completed 'Elm' about the 'mad, self-destructive world' in which they lived. This atmosphere may also have contributed to the imagery of the poem, especially in stanza 5 where it suggests the aftermath of a nuclear bomb.

Form of the poem

Compared with the careful structure of 'Pheasant', 'Elm' is written in a looser manner, with lines of varying lengths. The lack of formal certainty mirrors the swarming content of the poem. Interestingly, the critic Hugh Kenner believes that Plath's abandonment of formal structures in her later poetry encouraged her to explore states of mind and emotions that were unsafe and which, ultimately, contributed to her suicide.

Thinking about the poem

1   What impression of the elm is created by its statements in the first stanza?

2   Examine the questions posed by the elm in stanza 2. What do they suggest about the elm and the person it addresses?

3   What image of love is created in stanzas 3 and 4? Is the elm comforting or cruel in these stanzas? Explain your answer.

4   Stanzas 5 to 9 describe the elements of rain, sun, wind and moon and their relationship to the elm. What aspect of each is emphasised? How does each affect the elm? What, in your view, is the most striking image in these stanzas?

5   What is the elm's attitude to the moon? Where is this attitude most apparent?

6   What do stanzas 5 to 9 suggest about the nature of the elm's existence? Select the words or phrases that strike you most forcefully.

7   What relationship is suggested between the elm and the 'you' of the poem in the statement: 'How your bad dreams possess and endow me' (line 27)? The line can be read as either the elm addressing the woman or the woman addressing the elm. What is the effect of each reading? How do you read it?

8   The last five stanzas are rich, complex and difficult. How does the narrator view herself? What images strike you as particularly disturbing or vivid? What is your reaction to the use of the word 'faults' (line 41)? What is the tone of the extraordinary last line of the poem?

9   'In "Elm" the boundary between outside and inside is blurred. It is as if the "you", the poetic persona, takes the elm into herself.' In the light of this statement, describe the poetic personae of 'Elm' and the nature of the world, physical and psychological, that they inhabit. Refer to the imagery and vocabulary of the poem in your answer.

10 There is no single reading of 'Elm' that will do justice to its rich complexity. Here are three of the many readings proposed for the poem. Give your opinion of each.

(a)   *The poem's narrator confesses that she is searching desperately for someone to love. Because of this hysteria, she realises that some deadly force within her has been triggered into action by the loss of love. The disintegration of love, the poem says, is a sure death warrant for the speaker.* (Paul Alexander)

(b)   *'Elm' describes the effects of nuclear and chemical damage upon a tree and a woman. 'I have suffered the atrocity of sunsets', the speaker explains, and further, 'My red filaments burn and stand, a hand of wires.' . . . 'Elm' is one of the many poems in which Plath explores the consequences of isolation, and argues against the impulse to hold oneself as separate from the rest of the world.* (Tracy Brain)

(c)   In the poem, originally titled, 'The Elm Speaks', wych elm becomes witch elm, a frightening mother-double of the poet, who offers death as the only possible love substitute. Between the taproot of the tree and the murderous face of the moon, the poet, 'incapable of more knowledge' is forced into a terrible acknowledgement of 'faults' – suddenly a new word in Sylvia's poetic lexicon. The poem suggests them as somehow built into her nature, bent like a crooked tree by traumatic childhood events: 'These are the isolate slow faults / That kill, that kill, that kill.' (Anne Stevenson)

11   'The poem vividly conveys suffering, self-doubt and despair.' Give your response to this assessment of 'Elm', supporting the points you make by quotation from the poem.

12   'Elm' is a poem with many striking visual images. Perhaps you might like to offer your own creative response to, or interpretation of, the poem, in visual form.

Personal response

1   Imagine that you are editing this poem, you can make any changes to the poem you deem necessary. What changes would you make and why?

2   'Elm' is a poem with many striking visual images. Perhaps you might like to offer your own creative response to, or interpretation of, the poem, in visual form.

Before you read 'Poppies in July'

Did you ever feel caught between rage and helplessness? Has your mood ever swung from feeling energetic to feeling exhausted? If the answer to either of these questions is 'yes', then you will sympathise with the speaker in 'Poppies in July' below.

Death wish.

1962
Poppies in July

colour
Little poppies, little hell flames,
Do you do no harm? _not innocent_

knows they're harmful
You flicker. I cannot touch you.
I put my hands among the flames. Nothing burns.   _desire for self harm but dissapointed._

depressed
And it exhausts me to watch you   _lethargic (no energy)_
Flickering like that, wrinkly and clear red, like the skin of a mouth.   5
contrast with "But colourless. colourless"

[annotation: attracts → her]

[annotation: Naturally we are repelled by pain + blood but plath is attracted to it in her desire for self harm.]

A mouth just bloodied.

Little bloody skirts! *[annotation: poppy]*

[annotation: opium]

There are fumes that I cannot touch. *[annotation: synaesthesia (mixing up senses, describing a sense that is more appropriate for another sense. 10]*

Where are your opiates, your nauseous capsules? *[annotation: wants sickness, sense of yearn for something bad.]* 10

[annotation: pain (feeling) (exhausted)]

If I could bleed, or sleep! — *[annotation: on escape from present feeling.]*

If my mouth could marry a hurt like that! *[annotation: want pain.]*

[annotation: Juices of poppies = liquors.] *[annotation: intoxicating]*

Or your liquors seep to me, in this glass capsule, *[annotation: suicidal thoughts?]*

Dulling and stilling.

[annotation: too exhausted] *[annotation: NO escape Feels trapped]*

But colourless. Colourless. *[annotation: she feels colourless.]* 15

[annotation: Nothing dead about poppies, opposite of herself.]

Glossary		
10	*opiates*: opium comes from the unripe seed of the poppy
10	*nauseous capsules*: tablets that cause sickness or discomfort
13	*liquors*: a solution of a drug or chemical in water
13	*glass capsule*: a bell jar, of the kind used in scientific experiments or to hold a specimen

Guidelines

Plath wrote 'Poppies in July' in July 1962, at Court Green in Devon, during the break-up of her marriage. The poetic persona addresses the flowers in a voice that is overwrought and anguished. Anne Stevenson, Plath's biographer, sets the poems that Plath wrote in the final months of her life in a biographical context. She says that these poems report on 'the weather of her inner universe' and the two poles that governed it: rage and stasis. 'At the depressed pole there was a turning in on herself, a longing for non-being as in "Poppies in July".'

Commentary

Title

Red poppies are a common sight in the English countryside in summer. The poppy is also a flower of remembrance for the war dead. In Keats' poem 'To Autumn', the poppy is associated with sleep and ease. As Plath develops the symbolism of the poppy, it takes on a dark and destructive resonance, indicative of a troubled state of mind.

Couplets 1–4

From the first line we realise that the speaker of the poem is troubled. The opening line greeting the poppies – 'Little poppies, little hell flames' – seems to be spoken by two different people. 'Little poppies' suggests a sentimental relationship to the flowers. However, this impression is immediately destroyed by the negative energy of 'little hell flowers' and the association that the speaker makes between the red poppies and the flames of hell. After only one line, we suspect that the poem is not really about the poppies. It is about someone in an excited and disturbed psychological state.

This disturbance is carried into the second line, where the speaker asks: 'Do, you do no harm?' **The word 'harm' is striking and from here on the speaker explores and contemplates the different kinds of harm that she associates with the flowers.** The poppies are associated with danger and death.

The second couplet (lines 3 and 4) continues the imagery of 'flames' begun in line 1. The movement of the red petals is like the flickering of flames. The speaker says she puts her hands among the flames (the petals of the flowers) but 'Nothing burns' (line 4). It is as if the speaker is cut off from feeling and sensation, an idea taken up later in the fifth couplet and linked to the imagery of being contained in the glass jar.

The speaker cannot touch the poppies but she can watch them, though she finds their movement exhausting (line 5). In a striking visual image, she compares the poppies to a mouth and immediately develops the comparison to bloodied mouths and bloodied skirts. The bloodied mouth may suggest violence. Plath often associated red with love, and love with violent emotion that incorporated danger, excitement and vitality. Famously, in her first meeting with Ted Hughes, she bit him on the cheek and he left with blood running down his face.

In poetry, blood is a complex symbol, suggesting hurt, violence, danger, excitement and vitality. The reference to 'little bloody skirts' (line 8) may suggest the stain of menstrual blood and the association of female sexuality with a wound. The tone of 'little bloody skirts' suggests disgust or irritation. It could also be an indirect and derogatory reference to Assia Wevill, the woman with whom Hughes was having an affair. Indeed, Ronald Hayman, one of Plath's biographers, suggests that 'Poppies in July' is directed at Assia Wevill.

Couplets 5–7

In the fifth couplet **the speaker changes tack and focuses on the by-products of poppies: the colourless fumes, their opiates.** She seems frustrated that she cannot inhale the fumes that bring drowsiness and ease, or find the opium tablets that make you feel sick or unwell.

In the sixth couplet we realise how distressed the speaker is. She expresses the wish that she could either bleed or sleep, suffer or escape. In other words, **the speaker seems trapped, unable to live life to the full or escape from it.** Either suffering or sleeping, it seems, would bring relief to her. The couplet concludes with the startling and passionate exclamation, 'If my mouth could marry a hurt like that' (line 12). It is a strange, wild and fascinating statement of longing and captures the desperation of the speaker to live life in a different way from the way she is living it now. It encompasses all the related imagery at work in the poem: life, death, violence, sexuality, addiction, sickness.

The seventh couplet (lines 13 and 14) expresses an alternative wish, namely that the fumes of the poppy will seep into the glass jar where she is trapped, dulling and stilling her senses. This is a death wish, which involves no blood or violence just a colourless fume that will drain the colour out of life. The image of the 'glass capsule' (the bell jar) is a recurrent one in Plath's work. References to bell jars and liquor suggest hospital and museum specimens kept in chemical solutions. Plath witnessed such specimens when she posed as a medical student and observed an anatomical dissection. The experience proved traumatic. In this case, the imagery suggests that the speaker sees herself as trapped in a glass jar, like an exhibit in a museum.

The poem concludes with a chilling wish for annihilation in place of her present inability to feel or experience life.

Interpreting the poem

The poem is complex and invites a variety of interpretations and you may not fully agree with the one offered here. It is clear that the speaker is distressed and acting out a psychological drama in her words. She is deeply unhappy and feels trapped. She wants something to change in her life or she wants her life to end. There are two impulses at work in the poem, one associated with the vibrant colour red and the other with the absence of colour. One symbolises a life of physical, even violent, intensity and the other the total annihilation of consciousness.

Style and form of the poem

The poem is dramatic. It progresses in short dramatic statements, governed by careful punctuation, which are organised into unrhymed, irregular couplets. The use of exclamation marks and question marks adds to the dramatic impact and the poem moves through a range of tones in its short fifteen lines, including fascination, frustration, disgust and repulsion, intense desire and longing. Plath is brilliant at weaving intricate patterns of sound that mirror the sense of the lines. You can almost hear the crackle of the flames in the opening six lines. This is achieved by the onomatopoeic effect of the 'c' and 'k' sounds used. A completely different effect is achieved in the final three lines of the poem where the soft 's' sounds and the long 'u' and 'ou' vowels create a sense of ease and quiet.

Thinking about the poem

1   Based on the first two lines of the poem, what is the state of mind of the speaker?

2   Why, in your view, does the speaker want to experience the sensation of burning by putting her 'hands among the flames' (line 4)?

3   In the fourth couplet, the speaker compares the poppies to 'a mouth just bloodied' and 'little bloody skirts'. What is the impact of these comparisons?

4   In the fifth couplet, the speaker says she cannot touch the fumes of the poppies. Why, in your view, can she not touch them?

5   The speaker asks about opiates and tablets in line 10. What do her questions tell us about what she is thinking?

6   'If I could bleed or sleep!' (line 11). If the speaker is neither bleeding nor sleeping, what kind of existence is she experiencing? Explain your answer.

7   What does the reference to 'this glass capsule' (line 13) say to you about how the speaker views her life?

8   What is the wish expressed by the speaker at the end of the poem? How does the wish make you feel?

9   Which **two** of the following statements best describe your view of the poem?
   ● It is a poem about feeling trapped.
   ● It is a poem about wanting to escape.
   ● It is a poem abut feeling numb.
   ● It is about wanting to live life to the full.
   ● It is a poem about annihilation.
   Explain your choice using reference to the text.

10 Which of the following statements is closest to your own feelings for the speaker of the poem?
   ● I admire the speaker.
   ● I feel sorry for the speaker.
   ● I am fascinated by the speaker.
   Explain your choice.

11 Comment on the phrase 'little hell flames' (line 1) – considering each of the three words – and its impact upon you.

12 The phrase 'I cannot touch' is used twice in the poem (lines 3 and 9). How does it add to your understanding of the predicament of the speaker?

13 'If my mouth could marry a hurt like that!' (line 12). In your opinion, what longing is expressed in this line?

14 'The poem 'Poppies in July' has little to do with poppies and a great deal to do with the mind that perceives them.' Give your response to this statement, supporting the points you make by quotation from the poem.

Personal response

1 Imagine that you are asked to make a short film to accompany a reading of the poem. Explain how you would use music, sound effects, colour, images, etc. to capture the atmosphere of the poem.

2 Imagine that you are the poet. Write **two** diary entries that give your reaction to the poem a long time after you first wrote it.

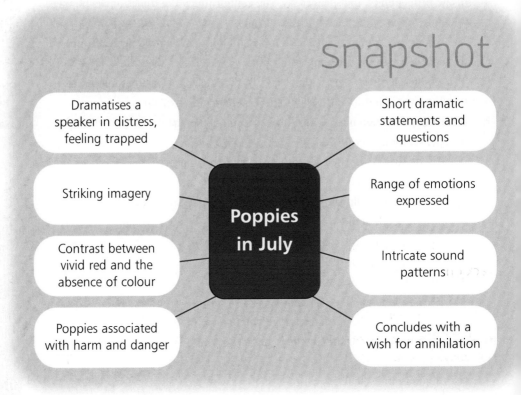

snapshot

Dramatises a speaker in distress, feeling trapped

Striking imagery

Contrast between vivid red and the absence of colour

Poppies associated with harm and danger

Poppies in July

Short dramatic statements and questions

Range of emotions expressed

Intricate sound patterns

Concludes with a wish for annihilation

Bees. What side are you on: for or against? Do they fascinate you? Are you afraid of them? Would you put your hand in a bee hive? Do you like the sound of bees? Would you be happy to see a swarm land in your garden? Share your reaction and experience of bees with a partner before reading this poem.

The Arrival of the Bee Box

Sylvia Plath

I ordered this, this clean wood box
Square as a chair and almost too heavy to lift.
I would say it was the coffin of a midget
Or a square baby
Were there not such a din in it.   5

The box is locked, it is dangerous.
I have to live with it overnight
And I can't keep away from it.
There are no windows, so I can't see what is in there.
There is only a little grid, no exit.   10

I put my eye to the grid.
It is dark, dark,
With the swarmy feeling of African hands
Minute and shrunk for export,
Black on black, angrily clambering.   15

How can I let them out?
It is the noise that appals me most of all,
The unintelligible syllables.
It is like a Roman mob,
Small, taken one by one, but my god, together!   20

I lay my ear to furious Latin.
I am not a Caesar.
I have simply ordered a box of maniacs.

They can be sent back.
They can die, I need feed them nothing, I am the owner.   25

I wonder how hungry they are.
I wonder if they would forget me
If I just undid the locks and stood back and turned into a tree.
There is the laburnum, its blond colonnades,
And the petticoats of the cherry.   30

They might ignore me immediately
In my moon suit and funeral veil.
I am no source of honey
So why should they turn on me?
Tomorrow I will be sweet God, I will set them free.   35

The box is only temporary.

Glossary	
13	*swarmy*: moving in large numbers
22	*Caesar*: Roman emperor
29	*colonnades*: row of columns, in this case ringlets
32	*moon suit*: spacesuit, protective clothing worn by astronauts

Guidelines

In 1962 Plath and Hughes decided to take up beekeeping. (Plath's father had been an expert on bees.) In October, following their separation, Plath wrote a sequence of bee poems that explore the nature of the self and self-identity; personal fears; complex relations and attitudes towards freedom and control. Of the five poems in the sequence, 'The Arrival of the Bee Box' is the one that can stand on its own.

The poem may be taken at face value: it describes the arrival of the bee box and the speaker's response to it. **The box both frightens and fascinates the speaker of the poem. However, the bee box is often read as a symbol for the inner life of the speaker or a symbol for poetry itself, a formal shape which contains a swarm of ideas and feelings.**

Commentary

Stanza 1

The poem opens on a note of wonderment as the speaker seems surprised by the bee box and by the fact that she is responsible for its presence, 'I ordered this'. The verb 'ordered' introduces a major theme of the poem: the question of power and control.

Lines 3 and 4 introduce the first of the surreal images that run through the poem. The speaker says she would compare the box to 'the coffin of a midget / Or a square baby' except for the noise coming from it. The box, like the bell jar imagery that is evident in much of Plath's work, symbolises entrapment and confinement and, as the poem progresses, the noise coming from it is the sound of the bees agitating for release.

Stanza 2

The second stanza is the most straightforward in the poem. It opens with two direct statements: 'The box is locked. It is dangerous.' The speaker says she has to live with the box overnight and cannot keep away from it. Lines 9 and 10 describe the box in terms that bring to mind a windowless prison cell. **This stanza reveals the speaker's fascination with the contents of the box.** In Greek mythology, Pandora, out of curiosity, opened a container and released harm and sickness into the world. All the contents of the box escaped except hope. The box in this poem resembles Pandora's in the mixture of fear and hope that it excites in the speaker.

Stanza 3

Plath was influenced by the surrealist painter Giorgio de Chirico, and his use of symbols taken from the subconscious to create ominous, disturbing images. She was also interested in African sculpture and folktales. Both interests – surrealism and Africa – come together in the imagery of the third stanza.

The speaker tells us that she can see only darkness when she puts her eyes to the grid. It is not an empty darkness but one which the speaker associates with 'African hands' (line 13), a reference to the Black slave-workers exported from Africa on slave ships to work as manual labourers on plantations. In a surreal, disturbing image, the speaker sees these 'hands' as 'minute and shrunk' (line 14).

Like the African slaves, the bees are workers and they must clamber over each other to move around in their cramped conditions. The use of the word 'angrily' (line 15) suggests the danger and aggression that the speaker senses within – the threat posed by the contained but angry bees. Some commentators have suggested that the series of images linking the bees to African slaves could only have been made by a White writer.

Stanza 4

The opening line of the fourth stanza, 'How can I let them out?', is ambiguous. Given the anger of the bees the question may mean 'How can I let them out *safely?*' On the other hand, it could mean 'How can I *possibly* let them out *now that I know what they are like?*' **It is as if the speaker doubts her capacity to cope with the bees, and their dangerous potential.** She tries to identify the source of her dismay and attributes it to the noise and its incomprehensibility: she fears what she does not understand. The potential for destruction that she senses in the bee box is captured in the comparison to the mob which, in Roman times, demanded public killings for their amusement (line 19).

Stanza 5

Listening to the 'furious Latin' (line 21), the speaker feels unable to control the mob, as Caesar did, by the power of his words. Their language is, after all, 'unintelligible' (line 18) to her. But then **the speaker grows more confident. She defines the situation and the solution to the problem with a new clarity** in lines 23–24: 'I have simply ordered a box of maniacs. / They can be sent back.' The situation is not out of control. In the final line of the stanza, another possibility occurs to her. The bees might be left in their box, without food. Then it will become a coffin. Ownership gives her the power of life and death. She is like a slave owner.

Stanza 6

The sixth stanza brings a change of tone. The possibility of allowing the bees to die is no longer entertained. Instead, she thinks of how they might be released without causing harm to herself. **The speaker is calmer, although still curious.** She wonders if the bees will forget her. It is an intriguing question. Does she mean 'forget' in the sense of not wanting to exact revenge upon her for bringing them there in the first place?

She thinks of the idea of escaping by becoming a tree. In Greek mythology, the God Apollo, mad with love and desire, pursued the nymph Daphne, who called on her father, Peneus, for help and was turned into a laurel tree.

The speaker seems to suggest that the laburnum and cherry trees may well be the result of a similar transformation. The drooping flower-covered branches of the laburnum are likened to blond ringlets and the blossom of the flowering cherry tree to the ruffled petticoats that were popular in the 1950s and 1960s (lines 29 to 30).

Stanza 7

The seventh stanza presents another possibility: the bees might ignore her in her beekeeper's suit, which she describes as a spacesuit topped with the type of veil traditionally worn by women mourners at a funeral, another comparison which shows that the speaker's mind swarms with ideas and associations.

Line 33 is a simple statement – 'I am no source of honey' – and it prompts the question, 'So why should they turn on me?' **This reveals the speaker's fear that the bees might hurt her**. The question is really an attempt by the speaker to persuade herself that the bees will not harm her. And taking comfort, she speaks with calm authority in line 35: 'Tomorrow I will be sweet God. I will set them free.' **She anticipates the pleasure of exercising her power in a generous way, though the action itself is postponed.**

Final line
There is a note of optimistic triumph in the final line of the poem, 'The box is only temporary.'

Interpreting the poem

The poem can be read as the story of an inexperienced beekeeper who orders a box of bees and is then afraid to release them. However, because Plath employs symbols and works by association, and because she was interested in the unconscious, her poems tend to be interpreted in a variety of ways. Here are examples of how some readers have interpreted this poem:

- The White female beekeeper wants to free the Black bees but she is appalled by them and frightened of what they might do to her.
- The poem depicts a psychological drama between the inner turmoil of the speaker, who is a version of Plath, and the outer, formal control that the speaker exerts on her feelings.
- It is about the kind of poetry that Plath wrote and the dangers involved in writing it. The bees represent her mind and all the repressed feelings, memories and ideas it contains. This is the dangerous subject-matter that both fascinates and appals her. The box represents the poem, the structure that contains and controls the dangerous swarming content of her mind.
- The beekeeper opening the box is like a person releasing repressed feelings or a poet exploring dark themes: all are likely to get hurt.

Style and form of the poem

The poem is written in five-line unrhymed stanzas. The language is direct and powerful. From the opening 'this', the speaker utters her words in short, sharp bursts. The dramatic impact is heightened by the repetition of key words such as 'dark', 'black' and 'I' ('I' appears five times in the fifth stanza alone).

The run-on lines and conversational words create the impression of someone telling a personal story. Look, for example, at the way the sound echoes in the first stanza in the words 'square', 'chair', 'were' and 'there'. The 'r' sound is repeated throughout the poem and occurs in the final word: 'temporary'. As always in Plath's poetry, there is an intricate pattern of sound woven through the text.

Because of the narrative structure and the use of the present tense, we get a sense of the flow of time and live the experience with the speaker.

Interestingly, the last line of the poem falls outside the five-line stanza structure. The speaker announces her intention to free the bees in a line that seems to escape the formal structure of the poem.

Thinking about the poem

1   How does the speaker describe the bee box in the first stanza? Do you find the imagery of the first stanza strange, disturbing or amusing? Explain your answer.

2   Based on the evidence of stanza 2, what is the speaker's attitude to the bee box?

3   Explain as clearly as you can the reference to 'African hands' (line 13) and the comparison the speaker makes between them and the bees.

4   What, according to the speaker in stanza 4, appals her most of all about the bees?

5   In stanza 5, the speaker grows more confident. Speaking as the 'owner' what actions are open to her?

6   In stanza 6, the speaker considers ways in which the bees might be released without causing harm to herself. What options does she consider?

7   What announcement does the speaker make in stanza 7? What is the tone of this announcement?

8   What, in your view, does the final line add to the poem? Does the poem end on a note of optimism?

9   Which one of the following statements best describes your view of the poem?
   ● It is a poem about bees.
   ● It is a poem about psychological fears.
   ● It is a poem about writing poetry.
   Explain your choice using reference to the text.

10   What impression of the poet do you form from reading the poem? What words or phrases help to create this impression of Plath?

11   'The box is locked, it is dangerous' (line 6). Comment on Plath's use of the word 'dangerous' and what you think it adds to the poem.

12 'With the swarmy feeling of African hands' (line 13). Describe the impact of this line on you.

13 'I will be sweet God' (line 35). Write a note on this statement and what it means in the context of the poem.

14 'In the poem, there is both a desire to trust the bees and a fear of trusting them, but in the end, the fear is overcome.' Do you agree with this reading of the poem? Explain your answer.

Personal response

1 You are the speaker of the poem. Write a diary entry describing your experience of having the bee box in your possession overnight. The entries should catch some of the conflicting feelings evident in the poem: fear, fascination, repulsion, intended kindness, etc.

2 Choose a song or a film that, in your opinion, has a similar atmosphere to that created in the 'The Arrival of the Bee Box'. Explain your choice.

3 Suggest an alternative title for the poem. Explain your suggestion.

snapshot

Box frightens and fascinates the speaker

Theme of power and control

Images of entrapment and confinement

Growing sense of calm in the poem

The Arrival of the Bee Box

Ends on a note of optimism

Language is direct and powerful

Surreal imagery

Last line falls outside formal pattern of the poem

Before you read 'Child'

Picture a young mother talking to her one-year-old son. What will she say to him? What will she talk to him about? What feelings will the mother and son share? Share your thoughts with a partner before reading this poem in which a mother speaks to her baby son.

Child

written in 1963.

analysing as a work of art

unconditional love

innocent   better vision of the world

Your clear eye is the (one absolutely beautiful thing.)

I want to fill it with colour and ducks.   *simple   basic   yellow.*

The zoo of the new   *everything is new*

absorb

Whose names you meditate –

spring new life

April snowdrop, Indian pipe,   *flower culture*   5

Little

flower for possibility growth   flawless love.

Stalk without wrinkle,

typical plath reference to reflection

Pool in which images

(Should) be grand and classical   *value enduring*

(negative)

disturbed

Not this troublous   10

nervous Wringing of hands, this dark   *depression*

Ceiling without a star. *(darkness)*

doesn't want the/these child to see her depression

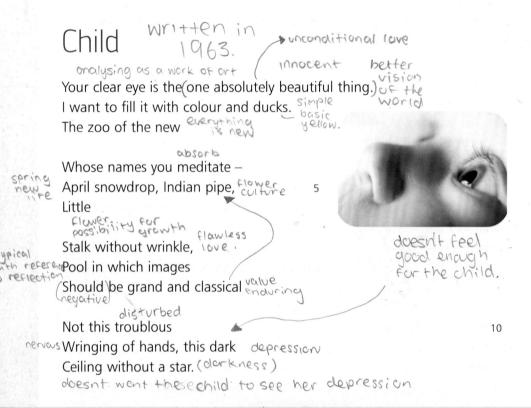

doesn't feel good enough for the child.

Glossary	
4	*meditate*: reflect upon; this is picking up the imagery of reflection
5	*snowdrop*: small, white-flowering plant that blooms in spring
5	*Indian pipe*: small, woodland flower
10	*troublous*: agitated, unsettled, disturbed; taking up the idea of classical and grand in the preceding line, Plath uses an old-fashioned, literary word

Guidelines

'Child' appeared in Plath's collection *Winter Trees*, published in 1971, eight years after her death. It was written at the end of January 1963, shortly after her son's first birthday and less than two weeks before she took her life at the age of thirty. It is a beautifully phrased and composed poem in which a mother expresses her frustrated wishes for her child.

Commentary

Stanza 1

'Child' opens dramatically with the mother addressing her child in what is the longest line in the poem. **She tells the child that its eye is the one thing in her life that is beautiful:** 'Your clear eye is the one absolutely beautiful thing.' The line tells us as much about the mother and the world she inhabits as it does about the child.

The mother then expresses her wishes for her child. She wants to create a world of excitement and colour to fill the child's eye: 'I want to fill it with colour and ducks. / The zoo of the new'. These lines work brilliantly. The random progression from 'colour' to 'ducks' captures the unpredictability and pleasure of the world she wants to show her child. The phrase 'the zoo of the new' expresses not only the potential of the world to delight, but also the humour and inventiveness of the mother who wants to bring this world to her child.

Stanza 2

The mother begins to describe the joyful world she wants to offer to her child: 'April snowdrop, Indian pipe' (line 5). The verb 'meditate' (to reflect upon, line 4) suggests that the child has not yet seen these beautiful flowers. The placing of the word 'Little' on its own in line 6 emphasises the smallness of the child. **For the mother, the child is her April snowdrop, the symbol of spring and new beginnings.**

Stanza 3

The child is also 'Little / Stalk without wrinkle' (lines 6–7) – delicate, young and unblemished like the flowers. Line 8 picks up on the imagery of reflection, which began with 'clear eye' in the opening line and continued in line 4 with 'meditate'. **Now the child's eye is a 'pool'. The mother thinks that 'grand and classical' images should fill it.** The image of a pool creates a different set of associations from the image of an eye: the world reflected in a pool is an unstable one that can quickly lose its shape and dissolve into formlessness.

Stanza 4

The final stanza gives us the image that fills the child's eye. It is a classic image of despair: the 'wringing of hands' (line 11). It symbolises the mother's anguish. Her anguish is intensified by her inability to give her child what she feels the child deserves. **The speaker is reduced to expressing her own anguish.** Her failure to fill the child's world with joy adds to her gloom: her world is now a 'dark / Ceiling without a star' (lines 11–12).

Interpreting the poem

It is difficult not to read this poem in the biographical context in which it was written – two weeks before Plath took her life. The poem presents a speaker who has lost confidence in her ability to create joy, a mother unable to escape her own anguish and despair, but anxious to spare her child the sight of it. She does not want the child's clear eye to witness the pain she endures, yet she lacks the strength and self-belief – not the humour, imagination or inventiveness – to make things otherwise.

Style and form of the poem

The poem is written in unrhymed, three-line stanzas. 'Child' is a testimony to Plath's skill and judgement as a poet. Every word is carefully chosen. The words 'Little' (line 6) and 'dark' (line 11), for example, are perfectly placed. The despair that underlies the poem is managed and controlled.

Thinking about the poem

1 'The first line of the poem shows the mother's love for her child.' Do you agree? Explain your answer.

2 On the evidence of lines 2 and 3, what kind of world does the mother want to create for her child?

3 What is the effect of the flower names mentioned in the second stanza? Explain your answer.

4 What are the conditions in which the images in a pool might appear 'grand and classical' (line 9)? Do these conditions exist in the child's life?

5 What does stanza 4 tell us about the mother? What feeling does the mother have for her child? What feeling do you have for the mother?

6 This poem presents us with a picture of a woman who is deeply troubled.' Do you agree with this assessment of the poem? Explain your answer.

7   Which of the following statements is closest to your own view of the poem?
    ●   It is a poem about love.
    ●   It is a poem about despair.
    ●   It is a poem about innocence.
    Explain your choice.

8   'Your clear eye' (line 1). Comment on Plath's use of the adjective 'clear' at the beginning of the poem.

9   Comment on the use of the word 'zoo' (line 3) and the mood and ideas it generates.

10 Consider the phrase 'grand and classical' in line 9. Write a note on both words and the kind of images you associate with each.

11 Comment on the placing of the words 'Little' in line 6 and 'dark' in line 11.

Personal response

1   If you could write a letter to Sylvia Plath, after reading 'Child', what would you say to her?

2   What music would you select to accompany a reading of this poem? Explain your choice.

snapshot

Mother caught between love and despair

Mother's love is evident

Humour and inventiveness in the wishes expressed by the mother

Lyrical language

Child

Imagery of reflection

Carefully phrased poem

Troubled ending

Speaker has no confidence in her ability to create joy

Exam-Style Questions

1   Give your personal response to the poetry of Sylvia Plath, describing the impact of the poems upon you. Support your answer by relevant quotation from the poems you have studied.

Here are some possible areas that you might focus on in your answer:

- Her themes, for example love and despair.
- The anguished voice of some of her poems.
- The startling imagery and symbolism employed in the poems.
- Her skill as a poet.
- The relationship between her life and her poetry.

2   What in your view are the emotions and the emotional experiences explored in Plath's poetry and how are these conveyed in the language and imagery of the poems? Support the points you make by quotation from the poems you have studied.

3   'The poetic techniques employed by Plath succeed in making the world of her poetry a strange and terrifying one.' In the light of this statement, discuss the world of Plath's poetry. Support your answer by quotation from the poems you have studied.

4   'Plath's poems make most sense when they are read as biographical.' Do you agree with this view of Plath's poetry? Explain your answer, supporting the points you make by quotation from the poetry by Plath on your course.

5   'Death and annihilation are the themes that dominate Plath's poetry.' Is this an accurate assessment? Support your point of view by quotation from the poems you have studied.

6   'Plath's poetry presents a vivid portrait of an individual whose life is tormented and anguished.' Do you agree with this reading of Plath's work? Support the points you make by quotation from the poems by Plath on your course.

7   Write an essay in which you outline your reasons for liking or not liking the poetry of Sylvia Plath. You must refer to the poems of Plath on your course.

Possible reasons for liking the poetry include:

- The uniqueness of the poetic voice.
- The striking imagery and symbolism.
- The vitality and energy of the writing.
- The exploration of emotions and extreme states of mind.
- The exploration of women's experiences.
- The impact of the poetry upon the reader.
- The variety of themes.
- Plath's skill as a poet.

Possible reasons for not liking the poetry include:

- The themes of isolation and estrangement.
- The cruelty of the world of many of the poems.
- The absence of happiness in many of the poems.
- The obscurity of the imagery.
- The troubled nature of the poetic persona.
- The complexity of the relationship explored in the poetry.
- The feeling of despair in many of the poems.
- The effect of the poems upon the reader.

8   'The movement of Plath's poetry is from the outside world to the inner world, from landscape to mindscape.' Discuss this statement in relation to **two** of the poems by Plath on your course.

9   Select your favourite poems by Plath and explain what it is you admire about them. Support the points you make by quotation from the chosen poems.

10   'In Plath's poetry, of course, this slightly old-fashioned point of view of the sanctity of domesticity is wedded to a tormented modern consciousness.' (Margaret Dickie)

'For all her harrowing and courageous record of suffering, Sylvia Plath died in the end because she could not sustain confidence in her true potentialities which could free her.' (David Holbrook)

Write an essay on Plath's poetry in support of **one** of the views above. Support the points you make by quotation from the poems you have studied.

Sample Essay

What in your view are the emotions and the emotional experiences explored in the poetry of Sylvia Plath and how are these conveyed in the language and imagery of the poems? Support the points you make by quotation from the poems you have studied.

Sylvia Plath's poetry is a poetry of emotional extremes and while there are moments of joy and optimism in her poems, the prevailing mood is dark and filled with fear, suffering and despair. The mood of her poetry is conveyed in dramatic monologues in which the speakers use memorable, haunting and sometimes terrifying imagery to convey their feelings.

[Opening paragraph sets up answer]

'Black Rook in Rainy Weather' was published during the time Plath spent in Cambridge as a student and probably captures the contrast between the sunny weather of Plath's Boston and the wet and dark atmosphere of autumn in England. The 'black' and 'rainy' adjectives of the title tell us all we need to know about the kind of experience that inspired the poem. However, the poem uses the dark colours of the bird and the gloomy atmosphere as symbols to represent the emotional mood of the speaker, the poetic persona of the poem. The landscape is described as 'dull, ruinous'. The autumn weather is now a 'season of fatigue' where the speaker is 'trekking stubborn'. The double consonant sounds and the long vowels capture the effort required by the speaker just to keep going. The speaker hopes for a break in the weather, for 'spasmodic tricks of radiance' that might give her 'A brief respite from fear / Of total neutrality'. Almost out of nowhere a poem that began by describing a bird in the rain gathers together all its imagery and poetic energy to announce its theme: the speaker's fear of a complete loss of identity. This theme runs through Plath's poetry and is expressed in striking imagery.

[Important theme introduced; first poem discussed]

Consider, for example, the museum imagery of 'Morning Song', where the newborn is described as a museum exhibit and the parents 'stand round blankly as walls'. The word 'blankly' is particularly striking. And it is immediately followed by the speaker of the poem announcing that she feels no more the mother of a child than a cloud is mother to a pool of water that shows the cloud 'its own slow / Effacement at the wind's hand.' As a reader, you want to shout 'Stop'. How can a poem that begins with the birth of a child move so quickly to the loss and disappearance of the mother? And while the poem ends on an optimistic note, it is the imagery of effacement and the word 'blankly' that stay in the mind.

[Reader response introduced; second poem discussed]

'Finisterre' is one of the few Plath poems that does not have a poetic persona or narrator and this results in the poem being less emotionally engaging than some of the others. However, what is clear is that the poem circles the theme of identity and fixed forms versus formlessness. The poem describes the statue of Our Lady of the Shipwrecked and says that 'She is in love with the beautiful formlessness of the sea'. It is a line that requires a bit of teasing out. What it seems to convey is an attraction to the loss of identity that was feared in the poems I have already discussed. The attraction is revealed in the long vowels and the soft sibilant sounds of the line, which reflect the seductive power of the formless sea. It is a dangerous form of seduction. This ambiguity towards annihilation becomes more pronounced in the poems that Plath wrote towards the end of her life.

[Third poem widens the discussion]

Of course, it is always dangerous to generalise about a poet's work, for as soon as we do, a poem appears that questions the validity of what we have claimed. Take,

'Pheasant', for example. The poem is brilliantly dramatic, with a woman pleading to a man to spare a pheasant he has threatened to kill. The basis of her plea is the definite shape and identity of the bird. Its solidity attracts her: 'it is such a good shape, so vivid.' And the poem itself is a good shape, written in carefully constructed three-line stanzas. The speaker sees the bird as belonging where it is. It is she who feels like a trespasser and pleads for the pheasant to be left alone: 'I trespass stupidly. Let be, let be.' Interestingly, the simplicity of the language indicates the heart-felt nature of the plea.

[Fourth poem introduced to show awareness of other aspects of the poet's work]

The repetition of 'Let be' at the end of the poem, suggests that the speaker is emotional and overwrought. The emotion is held in check by the tight structure of the poem. Certainly the speaker who addresses the poppies in 'Poppies in July' is anguished and emotional. The imagery is terrifying. The speaker sees the poppies as 'hell flames' and is disappointed that 'nothing burns' when she places her hands among them. The sinister, surreal imagery of the poem, conveys the distress of the speaker, who addresses the flowers as 'A mouth just bloodied' and 'Little bloody skirts'. Unable to feel pain or inflict harm upon herself, the speaker expresses a chilling wish for annihilation, where the fumes of the poppies would seep into her in her 'glass capsule' and dull and still her senses until life was drained of all its colour. The reference to a glass capsule suggests that the speaker feels trapped, and is so dissatisfied with life that death seems to be an attractive alternative to her current situation.

[Argument in new paragraph follows on from discussion in previous one; fifth poem discussed]

Of course at this stage the reader is asking, 'Why?' Why are the speakers in Plath's poems so fearful and afraid? Three poems offer two different answers. In 'Child', one of the last poems she completed before taking her own life, it is because the mother has lost confidence in herself and in her ability to create the kind of joyful world she would like for her child. She wants to fill her child's eye with 'The zoo of the new'. It is such a brilliant phrase – simple, zany, unforgettable. It shows a mother who is inventive and fun. But this is not enough for the speaker. She is anxious and in despair and does not want her child's 'clear eye' to witness her pain and distress. The speaker does not believe herself capable of being the mother she would like to be. It is such a sad poem.

[Sixth poem discussed; notice how short quotations are used throughout the answer]

In 'Elm', the speaker's terror is related to 'this dark thing / That sleeps in me.' This is the darkest imagery in all her poems, full of terror and self-hatred. The dark thing inside her is malignant and the poem concludes with an image of poisonous acids killing the self. The repetition of the verb 'kill' at the end of the poem suggests a frenzy of uncontrollable violence. This is a poem on the furthest edge of emotion and self-analysis.

[New paragraph continues the thread of argument running through the essay]

The idea of the uncontrollable violence and darkness that the speaker senses within herself is also evident in 'The Arrival of the Bee Box', where the bees represent a fascinating dark force that she senses within but which she does not understand. They speak in 'unintelligible syllables' and 'furious Latin'. The bees 'appal' her but she tells us that she 'can't keep away' from them. The box contains them but the speaker wants to see them free, even though she understands they could harm her, turn on her, just as the slow faults referred to in 'Elm' have the capacity to kill. However, 'The Arrival of the Bee Box' concludes with the speaker determined to release the bees. The last triumphant statement declares: 'The box is only temporary.' As a reader you fear for the safety of the speaker who would release such dark and dangerous things upon herself.

[Begins to draw entry to conclusion]

To read the poetry of Sylvia Plath is to encounter a succession of speakers who live on the edge, who seem on the point of being overwhelmed by doubt and fear and a lack of belief. The wonder of the poetry is that out of such dark material Sylvia Plath makes such beautifully crafted poems. The tragedy for the poet was that, in her own life, she was not able to contain her personal fears within such tightly controlled structures.

[Strong conclusion]

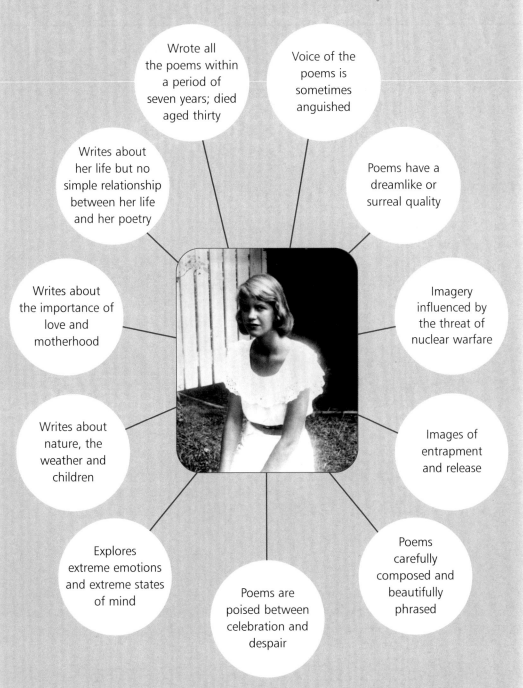

Wrote all the poems within a period of seven years; died aged thirty

Voice of the poems is sometimes anguished

Writes about her life but no simple relationship between her life and her poetry

Poems have a dreamlike or surreal quality

Writes about the importance of love and motherhood

Imagery influenced by the threat of nuclear warfare

Writes about nature, the weather and children

Images of entrapment and release

Explores extreme emotions and extreme states of mind

Poems are poised between celebration and despair

Poems carefully composed and beautifully phrased

William Butler Yeats

1865–1939

Biography

William Butler Yeats was born on 13 June 1865 in Sandymount, Dublin. His father was the artist John Butler Yeats; his mother, Susan, was a member of a well-to-do Sligo merchant family. When Yeats was nine the family moved to London, where Yeats attended the Godolphin School, Hammersmith. In 1880 the family returned to Ireland and settled in Howth, where Yeats attended the High School in Dublin. He later studied at the College of Art in Dublin. Soon, however, his interest in art gave way to his enthusiasm for literature.

From his late teens he was writing poetry with the active encouragement of his father. Early in his career he began to explore mysticism and the occult, particularly Indian mysticism. This interest was to remain central to his outlook throughout his life. More significantly, however, he became active in helping to launch the movement known as the Irish Literary Renaissance, which saw a revival of interest in Ireland's literary heritage and was inspired by political and cultural nationalism.

In 1888 he met Maud Gonne, a committed Irish nationalist, whose influence on his personal life and work was to be considerable; she inspired his play *The Countess Kathleen* (1892) and a number of his great poems. He proposed marriage to her on several occasions. In 1896 he met Lady Augusta Gregory, the mistress of Coole Park estate in Co. Galway, where he composed many of his best poems, including the one that gives its name to his 1919 collection, *The Wild Swans at Coole*. In 1917 he bought an old Norman tower at Ballylee, close to Lady Gregory's house.

Yeats again proposed marriage to Maud Gonne following the execution of her husband, Major John MacBride, for his involvement in the 1916 Rising. Having been turned down by her, he proposed to her daughter, Iseult, again without success. In October 1917 another of his proposals of marriage was accepted by Georgie Hyde-Lees; he was fifty-two and she was twenty-five. The couple had two children: Anne, born in 1919, and Michael, born in 1921.

Following the establishment of the Irish Free State in 1922, Yeats took a lively interest in politics, becoming a member of the Irish Senate, and taking up such unpopular causes as divorce. In 1923 he was awarded the Nobel Prize for Literature. In the 1920s and 1930s he spent much of his time abroad, mainly for the sake of his health. He took a sympathetic interest in fascism during the 1930s, particularly in its Irish variety: the Blueshirt movement.

There is an important sense in which Yeats is the most remarkable of all poets who have written in English. There is no record in English literary history of another poet who produced his greatest work between the ages of fifty and seventy-four. Wordsworth represents the norm among poets in this regard: although he lived to be eighty, all his really significant work belongs to the first productive period of his life, between 1798 and 1810, that is before the age of forty. In the case of Yeats, there is constant renewal, experimentation and utter dedication to the craft of poetry, leading to the ultimate command of words and images characteristic of his mature work.

Yeats became seriously ill in France at the beginning of 1939 and died on 28 January of that year. He was buried in France, but in 1948 his body was taken to Drumcliffe Churchyard near Sligo.

Social and Cultural Context

Irish literary heritage

For convenience, Yeats's poetry is generally divided into three main phases. Only one of the poems in this anthology, 'The Lake Isle of Innisfree', belongs to the first phase, which extended from 1889 to 1909. Encouraged by the veteran Fenian John O'Leary, Yeats had broadened his knowledge of Irish history and folklore and during this phase his poetry is dominated by Celtic myths and motifs and much of it is escapist. During his visits to his uncle George Pollexfen in Sligo, he absorbed fairy lore and folk tales. He read, in translation, Irish legends such as the Cúchulainn saga and the stories of the Fianna, which inspired the poems in *The Rose* (1893), one of his early collections. The publication of *The Wanderings of Oisin and Other Poems* in 1889 established him as a literary figure. In the 1890s he was active in promoting the idea of a distinctively Irish literature for an Irish public.

Revolutionary Ireland

The transitional years, 1909 to 1914, represented in this anthology by 'September 1913', marked a change in Yeats's poetry, as well as in his life. He gradually ceased to be a Romantic poet and his work became less decorative and musical, more harsh and realistic and, above all, more in tune with contemporary realities and public issues. The Easter Rising of 1916 and the revolutionary turmoil that followed it had a profound effect on his mind and writings.

The 1916 Rising and the subsequent Irish Civil War inspired some of his finest poems. He invested these great and terrible public events and those who took part in them – such as Patrick Pearse, James Connolly, Maud Gonne, Countess Markiewicz, Kevin O'Higgins – with a mythic significance. In one of his Last Poems, called 'Beautiful Lofty Things', he shows how a commonplace, everyday happening can transform itself into an episode from a great personal mythology in which a woman he admires suddenly takes her place with great figures of ancient Greece:

> Maud Gonne at Howth Station waiting for a train
>
> Pallas Athene in that straight back and arrogant head
>
> All the Olympians, a thing never known again.

Political events in Ireland from 1916 onwards confronted Yeats with a series of acute personal dilemmas. On the one hand, his instinctive Irish nationalism responded with pride to the patriotic surge and heroic endeavour that inspired the 1916 Rising. On the other, he knew that triumphant nationalism was bound to destroy the Anglo-Irish civilisation that he regarded as the ideal embodiment of the aristocratic way of life. This explains the deep ambivalence that marks such poems as 'Easter 1916'.

Complex personal mythology

Yeats's great period dates from 1919 to the year of his death, 1939. This period witnessed the publication of his four outstanding books of poetry: *The Wild Swans at Coole* (1919), *Michael Robartes and the Dancer* (1921), *The Tower* (1928) and *The Winding Stair* (1933). The poems in these collections feature a comprehensive mythology of persons in which contemporaries who impressed Yeats appear larger than life. Yeats also draws from the great deposit of history and philosophy (the work of Plato and the art of the Byzantine empire) and universal symbolism (the tower, the moon and the swan, for example). The complex personal mythology behind these poems is elaborated at length in his prose work, *A Vision* (1925).

The Civil War led to Yeats's increasing disillusionment with Irish public life and caused him to question the patriotic, often fanatical, strivings of friends who had involved themselves in the nationalist cause. 'In Memory of Eva Gore-Booth and Con Markiewicz' is a splendid lament for the vanishing Anglo-Irish world and an exposure of the destructive effects of what Yeats regarded as misguided political activity on the minds and bodies of two once beautiful and elegant women.

The poetry written during the final twenty years of his life is notable for its vigorous rhythms within a generally plain, unornamented style with few adjectives and few, if any, of the luxuriant trappings of his earlier work. Even in his *Last Poems* (1939) Yeats retains his energy: the language and manner of 'An Acre of Grass' and 'Under Ben Bulben' are as emphatic as ever.

Timeline

1865	Born on 13 June in Sandymount, Dublin
1867	Moves to London
1880	Yeats family returns to Ireland
1884/5	Attends Metropolitan School of Art, Dublin
1886	Meets John O'Leary, mentioned in 'September 1913'
1889	Publishes *The Wanderings of Oisin and Other Poems*; meets Maud Gonne
1896	Meets Lady Gregory; meets John Millington Synge in Paris
1905	Abbey Theatre founded, with Yeats as a founder member
1917	Marries Georgie Hyde-Lees
1919	Birth of daughter, Anne; publishes *The Wild Swans at Coole*
1921	Birth of son, Michael; publishes *Michael Robartes and the Dancer*
1922	Made a senator
1923	Awarded the Nobel Prize for Literature
1928	Publishes *The Tower*
1933	Publishes *The Winding Stair*
1939	Dies at Cap Martin, France
1948	Body reinterred in Drumcliffe, Co. Sligo

The Lake Isle of Innisfree

I will arise and go now, and go to Innisfree,
And a small cabin build there, of clay and wattles made;
Nine bean-rows will I have there, a hive for the honey-bee,
And live alone in the bee-loud glade.

And I shall have some peace there, for peace comes dropping slow,   5
Dropping from the veils of the morning to where the cricket sings,
There midnight's all a glimmer, and noon a purple glow,
And evening full of the linnet's wings.

I will arise and go now, for always night and day
I hear lake water lapping with low sounds by the shore;   10
While I stand on the roadway, or on the pavements grey,
I hear it in the deep heart's core.

William Butler Yeats

Glossary	
title	*Innisfree:* an island in Lough Gill, Co. Sligo; the English version of the name of the island is derived from two Irish words: Inis (island) and fraoch (heather)
1	*I . . . now:* Yeats seems to have had the Gospel of Luke, chapter 15, verse 18 in mind: 'I will arise and go to my father', where the prodigal son in the parable wants to return home, just as the speaker in the poem does
2	*wattles:* flexible rods that can be interwoven and plastered with mud to form a building material
4	*glade:* open space in a wood
7	*Noon a purple glow:* heather grows profusely on the island and gives a purple glow to the light in the middle of the day
9	*always night and day:* an echo of the Gospel of Mark, chapter 5, verse 5: 'And always night and day, he was in the mountains'

Guidelines

Yeats wrote 'The Lake Isle of Innisfree' in London when he was twenty-five years of age. As he walked through Fleet Street, a fountain in a shop window reminded him of the sound of lake water and thus revived his dream of living alone on the island in Lough Gill, finding wisdom and peace in the tradition of the ancient hermits.

Yeats provided further background information on the inspiration behind the poem. He explained that early in life he was influenced by the example of the nineteenth-century American essayist and poet Henry David Thoreau (1817–62), popularly known as the 'hermit of Walden'. In 1845 Thoreau abandoned conventional living and built himself a shanty (or shack) in the woods near Walden Pond. There he wrote his classic work *Walden; or, Life in the Woods* (1854). Yeats recalled that his father read him a passage from this book. He came to the conclusion that, in imitation of Thoreau, he should live 'in a cottage on a little island called Innisfree', where he would seek wisdom in isolation from the rest of humankind. The window display in London reminded him of this youthful hope and prompted him to write 'The Lake Isle of Innisfree'.

Yeats had earlier written a short novel entitled *John Sherman*, in which one of the characters, when in trouble, wants to go away and live in solitude on Innisfree. Many of the details in *John Sherman* anticipate this poem. For example, the island covered in bushes, the building of a hut and the ripple of the water.

Commentary

Yeats told a friend that the speaker of the poem is a persona, or a character distinct from the poet himself, although the feelings expressed were related to the poet's own.

The poem belongs to the Romantic phase of Yeats's early career, which was dominated by a quest for beauty in nature and in life. It celebrates a common and deep human impulse: the desire to find a way of escape from the sordid realities of city life into a pastoral Utopia where, free from care, the fortunate recluse can enjoy the simple, peaceful life amid the beauties of a natural landscape. The attractions of the ideal island of Innisfree are heightened by the contrast with the drabness of London, with its 'pavements grey' (line 11).

It is easy to see why this became one of Yeats's most popular poems and why it has remained so. It is pleasant, fluent, not particularly demanding and rich in texture. It is remarkable for its beauty of sound and its relaxed rhythms. The movement, rhythm, repetition, alliteration and assonance combine to give the poem a soporific, dreamy quality, reminiscent of much Victorian escapist poetry in which ideal landscapes and states of living are evoked as alternatives to the unpleasantness of the real world.

After a time, the remarkable popularity of the poem began to embarrass Yeats. Ezra Pound wrote a parody called 'The Lake Isle': 'Lend me a little tobacco shop / Or install me in any profession / Save this damned profession of writing / where one needs one's brains all the time.' In a humorous letter to Yeats, a relative, referring to some purchases of land in 1938 near Innisfree, issued a mock warning that notices would be put up on the land saying 'this way to the bee glade . . . anyone interfering with the bees will be severely dealt with . . . the beans must not be eaten. They are the property of the Land Commission.' In more recent times an imaginative journalist wrote a piece featuring a planning application by Yeats to Sligo County Council for permission to build a small cabin of clay and wattles on Innisfree, to grow nine rows of beans and to have a bee hive. The planning application is rejected because the cabin would be in breach of building regulations, the bees might represent a danger to passing tourists and the noise coming from 'the bee-loud glade' would disturb the peace of the lake.

Thinking about the poem

1   Consider the poem as a pleasant piece of escapism. What does the speaker want to escape from?

2   The poem is remarkable for its beauty of sound and leisurely rhythms. How do such features help to convey the theme?

3   In what ways, do you think, might the kind of life imagined in the poem prove satisfactory? Would you enjoy the kind of life the speaker wants to create for himself?

4   This is perhaps the most popular of all Yeats's poems. Suggest possible reasons for this.

5   Over time, Yeats came to dislike the poem. Suggest reasons why.

6   In 'Sailing to Byzantium', Yeats imagines another ideal world. How do the two worlds compare? Which would you choose, and why?

7   Suggest an alternative title for the poem, and explain the reason or reasons for your choice.

8   Which of the following statements best describes your view of the speaker of the poem?
    ● The speaker is a wise man.
    ● The speaker is not a very practical man.
    ● The speaker shows good judgement.
    Explain your choice.

9   'In this poem, sound is more important than meaning.' Do you agree with this point of view? Give a reason for your opinion.

William Butler Yeats

Personal response

1   Compose a reply to the writer of a review of this poem who argues that it has nothing to offer a modern reader.

2   Imagine that you have been living on the Lake Isle of Innisfree, with all the amenities Yeats describes in the poem. Write a report on your experiences to date.

3   Yeats often revised his poems. The following is his first version of 'The Lake Isle of Innisfree' (lines 1–8):

> I will arise and go now and go to the island of Innis Free
> And live in a dwelling of Wattles – of woven wattles and wood work made,
> Nine bean rows will I have there, a yellow hive for the honey bee
> And his old care shall fade.
> There from the dawn above me peace will come down dropping slow
> Dropping from the veils of the morning to where the household cricket sings.
> And noontide there be all a glimmer, midnight a purple glow,
> And evening full of the linnet's wings.

(a)   Do you think the present version is an improvement on the first one? Explain your answer.

(b)   What do the changes do for the poem? How do they alter the rhythm? Choose some words or phrases Yeats was well advised to omit and explain why.

Before you read 'The Wild Swans at Coole'

Swans are a common subject in poetry, as well as mythology, folklore and fairy tales. With a partner, think of as many examples as you can of their presence in popular culture. Discuss why swans feature in such works and what they represent or stand for.

The Wild Swans at Coole

The trees are in their autumn beauty
The woodland paths are dry,
Under the October twilight the water
Mirrors a still sky;
Upon the brimming water among the stones   5
Are nine-and-fifty swans.

The nineteenth autumn has come upon me
Since I first made my count;

I saw, before I had well finished,
All suddenly mount   10
And scatter wheeling in great broken rings
Upon their clamorous wings.

I have looked upon those brilliant creatures,
And now my heart is sore.
All's changed since I, hearing at twilight,   15
The first time on this shore,
The bell-beat of their wings above my head,
Trod with a lighter tread.

Unwearied still, lover by lover,
They paddle in the cold   20
Companionable streams or climb the air;
Their hearts have not grown old;
Passion or conquest, wander where they will,
Attend upon them still.

But now they drift on the still water,   25
Mysterious, beautiful;
Among what rushes will they build,
By what lake's edge or pool
Delight men's eyes when I awake some day
To find they have flown away?   30

Glossary	
title:	*Coole:* Coole Park, the Co. Galway home of Yeats's patron and friend Lady Augusta Gregory and her husband, Sir William Gregory, a local landlord. Yeats was a frequent visitor to Coole Park. The poem records an experience he had during one of these visits
3	*twilight:* soft light at dusk, after the sun has gone down
11	*wheeling:* circling around
12	*clamorous:* noisy
18	*Trod . . . tread:* he walked with a lighter step (nineteen years ago, the first time that he saw these wild swans)
21	*companionable streams:* the streams at Coole Park provide a friendly atmosphere for the swans to enjoy a sense of companionship with each other

Guidelines

This is the title-poem of a collection first published in 1917, when Yeats was aged fifty-two and had become concerned about the exhausting effect of age on his imaginative powers. In the poem he reflects that he has been enjoying the beauty of the swans at Coole Park, the residence of his friend Lady Gregory, for nineteen years: his habit of counting them over that period reminds him of his own age. Yeats is conscious of the gulf opening up between himself as the slave of time and timeless nature represented by the swans. He ends the poem on a note of fear: one day the swans, which embody his creative relationship with nature, will have gone elsewhere, leaving him desolate.

Commentary

The poem is deeply symbolic. Like the subject of Keats's 'Ode to a Nightingale', Yeats's swans seem to defy time. They may age like the speaker, but they give the illusion of immortality. They are a Yeatsian symbol of eternity as they rise from the lake to wheel above him 'in great broken rings' (line 11).

The meaning of the poem depends to a large extent on the relationship the speaker establishes between the swans and himself. The speaker, conscious of his advancing age, looks at the fifty-nine swans. He has been counting these swans for nineteen years. Over all that time they, as if by a miracle, seem to have defied time ('Their hearts have not grown old', line 22). The speaker knows that individual swans are just as mortal as himself, but suggests they give the illusion of immortality: the pattern they establish survives.

Any interpretation of the poem must focus on the symbolism of the swans, without being over-precise about the meaning they generate. They anticipate the pattern of eternity as, before the speaker has finished counting them, they rise from the lake to wheel above him. They link the 'still water' (line 25) to the 'still sky' (line 4) that is mirrored in it. Unlike people, they are able to live in two elements: air and water. More importantly, they are able to live (in the symbolic sense created by the poem) on earth as well as in eternity. They are mortal – 'lover by lover' – and yet give the impression of immortality – 'Unwearied still' (line 19).

Throughout the poem, we are conscious of the contrast between the speaker's sense of his own mortality and the perpetual youth and vitality enjoyed by the swans. In stanza 2, for example, the swans resist the speaker's attempt to define them in terms of their number and to make them finite beings; instead, they assert their independence in a ritual flight symbolising their freedom from the constraints of time: 'All suddenly mount / And scatter wheeling in great broken rings' (lines 10–11).

The emphasis of the third stanza is on the changeless character of the swans and the all too evident decline in the speaker's vitality, which their animated movements underline for him. The speaker's response to the contrast between his sense of mortality and the ageless vitality of the swans is a self-regarding sorrow: his 'heart is sore' (line 14). By the end of the poem, however, he has come to terms with his own ageing and the eternity symbolised by the swans, who are outside time.

The final stanza raises complex questions, suggested in the speaker's description of the swans as 'mysterious' (line 26). The contemplation of these mysterious creatures leads him to wonder where they will be, to delight men's eyes, when some day he finds 'they have flown away' (line 30). The expression 'when I awake some day' in line 29 cannot be taken literally. The speaker is not simply saying that some day he will awake to find that the swans have gone. The question then arises: what kind of awakening is he describing? Is he talking about awakening into death to find that the pattern of immortality represented by the swans has vanished, as he himself has become immortal? Or, given that the swans symbolise youthfulness, is he saying that their eventual flight from his life will signal his decline into old age and approaching death?

The poem's references to autumn and the passage of time ('The nineteenth autumn has come upon me', line 7) may suggest that the swans represent his passionate youth, or at least mirror that part of his past. The final stanza may, in the light of this, imply that when the speaker is old, perhaps dead (having awakened in eternity), the swans will delight other men in other places who enjoy the youth and passion that he has lost. Lines 23 and 24 suggest that the 'passion or conquest' associated with youth and vitality are an intimate part of their significance, that wherever they wander, these 'Attend upon them still'. Those human beings whose youth makes them capable of passion or conquest will always ('still') find in the swans a symbolic representation of their feelings and impulses.

Different interpretations

The poem ends on the optimistic notion that the swans will always be symbols of beauty, love, youth and vitality. The poet finally comes to terms with the swans' freedom and with his own ageing. This reading is not universally accepted. Some interpreters see the poem as ending on a note of pessimism, and expressing the fear that the day will come when the swans, symbolising the speaker's creative relationship with nature, will desert him, leaving him bereft of inspiration and creativity.

Thinking about the poem

1. The autumn setting is important. Why?
2. What does the counting of the swans signify?
3. What meaning do the swans have for the speaker?
4. The poem is partly based on a contrast between the speaker and the swans. What is this contrast? Mention some other contrasts in the poem.
5. Why is the speaker troubled as he contemplates the swans?
6. Does the speaker have reason to envy the swans?
7. Describe the impression the poem has made on you.
8. Choose your favourite image from the poem, and explain why you have chosen it.
9. There are changes in the poet's feeling and attitude in the course of the poem. Describe these changes.
10. Yeats explained that lonely birds such as the heron, hawk, eagle and swan are the natural symbols of subjectivity. In 'The Wild Swans at Coole', do the swans symbolise other things?
11. In this poem Yeats commemorates the passing of time. Which details help to convey this?
12. In the first printed version of the poem, Yeats had arranged the stanzas in a different order from the one we find in the present version. The current stanza 5 was then stanza 3, making the old order: 1, 2, 5, 3, 4. Yeats's decision to change the order of the stanzas changed the entire emphasis of the poem and its main themes. Identify two significant changes.

Personal response

1. You have been asked to make a short film to accompany a reading of this poem. Say how you would use music, sound effects, colour, images, etc. to convey the atmosphere of the lake.
2. Write a response to a landscape you are familiar with, emphasising its features and what they mean to you.

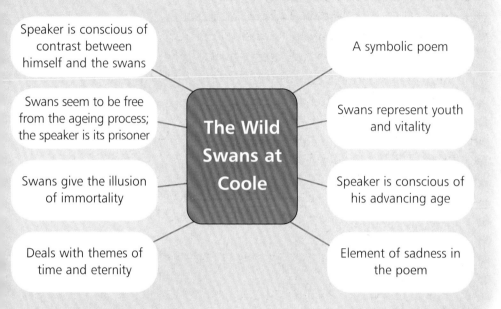

The Wild Swans at Coole

Speaker is conscious of contrast between himself and the swans

Swans seem to be free from the ageing process; the speaker is its prisoner

Swans give the illusion of immortality

Deals with themes of time and eternity

A symbolic poem

Swans represent youth and vitality

Speaker is conscious of his advancing age

Element of sadness in the poem

Before you read 'An Irish Airman Foresees His Death'

'An Irish Airman Foresees His Death' by William Butler Yeats (on page 410) is about an Irishman who volunteered to fight in the First World War as a fighter-pilot in the British Air Force. He was one of tens of thousands of Irishmen who joined the British forces in the course of the war. Find out  what you can about why so many joined, and about the people who encouraged them to do so. You might like to look for information on the Meath poet Francis Ledwidge, who joined the British Army, and who, like Robert Gregory, the Irish airman in Yeats's poem, was killed in action.

An Irish Airman Foresees His Death

I know that I shall meet my fate
Somewhere among the clouds above;
Those that I fight I do not hate,
Those that I guard I do not love;
My country is Kiltartan Cross,   5
My countrymen Kiltartan's poor,
No likely end could bring them loss
Or leave them happier than before.
Nor law, nor duty bade me fight,
Nor public men, nor cheering crowds,   10
A lonely impulse of delight
Drove to this tumult in the clouds;
I balanced all, brought all to mind,
The years to come seemed waste of breath,
A waste of breath the years behind   15
In balance with this life, this death.

Glossary	
title	*Irish Airman:* the subject of this poem is Major Robert Gregory (1881–1918), the only child of Lady Gregory
1–2	*I know . . . above:* Yeats makes Gregory 'know' what the future holds for him. To understand this we have to bear in mind that Gregory was reputed to possess psychic second sight, which gave him a premonition of death; Yeats believed that people could possess this faculty, and admired it
4	*Those . . . I guard:* the Allied peoples in World War 1
5–6	*My country . . . poor:* the Gregorys lived on the Coole Park estate, Kiltartan, Co. Galway; Kiltartan Cross is a few miles from Coole
7	*end:* result of the war
9	*Nor . . . fight:* I enlisted neither because I was legally compelled to do so, nor out of a sense of patriotic duty
10	*public men:* politicians whose warlike oratory encouraged young men to fight
11	*lonely impulse:* his impulse to join in the fight is lonely because it comes from within himself; he will choose a hero's death in a war that is otherwise without meaning for him.

Guidelines

This poem is part of Yeats's 1919 volume, *The Wild Swans at Coole*. Its subject is Major Robert Gregory, the only son of Lady Gregory. Like his mother, Robert had been extremely close to Yeats. He learned Irish at Coole, his mother's home, and was a stage designer for Yeats at the Abbey Theatre in Dublin. An accomplished artist, he became a member of the Royal Flying Corps during World War 1. In January 1918 he was shot down as he returned to base in northern Italy.

Commentary

The sixteen lines of this poem are not a conventional lament for a dear friend, but a presentation, or definition, of Gregory as the perfect man of Yeats's imagination.

Lines 1–8

From Yeats's point of view, the quality that best defined the perfect man was balance, and this quality is central to his presentation of Gregory. From his lofty position in the clouds, Gregory is able to view the war with detachment and poise. He is not motivated to fight by partisan political emotions: he neither hates the Germans nor loves the Allies (lines 3–4). He balances the future prospects of his poor countrymen living on or near his family estate at Kiltartan, Co. Galway, against the outcome of the war, concluding that, regardless of the war's outcome, they will neither lose nor gain (lines 7–8).

Lines 9–16

Gregory's detachment is further shown in his indifference to the cheering crowds encouraging men such as himself to go to war and to the warlike speeches of politicians (line 10). Instead, he is able to resolve the tensions of his life by finding fulfilment in the 'tumult in the clouds' (line 12), which will inevitably lead to his extinction. There is a sense in which Yeats presents the war purely as an opportunity for Gregory to gratify his impulse and to resolve his personal problems. Yeats sees Gregory as a man fated to find his ultimate delight in the experience of death in life. Given his hero's impulse to balance 'all' at the expense of life itself, it is appropriate that Yeats should ask in another poem, 'In Memory of Major Robert Gregory': 'What made us dream that he could comb grey hair?'

The structural impulse behind the poem is indicated in line 13: 'I balanced all, brought all to mind'. Yeats makes his speaker take a balanced, unemotional view of his involvement in the war. This involvement is explained in lines 9 to 12, which are all the more remarkable when we consider the historical background against which they were written. Young men went to war because they were conscripted (by 'law') or because they saw it as their 'duty' to fight for their country. Alternatively, many of them were caught up in a patriotic surge, created by the passionate speeches of politicians ('public men'), who had launched the war and were willing to sacrifice the youth of all nations to keep it going. This patriotic nationalism was further inflamed by the multitudes who cheered the doomed young men on to their deaths.

The speaker of Yeats's poem is unmoved by the emotions generated by the public rhetoric of war and the mass hysteria of patriotic crowds. These themes were rehearsed in innumerable war poems – many poets were prepared to debase their art in the service of propaganda by supplying recruiting verses to correspond to the government's recruiting posters. Most of the pro-war poetry is simple-minded in the extreme. The following from 'To You Who Have Lost' in John Oxenham's *All's Well: Some Helpful Verse for these Dark Days of War* is typical:

> He died as a few men get the chance to die –
> Fighting to save a world's morality.
> He died the noblest death a man may die,
> Fighting for God, and Right, and Liberty –
> And such a death is Immortality.

The speaker's participation in the war has nothing to do with such impulses, or with a belief in whatever goal the war was supposed to achieve, or with the notion that one side was right and the other wrong. He is above and beyond such absurd oppositions.

The war has, however, a purpose for the speaker. It gives him a splendid opportunity to resolve his own tensions, to live with the utmost intensity and to experience the paradox of death in life, which will give him his greatest fulfilment. His decision to fight, and die, in the skies is made coldly, rationally and without passion. Yeats makes Gregory see life and death as equivalent to each other: he will find his life's meaning in the manner of his death (line 16). His experience of death will not, however, be without passion: it will involve both 'delight' (line 11) and 'tumult' (line 12). Gregory thus becomes the kind of man Yeats most admired: one who can combine passion and detachment, joy and loneliness.

Second thoughts

Yeats wrote a sequel to 'An Irish Airman Foresees His Death' in 1921, but the sequel, 'Reprisals', was suppressed until 1948, nine years after Yeats's death, for fear of offending the Gregory family. 'Reprisals' was written during the Irish War of Independence, when British soldiers were shooting tenants on the Gregory estate. Yeats imagined Robert Gregory's ghost visiting Kiltartan, bitterly contemplating what the soldiers of the country he had fought for are now doing to his own people. Yeats addresses Gregory's ghost:

Yet rise from your Italian tomb,

Flit to Kiltartan Cross and stay

Till certain second thoughts have come

Upon the cause you served, that we

Imagined such a fine affair:

Half-drunk or whole-mad soldiery

Are murdering your tenants there.

Men that revere your father yet

Are shot at on the open plain.

Then close your ears with dust and lie

Among the other cheated dead.

Thinking about the poem

1   Describe the speaker's attitude to the war. Does he think it is worthwhile?
2   Consider the idea of balance as central to the poem.
3   Yeats greatly admired Major Robert Gregory, the subject of the poem. Does the poem suggest why?
4   Does the speaker emerge as a self-centred, even selfish man? Give reasons for your answer.
5   Does the poem give the impression of a man who feels superior to those around him? Give reasons for your answer.
6   How would you describe the tone of the poem?
7   How would you describe the language of the poem?
8   Might the poem be described as an anti-war poem? Give reasons for your answer.
9   Write a short piece outlining your response to the poem and its speaker.
10 Given his attitude to the parties fighting the war, was the speaker justified in becoming involved? Give reasons for your answer.
11 'An Irish Airman Foresees His Death' and 'Easter 1916' both deal with conflict from different points of view. Comment on the features that the two poems have in common, and on the differences between them. Which of them do you find the more convincing? Explain your choice.
12 What do the two poems mentioned in question 11 tell you about Yeats's attitude to war?

Personal response

1   Imagine that you are a newspaper reporter. Using details from the poem, write a brief account of the airman's approach to life and death, as if you had interviewed him.

2   Imagine you were one of those Irishmen who fought in the First World War. Explain your motives for doing so.

3   This poem has been described as a work of 'pure joy'. Would you agree with this description? Explain your answer.

snapshot

The outcome of the war will make no greater difference to him than it will to the poor people of Kiltartan

War gives the speaker an opportunity to resolve his own tensions

An original view of war

An Irish Airman Foresees His Death

Speaker's participation in the war is not motivated by patriotism

Speaker takes a balanced view of the conflict

Speaker lacks passion

September 1913

What need you, being come to sense,
But fumble in a greasy till
And add the halfpence to the pence
And prayer to shivering prayer, until
You have dried the marrow from the bone?   5
For men were born to pray and save:
Romantic Ireland's dead and gone,
It's with O'Leary in the grave.

Yet they were of a different kind,
The names that stilled your childish play,   10
They have gone about the world like wind,
But little time had they to pray
For whom the hangman's rope was spun,
And what, God help us, could they save?
Romantic Ireland's dead and gone,   15
It's with O'Leary in the grave.

Was it for this the wild geese spread
The grey wing upon every tide;
For this that all that blood was shed,
For this Edward Fitzgerald died,   20
And Robert Emmet and Wolfe Tone,
All that delirium of the brave?
Romantic Ireland's dead and gone,
It's with O'Leary in the grave.

Yet could we turn the years again,   25
And call those exiles as they were
In all their loneliness and pain,
You'd cry, 'Some woman's yellow hair
Has maddened every mother's son':
They weighed so lightly what they gave.   30
But let them be, they're dead and gone,
They're with O'Leary in the grave.

Glossary

1	*you:* the Irish merchant and business classes of the early twentieth century
5	*dried . . . bone:* lost all human feeling, allowed emotion to wither
8	*O'Leary:* John O'Leary (1830–1907), a Fenian veteran whose devotion to Irish independence forced him into exile in France, where Yeats came to know him
9	*they:* self-sacrificing Irish patriots
17	*wild geese:* Irish soldiers who served in foreign armies in the seventeenth and eighteenth centuries; these included such patriotic leaders as Patrick Sarsfield
20	*Edward Fitzgerald:* (1763–98) Lord Edward Fitzgerald took part in the 1798 Rebellion; he died of wounds sustained while he was being arrested for treason
21	*Robert Emmet:* (1778–1803) Irish revolutionary who spent his personal fortune on weapons to be used against the British government in Ireland; he was hanged in September 1803 following the failure of the rising he led
21	*Wolfe Tone:* (1763–98) Theobald Wolfe Tone organised a French military expedition to Ireland in support of a planned revolution; he was captured, tried and condemned to death as a traitor, but committed suicide in prison while waiting to be hanged. Line 13 ('For whom the hangman's rope was spun') is especially appropriate to Tone, as well as to Emmet

Guidelines

An angry speaker is addressing people he dislikes. These are middle-class Irish merchants, whose lives, he suggests, are focused on two occupations: praying and saving. They have no love for their country and have made Ireland a selfish, materialistic society. As always with Yeats, there is a contrast. This is provided by the unselfish, patriotic heroes of the past, who were prepared to die for the freedom of their country. The speaker recognises that these past idealists would be regarded by leaders of modern opinion as foolish, even mad, and best forgotten.

Commentary

Stanza 1

The central impulse behind the poem is the disparagement of the present by setting it in opposition to a romanticised past. The 'you' of line 1 is the group to whom the poem is mockingly and ironically addressed: the nationalist merchant class, characterised here by the qualities of religious devotion and attachment to money. The speaker is asking the people he despises, 'What more do you need than to spend your time praying and saving, and so dehumanising yourselves? What else, after all, were men born for?' The rhetoric is all the more effective for its vivid, concrete imagery. The image of the merchant fumbling 'in a greasy till' (line 2) conveys just the right note of contempt for the whole class he represents, making its activities appear sordid, mean and squalid.

Refrain

Against this presentation of crass materialism allied to debased religious practice, the speaker offers a nobler vision of Ireland represented by the Fenian John O'Leary, who had a vital influence on Irish cultural nationalism. When Yeats first met him, O'Leary was a venerable Fenian. He had served five years in prison and fifteen years in exile in Paris. He introduced Yeats to the work of such Irish nationalist poets as Thomas Davis and James Clarence Mangan. In Yeats's personal mythology, O'Leary represented all that was finest and most idealistic in the Irish poetic tradition. In the scheme of the poem, the tradition represented by the dead O'Leary belongs to a vanished age.

Stanzas 2 and 3

The 'they' at the beginning of Stanza 2 are the patriots of the heroic past, whose mere names are enough to bring the play of children to a halt, and who are universally honoured. Line 12 ('But little time had they to pray') and line 14 ('And what, God help us, could they save?') contrast sharply with the preoccupations of the speaker's contemporaries described in stanza 1. The 'this' of line 17 is contemporary Ireland with all its imperfections. The 'wild geese' were the Irish soldiers who served in the armies of Europe after the Treaty of Limerick in 1691. The speaker wonders whether their sacrifice, or the sacrificial deaths of Fitzgerald, Emmet and Tone, were worthwhile if the only result is a nation of prayerful materialists.

His choice of models of Irish patriotism, apart from O'Leary, is significant. The three he mentions in lines 20 and 21 – Fitzgerald, Emmet and Tone – were all members of the Anglo-Irish Protestant Ascendancy, a class to which Yeats was proud to belong.

The phrase 'delirium of the brave' (line 22) is not intended to suggest that the Irish heroes of the past were delirious, but that their sacrifice was emotional and instinctive rather than calculating and rational. Had they been rational they would, presumably, have prayed and saved like merchants: instead, they gave their lives for a dream.

Stanza 4

The ironic tone persists in the final stanza. Yeats is imagining a return to life of the heroic dead to confront the unheroic living, who would probably dismiss the sacrifices of the past as mere madness, inspired by romantic love for a woman (or for Ireland in the traditional guise of a woman). The calculating merchants who now hold sway would find the activities of patriotic Irishmen ridiculous because they gave everything they had without counting the cost. The final two lines set a seal on the mocking irony to which Yeats has exposed his contemporaries throughout the poem. The speaker imagines his merchants thinking that past heroes are best forgotten since they are safely dead and buried with O'Leary.

Dispiriting vision

'September 1913' offers a dispiriting vision of an Ireland lacking in spiritual values, 'a little greasy huxtering nation groping for halfpence in a greasy till', as Yeats expressed it elsewhere. The poem is a rousing celebration of past patriotic glory, but it also reflects Yeats's strong anti-democratic feelings, his elitist view of Irish history and his lack of faith in the possibility of a wise and civilised democratic government. Less than three years later, in 'Easter 1916', he was to discover and record a more optimistic vision of Ireland.

Inspiration for the poem

This poem was mainly prompted by a bitter controversy that had developed over the issue of building an art gallery in Dublin. Those, including Yeats, who were pressing for the provision of such a gallery, were influenced by the offer made by Sir Hugh Lane, Lady Gregory's nephew, to present his important collection of French impressionist paintings to the City of Dublin provided that a gallery was built in which to house them. The project met with a poor response from Dublin Corporation, and disagreement arose over the possible location of the gallery. There was much public indifference and opposition. Subscriptions to a gallery fund were inadequate. Yeats responded with this condemnatory poem, which was first published in *The Irish Times* on 8 September 1913, under the odd title, 'Romance In Ireland (on reading much of the correspondence against the Art Gallery)'.

Thinking about the poem

1   There is a clear contrast in the poem between past and present. Show how Yeats manages this contrast. Mention other contrasts in the poem.

2   Irony plays a significant part in the poem with one thing being said but another meant. Give examples of this feature. Is it effective?

3   How does Yeats convey the modern absence of human feelings and idealism?

4   Does Yeats present an ideal for his readers' approval? If so, how can it be described?

5   What does 'Romantic Ireland' mean in the context of this poem?

6   Does the poem have a significance for the Ireland of the present day? Are the issues it raises of interest to you?

7   Do you think that the patriots mentioned in the poem were fools? Did the poet think so?

8   Yeats lists a number of patriots in the poem. What did they have in common?

9   There is a suggestion in the poem that extreme patriotism might be seen as a form of madness. Do you think that the poet agrees with this view? Explain your answer with reference to the poem.

10   Comment on the reference to 'Some woman's yellow hair' (line 28). Who do you think the woman might be?

11   The poem gave some memorable lines and phrases to the language. Mention those you can identify.

12   This is a poem of protest and complaint. What exactly is Yeats protesting and complaining about? Explain your answer.

Personal response

1   Describe the effect that this poem has on you.

2   Do you think that this poem is suitable or unsuitable for inclusion in a school anthology? Give reasons for your answer.

Before you read 'Easter 1916'

The Easter Rising of 1916 has long been regarded as a major turning point in Irish history. To arrive at a fuller understanding of the poem 'Easter 1916' on page 420, find out as much as you can about the events of Easter week 1916: what led to these events and what happened immediately afterwards? Do some research on the leaders of the Rising, their characters and motives, and their fate. Such information is available in any good history of the period.

Easter 1916

I have met them at close of day
Coming with vivid faces
From counter or desk among grey
Eighteenth-century houses.
I have passed with a nod of the head   5
Or polite meaningless words,
Or have lingered awhile and said
Polite meaningless words,
And thought before I had done
Of a mocking tale or a gibe   10
To please a companion
Around the fire at the club,
Being certain that they and I
But lived where motley is worn:
All changed, changed utterly: 15
A terrible beauty is born.

That woman's days were spent
In ignorant good-will,
Her nights in argument
Until her voice grew shrill.   20
What voice more sweet than hers
When, young and beautiful,
She rode to harriers?
This man had kept a school
And rode our winged horse: 25
This other his helper and friend
Was coming into his force;
He might have won fame in the end,
So sensitive his nature seemed,
So daring and sweet his thought.   30
This other man I had dreamed
A drunken, vainglorious lout.
He had done most bitter wrong

To some who are near my heart.
Yet I number him in the song; 35
He, too, has resigned his part.
In the casual comedy;
He, too, has been changed in his turn,
Transformed utterly:
A terrible beauty is born. 40

Hearts with one purpose alone
Through summer and winter seem
Enchanted to stone
To trouble the living stream.
The horse that comes from the road, 45
The rider, the birds that range
From cloud to tumbling cloud,
Minute by minute they change;
A shadow of cloud on the stream
Changes minute by minute; 50
A horse-hoof slides on the brim,
And a horse plashes within it;
The long-legged moor-hens dive,
And hens to moor-hens call;
Minute by minute they live: 55
The stone's in the midst of all.

Too long a sacrifice
Can make a stone of the heart.
O when may it suffice?
That is Heaven's part, our part 60
To murmur name upon name,
As a mother names her child
When sleep at last has come
On limbs that had run wild,
What is it but nightfall? 65
No, no, not night but death;
Was it needless death after all?
For England may keep faith

For all that is done and said.
We know their dream; enough   70
To know they dreamed and are dead;
And what if excess of love
Bewildered them till they died?
I write it out in a verse –
MacDonagh and MacBride   75
And Connolly and Pearse,
Now and in time to be,
Whenever green is worn,
Are changed, changed utterly:
A terrible beauty is born.   80

Glossary

1	*them:* the people who secretly planned the 1916 Rising
4	*Eighteenth-century houses:* many of the houses in central Dublin date from the Georgian era (1714–1830) when the city experienced rapid growth
14	*motley:* the dress of the fool in a play
17	*That woman:* Constance Markiewicz (1868–1927), one of the daughters of the Gore-Booth family of Lissadell House, Co. Sligo, and a Volunteer officer during the 1916 Rising (see also 'In Memory of Eva Gore-Booth and Con Markiewicz')
24	*This man:* Patrick Pearse (1879–1916), schoolmaster, lawyer and poet, President of the Republic declared in 1916, who was executed as a leader of the Rising
24	*a school:* St Enda's in Rathfarnham, Dublin, where the pupils were taught to value their Gaelic heritage
25	*winged horse:* Pegasus, traditionally associated with poetic inspiration
26	*This other:* Thomas MacDonagh (1878–1916), poet, teacher, dramatist and critic, who was executed as a leader of the Rising
31	*This other man:* Major John MacBride (1868–1916), estranged husband of Yeats's muse Maud Gonne; he was executed for taking part in the Rising

33–4	*He had . . . heart:* for a long time Yeats had despised MacBride for betraying Maud Gonne and, as he believed, molesting her daughter, Iseult. When he was writing this poem, both mother and daughter were 'near to his heart'. He was in love with both of them, and proposed marriage to each of them at different times. Both turned him down
67–9	*Was it . . . said:* Yeats is suggesting that the 1916 rebels perhaps died in vain. In 1914 the British government had undertaken to grant Home Rule to Ireland when hostilities in the First World War ended. If this were to come about, it would satisfy the demands of many Irish nationalists. Yeats is arguing that it was possible that the British government might honour its undertaking and settle the Irish question without bloodshed. Hence, those who died in the 1916 Rising may have shed their blood needlessly
76	*Connolly:* James Connolly (1870–1916). His Citizen Army, the military force of the labour movement, took part in the 1916 Rising. Although severely wounded, he was executed as a leader of the Rising while in a wheelchair. The manner of his killing brought the British government and the military authorities into disrepute

Guidelines

The subject of this poem is the Easter Rising of 1916, the central event in twentieth-century Irish history, whose consequences are still felt. On 24 April 1916 a small group of Irish republicans occupied buildings in the centre of Dublin and their leaders proclaimed an Irish Republic. The Rising collapsed within a week and its leaders were executed by firing squad. Their idealism, bravery and chivalry impressed even their enemies. They were soon seen as martyrs and as heroic champions of the cause of Irish freedom.

Yeats was with Maud Gonne in France when he heard the news, and was at first shocked, believing that what the patriots had died for might be conceded peacefully by the British. Against this, he acknowledged that Maud Gonne might have been justified in arguing that with the Rising, in which her estranged husband died, 'tragic dignity has returned to Ireland', an idea expressed in the poem's most memorable line, 'A terrible beauty is born'. The Rising, which he saw as a tragic drama, moved Yeats as no other public event ever did. The first manuscript of the poem is dated 25 September 1916.

'Easter 1916' may be read as a retraction of the more cynical view of Irish public life expressed in 'September 1913'. Maud Gonne recalled that when Yeats read the newly composed 'Easter 1916' to her in France, he urged her to abandon her patriotic intensity, imploring her 'to forget the stone and its inner fire for the flashing, changing joy of life'. See lines 41 to 56 of the poem for the context of Yeats's plea.

Commentary

Like 'September 1913', this poem is based on contrast and antithesis (a balancing of opposing ideas). The central antithesis is between the speaker's attitude to the people who were secretly planning the 1916 Rising and his attitude to the same people after they had displayed an unexpected heroism and become nationalist martyrs.

Stanza 1

Yeats evokes the spirit of pre-revolutionary Ireland, when he could detect no serious commitment to patriotism, which seemed a matter of show rather than substance. Before 1916, he could not take either the patriots or their cause seriously, as the first fourteen lines make clear. They seemed to be merely posing as revolutionaries. He characterises their seemingly ineffectual activities as no more significant than those of well-meaning patriots who might dress in bright colourful costumes for a pageant, the 'motley' of line 14 being the multi-coloured dress of a clown or the fool in a play, a way of suggesting that the planners of revolution were merely playing at it, without any real intention of carrying it out. He had even thought of making fun of them with his sophisticated friends at the gentleman's club to which he belonged.

Refrain

'Easter 1916' is a profoundly ambiguous poem as suggested by the refrain in three of the four stanzas: 'A terrible beauty is born'. The poem is not a single-minded celebration of what the leaders of the Rising have done. The key phrase 'terrible beauty' suggests that the beauty of what has been achieved has been purchased at the expense of life. The patriots have transcended the changing world, but only by making themselves immune from normal human impulses; their concentration on 'one purpose alone' (line 41) has turned their hearts to stone.

Stanza 2

The second stanza is a catalogue of the revolutionary men and women the speaker had so seriously undervalued in the years before the Rising. His presentation of the first of these, his friend Countess Markiewicz, is based on an antithesis: Yeats contrasts her younger days as a beautiful aristocratic woman of leisure with her later ones as a fanatical nationalist. The revolutionary countess had allowed her voice to become shrill in political argument, thus becoming a different, and less attractive, person from her earlier self who enjoyed aristocratic sports and had a sweet voice. There is loss and gain: her earlier good will was 'ignorant', but her later patriotism involves a coarsening of voice and appearance. The speaker next introduces two men: Patrick Pearse and Thomas MacDonagh, both of them teachers and poets. MacDonagh, as the speaker remarks with some regret, had the qualities of mind and imagination that might have brought him fame as a writer had he lived. The speaker's fourth figure is quite different. He is Major John MacBride, the husband of Maud Gonne, the woman Yeats loved in vain. He is characterised as a drunken, boastful lout who had wronged people whom Yeats holds dear.

In lines 36 to 41, these four figures are considered as characters in a drama, with the speaker returning to the earlier suggestion that before 1916 they had been acting out trivial parts in the play of life. Now, as he recognises, they have 'resigned' the parts assigned to them in 'the casual comedy' and transformed themselves into noble, beautiful actors in a new drama. This new drama is tragic rather than comic – it is the drama of violent, redemptive revolution leading to the deaths of all but the Countess. No longer half-hearted or faintly ridiculous casual patriots, they became noble, tragic participants, terrible and violent but beautiful in their self-sacrifice. The Rising is characterised by the speaker as 'terrible' as well as beautiful, since it involves great loss and waste as well as the regeneration of Ireland's soul.

In the first two stanzas, the idea of change has been dominant. The change in question is also one affecting the speaker: his perception of the participants in the Rising has changed. Yeats must even revise his opinion of his rival MacBride, whose sacrifice of his life in the cause of the Republic is evidence of his commitment and genuine patriotism.

Stanzas 3 and 4

The notion of change (or the appearance of change) gives way in stanza 3 to its opposite: the unchanging reality of patriotic devotion. The patriots of the poem have dedicated themselves exclusively and obsessively to the cause of Irish freedom. The price of this is that they become stone-hearted, devoid of everyday human emotion. The relation of the 1916 martyrs to the world around them is conveyed in the images of the stream and the stone.

The stone in the midst of the flowing stream is a powerfully effective image: the patriots remain unchanging, inflexible, immovable in a world of contrast and change. Pearse and his followers have turned their backs on life (the stone is a dead thing) in their fanatical concentration on a single cause. These lines are based on a powerful contrast between the constantly changing face of nature in a world of flux (whose image is the 'living stream', line 44) and the obsessive resistance to change that characterises the patriots, whose hearts, 'with one purpose alone' (line 41), are the only fixed objects.

The onward movement of daily life, in which all things alter from minute to minute, is the living stream, around and in which the rider and his horse, the birds, the cloud, the moor-hens and moor-cocks are part of a constant process of change. The stone stands firm in the midst of all this movement, to trouble and challenge it, as the patriotic rebels confront the changes and compromises of their world with their inflexible principles. This inflexibility exacts a terrible price: 'Minute by minute they live: / The stone's in the midst of all' (lines 55–56). The stone is a dead thing in the midst of the living things around it. This idea is clarified in the following lines. The heroic dreams of the patriots have deprived them of life. The metaphor becomes a reality: they are as dead as stones as a result of their inflexible heroism: 'Too long a sacrifice / Can make a stone of the heart' (lines 57–58).

The third stanza is a celebration of the joy of life to which the patriots have deliberately blinded themselves and makes us wonder whether they sacrificed too much. The speaker raises a more disturbing question in lines 67 to 69: 'Was it needless death after all? / For England may keep faith / For all that is done and said'. The 1916 patriots, in other words, may have wasted their lives in the cause of Irish independence, something the speaker suggests might have been granted by England in any case, even had there been no 1916 Rising. Yeats is here referring to the belief at the time that the British authorities would soon give Ireland a measure of freedom, as promised in the Home Rule Bill.

Yeats's speaker retains an impersonal attitude and refuses to pass judgement on the prudence or otherwise of what the rebels have done, preferring to leave this to the deeper wisdom of providence ('That is Heaven's part', line 60). The speaker is content to assume the role of chorus: 'To murmur name upon name, / As a mother names her child' (lines 61–62).

Thinking about the poem

1 Two worlds clash in 'Easter 1916'. Describe these two worlds. In what ways do they clash?

2 Discuss Yeats's evolving attitudes to the people who participated in the 1916 Rising.

3 Yeats expresses reservations about the people who sacrificed their lives in the Rising. What are these reservations? How does he express them?

4 Comment on the symbols used in the poem (the stone and the stream, for example). Consider the function of these symbols. How do they contribute to the meaning of the poem?

5 Having read the poem carefully, do you get the impression that Yeats, on the whole, approves of the Rising? Is 'Easter 1916' a patriotic poem? Explain your answer.

6 The poem has many striking images. Choose **two** of these and explain how they contribute to the effect of the poem.

7 What kind of person is the speaker of the poem? Support your answer with reference to **three** phrases or lines from the poem.

8 Consider the relationship between 'Easter 1916' and some of Yeats's other 'political' poems, such as 'September 1913', 'The Stare's Nest by My Window', 'In Memory of Eva Gore-Booth and Con Markiewicz'. Outline some resemblances and differences of outlook and treatment of political issues in these.

9 'Easter 1916' and 'An Irish Airman Foresees His Death' both deal with war. Are the attitudes expressed in both similar or are there differences?

10 "Easter 1916" offers a balanced view of the Rising and of those who participated in it.' Would you agree with this verdict on the poem? Explain your answer.

11 Why does Yeats repeat the notion that the Rising has given birth to 'a terrible beauty'? What does this beauty consist of? How can it be described as 'terrible'?

12 In the last stanza the poet raises a number of questions. What are these questions and what do they suggest about his attitude to his theme?

13 It has been remarked that 'Easter 1916' is a dialogue with, and within, the poet's uncertain self. Comment on the issues raised in this dialogue.

14 Yeats believed that all achievements are won by compromise. How is this belief reflected in the poem?

15 Six years before he wrote 'Easter 1916', Yeats wrote of the sterility that results when people give themselves to an abstract idea of the nation, and allow themselves to sacrifice their natural impulses to a morbid attachment to some fixed idea. Comment on the poem as an exploration of these ideas.

Personal response

1 With 'Easter 1916' in mind, write about the usefulness or futility of self-sacrifice and the dangers of fanaticism when political aims are being pursued.

2 Having read the poem, how does it make you feel about those who took part in the 1916 Rising? Do you feel (a) like condemning them; (b) like admiring them; or (c) that they were brave but foolish? Give reasons for your choice.

The Second Coming

Turning and turning in the widening gyre
The falcon cannot hear the falconer;
Things fall apart; the centre cannot hold;
Mere anarchy is loosed upon the world,
The blood-dimmed tide is loosed, and everywhere   5
The ceremony of innocence is drowned;
The best lack all conviction while the worst
Are full of passionate intensity,

Surely some revelation is at hand:
Surely the Second Coming is at hand,   10
The Second Coming! Hardly are the words out
When a vast image out of Spiritus Mundi
Troubles my sight: somewhere in sands of the desert
A shape with lion body and the head of a man,
A gaze blank and pitiless as the sun,   15
Is moving its slow thighs, while all about it
Reel shadows of the indignant desert birds.
The darkness drops again; but now I know
That twenty centuries of stony sleep
Were vexed to nightmare by a rocking cradle   20
And what rough beast, its hour come round at last,
Slouches towards Bethlehem to be born?

Glossary

title	*The Second Coming:* here Yeats combines two elements of Christian scripture: the Second Coming of Christ to judge humankind on the Day of Judgement, and the coming of the Antichrist, foretold in the Apocalypse
1	*gyre:* in Yeats's mythology, gyres are conical spirals of history through which events and people move; he saw history in terms of cycles, each lasting for two thousand years, and this poem visualises the destruction of the two-thousand-year Christian cycle
5	*blood-dimmed tide:* bloody wars
10	*Second Coming:* not the coming of Christ but of His opposite, the Antichrist
12	*Spiritus Mundi (Spirit of the World):* a storehouse or reservoir of images built up in the course of human history; such images can have a universal meaning
14–16	*shape . . . thighs:* the Sphinx-like beast represents the horrors to come

Guidelines

'The Second Coming' was written out of Yeats's reaction to the First World War and the brutalities and massive loss of life, as well as the material destruction, involved in that struggle. The poem makes no specific reference to the war, although this and other violent episodes in modern history may be seen as forerunners of the terrible future Yeats foresees for humankind. An early draft of the poem shows that it was written as a direct response to the war (in that draft Yeats refers to the Germans and Russians).

Commentary

The title of the poem is drawn from a fundamental Christian belief that after a second coming, Christ will establish on Earth a holy kingdom of happiness. Yeats did not believe in the Christian version of a second coming. He simply uses it as a convenient model for suggesting a world that shows signs of coming to a close. The Christian model is convenient because it is widely familiar, and was even more so in 1919 when the poem first appeared.

Although the Christian story frames the poem, in its allusions to the birth of Christ (Bethlehem, the traditional birthplace) and Christ's second coming in judgement, the world of Christian scripture dissolves into a quite different one, when the speaker's sight is troubled by 'a vast image out of Spiritus Mundi' (line 12) or the world's soul, the treasure house of images not invented by human beings but given to them from beyond. Yeats uses the term for the collective memory of the human race, a reservoir out of which he believed he received signals by way of images and symbols that he put to use in his poetry. In the case of this poem, the 'vast image' he receives is ugly and threatening, with an appearance like that of an Egyptian sphinx. This terrifying figure struggles out of the womb of time, with a lion's body and the head of a man, and slouches in monstrous birth to Bethlehem.

The second coming of this poem is not to be the final coming, and not the Last Judgement in the Christian sense. Instead, it is a terrifying incarnation of horrors that will face humanity in the two thousand years following the end of the Christian cycle.

To understand what is going on in the poem, it is necessary to understand Yeats's system of gyres, glanced at in the first line of the poem, on which his philosophy of history was based. This philosophy is outlined in his prose work, *A Vision*. Yeats believed that every two thousand years or so (see line 19 of the poem) the dominant civilisation is convulsed, and in a violent upheaval, a new kind of civilisation replaces the old one. The new one is the reverse of the old, its antithesis.

429

This idea is expressed in the lines: 'but now I know / That twenty centuries of stony sleep / Were vexed to nightmare by a rocking cradle' (lines 18–20). The twenty centuries referred to here were the two thousand years before the birth of Christ, represented by the rocking cradle. The 'rough beast' of line 21, with its sphinx-like appearance, suggests the Egyptian civilisation, which antedated those of pagan Greece and Christian Rome. The power that Yeats sees as replacing Christianity will be brutal and beastly in nature, with 'A gaze blank and pitiless as the sun' (line 15). It will destroy all things associated with Christianity. The Christian era will be replaced by an alien force. This force will be as opposite to Christianity as Christianity was to the spiritual forces that dominated the Greco-Roman world.

The poem gives a frightening account of the fate in store for the post-Christian world. As the gyre widens and there is a collapse of order, 'Things fall apart; the centre cannot hold' (line 3). The end of the Christian age is granted the revelation of the character of the next age. The tide of violence and personal and social revolution has already begun to move, and as it does, it begins to drown the 'ceremony of innocence' (line 6), which, in Yeats's symbolic system, stands for order, obedience and harmony (i.e. established institutions such as monarchies and empires). Social anarchy and massive destruction are made worse by the collapse of moral values among the leaders of nations: good people (the 'best', line 7) have grown cynical and sceptical and lack the strength and commitment to resist the fanatics (the 'worst', line 7) who have seized power. Evil will triumph in the public sphere because those leaders who might be expected to defend humane values lack the determination to resist those who preach violence and intolerance.

The more terrible events associated with the Antichrist are yet to come, but in lines 3 to 8 Yeats makes it clear that the world is already experiencing a foretaste of the grim future heralded by the birth of the rough beast. The year of the composition of 'The Second Coming' was an appropriate one in which to contemplate the effects of the anarchy that war and revolution had loosed upon the world: war, revolution and the collapse of great empires and dynasties were very recent events in 1919, while the Irish War of Independence was threatening to uproot the Anglo-Irish Ascendancy and the civilisation it represented, many elements of which appealed to Yeats.

'The Second Coming' does not offer a simple contrast between a peaceful Christianity and a violent paganism. It should be noted that Yeats associates the emergence of each new two-thousand-year cycle with violent upheaval and turbulence. Yeats was convinced that revelation from the other world, whatever the nature of this revelation might be, is always felt as a spiritual shock. Thus, he imagines that expiring pagan world as having been 'vexed to nightmare' (line 20) by the arrival of Christianity.

Similarly, he imagines the expiring Christian world shocked by the terrifying spectre of the 'rough beast' (line 21).

For the purposes of this poem, Yeats places pagan and Christian accounts of reality on the same level of importance, making brutal imagery central to both. Christian and pagan mysteries intrude into the visible human world and do it violence. "The Second Coming" expresses Yeats' conviction that each new cycle of revelation from the other world, no matter what the nature of this revelation may be, is bound to be shocking and violent. Pagans saw their world being threatened by the spiritual violence represented by the image of a condemned man nailed to a cross. In like manner, as Yeats's poem suggests, later Christians would have to face the threat to their world presented by the 'rough beast' (line 21) about to usher in the era of the Antichrist.

Yeats was unable to accept any of the orthodox versions of Christianity and was never a member of any Christian denomination. On the other hand, he did not think he could live without religion. The spirit world was always more real to him than the material world. He sensed a spiritual reality behind the world of physical appearances. All his life, he was seeking for a concrete proof of the supernatural. This quest led him to explore and experiment with every kind of mystical cult. He studied Greek mystery cults and Hindu scriptures. He dabbled in spiritualism. He dreamed of resurrecting the pagan Gods of ancient Ireland. He participated in séances. In this way he became a religious magpie, choosing what appealed to him and rejecting what did not. It was thus that he evolved a religious system all his own, expressed in his work in the language of symbol and myth, interweaving Christian and pagan motifs, as he does in 'The Second Coming'.

Thinking about the poem

1   The poem dramatises a clash between two contrasting ways of life. Describe these and discuss the poet's attitude to them.
2   In 'The Second Coming', Yeats presents his ideas in terms of images. Describe the kinds of images that dominate the poem and discuss their effect on the reader's imagination.
3   This is a political poem. What kind of political vision does it convey?
4   How does Yeats convey the idea that good is about to be overcome by evil?
5   In 'The Second Coming', Yeats suggests a reason why the forces of evil will overcome the forces of good. What is this reason?
6   Why does Yeats refer to Bethlehem in the final line of the poem?

7   How does Yeats work out the implications of the title of his poem?

8   Bearing in mind that the poem was written early in the twentieth century, can it now be seen as prophetic? Why do you think it is so often quoted? Mention some features of present-day civilisation to which the poem seems to look forward.

9   How would you describe the mood or tone of the poem?

10   Is the speaker in this poem more or less detached from his subject matter than the speakers in Yeats's other 'political' poems? Does he offer a murderous, despairing vision, unrelieved by any kind of hope?

11   What does the poem suggest to you about Yeats's view of Christianity?

12   'The Second Coming' has been described as 'a poem about history', and also as 'a poem about image-making' and as 'an occult experiment in imagination'. Which of these three descriptions best represents your own impression of the poem? Give reasons for your choice.

Personal response

1   The poem is partly based on the idea that in the year 2000, a new world would be summoned into existence by the mass imagination of the human race. Does the poem provide convincing evidence to support this idea? Explain your answer.

2   If you were asked to give a talk outlining the main ideas in this poem, what points would you emphasise?

3   'The Second Coming' is often described as a prophetic poem. Would it be more accurate to describe it as a work of fantasy, with little or no basis in the real world? Explain your answer.

Before you read 'Sailing to Byzantium'

Before reading 'Sailing to Byzantium' by William Butler Yeats on page 433, it may be helpful to consult a good book on art history, paying special attention to the wonderful mosaics for which Byzantine civilisation was noted. This will help you to enter into the spirit of the poem. Before writing the poem, Yeats made himself familiar with the art and history of Byzantium, and studied Byzantine artworks in the Italian city of Ravenna, in particular the church mosaics.

Sailing to Byzantium

That is no country for old men. The young
In one another's arms, birds in the trees
Those dying generations – at their song,
The salmon-falls, the mackerel-crowded seas,
Fish, flesh, or fowl, commend all summer long   5
Whatever is begotten, born and dies
Caught in that sensual music all neglect
Monuments of unageing intellect.

An aged man is but a paltry thing,
A tattered coat upon a stick, unless   10
Soul clap its hands and sing, and louder sing
For every tatter in its mortal dress,
Nor is there singing school but studying
Monuments of its own magnificence;
And therefore I have sailed the seas and come   15
To the holy city of Byzantium.

O sages standing in God's holy fire
As in the gold mosaic of a wall,
Come from the holy fire, perne in a gyre,
And be the singing-masters of my soul.   20
Consume my heart away; sick with desire
And fastened to a dying animal
It knows not what it is; and gather me
Into the artifice of eternity.

Once out of nature I shall never take   25
My bodily form from any natural thing,
But such a form as Grecian goldsmiths make
Of hammered gold and gold enamelling
To keep a drowsy Emperor awake;
Or set upon a golden bough to sing   30
To lords and ladies of Byzantium
Of what is past, or passing, or to come.

Glossary

title	*Byzantium:* this ancient city, later called Constantinople and then Istanbul, was a famous centre of religion, art and architecture. Yeats, who dreamed of a world free from the common sadness of everyday life, imagines that ancient Byzantium might have corresponded to this ideal. He wrote that if he could be given a month in an ancient place, he would choose to spend it in Byzantium
1	*country:* the country is Ireland and there is a hint also of Tír na nÓg, the land of the young, the old Irish name for a paradise where nobody grows old. Nine years after the poem was published, Yeats considered changing the first line to: 'Old men should quit a country where the young'
3	*dying generations:* not only the birds at their song, but also the fish, flesh and fowl, which, along with the young of line 1, are part of what is 'begotten, born and dies' (line 6)
7–8	*Caught . . . intellect:* in the general enjoyment of the pleasures of the senses, the life of the intellect, represented by such notable monuments to human achievement as the art and architecture of Byzantium, is neglected
9	*paltry:* mean, trashy, not worth considering
10	*tattered . . . stick:* the ageing process renders an old man fleshless, a mere mockery of a human being, like a scarecrow dressed in cast-off clothes
11	*Soul clap its hands:* an image of the spiritual and artistic side of man rejoicing
12	*its mortal dress:* the body; in this case the body is old and tattered. Since the body can only cause its owner to despair, the soul should celebrate intellectual and spiritual achievement
13–14	*Nor . . . magnificence:* there is no more perfect way of passing the time than for the soul to give itself over to the contemplation of the timeless art of earlier periods, which is the glory of the human race
13	*singing school:* Yeats's term for an ideal or perfect exercise
15	*sailed the seas:* the voyage mentioned here is not a physical one, but a voyage of the spirit and of the imagination

17–18	*O sages . . . wall*: Yeats may have had in mind a mosaic in a church in Ravenna, Italy, which he visited in 1907, or some Byzantine mosaics in Sicily, which he saw in 1925, shortly before he wrote the poem. These mosaics depicted processions of Christian martyrs. Yeats told a correspondent that a medium he had consulted influenced him to associate the sages of this poem with a picture by the poet Blake of the poet Dante 'entering the Holy Fire' of purgatory
19	*perne in a gyre:* spin in a spiral
20	*be . . . my soul:* the speaker is asking the wise, holy men, now immune from decay, to enter the physical world and bring him away to their spiritual domain
21–4	*Consume . . . eternity:* the emotional side of the speaker (represented by the heart) wants to be separated from the body (the 'dying animal'). The separation will be achieved when he becomes part of an eternity of artistic beauty (gathered into 'the artifice of eternity')
25	*Once out of nature:* once I have left the physical world
26	*My bodily form:* Yeats suggested in his prose work, *A Vision*, that the visible forms taken by dead souls are extremely plastic (liable to radical changes of shape) under pressure from the imagination. This is why he feels able to determine the shape his soul will take when he abandons his human existence and casts off his scarecrow body
26	*natural:* living
27–8	*form . . . enamelling:* Yeats had read that in the emperor's palace at Byzantium there was a tree made of gold and silver, with artificial birds that sang
29–31	*To keep . . . Byzantium:* Yeats's imagination was always haunted by the image of man who turns into a bird as he passes into the other world and into a higher state of being. These lines may have been suggested to Yeats by Hans Christian Andersen's fairy tale 'The Nightingale', which tells of a singing-contest between a live bird and a mechanical one. The mechanical bird wins the loudest applause, but only the live bird can revive the emperor when he seems to be dying. Many critics doubt that Yeats wanted to become a mechanical bird after death
32	*Of . . . come:* in eternity the mechanical bird sings to the lords and ladies of Byzantium about history ('what is past') about time ('what is passing') and the future (what is 'to come') perhaps it is not too fanciful to suggest that the future may involve the rebirth of the speaker's soul in the form of some 'natural thing' after he has wearied of being a mechanical bird

Guidelines

'Sailing to Byzantium' confronts the problems posed by advancing age. Yeats found the idea of bodily decay and decrepitude intolerable and in this poem he outlines a means of escape: to travel in the imagination to an ideal place in which he will be exempt from decay or death, a civilisation in which he can spend his eternity as a work of art. See 'The Lake Isle of Innisfree' for another version of a happy future.

Commentary

Title

The title of the poem expresses the notion of a voyage to perfection: in many of Yeats's works sailing is a symbol of such a voyage. In this case, the voyage is to a country of the mind, firmly situated in an ideal past: the ancient city of Byzantium. This inner voyage is prompted by the speaker's consciousness of increasing age and decrepitude. The ageing man, falling victim to the ravages of time, is in a quest for a timeless existence in a timeless paradise of art.

Stanza 1

The country of this stanza is Ireland, with its 'salmon-falls' and 'mackerel-crowded seas' (line 4). Yeats probably had Co. Sligo or Co. Galway in mind. However, the geographical location is not really important. What does merit attention here is the imagery of full and abundant natural life: the 'sensual music' (line 7) of the birds sounding mockingly in the ears of an old man whose waning physical powers make him feel out of place in a world in which vitality and energy are the supreme values. The real birds singing in real trees, with which the speaker contrasts the artificial golden birds and boughs of Byzantium in the final stanza, are, for all their joyful music, symbols of the transience of natural life: they are the 'dying generations' (line 3). So, too, are the other creatures, 'Fish, flesh, or fowl' (line 5): all are doomed to death and decay.

As a result of this transformation, he will see into the nature of reality. Being out of nature he will no longer be time-bound and subject to decay, but absorbed into art, which is timeless. The contrast is between the sensual music of the first stanza, which merely celebrates 'Whatever is begotten, born and dies' (line 6), and the eternal music of the golden bird, which will sing of 'what is past or passing, or to come' (line 32).

There are variations within the general pattern of the poem. From the old men in stanza 1, we move to the image of an aged man as a scarecrow in stanza 2 and as a dying animal in stanza 3. There is the parallel pattern of movement from the natural birds in stanza 1 to the birds as artefacts in stanza 4. We also experience the movement from the young in stanza 1, who devote themselves to sensual enjoyment, to the old in the subsequent stanzas, who are driven to seek spirituality because the life of the senses has ceased to hold any attraction for them.

Against these, the speaker sets up the uncompromising contrast of 'Monuments of unageing intellect' (line 8), symbols of the life of the spirit, of contemplation, of art. In their preoccupation with the life of the senses, the inhabitants, whether human or animal, of the natural world that the speaker rejects, and is about to abandon, ignore ('all neglect', line 7) the inner life (of the mind and spirit that can create the enduring works of art associated with Byzantium).

Stanza 2

In the second stanza the speaker develops the theme of the uselessness of the old in relation to the life of the senses. Confronted by the teeming life of youth, an old man is no better than a poor scarecrow (lines 9–10). The images of the ageing body, the soul's 'mortal dress' (line 12) in tatters, become more cruel as the poem progresses: the speaker is one of the 'old men' in the first stanza, a decrepit scarecrow in the second and 'a dying animal' in the third.

But if the condition of the body is a source of despair, the soul can rise above the sad condition of its 'mortal dress' (lines 10–12). It must listen, not to the 'sensual music' of the first stanza, but to the immortal singing of the holy sages of Byzantium. There is no more perfect exercise ('singing school', line 13) for the soul than to assert itself and break free from the limitations of bodily life and lose itself in the study of the timeless art of previous generations ('Monuments of its own magnificence', line 14). With this purpose in view, the speaker will undertake his inner voyage to Byzantium, the beautiful world where human limitations are transcended.

Stanza 3

Here the speaker addresses Byzantine sages who are also martyrs ('Come from the holy fire', line 19). These sages are exemplars of spiritual wisdom and perfection. The scene described in the first three lines of this stanza is of the kind Yeats admired on the Byzantine mosaics in Ravenna. To 'perne in a gyre' (line 19) means to move in a circular, spinning motion. These Byzantine sages will heal the speaker's sufferings and agonies ('Consume my heart away', line 21), and having instructed him in their kind of perfection (having been his 'singing-masters', line 20), will absorb ('gather', line 23) his soul, now artificially joined to a wasting body ('dying animal', line 22) into an eternity of beauty. The sages are being asked to re-enter this world of change and decay long enough to take him away to their world, which, like them, is immune from decay.

Stanza 4

Having shaken off his human nature and become an inhabitant of the heavenly city of Byzantium, the speaker will take on a shape that will ensure him an eternity of freedom from change and decay. The golden bird on the golden bough of the final stanza is an ageless, incorruptible thing, the antithesis of the 'dying animal' (the body he must occupy) of the third stanza.

Contradictory emotions

The 'official' theme of the poem is that the speaker feels obliged to make a choice between two worlds. The world he rejects is the cruel world of birth, generation and death, splendidly evoked in the richly concrete first stanza, where life is celebrated. The world he embraces as he turns away from life is a timeless world of art. He longs to spend eternity, after he has cast away his mortal body, in a Byzantine palace of art, taking the form of an imperishable artefact, a golden bird perched on a golden bough, which will sing as a way of passing the time for the nobility of this ideal place.

The feeling of the poem, however, reflected in its imagery and rhythms, suggests that the speaker, despite his longing to escape from reality, finds that the alternative fails to compensate for the vigorous excitement of actual life. Another look at the first stanza, notable for its rhythmic vitality and 'sensual music', confirms this impression. **The real theme of the poem is that art is not a substitute for life. The speaker's metamorphosis into a golden bird at the end seems an elaborate triviality when compared with the scenes from the real world presented in stanza 1.**

Development of ideas: the pattern

The overall impulse of the poem is suggested in the title, 'Sailing to Byzantium'. The speaker wants to sail, or make a journey of the mind, from the sensual music made by the birds to the ethereal, or heavenly, music made by the Byzantine birds 'Of hammered gold and gold enamelling' (line 28). The singing of the birds on natural trees in the first stanza is not the kind of singing the soul needs to learn. Instead, the speaker appeals to the Byzantine wise men to be his 'singing-masters' (line 20). Once he has been taken up by them and made a part of an eternity of artistic beauty, and thus taken out of the natural world, he will be transformed into a golden bird singing on a golden bough.

Thinking about the poem

1 Many of the poem's images suggest that the soul is superior to the body. List these. Do these images tend to make us see Yeats's point of view?

2 Is there anything in the poem to suggest that the ageing speaker regrets his bodily decay? Explain your answer.

3 Choose **two** images from the poem that strike you as particularly impressive. Say why you admire these images.

4 Choose an alternative title for the poem, and explain the reason for your choice.

5   Is this a religious poem? Could a Christian poet write as Yeats does here?

6   Is this a sad or a happy poem? Explain your answer with reference to the text.

7   'This poem is a powerful exercise in imagination'. Agree or disagree with this statement. Refer to features of the poem in your answer.

8   Consider the poem as a splendid exercise in escapism.

9   The poem is an attempt to overcome the horrors associated with old age. What does this attempt involve? Compare the response to old age offered in this poem to that offered in 'An Acre of Grass'. Which of the responses makes more sense to you?

10 Discuss the poem as a meditation on time and eternity.

11 The poem is built on contrasts between different states of being. Examine it in this light.

12 Why do the 'dying generations' of Stanza 1 neglect 'Monuments of unageing intellect'. Why does the speaker take a different view of them?

13 One of the themes of the poem is the relationship of art and life. Develop this idea.

14 'This poem is Yeats's vision of an anti-world'. Is this a good description? Explain your answer.

15 Yeats wrote this poem when he was sixty-one. Do you think this might account for the attitude to life expressed in it? Support your comments by reference to the text.

Personal response

1   Two kinds of life are described in this poem: real life and imagined life. As Yeats presents them, which of the two do you find more appealing? Give reasons for your choice.

2   'The purpose of poetry is to enhance the enjoyment and understanding of the reader'. Does this poem do this in your case? Explain your answer.

Before you read *from* 'Meditations in Time of Civil War: IV: The Stare's Nest by My Window'

from 'Meditations in Time of Civil War: IV: The Stare's Nest by My Window' on page 440 deals with some of the horrors unleashed throughout the country by the Irish Civil War (1922–23). There are many books and articles on that war, which is also discussed in surveys of modern Irish history. Any of these will give you an understanding of the background to Yeats's poem.

from Meditations in Time of Civil War: VI: The Stare's Nest by My Window

The bees build in the crevices
Of loosening masonry, and there
The mother birds bring grubs and flies.
My wall is loosening; honey-bees,
Come build in the empty house of the stare.   5

We are closed in, and the key is turned
On our uncertainty; somewhere
A man is killed, or a house burned,
Yet no clear fact to be discerned:
Come build in the empty house of the stare   10

A barricade of stone or wood;
Some fourteen days of civil war;
Last night they trundled down the road
That dead young soldier in his blood:
Come build in the empty house of the stare.   15

We had fed the heart on fantasies,
The heart's grown brutal from the fare;
More substance in our enmities
Than in our love; O honey-bees,
Come build in the empty house of the stare.   20

Glossary

title	*Stare:* starling
1	*crevices:* cracks, narrow openings
4	*My wall is loosening:* the tower seems to be collapsing
6–7	*the key . . . uncertainty:* there is a similar image in T. S. Eliot's 'The Waste Land' (1922): 'I have heard the key / turn in the door once and then turn once only / we think of the key, each in his prison' (lines 12–14). The context of Eliot's lines is somewhat similar as they refer to a thirteenth-century Italian nobleman imprisoned in a tower with members of his family. When the prisoners were inside and the door locked, the key was thrown into a river and the prisoners left to starve. In Yeats's poem, the poet-speaker is another kind of prisoner, powerless to cope with the terrible circumstances of the Civil War raging all around him
9	*Yet . . . discerned:* isolated in his tower, the speaker has no access to reliable information about outside events
10	*Come build . . . stare:* this repeated line seems to have been inspired by an experience recorded by Yeats: 'presently a strange thing happened: I began to smell honey where honey could not be'. He sees the bees as representing hope in the midst of chaos and ruin. Also, Yeats believed that history was characterised by contrasting cycles: a cycle of despair would therefore be followed by one of hope
14	*soldier:* a member of the Free State army, killed by republicans
16–17	*We had . . . fare:* the background to these lines is the Irish struggle for freedom. The lines suggest that Irish patriots had taught their followers that only violent action could make freedom possible. The result of putting this teaching into practice was to be seen in the brutality of the Civil War. Compare 'Easter 1916' for Yeats's reservations about such teaching
17	*brutal:* violent doctrines have hardened the hearts of those who have taken them seriously, and led them to behave savagely towards those who refuse to accept their point of view; there are overtones of cannibalism here
18–19	*More substance . . . love:* hatred now carries more weight, and has greater influence on our actions, than love does

Guidelines

The setting of the poem is the Tower, Thor Ballylee, near Gort in south Co. Galway, which Yeats used as a retreat. In a time of Civil War, the tower, as the poem makes clear, could offer no sanctuary from the harsh realities outside. Word of killings and burnings reaches him in his tower, as well as accounts of terrible incidents such as that involving the dead young soldier (lines 13–14). The reality of this young man's fate was much more terrible than the poem suggests. He had been dragged down a road near the tower, his body so mangled that his mother could recover only his torn, disembodied head. **The poem is a vision of a disintegrating society (note the symbolism of the 'loosening masonry' of line 2).**

Commentary

In 'The Stare's Nest by My Window' there is a sense that the poet-speaker is overawed by the crude power of the men who fight the Civil War, compared with whom he is a powerless dreamer. In the first stanza he expresses his consciousness of the disintegration of his personal values in the midst of the war. This consciousness is conveyed in terms of symbolism, as he calls on the honey-bees, emblems of sweetness, to build in the 'loosening masonry' (line 2) of his tower, swept by violence and bitterness. **The loosening of the wall of the tower is an image of the collapse of order in the world outside, reminding us of the descent into anarchy visualised in 'The Second Coming'.**

As the speaker sees the bees building in the masonry, he senses that he must rebuild his imagination and that he must do this on a foundation of love rather than on a dangerous fantasy, the cause of the destructive bitterness that underlies the Civil War (lines 16–19). The consequences of this diet of fantasy are made real in the poem by means of images of war: 'A man is killed, or a house burned' (line 8) and 'Last night they trundled down the road / That dead young soldier in his blood' (lines 13–14).

The tower in which the speaker lives might have been a sanctuary, a place of detachment from the imperfect, troublesome world outside. During the Civil War, however, it offers the speaker no protection from reality. This is because stories of killings and burnings continue to intrude on his peace of mind. All these outside horrors force their way into the speaker's consciousness even though: 'We are closed in, and the key is turned / On our uncertainty' (lines 6–7).

Thinking about the poem

1 What kind of atmosphere does the poem convey?

2 Why does Yeats introduce the image of the honey-bees? What do they represent?

3 This poem deals with the collapse of a civilisation and of its values. How does the speaker convey this collapse? Refer to relevant details from the poem in support of your answer.

4 Comment on the relevance to the speaker of what is described in the poem.

5 Judging from what he says in this poem, what kind of Ireland would the speaker like? How would it differ from the Ireland he describes?

6 In stanza 2, the speaker makes the point that living in his tower does not protect him from sharing in the horrors of the world outside. How does he convey this idea?

7 Yeats connects the 'fantasies' (line 16) on which Irish hearts have been fed with the events described in the poem? Consider the nature of the connection.

8 The poem raises questions about the nature of nationalism, particularly in its extreme forms. What are these questions? Are they still topical in Ireland or elsewhere?

9 What has this poem in common with 'The Second Coming'? Does it offer a more balanced account of evil?

10 What, in your opinion, do the images of nature in the poem represent?

11 In poems such as this one, Yeats is meditating on the tragedy of beauty and grace distorted by politics, arrogance and intellectual hatred. Mention some details in the poem which convey this tragedy.

12 Other poems on your course deal with the issues dealt with in 'The Stare's Nest by My Window', and mentioned in the question above. Select two of these poems, and discuss their similarities with this poem.

Personal response

1 Give your response to the poem, recording its effect on you, the feelings it arouses in you, and your views on the kind of events it describes.

 2 Your class has been asked to make a video to accompany a reading of this poem. In pairs or groups, describe how you would use setting, lighting, music, etc. to convey the atmosphere to the audience.

In Memory of Eva Gore-Booth and Con Markiewicz

The light of evening, Lissadell,
Great windows, open to the south,
Two girls in silk kimonos, both
Beautiful, one a gazelle.
But a raving autumn shears   5
Blossom from the summer's wreath;
The older is condemned to death,
Pardoned, drags out lonely years
Conspiring among the ignorant.
I know not what the younger dreams –   10
Some vague Utopia – and she seems,
When withered old and skeleton-gaunt,
An image of such politics.
Many a time I think to seek
One or the other out and speak   15
Of that old Georgian mansion, mix
Pictures of the mind, recall
That table and the talk of youth,
Two girls in silk kimonos, both
Beautiful, one a gazelle.   20
Dear shadows, now you know it all,
All the folly of a fight
With a common wrong or right,
The innocent and the beautiful
Have no enemy but time: 25
Arise and bid me strike a match
And strike another till time catch;
Should the conflagration climb,
Run till all the sages know.
We the great gazebo built,   30
They convicted us of guilt;
Bid me strike a match and blow.

Glossary

1	*Lissadell:*	the early nineteenth-century mansion near Sligo that was the home of the Gore-Booth sisters, Constance and Eva; Yeats visited the house as a young man in the winter of 1894/95
3	*kimonos:*	Japanese ankle-length, wide-sleeved garments that wrap around the body and are secured with a sash
7	*The older:*	Constance Markiewicz (1868–1927) (see also 'Easter 1916')
11	*Utopia:*	an ideal place or state; Yeats shows his scorn for political Utopias by invoking Eva's old, withered body as an image of them
16	*Georgian mansion:*	Lissadell
21	*shadows:*	ghosts; here means the dead women, Constance and Eva, who are now in a position to know what they could not know on earth
27	*catch:*	here means 'catch fire'
28	*conflagration:*	massive fire
29	*sages:*	wise people
30	*gazebo:*	a building commanding a view, probably a summer-house

Guidelines

The poem was written after the two Gore-Booth sisters, Eva and Constance, had died, the first in 1926, the second in July 1927. The poem was completed in October 1927.

The 'gazelle' (line 4), an image of graceful femininity, was Eva, the younger sister who, in Yeats's opinion, showed 'some promise as a writer of verse'. She was, like Yeats, interested in mysticism. She later rejected her privileged lifestyle and devoted herself to the service of the poor. She moved to England in 1897 to be with her partner, Esther Roper, and together they were involved in the trade union movement and the campaign for the emancipation of women.

Constance became a painter, married a Polish Count called Casimir Markiewicz, and settled in Dublin. A disciple of James Connolly, the Dublin Labour leader, she had joined his Citizen Army. She was second-in-command of a group that fought in St Stephen's Green during the 1916 Rising (see 'Easter 1916'). She was condemned to death, but later pardoned, for her part in the Rising. On her release, she became involved once more in revolutionary politics. She was elected to the British parliament, but did not take her seat. She became Minister for Labour in the first Dáil Éireann cabinet. She supported the republican cause in the Civil War of 1922/23.

Commentary

'folly of a fight'

This poem is built on a striking contrast between two ways of life. The first belongs to the elegant, beautiful civilisation in which the sisters grew up, which Yeats found immensely attractive. The second began when they took up another kind of living as servants of the cause of Irish freedom and of social reform, or as Yeats contemptuously puts it, spent their time 'Conspiring among the ignorant' (line 9) and dreaming of 'Some vague Utopia' (line 11). Their youth and beauty were spoiled in their struggle. Revolutionary politics made them appear crude and ugly. Yeats's terrible 'image of such politics' (line 13) is that of Eva, 'withered old and skeleton-gaunt' (line 12). The poem marks the disappearance of a civilisation whose images are two beautiful sisters elegantly dressed, and a pleasant gazebo. This civilisation, Yeats suggests, has given way to democratic ignorance and ugliness.

The poem is less a memorial to the Gore-Booth sisters than a nostalgic recollection of what they had been when the young Yeats had visited them at Lissadell in their youth, before they involved themselves in political and social agitation. The poem contemplates with bitterness the radical change undergone by the two sisters: two once beautiful, elegant aristocratic women grew prematurely old and miserable by devoting themselves to what the speaker sees as pointless, futile political activity. Yeats had no faith in the efforts of liberal aristocrats such as the Gore-Booths to build a world for the benefit of the lower orders of society. And he abhorred their 'folly' (line 22) in wasting their youth and beauty in violent acts.

'no enemy but time'

The speaker, however, has another target. Lines 5 to 6 offer a beautiful image of the destruction of human beauty by its enemy, time. The violence of time is the 'raving autumn' (line 5) that shears off youth from the 'innocent and the beautiful' (line 24). Time converts the sisters into 'Dear shadows' (line 21) of the selves they once were, ghosts clinging to withered bodies. The final seven lines of the poem are addressed to these 'Dear shadows' or ghosts, both those of the sisters and of the speaker's younger self. The task of these ghosts is not made totally clear and has been interpreted in a variety of ways.

Lines 26 to 32 are so difficult to interpret because the poem offers no obvious context for the command to set the 'great gazebo' alight. However, the key to the passage may be found in Yeats's view of time, life and death. For example, he believed that time was merely a construction of the human mind, and not an independent reality. He called pure time and pure space 'abstractions or figments of the mind'. In 'The Tower' (part III: lines 28–29) he wrote that 'Death and life were not / Till man made up the whole'. Another reference to time is helpful: 'Time drops in decay, / Like a candle burnt out' ('The Moods', lines 1–2). If time is only a construction of the human mind, or the human imagination, it can also be deconstructed, or burnt away, as the first two lines of this passage suggest: 'Arise and bid me strike a match / And strike another till time catch [fire]'.

By burning up the time that is the enemy of youthful innocence and beauty, the poet can restore these qualities, bringing back to life the 'Two girls in silk kimonos, both / Beautiful, one a gazelle' (lines 3–4 and 19–20). In other words, Yeats uses the power of his poetic imagination to re-create the former beauty of Constance and Eva. Thus, his achievement in this poem is to undo the ravages of time: to restore the blossom of summer (youthful beauty) that a 'raving autumn' (the passage of time) has sheared away (lines 5–6).

'the great gazebo'

A gazebo is generally a building commanding a view and here probably refers to a summer-house. If we take lines 30 to 32 literally, they refer to an arsonist setting fire to such a building. However, it seems more appropriate to interpret the gazebo as a reference to the dreams and ambitions of youth associated with the Gore-Booth sisters and their involvement in the 'folly of a fight' (line 22). Yeats is here returning to his theme of the damaging effect of political fanaticism on the sisters, and the hopelessness of the causes they followed. The 'We' in line 30 seems to unite Yeats with the two sisters in a common cause: that of building up a 'great gazebo' of youthful hopes. The 'They' of line 31 would thus seem to be their critics, the would-be 'sages' or wise people of line 29, who found them guilty of entertaining such hopes.

In his monumental biography of Yeats, R.F. Foster has offered an alternative interpretation. This interpretation is partly prompted by the fact that in an early draft of the poem Yeats had written: 'I the great gazebo built / They brought home to me the guilt'. To Foster's mind, the 'great gazebo' is an image of the achievement of the Anglo-Irish Ascendancy of which Yeats was always proud, and to which he and the Gore-Booth sisters belonged. He goes on to suggest that the people who convicted 'us' of guilt are not the sages but the Gore-Booth sisters themselves, who denounced the Anglo-Irish world from whence they came, and to which Yeats still felt loyal and for which he expressed public admiration, as he does for the Anglo-Irish patriots in 'September 1913': Tone, Fitzgerald and Emmet.

Thinking about the poem

1   This is a poem of contrasts. Develop this idea.

2   Comment on the tone of the poem. Does the tone change as the poem progresses?

3   Does Yeats approve of politics as a career for beautiful women? Give reasons for your answer.

4   Is this an optimistic or a pessimistic poem? Give reasons for your answer.

5   This poem has some impressive images. Select **three** of these and comment on their effectiveness in the context of the poem.

6   This poem has elements in common with 'The Stare's Nest by My Window'. Comment on this idea with reference to both poems.

7   On the evidence supplied by the poem, how would you describe Yeats's attitude to the two sisters? Can you sympathise with this? Why did the sisters give up their pampered way of life?

8   The passing of time and its effects are at the heart of the poem. Show how Yeats deals with this idea.

9   The poem betrays Yeats's social and political attitudes. How would you describe these on the evidence it provides? Consider also the insight offered by 'Politics'.

10 Like 'September 1913' and 'Easter 1916', this a political poem. How does it fit into the context created by each of the others?

11 The speaker's main objective in the poem is to bring back the delights of the past. How does he do this?

Personal response

1   If Eva Gore-Booth and Constance Markiewicz could be conjured back to life and were shown Yeats's poem, what might they say?

2   Imagine you are Yeats. Based on what you say about the two subjects of the poem, how would you like them to behave?

3   Do you think Yeats's treatment of the two women is appropriate? Give reasons for your answer.

4   At the time Yeats wrote this poem, he was angered by the political assassination of his friend Kevin O'Higgins, the Free State Minister for Justice. The people responsible were widely assumed to be republicans. He thought that Con Markiewicz, at that time a dedicated republican, was driven by the same bitter hatred for the Free State that the killers of O'Higgins had felt. Do you think that these circumstances might help to account for the poet's comments on the sisters?

Swift's Epitaph

Swift has sailed into his rest;
Savage indignation there
Cannot lacerate his breast.
Imitate him if you dare,
World-besotted traveller; he   5
Served human liberty.

Glossary	
title	*Swift's Epitaph:* Jonathan Swift (1667–1745), best known as the author of *Gulliver's Travels* and Dean of St Patrick's Cathedral, Dublin. An epitaph is a commemorative inscription on a tombstone or on a plaque. Swift wrote his own epitaph in Latin, which may be seen in St Patrick's Cathedral. In this poem, Yeats offers a poetic translation of Swift's Latin text
1	*Swift has sailed:* Yeats commonly described any kind of journey in terms of sailing, as for example in 'Sailing to Byzantium'; here, the line means: Swift has gone to his eternal rest
2	*Savage indignation:* a reference to Swift's satirical treatment of the follies of humankind
2	*there:* in the next world
3	*lacerate his breast:* wound his heart
5	*World-besotted:* over-attached to worldly things

Guidelines

The first line of the poem is by Yeats. The remainder is Yeats's translation of Swift's Latin epitaph, now in St Patrick's Cathedral, Dublin, where Swift was Dean. Yeats was particularly attracted to the notion that Swift had fought for the cause of human liberty, but he interpreted this in a sense that suited his own aristocratic view of society. Yeats had little respect for popular opinion, or the liberty of expression linked to democracy, which he tended to associate with organised mobs of ignorant people.

Swift had a strong hold on Yeats's imagination. Yeats liked to 'wander and meditate' in St Patrick's Cathedral, or sit beside Swift's monument on which his epitaph was carved, sensing that Swift was 'always just round the next corner'.

Commentary

Swift was a moralist, who advocated a society in which vice should be punished and virtue rewarded. Vices such as cruelty, hypocrisy, selfishness and aggression aroused his intense anger or, as Yeats puts it, 'Savage indignation' (line 2). This reaction found ironical expression in some of the greatest satires written in the English language, among them Gulliver's Travels.

The meaning of Yeats's poem can be seriously misunderstood, particularly the significance of the ending: 'he / Served human liberty' (lines 5–6). The sense in which this was true for either Swift or Yeats is limited. It is true that both Swift and Yeats were devoted to some forms of liberty, particularly the liberty of the artist. Both defended the liberty of Ireland, or at any rate of the Anglo-Irish Ascendancy, against English domination. Neither Yeats nor Swift, however, had much faith in the liberty of the masses. Yeats admired Swift for isolating himself from the mass of common men to give voice to the human spirit. **As Yeats saw it, Swift served human liberty by freeing the artist from the mob and not by being a champion of the rights of all the people.** In 1930 Yeats recorded in his diary that he interpreted Swift's epitaph as meaning that 'the liberty he served was that of intellect, not liberty for the masses but for those who could make liberty visible'.

Yeats's political outlook in the 1930s helps to account for his admiration for Swift's elitist position. In April 1934, with Hitler in power in Germany and Mussolini in Italy, Yeats was advocating 'force, marching men' to 'break the reign of the mob' in Ireland. Here he was thinking of a role for the Blueshirts, the Irish movement modelled on continental fascism, for which he wrote anti-democratic songs ('What is equality? Muck in the yard'). Yeats lost interest in Irish fascism only when it became evident that it was a lost cause. The Irish politician he admired most, indeed without qualification, was Kevin O'Higgins, the ruthless 'strong man' of the 1920s, and he associated this admiration with the rise of fascism in Europe.

As an Anglo-Irishman, Yeats felt that he belonged to a superior caste. In a famous speech in the Senate in 1925, he denied the right of the elected majority to make laws affecting the rights of people such as himself. Speaking of the members of the Protestant Ascendancy, he told his fellow-senators, 'We are one of the great stocks of Europe. We are the people of Burke; we are the people of Grattan; we are the people of Swift, the people of Emmet, the people of Parnell. We have created the most of the modern literature of this country. We have created the best of its political intelligence.' These sentiments are reflected in many of Yeats's poems (see especially 'September 1913' and 'In Memory of Eva Gore-Booth and Con Markiewicz').

Thinking about the poem

1 Compare this epitaph with the one Yeats chose for himself in 'Under Ben Bulben'.
2 On the evidence of the epitaph, what kind of man was Swift?
3 Why is the 'World-besotted traveller' being addressed in the epitaph?

Personal response

1 Based on the poem, what kind of person do you imagine Jonathan Swift to have been?
2 Prepare a short epitaph (three to six lines) for a well-known person who died during the last twenty years. Begin with the person's name (as Yeats began with 'Swift').

An Acre of Grass

Picture and book remain,
An acre of green grass
For air and exercise,
Now strength of body goes;
Midnight, an old house   5
Where nothing stirs but a mouse.

My temptation is quiet,
Here at life's end
Neither loose imagination,
Nor the mill of the mind   10
Consuming its rag and bone,
Can make the truth known.

Grant me an old man's frenzy,
Myself must I remake
Till I am Timon and Lear   15
Or that William Blake
Who beat upon the wall
Till Truth obeyed his call:

A mind Michael Angelo knew
That can pierce the clouds,   20
Or inspired by frenzy
Shake the dead in their shrouds;
Forgotten else by mankind,
An old man's eagle mind.

Glossary

9	*loose*: relaxed
11	*rag and bone*: the flesh, or body, the emotions
15	*Timon and Lear*: Shakespearean tragic heroes; Timon of Athens rages against humanity in frenzied language and King Lear attacks vice, hypocrisy and injustice during his spell of madness
16	*William Blake*: (1757–1827) mystic, poet, printmaker and prophetic figure
19	*Michael Angelo*: Michelangelo Buonarroti (1475–1564), one of the supreme artists and figures of the Renaissance
24	*eagle mind*: sharp, penetrating mind

Guidelines

The main themes of 'An Acre of Grass' have something in common with those of 'Sailing to Byzantium'. The speaker is preoccupied with old age. He wants to associate himself with those figures from art and life who retained powerful creative energy as they aged, who refused to remain quiet and passive. He insists on his right to break free of the limits of old age, to experience the whole of life and living and to have visions and dreams so compelling that they will shake the dead in their shrouds.

Commentary

Stanza 1

In the opening stanza the speaker expresses anger at the restraints imposed on old men by society. He imagines himself like a harmless, superannuated horse, and is reluctant to be put out to pasture on 'An acre of green grass / For air and exercise' (lines 2–3) as if he were in need of rest and quiet.

Stanza 2

He is tempted to adopt the attitude of philosophical detachment ('My temptation is quiet', line 7) that might be considered appropriate to an old man's retirement. In this kind of quiet condition, however, he cannot produce any work of lasting merit. Living a quiet life may give the speaker truth, but it cannot help him to work that truth into poems. Neither his relaxed imagination nor its casual focus on the body (the 'rag and bone' it consumes, line 11) 'Can make the truth known' (line 12).

Stanzas 3 and 4

If he wants to assert himself as a great poet and write 'true' poetry, he must achieve mystical insight, which will come only if he can model himself on those inspiring figures from art (such as Timon and Lear) and life (such as William Blake and Michelangelo) who retained creative energy (were 'inspired by frenzy', line 21) well into old age. What the speaker needs is indicated in his account of Blake 'Who beat upon the wall / Till Truth obeyed his call' (lines 17–18). He must cease to be the quiet man he has become in old age and remake himself in the form of a mad old prophet. Possessed and inspired by this frenzy, his quiet, relatively uninspired self will give way to an impassioned, prophetic self with 'An old man's eagle mind' (line 24) that can excite the world or 'Shake the dead in their shrouds' (line 22). He insists on his right, in spite of old age, to experience the fullness of life, and will not be forced to live the quiet, limited life normally associated with someone 'at life's end' (line 8).

Thinking about the poem

1. What kind of condition is suggested in the first stanza?
2. How would you describe the tone of lines 2 to 3: 'An acre of green grass / For air and exercise'?
3. Why is the speaker dissatisfied with his quiet life?
4. In the third and fourth stanzas, the poem becomes a kind of prayer. What kind of prayer?
5. How would the speaker like to pass his old age? Explain the significance of the title.
6. Reread the first four lines of the second stanza of 'Sailing to Byzantium' (lines 9–12) and explore the common elements of that poem and 'An Acre of Grass'. Does the latter poem offer any new insights?
7. Yeats mentions four names in the poem. What do these names mean to him? What purpose do they serve in the poem?
8. In stanza 3, the speaker writes: 'Myself must I remake' (line 14). For what purpose must he 'remake' himself?
9. Choose **two** images from the poem that strike you as particularly effective. Explain your choice.

William Butler Yeats

10 Do you think that the speaker deserves our admiration? Give reasons for your answer.

11 In 'An Acre of Grass', Yeats rages against the limits that society tries to impose on old men. What exactly are these limits? How does he propose to go beyond them? Explain your answers by referring to the text.

Personal response

1 The celebrated critic Samuel Johnson claimed that 'the only end [purpose] of writing is to enable the readers better to enjoy life, or better to endure it'. In the case of 'An Acre of Grass', do you think Yeats fulfilled this purpose by contributing to your enjoyment of life, or by helping you to endure your present condition better? Give reasons for your answer.

2 Suppose Johnson had written 'the writers' instead of 'the readers' in the comment quoted above. Might this have suited Yeats better, to judge from what he has to say in 'An Acre of Grass'?

Politics

'In our time the destiny of man presents its meaning in political terms.'
Thomas Mann

How can I, that girl standing there,
My attention fix
On Roman or on Russian
Or on Spanish politics?
Yet here's a travelled man that knows   5
What he talks about,
And there's a politician
That has read and thought,
And maybe what they say is true
Of war and war's alarms,   10
But O that I were young again
And held her in my arms!

Glossary

| epigraph | *Thomas Mann:* (1875–1955) German writer |

Guidelines

Yeats wrote this poem as an answer to an article about his work that had appeared in an American journal, the *Yale Review*. The article suggested that Yeats should devote his attention to political subjects. The poem is also an answer to the claim made by Thomas Mann in the epigraph. The poem shows how insignificant the great issues of Italian, Russian or Spanish politics can seem when human realities (in this case represented by the sight of a beautiful girl) intrude on the poet's consciousness.

Commentary

Yeats originally called this poem 'The Theme', and wrote it as an answer to the Yale Review article about his work written by the poet and playwright Archibald MacLeish, who praised the language of Yeats's poetry for being 'public'. This pleased Yeats, whose constant desire was to communicate with a popular audience and 'to move the common people'. However, he disagreed with MacLeish's claim that his public language might have more profitably been used on political themes.

Yeats had long considered politics as fundamentally dishonest and superficial, defining the activities of professional politicians as 'the manipulation of popular enthusiasm by false news'. This attitude explains the ironic contemplation in the poem of his experience of their public pronouncements: 'And maybe what they say is true' (line 9).

In contrast to this display of half-truth and pretended expertise, Yeats presents another kind of truth, one which makes Roman, Russian and Spanish politics appear of little importance. The essential truths are those involving live human relationships, not the abstractions mediated by politicians. The girl in the poem is of considerably more significance in the scheme of reality than all the politicians in the world, which is why the sight of her can make the speaker forget about politics and focus exclusively on her: 'O that I were young again / And held her in my arms!' (lines 11–12).

Thinking about the poem

1   This poem can be considered in relation to Yeats's other 'political' poems. What has it in common with them?

2   Does Yeats make a convincing point in the poem? Give reasons for your answer.

3   What does the young girl in the poem represent?

4   Is the speaker in this poem impressed by world affairs and by what people say about these?

Personal response

1   Did you enjoy reading 'Politics'? Give a reason for your opinion.
2   Suggest an alternative title for the poem and give reasons for your suggestion.

from Under Ben Bulben: V and VI

V

Irish poets, learn your trade,
Sing whatever is well made,
Scorn the sort now growing up
All out of shape from toe to top,
Their unremembering hearts and heads   5
Base-born products of base beds,
Sing the peasantry, and then
Hard-riding country gentlemen,
The holiness of monks, and after
Porter-drinkers' randy laughter;   10
Sing the lords and ladies gay
That were beaten into the clay
Through seven heroic centuries;
Cast your mind on other days
That we in coming days may be   15
Still the indomitable Irishry.

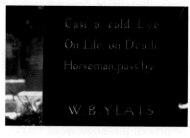

VI

Under bare Ben Bulben's head
In Drumcliff churchyard Yeats is laid,
An ancestor was rector there
Long years ago, a church stands near,   20
By the road an ancient cross.
No marble, no conventional phrase;
On limestone quarried near the spot
By his command these words are cut:
Cast a cold eye   25
On life, on death.
Horseman, pass by!

Glossary

2	*Sing*: write about
6	*Base-born . . . beds*: low-born descendants of low-born parents; this idea may reflect Yeats's interest in contemporary theories of improving the racial stock, morally, mentally and physically, by means of selective breeding, and the elimination of people deemed unfit or inferior – such ideas were popular in Hitler's Germany
13	*seven heroic centuries*: the seven centuries that followed the Norman invasion of Ireland in 1169
16	*indomitable*: unconquerable
17	*Ben Bulben*: the mountain that dominates the landscape around Drumcliffe churchyard, Co. Sligo, where Yeats was later buried

Guidelines

This poem is generally read as Yeats's farewell to the world, his poetic last will and testament. Section V expresses his hopes for the future course of Irish poetry, and provides advice for Irish poets on the themes they should choose and on the proper way to give them expression. Section VI gives his reasons for being buried at Drumcliffe and provides the words for his tombstone.

Yeats died at Cap Martin, on the French Riviera, on 28 January 1939 and was buried there. In September 1948 his body was reinterred in Drumcliffe churchyard, and his chosen epitaph was engraved on his tombstone.

Commentary

Throughout his career, Yeats wrote many elegies, that is, poems celebrating the significance and achievements of dead friends. This poem is his own elegy, a statement of his beliefs as he approaches death and of the inscription he wanted on his gravestone as an epitaph.

Section V

Yeats offers a pessimistic comment on contemporary poetry: the great poetic tradition represented by such visionary poets as William Blake had, in the course of time, become corrupted. He believed that modern poetry was the product of a historical cycle nearing its end and was thus confused, formless and unworthy of imitation. (For Yeats's more detailed exploration of the end of the two-thousand-year

Christian cycle, see 'The Second Coming'.) Modern poets had forgotten or neglected the great tradition of poetry so that their language had become awkward and their themes degraded. For these reasons, the poem encourages Irish poets to ignore their modern contemporaries and become technically competent.

Yeats advises the Irish poets who will succeed him to feel contempt for the shapeless, badly constructed work of the latest generation of writers. The 'sort now growing up' (line 3) are the middle-class makers of post-independence Ireland, for whom Yeats had little respect. Instead, he encourages new Irish poets to learn their craft by turning to the past and dealing with themes associated with peasants and aristocrats, which will impart vigour and authenticity to their poems.

Section VI

In contrast to the rhetorical, dogmatic, even shrill tone of section V, section VI is a tranquil lyric in which Yeats gives reasons for being buried at Drumcliffe. His grandfather John Yeats had been Rector at Drumcliffe church. Yeats refers to himself in the third person as a dead man ('In Drumcliff churchyard Yeats is laid') and provides a short and simple but enigmatic epitaph.

It is not clear what the epitaph means, and we cannot be sure to whom it is addressed. The horseman may be one of the visionary beings of local folklore, described for Yeats by Sligo people. It has also been suggested that the horseman is Yeats's ghost, or any passing rider. The injunction given to the passer-by, to 'Cast a cold eye / On life, on death' (lines 25–26) is characteristic of Yeats's thinking and of his fondness for balancing opposites. Notice that the sentiments expressed here echo those of the speaker in 'An Irish Airman Foresees His Death' (lines 13–16). The reader of the epitaph is encouraged to see life and death as coldly, if paradoxically, balanced.

We can also view the epitaph as belonging to an ancient tradition. Since classical times, passing travellers have been encouraged by those who carved inscriptions on monuments to the dead to pause or stop, if only to consider their own mortality, and to recognise that as the dead man is, they will some day be. The brevity of Yeats's epitaph is such that the horseman would be able to read it as he passed. Many commentators have suggested that Yeats should have retained his earlier version of the final line, which was 'Draw rein, Draw breath', thus asking the horseman to pause and contemplate the words.

There is an interesting parallel between Yeats's epitaph in this poem and his version of Jonathan Swift's epitaph, where the traveller is encouraged to imitate Swift if he dare. Yeats's epitaph may offer a similar inducement to the horseman to imitate its author's dispassionate attitude to life and death.

Thinking about the poem

1   What attitude to contemporary writers does Yeats express here?
2   What kind of Irish poetry would he like to see in the future?
3   Does Yeats see himself as an Irish patriot?
4   How would you describe the tone of section V of the extract?
5   Why has Yeats chosen the three-line epitaph at the end of section VI? What does it tell us about him?

Personal response

1   Describe the impression the poem has made on you.
2   Write a letter (or poem) to W. B. Yeats in which you either agree or disagree with his advice in this poem.

Exam-Style Questions

1   Yeats's poetry presents a consistent tension between projected ideal states and actuality. Is this an accurate generalisation?
2   Consider various versions of the past as central themes of Yeats's poetry. Why do you think he usually makes the past seem better than the present?
3   Discuss the ways in which Yeats uses his poetry as a means of escape from unpleasant realities such as old age and decay.
4   Examine the versions of Ireland that emerge from Yeats's poems. Do these versions form a consistent pattern?
5   Consider Yeats as a poet of conflict.
6   Explore the significance of art in the poetry of Yeats.
7   Comment on the ways in which many of Yeats's poems convey a sense of loss.
8   Discuss Yeats's quest for a sense of permanence in the midst of change.
9   Do his poems as a whole suggest that Yeats was a pessimist?
10 It has been remarked that Yeats conveys his meanings by means of images and symbols to a greater extent than through statement and argument. Would you agree? Give reasons for your answer.
11 What do Yeats's poems, taken as a whole, tell us about the man who wrote them?
12 Outline the qualities of Yeats's poetry you admire or dislike. You might discuss Yeats's ideas, his images, his descriptive power, his power of suggestion, his relevance for our time, his emotional and intellectual power, his patriotism, his honesty, his skilful depiction of human beings.

13   Write an essay in which you give your reasons for liking and/or not liking the poetry of W.B. Yeats. You must support your points by reference to, or quotation from, the poems that are on your course.

The following are reasons you might give for liking Yeats's poetry:

- The subject matter of the poems is of interest to Irish readers.
- The poems deal with an interesting variety of subjects.
- Many of the poems enable us to understand history and politics, especially Irish politics.
- The poems are full of powerful images and impressive descriptions.
- The poems are remarkable for their profound and original ideas, etc.

Here are some reasons you might give for not liking Yeats's poetry:

- Some of the allusions in the poems are extremely obscure.
- The poems seldom convey a sense of happiness.
- There is an undue emphasis on the poet in Yeats's poems.
- Younger readers may be alienated by the emphasis on old age in the poems.
- Too much background reading is required for an understanding of Yeats's philosophical themes.

Sample Essay

'Much of the poetry of W.B. Yeats is based on contrast'.

Discuss this comment with reference to, and quotation from, some of the poems by Yeats on your course.

The first kind of contrast I would like to discuss is that between past and present in two of Yeats's 'patriotic' poems: 'September 1913' and 'Easter 1916'. The main structural feature of 'September 1913' is the opposition created by Yeats between an unattractive present and an admirable past. The present is unattractive because it is inhabited by a set of people with little or no concern for the welfare of their country. Instead, they are content to occupy themselves with accumulating money: they 'fumble in a greasy till' and they 'add the halfpence to the pence'. They spend the rest of their time praying: they add 'prayer to shivering prayer', as if people were born for no other reason than to 'pray and save'.

[First sentence of answer immediately addresses the point of the question]

Then comes the contrast with these selfish, unpatriotic people. The contrast is provided by a number of patriotic Irishmen of the past, who fought for the freedom of their country. They had little time to pray because they were in constant danger of death:

the 'hangman's rope' had been spun specially for them. They were too busy fighting to think of saving: 'And what, God help us, could they save'. Yeats sees that the 'Romantic Ireland' of these patriots, Edward Fitzgerald, Robert Emmet, Wolfe Tone and John O'Leary, belongs strictly to the past, while the materialists dominate the present. These unpatriotic cynics are given the last word, as they dismiss the dead patriots as foolish individuals who 'weighed so lightly what they gave' and failed to consider their own interests. The patriots can now safely be forgotten: 'But let them be, they're dead and gone'.

[Contrast has been outlined between past and present in the case of one poem]

The contrast between past and present in 'Easter 1916' is different. It relates to the difference between the poet's opinion of the leaders of the 1916 Rising before and after its outbreak. For the purposes of the poem, the Rising marks a dividing line between past and present. In the past (the period preceding the Rising), Yeats had found it difficult to take the leaders of the Rising seriously, to the extent that he considered mocking their efforts when he spoke to friends at his gentlemen's club, thinking that Patrick Pearse, Thomas MacDonagh, James Connolly and John MacBride were not serious revolutionaries, but merely play-acting. When the Rising did take place, and when those who planned and took part in it showed themselves to be agents in the regeneration of Ireland's soul, Yeats was obliged to acknowledge that what they had done would change the course of Irish history. Pearse and the rest of the revolutionaries, now and in future time, are, and will be seen as having been, 'changed, changed utterly'. They took part in a terrible, violent event, which their nobility and self-sacrifice made beautiful. The contrast between the earlier opinion of the poet that they were simply playing games, and his subsequent view of them as heroes in a great national event, could not be more stark.

[Another contrast has been discussed, using a different poem]

A second kind of contrast in Yeats's poetry is between ideal, imagined states of being and realities. Here, a good example is to be found in 'Sailing to Byzantium'. One side of the contrast is presented in the first two stanzas of the poem. These reveal the reality of old age lived out in an Ireland 'that is no country for old men'. The body of an old, or ageing, man is no better than a scarecrow, 'a tattered coat upon a stick'. At this stage of life, the old can find consolation for their physical decay only if their souls rise to the contemplation of an ideal world presented through the medium of great works of art. An escape from the physical reality of bodily decay can be achieved by making an imaginative voyage to some ideal country of the mind like Byzantium. On this voyage, the soul will no longer be fastened to the 'dying animal', which is the body, but will be gathered 'into the artifice of eternity'. In eternity ('out of nature') the poet would like to take on a new 'bodily form', not that of the ageing man he now is, but that of a beautiful, incorruptible golden bird made by Grecian goldsmiths, perched on a 'golden bough', singing forever to the immortal 'lords and ladies of Byzantium'. The contrast between real and ideal is reinforced by the opposing images of the body as a scarecrow and the soul escaping from that body to join itself to a splendid everlasting work of art.

[A new example of contrast has been outlined, with reference to a third poem]

'The Second Coming' deals with the stark contrast between two cycles, or periods, of human history, each two thousand years long. The first of these cycles, the Christian one, Yeats sees as soon coming to an end, as humanity, symbolised by the falcon, is rapidly losing touch with Christ, the falconer ('the falcon cannot hear the falconer'). Yeats implies that Christianity stood for order, peace and harmony. The imminent destruction of its two-thousand-year cycle, in contrast, will be marked by a new cycle of disorder. It will be a period during which 'mere anarchy is loosed upon the world'. Christ's rule will be followed by that of his opposite, the Anti-Christ, who will preside over a time of bloody war and revolution against established governments and institutions and the general collapse of order throughout the world. The reign of the Anti-Christ will signal the collapse of civilised values:

The blood-dimmed tide is loosed, and everywhere

The ceremony of innocence is drowned.

Just as the pagan cycle ended with Christ's birth ('twenty centuries of stony sleep' vexed by a 'rocking cradle'), the cycle of the Anti-Christ is heralded in a fearful image:

And what rough beast, its hour come round at last,

Slouches towards Bethlehem to be born?

[A fourth poem is used to provide another example of contrast]

In other poems, the principle of contrast is maintained. In 'The Lake Isle of Innisfree', we have a contrast between the commonplace, uninspiring realities of city life, indicated in images of the roadway and 'the pavements grey', and the contrasting beauties of a natural landscape to be enjoyed on a lake island by a solitary lover of nature, whose senses are continually stimulated by lovely sights and sounds, the 'purple glow' of noon and the 'lake water lapping with low sounds by the shore'. In 'The Wild Swans at Coole', Yeats is conscious of the troubling constrasts between the swans and himself. He is conscious of ageing and the passage of time. In contrast the swans give the illusion of immortality. They are, for Yeats, a symbol of eternity as they rise 'in great broken rings'. In 'In Memory of Eva Gore-Booth and Con Markiewicz', there is a painful, moving contrast between two phases in the lives of these women. In their early lives they were 'two girls in silk kimonos, both beautiful, one a gazelle'. Their beauty soon fades, as time, in the form of 'a raving autumn', shears away the blossoms of youth. The fate of the beautiful younger sister is to become 'withered old and skeleton-gaunt'.

[Summary of other examples of contrast from other poems on the course]

As this essay has illustrated, much of the poetry of W.B. Yeats is indeed based on contrast. We find this both within individual poems and between one poem and another.

[Brief concluding paragraph referring back to the question]

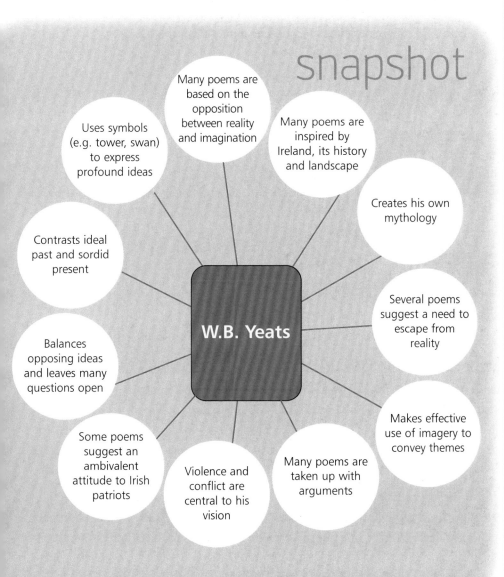

snapshot

- Uses symbols (e.g. tower, swan) to express profound ideas
- Many poems are based on the opposition between reality and imagination
- Many poems are inspired by Ireland, its history and landscape
- Creates his own mythology
- Contrasts ideal past and sordid present
- Several poems suggest a need to escape from reality
- Balances opposing ideas and leaves many questions open
- **W.B. Yeats**
- Makes effective use of imagery to convey themes
- Some poems suggest an ambivalent attitude to Irish patriots
- Violence and conflict are central to his vision
- Many poems are taken up with arguments

W. H. Auden

1907–7

FUNERAL BLUES

Biography

Wystan Hugh Auden was born in York, England, in 1907. He was educated as a boarder at St Edmund's School, Surrey, and at Christ Church College, Oxford. During his time at Oxford he was part of a group of young intellectuals and writers that included Louis MacNeice, Cecil Day-Lewis and Stephen Spender. As a young man he worked as a schoolmaster in England. During the 1930s he also lived in Berlin, where he wrote some verse plays with the writer Christopher Isherwood, amongst them *The Dog Beneath the Skin*.

In 1935 Auden married Erika Mann, who was the daughter of the German novelist Thomas Mann. It was a marriage of convenience that enabled her to gain British citizenship and escape Nazi Germany. Auden was homosexual. In 1937 he went to Spain, where, as a stretcher-bearer, he supported the Republican side in the Spanish Civil War.

In 1939 Auden and Christopher Isherwood emigrated to the United States. This was a controversial move. Some people regarded it as a bid to escape the war in Europe and saw Auden as having betrayed his country. In New York Auden met the poet Chester Kallman, who became his lifelong partner.

Auden taught at a number of American universities and became a US citizen in 1946. From 1956 to 1961 he was Professor of Poetry at Oxford. In 1972, with his health declining, he decided to leave America and return to Oxford, where he lived in a cottage belonging to his old college, Christ Church. He spent the summer months in his house in Austria, where he died in September 1973.

Auden's poems confront many of the political issues of the 1930s, from rising unemployment to the threat of fascism. In his younger years he was attracted to Marxism, but in the early 1940s he reconverted to Christianity and introduced religious themes into his work. His poetry also deals with more intimate themes such as alienation and loneliness, of which he had personal experience since his own life was often unhappy. As a homosexual he was forced, due to the conventions of the times, to conceal the sex of the beloved in his poems.

Auden's intellectual gifts and his ability to write poetry in almost every form were extraordinary. His output ranges from light verse, ballads and songs to serious meditative work and political commentary. He was also involved in writing opera libretti, among them *The Rake's Progress* with music by Stravinsky. In his work as a critic he edited a huge anthology entitled *Poets of the English Language*, which was published in New York in 1950. By the time of his death in 1973 he was regarded as one of the leading poets of the twentieth century.

Before you read 'Funeral Blues'

What are the implications of the word 'blues' in the title 'Funeral Blues' in the poem on page 466? What possible different meanings of the word are there? How might these meanings relate alongside the word 'funeral'?

Funeral Blues

Stop all the clocks, cut off the telephone,
Prevent the dog from barking with a juicy bone,
Silence the pianos and with muffled drum
Bring out the coffin, let the mourners come.

Let aeroplanes circle moaning overhead   5
Scribbling on the sky the message He Is Dead,
Put the crêpe bows round the white necks of the public doves,
Let the traffic policemen wear black cotton gloves.

He was my North, my South, my East and West,
My working week and my Sunday rest,   10
My noon, my midnight, my talk, my song;
I thought that love would last for ever: I was wrong.

The stars are not wanted now: put out every one;
Pack up the moon and dismantle the sun;   15
Pour away the ocean and sweep up the wood;
For nothing now can ever come to any good.

Glossary		
1	*Stop all the clocks:* it used to be the custom to stop all the clocks in a house where someone had died
3	*muffled drum:* the loud sounds of the drum were sometimes deadened on solemn occasions
5	*aeroplanes circle:* an aerial salute or 'flypast' is sometimes performed as part of major events or state occasions and funerals
7	*crêpe bows:* bows made of a thin, silky crinkled material, dyed black in times of mourning (also called 'crape')
7	*public doves:* flocks of doves were often let loose to mark public occasions of celebration or mourning
14	*dismantle:* pull down, take apart

Guidelines

This poem is the ninth song from 'Twelve Songs', 1936. The first two stanzas were used initially in a play written by Auden and Christopher Isherwood, *The Ascent of F6*. The context was political and the lines satirised the love of a people for a dead leader. While working with the composer Benjamin Britten in 1936, Auden decided to use them as the start of this more personal love song. The poem is also an elegy (a poem written about the death of someone).

Commentary

The grief expressed in this poem at the death of the beloved is so intense that it seems the world should almost come to an end because he is no longer alive. Each of the four stanzas expresses this sense of loss.

Stanza 1

The speaker says that time should be stopped and all the sounds of life should be silenced – the ringing of the phone, the barking of the dog, the playing of a piano. All he wishes to hear is the muted sound of the drum as it accompanies the coffin and the mourners.

Stanza 2

The speaker expresses his desire for public mourning in recognition of how devastating his loss is. He wants planes to fly overhead as a mark of respect; he wants a release of mourning doves; he wants the traffic police to be dressed in black. Each of these displays of mourning has accompanied the death of a public figure or someone important in society.

Stanza 3

The speaker now expresses his feelings in a more personal way. He uses moving metaphors to convey what his beloved meant to him. His beloved gave direction to and influenced every aspect of his life, from what time of day it was, to how he worked, to how he played: 'my talk, my song' (line 11).

The effect of these lines is to pay a remarkable tribute to the loved one, who meant everything to him. There is a tremendous sense of loss when he says in simple language that he 'thought that love would last for ever – I was wrong' (line 12).

Stanza 4

Elemental images in the final stanza reinforce the sense of bereavement. He has no longer any use for the sun, moon and stars, nor for oceans and woods. There is nothing left in the world to give him any pleasure.

W. H. Auden

Rhythm and language of the poem

A 'blues' song is a slow, sad song. The rhyming couplets in each stanza also have a musical effect.

In the first two stanzas the tone is stately and commanding, with its many verbs: 'stop', 'prevent', 'silence', let', etc. This use of language seems to emphasise the public aspect of the speaker's loss and his desire that it should be recognised by others.

In the third stanza the language becomes more personal. The emphasis is on 'he' and 'my', ending in line 12 with the even more personal 'I'.

The language in the final two stanzas is largely metaphorical. That is, the speaker makes use of comparisons to show how much his beloved meant to him. For example, in the final stanza he chooses images from the natural world to express the extent of his great loss. Images of the sun, moon and stars have always been important in love poems.

Auden expresses his grief largely through hyperbole (exaggeration used for effect).

Exam-Style Questions

Thinking about the poem

1   How does the speaker express his feelings of grief in the first and second stanzas?
2   Do you think the speaker succeeds in conveying what his lover meant to him in the third and fourth stanzas? Give reasons for your view.
3   Do you like the way the poet expresses sadness at the death of his beloved? Give a reason for your opinion.
4   How does the title of the poem suit the feelings expressed?
5   Having read the poem, what title would you have given it?
6   Look at the sound patterns of the poem: assonance and rhyme. How do they contribute to the poem?
7   From your reading of the poem, what did you learn about the poet W. H. Auden?
8   What features of the poem are particularly song-like, in your opinion? Refer to the poem in your answer.
9   From the statements below, choose the one that you believe best describes this poem:
    ● The speaker exaggerates his feelings.
    ● The speaker feels utterly devastated at the loss of his beloved.
    ● The speaker is asking for impossible things to be done.
    Explain your answer with reference to the poem.

Taking a closer look

1 'Stop all the clocks' (line 1). Is this a good way to start a poem? Give reasons for your answer.

2 Choose two lines from the poem that especially appeal to you and explain your choice.

3 'He was my North, my South, my East and West, / My working week and my Sunday rest' (lines 9 and 10). Do you think these images are effective in conveying the speaker's love? Explain your answer.

Personal response

1 Someone asks you to suggest a poem for a collection of love poems. You recommend this one. Explain why you have chosen it.

2 Your class has decided to make a video version of this poem for YouTube. In pairs or groups, discuss the sort of atmosphere you would like to create, and say what music, sound effects and images you would use.

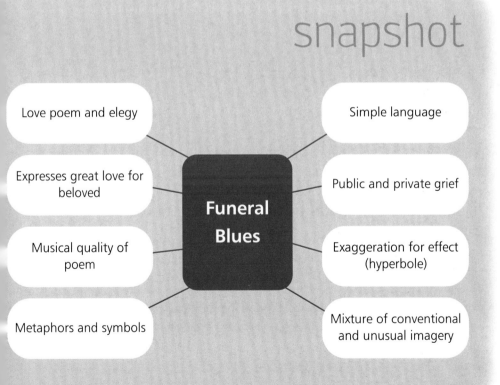

snapshot

Love poem and elegy

Simple language

Expresses great love for beloved

Public and private grief

Funeral Blues

Musical quality of poem

Exaggeration for effect (hyperbole)

Metaphors and symbols

Mixture of conventional and unusual imagery

W. H. Auden

Colette Bryce

b. 1970

SELF-PORTRAIT IN THE DARK (WITH CIGARETTE)

Biography

Colette Bryce was born in Derry in 1970. She moved to England as a teenager and was educated at St Mary's, Twickenham. She lived in London and Spain before moving to Scotland in 2002, where she held the fellowship in creative writing at the University of Dundee.

In 2003 Bryce was appointed to the North East Literary Fellowship and moved to Newcastle upon Tyne. This creative writing fellowship is jointly hosted by the universities of Durham and Newcastle.

She divides her time between Newcastle and London in her work as a freelance writer and editor. She teaches for various creative writing organisations, including the Arvon Foundation, The Poetry School and the University of Newcastle. She was the editor of Britain's bestselling poetry magazine, *Poetry London*, from 2009 to 2012.

Bryce's poems were first published by Carol Ann Duffy for Anvil Press in 1995. Her poetry collections are: *The Heel of Bernadette* (2000), *The Full Indian Rope Trick* (2004) and *Self-Portrait in the Dark* (2008). She also published a pocketbook of nineteen poems in 2007 entitled *The Observations of Aleksandr Svetlov*.

In 2002 Bryce was one of five poets commissioned by the Victoria and Albert Museum in London and the Poetry Book Society to create new works inspired by the objects on display in the British Galleries 1500–1900. Her poem was inspired by a peacock-shaped necklace designed in 1901.

Bryce has received several awards for her books, including the Aldeburgh Prize and the Strong Award. For individual poems, she has won both the National Poetry Competition (2003) and the Academi Cardiff International Poetry Competition (2007). She received the Cholmondeley Award in 2010.

Before you read 'Self-Portrait in the Dark (with Cigarette)'

If you have access to the Internet, search it for works of art (mainly paintings) with an identical or similar title to the name of the poem below, and see how many artists have had similar inspiration.

In small groups, discuss the idea of a 'self-portrait'. What does it suggest to you? Would it suggest someone vain enough to paint themselves in a flattering way, or someone who is trying to be honest? Keep these ideas in mind when you read Bryce's poem.

Self-Portrait in the Dark (with Cigarette)

To sleep, perchance
to dream? No chance:
it's 4 a.m. and I'm wakeful
as an animal,
caught between your presence and the lack.   5
This is the realm insomniac.
On the window seat, I light a cigarette
from a slim flame and monitor the street –

a stilled film, bathed in amber,
softened now in the wake of a downpour.   10

Beyond the daffodils
on Magdalen Green, there's one slow vehicle
pushing its beam along Riverside Drive,
a sign of life;
and two months on   15
from 'moving on'
your car, that you haven't yet picked up,
waits, spattered in raindrops like bubble wrap.
Here, I could easily go off
on a riff   20

on how cars, like pets, look a little like their owners
but I won't 'go there',
as they say in America,
given it's a clapped-out Nissan Micra . . .
And you don't need to know that   25
I've been driving it illegally at night
in the lamp-lit silence of this city
– you'd only worry –
or, worse, that Morrissey
is jammed in the tape deck now and for eternity;   30

no. It's fine, all gleaming hubcaps,
seats like an upright, silhouetted couple;
from the dashboard, the wink
of that small red light I think
is a built-in security system.   35
In a poem
it could represent a heartbeat or a pulse.
Or loneliness: its vigilance.
Or simply the lighthouse-regular spark
of someone, somewhere, smoking in the dark.   40

Glossary

1–2	*To sleep . . . dream:* quotation from Hamlet's famous 'To be or not to be' soliloquy (Hamlet, Act 3, Scene 1)
3	*wakeful:* unable or unwilling to sleep
6	*realm:* kingdom; here it means zone or area
6	*insomniac:* someone who is unable to sleep
9	*amber:* brownish-yellow/orange colour
12	*Magdalen Green:* Dundee's oldest city park
13	*Riverside Drive:* address of the University of Dundee Botanic Gardens
18	*bubble wrap:* type of material used for packaging
20	*riff:* here, repetitive speech
24	*clapped-out:* useless
29	*Morrissey:* singer songwriter, lead vocalist with The Smiths in the 1980s
32	*silhouetted:* outlined in shadow
38	*vigilance:* watchfulness

Guidelines

This poem is from the collection of the same name, *Self-Portrait in the Dark*, published in 2008. As the title suggests, the poem reveals a great deal about the speaker as she sits, alone and sleepless, smoking and looking out the window.

Commentary

Stanza 1

The poem opens with a quotation from Shakespeare's *Hamlet*: 'To sleep, perchance / to dream?', which is answered wryly with the colloquial 'No chance'. The speaker describes her situation clearly: it is four in the morning and she cannot sleep, caught up as she is between thinking of her lover's 'presence' (line 5) and the fact that her lover is no longer with her. This is the first indication we have that the poem is about a love relationship that has ended.

When the speaker ruefully says that she is in the 'realm insomniac' (line 6), we may assume that she has experienced this sleeplessness before. She has her own ways of coping with it: smoking a cigarette, looking out the window to 'monitor' (line 8) the street (the word 'monitor' suggests inspection or careful watching). All of her senses are heightened, as can happen during insomnia. She sees the street as a 'stilled film, bathed in amber' (line 9), and now soft 'in the wake of a downpour' (line 10). These last words of the first part of the poem seem to suggest sorrow and death.

Stanza 2

The speaker makes us aware of where exactly she is by mentioning directly places found in the Scottish city of Dundee, where Bryce lived for a time (Magdalen Green, Riverside Drive). **Perhaps these are places that evoke particular memories of her lover and their relationship.** The car she sees 'pushing its beam' (line 13) along the road is a 'sign of life' (line 14) in the quietness of night, but the phrase leads her to the painful awareness that her lover has moved on (like the car that is moving outside).

By association of ideas she thinks of her lover's car that still waits to be picked up, two months later. She describes it now as 'spattered in raindrops like bubble wrap' (line 18), but bubble wrap is something used to package something, perhaps to send it away? The choice of comparison may say something about how she sees their relationship now.

At this point the image of the lover's car takes on an extended life as she says she could go on a 'riff' (line 20), or a long repetitive speech. In fact she does go on a 'riff' in an extended image of the car as a metaphor for her relationship and her present feelings.

Stanza 3

Lines 21 to 24 are quietly humorous and as such may also suggest something about the honest and playful relationship the speaker has had with her beloved. But the car, left behind by her lover, probably because it was 'clapped-out' (line 24) (is this also a comment on the end of their relationship?), has obviously got an emotional association for the speaker.

She admits to driving it illegally at night through the city. Is this because she wishes to keep alive memories of her beloved? When she says that her lover would 'worry' (line 28), is she trying to convince herself that there are some feelings left between them? Or is she acknowledging the strength of the feelings that did exist, and therefore remain in spite of their absence from one another?

The speaker then goes on to joke that 'worse' (line 29), a tape by the singer Morrissey has become stuck in the tape deck. Whatever associations Morrissey had for the couple, the tape has been left in the car 'for eternity' (line 30). **The word 'eternity' may be an ironic comment on the relationship, which has not lasted forever.**

Stanza 4

Instead of telling her beloved the truth about the car, the speaker decides to put a gloss on what it looks like, with 'gleaming hubcaps' and the seats 'like an upright, silhouetted couple' (lines 31 and 32). The simile is interesting in the context of their relationship, which is clearly not that of a 'couple' any longer. She pictures the 'small red light' of the 'built-in security system' (lines 34 and 35), which is another evocative image, suggesting the security they obviously now lack as a couple.

When she says 'In a poem / it could represent . . .' it is as if she is trying to distance herself from the true heartbreak of what the 'small red light' really means: 'a heartbeat or a pulse. / Or loneliness: its vigilance' (lines 36–38). Here, the image of 'security' gives way to the more sinister 'vigilance' of someone who is alone and lonely at night.

The poem echoes in its closing lines the earlier idea of being 'wakeful' (line 3). This feeling is reinforced by the image of the lighted cigarette in the dark as a 'lighthouse-regular spark' (line 39), an image that evokes the bleakness of being alone. **If we think back to the quotation from *Hamlet* in the first line, we might recall that it is from a speech in which Hamlet expresses deep despair and a possible desire for suicide.**

Language of the poem

The poem is a blend of colloquial language and poetic simile and metaphor. The first sentence, a quotation from Shakespeare and clearly not written in everyday speech, is followed by the more ordinary 'no chance' as the speaker accepts her insomnia. There are similes such as 'wakeful as an animal' or 'seats like an upright, silhouetted couple'; and metaphors such as the street as a stilled film, or the light in the car as a heartbeat or a pulse. Alongside this imaginative use of language there are colloquial expressions: 'I could easily go off on a riff', 'clapped-out Nissan Micra' and the Americanism I won't 'go there'.

The effect created is of someone thinking aloud, addressing her thoughts to an absent 'you' and not necessarily expecting to be heard. The blend of the ordinary and the poetic also prevents the tone of the poem from becoming too solemn or gloomy.

Form of the poem

Although the poem's tone is at times casual, as if the speaker is simply putting into words what she is thinking, the poem is nonetheless divided quite formally into four distinct sections, each of ten lines. The line lengths vary, reflecting the speaking voice.

Each of the sections contains a central idea. In the first section, the speaker places herself in a particular time and place. In the second, she gives us an insight into the reason for her unease. In the third, she extends the 'riff' she mentions by describing the car, which clearly played a pivotal role in their relationship. In the fourth, the light in the car becomes a symbol of the poet's nightly vigil and of her loneliness.

Sound patterns in the poem

Bryce uses sound patterns to create a musical effect in the poem. Look at the endings of each line, for example, and her use of half-rhyme with words such as 'up' and 'wrap' or 'off' and 'riff'. There are also examples of assonance: 'slim' and 'stilled film' or 'spattered' and 'wrap'; and of alliteration: 'someone, somewhere, smoking'. The full rhyme in the last two lines ('spark' and 'dark') could be said to give a sense of closure to the poem.

Exam-Style Questions

Thinking about the poem

1   What is the speaker's situation, as described in the first few lines?

2   Why, according to herself, is she unable to sleep?

3   What does she see from her window? How does the scene she sees add to the atmosphere she creates in the poem?

4   What does she tell us about her relationship with her lover?

5   Do the lines about the Nissan Micra reveal anything further about the relationship between the speaker and her lover?

6   Would you agree that the poem tells us more about the speaker than about the lover? Give a reason for your answer.

7   What insight does the poem give us about Bryce's life and feelings?

8   Which of these statements most closely represents your opinion?

   ● The speaker expresses a great sense of loneliness and regret.

   ● The speaker would like to hide her true feelings, even from herself.

   Explain your choice.

9   Do you think the combination of everyday speech and poetic images is successful in the poem? Give reasons for your answer.

Taking a closer look

1   'no. It's fine, all gleaming hubcaps, / seats like an upright, silhouetted couple' (lines 31 and 32). Why, in your opinion, does the poet pretend to her lover that the car is 'fine'? What does this suggest about her feelings about the end of the relationship?

2   What would you say is the main feeling expressed in the last three lines of the poem?

3   Give possible reasons for the poet's inclusion of real names of places (Magdalen Green and Riverside Drive) and of a model of car (Nissan Micra) in her poem.

1 Imagine you are the 'you' to whom the poem is addressed. Write down the thoughts you have when you read the poem.

2 'Bryce reveals a great deal about herself in this poem. It is a true self-portrait.' Write a paragraph in which you either agree or disagree with this point of view.

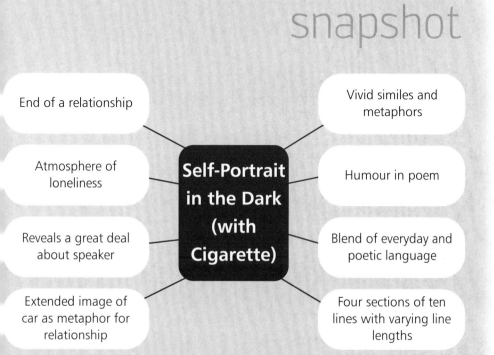

snapshot

End of a relationship

Atmosphere of loneliness

Reveals a great deal about speaker

Extended image of car as metaphor for relationship

Self-Portrait in the Dark (with Cigarette)

Vivid similes and metaphors

Humour in poem

Blend of everyday and poetic language

Four sections of ten lines with varying line lengths

Colette Bryce

Greg Delanty

b. 1958

AFTER VIEWING *THE BOWLING MATCH AT CASTLEMARY, CLOYNE* (1847)

Biography

Greg Delanty was born in Cork city in 1958 and is the son of a master-printer. He enjoyed sport growing up and he was a champion swimmer. He was educated at University College Cork.

He lived in Cork until 1986, when he emigrated to the United States. He spends most of the year in Burlington, Vermont, where he teaches literature in St Michael's College. For three months of each year, however, he returns to his Irish home at Derrynane, Co. Kerry.

Delanty became a US citizen in 1994. He has an active interest in American politics and has run for election for the Vermont Green Party.

His poems have appeared in numerous anthologies and magazines. Among his poetry collections are: *Cast in the Fire* (1986), *Southward* (1992), *American Wake* (1995), *The Hellbox* (1998) and *The Ship of Birth* (2003). His *Collected Poems 1986–2006* was published in 2006.

He has translated plays from Ancient Greece, including *The Suits* by Aristophanes and *Orestes* by Euripides. He edited *The Word Exchange*, which is a book of translations from Anglo-Saxon. In 2007 he published his translations of the work of Irish poet Seán Ó Ríordáin.

Agenda magazine issued a fiftieth-birthday supplement in Delanty's honour in 2008. It featured examples of his work and also essays from leading critics. The *Independent* (UK) newspaper said that the supplement showed Delanty 'to be an important voice for today and the future'.

Delanty has received numerous awards for his poetry, including the Patrick Kavanagh Award in 1983, the Allan Dowling Poetry Fellowship in 1986, the Austin Clarke Centenary Poetry Award in 1997 and the National Poetry Competition in 1999.

In 2007 he was awarded a Guggenheim Fellowship for Poetry. These fellowships are intended for men and women who have demonstrated exceptional creative ability in the arts.

In his poems Delanty explores themes of family life, love and friendship, as well as his experience of the natural and political world.

Delanty recalls being sent as a child for art lessons to the Crawford Municipal Art Gallery in Cork, where it is likely he saw Daniel MacDonald's painting *The Bowling Match at Castlemary, Cloyne* (1847), which inspires this poem.

Before you read 'After Viewing *The Bowling Match at Castlemary, Cloyne* (1847)'

Look carefully at the picture 'The Bowling Match at Castlemary, Cloyne (1847)' on page 480. It shows a painting by Daniel MacDonald (1821–53) that can be viewed at the Crawford Municipal Art Gallery, Cork. In a short paragraph, describe what you see. Do you find the scene painted surprising, given that it took place in Ireland in 1847?

Now read Delanty's poem in response to the painting.

After Viewing *The Bowling Match at Castlemary, Cloyne* (1847)

I promised to show you the bowlers
  out the Blarney Road after Sunday mass,
you were so taken with that painting
  of the snazzy, top-hatted peasant class
    all agog at the bowler in full swing,   5
    down to his open shirt, in trousers
as indecently tight as a baseballer's.

You would relish each fling's span
  along blackberry boreens, and delight
in a dinger of a curve throw   10
  as the bowl hurls out of sight,
    not to mention the earthy lingo
    && antics of gambling fans,
giving players thumbs-up or down the banks.

It's not just to witness such shenanigans   15
  for themselves, but to be relieved
from whatever lurks in our background,
  just as the picture's crowd is freed
    of famine & exile darkening the land,
      waiting to see where the bowl spins   20
off, a planet out of orbit, and who wins.

Glossary	
title	*Cloyne:* a village in east Co. Cork
1	*bowlers:* people playing the sport of road bowling
2	*Blarney road:* the road to Blarney, outside Cork city
4	*snazzy:* attractive, fashionable
4	*peasant class:* small farmers and country people

5	*agog:* excited, eager
8	*span:* here, the length of the throw
9	*boreens:* lanes
10	*dinger:* slang word meaning great, wonderful
12	*lingo:* jargon, language
14	*down the banks:* to criticise
15	*shenanigans:* antics, larking about
19	*famine & exile:* in 1847 the failure of the potato crop had brought about a devastating famine in Ireland. It is estimated that almost one million people died and one million more were forced to emigrate

Guidelines

This poem is from the collection *American Wake* (1995). Although the poem deals lightly with its topic – a picture and a bowling game – it also raises some deeper issues. The speaker touches on the tragedy that befell the people of Ireland in the 1840s, the Great Famine, caused by the failure of the potato crop, and the wave of emigration that occurred as a result. There are also hints that the speaker and his friend are not without their own worries at the present time.

Road bowling is an Irish sport in which competitors attempt to take the fewest throws to propel an iron ball along a three-mile stretch of country roads. The sport originated in Ireland and is mainly played in counties Armagh and Cork. There are two or more players or teams in a match or 'score'. The one with the fewest shots to the finish line wins. Spectators often bet on the outcome and give advice to their favoured competitor in the course of a match or 'score'.

Commentary

Stanza 1
The opening lines are direct and casual, like a conversation. The speaker refers to a promise he had made to his friend to show him (or her – we are not told) a bowling match being played close to Cork city on a Sunday afternoon.

We hear that the companion had enjoyed looking at a famous painting entitled *The Bowling Match at Castlemary, Cloyne* (1847). The speaker starts to describe the picture: the local farmers in their top hats, looking with eager interest at the bowler about to throw the ball. The bowler's open shirt indicates the effort he is making, while the tightness of his trousers seems to give some amusement to the viewers.

The comparison with the baseball player suggests that the speaker's friend may be American.

Stanza 2

The speaker is clearly talking to a fan of sport who would enjoy the length and skill of each throw. His own appreciation of the sport can be seen in the language he uses to describe it. Words such as 'relish', 'delight' and 'dinger' (lines 8–10) convey his enthusiasm. He tells his companion that he would also enjoy the atmosphere of the sporting occasion, listening to the talk of the fans who gamble on the result and comment on each move in the game.

Stanza 3

At this point in the poem the tone becomes less descriptive and more reflective. The speaker recognises the enjoyment of looking at sport and savouring the atmosphere for its own sake. But he also sees that losing yourself in the enjoyment of the occasion can help you to escape from whatever 'lurks in our background' (line 17); these worries are not specified.

He then returns to the picture that was the poem's starting point. He places it in its historical context. Line 19, 'famine & exile darkening the land', sums up the situation that faced Ireland in 1847. Despite these major threats, the men and women in this picture were able to lose themselves for a moment in wondering about the outcome of the game. Where would the bowl spin, and who would win?

When he compares the bowl to a 'planet out of orbit' (line 21) it is as if he is widening the frame of reference in the poem. We see the bowl, for a moment, as a little world in itself. As in the wider world, it is not known what will happen. In life itself, it is never clear who will be a winner or a loser. By leaving us with this thought, the poet links past and present together. The people in the picture, caught in a moment of time, had no way of knowing what would happen in the future. Just as in the present, the speaker and his companion have no way of knowing their futures.

Tone of the poem

The final lines of the poem describe the reaction of the spectators as they watch the spin of the ball and await the outcome of the game. They may also remind us that life is like sport in many ways. We do not know how chance (the curve of the bowl and where it spins) may affect us. Life may set us on an unexpected course, like a 'planet out of orbit'. We do not know who will win and who will lose. If we apply this idea to the picture we could say that the spectators (or the players) had no way of knowing whether they would survive or die in the famine or leave their country for ever. In the same way, he and his friend are in the dark about what will happen in the future.

Language of the poem

The poet uses a mixture of conversational and more formal language. Colloquial words such as 'snazzy', 'dinger', 'lingo' and 'shenanigans' remind us that the poet is speaking to someone, the 'you' of the poem. This person is probably from the United States, as is suggested by the Americanism 'dinger' and the comparison with a baseball player. But we are also reminded of the poem's Cork setting through the game being played (road bowling) and echoes of Cork idiom in 'the banks' (as in the song 'The banks of my own lovely Lee').

Alongside this informal language, there are poetic images such as 'famine & exile darkening the land'. The poet also makes use of metaphors, for example when he describes the bowl as a 'planet out of orbit'.

Perhaps the most striking thing about the language is how precisely it evokes appreciation of sporting skill and enjoyment of a sporting occasion in words such as 'relish', 'delight' and 'antics', and in images such as 'each fling's span / along blackberry boreens'.

Sound patterns in the poem

The sounds used in the poem have an attractive, harmonious quality. There is a mixture of full rhyme such as 'mass' and 'class'; assonance such as 'taken' and 'painting'; consonance such as 'lurks' and 'darkening'; and alliteration such as 'blackberry boreens'. The full rhyme in the final two lines ('spins' and 'wins') gives a sense of closure to the poem.

Exam-Style Questions

Thinking about the poem

1 What reaction did his companion have to the painting, as described by the speaker?
2 According to the speaker, what would his companion enjoy about seeing a bowling match?
3 What hints are there that the speaker's companion is not Irish-born?
4 Apart from enjoyment of the game, how might the speaker and his companion gain from being there?
5 In stanza 3 how does the poet link the present day with the past as depicted in the picture?
6 What contrast between what is happening in the picture and the experience of those who lived at that time is suggested in the poem?
7 Do you think sport has lessons for life, or is it just 'shenanigans' as the poet says?
8 Do you think the last two lines apply only to a sporting occasion, or might they be relevant to life in general? Explain your answer.

9   Which of the following statements is closest to your understanding of the poem?

●   It is a poem about a picture.

●   It is a poem about sport.

●   It is a poem about how the poet feels about life.

Explain your answer.

10   Look again at the picture that accompanies this poem. Does the poem describe it well, in your opinion?

Taking a closer look

1   What sort of person is the 'You' referred to in stanza 2, in your view?

2   'just as the picture's crowd is freed / of famine & exile darkening the land' (lines 18 and 19). What picture of life in 1847 is suggested by these lines?

3   'waiting to see where . . . and who wins' (lines 20 and 21). Do you think these lines make a good ending to the poem? Explain your answer.

Personal response

1   Your class has been asked to compile a list of poems for a book to be called *The Pleasures of* Sport. In pairs or groups, discuss whether or not you would include this poem.

2   Choose two lines from the poem that especially appeal to you. Explain your choice.

3   Write a paragraph giving your views on the role of sport in our lives.

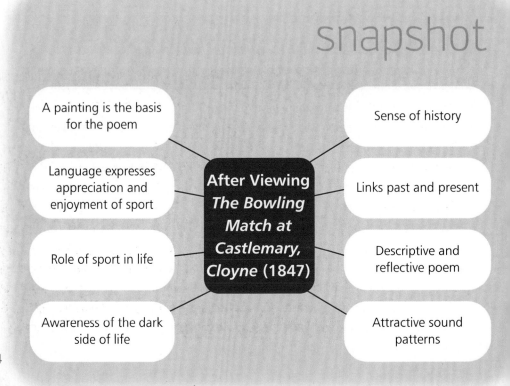

snapshot

A painting is the basis for the poem

Sense of history

Language expresses appreciation and enjoyment of sport

After Viewing *The Bowling Match at Castlemary, Cloyne* (1847)

Links past and present

Role of sport in life

Descriptive and reflective poem

Awareness of the dark side of life

Attractive sound patterns

Carol Ann Duffy

b. 1955

VALENTINE

Biography

Carol Ann Duffy was born in Glasgow in December 1955. She grew up in Staffordshire and was educated at Stafford Girls' High School. She has described her upbringing as 'left wing, Catholic, working class'.

Duffy studied philosophy at university in Liverpool before moving to London to work as a freelance writer. She has written plays as well as poems, edited books of poetry and been a writer in residence at the Southern Arts, Thamesdown.

When her first volume of poetry, *Standing Female Nude*, was published in 1985, it was praised as 'the debut of a genuine and original poet'. Since then she has achieved both critical and commercial success.

Duffy's other early collections include *Selling Manhattan* (1987), *The Other Country* (1990) and *Mean Time* (1993). In 2000 she published *The World's Wife*, a collection of dramatic monologues in the voices of the wives of famous men (Mrs Midas and Mrs Aesop, for example). She has written picture books for children and edited two anthologies for teenagers: *I Wouldn't Thank You for a Valentine* and *Stopping for Death*.

More recently, *Rapture* was published in 2006, and *New and Collected Poems for Children* appeared in 2009. *The Bees* (2011) won the Costa Poetry Award and the T. S. Eliot Prize.

In 1999 Duffy became a fellow of the Royal Society of Literature. She was awarded an OBE (Officer of the British Empire) in 1995 and a CBE (Commander of the British Empire) in 2001.

She was appointed as Britain's Poet Laureate in May 2009, becoming the first woman, the first Scot and the first openly gay person to hold the position in its 300-year history. At her first press conference as laureate, she said:

> Poetry matters to people . . . poetry is a place we can go to for comfort, celebration, when we're in love, when we're bereaved and sometimes for events that happen to us as a nation.

> Poetry comes from the imagination, from memories, from experience, from events both personal and public, so I will be following the truth of that and I will write whatever needs to be written.

In 2012 she compiled *Jubilee Lines*, a collection of sixty poems from sixty poets to mark the sixtieth year of the reign of Queen Elizabeth II.

Duffy lives in Manchester, where she is Creative Director of the Writing School at Manchester Metropolitan University.

Before you read 'Valentine'

We are all familiar with 'Valentine' cards and wishes. In pairs or groups, discuss what feelings are usually expressed on Valentine's Day. How is this done? What objects and images do you associate with Valentine's Day?

Valentine

Not a red rose or a satin heart.

I give you an onion.
It is a moon wrapped in brown paper.
It promises light
like the careful undressing of love.   5

Here.
It will blind you with tears
like a lover.
It will make your reflection
a wobbling photo of grief. 10

I am trying to be truthful.

Not a cute card or a kissogram.

I give you an onion.
Its fierce kiss will stay on your lips,
Possessive and faithful 15
As we are,
for as long as we are.

Take it.
Its platinum loops shrink to a wedding-ring,
if you like. 20
Lethal.
Its scent will cling to your fingers,
Cling to your knife.

Glossary

| 19 | *platinum:* valuable white metal used in jewellery |
| 21 | *Lethal:* deadly, dangerous |

Guidelines

'Valentine' is from the collection *Mean Time* (1993). Like a traditional valentine, the poem contains a proposal of marriage. But unlike a traditional valentine, the proposal is expressed in unromantic terms and Duffy's version does not try to rhyme.

The title prepares us for a romantic love poem, but in fact Duffy rejects traditional symbols of love.

Commentary

The poem is honest about love. It sees love as sexual, passionate and hopeful. But it also sees that love can cause pain and grief and that it may not last: it will only be 'possessive and faithful' (line 15) for as long as the lovers remain true to each other. This is a more realistic view of love than is usually found in a valentine.

Lines 1–10

Instead of the usual gifts a lover gives to a beloved – red roses or satin hearts – this poem offers an onion.

The speaker makes a case for the onion as an appropriate gift. She proceeds to use the image of **the onion as a metaphor for love**, keeping the extended metaphor going throughout the poem. She mixes romantic images (the onion is a 'moon' in shape) with ordinary things: an onion comes 'wrapped in brown paper' (i.e. onion skin) (line 3). Yet underneath its dull appearance, an onion 'promises light' (hope? happiness?) (line 4) just as love does. It can be peeled to reveal beauty, just as lovers also undress each other. The different layers of the onion are also like the layers of someone's personality as it is discovered in a relationship.

As an onion may do, love may cause tears that will blind your eyes. Your reflection will become 'a wobbling photo of grief' (line 10). Here the poet cleverly plays on the 'wobbling' or blurring of vision that occurs as our eyes water when we peel an onion.

Lines 11–20

The speaker thinks that an onion is a more 'truthful' (line 11) symbol of love than other more conventional Valentine's Day gifts, a 'cute card' or a 'kissogram' for instance (line 12). 'I give you an onion' echoes the ceremony of marriage ('I give you this ring'). The smell and taste of the onion, its 'fierce kiss' (line 14), will last on the lips of the beloved, just as the speaker's love will last as long as the love they share lasts.

An onion, too, has rings, and this brings the speaker to compare its 'platinum loops' to a 'wedding-ring', adding hesitantly, 'if you like' (lines 19 and 20). Here now is the proposal for a long-term relationship, even if it is expressed in a rather casual and off-hand manner. The speaker does rather undermine this proposal by using the word 'shrink' (line 19). Might she be suggesting that marriage can be experienced as something negative, something less than love itself?

Lines 21–23

Throughout the poem the speaker has stressed her desire to be honest about love. We can read the final three lines in a number of ways. 'Lethal' (line 21) might suggest the fierceness of love, but it has underlying connotations of destruction. And is there a threatening tone in the image of the onion's scent that 'will cling to your fingers / cling to your knife' (lines 22 and 23)? 'Knife' is a strange word to end a poem about love. It has suggestions of bitterness and betrayal.

Tone of the poem

The mixture of ordinary and romantic images gives 'Valentine' its ironic, bittersweet tone, so that we are never quite sure what the feelings of the speaker are. Duffy creates a sense of an intimate conversation taking place between the 'I' and 'you' of the poem. The abrupt tone of the first line, 'Not a red rose or a satin heart', gives the impression of an exchange that has been going on for some time. It is as if the gift is being given at this present moment ('Here') and the reader is witnessing the event.

At times the speaker seems confident and in control ('Take it'), at other times she seems unsure ('if you like'). It is possible to read the final lines as expressing doubts about the future of the relationship (a 'knife' may make sense in terms of an onion, but it suggests pain and betrayal in terms of a relationship). Despite the casual and even slightly comical tone of the poem, it is clear that the speaker is not avoiding the darker side of love.

How we respond to the poem may depend on our personal experiences, but we cannot fail to see how original and honest it is.

Exam-Style Questions

Thinking about the poem

1 Why, according to the speaker, is the onion suitable as a gift for the beloved on Valentine's Day?
2 Which of the metaphors and similes that the poet uses do you find the most unusual and effective?
3 Do you think the relationship between the lovers in this poem is a happy one?
4 What attitude to love and relationships in general is suggested in this poem?
5 With which of these statements would you most agree?
    ● The speaker is very honest about love.
    ● The speaker is very bitter about love.
    ● The speaker's attitude to love is refreshing and enjoyable.
    Give reasons for your view.
6 Suggest reasons for the poem's arrangement on the page (with short lines and spaces).
7 Describe the proposal that is contained within the poem.
8 Do you think this is a good love poem? Explain your answer.

Taking a closer look

1   Write down one line or phrase from the poem that tells you most about the kind of relationship the lovers have. Say why you think it is an important line.

2   'Its fierce kiss will stay on your lips, / Possessive and faithful / As we are, / for as long as we are' (lines 14–17). What do these lines suggest to you about the speaker's view of love?

3   'It's scent will cling to your fingers, / Cling to your knife' (lines 22 and 23). How do these lines affect your reading of the poem? Give a reason for your view.

Personal response

1   Imagine you are the person who has received the onion (and the poem) as a valentine. Write out the response you would make.

2   Write out, in dialogue form, the conversation that may have taken place after the onion was given as a gift.

3   In pairs or groups, discuss how your expectations about valentines were changed by the poem.

snapshot

Extended metaphor of onion as a metaphor for love

Mixture of ordinary and romantic images

Complex vision of love

Written in unrhymed, conversational language

Valentine

Tone changes throughout

Rejects traditional 'valentines'

Creates sound of speaking voice

Clever and original love poem

Kerry Hardie

b. 1951

DANIEL'S DUCK

Biography

Kerry Hardie was born in 1951 in Singapore and grew up in Co. Down. She studied English at York University in England before returning to Ireland to work as a researcher and radio interviewer for the BBC in Belfast and Derry:

> This period coincided with the most violent years of the Troubles, and through my job I had access to situations and people I might not otherwise have known. I became fascinated with people who found themselves in a hard place and with how they reacted to this place. Some people adapted astonishingly fast to their new realities, but others spent their energies resisting and could only change to meet them when they had in some way been broken by them.

Hardie has published several collections of poetry, including her *Selected Poems* (2011). Her first novel, *A Winter Marriage*, was published in 2002, and her second novel, *The Bird Woman*, followed in 2006.

A Furious Place (1996) includes poems that record people in their own landscapes and explores the way in which landscape permeates their lives. Other poems dwell on the hardships and lessons of a chronic illness. Hardie suffers from ME (Chronic Fatigue Syndrome):

> Being chronically sick makes you an observer rather than a participant. Before I was sick, I lived very hard and my life was very outgoing; now my life is quiet and disciplined and reflective. . . . It took me a long time to come to terms with the change, but now I find my life immensely rich and rewarding.

Many of the poems in *The Sky Didn't Fall* (2003), from which 'Daniel's Duck' is taken, deal with grief and loss and the contrast between the outside world and our inner feelings.

Hardie has won major literary awards and she is a member of Aosdána, the national arts organisation. Her writing has taken her to various countries, including Spain, France, Australia, China and Moldova. She represented Ireland at the International Meeting of Poets in Portugal in 2001.

She lives in Kilkenny with her husband, Sean Hardie, who is a writer and television director.

Before you read 'Daniel's Duck'

Have you ever come across a wild animal or bird shortly after it died? What feelings did you have? Maybe you felt uneasy, fascinated, sad, afraid, admiration, or something else? Is it easy to put your reaction into words? Discuss your thoughts with a partner, before sharing your ideas with the rest of the class.

Daniel's Duck

for Frances

I held out the shot mallard, she took it from me,
looped its neck-string over a drawer of the dresser.
The children were looking on, half-caught.
Then the kitchen life – warm, lit, glowing –
moved forward, taking in the dead bird,   5
and its coldness, its wildness, were leaching away.

The children were sitting to their dinners.
Us too – drinking tea, hardly noticing
the child's quiet slide from his chair,
his small absorbed body before the duck's body,   10
the duck changing – feral, live –
arrowing up out of black sloblands
with the gleam of a river
falling away below.

Then the duck – dead again – hanging from the drawer-knob   15
the green head, brown neck running into the breast,
the intricate silvery-greyness of the back;
the wings, their white bars and blue flashes,
the feet, their snakey, orange scaliness, small claws, piteous webbing,
the yellow beak, blooded,   20
the whole like a weighted sack –
all that downward-dragginess of death.

He hovered, took a step forward, a step back,
something appeared in his face, some knowledge
of a place where he stood, the world stilled,   25
the lit streaks of sunrise running off red
into the high bowl of the morning.

She watched him, moving to touch, his hand out:
What is it, Daniel, do you like the duck?
He turned as though caught in the act,   30
saw the gentleness in her face and his body loosened.
I thought there was water on it –
he was finding the words, one by one,
holding them out, to see would they do us –
But there isn't.   35
He added this on, going small with relief
that his wind-drag of sound was enough.

Glossary

1	*mallard:* a wild duck (the male or drake has the markings described in the poem)
6	*leaching away:* seeping or draining away; disappearing
11	*feral:* wild; not tame or domesticated but fending for itself
12	arrowing up: flying upwards with wings outstretched the duck resembles an arrow shape
12	*sloblands:* mudflats or land reclaimed from the sea
19	*scaliness:* the quality of being covered in scales or scab-like, thin plates that provide protection on the legs of birds and the skin of fish and reptiles
19	*piteous:* deserving or giving rise to pity; heartrending; pathetic
37	*wind-drag:* when birds fly they use their wings to push the air out of the way and the sound made by their wings is the result of the drag or resistance of the wind

Guidelines

The poem tells a story, a little drama from daily life. In a kitchen, where the children sit down to their dinner and the adults drink tea, **a young boy encounters death in the form of a shot mallard and tries to make sense of his experience.** The poem focuses on the moment when the boy begins to understand something, though he has not the words to express his new knowledge. Standing before the bird, he enters a private world and feels something like guilt when he becomes aware of the attention of the adults. To his relief, the adults are satisfied by the words he finds to explain his fascination for the duck.

Commentary

Within the narrative, the poem encompasses many ideas and contrasting themes: the contrast between the living wild duck and the dead bird hanging in the kitchen; the contrast between the duck 'arrowing up out of black sloblands' (line 12) and the force of death dragging the body down; childhood innocence versus the dawning of knowledge; the busy kitchen versus the private, interior world of the child; the contrast between things we can describe and those experiences for which we struggle to find words.

Stanzas 1 and 2

The narrator tells us that the handing over of the duck to the woman of the house and the hanging of the bird on the dresser was something that 'half-caught' (line 3) the attention of the children before the life of the kitchen, the warm domestic life of the household, moved on and the duck began to lose its 'wildness' (line 6).

We learn that one child, the Daniel of the title, has slid from the chair and is standing in front of the duck. Reading between the lines, the poem suggests that Daniel is seeing the duck as though it was still alive and in its wild or feral state.

Stanzas 3 and 4

There is a detailed description of the duck as it is now, hanging dead on the drawer-knob. The description emphasises its intricate colouring, including the blood on its 'yellow beak' (line 20), and the way in which the duck is weighed down and dragged down by death.

The young boy tries to make sense of what he sees. The verb 'hovers' suggests that his thoughts are moving back and forth and he is absorbed in the moment, so much so that the world is 'stilled' (line 25). **The idea that he understands something for the first time is suggested in the imagery of the dawn and the sun rising.**

Stanza 5

As he reaches out his hand to touch the dead duck, the boy is interrupted by a woman's voice. He seems almost guilty, 'as though caught in the act' (line 30), but he relaxes when he sees 'the gentleness in her face' (line 31). **He tries to find the words to explain himself and is relieved when no more questions are asked.**

Narrative voice

The story is narrated by an adult, possibly the person who shot the duck. Clearly the narrator's account is sympathetic to Daniel and, arguably, parts of the poem are written as if seen through the child's eyes. 'Daniel's Duck' brings us into the middle of a small drama, but intriguingly it leaves a number of questions unanswered. Who speaks the words: the poet or a persona like a narrator in a novel? Is it a man or a woman? What is the speaker's relationship to the 'she' of the poem and to Daniel? Is the 'she' Daniel's mother?

Form and language of the poem

Although the poem is written in irregular stanzas with no rhyme scheme, Hardie pays great attention to sound and rhythm and there are many examples of alliteration as well as consonance and assonance. Look, for example, at how the 'l' sound is repeated throughout the first stanza, or how 'b' and 'd' sounds echo through the second stanza and into the first lines of stanza 3. You will also notice the words that end with '-ness'. Note, too, the succession of noun phrases that are used to great effect in stanza 3 to describe the duck.

Kerry Hardie

Exam-Style Questions

Thinking about the poem

1   According to the first stanza, what happened to the duck once it was hung from the dresser?

2   There is a reference in stanza 2 to 'the duck changing' (line 11). Where and how does the duck change?

3   The third stanza is a detailed description of the appearance of the shot duck. Comment on each detail and its significance.

4   The fourth stanza focuses on the young boy. In your own words explain what happens to the boy and the 'something' that 'appeared in his face' (line 24).

5   What was Daniel's initial reaction, in the final stanza, when the woman called out to him?

6   Think about the meaning of the last word of the poem, 'enough'. In what sense was Daniel's answer 'enough'?

7   There are many contrasts in the poem. Identify as many of them as you can and comment on each.

8   Having read the poem, what age is Daniel, in your opinion? Give a reason for your answer.

9   Here are three views of what the poem is about. Which one of them is closest to your view?
    ●   A child's first encounter with death.
    ●   The difference between the things we can describe and those which are beyond words.
    ●   The difference between the private world of children and the world of adults.
    Explain your choice.

10 'Good poetry creates vivid pictures in our minds.' In your opinion, is this true of 'Daniel's Duck'? Support your view by reference to the poem.

Taking a closer look

1   Give your views on the effectiveness of the phrase 'that downward-dragginess of death' (line 22).

2   'the lit streaks of sunrise running off red / into the high bowl of the morning' (lines 26 and 27). In your view, why has the poet included these lines at this point in the poem?

3   Comment on the phrase 'his wind-drag of sound' in the final line of the poem.

4   There are many interesting uses of words in this poem. Select two that you like and say why you like them.

Personal response

1 Imagine you are Daniel. You are now a young man. Write a diary entry in which you record your experiences and feelings on the day described in the poem.

2 If you were to make a film that interprets the poem, what images would you include and what would you select for the musical score?

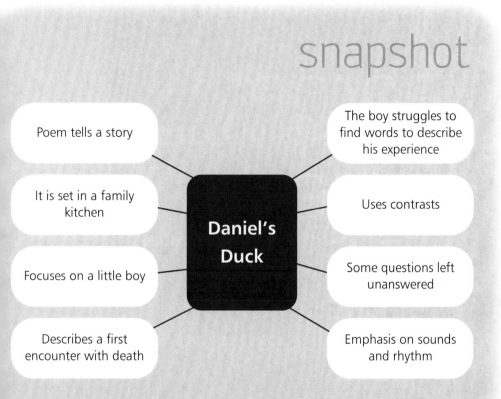

snapshot

Kerry Hardie

Poem tells a story

It is set in a family kitchen

Focuses on a little boy

Describes a first encounter with death

Daniel's Duck

The boy struggles to find words to describe his experience

Uses contrasts

Some questions left unanswered

Emphasis on sounds and rhythm

George Herbert

1593–163[

THE COLLAR

Biography

George Herbert was born in Montgomery Castle, Wales. He was a member of one of the most aristocratic families of the Welsh border country. His eldest brother was a leading statesman, philosopher and poet, and became Lord Herbert of Cherbury. His mother was a close friend of John Donne, whose poetry had a strong influence on his work.

Herbert was first educated at home, and then at Westminster School and Trinity College, Cambridge. In 1620 he was elected orator in the university. This position gave him the opportunity to meet and greet important visitors, including the monarch. In 1624 he became a member of parliament for Montgomery.

During his time at Cambridge, Herbert enjoyed the patronage of James I and the company of royal courtiers. He seemed destined for an outstanding career as a public figure, but circumstances began to change for him in 1625, following the death of the king. Many of Herbert's influential friends were out of favour with the new king, Charles I.

It had long been understood by his family that he would dedicate himself to the service of the Church of England. In or before 1626 he was ordained deacon. For some time he lived with friends. His mind was unsettled, and his physical health disimproved. He resigned from his position as university orator.

In 1629 he married and in 1630 he finally made up his mind to devote his talents to the Church of England. He was offered 'a living' at Bemerton, near Salisbury, which he accepted. A living was a position as a rector or vicar of a parish with an income or property, or both. To occupy this position he had to be ordained, which he duly was in September 1630. He had only three years to live.

His three years as a humble parson were notable for his dedication to his work. He made an exceptional impression on the parishioners he served. He had sacrificed a great deal in devoting his life to the service of the Church of England in an obscure parish. It was most unusual for someone so well born to take on this kind of role, especially as he was well qualified to take on a career at court or in politics.

Herbert explained his choice to abandon public life and become a clergyman, saying: 'The Court is made up of fraud, and titles and flattery, and many such empty, imaginary, painted pleasures, but in God and his service is a fullness of all joy and pleasure'. It is interesting to note that all his surviving poems deal with religious subjects.

Herbert did not publish his English poems, although he had published some in Latin. His friend Nicholas Ferrar, however, published them in 1633, the year of Herbert's death. The volume was entitled *The Temple*. By 1709 thirteen editions of *The Temple* had been published. The poems' popularity can partly be explained by the fact that religious matters occupied the minds of great numbers of English people at that time.

Herbert is notable for his ability to express profound ideas in plain language.

Before you read 'The Collar'

The poem on page 500 is entitled 'The Collar'. What does this title make you think of? Form small groups and compare your lists.

The Collar

I struck the board, and cry'd, No more.
   I will abroad.
  What? shall I ever sigh and pine?
My lines and life are free; free as the road,
   Loose as the winde, as large as store.   5
    Shall I be still in suit?
  Have I no harvest but a thorn
  To let me blood, and not restore
What I have lost with cordiall fruit?
    Sure there was wine   10
  Before my sighs did drie it: there was corn
   Before my tears did drown it.
  Is the yeare onely lost to me?
   Have I no bayes to crown it?
No, flowers, no garlands gay? all blasted?   15
   All wasted?
  Not so, my heart: but there is fruit,
   And thou hast hands.
  Recover all thy sigh-blown age
On double pleasures: leave thy cold dispute   20
Of what is fit, and not; forsake thy cage,
   Thy rope of sands,
Which pettie thoughts have made, and made to thee
  Good cable, to enforce and draw,
   And be thy law,   25
  While thou didst wink and wouldst not see
   Away; take heed:
   I will abroad.
Call in thy death's-head there: tie up thy fears.
   He that forbears   30
   To suit and serve his need,
   Deserves his load.
But as I rav'd and grew more fierce and wilde
   At every word,
Methought I heard one calling, *Childe*!   35
   And I reply'd, *My Lord*.

Glossary

1	*board:* the altar or the table of the father's house
2	*abroad:* away from home
5	*store:* plenty, an abundance
6	*in suit:* in service to the will of God
8	*let me blood:* spill my blood
9	*cordiall:* life-giving
10–11	*wine; corn:* these stand for lawful pleasures
14–15	*bayes; garlands:* symbols of achievement
17	*there is fruit:* life has its pleasures
19–20	*Recover . . . pleasures:* compensate yourself for your period of misery by enjoying a double share of pleasure
20	*cold dispute:* debate that brings no comfort
22	*rope of sands:* bonds that are liable to come apart easily, so ending the heart's imprisonment
23	*pettie:* petty, childish
29	*death's-head:* a skull, which served as a reminder to religious people of the certainty of death and was intended to ensure strict behaviour
30–31	*He . . . need:* the man who fails to put his own needs first
32	*his load:* the burdens others place on his shoulders
35	*Methought:* it seemed to me

Guidelines

The speaker of this poem is a Christian priest. **The poem is mainly concerned with a conflict between the speaker's heart and the will of God.** The title expresses discipline, control and service to God. For the priest-speaker this service is performed through following his religious vocation. He makes it clear that this vocation means that he must suffer a certain loss of freedom. He is strongly tempted to regain his freedom by giving up the priesthood and leaving for some unnamed region.

The more he thinks of the opportunities for pleasure he is missing and of the narrowness of his way of life, the more angry and frustrated he becomes. He talks wildly and excitedly, like a child who has been deprived of something he badly wants. At the height of his angry outburst, the voice of God sounds in his ears, calling him back. The speaker immediately submits to God's demand. The rebellion is over.

Commentary

Lines 1–16

The speaker expresses the complaints of his heart against his unhappy life of service to God. He is determined to find happiness and freedom in some unnamed place: 'abroad' (line 2). He feels that the courses of action open to him are without limit: his 'lines and life are free' (line 4). The road and the wind suggest freedom. The world outside is full of possible benefits, having plenty, 'store' (line 5), to offer him.

He wonders why he must always be a slave 'in suit' (line 6) to God's will. He has given up the pleasures of the world, represented in the poem by corn and wine. All he has got in return is a harvest of pain and sorrow: 'thorn . . . blood . . . sighs . . . tears' (lines 7–12). The 'bayes', 'flowers' and 'garlands' of lines 14 and 15 are symbols of success and achievement. He has none of these rewards because he has wasted his talents on a vocation that has given him only misery and disappointment.

Lines 17–26

The speaker's will answers the complaints made by the heart in the first section of the poem. The will suggests strongly that there is no need for the heart to despair. Life has its pleasures, its 'fruit' (line 17), but the speaker must reach out for them. He will be able to do so because he 'hast hands' (line 18), that is, he has the means to do so.

He can even make up for all the miseries he has suffered so far ('thy sigh-blown age', line 19). He can do this by enjoying increased or 'double pleasures' (line 20). He must give up his useless debate ('cold dispute', line 20) about what may be right or wrong for him ('what is fit, and not', line 21). His conscience is a prison from which he must break free, as a bird or animal might escape from its cage. His doubts and fears have bound him like a rope, which is not as strong as he thinks: it is merely a 'rope of sands' (line 22). He has refused to accept the means of escape, which have always been there.

Lines 27–32

These lines belong to the speaker's heart, which repeats the complaints it made in lines 1 to 16. It is now determined to break free. Up to now the speaker's life has been controlled by thoughts of death. The 'death's-head' (line 29), or skull, was a constant reminder of death. When he casts this skull aside, he will be able to enjoy himself without fear. He has been tied up by his fears; now he will be able to tie up those fears instead. He decides that he will serve his own needs rather than serve God. A slave deserves whatever burdens his master places on his shoulders. Here, the master is God.

Lines 33–36

The speaker's language has been growing more and more excitable and wild. In the final four lines, **the voice of God restores peace and calm to his soul, and the speaker addresses God as a child would address a father.** The final two lines express the traditional Christian idea that human beings are God's children. The speaker puts aside his complaints and is ready to follow his vocation as a priest.

Deeper meanings

'The Collar' offers new layers of meaning on each new reading. God is presented as a father, and the speaker as a child who wants to leave home. Here, Herbert is glancing at Christ's parable of the prodigal son. 'Board' in the first line can mean 'altar' as well as 'table'. Since the man striking the board is a priest, his action in striking the board is a sacrilege. The priest's collar of the title is a symbol of service and even enslavement. There may also be a pun on 'choler' (anger), which would fit the speaker's state of mind.

At first glance it might be difficult to tell from the imagery that this is a deeply Christian poem. This is because the Christian imagery on which the poem is based can be read as the imagery of nature, food and drink. The wine and corn of lines 10 and 11 are the bread and wine of the Eucharist. The thorn and blood of lines 7 and 8 are intended to recall Christ's crowning with thorns. The child and lord of the two final lines are the Christian and God, in this case the Christian priest and his heavenly Father.

Form and language of the poem

'The Collar' is one of the finest of all Herbert's poems. The diction is simple and commonplace as it often is in Herbert's poetry, since he believed that 'the highest truth must be plainly dressed'. However, the arrangement of the words and lines on the page is far from simple. The poem deals with disorder and confusion in the speaker's mind, and Herbert makes his language enact this disorder and confusion.

The structure of the poem offers a representation of the disorder it is communicating. As the feelings of the speaker become 'more fierce and wild', the organisation of the poem becomes more chaotic: the imagery grows more confusing, the lines are varied in length, and the speaker is so troubled that he does not seem to be able to find proper rhymes. For example, 'board' is supposed to rhyme with 'abroad', and both with 'road'. The speaker in one line thinks of himself as imprisoned in a cage, which in the next line becomes 'a rope of sands' created by 'pettie thoughts'.

Imagery has a vital part to play in expressing the speaker's thoughts and feelings. Until the final two lines the speaker's mind is disordered, even chaotic. The imagery reflects this. The board of the first line is the altar, normally a focus of peace and quietness. 'The Collar' opens with an image of a rebel priest violently striking the altar with his hand in a gesture of defiance. As the poem proceeds, the speaker's anger increases, and the imagery becomes more violent. The early lines feature pleasant images of 'cordiall' fruit, wine, flowers and garlands. These give way to the menacing images of the 'cage', the 'rope of sands', the 'cable' and the 'death's head'.

Rhymes and rhythms of the poem

The rhymes and rhythms of the 'The Collar', like its imagery, mirror the chaos and confusion of the speaker's mind. The arrangement of the lines and rhymes provides a perfect image of revolt. Notice the irregular appearance of the poem as you look at it on the page. Notice that as you read it aloud, it lacks an even, rhythmic pattern. The very first rhyme we hear is 'board' – 'abroad'. It is as if the speaker is too impatient and angry to find a proper rhyme. This is deliberate on Herbert's part.

The chaotic rhythms match the chaos in the speaker's mind and spirit. In lines 1 to 32 there are six different patterns of rhyme and seven different line lengths. The rhyming scheme lacks any kind of pattern. Of the nine groups of four lines, only the final one has a regular rhyming scheme ('wilde' and 'Childe'; 'word' and 'Lord'). This return to normal rhyming pattern comes only when the speaker returns to an orderly state of mind from his earlier confusion.

Exam-Style Questions

Thinking about the poem

1 For almost the entire poem, the speaker is in a state of revolt. What is he revolting against? Explain your answer with reference to the poem.

2 Why does the speaker submit at the end of the poem?

3 The speaker is a Christian priest. Comment on some details in the poem that suggest this.

4 'The poem as a whole is a depiction of violence and disorder.' Comment on this idea with reference to the poem.

5 The poem is based on a dialogue between the speaker's heart and his will. Comment on it from this point of view.

6 In what way does the speaker blame himself for his problems? Refer to relevant details of the poem in your answer.

7 Some of the images in the poem convey the idea that the speaker is in captivity. Explain how these images work.

8 What impression of the speaker do you get from reading this poem? Refer to the text in support of your answer.

9 Describe the relationship between God and the speaker. Support your answer with reference to the text.

10 'In Herbert's opinion, harmony and order represented God and goodness.' Comment on 'The Collar' in the light of this opinion.

11   In which part of the poem is harmony restored? Explain how this is done.
12   'Throughout the body of the poem, God's love has been working within the speaker despite his rebellious agitation.' Consider the evidence provided in 'The Collar' for this point of view.

Taking a closer look

1   Choose two phrases or lines from the poem that impressed you. Explain your choice.
2   Suggest reasons why Herbert chose 'The Collar' as the title of his poem. Then suggest an alternative title in keeping with the subject matter of the poem.

Personal response

1   Some commentators have suggested that the speaker overcomes the problems he outlines too easily, and that his sudden acceptance of God's will in the final lines is not convincing. Agree or disagree with this view, basing your answer on the text.
2   'The Collar' provides a dramatic account of a dilemma faced by the speaker: whether he should continue to devote his life to the service of God, or seek an easier life elsewhere. Mention some dilemma or difficult choice that you have faced, and give an account of how you dealt with it.

snapshot

Angry, violent imagery reflects the disorder of the speaker's mind

God is seen as a master, and the speaker as a slave

Dramatic dialogue between the speaker's heart and his will

The speaker becomes a child being spoken to by a father

The Collar

Christian imagery is homely and pleasant

Deals with the conflict between the speaker and God

Images of rebellion are menacing and unpleasant

Can be read as a cry for freedom

Ted Hughes

1930–98

THE STAG

Biography

Ted (Edward James) Hughes was born in 1930 in Mytholmroid, West Yorkshire, England. When he was seven his family moved to Mexborough in South Yorkshire, where his parents opened a stationery and tobacco shop.

He was a bright student, and won a scholarship to Pembroke College, Cambridge. He intended to study English literature, but soon switched to archaeology and anthropology.

Hughes admired the poetry of D. H. Lawrence, Gerard Manley Hopkins and the later work of W. B. Yeats. Like Hopkins, Hughes rejoiced in the survival of the natural world in an age of massive industrial and urban development. He respected the cunning and brutal instincts that enable animals to survive in a world that has little or no pity for weakness.

Unusually for a Cambridge graduate, his early jobs were in turn a zookeeper, a gardener and a nightwatchman. He was also still publishing poems in university magazines.

In 1956 Hughes married Sylvia Plath, an American poet, and they lived in Cambridge, where Hughes taught and Plath studied. He also won a major poetry prize in 1956. His first collection, *The Hawk in the Rain*, was published in 1957 to much critical acclaim. Hughes and Plath both taught in America for a while, before returning to England in 1959. His 1960 collection of poems, *Lupercal*, won two important awards.

His poems on human topics emphasise some of the basic instincts people share with animals. Qualities such as cruelty, selfishness and the ability to destroy and inflict suffering for enjoyment. Many readers dislike the primitive violence of some of his work. 'Thrushes' is one of his most popular poems. It conveys the power, violence and deadly precision of the bird as it drags out its wriggling victim. Hughes depicts his thrush as a perfect, horrifying killing machine, having reached its present state of efficiency as a result of millions of years of evolution.

Hughes showed his own capacity to inflict suffering, particularly in his treatment of his mentally fragile first wife, Sylvia Plath. The couple separated in 1962 as a result of his affair with Assia Wevill. Plath's mental and physical health declined and she took her own life in 1963. Wevill also developed a serious depression, and in 1969 she killed herself and their four-year-old daughter. Hughes became a target of hatred, attracting blame for the suicides of the two women. Plath's gravestone was repeatedly defaced by persons seeking to chisel off his name. In 1970 Hughes married Carol Orchard and they remained together until his death.

Hughes published many collections of poetry. Notable among these are *Selected Poems 1957–1967*; *Flowers and Insects* (1986); *New Selected Poems 1957–1994*; and *Birthday Letters* (1998). He became Britain's Poet Laureate in 1984, and was appointed a member of the Order of Merit by Queen Elizabeth II shortly before his death in October 1998. His *Collected Poems* appeared in 2003 in an edition of over 1,300 pages.

Before you read 'The Stag'

Before reading 'The Stag' by Ted Hughes on page 508 do some research on stag hunting. Find out what happens in a stag hunt. What kind of people take part? Find out about groups who think stag hunting is wrong and should be banned. Try to discover what action such groups took in Ireland, and what results their action had.

The Stag

While the rain fell on the November woodland
  shoulder of Exmoor
While the traffic jam along the road honked
  and shouted
Because the farmers were parking wherever they could
And scrambling to the bank-top to stare through the tree-fringe
Which was leafless,   5
The stag ran through his private forest.

While the rain drummed on the roofs of the parked cars
And the kids inside cried and daubed their chocolate and fought
And mothers and aunts and grandmothers
Were a tangle of undoing sandwiches and
  screwed-round gossiping heads   10
Steaming up the windows,
The stag loped through this favourite valley.

While the blue horsemen down in the boggy meadow
Sodden nearly black, on sodden horses,
Spaces as at a military parade,   15
Moved a few paces to the right and a few to the left
  and felt rather foolish
Looking at the brown impassable river,
The stag came over the last hill of Exmoor.

While everybody high-kneed it to the bank-top all along the road
Where steady men in oilskins were stationed at binoculars,   20
And the horsemen by the river galloped anxiously this way and that
And the cry of hounds came tumbling invisibly with their echoes down
  through the draggle of trees,
Swinging across the wall of dark woodland,
The stag dropped into a strange country.

And turned at the river   25
Hearing the hound-pack smash the undergrowth,
   hearing the bell-note
Of the voice that carried all the others,
Then while his limbs all cried different directions to his lungs,
   which only wanted to rest,
The blue horsemen on the bank opposite
Pulled aside the camouflage of their terrible planet.   30

And the stag doubled back weeping and looking for home
   up a valley and down a valley
While the strange trees struck at him and the bramble lashed him,
And the strange earth came galloping after him carrying the
   loll-tongued hounds to fling all over him
And his heart became just a club beating his ribs and his own hooves
   shouted with hounds' voice,
And the crowd on the road got back into their cars   35
Wet-through and disappeared.

Glossary	
1	*woodland shoulder:* wooded slopes
1	*Exmoor:* a hilly area of moorland and ancient forestry in Somerset and Devon, which became a national park in 1954. Red deer inhabit the area, particularly the remote hillsides
12	*loped:* ran with a long stride
13	*blue horsemen:* members of one of the local stag hunts who wear blue coats
17	*impassable river:* the river is in flood and cannot be crossed
19	*high-kneed it:* moved swiftly
22	*draggle:* the dismal weather is making the trees wet and dirty
26	*bell-note:* the cry of a stag is called a bell
28	*the limbs:* the stag's legs
30	*camouflage:* a means of disguising or concealing
33	*loll-tongued hounds:* the tongues of the hounds are hanging down loosely

Ted Hughes

Guidelines

This poem, written entirely in the past tense, tells the story of a stag hunt. A poem that tells a story is called a **narrative poem**.

'The Stag' also has **some of the features of a literary ballad**:

(a)   It has an abrupt opening, which sets the scene immediately.

(b)   It has generally plain and simple language.

(c)   It tells a story through action.

(d)   Its theme is often sad, sometimes even tragic.

(e)   There is a refrain (a phrase or line repeated at intervals during the poem, usually at the end of a stanza). There are six stanzas, or units of verse, in this poem and four of them end with similar sentences describing the movements of the stag.

(f)   The narrator does not intervene to give a view on what is happening, and allows the events of the story to speak for themselves. In this way, the narrative proceeds from beginning to end without interruption.

Commentary

One of the most notable features of 'The Stag' is that **the way in which the words are arranged (the syntax) keeps the narrative moving at a rapid pace.** Read the poem aloud and you will notice that if you pause at the end of each line it is difficult to keep track of the meaning. For example, consider the order of the words in Stanza 1. This stanza, like the other five, has six lines, but it consists of only a single sentence with one main verb. This main verb ('ran') does not appear until line 6, which means that the meaning of the stanza is suspended over the course of five lengthy lines until we reach the third word of the sixth line. It is only natural that the reader will move quickly through the connected clauses of the first five lines to arrive at the full meaning of the sentence revealed in line 6.

The opening words of the first five lines ('While', 'While', 'Because', 'And', 'Which') help to speed up the process of reading. 'While' is the first word of the first four stanzas. The word 'And' is the first word in ten of the poem's thirty-six lines. These words create a sense of forward motion and maintain the poem's fast pace.

In stanza 2 we must again work through a series of subordinate clauses before the main verb, 'loped', appears in line 12.

The stag's progress towards his doom is recorded in the last line of each of the first four stanzas. Hughes creates a sense of menace by using these four progress reports (lines 6, 12, 18 and 24) to suggest less and less favourable circumstances for the stag. In line 6 he is running through the private forest, where the huntsmen are forbidden to go, and he is therefore safe from them and their hounds. In line 12 he is still loping through his favourite valley, although he has left the safety of the private forest. In line 18 he has left his favourite valley and is coming into public view, over the last hill of Exmoor. Then, in line 24 with the cries of the hounds echoing through the trees, the stag finds himself dangerously exposed in strange country.

In the final two stanzas the rhythms of the verse become more urgent. The hounds were invisible in stanza 4, and only the echoes of their baying could be heard. By stanza 5 the full hound-pack is smashing its way through the undergrowth, while the stag is becoming exhausted, only wanting to rest. Stanza 6 shows the stag unable to find his way home to safety, being struck by unfamiliar trees and torn by brambles, 'weeping' (line 31) in terror as the hounds prepare to 'fling' themselves 'all over him' (line 33). The climax of the stag's terror comes in line 34 as his heart beats against his ribs like a club and the baying of the hounds overwhelms him. **We are left to imagine his cruel end**, as the spectators, having enjoyed their sport, get back to their cars and disappear.

Exam-Style Questions

Thinking about the poem

1   How does the poem make you feel about the stag? Support your answer by referring to relevant words or phrases from the text.

2   Based on what you have read about the subject in this poem, write a piece on stag hunting.

3   Do you think this poem could be used as propaganda by groups of people opposed to stag hunting? If so, choose three quotations from the poem that you think might be particularly effective. If not, explain why.

4   Do you get the impression that the huntsmen and spectators care about what happens to the stag? Refer to the poem in support of your answer.

5   Do the events described in 'The Stag' suggest that those present enjoy the stag hunt? In your answer refer to details from the poem.

6   There is a sense of excitement in this poem. Mention three details that convey this excitement.

7   Do you think 'The Stag' is a good title for this poem? If you do, explain why. If you do not like the title, suggest an alternative one, giving your reason(s) for your choice.

8   This poem has been admired for its good descriptions of details. Choose three examples from the poem and say why you have chosen them.

Taking a closer look

1 Choose two phrases or lines from the poem that impressed you. Explain your choice.

2 Comment on the expression 'high-kneed it' (line 19). What does it tell you about the spectators?

3 Comment on the use of the word 'weeping' (line 31) and its contribution to the meaning of the poem.

Personal response

1 Imagine you are a reporter for the *Exmoor Times* and you have been asked to file a report on the hunt described in 'The Stag'. What would you write?

2 Imagine you are the stag and have escaped from the pursuing huntsmen and their hounds. Describe your experience of the hunt.

3 Write an account of the events of this poem from the point of view of one of the huntsmen.

4 In small groups, discuss, based on the details of this poem, whether stag hunting should be illegal, or should be permitted as an entertaining country sport.

snapshot

Causes readers to think about stag hunting as a sport

Good descriptions

Has many features of a ballad

Skilfully builds up atmosphere and tension of a hunt

The Stag

A lively narrative poem

Uses plain and simple language

Moves at a fast pace

Creates sympathy for the stag

Brendan Kennelly

b. 1936

A GLIMPSE OF STARLINGS

Biography

Brendan Kennelly was born in Ballylongford, Co. Kerry, in 1936. He was educated at St Ita's College, Tarbert and Trinity College, Dublin. He also studied at Leeds University in England.

He has lectured at the University of Antwerp; at Barnard College, New York; and at Swarthmore College, Pennsylvania. He was Professor of Modern Literature at Trinity College, Dublin, for over thirty years, and retired from that post in 2005. He lives in Dublin and occasionally teaches in American universities.

Kennelly has published over thirty books of poetry, among them *My Dark Fathers* (1964), *Cromwell* (1983), *Breathing Spaces: Early Poems* (1992), *Poetry Me Arse* (1995), *Familiar Strangers: New and Selected Poems 1960–2004* (2004), *Now* (2006) and *Reservoir Voices* (2009).

Kennelly's *The Book of Judas*, a long poem that ran to over four hundred pages and gave Judas a voice, topped the bestseller lists in Ireland in 1991. It inspired 'Until the End of the World', a track on U2's 1991 album *Achtung Baby*.

He has translated poems from Irish, collected in the volume *Love of Ireland* (1989), and edited a number of anthologies, notably *The Penguin Book of Irish Verse* (1981). At Trinity he was the editor of the student literary magazine *Icarus*.

He has written two novels, *The Crooked Cross* (1963) and *The Florentines* (1967). He has also written versions of the Greek plays *Antigone, Medea* and *The Trojan Women*. These plays were produced successfully by the Peacock Theatre, Dublin. He used the plays to comment on modern Irish society and the position of women.

An accomplished performer of his own work and the works of others, he can be heard regularly on radio and television.

In a 2001 interview on poetry and teaching Kennelly said:

> If I had to define what is the nature of education I would say it's asking questions. All your life don't ever settle for answers. And you've got to keep on asking questions, and secondly, you've got to keep on having fun with life.

The Essential Brendan Kennelly: Selected Poems was published in 2011 to mark Kennelly's seventy-fifth birthday.

Before you read 'A Glimpse of Starlings'

What do you expect a poem with the title 'A Glimpse of Starlings' to be about? Would you expect a poem about nature? Might it be happy, or sad?

A Glimpse of Starlings

I expect him any minute now although
He's dead. I know he has been talking
All night to his own dead and now
In the first heart-breaking light of morning
He is struggling into his clothes,   5
Sipping a cup of tea, fingering a bit of bread,
Eating a small photograph with his eyes.
The questions bang and rattle in his head
Like doors and canisters the night of a storm.
He doesn't know why his days finished like this   10
Daylight is as hard to swallow as food
Love is a crumb all of him hungers for.
I can hear the drag of his feet on the concrete path

The close explosion of his smoker's cough
The slow turn of the Yale key in the lock   15
The door opening to let him in
To what looks like release from what feels like pain
And over his shoulder a glimpse of starlings
Suddenly lifted over field, road and river
Like a fist of black dust pitched in the wind.   20

Glossary

title:	*Starlings:* small black-brown birds; there is a superstition that associates them with death
9	*canisters:* small boxes, usually made of metal
20	*pitched:* thrown

Guidelines

'A Glimpse of Starlings' can be found in *Familiar Strangers: New and Selected Poems 1960–2004.* It is a deeply moving poem written about the death of the poet's father.

Commentary

Lines 1–12

The opening lines of the poem express the sense that the bereaved often have that the person who has died is still alive. It begins with the rather startling statement that he expects him 'any minute now although / He's dead' (lines 1 and 2). The speaker is sure that the dead man – his father, although he is not directly referred to as such – has spent the night merely talking to those who have died before him, perhaps his wife and other relatives: 'his own dead' (line 3). The speaker wants to think that at any moment now his father will return and do all the things he has been used to doing in his life, ordinary things such as drinking tea or getting dressed. The speaker imagines the thoughts of the dead man, all the questions he is having about his new experience, questions too about the end of his days.

Lines 13–20

To the speaker it is as if he is still alive: he can hear him walking on the path, hear him coughing, hear the sound of his key in the door. He sees the dead man entering through the door, but perhaps this is the door between this world and the next, a world in which all his pain is over.

The final image of the starlings 'like a fist of black dust pitched in the wind' (line 20) is a beautiful and accurate description of their sudden flight. But starlings have often been associated with death, and so this image fittingly reminds us of the finality of death, despite the vivid evocation of the dead man as he was when he lived.

Sound patterns in the poem

Although the poem does not rhyme, the sound patterns used are pleasing to the ear. Repeated vowel sounds (assonance) and consonant sounds (alliteration) can be heard throughout. From the beginning, the 'ing' sound in the title ('starlings') is repeated: 'talking', 'breaking', 'morning', 'struggling', 'sipping'. Vowel sounds repeated internally occur in words such as 'bang' and 'rattle'; 'love', 'crumb' and 'hungers'; 'close', 'explosion' and 'smoker's'. Alliteration, such as 'bit of bread', 'starlings / Suddenly' or 'road and river', adds to the harmonious effect.

Exam-Style Questions

Thinking about the poem

1   'I expect him any minute now although / He's dead.' Explain the opening lines of the poem.

2   What sort of life did the dead man have, as described in the poem?

3   What sort of person was the dead man, as conveyed by the poem?

4   Comment on the image of the starlings in the last three lines of the poem.

5   Do you think the speaker had a good relationship with his father? Give a reason for your answer.

6   From your reading of the poem, which of the following best reveals the speaker's feelings about the death of his loved one?
   ● He cannot believe he is dead.
   ● He has expected it for some time.
   ● He accepts that he is dead.
   Explain your answer.

7   Which of these words best describes the atmosphere of this poem, in your view: mysterious, sad or pessimistic? Give a reason for your choice.

8   The poem is written in the present tense. What effect does this have on the reader?

9   Suggest a new title for this poem. Give reasons for your choice of title, supporting them by reference to the poem.

Taking a closer look

1 Choose two details from the poem that appeal to you as a reader. Explain why you chose them.
2 What might the poet be suggesting in line 12, 'Love is a crumb all of him hungers for'?
3 In your opinion, what does the speaker mean when he says 'he has been talking / All night to his own dead' (lines 2 and 3)?

Personal response

1 'The poem gives us great insight into grief.' Would you agree with this view?
2 Did you enjoy reading this poem? Give a reason for your opinion.

3 Your class wishes to make a video of this poem. In pairs or groups, describe how you would use setting, lighting, music, etc. to convey the atmosphere to the audience.

snapshot

Vivid images evoke father's life

Poet's relationship with father

Starlings as image of death

Grief as theme of poem

A Glimpse of Starlings

Imaginative description of death

Deep feelings in poem

Sense of mystery

Repeated vowel and consonant sounds

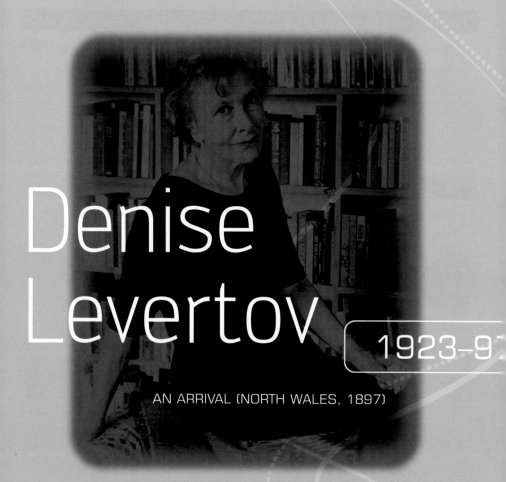

Denise Levertov

1923–9?

AN ARRIVAL (NORTH WALES, 1897)

Biography

Denise Levertov was born in Ilford, Essex, England. Her father, who taught at the German university of Leipzig, was a Russian Jew. After the First World War he converted to Christianity and moved to England. By the time of Denise's birth, her father was an Anglican parson, settled in London. Her mother, Beatrice Adelaide Spooner-Jones, was Welsh and traced her ancestry back to a Welsh mystic. Not surprisingly, given her family background, Levertov's poetry often has a spiritual, mystical quality, which celebrates the sacredness of all living things.

Levertov was educated at home by her mother, and began writing poetry at an early age. She also studied ballet, art, piano and French. She grew up in a house surrounded by books and people talking about books. She knew that she wanted to be a writer and sent some of her poems to T. S. Eliot, who replied with an encouraging letter. She said that growing up part Jewish, German, Welsh and English made her feel special.

Her mother and father, as well as her older sister, Olga, were political activists and Levertov was involved in many civil rights struggles throughout her life. During the Second World War she worked as a nurse in London. Her first book of poetry, *The Double Image*, was published immediately after the war, to wide acclaim. In 1947 she married the American writer Mitchell Goodman, and moved to the United States, becoming a naturalised citizen in 1955. The couple had one son, Nikolai, and lived in New York.

Levertov's poems, published throughout the 1950s and 1960s, brought recognition from critics and writers, including William Carlos Williams, with whom she corresponded. During the 1960s the Vietnam War and feminism became central concerns in her work. Her 1967 collection, *The Sorrow Dance*, is among her finest books. It brings together the political and the personal.

In the 1970s and 1980s she taught at a number of American universities, including Stanford in California. On the subject of poetry, she said:

> Poetry's basic root is in magic, in incantation and primal song. Poetry should be heard out loud; it should be read in a way to bring out its music. One should also read it silently for nuance. Take the necessary time with the poem.

Levertov had always had an interest in religious belief. In 1989 she became a Roman Catholic and this influence could be seen in her writing.

Up to the time of her death in 1997 she continued to write and publish poetry, translations and essays.

Before you read 'An Arrival (North Wales, 1897)'

Before reading 'An Arrival (North Wales, 1897)' on page 520 think of a time when you made your first visit to a new place. It may be somewhere in Ireland or elsewhere. What were your first impressions of that place? What things were different from what you were used to?

An Arrival
(North Wales, 1897)

The orphan arrived in outlandish hat,
proud pain of new button boots.
Her moss-agate eyes
photographed views of the noonday sleepy town
no one had noticed. Nostrils flaring,   5
she sniffed odours of hay and stone,
                    absence of Glamorgan coaldust,
and pasted her observations quickly
into the huge album of her mind.

Cousins, ready to back off like heifers   10
Were staring:
                    amazed, they received
the gold funeral sovereigns she dispensed
along with talk strange to them as a sailor's parrot.

Auntie confiscated the gold;   15
The mourning finery, agleam with jet,
was put by to be altered. It had been chosen
by the child herself and was thought
unsuitable. She had to be
the minister's niece, now,   20
not her father's daughter.
                    Alone,
She would cut her way through a new world's
graystone chapels, the steep and sideways
rockface cottages climbing   25
mountain streets,

enquiring, turning things over
in her heart,
                    weeping only in rage or when
the choirs in their great and dark and   30
golden glory broke forth and the hills
skipped like lambs.

Glossary

2	*button boots:* formal boots worn in the late nineteenth and early twentieth centuries, they were fastened by buttons rather than laces and a hook was used to pull the buttons through the holes
3	*moss-agate eyes:* moss agate is a semi-precious gem that is often used in rings. The stone is white in colour and has green markings, which give it a moss-like appearance
7	*Glamorgan coaldust:* Glamorgan is an area in south Wales that is rich with coal deposits and where mining was a major industry until the 1980s
10	*heifers:* young cows
13	*funeral sovereigns:* there is a tradition of mourners handing out coins at a funeral. What makes this unusual is that the coins are gold sovereigns, and the chief mourner is a little girl. A sovereign was worth one pound
16	*agleam with jet:* the girl's clothes are decorated with shiny black beads or buttons. Jet is a polished black stone used in jewellery
24	*chapels:* in Wales, churches were associated with the Anglican Church, whose priests were often English, and chapels with a wide range of non-Anglican congregations such as Methodists, Presbyterians and Baptists. There is a great tradition of choral singing in Welsh chapels
31–32	*the hills . . . lambs:* the lines come from Psalm 114, 'When Israel went out of Egypt', in which the mountains and the hills seem to celebrate God's power in rescuing the chosen people. Levertov would have heard psalms sung during services

Guidelines

The poem re-creates the arrival of a young girl in north Wales. She is an orphan and is dressed in mourning clothes. She has come from the mining area of Glamorgan in south Wales. The poem captures the strangeness of the experience and the loneliness the girl feels as she comes to live among cousins whom she scarcely knows. The poem is most likely based upon the experience of Levertov's mother, Beatrice Adelaide Spooner-Jones.

Commentary

Stanza 1

The first stanza focuses on the girl and her impression of her new surroundings. The orphan girl makes quite an impression when she arrives dressed in her 'outlandish hat' and 'new button boots' (lines 1 and 2). Not only does her dress

521

make her stand out, but also her eyes are the colour of 'moss-agate' (line 3). She is alert, like a nervous pony, nostrils flaring, eyes on the move, taking in everything. She is quick and observant, noting the absence of the coaldust, which was such a feature of her former life. She takes everything in and pastes her observations 'into the huge album of her mind' (line 9).

Stanza 2

The focus shifts to the cousins who meet her. If she is like a horse in stanza 1, all nervous energy and alertness, they are compared to 'heifers' (line 10), staring in amazement at this young girl, who gives them 'funeral sovereigns' (line 13). Her voice is as unfamiliar to them as a 'sailor's parrot' (line 14). Is there is a hint of mockery in this stanza towards the cousins?

Stanza 3

In the first seven lines of stanza 3 the perspective shifts to that of the aunt, who confiscates the gold coins. She puts the 'mourning finery' (line 16) aside so that it can be altered. Levertov manages to suggest the aunt's disapproval of the child and the child's father by implication rather than direct statement. Although written in the third person, we can almost hear the aunt saying the words of the stanza: 'She had to be / the minister's niece, now / not her father's daughter' (lines 19–21).

The word 'Alone', standing alone (line 22), emphasises the child's isolation. The child is determined, independent and resilient. Just like the villages cut into rock, she cuts her way through her new world, investigating it.

Stanza 4

The suggestion in the final stanza is that her exploration of her new surroundings is a solitary activity. She mulls 'things over in her heart' (lines 27 and 28). The break in the line after 'heart' mirrors the child turning things over. The word 'heart' is followed in the next line by 'weeping', though we are told the child wept 'only in rage' (line 29) or when she was moved by the beauty of the choirs singing in the chapels.

The description of 'the choirs in their great and dark / and golden glory' (lines 30 and 31) is magnificent, with the phrasing capturing the richness of choral singing, even when some of the hymns refer to dark and gloomy subjects. It is not hard to imagine how the beauty of the words of the psalm, as captured in the final line, might have moved the soul of a sensitive and artistic child. The final line of the poem gives a sense of joy and optimism that is, in many ways, at odds with the rest of the poem.

Form and tone of the poem

The poem is written in four irregular stanzas. It is carefully phrased. The phrases are full sounding. Read, for example, the first stanza. Note the long vowel sounds. Note the alliteration on 'p' and 'b' in line 2. Note the number of words that finish in 't' or 'd', which give a definite ending to the sound of the words. Note the number of times the sounds 'l', 'r' and 's' appear. These are among the most musical sounds in the language.

The tone of the poem is influenced by the girl's careful observation. For the most part it is detached, though we can sense the poet's sympathy for the girl. The final three lines of the poem suggest the emotional energy contained within the child.

Exam-Style Questions

Thinking about the poem

1. In whose eyes was the orphan's hat 'outlandish' (land 1)? Explain your answer.
2. What impression of the orphan do you form from stanza 1? Is she: curious, observant, cheeky, shy? Explain your answer.
3. How is the difference between the orphan girl and her cousins suggested in stanza 2? Describe the tone of this stanza.
4. What words in stanza 3 suggest the aunt's attitude to the orphan girl? On the basis of this stanza, what kind of relationship will there be between the aunt and her niece from Glamorgan?
5. Based on lines 22 to 32, what combination of words best describes the girl's life in north Wales? Choose from: lonely, exciting, solitary, adventurous, sad, frustrating, joyous. Explain your choices.
6. Which of these three statements is closest to your understanding of the poem?
   - It is a poem about the inner life of a child.
   - It is a poem about the absence of love.
   - It is a poem about arriving in a new place.
   Explain your choice.
7. 'The choirs in the poem can shake the heart and soul of the child.' Give your response to this reading of the poem.
8. 'The child in the poem is like an exile, taking photographs of a strange land, as she waits to return home.' Give your response to this reading of the poem.

Taking a closer look

1. 'moss-agate eyes' (line 3). Comment on the impact of this phrase. You can refer to both the sound and the sense of the phrase.
2. 'Auntie confiscated the gold' (line 15). Comment on the impact of the verb 'confiscated' in this line. Explain your thinking.

3   'turning things over / in her heart' (lines 27 and 28). Comment on these lines from the poem. What do they tell us about the orphan girl?

4   Working in pairs, take one stanza and read it aloud, paying attention to every word. Note as many sound repetitions as you can and discuss their effect in the poem.

Personal response

1   What might the locals in north Wales think about the orphan girl? Working in pairs, write a dialogue between the girl's aunt and a neighbour in which they discuss the new arrival.

2   You are the child in the poem. You are now an adult with children of your own. Tell your children about any three of the following:

- Your arrival in north Wales
- Losing your 'mourning finery'
- Being the minister's niece and not your father's daughter
- Turning things over in your heart
- Weeping in rage
- The choirs and their music.

3   Suggest a piece of music or a set of images to accompany a reading of the poem. Explain your choice.

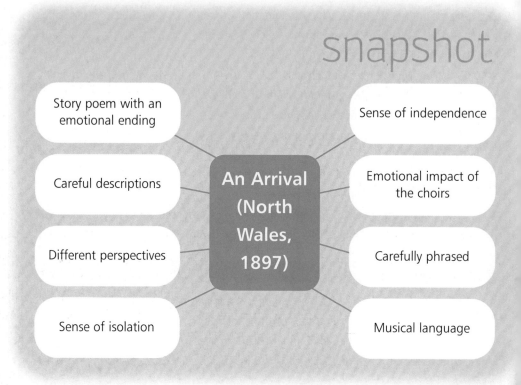

snapshot

Story poem with an emotional ending

Careful descriptions

Different perspectives

Sense of isolation

An Arrival (North Wales, 1897)

Sense of independence

Emotional impact of the choirs

Carefully phrased

Musical language

Liz Lochhead

b. 1947

REVELATION

Biography

Liz Lochhead was born in Motherwell in Scotland in 1947. She studied at the Glasgow School of Art between 1965 and 1970. She was a teacher of fine art in Glasgow and Bristol for over eight years, a career which she claims to have been a total disaster.

In the early 1970s she joined Philip Hobsbaum's Glasgow writers' group. Hobsbaum was a poet, a critic and a charismatic teacher. While living in Belfast in the 1960s he had set up a writing group from which emerged poets such as Seamus Heaney, Michael Longley and Derek Mahon. The Glasgow group was no less impressive and included such poets and writers as Alasdair Gray, James Kelman and Tom Leonard. This writing group may have given Lochhead the confidence she needed to publish her first book of poetry, *Memo for Spring* (1972), which won a Scottish Arts Council Award.

In 1978 Lochhead was elected for a Scottish/Canadian Writer's Exchange Fellowship and she decided to abandon her teaching career, travel to Canada and become a full-time performance poet, writer and broadcaster. A performance poet writes poems to be performed before a live audience in pubs, clubs, theatres and at festivals.

On her return to Britain in 1986 she became the writer in residence at the University of Edinburgh. In 1988 she became writer in residence at the Royal Shakespeare Company, which is based in Stratford upon Avon.

In 1986 she married the architect Tom Logan and they settled in Glasgow. She has written many award-winning plays and scripts for radio and television, including some translations and adaptations.

Lochhead is quoted as saying, 'when somebody asks me what I do I usually say writer. The most precious thing to me is to be a poet. If I were a playwright I would like to be a poet in the theatre.'

Her collection of poetry *The Colour of Black and White: Poems 1984–2003* was published in 2003. In 2000 she was awarded an honorary degree by the University of Edinburgh. In 2005 she was made Poet Laureate of Glasgow and in 2011 she became Scots Makar (Scotland's national poet). *A Choosing: The Selected Poetry of Liz Lochhead* was published in 2011.

Lochhead has described herself as 'female-coloured as well as Scottish-coloured'. Her poetry celebrates women as a marginalised community within Scottish society. When announced as Glasgow's Poet Laureate she was described as someone who is 'generous in her sympathies, sharp in her observation, and moves her audience to tears and laughter'.

Before you read 'Revelation'

What is a revelation? What connotations does this word conjure up for you? When might someone experience a revelation? Have you ever experienced a revelation? Now read 'Revelation' by Liz Lochhead on page 527.

Revelation

I remember once being shown the black bull
when a child at the farm for eggs and milk.
They called him Bob – as though perhaps
you could reduce a monster
with the charm of a friendly name.   5
At the threshold of his outhouse, someone
held my hand and let me peer inside.
At first, only black
and the hot reek of him. Then he was immense,
his edges merging with the darkness, just   10
a big bulk and a roar to be really scared of,
a trampling, and a clanking tense with the chain's jerk.
His eyes swivelled in the great wedge of his tossed head.
He roared his rage. His nostrils gaped like wounds.

And in the yard outside,   15
oblivious hens picked their way about.
The faint and rather festive tinkling
behind the mellow stone and hasp was all they knew
of that Black Mass, straining at his chains.
I had always half-known he existed –   20
this antidote and Anti-Christ his anarchy
threatened the eggs, well rounded, self-contained –
and the placidity of milk.

I ran, my pigtails thumping on my back in fear
past the big boys in the farm lane   25
who pulled the wings from butterflies and
blew up frogs with straws.
Past thorned hedge and harried nest,
scared of the eggs shattering –
only my small and shaking hand on the jug's rim   30
in case the milk should spill.

Glossary

title	*Revelation:* the act of revealing or disclosing something that previously was secret or obscure, especially something true in a dramatic or surprising way. 'Revelations' is the name of the last book of the New Testament, which contains visionary descriptions of heaven, of conflicts between good and evil and of the end of the world
6	*threshold:* any doorway or entrance; also the starting point of an experience
9	*reek:* strong and unpleasant smell; also to give off steam, to be wet with sweat
12	*clanking:* a sharp, hard, non-resonant sound, like that produced by two pieces of metal striking against each other
16	*oblivious:* unaware, unconscious
17	*festive:* joyous or merry
18	*hasp:* a slotted hinged metal plate that forms part of a fastening for a door or lid and is fitted over a metal loop and secured with a pin or a padlock
19	*Black Mass:* a blasphemous ceremony mocking the Christian Mass, especially one by an alleged worshipper of Satan
21	*antidote:* remedy to counteract the effects of poison; something that relieves or prevents something bad
21	*anarchy:* general lawlessness and disorder
23	*placidity:* calm, peacefulness
28	*harried:* troubled persistently with petty annoyances

Guidelines

'Revelation' is from *Dreaming Frankenstein and Collected Poems 1967–1984*. This free-verse poem retells the speaker's vivid experience of visiting a farm as a child. On the farm she comes face to face with a ferocious black bull that reveals a world to her that she was never really fully aware of. Lochhead's use of rich imagery, contrast and tone allow us to gain an insight into her views of sexuality and of the darkness that not only exists but is also necessary in the world around us.

Commentary

Lines 1–7

The poem opens with the persona (the person speaking in the poem) remembering a visit to a farm where she went to get eggs and milk and was 'shown' (line 1) a black bull for the first time. This remembrance illustrates to us that this poem has been written with the benefit of mature reflection. The poem's title 'Revelation' suggests that this visit marked a turning point in a young girl's life, a transition from innocence to awareness and experience, almost like a rite of passage.

In the first two lines we are introduced to the poem's two reoccurring symbols: the 'black bull' and the 'eggs and milk'. The bull symbolises male sexuality, aggression, violence and strength. It is in direct contrast with the purity of the milk and eggs, which are emblems of femaleness and symbols of fertility, nurturing, innocence and fragility.

The bull is introduced as 'Bob'. The connotations of this name are of something jolly, gentle, calm and familiar, but the character of the bull is the antithesis of this and the name seems incongruous and inappropriate. We are given an insight into the speaker's feelings about the bull. She knows that it is impossible to diminish this beast by calling him an innocuous name and she renames him a 'monster' (line 4), which connotes something threatening, sinister and menacing.

The child is led to the bull's outhouse and encouraged to take a closer look at him. She goes to the 'threshold of his outhouse' (line 6). The word 'threshold' is important, it can simply mean the entrance of the outhouse or it can metaphorically mean that the she is on the 'threshold' of losing her innocence.

Someone is holding her hand, indicating that she feels insecure about entering the bull's domain. She needs a comforting presence while she peers inside. The word 'peer' (line 7) tells us that she struggles to see into the unknown. She is being introduced to adulthood and the details of this are gradually being presented to her. She continues to watch.

Lines 8–14
There is rich imagery in the description of the bull that follows. The poet uses lots of sensory adjectives to enable us to share in the child's first experience of this animal. At first all she can see is 'black' (line 8) and she must rely on her sense of touch and smell to get a sense of the animal: 'the hot reek of him' (line 9). This merging of senses is called synesthesia and Lochhead uses it to convey the power of the girl's vivid first memory of the bull.

As her eyes adjust to the dark – the caesura (a pause in a line of poetry indicated by punctuation) here creates a dramatic pause – the 'monster' begins to emerge. He is 'immense' (line 9), his outline merges with the darkness, he is a 'big bulk' (line 11) that roars, tramples and jerks at his chains. These descriptions incite dread and panic. We are reminded that this is a young girl's perspective when she uses the phrase 'really scared of' (line 11).

Onomatopoeic verbs such as 'trampling' and 'clanking' (line 12) focus our attention on the bull's powerful hooves and the necessity of the chains that are restraining him. The poet's use of present participles of the verbs (ending '-ing') makes the movement of the bull more immediate and threatening.

The last two lines of the stanza reveal the wildness and ferocity of the bull. His eyes 'swivelled' in his 'tossed' head and his 'nostrils gaped like wounds' (lines 13 and 14). The alliterative 'roared his rage' (line 14) adds extra intensity to this scene. If we look at the poem so far and imagine the bull as a symbol of male sexuality, how does it change or enhance our reading of the poem?

Stanza 2

The second stanza is in stark contrast to the first. The girl has turned her attention to the 'yard outside' (line 15) where 'oblivious hens' (line 16) pick around. **The hens' dainty vulnerability, size and movements stand out against the powerful and immense presence of the bull.**

Unlike the girl, the hens don't know of the dark forces that threatens them, they are 'oblivious'. They are like children: still innocent and naïve, unaware of the malevolence that exists around them.

There is a pun on the words 'Black Mass', which refer to the size and colour of the bull but also to a ceremony worshipping the dark forces and Satan. This 'Black Mass' is 'straining at his chains' (line 19) waiting for an opportunity to escape to unleash his power. She calls him 'this antidote and Anti-Christ' (line 21), the bull represents the opposite ('anti-') of goodness and of Christian teaching.

This is the start of her revelation. **She realises that there are frightening and dangerous forces in the world,** though interestingly she 'had always half-known he [they] existed' (line 20). Such forces threaten 'the eggs, well rounded, self-contained' (line 22) and milk. The eggs and milk refer to her secure, safe world as they represent nurturing and maternal love. We cannot ignore the symbolism of 'well rounded' eggs representing the female body and fertility, and the black bull as a symbol for male sexual prowess.

Stanza 3

The girl's response is to run away from the outhouse, the evil bull and the farmyard back into her own secure world, but now that she has experienced this 'revelation' she is aware of all the dangers around her. **She has begun the journey from childhood to womanhood.**

Her 'pigtails', a symbol for childhood innocence, become animated with fear and violence 'thumping' on her back (line 24). She encounters the 'big boys' (line 25) – reminiscent of the alliteration earlier 'black bull' and 'big bulk', which links them. These boys have demonstrated wanton cruelty and savage actions, pulling off butterflies' wings (butterflies are associated with femininity and beauty) and using straws to blow up frogs. She is now seeing the evil, anarchy and chaos that she associated with the bull elsewhere in her world.

She sees male violence towards innocent nature. There are thorns in the hedges, barbs that can scratch and hurt. She sees a nest (a symbol of warmth and comfort) as being hassled and 'harried' (line 28). Her instinct is to protect the eggs and milk. She is vulnerable and defenceless, with only her 'small and shaking hand' (line 30) to guard against dangers. The repetition of the 's' sound here highlights the fact that she is young and scared, and gives these lines a sympathetic tone. The boys have the potential, not just to spill her milk but to shatter her eggs, causing irreversible damage. In these images we are reminded of a female trying to keep the house (or 'nest', line 28) together in the face of male violence that threatens to ruin everything.

Secondary theme
All that the girl has witnessed is understandably frightening and intimidating for someone on the threshold of adolescence. She has caught a glimpse of male desire and sexuality, but perhaps she is also frightened of a desire for the male that she recognises within herself, 'half-known' (line 20) but never fully revealed until now. The milk that she fears spilling is a wholesome everyday product that could not exist without the dark sexual world of the bull. She may be beginning to understand this and all the complexities that are involved with this level of awareness.

Exam-Style Questions

Thinking about the poem

1   In your opinion, is the first-person narrative effective? Give reasons for your answer.
2   Do you think that the title of the poem is appropriate? Suggest an alternative.
3   How would you feel if you were the young girl in the poem 'being shown' (line 1) the bull in the outhouse?
     ● I would feel afraid.
     ● I would feel excited.
     ● I would feel anxious but curious.
     ● I would feel under pressure.
     Explain your choice.
4   What impression do you get of the poet's views of women and men from this poem?

Liz Lochhead

5   Which of the following statements would best describe your view of the poem?

● It is a poem about the different animals in a farmyard.

● It is a poem about growing up.

● It is a poem about male stereotyping.

● It is a poem about sexual awakening.

● It is a poem about loss of innocence.

Explain your choice.

6   The title of the poem means that the persona of the poem has realised something. In your opinion, what has been revealed to her and what effect has this had on her?

7   Discuss the use of language and poetic devices in this poem.

8   'This poem's effectiveness relies heavily on contrasting images.' Identify two such contrasts and outline whether they are effective or not.

Taking a closer look

1   The description of the bull in the first stanza is particularly vivid, how is this achieved?

2   Identify the symbols or emblems of femininity in the poem, choose your favourite one and outline why.

3   After she runs away from the farmyard, the girl views the world differently. How do we see this in the final stanza?

4   'small and shaking hand' (line 30). What is the effect of this image on the reader?

Personal response

1   This poem was written from a child's perspective by an adult. Can you remember any 'revelations' that you experienced as a child? Write a short account or poem of one example and the effect it had on you.

2   Imagine that you are the young girl in the poem. You have arrived home safely with the eggs and milk, your mother asks how you got on and you say fine but you go up to your room and reveal all to your diary. What do you write?

3   In small groups, imagine that you are making a short film to accompany a reading of the poem. Agree how you would use music, sound effects, colour, images, etc. to capture the atmosphere of the poem.

snapshot

A journey from innocence to experience

Vivid experience of seeing a bull for the first time

Simple, ordinary language

First-person narrative, free verse

Revelation

Rich in sensuous language and contrasting imagery

Speaker as a young girl and as a mature reflector

No rhyme or regular beat

Nature as a source of truth in the world

Liz Lochhead

Edwin Morgan

1920–201

STRAWBERRIES

Biography

Edwin Morgan was born in Glasgow in 1920. He was the only child of his Presbyterian parents, Stanley and Madge Morgan. He did not grow up in a reading household, though he was considered a 'swot' at school. He entered the University of Glasgow in 1937 and studied French and Russian.

Morgan was studying at university when the Second World War broke out in 1939. Although he registered as a conscientious objector, he left his studies and joined the Royal Army Medical Corps. He served in Egypt, Palestine and Lebanon between 1940 and 1946.

He eventually completed his degree in 1947 and then worked as a lecturer in the English Department of Glasgow University. He remained there until his retirement in 1980.

In the late 1950s and early 1960s Morgan looked to American and Russian writers for inspiration. He drew on the example of poets who wrote of ordinary life, using direct and everyday language. He also made contact with a number of Brazilian poets, whose work he admired for their use of ordinary language and humour, and their focus on political concerns.

Morgan published his first collection in 1949. His last collection, his seventeenth, was published in 2010, shortly before he died. His poetry covers a wide range of styles and subject matter, from epic sea poems to his later science fiction narratives. He also wrote for the stage and translated poetry from twelve languages.

He was one of the great innovators and jokers of poetry, playing with language, ideas and the latest forms of information technology. Like many contemporary poets, Morgan was also at home in the more traditional forms.

His Glasgow sonnets are an impressive set of poems about his native city. He used the dialect of the city for many of his poems. He became Glasgow's first Poet Laureate in 1999, and was awarded the Queen's Gold Medal for Poetry in 2000. In 2004 he was appointed Scotland's first national poet, or Scots Makar.

He won many awards for his poetry. On one occasion he blew his prize money on a trip to the North Pole. He travelled on Concorde and met Father Christmas on this expensive daytrip!

'Strawberries' is one of a number of intense, personal love poems that he has written, noted for their directness and honesty.

Before you read 'Strawberries'

Working with a partner, brainstorm all the associations brought to mind by the word 'strawberries'. Read on to see how many of these find their way into Edwin Morgan's poem of the same name on page 536.

Edwin Morgan

Strawberries

There were never strawberries
like the ones we had
that sultry afternoon
sitting on the step
of the open french window   5
facing each other
your knees held in mine
the blue plates in our laps
the strawberries glistening
in the hot sunlight   10
we dipped them in sugar
looking at each other
not hurrying the feast
for one to come
the empty plates   15
laid on the stone together
with the two forks crossed
and I bent towards you
sweet in that air
in my arms   20
abandoned like a child
from your eager mouth
the taste of strawberries
in my memory
lean back again   25
let me love you

let the sun beat
on our forgetfulness
one hour of all
the heat intense   30
and summer lightning
on the Kilpatrick hills

let the storm wash the plates

Glossary	
3	*sultry:* hot and humid; also means full of pleasure
5	*french window:* a pair of glass doors, usually opening to a garden or balcony
32	*Kilpatrick hills:* a range of hills west of Glasgow

Guidelines

'Strawberries' appeared in Morgan's 1968 collection, *The Second Life.* **In this poem the speaker addresses his beloved, recalling an afternoon they shared and inviting a renewal of their passionate love.**

Commentary

The poem succeeds in re-creating and celebrating a remembered moment of love and conveys that moment in vivid, immediate terms.

Title

The word 'strawberries' is loaded with meaning and association. It conjures up the sweetness of summer days. The red of the strawberries and the sweet taste of their soft flesh make the fruit an apt symbol for the pleasures of sensual love. The word is musical, with its long vowels, its rolling 'r' and its gentle 's'. **As symbols of love, strawberries suggest warmth and pleasure.** In this poem they represent a delicious afternoon of warm, passionate love, shared by the lovers.

Lines 1–17

The first seventeen lines of the long first stanza set the scene. The two lovers sit facing each other, joined together, 'your knees held in mine' (line 7). The day is warm and sunny, the strawberries glisten in the 'hot sunlight' (line 10). **There is a sense of leisure, of unhurried enjoyment.**

Just as the strawberries represent the sweetness of food and the sweetness of love, so the word 'sultry' in line 3 demonstrates the way in which **the poem uses words that are descriptive of one thing, in this instance weather (hot and humid), but which also suggest the passion between the lovers.**

The lovers remain seated after the plates and the glasses have been emptied, lingering in the moment, that is both an ending and a beginning, 'not hurrying the feast / for one to come' (lines 13 and 14). The feast of food will be followed by a feast of passionate love. The sense of leisure is caught, paradoxically, in the long vowel sounds of the word 'hurrying'. The soft 'h' sound, the long vowel and the trailing '-ing' all convey a sense of ease that runs counter to the word's meaning. **Here, as elsewhere, the sounds of the poem are lush, with harmonious echoes, which imitate, in sound, the feast of food and love.**

In line 17 **the two forks crossed form an x, a symbol of love.** They also suggest that the feast is not over (crossing cutlery on your plate is a sign that you have not finished eating), a playful hint that the lovers will continue to feast on each other through their loving looks and actions. X is also the symbol for prohibition and some commentators suggest that the two forks hint that the love described in the poem is same-sex love. Homosexuality was illegal in Scotland until 1980, and Morgan was an activist for gay rights.

Every image in the first seventeen lines creates a sense of love and its rich sensual possibility, from the heat of the sun, the sultry afternoon weather, the open window, the glistening strawberries, to the sweet sugar-coated taste of the strawberries. The senses of taste, touch and sight are invoked. Even the placing of the plates side by side, and the crossing of the forks, has a romantic resonance. **This suggests that one of the themes of the poem is the way in which everything, including otherwise trivial details, is transformed in the eye of love.**

Lines 18–26

In lines 18 to 26, which almost form a stanza, there is a sense of the lovers progressing towards making love. Now the feast of food and the feast of love have become one in the taste of strawberries that the speaker takes from the lover's kisses. There is an interesting play on the idea of the lover as a child lost or 'abandoned' (line 21) in love.

There is a confusion or ambiguity in the tenses so that the lovers seem to belong to the past, to memory ('I bent towards you', line 18) and at the same time to exist in the present ('lean back again / let me love you', lines 25 and 26), as if the memory of that sultry afternoon works to create another occasion of love. The absence of punctuation in the poem also contributes to the confusion of time and further blurs the distinction between the past and the present.

There is a wonderful effect achieved in the repetition in the short lines 'in my arms' (line 20) and 'in my memory' (line 24) and in the rhythm of the final lines of this stanza. **The hypnotic combination of words and rhythm suggests the absorbed passion of the lovers.**

Stanza 2

The second stanza appears to move the poem into the present, though whether this is the vivid present of memory or the present of real time is hard to decide. Perhaps it is both. The poet plays on the idea of memory and forgetfulness in this stanza. He plays on the idea that the lovers remember the hour in which they forgot everything else except each other, as they were (are?) abandoned in love.

The image of 'summer lightning' (line 31) can be read as a symbol of the lovers' passion: warm and electrifying. It may also be read in a darker light, suggesting that their love is subject to destructive forces.

Final line

It is arguable that the final line of the poem, 'let the storm wash the plates', is unnecessary and takes away from the effect of the lightning. Is this a valid criticism? Or does the line catch the carefree attitude of the lovers, lost as they are in each other's presence? Perhaps the reference to washing the plates suggests that the storm might wash away the love between them.

Sound and form of the poem

'Strawberries' is as much about the way thoughts and feelings are expressed as the thoughts and feelings themselves. Consider, for example, the first four words of the poem, 'There were never strawberries'. The rich sweetness of these words, with their musical 'er' sounds and their long vowels, establishes that the words in this poem, like the strawberries and the love that they symbolise, are to be savoured.

Read the poem out loud and note the number of 't', 'p' and 'b' sounds. We use the tongue and the lips to make these sounds, which imitate the savouring of food, and also suggest the savouring of kisses.

The irregular structure of the poem, the absence of any punctuation and the failure to observe poetic conventions reinforce the idea of passion, of a kind of love that cares little for rules and regulations. The poem appears stretched out on the page, supporting the leisurely, carefree atmosphere.

Edwin Morgan

Exam-Style Questions

Thinking about the poem

1 Comment on the title of the poem. Is it an appropriate one? Explain your answer.

2 In your opinion, what details are most vivid in this poem?

3 Identify where in the poem the speaker refers to the various senses: taste, touch, sight and smell. How effective is each image?

4 Examine Morgan's use of long vowels, soft sounds, rhymes and echoes to create a sensuous mood.

5 (a) Does the lack of punctuation add to or take from your enjoyment of the poem?

   (b) Indicate where you would place the most important pauses in the poem.

6 (a) Suggest reasons why the speaker recalls the afternoon of the strawberries. In your view, are the lovers still as united as they were on that day?

   (b) What line in the poem tells you the most about the relationship between the lovers?

7 Do you think the poem works as a love poem? Explain your answer.

8 Here are two views of the poem. Which one is closest to your reading of the poem?

   'Strawberries' is a celebration of a shared love.

   'Strawberries' is a lover's plea for a love that is fading.

   Explain your choice.

Taking a closer look

1 What, in your view, is the significance of the 'two forks crossed' (line 17)?

2 'let the storm wash the plates' (line 33). Is this a good ending to the poem? Explain your answer.

3 Find two examples of where sound and sense marry in the poem in a particularly effective way. Explain your choices.

4 Select your two favourite lines or phrases from the poem. Explain your choice.

Personal response

1 You have been asked to review this poem for a literary magazine. In less than 300 words try to capture your thoughts.

2 Select a piece of music that you think would make a good accompaniment to 'Strawberries' and explain your choice.

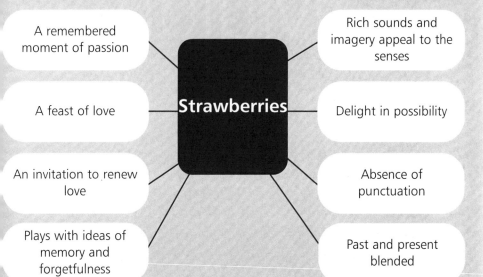

A remembered moment of passion

A feast of love

An invitation to renew love

Plays with ideas of memory and forgetfulness

Strawberries

Rich sounds and imagery appeal to the senses

Delight in possibility

Absence of punctuation

Past and present blended

Edwin Morgan

Paul Muldoon

b. 1951

ANSEO

Biography

Paul Muldoon was born in Portadown, Co. Armagh in 1951. His mother was a teacher, his father was a labourer and market gardener. He was educated at St Patrick's College, Armagh, and Queen's University, Belfast, where the poet Seamus Heaney was his English tutor.

Muldoon's first collection of poems, *New Weather,* was published in 1973. He was just twenty-two years of age and still a university student. It dealt with the violence in Northern Ireland at that time as well as with more personal themes.

Muldoon worked as a radio and television producer for BBC Northern Ireland until 1986. Since then he has held writing fellowships at various universities, including Cambridge University, Columbia University (New York) and the University of California at Berkeley. In 1990 he became Professor of Humanities and Creative Writing at Princeton University. In 1999 he was appointed Professor of Poetry at Oxford University.

He has received many awards for his poetry, including the Sir Geoffrey Faber Memorial Award in 1991, the T. S. Eliot Memorial Prize in 1994 for his collection *The Annals of Chile,* and the American Academy of Arts and Letters Award for Literature in 1996. His *New Selected Poems 1968–1994*, published in 1996, won the prestigious Irish Times Irish Literature Prize for Poetry in 1997. His collection *Moy Sand and Gravel* (2002) was awarded the Pulitzer Prize for Poetry in 2003.

Muldoon has been described as a storyteller. He has spoken of his interest in 'the story, and in wanting almost to write novels in the poem' and how he likes 'using different characters, to present different views of the world'.

Muldoon has also edited a number of poetry anthologies, among them *The Faber Book of Contemporary Irish Poetry* (1986). He has written a play for television, *Monkeys* (1989), and an opera libretto, *Shining Brow* (1993). In 2007 he became poetry editor of *New Yorker* magazine. He published *When the Pie Was Opened* in 2008, which includes his translations from Latin, Anglo-Saxon, Medieval Welsh, Greek and Irish. His eleventh poetry collection, *Plan B,* was published in 2009.

In 2008 he remarked:

> The point of poetry is to be acutely discomforting, to prod and provoke, to poke us in the eye, to punch us in the nose, to knock us off our feet, to take our breath away.

He lives in the United States with his novelist wife, Jean Hanff Korelitz, and their children.

Before you read 'Anseo'

The poem 'Anseo' on page 544 is written in English but has an Irish word for its title. Think of reasons why the poet might do this. What does it suggest to you? Does the fact that the poem is set in Co. Armagh give the decision to use an Irish word additional meaning?

Paul Muldoon

Anseo

When the Master was calling the roll
At the primary school in Collegelands,
You were meant to call back Anseo
And raise your hand
As your name occurred.   5
Anseo, meaning here, here and now,
All present and correct,
Was the first word of Irish I spoke.
The last name on the ledger
Belonged to Joseph Mary Plunkett Ward   10
And was followed, as often as not,
By silence, knowing looks,
A nod and a wink, the Master's droll
'And where's our little Ward-of-court?'

I remember the first time he came back   15
The Master had sent him out
Along the hedges
To weigh up for himself and cut
A stick with which he would be beaten.
After a while, nothing was spoken;   20
He would arrive as a matter of course
With an ash-plant, a salley-rod.
Or finally, the hazel-wand
He had whittled down to a whip-lash,
Its twist of red and yellow lacquers   25
Sanded and polished,
And altogether so delicately wrought
That he had engraved his initials on it.

I last met Joseph Mary Plunkett Ward
In a pub just over the Irish border.   30
He was living in the open,
In a secret camp
On the other side of the mountain.
He was fighting for Ireland,
Making things happen.   35
And he told me, Joe Ward,
Of how he had risen through the ranks
To Quartermaster, Commandant:
How every morning at parade
His volunteers would call back Anseo   40
And raise their hands
As their names occurred.

Glossary	
title:	*Anseo:* the Irish word for 'present', in answer to a roll call
2	*Collegelands:* an area in Co. Armagh near where the poet was brought up. It was once the property of Charles Stewart Parnell, who left it to Trinity College, Dublin, hence the name
9	*ledger:* register, roll book
10	*Joseph Mary Plunkett Ward:* the boy was clearly named after Joseph Mary Plunkett, one of the leaders of the 1916 Easter Rising and signatories of the Proclamation
13	*droll:* amusing
14	*Ward-of-court:* a play on the phrase 'ward of court', to be in the care of the courts
22	*salley-rod:* a type of stick cut from the salley tree
24	*whittled . . . whip-lash:* pared down until it became like a whip
25	*lacquers:* varnishes
27	*wrought:* made
30	*over the Irish border:* this suggests that it was in Co. Monaghan
38	*Quartermaster:* a staff officer in the army (here, the IRA)

Paul Muldoon

Guidelines

'Anseo' is from the volume *Why Brownlee Left* (1980). It was written when the Northern Ireland conflict, known as the 'Troubles', seemed to have no solution.

Commentary

Stanza 1

Irish children have often used the Irish word '*Anseo*', meaning 'present', during roll call at school, as the speaker and his classmates did at primary school in Collegelands, Co. Armagh. One of the boys in the class, Joseph Mary Plunkett Ward, was regularly absent, a fact remarked on quite sarcastically by the teacher.

The boy's name is significant in the context of Irish history (see Glossary for more information). As the poem is set in Northern Ireland it suggests that his parents' political views were those of Irish republicans. The reasons why he was absent from school are not explained. Nor are we given any explanation why the 'Master' (schoolteacher) reacted as he did, with his rather feeble pun on the boy's last name. The impression we get of the Master is of a sarcastic, insensitive man.

Stanza 2

The speaker remembers how the teacher would send Ward out to cut a stick with which he would beat him. He describes in an unemotional way how the boy became so used to being beaten that he would arrive at school with the stick already cut. The sticks are described as if they were objects of beauty, 'Sanded and polished' (line 26).

The boy himself seems immune to being punished – he has carved his own initials on the stick. **It is almost as if he is proud of being punished, which as we know is not a normal reaction.**

When you read these lines it is easy to gloss over the fact that corporal punishment was an accepted part of school life. Not only that, but to our modern minds it seems incredible that a child would be asked to prepare his own instrument of punishment, as Ward was. The speaker does not make any comment, underlining perhaps the fact that generations of children did not question the treatment they sometimes got at school.

Stanza 3

In this stanza it is suggested that his treatment at school had a profound effect on Ward's later career. We see him as an adult and as a member of the Irish Republican Army, involved in the violent conflict in Northern Ireland. He lives 'in the open' (line 31), a kind of outlaw from ordinary life.

It is clear that he is now in a position of power over others, as the teacher had once been over him. Ironically, he calls the roll in exactly the same way as the schoolmaster, so that the volunteers must answer *anseo*.

Theme of the poem

The speaker, or the poet, makes no direct comment on Joe Ward or his situation. The connection is clear, though, between the boy's treatment at school and his later life of violence. His experience has made him insensitive to the pain of others or the damage his actions may cause. But he had been brutalised in his turn by the schoolteacher. Perhaps this is one of the themes of the poem: what happens to us in childhood affects the way we live later on and what we do. Ironically, though, Ward seems unaware of this. He thinks merely that he is 'fighting for Ireland'. Is this the worst irony of all?

Exam-Style Questions

Thinking about the poem

1   What impression of primary school life does this poem give us?
2   Do you think experience of primary school has changed from the time in which the first part of the poem is set (in the 1950s)? Explain your answer.
3   What aspect of the story do you find most disturbing? Give reasons for your view.
4   In your opinion, why does the poet describe the hazel-wand in such detail in the second stanza?
5   In your opinion, is there a connection between Ward's early experiences at school and his activities in the IRA? Or is there a more complex reason for his activities, connected perhaps with his family?
6   Does the name given to him by his parents throw any light on Ward's later activities? Explain your answer.
7   Which of these words comes closest to describing the tone of the poem, in your opinion: angry, disappointed, bitter, disgusted, detached? Refer to the poem in support of your views.
8   What, in your opinion, is the main point the poem makes? Do you agree with it?
9   What would you say is the speaker of the poem's attitude to Joe Ward? Choose the lines that in your view best suggest this attitude.
10 What is the effect of the Irish language 'Anseo' in the poem?

Paul Muldoon

Taking a closer look

1   'At the primary school in Collegelands' (line 2). How does the setting of the poem affect your response to it?

2   'And was followed, as often as not, / By silence, knowing looks, / A nod and a wink, the Master's droll / 'And where's our little Ward-of-court?'' (lines 11–14) What do these lines reveal to you about the teacher in the poem? Explain your answer.

3   Choose the two images from the poem that had the most impact on you and give a reason for your choice.

Personal response

1   Imagine you are the young Joseph Mary Plunkett Ward. Write an entry from your diary describing your life at home and at school.

2   In small groups, imagine you are some of Joe Ward's 'volunteers' and discuss the life you lead and what you think of your leader.

3   Write a short paragraph in which you agree/disagree with the statement 'Corporal punishment (beating) is always harmful'.

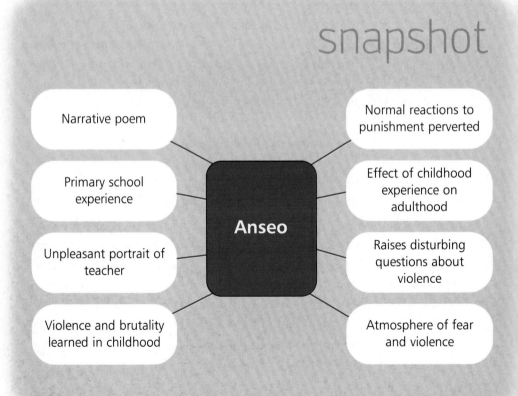

snapshot

Narrative poem

Normal reactions to punishment perverted

Primary school experience

Effect of childhood experience on adulthood

Anseo

Unpleasant portrait of teacher

Raises disturbing questions about violence

Violence and brutality learned in childhood

Atmosphere of fear and violence

Richard Murphy

b. 1927

MOONSHINE

Biography

Richard Murphy was born in Milford House, his family home in Galway. His father, Sir William Lindsay Murphy, was in the British Colonial Service, and Murphy spent part of his childhood in Ceylon (now Sri Lanka) and the Bahamas.

He was educated at boarding schools in Ireland and England, and won a scholarship to Magdalene College, Oxford at the age of seventeen. He studied English there under the author C. S. Lewis, who wrote *The Lion, the Witch and the Wardrobe*. He also studied in the famous Sorbonne University in Paris.

Murphy lived and worked in Crete before returning to Ireland in the early 1960s. He set up home on the island of Inisbofin, which lies seven miles off the west coast of Galway. He made his living from an old sailing boat, *Ave Maria*, which he restored and used to ferry visitors to and around the island. His 1963 collection, *Sailing to an Island*, won widespread acclaim.

Murphy's 1985 book entitled *The Price of Stone* charts his colourful life through the houses and buildings he has known. The book ranges over his colonial childhood, his English education and his life on a small island. An earlier book on the *Battle of Aughrim* (1968) is also of interest for many reasons, not least because his ancestors fought on both sides.

Murphy's work has always been highly regarded both at home and abroad. He has won many awards and has been writer in residence at several American universities.

Among his most famous literary friends were the poets Ted Hughes and Sylvia Plath. Their visit to him in Cleggan, Connemara, in September 1962, a short time before Plath's death, has received much attention from her biographers.

Murphy now divides his time between Dublin and Durban in South Africa, where his daughter Emily lives. His *Collected Poems* was published in 2000. In 2002 he published a memoir *The Kick – a Life among Writers*, which covers his life, family and the friendships from which his poetry sprang.

Before you read 'Moonshine'

The word 'moonshine' has many different meanings. What do you expect a poem entitled 'Moonshine' to be about? Share your thoughts with a partner and then read the poem to see if your expectations are correct.

'Moonshine'

To think
I must be alone:
To love
We must be together.

I think I love you   5
When I'm alone
More than I think of you
When we're together.

I cannot think
Without loving 10
Or love
Without thinking.

Alone I love
To think of us together:
Together I think 15
I'd love to be alone.

Guidelines

'Moonshine' is from Murphy's *Collected Poems*, published in 2000. For admirers of his work, 'Moonshine' is an example of Murphy's poised and dazzling style.

Commentary

This short, clever poem brings a lightness of touch to the age-old conflict between the need for love and the need to be alone. Witty and elegant, the poem hovers between nonsense and distilled wisdom, as suggested in its brilliant title. The clever arrangement of words (especially the last word of each line) suggests the nature of the conundrum.

Stanza 1

The poet sets out his conundrum in the first stanza in the form of two witty formulations. The first emphasises the need for the 'I' to be alone: 'To think / I must be alone'. The second emphasises the necessity of the 'We' to be together: 'To love / We must be together'. The rest of the poem is a playful meditation on the four terms: 'I', 'We', 'think' and 'love'. In the manner of a mathematical equation, the terms are moved around in an attempt to make them balance.

Stanza 2

The speaker poet makes an admission that, however playful, may sound insulting to the lover to whom it is addressed. He admits that he thinks more of the lover when he is alone than when they are together. It is hardly what a lover would want to hear.

Richard Murphy

Stanza 3

The speaker then considers the relationship between loving and thinking and thinking and loving. He declares that, for him, one cannot happen without the other.

Stanza 4

The fourth stanza, which risks exasperating the beloved to whom it is addressed, declares that when he is alone, he wants to be together and when they are together, he wants to be alone.

Significantly, the poem ends with the statement, 'I'd love to be alone' (line 16). Add this to the nine 'I's in the poem and you might be forgiven for concluding that the speaker is more than a little self-obsessed.

Form of the poem

This light-hearted poem is composed in a careful, witty way. Each short stanza is perfectly balanced. The structure of the poem therefore achieves what the speaker cannot.

The arrangement of the final word in each stanza echoes the meaning of the entire poem. The main technique in the poem is repetition.

Exam-Style Questions

Thinking about the poem

1   When does the speaker think he is in love?
2   When does the speaker love to think?
3   The four lines in the first and last stanzas end with the same four words. Comment on the significance (or otherwise) of the change in order from stanza 1 to stanza 4.
4   What, in your view, is the tone of the poem: playful, loving, teasing, selfish, or something else? Explain your choice
5   Which one of the following statements best describes your view of the speaker of the poem?
    ● The speaker is really clever.
    ● The speaker is really annoying.
    ● The speaker is really confused.
    ● The speaker is really charming.
    Explain your choice, with reference to the text.
6   Experiment with reading the poem in different ways. Mark the words that need to be stressed as well as any pauses and hesitations.

7   The final line of the poem is 'I'd love to be alone' (line 16). Is this an appropriate line on which to end? Explain your answer.

8   Which of these two statements is closest to your own reading of the poem?
    ●   This is a silly, playful poem and should not be taken seriously.
    ●   Although it is light-hearted, the poem deals with a real dilemma.
    Explain your choice.

Taking a closer look

1   Using the Glossary, consider the various meanings of the word 'moonshine' and the relevance of each to the poem.

2   Look at how the word 'I' is used in the poem. How does this affect your view of the speaker?

3   'The most important word in understanding the poem is the word 'must', as it is used in lines 2 and 4.' Do you agree with this point of view?

Personal response

1   Using the same range of words that Murphy used, write your own poem on a similar theme.

2   Imagine you are the person addressed in the poem. Write your response to the poem, choosing what you consider an appropriate tone.

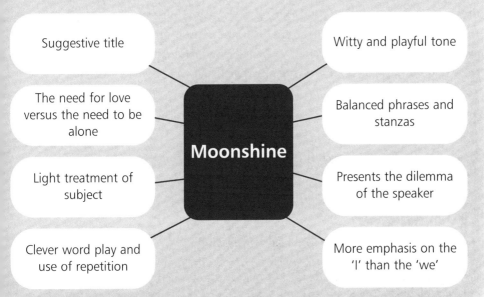

snapshot

Suggestive title

The need for love versus the need to be alone

Light treatment of subject

Clever word play and use of repetition

Moonshine

Witty and playful tone

Balanced phrases and stanzas

Presents the dilemma of the speaker

More emphasis on the 'I' than the 'we'

Julie O'Callaghan

b. 1954

THE NET

Biography

Julie O'Callaghan was born in Chicago in 1954 into an Irish-American family. She was the second child of seven and the oldest girl. The family lived five minutes from the beach at Lake Michigan and the children spent their summers swimming and playing in the sand.

Her father encouraged reading and the family made regular trips to the library. She attended a Catholic primary school and, later, Sullivan High School. English was her favourite subject and she enjoyed writing stories, articles and poetry.

O'Callaghan has lived in Ireland since 1974. She works in the library in Trinity College, Dublin, and was married to the poet Dennis O'Driscoll until his untimely death in December 2012. She described her husband as 'the best of teachers and editors'. She said she was always 'thrilled and happy' if one of her poems got past his eyes.

Other influences include the Irish poets Patrick Kavanagh and Seamus Heaney. On being a poet in Ireland, she says: 'Poetry in Ireland comes from an ancient tradition and is part of the culture. You don't have to apologise for it. I can't think of a better place to be writing.'

She has published several collections of poetry for children and young adults as well as her work for an adult audience, including *The Book of Whispers* (2006) for children, and *Tell Me This Is Normal* (2008). She has earned numerous distinctions and awards for her work, including the Michael Hartnett Poetry Award in 2001 and a number of Arts Council bursaries. She is a member of Aosdána, the national arts organisation.

Her advice for young writers is to:

> . . . read as many different kinds of poetry as possible: all eras, countries, types. If you need to write – you will. It isn't something that can be forced. I had no childhood dreams of being a writer, but I woke up one day to find I had published my first book.

Before you read 'The Net'

'Even if you want to, the social network sites on the Internet make it impossible to stay invisible and private.' Have a class discussion on this statement before reading Julie O'Callaghan's poem 'The Net'.

The Net

I am the Lost Classmate
being hunted down the superhighways
and byways of infinite cyber-space.
How long can I evade the class committee
searching for my lost self?   5

I watch the list
of Found Classmates
grow by the month
Corralled into a hotel ballroom
festooned with 70s paraphernalia,   10

bombarded with atmospheric
hit tunes, the Captured Classmates
from Sullivan High School
will celebrate thirty years
of freedom from each other.   15

I peek at the message board:
my locker partner,
out in California, looks forward
to being reunited with
her old school chums.   20

Wearing a disguise, I calculate
the number of months left
for me to do what I do best,
what I've always done:
slip through the net.   25

Glossary

2	*superhighways*: fast dual-carriageway roads
3	*byways:* secondary or side roads
3	*infinite:* vast, limitless
3	*cyber-space:* here, the Internet; generally, the environment or space in which communication takes place over computer networks
9	*Corralled:* herded in and confined as if in a corral or animal enclosure; it can also mean captured
10	*paraphernalia:* trappings, accessories
13	*Sullivan High School:* the second-level school in Chicago that O'Callaghan attended

Guidelines

'The Net' was inspired by a real event, when O'Callaghan saw that Sullivan High School was organising a thirtieth anniversary reunion for her class. In her words, 'It gave me the creeps having people hunting for me in the cyber-world.'

The poem deals with two interesting themes. **The first theme is the sinister nature of the Internet in terms of tracking and locating individuals and making it difficult to remain invisible. The second is the pressure on people to celebrate school reunions and subscribe to the myth that their school days were the best days of their life,** especially if, like the poet, you are shy and retiring by nature.

Commentary

The poem works by playing on the meaning of the word 'net'. In the poem, the 'Net' is not viewed as an exciting worldwide form of communication, but as a sinister worldwide form of entrapment and tyranny. The net catches people. However, the speaker of the poem does not want to be caught and hopes, as she says in the final line of the poem, 'to slip through the net'.

The poem is also a humorous account of the oppressive nature of school reunions where individuals are forced to celebrate their time in school. The poem employs a mock serious tone to make its point. In the first line the speaker declares herself 'the Lost Classmate'. She is a fugitive on the run.

Sinister air

The class committee takes on a sinister role in the poem, chasing down and capturing former classmates, like the intelligence service of a totalitarian state. For the speaker of the poem, the growing list of 'Found Classmates' (line 7) is not a cause for rejoicing. Like an escaped prisoner reading that her fellow escapees have been recaptured, the Lost Classmate feels the net tightening. However, she is determined to stay in hiding and slip through the net.

As portrayed in the poem, the Internet creates a nightmarish society in which the individual never feels safe and secure. There is the constant fear of being discovered and subjected to unwelcome attention.

Form of the poem

The poem is written in five stanzas, each of five lines. The stanzas are unrhymed and irregular, which gives a conversational feel to the poem. However, part of the pleasure of reading it is to recognise the many sounds that repeat and echo through the poem. Look, for example, at how the 'c' and 'l' sounds feature throughout.

Exam-Style Questions

Thinking about the poem

1   How does the speaker of the poem feel about the search for lost classmates? Where are her feelings most evident?
2   Trace the imagery of escape and capture, flight and pursuit, in the poem. Do you think the imagery is effective? Explain your answer.

Julie O'Callaghan

3   According to the poem, what will be the fate of 'Found Classmates' (line 7)?

4   Which of the following best describes the feelings of the speaker as she watches the list of found classmates?

- She is alarmed.
- She is determined.
- She is flattered.

Explain your choice.

5   The poem suggests that the Internet is part of the technology of surveillance and tracking. Do you agree with this point of view? Explain your answer.

6   Having read the poem, what, do you imagine, were the speaker's feelings on leaving Sullivan High School?

7   The poem is written in five-line stanzas. In your opinion, why has O'Callaghan broken the lines in the way that she has? You might find it helpful to read the poem aloud a number of times before answering the question.

8   What impression do you get of the class committee? Explain your answer.

Taking a closer look

1   Comment on the phrase 'the Lost Classmate' (line 1) and what it means to you.

2   Comment on the use of the verbs 'corralled' (line 9) and 'bombarded' (line 11) in the poem.

3   'celebrate thirty years / of freedom from each other' (lines 14 and 15). What is the speaker's attitude to school reunions? What does she expect them to be like?

Personal response

1   Write a letter to Julie O'Callaghan in which you either (a) encourage her to attend the class reunion or (b) offer support for the point of view she expresses in the poem.

2   Compose a short poem inspired by the phrase 'infinite cyber-space' (line 3).

3   You have been asked to make a short film version of the poem. Describe the atmosphere you wish to create. Outline the images, the shots and camera angles and the soundtrack you would use to create this atmosphere.

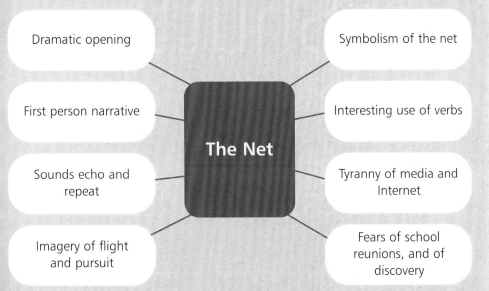

Dramatic opening

First person narrative

Sounds echo and repeat

Imagery of flight and pursuit

The Net

Symbolism of the net

Interesting use of verbs

Tyranny of media and Internet

Fears of school reunions, and of discovery

Julie O'Callaghan

Penelope Shuttle

b. 1947

JUNGIAN COWS

Biography

Penelope Shuttle was born in Middlesex, England, in 1947. Since 1970 she has lived by the sea in Falmouth, Cornwall, in south-west England. The weather, the landscape and the history of Cornwall have inspired her work and, in her own words, enlarged her imagination.

She was married to the poet Peter Redgrove, who died in 2003. With her late husband she wrote two books on women's menstrual cycles, which combine anthropology, poetry and Jungian psychology. Jungian psychology originates from the ideas of the Swiss psychiatrist Carl Jung (1875–1961). Jung was fascinated with the influence of our unconscious drives and feelings. 'Jungian Cows', which is set in Bollingen where Jung did most of his writing, is a humorous application of his ideas to that most Swiss of Swiss animals, the dairy cow.

Shuttle has also published novels and eleven poetry collections. Her poetry is highly regarded and appears in many anthologies. She won the Cholmondeley Award in 2007. In an interview she said:

> I follow my dreams as a poet, and draw from the deep reservoir of the images I find there and the places of the collective unconscious to which dreams lead. I always like that quote of Freud's – the craziest dreams are the most profound.

Redgrove's Wife (2006) is a book of laments on the deaths of her husband and her father, as well as a celebration of her husband's life and work. In 2010 she published *Sandgrain and Hourglass*, which continued to explore issues of loss and grief. That collection was followed by *Unsent: New and Selected Poems 1980–2012*.

She has a keen interest in yoga and has remarked on the importance of breath in determining the shape and form of a poem: 'For me it is the way the poem breathes that gives it form.'

On the importance of writing in her life, Shuttle says:

> With writing (and reading) active in my life, I can concentrate on the chaos, hold experience steady. I can explore, enjoy, mourn, comprehend within my own limits, and keep pushing them as far as I can.

A recurring feature of Shuttle's poetry is her humour and playfulness. Many of her poems deal with examples of the extraordinary (myth, magic or fantasy) as it is found in ordinary life. The narrative of a Shuttle poem often has a fantastical or surreal quality but it is delivered in a dead-pan tone.

Before you read 'Jungian Cows'

Before reading 'Jungian Cows' by Penelope Shuttle on page 562 consider these questions. Do you have a pet? Does your pet have dreams? Has your pet ever behaved in a way that made you wonder how did he or she know how to do that? Do animals inherit memories from their ancestors? Share your thoughts and experiences with your classmates.

Jungian Cows

In Switzerland, the people call their cows
Venus, Eve, Salome, or Fraulein Alberta,
beautiful names
to yodel across the pastures at Bollingen.

If the woman is busy with child or book,   5
the farmer wears his wife's skirt
to milk the most sensitive cows.

When the electric milking-machine arrives,
the stalled cows rebel and sulk
for the woman's impatient skilful fingers   10
on their blowzy tough rosy udders,
will not give their milk;

so the man who works the machine
dons cotton skirt, all floral delicate flounces
to hide his denim overalls and big old muddy boots,   15
he fastens the cool soft folds carefully,
wraps his head in his sweetheart's Sunday-best fringed scarf,
and walks smelling feminine and shy among the cows,

till the milk spurts hot, slippery and steamy
into the churns,   20
Venus, Salome, Eve, and Fraulein Alberta,
lowing, half-asleep
accepting the disguised man as an echo of the woman,
their breath smelling of green, of milk's sweet traditional climax.

Glossary

title	*Jungian:* relating to the theories of Carl Gustav Jung (1875–1961), the Swiss psychologist who developed the concept of the collective unconscious and its archetypes. The collective unconscious is that part of the unconscious mind which stores memories, instincts and experiences common to all humans and inherited from our ancestors. These are organised in archetypes and influence dreams and behaviour
1	*Switzerland:* the birthplace of Jung and a country where there is a strong tradition of farming and herding
2	*Venus, Eve, Salome:* all three names are associated with female power. Venus was the Roman Goddess of love; Eve exercised her power over Adam; Salome persuaded her stepfather, Herod, to give her the head of John the Baptist
2	*Fraulein:* German word for an unmarried woman, used as a form of address or a title similar to 'Miss' in English
2	*Alberta:* a once common girl's name
4	*yodel:* a style of singing or vocalisation that was developed in the Swiss Alps as a way of communicating between one mountain valley and another
4	*Bollingen:* a small village on the northern shore of Lake Zurich in Switzerland, where Jung built a country retreat and completed much of his writing
11	*blowzy:* flushed and full with milk
14	*dons:* puts on, wears
14	*flounces:* frills
20	*churns:* containers for collecting milk
22	*lowing:* mooing
24	*climax:* the high point or culmination of an experience or sequence of events

Guidelines

'Jungian Cows' is taken from Shuttle's 1988 collection, *Adventures with My Horse*.

The poem may be read as a playful suggestion that the physical process of milking is linked to a feminine principle that is deeply rooted in the unconscious of the cows. In order that the cows respond to 'the man who works the machine' (line 13) he has to take on the feminine persona of a milkmaid. Once the cows accept the man as an 'echo' (line 23) of the traditional milkmaid, they are content and give their milk happily.

This is a humorous version of an idea that occurs in different guises in Shuttle's work, namely, that **various forms of healing come not from masculine solutions but from an openness to feminine experience, know-how and wisdom.**

Commentary

Stanzas 1 and 2

The poem has a gentle, conversational tone with the speaker offering us some information on Switzerland. The speaker says the Swiss give names to their cows and remarks that the names are beautiful ones to call across the mountain pastures.

In the second stanza the speaker tells us that a Swiss farmer will put on his wife's skirt to milk the most sensitive cows if his wife is busy. **This information is given as fact, though we are not sure how seriously we are to take it.**

Stanzas 3 and 4

The speaker tells us that the cows are not happy when the milking machine replaces milking by hand. The cows sulk for a woman's touch and will not give their milk. So 'the man who works the machine' (line 13) puts on a skirt and his 'sweetheart's' good scarf (line 17) and then walks, 'smelling feminine' (line 18), among the cows until the milk comes because the cows accept the man 'as an echo of the woman' (line 23) and are content.

Form and style of the poem

The poem is written in irregular, unrhymed stanzas. The whole poem flows, aided by the run-on lines, the soft sounds and the long vowels. The poem is written in the present tense, which gives the impression of unhurried timelessness. The humour in the poem comes from the straight-faced telling of a story that sounds like a tall tale.

Exam-Style Questions

Thinking about the poem

1   What is your opinion of the names that the speaker says are given to cows in Switzerland? What kinds of personalities are suggested by the names?

2   What is your reaction to the information that the farmer puts on a skirt if his wife is 'busy with child or book' (line 5)?

3   How do the cows react to the arrival of the milking machine? Refer to the poem in your answer.

4   How does 'the man who works the machine' (line 13) make himself feminine? Why does he do this?

5   The man 'walks smelling feminine and shy among the cows' (line 18). What is your reaction to this image?

6   What happens when the cows accept the man 'as an echo of the woman' (line 23)?

7   Which two of the following statements best describe your view of the poem?
    ● It is a poem about cows.
    ● It is a poem about getting in touch with one's feminine side.
    ● It is a poem about the ingenuity of farmers.
    ● It is a poem about modern and traditional ways of farming.
    ● It is a poem about subconscious memories.
    ● It is a poem about the importance of the feminine.
    Explain your choice using reference to the text.

8   In your view, what is the connection between the title of the poem and the men dressing as women?

9   'Jungian Cows' has been described as 'an amusing and humorous poem'. Discuss this statement. Support the points you make with reference to the poem.

10 'Behind the humour, the poem reminds us of the need for openness to the feminine in life.' Give your response to this reading of the poem.

Taking a closer look

1   How, in the context of the poem, do you understand the phrase 'the most sensitive cows' (line 7)? What, in your opinion, is a Jungian cow?

2   Comment on the phrase 'the woman's impatient skilful fingers' (line 10).

3   Do you think the adjectives are well-chosen in 'blowzy tough rosy udders' (line 11)? Give reasons for your answer.

4   In the final line of the poem the breath of the cows is described as 'smelling of green, of milk's sweet traditional climax'. How do you interpret this line?

5   Shuttle has written on the relationship between breath and the shape and form of a poem. Read 'Jungian Cows' aloud. How would you describe the relationship between breath and the shape of the poem on the page.

Personal response

1   Imagine you are to make a video of 'Jungian Cows' to show to your class. What visual and sound effects would you use in the production? Explain your choices by reference to the poem.

2   Write a short letter to Penelope Shuttle, telling her about your thoughts and feelings on the poem. Refer to the text of the poem in your letter.

snapshot

Humorous and playful poem

Factual narrative voice

Straight-faced account of an unlikely story

Applies the ideas of Carl Jung to cows

Jungian Cows

Creates amusing pictures

Stresses the importance of the feminine

Sensuous and suggestive language

Poem concludes on the word 'climax'

William Wall

b. 1955

GHOST ESTATE

Biography

William Wall was born in Cork in 1955. He grew up in the coastal village of Whitegate. He was educated at University College Cork, where he obtained a degree in philosophy and English. He studied under the poet John Montague, about whom he has said, 'It would be impossible to overestimate his influence on the young writers who went to UCC at that time.'

Wall has remained in Cork, where he taught English and drama at Presentation Brothers College, Cork. He is married with two sons.

In an interview in 2011, Wall stated:

> When people ask me for a biographical statement I usually list the books I've published and say that I live in Cork. I don't believe that the details of my life have any relevance to a reading of my work. Besides, in many ways I lead a pretty boring life – I get up early and work as much as I can, I make coffee etc. What I want to say about my life, my thinking and my beliefs is in my books and other published materials. If I wanted to be a 'celebrity' (whatever the hell that is), whose every living moment is of vital interest to 'the public', I wouldn't be a writer. Writing is an essentially private business. I'd even go so far as to say that it's an intimate one.

Wall's three collections of poetry to date are *Mathematics & Other Poems* (1997), *Fahrenheit Says Nothing to Me* (2004) and *Ghost Estate* (2011). He has had numerous poems published in magazines and anthologies.

He has also written novels: *Alice Falling* (2000), *Minding Children* (2001), *The Map of Tenderness* (2002) and *This is the Country* (2005). His short story collection, *No Paradiso,* was published in 2006.

He was an Irish delegate to the European Writers' Parliament in Istanbul in 2010 and writer in residence at the Princess Grace Irish Library, Monaco, in the same year. He has won many awards for his poetry, including the Patrick Kavanagh Award.

Wall is a fan of publishing online and in journals and newspapers such as *The Irish Times*. He says this is because 'they reach readers who do not normally buy or even read poetry'.

In his work he explores contemporary Irish themes such as the political and economic crisis, as well as larger historical themes such as the Holocaust and the contemporary War on Terror.

Before you read 'Ghost Estate'

Have you heard the phrase 'ghost estate' before? What picture is formed in your mind by the phrase? Think also about the words 'ghost' and 'estate' separately. In pairs or groups, discuss what each of these words suggests to you.

With these ideas in mind, read the poem 'Ghost Estate' on page 569 and see whether your ideas have been reflected in what the poet says.

Ghost Estate

women inherit
the ghost estate
their unborn children
play invisible games
of hide & seek   5
in the scaffold frames
if you lived here
you'd be home by now

they fear winter
& the missing lights   10
of the unmade road
& who they will get
for neighbours
if anyone comes anymore
if you lived here   15
you'd be home by now

the saurian cranes
& concrete mixers
the rain greying into
the hard-core   20
& the wind
in the empty windows
if you lived here
you'd be home by now

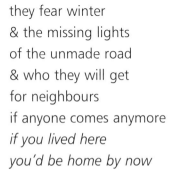

William Wall

the heart is open plan   25
wired for alarm
but we never thought
we'd end like this
the whole country
a builder's tip   30
if you lived here
you'd be home by now

it's all over now
but to fill in the holes
nowhere to go   35
& out on the edge
where the boys drive
too fast for the road
that old sign says
first phase sold out   40

Glossary

title:	*Ghost Estate:* partially finished housing estates, occupied by a few people, built in Ireland during the housing boom in the 2000s
17	*saurian:* like a lizard
20	*hard-core:* here, rubble used under foundations
25	*open plan:* having no internal walls or partitions, rooms run from front to back

Guidelines

In a short note to the collection *Ghost Estate* (2011), the poet says that the title refers to the 'thousands of housing estates, partially built and sometimes occupied by a few miserable souls who made the mistake of buying their new homes on the cusp of the Irish housing bubble, just before the developers went into liquidation'. However, as the poem progresses we can see Wall teasing out in more detail the implications of the words 'ghost estate' as he focuses on the eerie atmosphere in such places.

Stanza 1

It is 'women', he says in line 1, who 'inherit' such places. The word 'inherit' makes us aware of another meaning of 'estate', namely the possessions left by a person who has died (a ghost, in other words). Their children, some of them as yet 'unborn' (line 3), will play in completely inappropriate settings, among the 'scaffold frames' (line 6) that have been left behind as part of the half-built estate.

The refrain (lines 7 and 8) is heard now for the first time. At the time of the building boom it was a well-known advertising slogan, designed to entice buyers to a particular place. In the poem it takes on a number of different tones. Does it sound angry, in that it begs the question why would anyone wish to live among ghosts? Might it be ironic, in view of the fact that there are no real 'homes' here to be lived in?

Stanza 2

The poet lists the fears experienced by those unfortunate enough to have bought into these estates. They dread living through a harsh winter in such uncomfortable conditions, they are anxious about the danger of missing lights and unfinished roads. They fear that they will have unpleasant neighbours, or maybe even worse, no neighbours, as the poet says gloomily, 'if anyone comes anymore' (line 14). Now the refrain takes on an even more threatening tone: the safe 'home' that anyone would wish for is not to be found in this place.

Stanza 3

These lines describe the environment of these estates in strange and even alien terms. The cranes are like giant lizards ('saurian'; line 17). The images of concrete and the hard-core of rubble emphasise how harsh these surroundings are. Accompanied by the wind and rain through the empty windows, the picture painted is bleak and depressing. Once again the refrain highlights the emptiness of the original slogan that may have once sounded so hopeful.

Stanza 4

In this stanza the poet focuses on the feelings of those caught in this situation and also of those who have observed it. He applies the language of estate agents trying to sell houses, 'open plan' (line 25) and 'wired for alarm' (line 26), to the human heart: we can be hopeful even if aware of danger, but no one thought that the building boom would end in the way it did. No one thought that the 'whole country' would be 'a builder's tip' (lines 29 and 30). Of course the poet exaggerates here, but it is effective in expressing his anger at what happened in Ireland in the late 2000s. At this stage the refrain underlines this sense of anger at its fullest.

William Wall

Stanza 5

The tone of the final stanza is extremely bleak. 'It's all over now' could refer to the hopelessness of lives lived in these surroundings, almost a kind of 'death' that turns these people into 'ghosts' living 'out on the edge' (line 36) of life. It could also reflect the feelings of despair that were experienced by some people in Ireland when the building boom gave way to a recession.

The phrase 'to fill in the holes' (line 34) could be interpreted in a number of ways. The literal meaning in the context of finishing a building is clear. But might it also suggest the filling in of the hole that is the grave, and in this way reinforce the image of death and ghosts that runs through the poem?

Living 'out on the edge' is another phrase that has a literal and also metaphorical meaning. Ghost estates were generally built in the countryside, away from the communal safety of towns and cities. To live 'out on the edge' also suggests alienation from laws and social norms, which leads to the image of the joyriding boys who play with danger.

Instead of the refrain, the poet finishes with another advertising phrase that would have been familiar during the building boom: 'first phase sold out'. Here the phrase 'sold out' is a comment on the unfairness and indeed injustice that the inhabitants of these ghost estates have endured. The dream of owning a home that they once had has turned out to be a nightmare.

Tone of the poem

The tone of the poem is both compassionate and angry. The poet feels empathy for those people who have bought houses in these unfinished estates and who are now suffering, through no fault of their own. Running though the poem too is anger that someone somewhere made decisions that affected these people so badly. Truly, they have been 'sold out' by planners, developers and builders and by the advertising industry with its empty and deceptive slogans.

This sense of anger can be called political, in that it recognises that people themselves were not responsible for these mistakes. The political climate of the time failed to take the right action to prevent the situation from occurring. Although the poem stops short of naming the groups who might be to blame, the poet expresses his disgust when he describes the 'whole country' as 'a builder's tip'.

Form of the poem

Each of the five stanzas into which the poem is divided presents a specific image of the ghost estates and the concerns of those who live there. Each stanza consists of six lines and a refrain.

In stanza 1 the figures of the women who 'inherit' the estates are shadowy, themselves like ghosts. In stanza 2 their fears are expressed. In stanza 3 the alien aspects of their surroundings are described. Stanza 4 hints at the disappointment and alarm they have experienced as well as the general disillusionment of the 'whole country'. In the final stanza the sense of bleakness culminates in images of death and danger. The refrain links each of the stanzas, and the final words seem to sum up what the poet thinks has happened: these people have been 'sold out'.

There are no capital letters or punctuation marks in the poem. Wall has written that the lack of punctuation forces him to use short lines, each one a unit of sense in itself. He likes to use the ampersand (&) to link his lines, instead of the more usual 'and'. Even at the end of the poem, where we might expect a full stop, the poet leaves the words 'sold out' hanging in the air (perhaps rather like the people who are living in the no-man's-land of the ghost estates).

Exam-Style Questions

Thinking about the poem

1 In your opinion, why does the poet say that 'women inherit / the ghost estate' (lines 1 and 2)?
2 Which of the fears expressed in stanza 2 seem to you the most real? Give a reason for your opinion.
3 Look at the images in stanza 3: the saurian (lizard-like) cranes, the concrete mixers, etc. What sort of life do they suggest for the people who live in these estates?
4 How would you describe the tone of stanza 4? Which words or phrases create the tone?
5 In your opinion, why does the poet change the refrain in stanza 5?
6 What might the poet mean to suggest in the final two lines?
7 Pick out the words that suggest emptiness or non-existence throughout the poem ('ghost', 'unborn', 'invisible', etc.) and say what atmosphere they created for you as you read the poem.
8 From your reading of the poem, which of the following best reveals Wall's attitude?
   ● He is disgusted at what has happened in Ireland.
   ● He feels sorry for the people who live in ghost estates.
   ● He blames certain people for what has happened.
   Explain your answer.
9 In what sense could the poem be called a 'political' poem?

10   Which of these statements most closely corresponds to your view of the poem?
- It is a very depressing poem.
- It is a very realistic poem.
- It is quite a frightening poem.

Give a reason for your choice.

Taking a closer look

1   'if you lived here / you'd be home by now'. How might this advertising slogan have attracted potential buyers, in your opinion?

2   Do you think the refrain makes the poem more effective? Give a reason for your view.

3   Do you think the lack of punctuation – capital letters, commas, full stops – adds to or takes from the poem? Give a reason for your view.

Personal response

1   Did you like the poem 'Ghost Estate'? Give a reason for your opinion.

2   Write a newspaper report in which you describe a ghost estate in your locality, outlining the problems experienced by the people who live there.

3   You are living on a ghost estate, write a letter to your local representative or councillor, complaining about the conditions there and asking for something to be done about them.

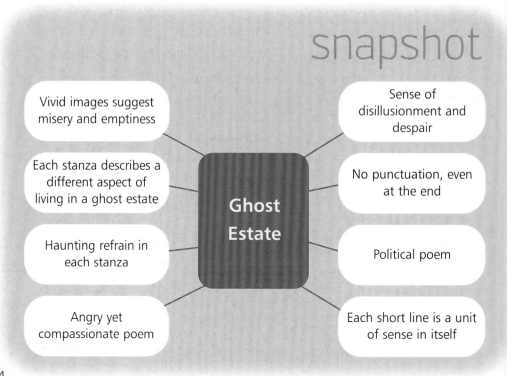

snapshot

Vivid images suggest misery and emptiness

Sense of disillusionment and despair

Each stanza describes a different aspect of living in a ghost estate

Ghost Estate

No punctuation, even at the end

Haunting refrain in each stanza

Political poem

Angry yet compassionate poem

Each short line is a unit of sense in itself

Reading Unseen Poetry

Reading the Unseen Poem

Reading a poem is an activity in which your mind, your beliefs and your feelings are called into play. As you read, you work to create the poem's meaning from the words and images offered to you by the poet. This process takes a little time, so be patient. However, the fact that poems are generally short – much shorter than most stories, for example – allows you to read and re-read a poem many times over.

As you read a poem, jot down your responses. These notes may take the form of words or phrases from the poem that you feel are important, although you may not be able to say at first why this is so. Write questions, teasing out the literal meaning of a word or a phrase. Write notes or commentaries as you go, expressing your understanding. Record your feelings. Record your resistance to, or your approval of, any aspect of the poem – its statements, the choice of words, the imagery, the tone, the values it expresses.

Begin with the title. What expectations does it set up in you? What does it remind you of?

Next, read the poem and jot down any ideas or associations brought to mind by any element of the poem, such as a word, a phrase, an image, the rhythm or the tone.

Be alert to combinations of words and patterns of repetition. Look for those words or images that carry emotional or symbolic force. Try to understand their effect.

Note other poems that are called to mind as you read the unseen poem. In this way, you create a territory in which the poem can be read and understood.

Poems frequently work by way of hints, suggestions or associations. The unstated may be as important as the stated. Learn to live with ambiguity. Learn to enjoy the uncertainty of poetry. Don't be impatient if a poem does not 'make sense' to you. Most readers interpret and work on poems with more success than they know or admit! Learning to recognise your own competence, and trusting in it, is an important part of reading poems in a fruitful way. Remember that reading is an active process and that your readings are provisional and open to reconsideration.

Do not feel that you have to supply all the answers asked of you by a poem. In a class situation, confer with your fellow students. Words and images will resonate in different ways for different readers. Readers bring their own style, ideas and experiences to every encounter with a poem. Sharing ideas and adopting a collaborative approach to the reading of a new poem will open out the poem's possibilities beyond what you, or any individual, will achieve alone.

In an examination situation, of course, you will not be able to talk with your fellow students or return to the poem many times over a couple of days. **Trust yourself.** The poem may be new to you, but you are not new to the reading of poems. Draw on your experience of creating meaning.

Poetry works to reveal the world in new ways. D. H. Lawrence said, 'The essential quality of poetry is that it makes a new effort of attention and "discovers" a new world within the known world.' In an examination answer, you are looking to show how a poem, and your reading of it, presents a new view of the world. Read the poem over, noting and jotting as you do so, and then focus on different aspects of the poem. **The questions set on the poem will help direct your attention.**

Possible Ways into a Poem

There are many ways to approach a poem, here are some suggestions.

The words of the poem

Remember that every word chosen by a poet suggests that another word was rejected. In poetry some words are so charged with meaning that everyday meaning gives way to poetic meaning. Often there are one or two words in a poem that carry a weight of meaning – these words can be read in a variety of ways that open up the poem for you. Think, for example, of how the words 'rocks' and 'sea' come to signify fixed forms and formlessness in Sylvia Plath's poem 'Finisterre'.

Here are some questions you might ask yourself:

- Are the words in the poem simple or complex, concrete or abstract?
- Are there any obvious patterns of word usage, for example words that refer to colours, or verbs that suggest energy and force?

- Is there a pattern in the descriptive words used by the poet?
- Are there key words – words that carry a symbolic or emotional force, or a clear set of associations? Does the poet play with these associations by calling them into question or subverting them?
- Do patterns of words establish any contrasts or oppositions, for example night and day, winter and summer, joy and sorrow, love and death?

The music and movement of the poem

In relation to the sounds and rhythms of the poem, **note such characteristics as punctuation, the length of the lines, or the presence or absence of rhyme**. A short line can create a feeling of compressed energy; a long line can create an impression of unhurried thought.

Look carefully at the punctuation in a poem and the way in which it affects your reading. Think of Emily Dickinson's 'I felt a Funeral in my Brain' and the way in which the punctuation works with the line endings and the repetition to influence the flow and energy of the poem.

Consider how sound patterns add to the poem's texture and meaning. For example, do the sound patterns create a sense of hushed stillness, or an effect of forceful energy?

Ask yourself the following questions:
- What is the pattern of line length in the poem?
- What is the pattern of rhyme?
- Is there a pattern to vowel sounds and length? What influence might this have on the rhythm of the poem or the feelings conveyed by the poem?
- Are there patterns of consonant sounds, including alliteration? What is their effect?
- Are there changes in the poem's rhythm? Where and why do these occur?
- What part does punctuation play in controlling or influencing the movement of the poem?

The voice of the poem

Each poem has its own voice. When you read a poet's work, you can often recognise a distinctive, poetic voice. This may be in the poetry's rhythms or in the viewpoint the poems express. Sometimes it is most evident in the tone of voice. Sometimes you are taken by the warmth of a poetic voice, or its coldness and detachment, or its tone of amused surprise.

Try to catch the distinctive characteristic of the voice of the poem, as you read. Decide if it is a man's voice or a woman's voice and what this might mean.

Try to place the voice in a context; for example, is it the voice of a child or an adult? This may help you to understand the assumptions in the poem's statements, or the emotional force of those statements.

The imagery of the poem

Images are the descriptive words and phrases used by poets to speak to our senses. They are mostly visual in quality (word pictures) but they can also appeal to our sense of touch, smell, taste or hearing.

Images and patterns of imagery are key elements in the way that poems convey meanings. They create moods, capture emotions and suggest or provoke feelings in the readers.

Ask yourself these questions:

- Are there patterns of images in the poem?
- What kind of world is suggested by the images of the poem – familiar or strange; fertile or barren; secure or threatening; private or public; calm or stormy; generous or mean? (Images often suggest contrasts or opposites.)
- What emotions are associated with the images of the poem?
- What emotions might have inspired the choice of images?
- What emotions do the images provoke in me?
- If there are images that are particularly powerful, why do they carry the force they do?
- Do any of the images have the force of a symbol? What is the usual meaning of the symbol? What is its meaning in the poem?

The structure of the poem

There are endless possibilities for structuring a poem, for example:

- The obvious structures of a poem are the lines and stanzas. Short lines give a sense of tautness to a poem. Long lines can create a conversational feel and allow for shifts and changes in rhythm.
- Rhyme and the pattern of rhyme influence the structure of a poem.
- The poem is also structured by the movement of thought. This may or may not coincide with line and stanza divisions. Words such as 'while', 'then', 'and', 'or' and 'but' may help you to trace the line of thought or argument as it develops through the poem.
- In narrative poems, a simple form of structure is provided by the story itself and the sequence of events it describes.
- Another simple structure is one in which the poet describes a scene and then records his or her response to it.

- A poem may be built on a comparison or a contrast.
- A poem may be structured around a question and an answer, or a dilemma and a decision.
- The structure may also come from a series of parallel statements, or a series of linked reflections.

The structure of a poem can be quite subtle, perhaps depending on such things as word association or changes in emotions. **Be alert to a change of focus or a shift of thought or emotion in the poem.**

Quite often there is a creative tension between the stanza structure (the visual form of the poem) and the emotional or imaginative structure of the poem. Think, for example, of the three-line stanza form of Sylvia Plath's 'Elm', which gives an impression of neat tidiness, and the alarming changes of tone that occur within this structure. For this reason, **look out for turning points in poems – these may be marked by a pause, a change in imagery or a variation in rhythm.**

If the poem is in a conventional form such as a sonnet or a villanelle, consider why the poet chose that structure for the subject matter of the poem. Also note any departures from the traditional structure and consider why the poet has deviated from the convention.

Five Poems for You to Try

In each case, answer **either** Question 1 **or** Question 2

'Thistles' by Ted Hughes

Thistles

Against the rubber tongues of cows and the hoeing hands of men
Thistles spike the summer air
Or crackle open under a blue-black pressure.

Every one a revengeful burst
Of resurrection, a grasped fistful   5
Of splintered weapons and Icelandic frost thrust up

From the underground stain of a decayed Viking.
They are like pale hair and the gutturals of dialect.
Every one manages a plume of blood.

Then they grow grey, like men.   10
Mown down, it is a feud. Their sons appear,
Stiff with weapons, fighting back over the same ground.

1   (a)   What in your view is the poet's attitude to thistles and where is it most
             evident? Refer to the text in support of your answer.

      (b)   Choose one image in the poem that appealed to you. Explain your choice.

OR

2   Give your personal response to the poem, highlighting the impact it made upon
     you. Support your answer with close reference to the text of the poem.

Eating Poetry

Ink runs from the corners of my mouth.
There is no happiness like mine.
I have been eating poetry.

The librarian does not believe what she sees.
Her eyes are sad   5
and she walks with her hands in her dress.

The poems are gone.
The light is dim.
The dogs are on the basement stairs and coming up.

Their eyeballs roll,   10
their blond legs burn like brush.
The poor librarian begins to stamp her feet and weep.

She does not understand.
When I get on my knees and lick her hand,
she screams.   15

I am a new man.
I snarl at her and bark.
I romp with joy in the bookish dark.

1   (a)   What in your view is the mood of the poem and how is it conveyed by the
           poet?
    (b)   Choose an image or idea from the poem that appealed to you and explain
           your choice.

OR

2   Write a response to the poem, explaining the impact it made on you. Support
    your answer with reference to the poem.

Lay Back the Darkness

My father in the night shuffling from room to room
on an obscure mission through the hallway.

Help me, spirits, to penetrate his dream
and ease his restless passage.

Lay back the darkness for a salesman   5
who could charm everything but the shadows,

an immigrant who stands on the threshold
of a vast night

without his walker or his cane
and cannot remember what he meant to say,   10

though his right arm is raised, as if in prophecy,
while his left shakes uselessly in warning.

My father in the night shuffling from room to room
is no longer a father or a husband or a son,

but a boy standing on the edge of a forest   15
listening to the distant cry of wolves,

to wild dogs,
to primitive wingbeats shuddering in the treetops.

1   (a)   What impression of the father–son relationship do you get from reading
            the poem?
     (b)   Briefly describe the mood or feeling you get from reading the poem.

OR

2   Write a personal response to the poem. Support your answer with close reference
     to the poem.

Dreams

Hold fast to dreams
For if dreams die
Life is a broken-winged bird
That cannot fly.

Hold fast to dreams   5
For when dreams go
Life is a barren field
Frozen with snow.

1   (a)   Give your response to the imagery in lines 3–4 and 7–8.

     (b)   In your view, does the poem create a mood of optimism or pessimism?

OR

2   Describe the impact that the poem makes on you. Refer to the poem in your
     answer.

A Blessing

Just off the highway to Rochester, Minnesota,
Twilight bounds softly forth on the grass.
And the eyes of those two Indian ponies
Darken with kindness.
They have come gladly out of the willows   5
To welcome my friend and me.
We step over the barbed wire into the pasture
Where they have been grazing all day, alone.
They ripple tensely, they can hardly contain their happiness
That we have come.   10
They bow shyly as wet swans. They love each other.
There is no loneliness like theirs.
At home once more,
They begin munching the young tufts of spring in the darkness.
I would like to hold the slenderer one in my arms,   15
For she has walked over to me
And nuzzled my left hand.
She is black and white,
Her mane falls wild on her forehead,
And the light breeze moves me to caress her long ear   20
That is delicate as the skin over a girl's wrist.
Suddenly I realize
That if I stepped out of my body I would break
Into blossom.

1   (a)   Do you think that the poem describes an interesting experience? Explain
            your answer.

     (b)   Comment on the image that most appeals to you in the poem.

OR

2   Give your personal response to the poem.

Exam Advice from the Department of Education and Skills

The Department of Education and Skills published this advice to students on answering on the unseen poem in the Leaving Certificate Examination.

> As the Unseen Poem on the paper will more than likely be unfamiliar to you, you should read it a number of times (at least twice) before attempting your answer. You should pay careful attention to the introductory note printed above the text of the poem.

It has also issued an explanation of the following phrases, which may be used in the exam questions on poetry:

'Do you agree with this statement?'

You are free to agree in full or in part with the statement offered. But you must deal with the statement in question – you cannot simply dismiss the statement and write about a different topic of your choice.

'Write a response to this statement.'

As above, your answer can show the degree to which you agree/disagree with a statement or point of view. You can also deal with the impact the text made on you as a reader.

'What does the poem say to you about . . . ?'

What is being asked for here is your understanding/reading of the poem. It is important that you show how your understanding comes from the text of the poem, its language and imagery.

Last Word

The really essential part in reading a poem is that you try to meet the poet halfway. Bring your intelligence and your emotions to the encounter with a poem and match the openness of the poet with an equal openness of your mind and heart. **And when you write about a poem, give your honest assessment.**

In responding to the unseen poem in the exam, never lose sight of the question you have been asked. Make sure that you support every point you make with clear references to the poem. Your answers do not have to be very long, but they must be clearly structured in a coherent way. For this reason, **write in paragraphs. Write as clearly and accurately as you can.**

Guidelines for Answering Questions on Poetry

Phrasing of Examination Questions

Questions may be phrased in different ways in the Leaving Certificate English examination. In the earlier years of the examination questions were usually phrased in a general way. Some examples include:

- Poet V: a personal response.
- What impact did the poetry of Poet W have on you as a reader?
- Write an introduction to the poetry of Poet X.

However, in recent years students have been presented with more specific statements about a poet, to which they are then invited to respond. Some examples include:

- 'The poetry of Sylvia Plath is intense, deeply personal, and quite disturbing.' Do you agree with this assessment of her poetry? Write a response, supporting your points with the aid of suitable reference to the poems you have studied. (2007)
- "John Montague expresses his themes in a clear and precise fashion." You have been asked by your local radio station to give a talk on the poetry of John Montague. Write out the text of the talk you would deliver in response to the above title. You should refer to both the style and subject matter. Support the points you make by reference to the poetry on your course. (2009)
- "Yeats can be a challenging poet to read, both in terms of style and subject matter." To what extent do you agree with this statement? Support your answer with suitable reference to the poetry on your course. (2011)

Answering the full question

You will notice that these questions refer to more than one aspect of the poet's work. For example both questions ask you to consider the 'themes' (ie the subject matter) of the poems as well as the poet's style, i.e. how he expresses these themes.

Pay special attention to the guidelines that follow the opening statement. Examiners will expect discussion of both aspects of the question, although it is not necessary to give exactly equal attention to both.

Do not neglect the final aspect of the questions asked, "Support your points with suitable reference to the poems on your course". This may take the form of direct quotation or paraphrasing of the appropriate lines.

Whatever way the question is phrased, you will need to show that you have engaged fully with the work of the poet under discussion.

Marking criteria

As in all of the questions in the examination, you will be marked using the following criteria:

- *Clarity of purpose* (30% of marks available). This is explained by the Department of Education and Skills as 'engagement with the set task' – in other words, are you answering the question you have been asked? Is your answer relevant and focused?
- *Coherence of delivery* (30% of marks available). Here you are assessed on your 'ability to sustain the response over the entire answer'. Is there coherence and continuity in the points you are making? Are the references you choose to illustrate your points appropriate?
- *Efficiency of language use* (30% of marks available). This concerns your 'management and control of language to achieve clear communication'. Aspects of your writing such as vocabulary, use of phrasing and fluency will be taken into account – in other words, your writing style.
- *Accuracy of mechanics* (10% of marks available). Your levels of accuracy in spelling and grammar are what count here. Always leave some time available to read over your work – you are bound to spot some errors.

Preparing for the Examination

In order to prepare well for specific questions such as those above, it is necessary to examine different aspects of the work of each poet on your course.

The poet's choice of themes

Be familiar with the issues and preoccupations of each poet on your course. **In writing about themes in the examination, you will need to know how the poet develops the themes, what questions are raised in the poems and how they may or may not be resolved.** Bear in mind that the themes may be complex and open to more than one interpretation.

Write about how you responded to the poet's themes. In forming your response, questions you should ask yourself include:

- Do the poet's themes appeal to me because they enrich my understanding of universal human concerns such as love or death?
- Do the themes offer me an insight into the life of the poet?
- Do I respond to the themes because they are unusual or unfamiliar?
- Do the themes appeal to me because they reflect my personal concerns and interests?
- Do I respond to themes that appeal to my intellect as well as to my emotions, for example politics, religion or history?

The poet's style or use of language

Any discussion of a poet's work will involve his or her style or use of language. In preparing for the examination you should study carefully the individual **images** or **patterns of imagery** used by each of the poets on your course.

When you write about imagery, try to analyse how the particular poet you are dealing with creates the effects he or she does (i.e. what the poet's unique or **distinctive style** is). Ask yourself the following questions:

- Do the images appeal to my senses – my visual, tactile and aural senses, and my sense of taste and of smell? How do I respond? Do I find the images effective in conveying theme or emotion?
- Are the images clear and vivid, or puzzling in an unusual or exciting way?
- Are the images created by the use of **simile** and **metaphor**? Can I say why these particular comparisons were chosen by the poet? Do I find them surprising, precise, fresh, painterly . . . ?

- Has the poet made use of **symbol** or **personification**? How have these devices added to the poem's richness?
- Does the poet blend poetic and conversational language? Has language been used to **denote** (to signify) and/or to **connote** (to suggest)?
- Does the poet use simple expression to convey his or her ideas or complex language to express complex ideas?

An exploration of language may include style, manner, phraseology and vocabulary, as well as imagery and the techniques mentioned above.

The sounds of poetry

Many people find that it is the sound of poetry that they respond to most. It is an ancient human characteristic to respond to word patterns like **rhyme** or musical effects such as rhythm. This may be one of the aspects of a poet's work that makes it unique or distinctive.

Sound effects such as **alliteration, assonance, consonance** and **onomatopoeia** may be used for many reasons – some thematic, some for emotive effect, some merely because of the sheer pleasure of creating pleasant musical word patterns.

Look carefully at how each of the poets you have studied makes use of sound. Your response will be much richer if it is based on close reading and attention to sound patterns and effects.

The poet's life, personality or outlook

Since poems are often written out of a poet's inner urgency, they can reveal a great deal about the personality of the poet. An examination question may ask you to discuss this aspect of a poet's work. (See, for example, the question on Sylvia Plath mentioned earlier.)

Poems can be as revealing as an autobiography. Read the work of each of the poets carefully with this in mind. Ask yourself the following questions:

- Can I build up a profile of the poet from what he or she has written, from his or her personal voice?
- Is this voice honest, convincing, suggesting an original or perceptive view of the world?
- Do I find the personal issues revealed to be moving, intense, disturbing? What reasons can I give for my opinion?

It may also be that you like the work of a particular poet for a contrasting reason: that he or she goes beyond personal revelation to create other voices, other lives. Many poets adopt a different persona to explore a particular experience. Might this enrich our understanding of the world? Your response may also take into account this aspect.

Poetry and the emotions

At their best, poems celebrate what it is to be human, with all that being human suggests, including confronting our deepest fears and anxieties. **Very often it is the emotional intensity of a poem that enables us to engage with it most fully.**

Questions to consider include:

- What is the tone of the poem? Tone conveys the emotions that lie behind the poem. All of the elements in a poem may be used to convey tone and emotion. Each stylistic feature – such as the poet's choice of imagery, language and sound patterns – contributes to the tone of the poem. Look at the work of the different poets with this in mind.

- What corresponding emotions does the work of each poet on the course create in you as a reader? Do you feel consoled, uplifted, disturbed, perhaps even alienated? Does the poet succeed in conveying his or her feelings effectively, in your view?

These are issues you should consider in preparing to form your response to a specific question in the examination.

Conclusion

It is worth remembering that you will be rewarded for your attempts to come to terms with the work of the poets you have studied in a personal and responsive way. This may entail a heartfelt negative response, too. But even a negative response must display close reading and should pay attention to specific aspects of the poems mentioned in the question. Do not feel that you have to conform to the opinions of others – even the opinions expressed in this book!

Read the question carefully. Some questions may direct your attention to specific aspects of a poet's work – make sure you deal with these aspects in your answer.

Some questions may simply invite you to include some aspects of a poet's work in your response. It would be unwise to ignore any hints as to how to proceed!

You will be required to support your answer by reference to or quotation from the poems chosen. The Department of Education and Skills has published the following advice to students on answering the question on poetry:

> It is a matter of judgement as to which of the poems will best suit the question under discussion and candidates should not feel a necessity to refer to all of the poems they have studied.

Remember that long quotations are hardly ever necessary.

Good luck!

Glossary
of Terms

Allegory: a story with a second symbolic meaning hidden or partially hidden behind its literal meaning.

Alliteration: repetition of consonants, especially at the beginning of words. The term itself means 'repeating and playing upon the same letter'. Alliteration is a common feature of poetry in every period of literary history. It is used mainly to reinforce a point. A good example is found in Emily Dickinson's 'I felt a Funeral in my Brain' where the speaker expresses her growing despair, "And I, and Silence, some strange Race / Wrecked, solitary here – "

Allusion: a reference to a person, place or event or to another work of art or literature. The purpose of allusion is to get the reader to share an experience that has significant meaning for the writer.

Ambiguity: ambiguous words, phrases or sentences that are capable of being understood in two or more possible senses. In many poems, ambiguity is part of the poet's method and is essential to the meaning of the poem. The title of Philip Larkin's celebrated poem 'Church Going' involves a suggestive ambiguity. It means both 'going to church' and 'the church going' (i.e. disappearing, going out of use, or becoming decayed).

Assonance: repetition of identical or similar vowel sounds, especially in stressed syllables, in a sequence of words. Assonance can contribute significantly to the meaning of a poem.

Ballad: concentrates on the story and the characters. They are usually composed in quatrains with the second and fourth lines rhyming. Their meaning can be easily grasped.

Colloquialism: using the language of everyday speech and writing. The colloquial style is plain and relaxed. In much poetry of the twentieth and twenty-first centuries, there is an acceptance of colloquialism, even slang, as a medium of poetic expression.

Consonance: repetition of consonant sounds that are not confined to the initial sounds of words, as in alliteration, though they may support and echo an alliterative pattern.

Convention: any aspect of a literary work that author and readers accept as normal and to be expected in that kind of writing. For example, it is a convention that a sonnet has fourteen lines that rhyme in a certain pattern.

Diction: the vocabulary used by a writer – his or her selection of words. Until the beginning of the nineteenth century, poets wrote in accordance with the principle that the diction of poetry had to differ, often significantly, from that of current speech. There was, in other words, a certain sort of 'poetic' diction, which, by avoiding commonplace words and expressions, was supposed to lend dignity to the poem and its subject. This is entirely contrary to modern practice.

Genre: a particular literary species or form. Traditionally, the important genres were epic, tragedy, comedy, elegy, satire, lyric and pastoral. Until modern times, critics tended to distinguish carefully between the various genres and writers were expected to follow the rules prescribed for each.

Imagery: this is a term with a very wide application. When we speak of the imagery of a poem, we refer to all its images taken collectively. The poet Cecil Day Lewis puts the matter well when he describes an image as 'a picture made out of words'. If we consider imagery in its narrow and popular sense, it signifies descriptions of visible objects and scenes. In its wider sense, imagery signifies figurative language, especially metaphor and simile.

Lyric: any relatively short poem in which a single speaker, not necessarily representing the poet, expresses feelings and thoughts in a personal and subjective fashion. Most poems are either lyrics or feature large lyrical elements.

Metaphor and simile: the two commonest figures of speech in poetry. A simile contains two parts – a subject that is the focus of attention, and another element that is introduced for the sake of emphasising some quality in the subject. In a simile, the poet uses a word such as 'like' or 'as' to show that a comparison is being made. Sylvia Plath's 'The Arrival of the Bee Box' features a striking metaphor in which the bee box is described as 'the coffin of a midget'. Metaphor differs from simile only in omitting the comparative word ('like' or 'as'). If in a simile someone's teeth are like pearls, in a metaphor they are pearls. While in the case of a simile the comparison is openly proclaimed as such, in the case of a metaphor the comparison is implied. A metaphor is capable of a greater range of suggestiveness than a simile and its implications are wider and richer. One advantage of metaphor is its tendency to establish numerous relationships between the two things being compared. In Sylvia Plath's 'Poppies in July', the poet compares the red flowers to 'little hell flames'.

Metre: the rhythm or pattern of sounds in a line of verse. The metrical scheme is determined by the number and length of feet in a line. A foot is a unit of poetic metre that has one unstressed syllable followed by one stressed syllable. The number of feet in a line determines the description of its length, for example a line of five feet (or five stresses) is described as a pentameter.

Onomatopoeia: the use of words that resemble, or enact, the very sounds they describe.

Paradox: an apparently self-contradictory statement, which, on further consideration, is found to contain an essential truth. Paradox is so intrinsic to human nature that poetry rich in paradox is valued as a reflection of the central truths of human experience.

Personification: involves the attribution of human qualities to an animal, concept or object.

Sestina: a poem with six stanzas of six lines each, followed by a three-line seventh stanza (known as an envoy). The poet uses six particular words throughout the poem as the end words of each line, but in a different order in each stanza.

Sibilance: the hissing sound associated with certain letters such as 's', 'sh'. The sound is used to good effect by the poet Mary Oliver when she tells us how the sun 'slides again / out of the blackness' in her poem 'The Sun'.

Simile: see 'metaphor and simile'.

Sonnet: a single-stanza lyric, consisting of fourteen lines. These fourteen lines are long enough to make possible the fairly complex development of a single theme, and short enough to test the poet's gift for concentrated expression. The poet's freedom is further restricted by a demanding rhyme scheme and a conventional metrical form (five strong stresses in each line). The greatest sonnets reconcile freedom of expression, variety of rhythm, mood and tone and richness of imagery with adherence to a rigid set of conventions. The Petrarchan sonnet, favoured by Milton and Wordsworth, falls into two divisions – the octave (eight lines rhyming *abba, abba*) and the sestet (six lines generally rhyming *cde, cde*). The octave usually presents a problem, situation or incident; the sestet resolves the problem or comments on the situation or incident. In contrast, the Shakespearean sonnet consists of three quatrains (groups of four lines rhyming *abab, cdcd, efef*) and a rhyming couplet (*gg*).

Style: the manner of expression characteristic of a writer – that is, his or her particular way of saying things. Consideration of style involves an examination of the writer's diction, use of figures of speech, order of words, tone and feeling, rhythm and movement. Traditionally, styles were classified as: high (formal or learned), middle and low (plain). Convention required that the level of style be appropriate to the speaker, the subject matter, the occasion that inspired the poem and the literary genre.

Symbol: anything that stands for something else. In this sense, all words are symbols. Literary symbolism, however, comes about when the objects signified by the words stand in turn for things other than themselves. Objects commonly associated with fixed ideas or qualities have come to symbolise these: for example, the cross is the primary Christian symbol, and the dove is a symbol of peace. Colour symbols have no fixed meaning, but derive their significance from a context: green may signify innocence or Irish patriotism or envy. In W.B. Yeats' 'Sailing to Byzantium', the golden bird symbolises the timelessness of art.

Tone: the expression of the speaker's attitude to the listener or the subject. When one is trying to describe the tone of a poem, it is best to think of every poem as a spoken, rather than a written, exercise. A poem has at least one speaker who is addressing somebody or something. In some poems, the speaker can be thought of as meditating aloud, talking to himself or herself. We, the readers overhear the words. Every speaker must inevitably have an attitude to the person or object being addressed or talked about, and must also see himself or herself in some relationship with that person or object. This attitude or relationship will determine the tone of the utterance.

Villanelle: a highly stylised formal poem. It has five stanzas of three lines (tercets) and a final stanza of four lines (quatrain). In the tercets the rhyme scheme is *aba*. Each of these three-line stanzas ends in a refrain and there are two refrains that alternate throughout the poem. In the quatrain the two refrains come together. It is often used for poems that deal with death and grief.

Poets Examined at Higher Level in Previous Years

2012
Thomas Kinsella
Adrienne Rich
Philip Larkin
Patrick Kavanagh

2011
Eavan Boland
Emily Dickinson
Robert Frost
W.B. Yeats

2010
T.S. Eliot
Patrick Kavanagh
Adrienne Rich
W.B. Yeats

2009
Derek Walcott
John Keats
John Montague
Elizabeth Bishop

2008
Philip Larkin
John Donne
Derek Mahon
Adrienne Rich

2007
Robert Frost
T.S. Eliot
John Montague
Sylvia Plath

2006
John Donne
Thomas Hardy
Elizabeth Bishop
Michael Longley

2005
Eavan Boland
Emily Dickinson
T.S. Eliot
W.B. Yeats

2004
G.M. Hopkins
Patrick Kavanagh
Derek Mahon
Sylvia Plath

2003
John Donne
Robert Frost
Sylvia Plath
Seamus Heaney

2002
Elizabeth Bishop
Eavan Boland
Michael Longley
William Shakespeare

2001
Elizabeth Bishop
John Keats
Philip Larkin
Michael Longley

Emily Dickinson Revision Chart

	Theme	Tone	Imagery	Language	Form	Mood	Effect
pe' is the ng with thers	Hope	Buoyant, solemn	Flight	Precise, metaphorical	Lyric, hymn-like	Optimism	Striking, vivid and Immediate
re's a tain Slant ight	Despair	Oppressive, authoritative	Blurring of senses	Solemn, weighty	Lyric statement	Affliction	Sobering
It a eral, ny Brain	Death, breakdown, the limits of the imagination	Intense, disoriented	Sounds, falling	Sparse, repetitive	Intense lyric	Incomprehension	Startling
ird came vn the k	Nature, harmony	Amused, whimsical, gentle	Movement, flight	Playful, gentle, metaphorical	Descriptive lyric	Grace	Calming
ard a Fly z – when ed	Death, faith	Ironic	Light and dark	Solemn, legal	Dramatic monologue	Ambiguity	Revelatory of the poet
Soul has daged nents	Elation/despair	Chilling, delirious,	Freedom, entrapment	Gothic	Lyric meditation	Oppression	Chilling
uld bring Jewels – l a d to	Love	Confident, playful	New world, treasures	Colourful, allusive	Love lyric	Assurance	Heartening
arrow w in the ss	Nature	Conversational, terrified fascination	Secrecy, unpredictability	Formal, poised	Lyric description	Wariness	Quietly chilling
ste a or never wed	Joys of summer	Joyful, rapturous	Intoxication, extravagant imagery	Playful, ornate	Lyric	Dizzy happiness	Cheering
er great a formal ing comes	Suffering	Dignified, solemn	Immobility, freezing	Formal, fragmented	Lyric meditation	Anguish	Sobering

John Donne Revision Chart

	Theme	Tone	Imagery	Language	Form	Mood	Effect
The Sunne Rising	Two lovers displacing the sun at the centre of the universe	Conversational, impertinent tone giving way to sympathetic one	A mixture of homely and learned images	Combination of colloquial speech with learned reference	Love poem	Celebratory	Stimulating
Song: Goe and Catch a Falling Starre	Inconstancy of women, especially beautiful ones	Provocative, mocking	From fable and folklore	Based on colloquial speech	Satire	Cynical	Dispiriting
The Anniversarie	Undying love	Exalted, celebratory, argumentative	Dominant image is that of kingship	Complex	Love poem	Optimistic	Stimulating
Song: Sweetest Love, I Do Not Goe	Temporary parting of lovers can serve useful purposes	Reassuring, at times sombre	Death; wasting effects of grief	Complex, difficult	Unconventional love poem with overtones of death	Thoughtful, serious	Thought-provoking
A Valediction: Forbidding Mourning	A poem about separation of loves	Serious, argumentative	Mainly drawn from science and mathematics	Learned, complex, featuring far-fetched comparisons	Love poem	Thoughtful	Admiration for poet's powers of invention and imagination
The Dreame	Blending of waking and sleeping	Urgent, argumentative	Sleeping, dreaming, waking	Subtle, complex	Love poem, but not a conventional one	Joyful	Confusing
The Flea	The wide implications of a fleabite	Flippant, witty	Drawn from marriage and religion	Ingeniously argumentative, informal, colloquial	A flea poem with a difference	Playful	Admiration for poet's skill
Batter My Heart	Search for assurance from God	Urgent, demanding, passionate	Drawn from war, marriage and theology	Remarkable for use of paradox and conceit	Sonnet	Anxious, insecure	Exciting, stimulating
At the Round Earth's Imagin'd Corners	Death and the fate of souls after death	Insistent, turning to submissive	Drawn mainly from New Testament	Energetic; breathless in octave, less so in sestet	Sonnet	Troubled, uncertain	Impressive
Thou Hast Made Me	Temptation to despair	Pessimistic	Drawn from Christian theology	Emphatic	Sonnet	Anxious, uncertain	Troubling

Robert Frost Revision Chart

	Theme	Tone	Imagery	Language	Form	Mood	Effect
The Tuft of Flowers	Human fellowship and relationships	Initially solitary then optimistic	Nature, flowers	Descriptive and symbolic	Lyric	Celebration	Uplifting
Mending Wall	Barriers to human understanding	Conversational, seemingly simple	Work, some supernatural images	Straight-forward, conversational	Lyric	Questioning	Thought-provoking
After Apple Picking	Feelings after apple-picking, writing poems	Joyful, sensuous	Rural setting, work, dreams, sleep	Sensuous, metaphorical	Lyric description	Suspended between wakefulness and sleep	Beautiful, celebratory
The Road Not Taken	Making a decision	Reflective, rueful	Roads in wood	Simple, symbolic	Lyric	Regret, wistfulness	Moving
Birches	Climbing birches, writing	Nostalgic, reflective	Trees, nature	Blend of prosaic and poetic, metaphorical	Lyric description	Celebration, insight	Uplifting
'Out, Out–'	Farm accident	Detached, almost cold	Rural setting, farm	Straight-forward, simple	Narrative	Tragic, horrifying	Disturbing
Spring Pools	Cycle of nature	Regretful	Plants, water	Metaphorical	Lyric	Sombre	Pessimistic
Acquainted with the Night	Alienation, depression	Hopeless, dreary	Urban life	Deliberately repetitive	Sonnet	Despair	Chilling
Design	Purpose in nature	Questioning	Spider, moth, plant	Descriptive	Sonnet	Puzzlement, cynicism	Thought-provoking
Provide, Provide	Need for self-reliance	Imperative, warning	Riches/poverty, power	Straight-forward, direct	Lyric	Disillusionment, cynicism	Depressing

Thomas Hardy Revision Chart

	Theme	Tone	Imagery	Language	Form	Mood	Effect
Drummer Hodge	Commemoration of soldier; destruction caused by war	Poignant, elegiac, quiet anger directed at army	Landscape and sky	Simple and direct with Afrikaans words	Lyric	Regret and sorrow	Induces sympathy and anti-war feeling
The Darkling Thrush	Absence of hope	Solemn, serious, resigned, admiring of the thrush	Desolate landscape, nature shrunken	Spare, hard-edged, literary and personal	Meditative lyric	Dejection	Sobering
The Self Unseeing	Happiness of family life; regret at taking happiness for granted	Loving, sorrowful	Homely, music and the hearth	Direct, simple	Lyric	Fond remembrance	Revealing of the poet, moving
The Convergence of the Twain	Fate, vanity	Sombre, pessimistic, ironic, ambiguous	Contrast between opulence of ship and its slimy resting place; marriage imagery	Descriptive, ornate; strong, insistent rhythm	Philosophical meditation with narrative elements	Sober judgement	Dramatic, thought-provoking
Channel Firing	Impending war, humanity's inability to learn	Blackly humorous, sarcastic	Graveyard, Judgement Day, animals and history	Conversational, colloquial	Dramatic lyric	Satiric	Amusing, sobering
When I Set Out for Lyonnesse	Transforming power of love	Magical, warm, mysterious	Taken from nature and myth	Heightened, poetic	Love lyric in rondeau form	Love	Enchanting
Under the Waterfall	The power of memory, love immortalised, love lost	Affectionate, sentimental, vivid	Picnic, water, symbol of lost glass	Musical, energetic, descriptive, onomatopoeic	Descriptive narrative	Sweet remembrance	Moving
During Wind and Rain	Change, memory and love, loss and regret	Celebratory, anguished, optimistic and regretful	Juxtaposition of family happiness and destructive force of nature	Simple, direct, repetitive	Lyric meditation	Loss	Moving, sobering
The Oxen	Longing for comfort of old beliefs	Gentle, wishful, affectionate	Taken from legend and religion	Simple, direct, with use of dialect words	Traditional ballad or hymn	Nostalgic, wishful	Moving, evocative
Afterwards	The wish to be remembered, the after-life as memory	Reflective, gentle, questioning, tentative, self-effacing	Closely observed nature	Richly descriptive and alliterative	Lyric meditation	Thoughtful reflection	Induces admiration

John Montague Revision Chart

	Theme	Tone	Imagery	Language	Form	Mood	Effect
Killing the Pig	Cruel slaughter of an animal	Matter of fact	Vivid, realistic, disturbing	Descriptive, simple	Narrative	Oppressive, grim	Chilling
The Trout	Relationship between human beings and other creatures	Restrained	Suggests God-like human being in control of natural world	Descriptive, sensuous	Narrative	Troubled	Disturbing, thought-provoking
The Locket	Mother–son relationship	Sad, but finally uplifting	Entrapment, claustrophobic suffering	Descriptive, relaxed movement, leisurely pace	Lyrical meditation	Rejection turning to sense of acceptance	Bittersweet
The Cage	Father's unhappy life	Sympathetic	Drawn from nature and mythology	Descriptive	Lyrical meditation	Sombre	Sad, evokes pity
Windharp	An Irish landscape	Cheerful	Images suggest symbolic meanings	Highly descriptive	Lyrical description	Happy	Affirming pleasing to the ear
All Legendary Obstacles	Separation of two lovers	Nervous anticipation	Images of light and gentle music associated with love	Rhythms reflect meaning	Lyrical meditation	Hopeful but not entirely secure	Challenging
The Same Gesture	Love	Optimistic	Vivid descriptive, realistic, sometimes disturbing	Descriptive	Lyrical meditation	Happy	Reassuring
The Wild Dog Rose	A misunderstood old woman who overcomes suffering through religious faith	Sympathetic	Vividly harsh, sordid	Emotional, evocative, vividly descriptive	Lyrical meditation	Sober subdued, later celebratory	Disturbing; God ultimately reassuring
Like Dolmens Round My Childhood, the Old People	A child's relationship with his elderly neighbours	Sympathetic	Realistic, cruel, revolting	Vividly descriptive	Meditation	Oppressive, fearful, later positive	Reassuring
A Welcoming Party	A young man's response to wartime horrors	Solemn, sombre, reflective, ironic		Descriptive, evocative	Narrative	Horror, sense of helplessness	Highly disturbing

Eiléan Ní Chuilleanáin Revision Chart

	Theme	Tone	Imagery	Language	Form	Mood	Effect
Lucina Schynning in Silence of the Nicht	Escape; healing power of nature	Peaceful, contemplative	Nature: hare, animals, moon, water	Metaphorical, symbolic	Monologue	Relaxed, optimistic	Calming
The Second Voyage	Longing for home; control of nature	Despairing	Water, wild and controlled journey	Unusual description, playful, heightened	Narrative	Anguish, fear	Trapped, no control
Deaths and Engines	Vulnerability of life	Reflective	Aeroplanes and wreckage; hospital	Simple, direct	Reflective lyric	Reflective	Instructive, affective
Street	Love, danger	Mysterious	Blood, beauty, butchery	Conversational	Narrative	Quirky	Questions the notions of attraction
Fireman's Lift	Remembrance, love, loss	Affectionate, caring	Heavenly bodies; strength and weakness	Powerful, symbolic	Reflective lyric	Hopeful	Hopeful
All for You	Getting what you thought you wanted	Ironic	Medieval, gothic; key buildings; fairy tale	Straightforward	Lyric	Unsettling	Thought-provoking
Following	Memory; following in his footsteps	Longing	Gothic, folkloric	Moves from concrete to mystical and allusive, disjointed, personal	Dramatic lyric	Lost	Heartening
Kilcash	Decline in Ireland post-1800s	Sorrowful, pessimistic	Nature, light and dark, apocalyptical	Plain, simple	Lyric	Nostalgic, despairing, forlorn	Devastating
Translation	Oppression, injustice, remembering	Sadness	Haunting, macabre, keys	Symbolic, metaphorical	Lyric of hurt and regret	Anguished, dark, unresolved	Deeply upsetting
The Bend in the Road	Remembrance, loss, passage of time	Deep hurt	Moves from the concrete to the abstract	Personal, straightforward	Lyric meditation	Philosophical	Quietly reassuring
On Lacking the Killer Instinct	Escape, self-questioning, self-recrimination; remembering her father	Nostalgic	Nature, vivid and descriptive escapes	Controlled, descriptive	Lyric	Reflective	Relief, acceptance
To Niall Woods and Xenya Ostrovkaia, married in Dublin on 9 September 2009	Celebration of love; universality of story	Personal yet detached; clear-eyed, honest	Folkloric, magical	Reassuring, loving	Epithalamium	Optimistic, encouraging	Celebratory

Sylvia Plath Revision Chart

	Theme	Tone	Imagery	Language	Form	Mood	Effect
Black Rook in Rainy Weather	Inspiration	Fearful, hopeful, cautious	Light and radiance; transformation	Heightened, metaphorical, controlled	Lyric meditation	Ambiguity	Exhilarating
The Times Are Tidy	Blandness of contemporary culture	Dismissive	Fairytale	Clear, patterned	Lyric, confident statements	Irony	Low-keyed
Morning Song	Motherhood, birth	Joyful amazed, protective	Museum, separation, baby's cry	Clear, direct, musical	Lyric, expressive	Elation	Surprising, elevating
Finisterre	Life and death	Anxious, calm	Surreal images of the ocean	Detailed, symbolic	Lyric-description and meditation	Heightened emotion	Fascinating
Mirror	Judgement, fear, ageing	Detached, cold	Personification rising fish	Precise, accurate	Dramatic monologue	Darkness	Disturbing
Pheasant	Preciousness of life, fear of destruction	Accusing, pleading, admiring	Visual, descriptive	Intense	Dramatic monologue in terza rima	Anguish	Revealing of the poet
Elm	Fear, love, self hatred	Mocking, fearful, threatening	Subconscious, dreams, nightmares	Powerful, symbolic, rich	Dramatic monologue	Terror	Overpowering
Poppies in July	Fear and longing	Dramatic, disturbed, emotional	Sickness, violence, annihilation	Intense, passionate, onomatopoeic	Concentrated lyric	Darkness	Unsettling
The Arrival of the Bee Box	Personal fears	Frightened, fascinated	Entrapment and freedom	Direct, powerful	Present tense narrative	Triumphant optimism	Unsettling
Child	Love and despair	Frustration, longing	Whimsical, images of reflection	Inventive, composed	Short lyric	Anguish	Heart-breaking

W. B. Yeats Revision Chart

	Theme	Tone	Imagery	Language	Form	Mood	Effect
The Lake Isle of Innisfree	Desire for peace amid beauty of nature	Celebratory	Beautiful sights and sounds	Fluent, descriptive	Pastoral lyric	Contentment	Relaxing
The Wild Swans at Coole	Time, death, immortality	Initially regretful, finally resigned	Symbolic	Musical, harmonious	Lyrical meditation	Reflective, wistful	Exhilarating
An Irish Airman Foresees His Death	One man's attitude to war, life and death	Detached, stoical	Drawn from common life	Unadorned, controlled	Reflective lyric	Detached, almost casual	Exhilarating
September 1913	Betrayal of a noble ideal	Ironical, mocking	Images of thrift and sacrifice	Energetic	Ballad	Resentful, bitter	Disturbing
Easter 1916	Transportation of casual patriots into heroes	Questioning, enquiring	Play-acting and sacrifice	Partly symbolic, partly descriptive	Meditation	Reflective	Thought-provoking
The Second Coming	End of order, coming of anarchy	Deeply pessimistic	Repulsive	Heightened, dramatic	A prophetic poem	Fearful	Terrifying
Sailing to Byzantium	Journey to ideal world, curse on old age	Passionate	Decaying nature and immortal art	Forceful, energetic	A lyric	From despair to celebration	Fascinating
from **Meditations in Time of Civil War: VI: The Stare's Nest by My Window**	Damaging influence of civil conflict	Disillusioned, fearful	Balance of repulsive and gentle images	Colloquial, drawn from nature and common life	Lyric, description and meditation	Depressed and bitter	Deeply depressing
In Memory of Eva Gore-Booth and Con Markiewicz	Past contrasted with present of two women	Critical	Decaying human nature and fashional social life	Descriptive	Analogy	Bitter, regretful	Disturbing closing lines
Swift's Epitaph	Swift as champion of liberty	Celebratory	Enemy of oppression	Dignified	An epitaph	Solemn	Challenging
An Acre of Grass	Limits imposed by old age	Emotional	Images of great artists of the past	Plain words, strong rhythms	A meditation	Frustration rage	Exhilarating
Politics	Regret over lost youth	Frustration, longing	Abstract images of politics	Colloquial	Lyric	Regret	Inducing nostalgia
from **Under Ben Bulben: V and VI**	Guidance for future Irish poets; desire for a plain monument	Celebratory, affirmative	Drawn from everyday life	Lively, energetic in Part V; obscure in Part VI	A valediction or farewell poem	Generally optimistic	Stimulating